Microeconomics
Custom Editon for UTSA

Roger A. Arnold

THOMSON

TM

SOUTH-WESTERN

Australia · Canada · Mexico · Singapore · Spain · United Kingdom · United States

THOMSON

SOUTH-WESTERN

Microeconomics
Custom Editon for UTSA

Executive Editors:
Michele Baird, Maureen Staudt &
Michael Stranz

Project Development Manager:
Linda deStefano

Sr. Marketing Coordinators:
Lindsay Annett and Sara Mercurio

Production/Manufacturing Manager:
Donna M. Brown

Production Editorial Manager:
Dan Plofchan

Pre-Media Services Supervisor:
Becki Walker

Rights and Permissions Specialist:
Kalina Ingham Hintz

Cover Image
Getty Images*

International Divisions List

Asia (Including India):
Thomson Learning
(a division of Thomson Asia Pte Ltd)
5 Shenton Way #01-01
UIC Building
Singapore 068808
Tel: (65) 6410-1200
Fax: (65) 6410-1208

Australia/New Zealand:
Thomson Learning Australia
102 Dodds Street
Southbank, Victoria 3006
Australia

Latin America:
Thomson Learning
Seneca 53
Colonia Polano
11560 Mexico, D.F., Mexico
Tel (525) 281-2906
Fax (525) 281-2656

Canada:
Thomson Nelson
1120 Birchmount Road
Toronto, Ontario
Canada M1K 5G4
Tel (416) 752-9100
Fax (416) 752-8102

UK/Europe/Middle East/Africa:
Thomson Learning
High Holborn House
50-51 Bedford Row
London, WC1R 4LS
United Kingdom
Tel 44 (020) 7067-2500
Fax 44 (020) 7067-2600

Spain (Includes Portugal):
Thomson Paraninfo
Calle Magallanes 25
28015 Madrid
España
Tel 34 (0)91 446-3350
Fax 34 (0)91 445-6218

Brief Contents

What Economics Is About

Setting the Scene — Jackie and Stephanie share an apartment about a mile from West Virginia University. Both are juniors at the university; Jackie is a history major, and Stephanie is an economics major. The following events occurred one day not too long ago.

7:15 A.M.

Jackie's alarm clock buzzes. She reaches over to the small table next to her bed and turns it off. As she pulls the covers back up, Jackie thinks about her 8:30 American history class. Should she go to class today or sleep a little longer? She worked late last night and really hasn't had enough sleep. Besides, she's fairly sure her professor will be discussing a subject she already knows well. Maybe it would be okay to miss class today.

11:37 A.M.

Stephanie is in the campus bookstore browsing through two economics books. She ends up buying both books. As she leaves the bookstore, she glances over at a blue jacket with the West Virginia University emblem on it. She knows that her brother, who is a junior in high school, would like to have a WVU jacket. Stephanie tells herself that she might buy him the jacket for his birthday next month.

1:27 P.M.

Jackie, who did skip her 8:30 American history class, is in her European history professor's office talking to him about obtaining a master's degree in history. Getting a master's degree is something that mildly interests her, but she's not sure whether she wants it enough or not.

9:00 P.M.

Stephanie has been studying for the past three hours for tomorrow's midterm exam in her International Economics course. She says to herself, I don't think more studying will do very much good. So she quits studying and turns on the television to watch a rerun of one of her favorite movies, *Sleepless in Seattle*.

? Here are some questions to keep in mind as you read this chapter:

- *Is Jackie more likely to miss some classes than she is to miss other classes? What determines which classes Jackie will attend and which classes she won't attend?*

- *What does a basic economic fact have to do with Stephanie's buying two books at her campus bookstore?*

- *Does whether or not Jackie will go on to get a master's degree have anything to do with economics?*

- *Stephanie stopped studying at 9:00 P.M. Would she have been better off if she had studied 30 more minutes?*

See analyzing the scene at the end of this chapter for answers to these questions.

A Definition of Economics

In this section, we discuss a few key economic concepts; then we incorporate knowledge of these concepts into a definition of economics.

Goods and Bads

Economists talk about *goods* and *bads*. A **good** is anything that gives a person **utility** or satisfaction. A good can be tangible or intangible. If a computer gives you utility or satisfaction, then it is a good. If friendship gives you utility or satisfaction, then it is a good. (A computer is a tangible good, and friendship is an intangible good.)

A **bad** is something that gives a person **disutility** or dissatisfaction. If the flu gives you disutility or dissatisfaction, then it is a bad. If the constant nagging of an acquaintance is something that gives you disutility or dissatisfaction, then it is a bad.

People want goods and they do not want bads. In fact, they will pay to get goods ("Here is $1,000 for the computer"), and they will pay to get rid of bads they currently have ("I'd be willing to pay you, doctor, if you can prescribe something that will shorten the time I have the flu").

Resources

Goods do not just appear before us when we snap our fingers. It takes resources to produce goods. (Sometimes *resources* are referred to as *inputs* or *factors of production*.)

Generally, economists divide resources into four broad categories: *land, labor, capital,* and *entrepreneurship*. **Land** includes natural resources, such as minerals, forests, water, and unimproved land. For example, oil, wood, and animals fall into this category. (Sometimes economists refer to this category simply as *natural resources*.)

Labor consists of the physical and mental talents people contribute to the production process. For example, a person building a house is using his or her own labor.

Capital consists of produced goods that can be used as inputs for further production. Factories, machinery, tools, computers, and buildings are examples of capital. One country might have more capital than another. This means that it has more factories, machinery, tools, and so on.

Entrepreneurship refers to the particular talent that some people have for organizing the resources of land, labor, and capital to produce goods, seek new business opportunities, and develop new ways of doing things.

Scarcity and a Definition of Economics

We are now ready to define a key concept in economics: *scarcity*. **Scarcity** is the condition in which our wants (for goods) are greater than the limited resources (land, labor, capital, and entrepreneurship) available to satisfy those wants. In other words, we want goods, but there are just not enough resources available to provide us with all the goods we want.

Look at it this way: Our wants (for goods) are infinite, but our resources (which we need to produce the goods) are finite. Scarcity is our infinite wants hitting up against finite resources.

Many economists say that if scarcity didn't exist, neither would economics. In other words, if our wants weren't greater than the limited resources available to satisfy them, there would be no field of study called economics. This is similar to saying that if matter and

---

Good
Anything from which individuals receive utility or satisfaction.

Utility
The satisfaction one receives from a good.

Bad
Anything from which individuals receive disutility or dissatisfaction.

Disutility
The dissatisfaction one receives from a bad.

Land
All natural resources, such as minerals, forests, water, and unimproved land.

Labor
The physical and mental talents people contribute to the production process.

Capital
Produced goods that can be used as inputs for further production, such as factories, machinery, tools, computers, and buildings.

Entrepreneurship
The particular talent that some people have for organizing the resources of land, labor, and capital to produce goods, seek new business opportunities, and develop new ways of doing things.

Scarcity
The condition in which our wants are greater than the limited resources available to satisfy those wants.

Thinking like
AN ECONOMIST   *The economist says that everyone in the world—no matter how rich—has to face scarcity. But what about Bill Gates, the cofounder of Microsoft and a billionaire? He may be able to satisfy more of his wants for tangible goods (houses, cars) than most people, but this doesn't mean he has the resources to satisfy all his wants. His wants might include more time with his children, more friendship, no disease in the world, peace on earth, and a hundred other things that he does not have the resources to "produce."*

economics 24/7

24

You are going to tell me what I want to know, it's just a matter of how much you want to hurt.

—Jack Bauer

The FOX show *24* is said to be one of the more suspenseful shows on television. The main character of the show, Jack Bauer (Kiefer Sutherland), is a CTU (Counter Terrorism Unit) field agent. His job is to stop whatever impending doom is hanging over the country—such things as nerve gas, a deadly virus being released on the American public, or a nuclear warhead directed at a major American city.

What is it that makes *24* as suspenseful as it is? The answer, we think, has a lot to do with "utility" and "disutility" and the chance of moving from one to the other. Essentially what the writers of *24* do, early in the series, is set up two different worlds for the viewers. The one world is the world of the status quo; it is the world that exists; it is the world where people are receiving utility in their daily lives. The second world—the world that "could be"—is the world where something awful happens, pushing hundreds of thousands, if not millions, of people into disutility. It is the world where the nerve gas has killed hundreds of thousands of people; it is the world where the nuclear warhead kills millions of people in a major American city; it is the world where millions die an excruciatingly painful death as the result of a fatal virus.

Then, after the writers of *24* have shown the audience the two worlds—the good (high-utility) world and the bad (high-disutility) world—they essentially tell the viewer that just one tiny slip-up can be the difference between living in the high-utility world and living in the high-disutility world. Sometimes, it is just a matter of Jack Bauer doing something five seconds earlier (instead of later) that makes the difference between which world we end up living in.

The same kind of suspense holds for things other than TV shows, of course. People who are avid sports fans, for example, will feel very nervous watching their favorite team. That's because who wins the game can mean the difference between utility and disutility for them. If their team wins—utility; if their team loses—disutility. And of course, the closer the two teams are in ability, the greater the suspense is. That's because the closer the two teams are in ability, the smaller the slip-up can be in deciding who wins and who loses.

Will the writers of *24* ever change the basic formula of the show? Probably not. It will most likely always be the same: Good (high-utility) world can turn into bad (high-disutility) world if just the tiniest mistake is made. Thankfully, Jack Bauer is never going to make that tiniest of mistakes.

---

motion didn't exist, neither would physics, or that if living things didn't exist, neither would biology. For this reason, we define **economics** in this text as the science of scarcity. More completely, economics is the science of how individuals and societies deal with the fact that wants are greater than the limited resources available to satisfy those wants.

Economics

The science of scarcity; the science of how individuals and societies deal with the fact that wants are greater than the limited resources available to satisfy those wants.

THINKING IN TERMS OF SCARCITY'S EFFECTS Scarcity has effects. Here are three: (1) the need to make choices, (2) the need for a rationing device, and (3) competition. We describe each.

Choices People have to make choices because of scarcity. Because our unlimited wants are greater than our limited resources, some wants must go unsatisfied. We must choose which wants we will satisfy and which we will not. Jeremy asks: Do I go to Hawaii or do I pay off my car loan earlier? Ellen asks: Do I buy the new sweater or two new shirts?

Rationing Device

A means for deciding who gets what of available resources and goods.

Need for a Rationing Device A **rationing device** is a means of deciding who gets what. Scarcity implies the need for a rationing device. If people have infinite wants for goods and there are only limited resources to produce the goods, then a rationing device must be used to decide who gets the available quantity of goods. Dollar price is a rationing device. For example, there are 100 cars on the lot and everyone wants a new car. How do we decide who gets what quantity of the new cars? The answer is "use the rationing device dollar price." Those people who pay the dollar price for the new car end up with a new car.

Is dollar price a fair rationing device? Doesn't it discriminate against the poor? After all, the poor have fewer dollars than the rich, so the rich can get more of what they want than can the poor. True, dollar price does discriminate against the poor. But then, as the economist knows, every rationing device discriminates against someone.

Suppose that dollar price could not be used as a rationing device tomorrow. Some rationing device would still be necessary because scarcity would still exist. How would we ration gas at the gasoline station, food in the grocery store, or tickets for the Super Bowl? Let's consider some alternatives to dollar price as a rationing device.

Suppose first come, first served is the rationing device. For example, suppose there are only 40,000 Super Bowl tickets. If you are one of the first 40,000 in line for a Super Bowl ticket, then you get a ticket. If you are the 40,001st person in line, you don't. Such a method discriminates against those who can't get in line quickly. What about slow walkers or people with a disability? What about people without cars who can't drive to where the tickets are distributed?

Or suppose brute force is the rationing device. For example, if there are 40,000 Super Bowl tickets, then as long as you can take a ticket away from someone who has a ticket, the ticket is yours. Who does this rationing method discriminate against? Obviously, it discriminates against the weak.

Or suppose beauty is the rationing device. The more beautiful you are, the better your chance of getting a Super Bowl ticket. Again, the rationing device discriminates against someone.

These and many other alternatives to dollar price could be used as a rationing device. However, each discriminates against someone, and none is clearly superior to dollar price.

In addition, if first come, first served, brute force, beauty, or another alternative to dollar price is the rationing device, what incentive would the producer of a good have to produce the good? With dollar price as a rationing device, a person produces computers and sells them for money. He then takes the money and buys what he wants. But if the rationing device were, say, brute force, he would not have an incentive to produce. Why produce anything when someone will end up taking it away from you? In short, in a world where dollar price isn't the rationing device, people are likely to produce much less than in a world where dollar price is the rationing device.

Scarcity and Competition Do you see much competition in the world today? Are people competing for jobs? Are states and cities competing for businesses? Are students competing for grades? The answer to all these questions is yes. The economist wants to know why this competition exists and what form it takes. First, the economist concludes, *competition exists because of scarcity.* If there were enough resources to satisfy all our seemingly unlimited wants, people would not have to compete for the available but limited resources.

Second, the economist sees that competition takes the form of people trying to get more of the rationing device. If dollar price is the rationing device, people will compete to earn dollars. Look at your own case. You are a college student working for a degree. One reason (but perhaps not the only reason) you are attending college is to earn a higher income after graduation. But why do you want a higher income? You want it because it will allow you to satisfy more of your wants.

Suppose muscular strength (measured by lifting weights) were the rationing device instead of dollar price. People with more muscular strength would receive more resources and goods than people with less muscular strength would receive. In this situation, people would compete for muscular strength. (Would they spend more time at the gym lifting weights?) The lesson is simple: *Whatever the rationing device, people will compete for it.*

SELF-TEST

(Answers to Self-Test questions are in the Self-Test Appendix.)

1. Scarcity is the condition of finite resources. True or false? Explain your answer.

2. How does competition arise out of scarcity?

3. How does choice arise out of scarcity?

Key Concepts in Economics

There are numerous key concepts in economics—concepts that define the field. We discuss a few of these concepts next.

Opportunity Cost

As noted earlier, people must make choices because scarcity exists. Because our seemingly unlimited wants push up against limited resources, some wants must go unsatisfied. We must therefore *choose* which wants we will satisfy and which we will not. The most highly valued opportunity or alternative forfeited when a choice is made is known as **opportunity cost**. Every time you make a choice, you incur an opportunity cost. For example, you have chosen to read this chapter. In making this choice, you denied yourself the benefits of doing something else. You could have watched television, e-mailed a friend, taken a nap, eaten a few slices of pizza, read a novel, shopped for a new computer, and so on. Whatever you *would have chosen* to do had you decided not to read this chapter is the opportunity cost of your reading this chapter. For example, if you would have watched television had you chosen not to read this chapter—if this was your next best alternative—then the opportunity cost of reading this chapter is watching television.

OPPORTUNITY COST AND BEHAVIOR Economists believe that a change in opportunity cost will change a person's behavior. For example, consider Bill, who is a sophomore at the University of Kansas. He attends classes Monday through Thursday of every week. Every time he chooses to go to class, he gives up the opportunity to do something else, such as the opportunity to earn $8 an hour working at a job. The opportunity cost of Bill spending an hour in class is $8.

Now let's raise the opportunity cost of attending class. On Tuesday, we offer Bill $70 to skip his economics class. He knows that if he attends his economics class, he will forfeit $70. What will Bill do? An economist would predict that as the opportunity cost of attending class increases relative to the benefits of attending class, Bill is less likely to attend class.

Opportunity Cost
The most highly valued opportunity or alternative forfeited when a choice is made.

Thinking like **AN ECONOMIST** *Economists are fond of saying that there is no such thing as a free lunch. This catchy phrase expresses the idea that opportunity costs are incurred when choices are made. Perhaps this is an obvious point, but consider how often people mistakenly assume there is a free lunch. For example, some parents think education is free because they do not pay tuition for their children to attend public elementary school. Sorry, but there is no such thing as a free lunch. Free implies no sacrifice, no opportunities forfeited, which is not true in regard to elementary school education. Resources that could be used for other things are used to provide elementary school education.*

Consider the people who speak about free medical care, free housing, free bridges ("there is no charge to cross it"), and free parks. None of these is actually free. The resources that provide medical care, housing, bridges, and parks could have been used in other ways.

economics 24/7

WHY LEBRON JAMES ISN'T IN COLLEGE

LeBron James was born on December 30, 1984. So, he is currently the age of many people attending college. But LeBron James is not attending college. He went directly from high school into the NBA. He is currently playing professional basketball.

Why isn't LeBron James in college? It's not because he cannot afford the tuition charged at most colleges. Also, it's not because he wouldn't be admitted to any college. LeBron James is not in college because it is more expensive for him than it is for most 18- to 25-year-olds to attend college.

To understand, think of what it costs you to attend college. If you pay $1,000 tuition a semester for eight semesters, the full tuition amounts to $8,000. However, $8,000 is not the full cost of your attending college because if you were not a student, you could be earning income working at a job. For example, you could be working at a full-time job earning $25,000 annually. Certainly, this $25,000, or at least part of it if you are currently working part time, is forfeited because you attend college. It is part of the cost of your attending college.

Thus, the *tuition cost* may be the same for everyone who attends your college, but the *opportunity cost* is not. Some people have higher opportunity costs for attending college

than others do. LeBron James has extremely high opportunity costs for attending college. He would have to give up the millions of dollars he earns playing professional basketball and endorsing products if he were to attend college on a full-time basis.

This discussion illustrates two related points made in this chapter. First, *the higher the opportunity cost of doing something, the less likely it will be done.* The opportunity cost of attending college is higher for LeBron than it (probably) is for you, and that is why you are in college and LeBron James is not.

Second, according to economists, *individuals think and act in terms of costs and benefits and only undertake actions if they expect the benefits to outweigh the costs.* LeBron James is likely to see certain benefits to attending college—just as you see certain benefits to attending college. However, those benefits are insufficient for him to attend college because benefits are not all that matter. Costs matter too. For LeBron James, the costs of attending college are much higher than the benefits, and so he chooses not to attend college. In your case, the benefits are higher than the costs, and so you have decided to attend college.

This is how economists think about behavior, whether it is Bill's or your own. *The higher the opportunity cost of doing something, the less likely it will be done.* This is part of the economic way of thinking.

Before you continue, look at Exhibit 1, which summarizes some of the things about scarcity, choice, and opportunity cost up to this point.

Benefits and Costs

If it were possible to eliminate air pollution completely, should all air pollution be eliminated? If your answer is yes, then you are probably focusing on the *benefits* of eliminating air pollution. For example, one benefit might be healthier individuals. Certainly, individuals who do not breathe polluted air have fewer lung disorders than people who do breathe polluted air.

But benefits rarely come without costs. The economist reminds us that while there are benefits to eliminating pollution, there are costs too. To illustrate, one way to eliminate all car pollution tomorrow is to pass a law stating that anyone caught driving a car

© BRAND X PICTURES / JUPITER IMAGES

economics 24/7

THE COSTS AND BENEFITS OF ATTENDING CLASS

Do you attend every single class in college? Probably, there are some days when you do not. For example, you might be sick one day and thus choose not to attend class. But are there days when you are well and could attend class but choose not to? If so, do you pick these days to be absent from class randomly? We think not. We think it has to do with the costs and benefits of attending class.

In southern California, some students choose not to attend class when the surf is particularly good. In other words, the benefits of going to class that day may be just as high as going any other day, but the costs—the opportunity costs—on that particular day are higher. That's because it is a particularly good day for surfing. In other words, the opportunity cost of going to class when the surf is good might be much higher for a surfing enthusiast on this particular day. If the opportunity costs are high enough on this day, they may just be greater than the benefits of going to class, and so the student chooses not to go to class but to surf instead.

Think of costs and benefits in dollar terms for the surfer. Usually, the surfer sees the benefits of going to class as equal to $40 and the costs as equal to $30. In other words, there is a net benefit of going to class, or benefits are greater than costs, and so he goes to class. But when the surf is good, the cost rises from $30 to $55. Now the costs of going to class are greater than the benefits—there is a net cost to attending class—and so he chooses to not attend class.

will go to prison for 40 years. With such a law in place, and enforced, very few people would drive cars, and all car pollution would be a thing of the past. Presto! Cleaner air! However, many people would think that the cost of obtaining that cleaner air is too high. Someone might say, "I want cleaner air, but not if I have to completely give up driving my car. How will I get to work?"

What distinguishes the economist from the noneconomist is that the economist thinks in terms of *both* costs *and* benefits. Often, the noneconomist thinks in terms of one or the other. There are benefits from studying, but there are costs too. There are benefits from coming to class, but there are costs too. There are costs to getting up early each morning and exercising, but let's not forget that there are benefits too.

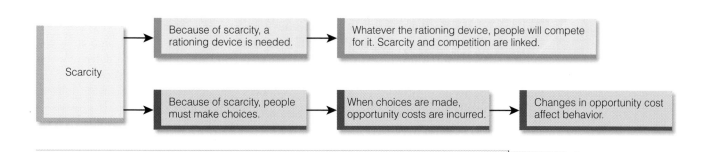

exhibit **1**

Scarcity and Related Concepts

Decisions Made at the Margin

It is late at night and you have already studied three hours for your biology test tomorrow. You look at the clock and wonder if you should study another hour. How would you summarize your thinking process? What question or questions do you ask yourself to decide whether or not to study another hour?

Perhaps without knowing it, you think in terms of the costs and benefits of further study. You probably realize that there are certain benefits from studying an additional hour (you may be able to raise your grade a few points), but there are costs too (you will get less sleep or have less time to watch television or talk on the phone with a friend). Thinking in terms of costs and benefits, though, doesn't tell us *how* you think in terms of costs and benefits. For example, when deciding what to do, do you look at the total costs and total benefits of the proposed action, or do you look at something less than the total costs and benefits? According to economists, for most decisions, you think in terms of *additional*, or *marginal*, costs and benefits, not *total* costs and benefits. That's because most decisions deal with making a small, or additional, change.

To illustrate, suppose you just finished eating a hamburger and drinking a soda for lunch. You are still a little hungry and are considering whether or not to order another hamburger. An economist would say that in deciding whether or not to order another hamburger, you will compare the additional benefits of the additional hamburger to the additional costs of the additional hamburger. In economics, the word *marginal* is a synonym for *additional*. So we say that you will compare the **marginal benefits** of the (next) hamburger to the **marginal costs** of the (next) hamburger. If the marginal benefits are greater than the marginal costs, you obviously expect a net benefit to ordering the next hamburger, and therefore, you order the next hamburger. If, however, the marginal costs of the hamburger are greater than the marginal benefits, you obviously expect a net cost to ordering the next hamburger, and therefore, you do not order the next hamburger.

What you don't consider when making this decision are the total benefits and total costs of hamburgers. That's because the benefits and costs connected with the first hamburger (the one you have already eaten) are no longer relevant to the current decision. You are not deciding between eating two hamburgers and eating no hamburgers; your decision is whether to eat a second hamburger after you have already eaten a first hamburger.

According to economists, when individuals make decisions by comparing marginal benefits to marginal costs, they are making **decisions at the margin**. The president of the United States makes a decision at the margin when deciding whether or not to talk another 10 minutes with the speaker of the House of Representatives, the employee makes a decision at the margin when deciding whether or not to work two hours overtime, and the college professor makes a decision at the margin when deciding whether or not to put an additional question on the final exam.

Efficiency

What is the right amount of time to study for a test? In economics, the "right amount" of anything is the "optimal" or "efficient" amount, and the efficient amount is the amount for which the marginal benefits equal the marginal costs. Stated differently, you have achieved **efficiency** when the marginal benefits equal the marginal costs.

Suppose you are studying for an economics test, and for the first hour of studying, the marginal benefits *(MB)* are greater than the marginal costs *(MC):*

$$MB \text{ studying first hour} > MC \text{ studying first hour}$$

Given this condition, you will certainly study for the first hour. After all, it is worthwhile: The additional benefits are greater than the additional costs, so there is a net benefit to studying.

Marginal Benefits

Additional benefits. The benefits connected to consuming an additional unit of a good or undertaking one more unit of an activity.

Marginal Costs

Additional costs. The costs connected to consuming an additional unit of a good or undertaking one more unit of an activity.

Decisions at the Margin

Decision making characterized by weighing the additional (marginal) benefits of a change against the additional (marginal) costs of a change with respect to current conditions.

Efficiency

Exists when marginal benefits equal marginal costs.

Suppose for the second hour of studying, the marginal benefits are still greater than the marginal costs:

MB studying second hour > *MC* studying second hour

You will study for the second hour because the additional benefits are still greater than the additional costs. In other words, it is worthwhile studying the second hour. In fact, you will continue to study as long as the marginal benefits are greater than the marginal costs. Exhibit 2 graphically illustrates this discussion.

The marginal benefit *(MB)* curve of studying is downward sloping because we have assumed that the benefits of studying for the first hour are greater than the benefits of studying for the second hour and so on. The marginal cost *(MC)* curve of studying is upward sloping because we assume that it costs a person more (in terms of goods forfeited) to study the second hour than the first, more to study the third than the second, and so on. (If we assume the additional costs of studying are constant over time, the *MC* curve is horizontal.)

In the exhibit, the marginal benefits of studying equal the marginal costs at three hours. So three hours is the efficient length of time to study in this situation. At fewer than three hours, the marginal benefits of studying are greater than the marginal costs; thus, at all these hours, there are net benefits from studying. At more than three hours, the marginal costs of studying are greater than the marginal benefits, and so it wouldn't be worthwhile to study beyond three hours.

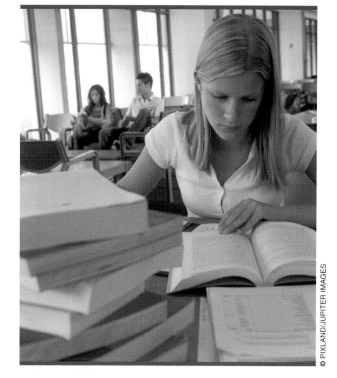

MAXIMIZING NET BENEFITS Take another look at Exhibit 2. Suppose you had stopped studying after the first hour (or after the 60th minute). Would you have given up anything? Yes, you would have given up the net benefits of studying longer. To illustrate, notice that between the first and the second hour, the marginal benefits curve (blue curve) lies above the marginal costs curve (red curve). This means there are net benefits to studying the second hour. But if you hadn't studied that second hour—if you had

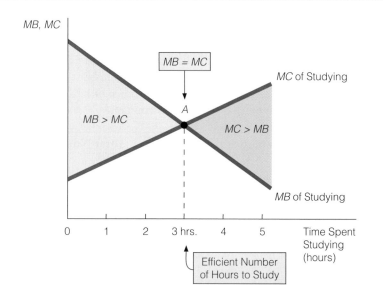

exhibit **2**

Efficiency

MB = marginal benefits and *MC* = marginal costs. In the exhibit, the *MB* curve of studying is downward sloping and the *MC* curve of studying is upward sloping. As long as *MB* > *MC*, the person will study. The person stops studying when *MB* = *MC*. This is where efficiency is achieved.

Does a person have to know about marginal costs and marginal benefits before he or she can achieve efficiency?

There may be people who do not know the definition of marginal cost and marginal benefit, but this doesn't prevent them from achieving efficiency in much the same way that a person who doesn't know much about how a car works can still drive a car. All the person has to "sense" is whether or not doing more of something comes with greater benefits than costs. As long as a person can do this—and there is plenty of evidence that people do this as naturally as they breathe air or walk—then efficiency can be achieved.

stopped after the first hour—then you would have given up the opportunity to collect those net benefits. (That's like leaving a $10 bill on the sidewalk.) The same analysis holds for the third hour. We conclude that by studying three hours (but not one minute longer), you have maximized net benefits. In short, efficiency (which is consistent with $MB = MC$) is also consistent with maximizing net benefits.

Unintended Effects

Has anything turned out differently from what you intended? No doubt, you can provide numerous examples. Economists think in terms of unintended effects. Consider an example. Andres, 16 years old, currently works after school at a grocery store. He earns $6.50 an hour. Suppose the state legislature passes a law specifying that the minimum dollar wage a person can be paid to do a job is $8.50 an hour. The legislators' intention in passing the law is to help people like Andres earn more income.

Will the $8.50 an hour legislation have the intended effect? Perhaps not. The manager of the grocery store may not find it worthwhile to continue employing Andres if she has to pay him $8.50 an hour. In other words, Andres may have a job at $6.50 an hour but not at $8.50 an hour. If the law specifies that no one will earn less than $8.50 an hour and the manager of the grocery store decides to fire Andres rather than pay this amount, then an unintended effect of the $8.50 an hour legislation is Andres' losing his job.

As another example, let's analyze mandatory seatbelt laws to see if they have any unintended effects. Many states have laws that require drivers to wear seatbelts. The intended effect is to reduce the number of car fatalities by making it more likely drivers will survive an accident.

Could these laws have an unintended effect? Some economists think so. They look at accident fatalities in terms of this equation:

Total number of fatalities = Number of accidents × Fatalities per accident

For example, if there are 200,000 accidents and 0.10 fatalities per accident, the total number of fatalities is 20,000.

The objective of a mandatory seatbelt program is to reduce the total number of fatalities by reducing the fatalities per accident. Many studies have found that wearing seatbelts does just this. If you are in an accident, you have a better chance of not being killed if you are wearing a seatbelt.

Let's assume that with seatbelts, there are 0.08 instead of 0.10 fatalities per accident. If there are still 200,000 accidents, this means that the total number of fatalities falls from 20,000 to 16,000. Thus, there is a drop in the total number of fatalities if fatalities per accident are reduced and the number of accidents is constant.

Number of Accidents	Fatalities per Accident	Total Number of Fatalities
200,000	0.10	20,000
200,000	0.08	16,000

However, some economists wonder if the number of accidents stays constant. Specifically, they suggest that seatbelts may have an unintended effect: *The number of accidents may increase.* This happens because wearing seatbelts may make drivers feel safer. Feeling safer may cause them to take chances that they wouldn't ordinarily take—such as driving faster or more aggressively, or concentrating less on their driving and more on

economics 24/7

WHY DID THE BRITISH SOLDIERS WEAR RED UNIFORMS?

When George Washington and the colonists fought the British, the colonists were dressed in rags, while the British troops were clad in fine bright red uniforms. Commenting on this difference, people often say, "The British were foolish to have worn bright red uniforms. You could see them coming for miles."

Economists would not be so quick to label the British as foolish. Instead, they would ask why the British troops wore bright red. For instance, David Friedman, an economist, thinks it is odd that the British, who at the time were the greatest fighting force in the world, would make such a seemingly obvious mistake. He has an alternative explanation, an economic explanation.

Friedman reasons that the British generals did not want their men to break ranks and desert because winning the war would be hard, if not impossible, if a lot of men deserted. Thus, the generals had to think up a way to make the opportunity cost of desertion high for their soldiers. The generals reasoned that the higher the cost of desertion, the fewer deserters there would be. The British generals effectively told their soldiers that if they deserted, they would have to forfeit their freedom or their lives.

Of course, the problem is that a stiff penalty is not effective if deserters cannot be found. Therefore, the generals had to make it easy to find deserters, which they did by dressing them in bright red uniforms. Certainly, it was possible for a deserter to throw off his uniform and walk through the countryside in his underwear alone, but in the harsh winters of New England, doing so would guarantee death. He had almost no choice but to wear the bright red uniform.

the music on the radio. For example, if the number of accidents rises to 250,000, then the total number of fatalities is 20,000.

Number of Accidents	Fatalities per Accident	Total Number of Fatalities
200,000	0.10	20,000
250,000	0.08	20,000

We conclude the following: If a mandatory seatbelt law reduces the number of fatalities (intended effect) but increases the number of accidents (unintended effect), it may, contrary to popular belief, not reduce the total number of fatalities. In fact, some economic studies show just this.

What does all this mean for you? You may be safer if you know that this unintended effect exists and you adjust accordingly. To be specific, when you wear your seatbelt, your chances of getting hurt in a car accident are less than if you don't wear your seatbelt. But if this added sense of protection causes you to drive less carefully than you would otherwise, then you could unintentionally offset the measure of protection your seatbelt provides. To reduce the probability of hurting yourself and others in a car accident, *the best policy is to wear a seatbelt and to drive as carefully as you would if you weren't wearing a seatbelt.* Knowing about the unintended effect of wearing your seatbelt could save your life

Exchange

Exchange or **trade** is the process of giving up one thing for something else. Economics is sometimes called the "science of exchange" because so much that is discussed in economics has to do with exchange.

Exchange (Trade)
The process of giving up one thing for another.

We start with a basic question: Why do people enter into exchanges? The answer is that they do so to make themselves better off. When a person voluntarily trades $100 for a jacket, she is saying, "I prefer to have the jacket instead of the $100." And of course, when the seller of the jacket voluntarily sells the jacket for $100, he is saying, "I prefer to have the $100 instead of the jacket." In short, through trade or exchange, each person gives up something he or she values less for something he or she values more.

You can think of trade in terms of utility or satisfaction. Imagine a utility scale that goes from 1 to 10, with 10 being the highest utility you can achieve. Now suppose you currently have $40 in your wallet and you are at 7 on the utility scale. A few minutes later, you are in a store looking at some new CDs. The price of each is $10. You end up buying four CDs for $40.

Before you made the trade, you were at 7 on the utility scale. Are you still at 7 on the utility scale after you traded your $40 for the four CDs? The likely answer is no. If you expected to have the same utility after the trade as you did before, it is unlikely you would have traded your $40 for the four CDs. The only reason you entered into the trade is that you *expected* to be better off after the trade than you were before the trade. In other words, you thought trading your $40 for the four CDs would move you up the utility scale from 7 to, say, 8.

SELF-TEST

1. Give an example to illustrate how a change in opportunity cost can affect behavior.

2. There are both costs and benefits of studying. If you continue to study (say, for a test) as long as the marginal benefits of studying are greater than the marginal costs and stop studying when the two are equal, will your action be consistent with having maximized the net benefits of studying? Explain your answer.

3. You stay up an added hour to study for a test. The intended effect is to raise your test grade. What might be an unintended effect of staying up an added hour to study for the test?

Economic Categories

Economics is sometimes broken down into different categories according to the type of questions economists ask. Four common economic categories are positive economics, normative economics, microeconomics, and macroeconomics.

Positive and Normative Economics

Positive Economics
The study of "what is" in economic matters.

Normative Economics
The study of "what should be" in economic matters.

Positive economics attempts to determine *what is*. **Normative economics** addresses *what should be*. Essentially, positive economics deals with cause-effect relationships that can be tested. Normative economics deals with value judgments and opinions that cannot be tested.

Many topics in economics can be discussed within both a positive framework and a normative framework. Consider a proposed cut in federal income taxes. An economist practicing positive economics would want to know the *effect* of a cut in income taxes. For example, she may want to know how a tax cut will affect the unemployment rate, economic growth, inflation, and so on. An economist practicing normative economics would address issues that directly or indirectly relate to whether the federal income tax *should* be cut. For example, she may say that federal income taxes should be cut because the income tax burden on many taxpayers is currently high.

This book mainly deals with positive economics. For the most part, we discuss the economic world as it is, not the way someone might think it should be. Keep in mind, too, that no matter what your normative objectives are, positive economics can shed some light on how they might be accomplished. For example, suppose you believe that absolute poverty should be eliminated and the unemployment rate should be lowered. No doubt you have ideas as to how these goals can be accomplished. But will your ideas work? For example, will a greater redistribution of income eliminate absolute poverty? Will lowering taxes lower the unemployment rate? There is no guarantee that the means you think will bring about certain ends will do so. This is where sound positive economics can help. It helps us see what is. As someone once said, "It is not enough to want to do good; it is important also to know how to do good."

Microeconomics and Macroeconomics

It has been said that the tools of microeconomics are microscopes, and the tools of macroeconomics are telescopes. Macroeconomics stands back from the trees to see the forest. Microeconomics gets up close and examines the tree itself, its bark, its limbs, and its roots. **Microeconomics** is the branch of economics that deals with human behavior and choices as they relate to relatively small units—an individual, a firm, an industry, a

Microeconomics
The branch of economics that deals with human behavior and choices as they relate to relatively small units—an individual, a firm, an industry, a single market.

A Reader Asks...

What's in Store for an Economics Major?

This is my first course in economics. The material is interesting, and I have given some thought to majoring in economics. Please tell me something about the major and about job prospects for an economics graduate. What courses do economics majors take? What is the starting salary of economics graduates? Do the people who run large companies think highly of people who have majored in economics?

If you major in economics, you will certainly not be alone. Economics is one of the top three majors at Harvard, Brown, Yale, the University of California at Berkeley, Princeton, Columbia, Cornell, Dartmouth, and Stanford. U.S. colleges and universities awarded 16,141 degrees to economics majors in the 2003–2004 academic year, which was up nearly 40 percent from five years earlier. The popularity of economics is probably based on two major reasons. First, many people find economics an interesting course of study. Second, what you learn in an economics course is relevant and applicable to the real world.

Do executives who run successful companies think highly of economics majors? Well, a *BusinessWeek* survey found that economics was the second favorite undergraduate major of chief executive officers (CEOs)

of major corporations. Engineering was their favorite undergraduate major.

An economics major usually takes a wide variety of economics courses, starting with introductory courses—principles of microeconomics and principles of macroeconomics—and then studying intermediate microeconomics and intermediate macroeconomics. Upper division electives usually include such courses as public finance, international economics, law and economics, managerial economics, labor economics, health economics, money and banking, environmental economics, and more.

According to the National Association of Colleges and Employers Salary Survey in Spring 2004, the average starting salary for a college graduate in economics was $43,000. For a college graduate in business administration, the average starting salary was $36,515, and for a college graduate in computer science, the average starting salary was $46,536. Also, according to the Economics and Statistics Administration of the U.S. Department of Justice, economics undergraduates have relatively higher average annual salaries than students who have majored in other fields. Specifically, of 14 different majors, economics majors ranked third. Only persons with bachelor's degrees in engineering or agriculture/forestry had higher average annual salaries.

Macroeconomics
The branch of economics that deals with human behavior and choices as they relate to highly aggregate markets (e.g., the goods and services market) or the entire economy.

single market. **Macroeconomics** is the branch of economics that deals with human behavior and choices as they relate to an entire economy. In microeconomics, economists discuss a single price; in macroeconomics, they discuss the price level. Microeconomics deals with the demand for a particular good or service; macroeconomics deals with aggregate, or total, demand for goods and services. Microeconomics examines how a tax change affects a single firm's output; macroeconomics looks at how a tax change affects an entire economy's output.

Microeconomists and macroeconomists ask different types of questions. A microeconomist might be interested in answering such questions as:

- How does a market work?
- What level of output does a firm produce?
- What price does a firm charge for the good it produces?
- How does a consumer determine how much of a good he or she will buy?
- Can government policy affect business behavior?
- Can government policy affect consumer behavior?

On the other hand, a macroeconomist might be interested in answering such questions as:

- How does the economy work?
- Why is the unemployment rate sometimes high and sometimes low?
- What causes inflation?
- Why do some national economies grow faster than other national economies?
- What might cause interest rates to be low one year and high the next?
- How do changes in the money supply affect the economy?
- How do changes in government spending and taxes affect the economy?

! analyzing the scene

Is Jackie more likely to miss some classes than she is to miss other classes? What determines which classes Jackie will attend and which classes she won't attend?

The lower the cost of not attending class, the more likely Jackie will not attend. On this particular day, Jackie is fairly sure that "her professor will be discussing a subject she already knows well." Therefore, the cost of missing this class is probably lower than missing, say, a class where the professor will be discussing an unfamiliar subject or a class in which a midterm exam will be given. Not all classes are alike for Jackie because the cost of attending each class isn't the same.

What does a basic economic fact have to do with Stephanie's buying two books at her campus bookstore?

Stephanie uses money to buy the two books. She pays the dollar price of each book. But what is dollar price? It is a rationing device. And why do we need rationing devices in

society? Because scarcity—a basic economic fact—exists. Both Stephanie *and* the long shadow of scarcity are together in the campus bookstore.

Does whether or not Jackie will go on to get a master's degree have anything to do with economics?

Jackie is undecided about whether or not she will pursue a master's degree. When she says she is not sure she wants it enough, she is really thinking about the costs and benefits of getting a master's degree. The benefits of getting the degree relate to (1) how much higher her annual income will be with a master's degree than without it, (2) how much she enjoys studying history, and so on. The costs relate to (1) the income she will lose while she is at graduate school working on a master's degree, (2) the less leisure time she will enjoy during the time she is studying, writing papers, and attending classes, (3) the tuition costs of the program, and so on. Are the benefits greater than the costs, or are the costs greater than the benefits? Jackie is thinking through an economic calculation, although she may know nothing about economics.

Stephanie stopped studying at 9:00 P.M. Would she have been better off if she had studied 30 more minutes?

Stephanie stopped studying after three hours. Studying for 30 more minutes might have provided some benefits for Stephanie, but she also would have incurred some costs.

Remember, Stephanie considers both the benefits *and* the costs of studying for 30 more minutes. If the costs are greater than the benefits, Stephanie is better off *not* studying for 30 more minutes. Stephanie likely believes she has studied the efficient amount of time—the amount of time at which the marginal benefits of studying equal the marginal costs of studying. It is possible to study too much ($MC > MB$), too little ($MB > MC$), or just the right amount ($MB = MC$).

chapter summary

Goods, Bads, and Resources

- A good is anything that gives a person utility or satisfaction.
- A bad is anything that gives a person disutility or dissatisfaction.
- Economists divide resources into four categories: land, labor, capital, and entrepreneurship.
- Land includes natural resources, such as minerals, forests, water, and unimproved land.
- Labor refers to the physical and mental talents that people contribute to the production process.
- Capital consists of produced goods that can be used as inputs for further production, such as machinery, tools, computers, trucks, buildings, and factories.
- Entrepreneurship refers to the particular talent that some people have for organizing the resources of land, labor, and capital to produce goods, seek new business opportunities, and develop new ways of doing things.

Scarcity

- Scarcity is the condition in which our wants are greater than the limited resources available to satisfy them.
- Scarcity implies choice. In a world of limited resources, we must choose which wants will be satisfied and which will go unsatisfied.
- Because of scarcity, there is a need for a rationing device. A rationing device is a means of deciding who gets what quantities of the available resources and goods.
- Scarcity implies competition. If there were enough resources to satisfy all our seemingly unlimited wants, people would not have to compete for the available but limited resources.

Opportunity Cost

- Every time a person makes a choice, he or she incurs an opportunity cost. Opportunity cost is the most highly valued opportunity or alternative forfeited when a choice is made. The higher the opportunity cost of doing something, the less likely it will be done.

Costs and Benefits

- What distinguishes the economist from the noneconomist is that the economist thinks in terms of *both* costs and benefits. Asked what the benefits of taking a walk may be, an economist will also mention the costs of taking a walk. Asked what the costs of studying are, an economist will also point out the benefits of studying.

Decisions Made at the Margin

- Marginal benefits and costs are not the same as total benefits and costs. When deciding whether to talk on the phone one more minute, an individual would not consider the total benefits and total costs of speaking on the phone. Instead, the individual would compare only the marginal benefits (additional benefits) of talking on the phone one more minute to the marginal costs (additional costs) of talking on the phone one more minute.

Efficiency

- As long as the marginal benefits of an activity are greater than its marginal costs, a person gains by continuing to do the activity—whether the activity is studying, running, eating, or watching television. The net benefits of an activity are maximized when the marginal benefits of the activity equal its marginal costs. Efficiency exists at this point.

Unintended Effects

- Economists often think in terms of causes and effects. Effects may include both intended effects and unintended effects. Economists want to denote both types of effects when speaking of effects in general.

Exchange

- Exchange or trade is the process of giving up one thing for something else. People enter into exchanges to make themselves better off.

Economic Categories

- Positive economics attempts to determine what is; normative economics addresses what should be.

- Microeconomics deals with human behavior and choices as they relate to relatively small units—an individual, a firm, an industry, a single market. Macroeconomics deals with human behavior and choices as they relate to an entire economy.

key terms and concepts

Good	Capital	Marginal Benefits	Positive Economics
Utility	Entrepreneurship	Marginal Costs	Normative Economics
Bad	Scarcity	Decisions at the Margin	Microeconomics
Disutility	Economics	Efficiency	Macroeconomics
Land	Rationing Device	Exchange (Trade)	
Labor	Opportunity Cost		

questions and problems

1   The United States is considered a rich country because Americans can choose from an abundance of goods and services. How can there be scarcity in a land of abundance?

2   Give two examples for each of the following: (a) an intangible good, (b) a tangible good, (c) a bad.

3   What is the difference between the resource labor and the resource entrepreneurship?

4   Explain the link between scarcity and each of the following: (a) choice, (b) opportunity cost, (c) the need for a rationing device, (d) competition.

5   Is it possible for a person to incur an opportunity cost without spending any money? Explain.

6   Discuss the opportunity costs of attending college for four years. Is college more or less costly than you thought it was? Explain.

7   Explain the relationship between changes in opportunity cost and changes in behavior.

8   Smith says that we should eliminate all pollution in the world. Jones disagrees. Who is more likely to be an economist, Smith or Jones? Explain your answer.

9   A layperson says that a proposed government project simply costs too much and therefore shouldn't be undertaken. How might an economist's evaluation be different?

10 Economists say that individuals make decisions at the margin. What does this mean?

11 How would an economist define the efficient amount of time spent playing tennis?

12 A change in X will lead to a change in Y; the predicted change is desirable, so we should change X. Do you agree or disagree? Explain.

13 Why do people enter into exchanges?

14 What is the difference between positive economics and normative economics? between microeconomics and macroeconomics?

Working with Diagrams

A picture is worth a thousand words. With this familiar saying in mind, economists construct their diagrams or graphs. With a few lines and a few points, much can be conveyed.

Two-Variable Diagrams

Most of the diagrams in this book represent the relationship between two variables. Economists compare two variables to see how a change in one variable affects the other variable.

Suppose our two variables of interest are *consumption* and *income*. We want to show how consumption changes as income changes. Suppose we collect the data in Table 1. By simply looking at the data in the first two columns, we can see that as income rises (column 1), consumption rises (column 2). Suppose we want to show the relationship between income and consumption on a graph. We could place *income* on the horizontal axis, as in Exhibit 1, and *consumption* on the vertical axis. Point *A* represents income of $0 and consumption of $60, point *B* represents income of $100 and consumption of $120, and so on. If we draw a straight line through the various points we have plotted, we have a picture of the relationship between income and consumption, based on the data we collected.

Notice that our line in Exhibit 1 slopes upward from left to right. Thus, as income rises, so does consumption. For example, as you move from point *A* to point *B*, income rises from $0 to $100 and consumption rises from $60 to $120. The line in Exhibit 1 also shows that as income falls, so does consumption. For example, as you move from point *C* to point *B*, income falls from $200 to $100 and consumption falls from $180 to $120. When two variables—such as consumption and income—change in the same way, they are said to be **directly related**.

Now let's take a look at the data in Table 2. Our two variables are *price of compact discs (CDs)* and *quantity demanded of CDs*. By simply looking at the data in the first two columns, we see that as price falls (column 1), quantity demanded rises (column 2). Suppose we want to plot these data. We could place *price* (of CDs) on the vertical axis, as in

exhibit 1

A Two-Variable Diagram Representing a Direct Relationship

In this exhibit, we have plotted the data in Table 1 and then connected the points with a straight line. The data represent a direct relationship: as one variable (say, income) rises, the other variable (consumption) rises too.

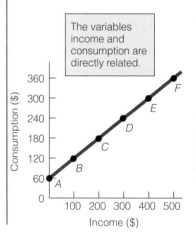

The variables income and consumption are directly related.

Directly Related

Two variables are directly related if they change in the same way.

table 1

(1) When Income Is:	(2) Consumption Is:	(3) Point
$ 0	$ 60	A
100	120	B
200	180	C
300	240	D
400	300	E
500	360	F

(1) When Price of CDs Is:	(2) Quanity Demanded of CDs Is:	(3) Point
$20	100	A
18	120	B
16	140	C
14	160	D
12	180	E

Exhibit 2, and *quantity demanded* (of CDs) on the horizontal axis. Point *A* represents a price of $20 and a quantity demanded of 100, point *B* represents a price of $18 and a quantity demanded of 120, and so on. If we draw a straight line through the various points we have plotted, we have a picture of the relationship between price and quantity demanded, based on the data in Table 2.

Notice that as price falls, quantity demanded rises. For example, as price falls from $20 to $18, quantity demanded rises from 100 to 120. Also as price rises, quantity demanded falls. For example, when price rises from $12 to $14, quantity demanded falls from 180 to 160.

When two variables—such as price and quantity demanded—change in opposite ways, they are said to be **inversely related**.

Inversely Related

Two variables are inversely related if they change in opposite ways.

Independent

Two variables are independent if as one changes, the other does not.

Slope

The ratio of the change in the variable on the vertical axis to the change in the variable on the horizontal axis.

As you have seen so far, variables may be directly related (when one increases, the other also increases), or they may be inversely related (when one increases, the other decreases). Variables can also be **independent** of each other. This condition exists if as one variable changes, the other does not.

In Exhibit 3(a), as the *X* variable rises, the *Y* variable remains the same (at 20). Obviously, the *X* and *Y* variables are independent of each other: as one changes, the other does not.

In Exhibit 3(b), as the *Y* variable rises, the *X* variable remains the same (at 30). Again, we conclude that the *X* and *Y* variables are independent of each other: as one changes, the other does not.

Slope of a Line

It is often important not only to know *how* two variables are related but also to know *how much* one variable changes as the other variable changes. To find out, we need only calculate the slope of the line. The **slope** is the ratio of the change in the variable on the vertical axis to the change in the variable on the horizontal axis. For example, if *Y* is on the vertical axis and *X* on the horizontal axis, the slope is equal to $\Delta Y/\Delta X$. (The symbol "Δ" means "change in.")

$$\text{Slope} = \frac{\Delta Y}{\Delta X}$$

Exhibit 4 shows four lines. In each case, we have calculated the slope. After studying (a)–(d), see if you can calculate the slope in each case.

Slope of a Line Is Constant

Look again at the line in Exhibit 4(a). We computed the slope between points *A* and *B* and found it to be -1. Suppose that instead of computing the slope between points *A* and *B*, we had computed the slope between points *B* and *C* or between points *C* and *D*.

A Two-Variable Diagram Representing an Inverse Relationship

In this exhibit, we have plotted the data in Table 2 and then connected the points with a straight line. The data represent an inverse relationship: as one variable (price) falls, the other variable (quantity demanded) rises.

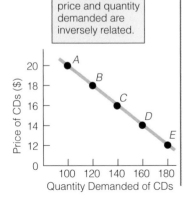

The variables price and quantity demanded are inversely related.

exhibit **3**

Two Diagrams Representing
Independence Between Two Variables

In (a) and (b), the variables X and Y
are independent: as one changes,
the other does not.

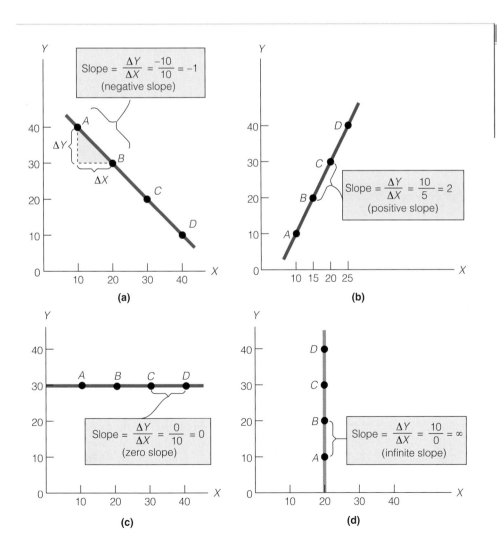

exhibit **4**

Calculating Slopes

The slope of a line is the ratio of the
change in the variable on the vertical
axis to the change in the variable on
the horizontal axis. In (a)–(d), we
have calculated the slope.

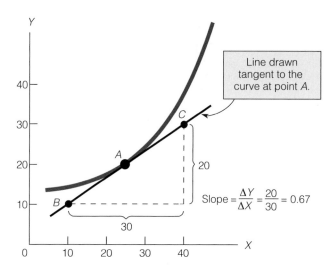

Calculating the Slope of a Curve at a Particular Point

The slope of the curve at point *A* is 0.67. This is calculated by drawing a line tangent to the curve at point *A* and then determining the slope of the line.

Would the slope still be −1? Let's compute the slope between points *B* and *C*. Moving from point *B* to point *C*, the change in *Y* is −10 and the change in *X* is +10. So, the slope is −1, which is what the slope was between points *A* and *B*.

Now let's compute the slope between points *A* and *D*. Moving from point *A* to point *D*, the change in *Y* is −30 and the change in *X* is +30. Again the slope is =1.

Our conclusion is that the slope between any two points on a (straight) line is always the same as the slope between any other two points. To see this for yourself, compute the slope between points *A* and *B* and between points *A* and *C* using the line in Exhibit 4(b).

Slope of a Curve

Economic graphs use both straight lines and curves. The slope of a curve is not constant throughout as it is for a straight line. The slope of a curve varies from one point to another.

Calculating the slope of a curve at a given point requires two steps, as illustrated for point *A* in Exhibit 5. First, draw a line tangent to the curve at the point (a tangent line is one that just touches the curve but does not cross it). Second, pick any two points on the tangent line and determine the slope. In Exhibit 5 the slope of the line between points *B* and *C* is 0.67. It follows that the slope of the curve at point *A* (and only at point *A*) is 0.67.

The 45° Line

Economists sometimes use a *45° line* to represent data. This is a straight line that bisects the right angle formed by the intersection of the vertical and horizontal axes (see Exhibit 6). As a result, the 45° line divides the space enclosed by the two axes into *two equal parts*. We have illustrated this by shading the two equal parts in different colors.

The major characteristic of the 45° line is that any point that lies on it is equidistant from both the horizontal and vertical axes. For example, point *A* is exactly as far from the horizontal axis as it is from the vertical axis. It follows that point *A* represents as much *X* as it does *Y*. Specifically, in the exhibit, point *A* represents 20 units of *X* and 20 units of *Y*.

The 45° Line

Any point on the 45° line is equidistant from both axis. For example, point *A* is the same distance from the vertical axis as it is from the horizontal axis.

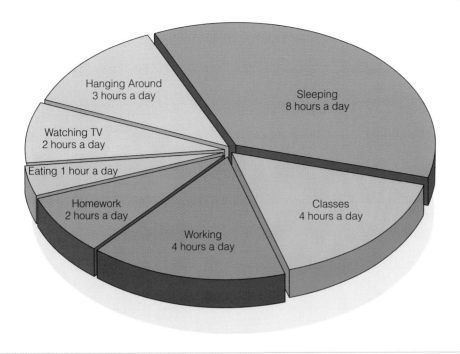

A Pie Chart

The breakdown of activities for Charles Myers during a typical 24-hour weekday is represented in pie chart form.

Pie Charts

In numerous places in this text, you will come across a *pie chart*. A pie chart is a convenient way to represent the different parts of something that when added together equal the whole.

Let's consider a typical 24-hour weekday for Charles Myers. On a typical weekday, Charles spends 8 hours sleeping, 4 hours taking classes at the university, 4 hours working at his part-time job, 2 hours doing homework, 1 hour eating, 2 hours watching television, and 3 hours doing nothing in particular (we'll call it "hanging around"). Exhibit 7 shows the breakdown of a typical weekday for Charles in pie chart form.

Pie charts give a quick visual message as to rough percentage breakdowns and relative relationships. For example, it is easy to see in Exhibit 7 that Charles spends twice as much time working as doing homework.

Bar Graphs

The *bar graph* is another visual aid that economists use to convey relative relationships. Suppose we wanted to represent the gross domestic product for the United States in different years. The **gross domestic product (GDP)** is the value of the entire output produced annually within a country's borders. A bar graph can show the actual GDP for each year and can also provide a quick picture of the relative relationships between the GDP in different years. For example, it is easy to see in Exhibit 8 that the GDP in 1990 was more than double what it was in 1980.

Gross Domestic Product (GDP)

The value of the entire output produced annually within a country's borders.

Line Graphs

Sometimes information is best and most easily displayed in a *line graph*. Line graphs are particularly useful for illustrating changes in a variable over some time period.

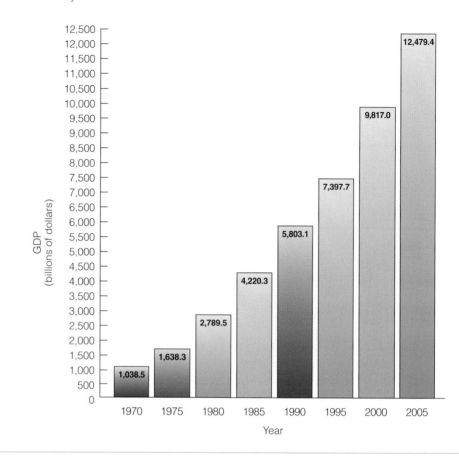

exhibit **8**

A Bar Graph

U.S. gross domestic product for different years is illustrated in bar graph form

Source: Bureau of Economic Analysis

Suppose we want to illustrate the variations in average points per game for a college basketball team in different years. As you can see from Exhibit 9(a), the basketball team has been on a roller coaster during the years 1994–2007. Perhaps the message transmitted here is that the team's performance has not been consistent from one year to the next.

Suppose we plot the data in Exhibit 9(a) again, except this time we use a different measurement scale on the vertical axis. As you can see in (b), the variation in the performance of the basketball team appears much less pronounced than in (a). In fact, we could choose some scale such that if we were to plot the data, we would end up with close to a straight line. Our point is simple: Data plotted in line graph form may convey different messages depending on the measurement scale used.

Sometimes economists show two line graphs on the same axes. Usually, they do this to draw attention to either (1) the *relationship* between the two variables or (2) the *difference* between the two variables. In Exhibit 10, the line graphs show the variation and trend in federal government expenditures and tax receipts for the years 1996–2007 and draw attention to what has been happening to the "gap" between the two.

(a)

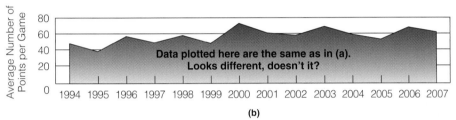

(b)

exhibit **9**

The Two Line Graphs Plot the Same Data

In (a) we plotted the average number of points per game for a college basketball team in different years. The variation between the years is pronounced. In (b) we plotted the same data as in (a), but the variation in the performance of the team appears much less pronounced than in (a).

Year	Average Number of Points per Game
1994	50
1995	40
1996	59
1997	51
1998	60
1999	50
2000	75
2001	63
2002	60
2003	71
2004	61
2005	55
2006	70
2007	64

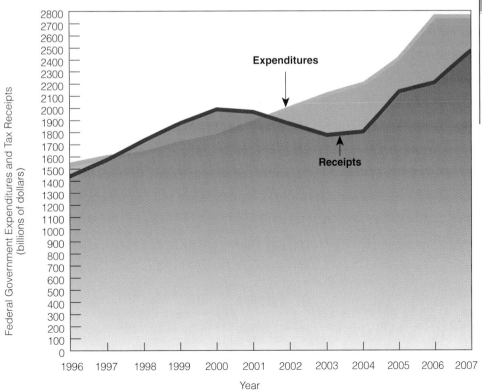

exhibit **10**

Federal Government Expenditures and Tax Receipts, 1996–2007

Federal government expenditures and tax receipts are shown in line graph form for the period 1996–2007. The data for 2006 and 2007 are estimates.

Source: Bureau of Economic Analysis

appendix summary

- Two variables are directly related if one variable rises as the other rises.
- An upward-sloping line (left to right) represents two variables that are directly related.
- Two variables are inversely related if one variable rises as the other falls.
- A downward-sloping line (left to right) represents two variables that are inversely related.
- Two variables are independent if one variable rises as the other remains constant.
- The slope of a line is the ratio of the change in the variable on the vertical axis to the change in the variable on the horizontal axis. The slope of a (straight) line is the same between every two points on the line.

- To determine the slope of a curve at a point, draw a line tangent to the curve at the point and then determine the slope of the tangent line.
- Any point on a 45° line is equidistant from the two axes.
- A pie chart is a convenient way to represent the different parts of something that when added together equal the whole. A pie chart visually shows rough percentage breakdowns and relative relationships.
- A bar graph is a convenient way to represent relative relationships.
- Line graphs are particularly useful for illustrating changes in a variable over some time period.

questions and problems

1   What type of relationship would you expect between the following: (a) sales of hot dogs and sales of hot dog buns, (b) the price of winter coats and sales of winter coats, (c) the price of personal computers and the production of personal computers, (d) sales of toothbrushes and sales of cat food, (e) the number of children in a family and the number of toys in a family.

2   Represent the following data in bar graph form.

Year	U.S. Money Supply (billions of dollars)
2001	1,182
2002	1,219
2003	1,304
2004	1,372
2005	1,369

3   Plot the following data and specify the type of relationship between the two variables. (Place "price" on the vertical axis and "quantity demanded" on the horizontal axis.)

Price of Apples ($)	Quantity Demanded of Apples
0.25	1,000
0.50	800
0.70	700
0.95	500
1.00	400
1.10	350

4   In Exhibit 4(a), determine the slope between points C and D.

5   In Exhibit 4(b), determine the slope between points A and D.

6   What is the special characteristic of a 45° line?

7   What is the slope of a 45° line?

8   When would it be preferable to illustrate data using a pie chart instead of a bar graph?

9   Plot the following data and specify the type of relationship between the two variables. (Place "price" on the vertical axis and "quantity supplied" on the horizontal axis.)

Price of Apples ($)	Quantity Supplied of Apples
0.25	350
0.50	400
0.70	500
0.95	700
1.00	800
1.10	1,000

Should You Major in Economics?

You are probably reading this textbook as part of your first college course in economics. You may be taking this course because you need it to satisfy the requirements in your major. Economics courses are sometimes required for students who plan to major in business, history, liberal studies, social science, or computer science. Of course, you may also be taking this course because you plan to major in economics.

If you are like many college students, you may complain that not enough information is available to students about the various majors at your college or university. For example, students who major in business sometimes say they are not quite certain what a business major is all about, but then they go on to add that majoring in business is a safe bet. "After all," they comment, "you are pretty sure of getting a job if you have a business degree. That's not always the case with other degrees."

Many college students choose their majors based on their high school courses. History majors sometimes say that they decided to major in history because they "liked history in high school." Similarly, chemistry, biology, and math majors say they chose chemistry, biology, or math as a college major because they liked studying chemistry, biology, or math in high school. In addition, if a student had a hard time with chemistry in high school and found it boring, then he doesn't usually want to major in chemistry in college. If a student found both math and economics easy and interesting in high school, then she is likely to major in math or economics.

Students also often look to the dollars at the end of the college degree. A student may enjoy history and want to learn more history in college but tell herself that she will earn a higher starting salary after graduation if she majors in computer science or engineering.

Thus, when choosing a major, students often consider (1) how much they enjoy studying a particular subject, (2) what they would like to see themselves doing in the future, and (3) income prospects.

Different people may weight these three factors differently. But no matter what weights you put on each of the factors, it is always better to have more information than less information, *ceteris paribus*. (We note *"ceteris paribus"* because it is not necessarily better having more information than less information if you have to pay more for the additional information than the additional information is worth. Who wants to pay $10 for a piece of information that only provides $1 in benefits?)

We believe this appendix is a fairly low-cost way of providing you with more information about an economics major than you currently have. We start by dispelling some of the misinformation you might possess about an economics major. Stated bluntly, some things that people think about an economics major and about a career in economics are just not true. For example, some people think that economics majors almost never study social relationships; instead, they only study such things as inflation, interest rates, and unemployment. Not true. Economics majors study some of the same things that sociologists, historians, psychologists, and political scientists study. We also provide you with some information about the major that you may not have.

Next, we tell you the specifics of the economics major—what courses you study if you are an economics major, how many courses you are likely to have to take, and more.

Finally, we tell you something about a career in economics. Okay, so you have opted to become an economics major. But the day will come when you have your degree in hand. What's next? What is your starting salary likely to be? What will you be doing? Are you going to be happy doing what economists do? (If you never thought economics was about happiness, you already have some misinformation about economics. Contrary to what most laypeople think, economics is not just about money. It is about happiness too.)

Five Myths About Economics and an Economics Major

MYTH 1: ECONOMICS IS ALL MATHEMATICS AND STATISTICS. Some students choose not to major in economics because they think economics is all mathematics and statistics. Math and statistics are used in economics, but at the undergraduate degree level, the math and statistics are certainly not overwhelming. Economics majors are usually required to take one statistics course and one math course (usually an introductory calculus course). Even students who say, "Math isn't my subject" are sometimes happy with the amount of math they need in economics. Fact is, at the undergraduate level at many colleges and universities, economics is not a very math-intensive course of study. There are many diagrams in economics, but there is not a large amount of math.

A proviso: The amount of math in the economics curriculum varies across colleges and universities. Some economics departments do not require their students to learn much math or statistics, but others do. Speaking for the majority of departments, we still hold to our original point that there isn't really that much math or statistics in economics at the undergraduate level. The graduate level is a different story.

MYTH 2: ECONOMICS IS ONLY ABOUT INFLATION, INTEREST RATES, UNEMPLOYMENT, AND OTHER SUCH THINGS. If you study economics at college and then go on to become a practicing economist, no doubt people will ask you certain questions when they learn your chosen profession. Here are some of the questions they ask:

- Do you think the economy is going to pick up?
- Do you think the economy is going to slow down?
- What stocks would you recommend?
- Do you think interest rates are going to fall?
- Do you think interest rates are going to rise?
- What do you think about buying bonds right now? Is it a good idea?

People ask these kinds of questions because most people believe that economists only study stocks, bonds, interest rates, inflation, unemployment, and so on. Well, economists do study these things. But these topics are only a tiny part of what economists study. It is not hard to find many economists today, both inside and outside academia, who spend most of their time studying anything but inflation, unemployment, stocks, bonds, and so on.

As we hinted earlier, much of what economists study may surprise you. There are economists who use their economic tools and methods to study crime, marriage, divorce, sex, obesity, addiction, sports, voting behavior, bureaucracies, presidential elections, and much more. In short, today's economics is not your grandfather's economics. Many more topics are studied today in economics than were studied in your grandfather's time.

MYTH 3: PEOPLE BECOME ECONOMISTS ONLY IF THEY WANT TO "MAKE MONEY." Awhile back we asked a few well-respected and well-known economists what got them interested in economics. Here is what some of them had to say:[1]

Gary Becker, the 1992 winner of the Nobel Prize in Economics, said: "I got interested [in economics] when I was an undergraduate in college. I came into college with a strong interest in mathematics, and at the same time with a strong commitment to do something to help society. I learned in the first economics course I took that economics could deal rigorously, à la mathematics, with social problems. That stimulated me because in economics I saw that I could combine both the mathematics and my desire to do something to help society."

Vernon Smith, the 2002 winner of the Nobel Prize in Economics, said: "My father's influence started me in science and engineering at Cal Tech, but my mother, who was active in socialist politics, probably accounts for the great interest I found in economics when I took my first introductory course."

Alice Rivlin, an economist and former member of the Federal Reserve Board, said: "My interest in economics grew out of concern for improving public policy, both domestic and international. I was a teenager in the tremendously idealistic period after World War II when it seemed terribly important to get nations working together to solve the world's problems peacefully."

Allan Meltzer said: "Economics is a social science. At its best it is concerned with ways (1) to improve well being by allowing individuals the freedom to achieve their personal aims or goals and (2) to harmonize their individual interests. I find working on such issues challenging, and progress is personally rewarding."

Robert Solow, the 1987 winner of the Nobel Prize in Economics, said: "I grew up in the 1930s and it was very hard not to be interested in economics. If you were a high school student in the 1930s, you were conscious of the fact that our economy was in deep trouble and no one knew what to do about it."

Charles Plosser said: "I was an engineer as an undergraduate with little knowledge of economics. I went to the University of Chicago Graduate School of Business to get an MBA and there became fascinated with economics. I was impressed with the seriousness with which economics was viewed as a way of organizing one's thoughts about the world to address interesting questions and problems."

Walter Williams said: "I was a major in sociology in 1963 and I concluded that it was not very rigorous. Over the summer I was reading a book by W.E.B. DuBois, *Black Reconstruction,* and somewhere in the book it said something along the lines that blacks could not melt into the mainstream of American society until they understood economics, and that was something that got me interested in economics."

Murray Weidenbaum said: "A specific professor got me interested in economics. He was very prescient: He correctly noted that while lawyers dominated the policy-making process up until then (the 1940s), in the future economics would be an important tool for developing public policy. And he was right."

Irma Adelman said: "I hesitate to say because it sounds arrogant. My reason [for getting into economics] was that I wanted to benefit humanity. And my perception at the time was that economic problems were the most important problems that humanity has to face. That is what got me into economics and into economic development."

Lester Thurow said: "[I got interested in economics because of] the belief, some would see it as naïve belief, that economics was a profession where it would be possible to help make the world better."

---

[1]See various interviews in Roger A. Arnold, *Economics, 2d edition* (St. Paul, Minnesota: West Publishing Company, 1992).

MYTH 4: ECONOMICS WASN'T VERY INTERESTING IN HIGH SCHOOL, SO IT'S NOT GOING TO BE VERY INTERESTING IN COLLEGE. A typical high school economics course emphasizes consumer economics and spends much time discussing this topic. Students learn about credit cards, mortgage loans, budgets, buying insurance, renting an apartment, and other such things. These are important topics because not knowing the "ins and outs" of such things can make your life much harder. Still, many students come away from a high school economics course thinking that economics is always and everywhere about consumer topics.

However, a high school economics course and a college economics course are usually as different as day and night. Simply leaf through this book and look at the variety of topics covered compared to the topics you might have covered in your high school economics course. Go on to look at texts used in other economics courses—courses that range from law and economics to history of economic thought to international economics to sports economics—and you will see what we mean.

MYTH 5: ECONOMICS IS A LOT LIKE BUSINESS, BUT BUSINESS IS MORE MARKETABLE. Although business and economics have some common topics, much that one learns in economics is not taught in business and much that one learns in business is not taught in economics. The area of intersection between business and economics is not large.

Still, many people think otherwise. And so thinking that business and economics are "pretty much the same thing," they often choose to major in the subject they believe has greater marketability—which they believe is business.

Well, consider the following:

1. A few years ago *BusinessWeek* magazine asked the chief executive officers (CEOs) of major companies what they thought was the best undergraduate degree. Their first choice was engineering. Their second choice was economics. Economics scored higher than business administration.
2. The National Association of Colleges and Employers undertook a survey in the summer of 2005 in which they identified the starting salary offers in different disciplines. The starting salary in economics/finance was $42,928. The starting salary in business administration was 7.8 percent lower.

What Awaits You as an Economics Major?

If you become an economics major, what courses will you take? What are you going to study?

At the lower-division level, economics majors must take both the principles of macroeconomics course and the principles of microeconomics course. They usually also take a statistics course and a math course (usually calculus).

At the upper-division level, they must take intermediate microeconomics and intermediate macroeconomics, along with a certain number of electives. Some of the elective courses include: (1) money and banking, (2) law and economics, (3) history of economic thought, (4) public finance, (5) labor economics, (6) international economics, (7) antitrust and regulation, (8) health economics, (9) economics of development, (10) urban and regional economics, (11) econometrics, (12) mathematical economics, (13) environmental economics, (14) public choice, (15) global managerial economics, (16) economic approach to politics and sociology, (17) sports economics, and many more courses. Most economics majors take between 12 and 15 economics courses.

One of the attractive things about studying economics is that you will acquire many of the skills employers highly value. First, you will have the quantitative skills that are important in many business and government positions. Second, you will acquire the writing skills necessary in almost all lines of work. Third, and perhaps most importantly, you will develop the thinking skills that almost all employers agree are critical to success.

A study published in the 1998 edition of the *Journal of Economic Education* ranked economics majors as having the highest average scores on the Law School Admission Test (LSAT). Also, consider the words of the Royal Economic Society: "One of the things that makes economics graduates so employable is that the subject teaches you to think in a careful and precise way. The fundamental economic issue is how society decides to allocate its resources: how the costs and benefits of a course of action can be evaluated and compared, and how appropriate choices can be made. A degree in economics gives a training in decision making principles, providing a skill applicable in a very wide range of careers."

Keep in mind, too, that economics is one of the most popular majors at some of the most respected universities in the country. As of this writing, economics is the top major at Harvard, Princeton, Columbia, Stanford, University of Pennsylvania, and University of Chicago. It is the second most popular major at Brown, Yale, and the University of California at Berkeley. It is the third most popular major at Cornell and Dartmouth.

What Do Economists Do?

Employment for economists is projected to grow between 21 and 35 percent between 2000 and 2010. According to the *Occupational Outlook Handbook:*

> Opportunities for economists should be best in private industry, especially in research, testing, and consulting firms, as more companies contract out for economic research services. The growing complexity of the global economy, competition, and increased reliance on quantitative methods for analyzing the current value of future funds, business trends, sales, and purchasing should spur demand for economists. The growing need for economic analyses in virtually every industry should result in additional jobs for economists.

Today, economists work in many varied fields. Here are some of the fields and some of the positions economists hold in those fields:

Education
College Professor
Researcher
High School Teacher

Journalism
Researcher
Industry Analyst
Economic Analyst

Accounting
Analyst
Auditor
Researcher
Consultant

General Business
Chief Executive Officer
Business Analyst
Marketing Analyst
Business Forecaster
Competitive Analyst

Government
Researcher
Analyst
Speechwriter
Forecaster

Financial Services
Business Journalist
International Analyst

Newsletter Editor
Broker
Investment Banker

Banking
Credit Analyst
Loan Officer
Investment Analyst
Financial Manager

Other
Business Consultant
Independent Forecaster
Freelance Analyst
Think Tank Analyst
Entrepreneur

Economists do a myriad of things. For example, in business, economists often analyze economic conditions, make forecasts, offer strategic planning initiatives, collect and analyze data, predict exchange rate movements, and review regulatory policies, among other things. In government, economists collect and analyze data, analyze international economic situations, research monetary conditions, advise on policy, and much more. As private consultants, economists work with accountants, business executives, government officials, educators, financial firms, labor unions, state and local governments, and others.

Median annual earnings of economists were $68,550 in 2002. The middle 50 percent earned between $50,560 and $90,710. The lowest 10 percent earned less than $38,690, and the highest 10 percent earned more than $120,440.

Places to Find More Information

If you are interested in an economics major and perhaps a career in economics, here are some places where you can go and some people you can speak with to acquire more information:

- To learn about the economics curriculum, we urge you to speak with the economics professors at your college or university. Ask them what courses you would have to take as an economics major. Ask them what elective courses are available. In addition, ask them why they chose to study economics. What is it about economics that interested them?

- For more information about salaries and what economists do, you may want to visit the *Occupational Outlook Handbook* Web site at http://www.bls.gov/oco/.

- For starting salary information, you may want to visit the National Association of Colleges and Employers Web site at http://www.naceweb.org/.

- To see a list of famous people who have majored in economics, go to http://www.marietta .edu/~ema/econ/famous.html.

Concluding Remarks

Choosing a major is a big decision and therefore should not be made too quickly and without much thought. In this short appendix, we have provided you with some information about an economics major and a career in economics. Economics may not be for everyone (in fact, economists would say that if it were, many of the benefits of specialization would be lost), but it may be right for you. Economics is a major where many of today's most marketable skills are acquired—the skills of good writing, quantitative analysis, and thinking. It is a major in which professors and students daily ask and answer some very interesting and relevant questions. It is a major that is highly regarded by employers. It may just be the right major for you. Give it some thought.

Economic Activities: Producing and Trading

Setting the Scene

The following events happened on a day in March.

8:25 A.M.

Two presidential advisors are in the West Wing of the White House discussing what Eduard Shevardnadze said in 1990. Shevardnadze had been the Soviet foreign minister before the collapse of the Soviet Union. He had said the Soviet Union collapsed because of the conflict between the Kremlin and the people. The Kremlin wanted "more guns," and the people wanted "more butter," but it was impossible to get more of both. Something had to give, and so it did: The Soviet Union imploded.

10:13 A.M.

Bob and Jim are roommates and students at the University of Missouri Kansas City. Bob says, "I have two final exams tomorrow—biology at 9 and calculus at 2. I think it's come down to choosing where I want to get an A. I don't have enough study time tonight to get As in both courses." Jim comments, "If we could

only produce 'more time' the same way people produce more watches or more cars. I bet we could sell *that* for a pretty penny."

5:55 P.M.

Karen and Larry have been married for eleven years. They have two children: a boy, James, nine years old, and a girl, Caroline, six years old. Every night, Karen cooks the dinner and Larry washes the dishes. Fact is, when Karen and Larry first got married, they decided to split the households tasks "right down the middle." To them, this meant that Karen and Larry would each do half of everything: Karen would do half the cooking, and Larry would do half the cooking; Karen would do half the cleaning, and Larry would do half the cleaning. It hasn't turned out that way, though. Each does 100 percent of certain tasks. In a way, each has specialized in performing certain tasks around the house.

6:25 P.M.

Jayant says to Helena. "What eBay did really wasn't that hard." Helena replies, "I just wish I had done it."

? **Here are some questions to keep in mind as you read this chapter:**

- *What does a point on a production possibilities frontier have to do with the collapse of the Soviet Union?*

- *Why can't Bob get As in both biology and calculus, and what does Jim's desire to produce "more time" tell us about life?*

- *What led Karen and Larry to specialize in doing certain tasks?*

- *What did eBay do that really wasn't that hard?*

See analyzing the scene at the end of this chapter for answers to these questions.

The Production Possibilities Frontier

This section discusses the production possibilities frontier (PPF) and numerous economic concepts that can be illustrated by it.

The Straight-Line PPF: Constant Opportunity Costs

Assume the following:

1. Only two goods can be produced in an economy: computers and television sets.
2. The opportunity cost of 1 television set is 1 computer.
3. As more of one good is produced, the opportunity cost between television sets and computers is *constant*.

Production Possibilities Frontier (PPF)

Represents the possible combinations of two goods that can be produced in a certain period of time under the conditions of a given state of technology and fully employed resources.

In Exhibit 1(a), we have identified six combinations of computers and television sets that can be produced in our economy. For example, combination *A* is 50,000 computers and 0 television sets, combination *B* is 40,000 computers and 10,000 television sets, and so on. We plotted these six combinations of computers and television sets in Exhibit 1(b). Each combination represents a different point in Exhibit 1(b). For example, the combination of 50,000 computers and 0 television sets is represented by point *A*. The line that connects points *A–F* is the production possibilities frontier. A **production possibilities frontier (PPF)** represents the combination of two goods that can be produced in a certain period of time under the conditions of a given state of technology and fully employed resources.

The production possibilities frontier is a *straight line* in this instance because the opportunity cost of producing computers and television sets is *constant*.

exhibit **1**

Production Possibilities Frontier (Constant Opportunity Costs)

The economy can produce any of the six combinations of computers and television sets in part (a). We have plotted these combinations in part (b). The production possibilities frontier in part (b) is a straight line because the opportunity cost of producing either good is constant: for *every* 1 computer not produced, 1 television set is produced.

Straight-line PPF = Constant opportunity costs

For example, if the economy were to move from point *A* to point *B,* from *B* to *C,* and so on, the opportunity cost of each good would remain *constant* at 1 for 1. To illustrate, at point *A,* 50,000 computers and 0 television sets are produced. At point *B,* 40,000 computers and 10,000 television sets are produced.

Point *A:* 50,000 computers, 0 television sets
Point *B:* 40,000 computers, 10,000 television sets

Combination	Computers	Television Sets	Point in Part (b)
A	50,000	0	*A*
B	40,000	10,000	*B*
C	30,000	20,000	*C*
D	20,000	30,000	*D*
E	10,000	40,000	*E*
F	0	50,000	*F*

(a)

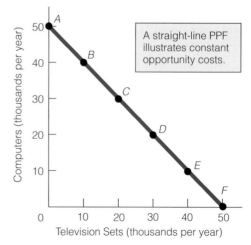

A straight-line PPF illustrates constant opportunity costs.

(b)

We conclude that for every 10,000 computers not produced, 10,000 television sets are produced—a ratio of 1 to 1. The opportunity cost—1 computer for 1 television set—that exists between points A and B also exists between points B and C, C and D, D and E, and E and F. In other words, opportunity cost is constant at 1 computer for 1 television set.

The Bowed-Outward (Concave-Downward) PPF: Increasing Opportunity Costs

Assume two things:

1. Only two goods can be produced in an economy: computers and television sets.

2. As more of one good is produced, the opportunity cost between computers and television sets *changes*.

In Exhibit 2(a), we have identified four combinations of computers and television sets that can be produced in our economy. For example, combination A is 50,000 computers and 0 television sets, combination B is 40,000 computers and 20,000 television sets, and so on. We plotted these four combinations of computers and television sets in Exhibit 2(b). Each combination represents a different point. The curved line that connects points A–D is the production possibilities frontier.

In this case, the production possibilities frontier is *bowed outward* (concave downward) because the opportunity cost of television sets *increases* as more sets are produced.

Bowed-outward PPF = Increasing opportunity costs

To illustrate, let's start at point A, where the economy is producing 50,000 computers and 0 television sets, and move to point B, where the economy is producing 40,000 computers and 20,000 television sets.

Point A: 50,000 computers, 0 television sets
Point B: 40,000 computers, 20,000 television sets

Q&A — *Opportunity cost and PPF seem like two economic concepts that are linked together somehow. Are they?*

Yes. When we move from one point on the PPF to another point on the PPF, we automatically incur an opportunity cost. To illustrate, suppose we move from point C in Exhibit 1(b) to point D. Notice what happens: We get more television sets but fewer computers. What we have to "give up" to get more television sets is the opportunity cost of those additional television sets.

exhibit 2

Production Possibilities Frontier (Increasing Opportunity Costs)

The economy can produce any of the four combinations of computers and televisions sets in part (a). We have plotted these combinations in part (b). The production possibilities frontier in part (b) is bowed outward because the opportunity cost of producing television sets increases as more television sets are produced.

Combination	Computers	Television Sets	Point in Part (b)
A	50,000	0	A
B	40,000	20,000	B
C	25,000	40,000	C
D	0	60,000	D

(a)

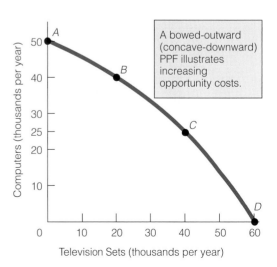

A bowed-outward (concave-downward) PPF illustrates increasing opportunity costs.

(b)

What is the opportunity cost of a television set over this range? We see that 20,000 more television sets are produced by moving from point *A* to point *B but at the cost of only 10,000 computers.* This means for every 1 television set produced, 1/2 computer is forfeited. Thus, the opportunity cost of 1 television set is 1/2 computer.

Now let's move from point *B*, where the economy is producing 40,000 computers and 20,000 television sets, to point *C*, where the economy is producing 25,000 computers and 40,000 television sets.

> Point *B:* 40,000 computers, 20,000 television sets
> Point *C:* 25,000 computers, 40,000 television sets

What is the opportunity cost of a television set over this range? In this case, 20,000 more television sets are produced by moving from point *B* to point *C but at the cost of 15,000 computers.* This means for every 1 television set produced, 3/4 computer is forfeited. Thus, the opportunity cost of 1 television set is 3/4 of a computer.

Law of Increasing Opportunity Costs
As more of a good is produced, the opportunity costs of producing that good increase.

What statement can we make about the opportunity costs of producing television sets? Obviously, as the economy produces more television sets, the opportunity cost of producing television sets increases. This gives us the bowed-outward production possibilities frontier in Exhibit 2(b).

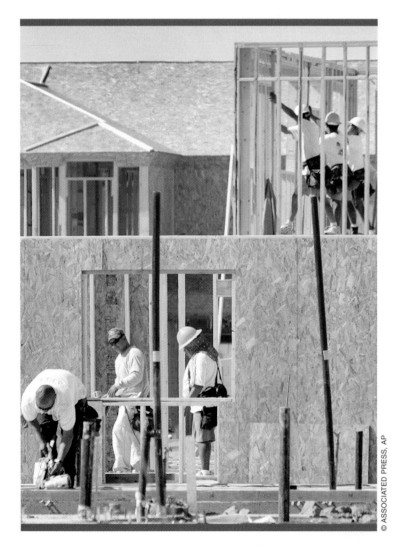

© ASSOCIATED PRESS, AP

Law of Increasing Opportunity Costs

We know that the shape of the production possibilities frontier depends on whether opportunity costs (1) are constant or (2) increase as more of a good is produced. In Exhibit 1(b), the production possibilities frontier is a straight line; in Exhibit 2(b), it is bowed outward (curved). In the real world, most production possibilities frontiers are bowed outward. This means that for most goods, the opportunity costs increase as more of the good is produced. This is referred to as the **law of increasing opportunity costs**.

But why (for most goods) do the opportunity costs increase as more of the good is produced? The answer is because people have varying abilities. For example, some people are better suited to building houses than other people are. When a construction company first starts building houses, it employs the people who are most skilled at house building. The most skilled persons can build houses at lower opportunity costs than others can. But as the construction company builds more houses, it finds that it has already employed the most skilled builders, so it must employ those who are less skilled at house building. These (less skilled) people build houses at higher opportunity costs. Where three skilled house builders could build a house in a month, as many as seven unskilled builders may be required to build it in the same length of time. Exhibit 3 summarizes the points in this section.

exhibit 3

A CLOSER LOOK

A Summary Statement About Increasing Opportunity Costs and a Production Possibilities Frontier That Is Bowed Outward (Concave Downward)

Many of the points about increasing opportunity costs and a production possibilities frontier that is bowed outward are summarized here.

We start with the assumption that not all people can build houses at the same opportunity cost. → When houses are first built, only the people who *can* build them at (relatively) low opportunity costs *will* build them. → As increasingly more houses are built, people with higher opportunity costs of building houses will start building houses. → This is the same as saying that as more houses are built, the opportunity cost of building houses increases.

And this is why the PPF for houses and good *X* is bowed outward (concave downward). See diagram at left.

Notice that when we go from building 60 to 70 houses (10 more houses), we forfeit 5 units of good *X*; but when we go from building 110 to 120 houses (again, 10 more houses), we forfeit 20 units of good *X*.

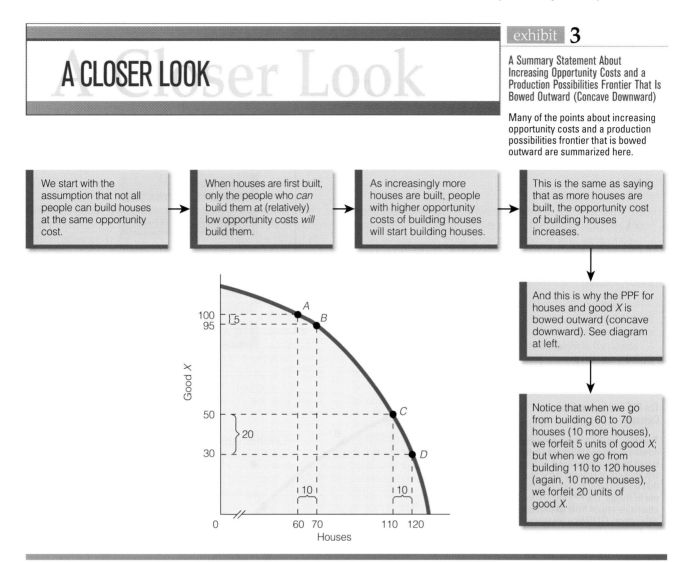

Economic Concepts within a PPF Framework

The PPF framework is useful for illustrating and working with economic concepts. This section discusses seven economic concepts in terms of the PPF framework (see Exhibit 4).

SCARCITY Recall that scarcity is the condition where wants (for goods) are greater than the resources available to satisfy those wants. The finiteness of resources is graphically portrayed by the PPF in Exhibit 5. The frontier (itself) tells us: "At this point in time, that's as far as you can go. You cannot go any farther. You are limited to choosing any combination of the two goods on the frontier or below it."

The PPF separates the production possibilities of an economy into two regions: (1) an *attainable region,* which consists of the points on the PPF itself and all points below it (this region includes points *A–F*) and (2) an *unattainable region,* which consists of the points above and beyond the PPF (such as point *G*). Recall that scarcity implies that some things are attainable and others are unattainable. Point *A* on the PPF is attainable, as is point *F*; point *G* is not.

exhibit 6

Economic Growth within a PPF Framework

An increase in resources or an advance in technology can increase the production capabilities of an economy, leading to economic growth and a shift outward in the production possibilities frontier.

Economic growth shifts the PPF outward.

PPF₂

PPF₁

Military Goods

0   Civilian Goods

Technology
The body of skills and knowledge concerning the use of resources in production. An advance in technology commonly refers to the ability to produce more output with a fixed amount of resources or the ability to produce the same output with fewer resources.

To illustrate, suppose we move from inefficient point *F* to efficient point *C*. We produce more television sets and no fewer cars. What if we move from *F* to *D*? We produce more television sets and more cars. Finally, if we move from *F* to *E,* we produce more cars and no fewer television sets. Thus, moving from F can give us more of at least one good and no less of another good. In short, *productive inefficiency implies that gains are possible in one area without losses in another.*

UNEMPLOYED RESOURCES When the economy exhibits productive inefficiency, it is not producing the maximum output with the available resources and technology. One reason may be that the economy is not using all its resources; that is, some of its resources are unemployed, as at point *F* in Exhibit 5.

When the economy exhibits productive efficiency, it is producing the maximum output with the available resources and technology. This means it is using all its resources to produce goods; its resources are fully employed, and none are unemployed. At the productive efficient points *A–E* in Exhibit 5, there are no unemployed resources.

ECONOMIC GROWTH Economic growth refers to the increased productive capabilities of an economy. It is illustrated by a shift outward in the production possibilities frontier. Two major factors that affect economic growth are (1) an increase in the quantity of resources and (2) an advance in technology.

With an increase in the quantity of resources (e.g., through a new discovery of resources), it is possible to produce a greater quantity of output. In Exhibit 6, an increase in the quantity of resources makes it possible to produce both more military goods and more civilian goods. Thus, the PPF shifts outward from PPF₁ to PPF₂.

Technology refers to the body of skills and knowledge concerning the use of resources in production. An advance in technology commonly refers to the ability to produce more output with a fixed quantity of resources or the ability to produce the same output with a smaller quantity of resources.

Suppose an advance in technology allows more military goods and more civilian goods to be produced with the same quantity of resources. As a result, the PPF in Exhibit 6 shifts outward from PPF₁ to PPF₂. The outcome is the same as when the quantity of resources is increased.

SELF-TEST

(Answers to Self-Test questions are in the Self-Test Appendix.)

1. What does a straight-line production possibilities frontier (PPF) represent? What does a bowed-outward PPF represent?

2. What does the law of increasing costs have to do with a bowed-outward PPF?

3. A politician says, "If you elect me, we can get more of everything we want." Under what condition(s) is the politician telling the truth?

4. In an economy, only one combination of goods is productive efficient. True or false? Explain your answer.

Exchange or Trade

Exchange (Trade)
The process of giving up one thing for something else.

Exchange or **trade** is the process of giving up one thing for something else. Usually, money is traded for goods and services. Trade is all around us; we are involved with it every day. Few of us, however, have considered the full extent of trade.

economics 24/7

LIBERALS, CONSERVATIVES, AND THE PPF

Liberals and conservatives often pull in different economic directions. To illustrate, suppose our economy is currently at point A in Exhibit 7, producing X_2 of good X and Y_2 of good Y. Conservatives prefer point C to point A and try to convince the liberals and the rest of the nation to move to point C. Liberals, however, prefer point B to point A and try to persuade the conservatives and the rest of the nation to move to point B. Thus, we have a political tug of war.

Is there a way that both groups can get what they want? Yes, if there is economic growth so that the production possibilities frontier shifts outward from PPF_1 to PPF_2. On the new production possibilities frontier, PPF_2, point D represents the quantity of X that conservatives want and the quantity of Y that liberals want. At point D, conservatives have X_3 units of good X, which is what they would have had at point C, and liberals have Y_3 units of good Y, which is what they would have had at point B. Through economic growth, both conservatives and liberals can get what they want. The political tug of war will cease—at least for a while.

We say "for a while" because even at point D, there is scarcity. The wants of liberals and conservatives are both greater than the resources available to satisfy those wants. Starting at point D, liberals might push for a movement up the production possibilities frontier and conservatives for a movement down it.

Question to ponder: Does an increase in a family's income have the same effect as economic growth in a society? Does it eliminate or reduce the family tug of war—at least for a while?

Through economic growth, shown here by a shift from PPF_1 to PPF_2, both liberals and conservatives can get more of what they want.

exhibit 7

Economic Growth May End Political Battles, for a While

The economy is at point A, but conservatives want to be at point C and liberals want to be at point B. As a result, there is a political tug-of-war. Both conservatives and liberals can get the quantity of the good they want through economic growth. This is represented by point D on PPF_2.

Periods Relevant to Trade

There are three time periods relevant to the trading process. We discuss these relevant time periods next.

BEFORE THE TRADE Before a trade is made, a person is said to be in the **ex ante** position. For example, suppose Ramona has the opportunity to trade what she has, $2,000, for something she does not have, a big-screen television set. In the ex ante position, she wonders if she will be better off with (1) the television set or with (2) $2,000 worth of other goods. If she concludes that she will be better off with the television set than with

Ex Ante

Phrase that means "before," as in before a trade.

$2,000 worth of other goods, she will make the trade. Individuals will make a trade only if they believe ex ante (before) the trade that the trade will make them better off.

AT THE POINT OF TRADE Suppose Ramona now gives $2,000 to the person in possession of the television set. Does Ramona still believe she will be better off with the television set than with the $2,000? Of course she does. Her action testifies to this fact.

Ex Post

Phrase that means "after," as in after a trade.

AFTER THE TRADE After a trade is made, a person is said to be in the **ex post** position. Suppose two days have passed. Does Ramona still feel the same way about the trade as she did before the trade and at the point of trade? Maybe. Maybe not. She may look back on the trade and regret it. She may say that if she had it to do over again, she would not trade the $2,000 for the big-screen television set. In general, though, people expect a trade to make them better off, and usually, the trade meets their expectations. But there are no guarantees that a trade will meet expectations because no one in the real world can see the future.

Trade and the Terms of Trade

Terms of Trade

How much of one thing is given up for how much of something else.

Trade refers to the process whereby "things" (money, goods, services, etc.) are given up to obtain something else. The **terms of trade** refer to *how much* of one thing is given up for *how much* of something else. For example, if $30 is traded for a best-selling book, the terms of trade are 1 bestseller for $30. If the price of a loaf of bread is $2.50, the terms of trade are 1 loaf of bread for $2.50. Buyers and sellers can always think of more advantageous terms of exchange. Buyers prefer lower prices, whereas sellers prefer higher prices.

Thinking like
AN ECONOMIST

A person buys a pair of shoes for $100. Later that day, the person says that he was "ripped off" by the shoe store owner; specifically, he says he paid too much for the shoes. Is this person arguing against trade or against the terms of trade? The economist knows that sometimes what sounds like a person arguing "against trade" is really his argument against the "terms of trade." Everyone can think of better terms of trade for himself. You buy a book for $40. Are there better terms of trade for you? Sure, you would have rather paid $30 for the book instead of $40. Sometimes, when it sounds as if we are arguing against trade, what we are really saying is this: "I wish I could have bought the good or service at better terms of trade than I did."

Costs of Trades

As always, economists consider both benefits and costs. They want to determine what costs are involved in a trade and whether the costs may prevent a trade from taking place.

UNEXPLOITED TRADES Suppose Smith wants to buy a red 1965 Ford Mustang in excellent condition. The maximum price she is willing and able to pay for the Mustang is $30,000. Also suppose that Jones owns a red 1965 Ford Mustang in excellent condition. The minimum price he is willing and able to sell the Mustang for is $23,000. Obviously, Smith's maximum buying price ($30,000) is greater than Jones's minimum selling price ($23,000), so a potential trade or exchange exists.

Will the potential trade between Smith and Jones become an actual exchange? The answer to this question may depend on the transaction costs. **Transaction costs** are the costs associated with the time and effort needed to search out, negotiate, and consummate a trade. To illustrate, neither Smith nor Jones may know that the other exists. Suppose Smith lives in Roanoke, Virginia, and Jones lives 40 miles away in Blacksburg, Virginia. Each needs to find the other, which may take time and money. Perhaps Smith can put an ad in the local Blacksburg newspaper stating that she is searching for a 1965 Ford Mustang in mint condition. Alternatively, Jones can put an ad in the local Roanoke newspaper stating that he has a 1965 Ford Mustang to sell. The ad may or may not be seen by the relevant party and then acted upon. Our point is a simple one: Transaction costs sometimes keep potential trades from turning into actual trades.

Transaction Costs

The costs associated with the time and effort needed to search out, negotiate, and consummate an exchange.

Consider another example. Suppose Kurt hates to shop for clothes because shopping takes too much time. He has to get in his car, drive to the mall, park the car, walk into the mall, look in different stores, try on different clothes, pay for the items, walk to and get back in his car, and drive home. Suppose Kurt spends an average of 2 hours when he shops, and he estimates that an hour of his time is worth $30. It follows, then, that Kurt incurs $60 worth of transaction costs when he buys clothes. Usually, he is not willing to incur the transaction costs necessary to buy a pair of trousers or a shirt.

Now, suppose we ask Kurt if he would be more willing to buy clothes if shopping was easier. Suppose, we say, the transaction costs associated with buying clothes could be lowered from $60 to less than $10. At lower transaction costs, Kurt says that he would be willing to shop more often.

How can transaction costs be lowered? Both people and computers can help lower the transaction costs of trades. For example, real estate brokers lower the transaction costs of selling and buying a house. Jim has a house to sell but doesn't know how to find a buyer. Karen wants to buy a house but doesn't know how to find a seller. Enter the real estate broker, who brings buyers and sellers together. In so doing, she lowers the transaction costs of buying and selling a house.

As another example, consider e-commerce on the Internet. Ursula can buy a book by getting in her car, driving to a bookstore, getting out of her car, walking into the bookstore, looking at the books on the shelves, taking a book to the cashier, paying for it, leaving the store, getting back in her car, and returning home. Or Ursula can buy a book over the Internet. She can click on one of the online booksellers, search for the book by title, read a short description of the book, and then click on 1-Click Buying. Buying on the Internet has lower transaction costs than shopping at a store because online buying requires less time and effort. Before online book buying and selling, were there potential book purchases and sales that weren't being turned into actual book purchases and sales? There is some evidence that there were.

TURNING POTENTIAL TRADES INTO ACTUAL TRADES Some people are always looking for ways to earn a profit. It would seem that one way to earn a profit is to turn potential trades into actual trades by lowering transaction costs. Consider the following example. Buyer Smith is willing to pay a maximum price of $400 for good X; Seller Jones is willing to accept a minimum price of $200 for good X. Currently, the transaction costs of the exchange are $500, evenly split between Buyer Smith and Seller Jones.

Buyer Smith thinks, "Even if I pay the lowest possible price for good X, $200, I will still have to pay $250 in transaction costs, bringing my total to $450. The maximum price I am willing to pay for good X is $400, so I will not make this purchase."

Seller Jones thinks, "Even if I receive the highest possible price for good X, $400, I will still have to pay $250 in transaction costs, leaving me with only $150. The minimum price I am willing to accept for good X is $200, so I will not make this sale."

This potential trade will not become an actual trade unless someone can lower the transaction costs. One role of an entrepreneur is to try *to turn potential trades into actual trades by lowering transaction costs.* Suppose Entrepreneur Brown can lower the transaction costs for Buyer Smith and Seller Jones to $10 each, asking $60 from each person for services rendered. Also, Entrepreneur Brown negotiates the price of good X at $300. Will the potential exchange become an actual exchange?

Buyer Smith thinks, "I am willing to pay a maximum of $400 for good X. If I purchase good X through Entrepreneur Brown, I will pay $300 to Seller Jones, $10 in transaction costs, and $60 to Brown. This is a total of $370, leaving me better off by $30. It is worthwhile for me to purchase good X."

Seller Jones thinks, "I am willing to sell good X for a minimum of $200. If I sell good X through Entrepreneur Brown, I will receive $300 from Buyer Smith and will have to pay $10 in transaction costs and $60 to Brown. That will leave me with $230, or $30 better off. It is worthwhile for me to sell good X."

Thus, an entrepreneur can earn a profit by finding a way to lower transaction costs. As a result, a potential exchange turns into an actual exchange.

Trades and Third-Party Effects

Consider two trades. In the first, Harriet pays 80 cents to Taylor for a pack of chewing gum. In this trade, both Harriet and Taylor are made better off (they wouldn't have traded otherwise), and no one is made worse off.

In the second trade, Bob pays $4 to George for a pack of cigarettes. Bob takes a cigarette, lights it, and smokes it. It happens that he is near Caroline when he smokes the cigarette, and she begins to cough because she is sensitive to cigarette smoke. In this trade, both Bob, who buys the cigarettes, and George, who sells the cigarettes, are made better off. But Caroline, who had nothing to do with the trade, is made worse off. In this exchange, a third party, Caroline, is adversely affected by the exchange between George and Bob.

These examples show that some trades affect only the parties involved in the exchange, and some trades have *third-party effects* (someone other than the parties involved in the exchange is affected). In the cigarette example, the third-party effect was negative; there was an adverse effect on Caroline, the third party. Sometimes economists call adverse third-party effects *negative externalities*. A later chapter discusses this topic in detail.

SELF-TEST

1. What are transaction costs? Are the transaction costs of buying a house likely to be greater or less than those of buying a car? Explain your answer.

2. Smith is willing to pay a maximum of $300 for good X, and Jones is willing to sell good X for a minimum of $220. Will Smith buy good X from Jones?

3. Give an example of a trade without third-party effects. Next, give an example of a trade with third-party effects.

Production, Trade, and Specialization

The first section of this chapter discusses production; the second section discusses trade. From these two sections, you might conclude that production and trade are unrelated activities. However, they are not: Before you can trade, you need to produce something. This section ties production and trade together and also shows how the benefits one receives from trade can be affected by how one produces.

Producing and Trading

To show how a change in production can benefit traders, we eliminate anything and everything extraneous to the process. Thus, we eliminate money and consider a barter, or moneyless, economy.

In this economy, there are two individuals, Elizabeth and Brian. They live near each other, and each engages in two activities: baking bread and growing apples. Let's suppose that within a certain period of time, Elizabeth can produce 20 loaves of bread and no apples, or 10 loaves of bread and 10 apples, or no bread and 20 apples. In other words, three points on Elizabeth's production possibilities frontier correspond to 20 loaves of bread and no apples, 10 loaves of bread and 10 apples, and no bread and 20 apples. As a consumer, Elizabeth likes to eat both bread and apples, so she decides to produce (and consume) 10 loaves of bread and 10 apples.

Within the same time period, Brian can produce 10 loaves of bread and no apples, or 5 loaves of bread and 15 apples, or no bread and 30 apples. In other words, these three combinations correspond to three points on Brian's production possibilities frontier. Brian, like Elizabeth, likes to eat both bread and apples, so he decides to produce and consume 5 loaves of bread and 15 apples. Exhibit 8 shows the combinations of bread and apples that Elizabeth and Brian can produce.

Elizabeth thinks that both she and Brian may be better off if each specializes in producing only one of the two goods and trading it for the other. In other words, Elizabeth should produce either bread or apples but not both. Brian thinks this may be a good idea but is not sure which good each person should specialize in producing.

An economist would advise each to produce the good that he or she can produce at a lower cost. In economics, a person who can produce a good at a lower cost than another person is said to have a **comparative advantage** in the production of that good.

Exhibit 8 shows that for every 10 units of bread Elizabeth does not produce, she can produce 10 apples. In other words, the opportunity cost of producing 1 loaf of bread *(B)* is 1 apple *(A)*:

$$\text{Opportunity costs for Elizabeth: } 1B = 1A$$
$$1A = 1B$$

As for Brian, for every 5 loaves of bread he does not produce, he can produce 15 apples. So, for every 1 loaf of bread he does not produce, he can produce 3 apples. It follows, then, that for every 1 apple he chooses to produce, he forfeits 1/3 loaf of bread.

$$\text{Opportunity costs for Brian: } 1B = 3A$$
$$1A = \tfrac{1}{3}B$$

Comparing opportunity costs, we see that Elizabeth can produce bread at a lower opportunity cost than Brian can. (Elizabeth forfeits 1 apple when she produces 1 loaf of bread, whereas Brian forfeits 3 apples when he produces 1 loaf of bread.) On the other hand, Brian can produce apples at a lower opportunity cost than Elizabeth can. We conclude that Elizabeth has a comparative advantage in the production of bread, and Brian has a comparative advantage in the production of apples.

Suppose each person specializes in the production of the good in which he or she has a comparative advantage. This means Elizabeth produces only bread and produces 20 loaves. Brian produces only apples and produces 30 apples.

Comparative Advantage

The situation where someone can produce a good at lower opportunity cost than someone else can.

Elizabeth		Brian	
Bread	**Apples**	**Bread**	**Apples**
20	0	10	0
10	10	5	15
0	20	0	30

exhibit **8**

Production by Elizabeth and Brian

This exhibit shows the combinations of goods each can produce individually in a given time period.

economics 24/7

JERRY SEINFELD, THE DOORMAN, AND ADAM SMITH

Oh, I get it. Why waste time making small talk with the doorman? I should just shut up and do my job, opening the door for you.

—The doorman, speaking to Jerry,
in an episode of *Seinfeld*

In a *Seinfeld* episode, Jerry comes across a doorman (played by actor Larry Miller) who seems to have a chip on his shoulder. While waiting for the elevator, Jerry sees the doorman reading a newspaper. Jerry looks over and says, "What about those Knicks?" (a reference to the New York Knicks professional basketball team). The doorman's response is, "What makes you think I wasn't reading the Wall Street page? Oh, I know, because I'm the uneducated doorman."

This exchange between the doorman and Jerry would be unlikely if Jerry had not lived in New York City or in some other large city. That's because doormen are usually found only in large cities. If you live in a city with a population less than 100,000, you may not find a single doorman in the entire city. There are few doormen even in cities with a population of 1 million.

This observation is not unique to us. It goes back to Adam Smith, who said that there is a direct relationship between the degree of specialization and the size of the market. Smith said:

> There are some sorts of industry, even of the lowest kind, which can be carried on nowhere but in a great town. A porter, for example, can find employment and subsistence in no other place. A village is by much too narrow a sphere for him; even an ordinary market town is scarce large enough to afford him constant occupation.[1]

Smith's observation that "some sorts of industry . . . can be carried on nowhere but in a great town" seems true. Some occupations and some goods can only be found in big cities. Try to find a doorman in North Adams, Michigan (population 514) or restaurant chefs who only prepare Persian, Yugoslavian, or Caribbean entrées in Ipswich, South Dakota (population 943).

[1] *An Inquiry into the Nature and Causes of the Wealth of Nations,* Adam Smith. Ed. Edwin Cannan, New York: Modern Library, 1965.

Thinking like AN ECONOMIST

We see many people specializing in the world in which we live. One person only works at accounting services, another only styles hair, a third only writes songs. Why do people specialize? Largely, it is because individuals have found that they are better off specializing in producing one good or service, selling that good or service for money, and then using the money to buy what they want. It is simply our story of Elizabeth and Brian occurring repeatedly with different pairs of individuals.

Now suppose that Elizabeth and Brian decide to trade 8 loaves of bread for 12 apples. In other words, Elizabeth produces 20 loaves of bread and then trades 8 of the loaves for 12 apples. After the trade, Elizabeth consumes 12 loaves of bread and 12 apples. Compare this situation with what she consumed when she didn't specialize and didn't trade. In that situation, she consumed 10 loaves of bread and 10 apples. Clearly, Elizabeth is better off when she specializes and trades than when she does not. But what about Brian?

Brian produces 30 apples and trades 12 of them to Elizabeth for 8 loaves of bread. In other words, he consumes 8 loaves of bread and 18 apples. Compare this situation with what he consumed when he didn't specialize and didn't trade. In that situation, he consumed 5 loaves of bread and 15 apples. Thus, Brian is also better off when he specializes and trades than when he does not.

Exhibit 9 summarizes consumption for Elizabeth and Brian. It shows that both Elizabeth and Brian make themselves better off by specializing in the production of one good and trading for the other.

	No Specialization and No Trade	Specialization and Trade	Gains from Specialization and Trade
Elizabeth Consumption of Loaves of Bread	10	12	+2
Consumption of Apples	10	12	+2
Brian Consumption of Loaves of Bread	5	8	+3
Consumption of Apples	15	18	+3

exhibit **9**

Consumption for Elizabeth and Brian With and Without Specialization and Trade

A comparison of the consumption of bread and apples before and after specialization and trade shows that both Elizabeth and Brian benefit from producing the good in which each has a comparative advantage and trading for the other good.

Profit and a Lower Cost of Living

The last column of Exhibit 9 shows the gains from specialization and trade. One way to view these gains is in terms of Elizabeth and Brian being better off when they specialize and trade than when they do not specialize and do not trade. In short, specialization and trade make people better off.

Another way to view these gains is in terms of *profit* and a *lower cost of living*. To illustrate, let's look again at Elizabeth. Essentially, Elizabeth undertakes two actions by specializing and trading. The first action is to produce more of one good (loaves of bread) than she produces when she does not specialize. The second action is to trade, or "sell," some of the bread for a "price" higher than the cost of producing the bread. Specifically, she "sells" 8 of the loaves of bread (to Brian) for a "price" of 12 apples. In other words, she "sells" each loaf of bread for a "price" of 1 1/2 apples. But Elizabeth can produce a loaf of bread for a cost of 1 apple. So she "sells" the bread for a "price" (1 1/2 apples) that's higher than her cost of producing the bread (1 apple). The difference is her profit.

Many people think that one person's profit is another person's loss. In other words, because Elizabeth earns a profit by specializing and trading, Brian must lose. But we know this is not the case. The cost to Brian of producing a loaf of bread is 3 apples. But he "buys" bread from Elizabeth for a "price" of only 1 1/2 apples. In other words, while Elizabeth is earning a profit, Brian's cost of living (what he has to forfeit to get a loaf of bread) is declining.

A Benevolent and All-Knowing Dictator Versus the Invisible Hand

Suppose a benevolent dictator governs the country where Brian and Elizabeth live. We assume that this benevolent dictator knows everything about almost every economic activity in his country. In other words, he knows Elizabeth's and Brian's opportunity costs of producing bread and apples.

Because the dictator is benevolent and because he wants the best for the people who live in his country, he orders Elizabeth to produce only loaves of bread and Brian to produce only apples. Next, he tells Elizabeth and Brian to trade 8 loaves of bread for 12 apples.

Afterward, he shows Exhibit 9 to Elizabeth and Brian. They are both surprised that they are better off having done what the benevolent dictator told them to do.

Now in the original story about Elizabeth and Brian, there was no benevolent, all-knowing dictator. There were only two people who were guided by their self-interest to specialize and trade. In other words, self-interest did for Elizabeth and Brian what the benevolent dictator did for them.

Adam Smith, the 18th-century Scottish economist and founder of modern economics, spoke about the *invisible hand* that "guided" individuals' actions toward a positive outcome that they did not intend. That is what happened in the original story about Elizabeth and Brian. Neither intended to increase the overall output of society; each intended only to make himself or herself better off.

SELF-TEST

1. If George can produce either (a) 10X and 20Y or (b) 5X and 25Y, what is the opportunity cost to George of producing one more X?

2. Harriet can produce either (a) 30X and 70Y or (b) 40X and 55Y; Bill can produce either (c) 10X and 40Y or (d) 20X and 20Y. Who has a comparative advantage in the production of X? of Y? Explain your answers.

A Reader Asks . . .

How Will Economics Help Me If I'm a History Major?

I'm a history major taking my first course in economics. But quite frankly, I don't see how economics will be of much use in my study of history. Any thoughts on the subject?

Economics often plays a major role in historical events. For example, many social scientists argue that economics played a large role in the collapse of communism. If communism had been able to produce the quantity and variety of goods and services that capitalism produces, perhaps the Soviet Union would still exist.

Fact is, understanding economics may help you understand many historical events or periods. If, as a historian, you study the Great Depression, you will need to know something about the stock market, tariffs, and more. If you study the California Gold Rush, you will need to know about supply, demand, and prices. If you study the history of prisoner-of-war camps, you will need to know about how and why

people trade and about money. If you study the Boston Tea Party, you will need to know about government grants of monopoly and about taxes.

Economics can also be useful in another way. Suppose you learn in your economics course what can and cannot cause inflation. We'll say you learn that X can cause inflation and that Y cannot. Then, one day, you read an article in which a historian says that Y caused the high inflation in a certain country and that the high inflation led to a public outcry, which was then met with stiff government reprisals. Without an understanding of economics, you might be willing to accept what the historian has written. But with your understanding of economics, you know that events could not have happened as the historian reports because Y, which the historian claims caused the high inflation, could not have caused the high inflation.

In conclusion, a good understanding of economics will not only help you understand key historical events but will also help you discern inaccuracies in recorded history.

! analyzing the scene

What does a point on a production possibilities frontier have to do with the collapse of the Soviet Union?

The former Soviet foreign minister said the Soviet Union had collapsed because of a conflict between the Kremlin and the Soviet people. What was the conflict? The conflict concerned where the economy of the Soviet Union chose to be located on its PPF. The Kremlin wanted a point that represented "more guns" (more military goods) and "less butter" (fewer civilian or consumer goods), whereas the people wanted a point that represented "fewer guns" and "more butter." In other words, the Kremlin wanted to be at one point on the PPF while the people wanted to be at another. It's unlikely the Soviet Union would have collapsed had the people and the Kremlin agreed on the point on the PPF to be at.

Why can't Bob get As in both biology and calculus, and what does Jim's desire to produce "more time" tell us about life?

Bob says he has to choose between an A in biology and an A in calculus. To make that statement, Bob must be thinking in terms of his PPF for "producing grades." His "grades PPF" would look like the straight line in Exhibit 1. Bob's likely biology grade is on the vertical axis (starting with an F at the origin and moving up to an A), and his calculus grade is on the horizontal axis (again starting with an F at the origin and moving across to an A). When Bob says that he must choose where he wants to get an A, he is saying that there is no point on his "grades PPF" that represents an A in both courses (given his resources, such as time, and his state of technology, such as his ability to learn the material). In other words, the point that represents two As is in his *unattainable region,* and the point that represents one A and, say, one B, is in his *attainable region.*

Jim's desire to produce "more time" tells us that he feels there is not enough of a particular resource (time) in which

to accomplish all his goals. More resources mean more goals can be met and fewer tradeoffs will be incurred.

What led Karen and Larry to specialize in doing certain tasks?

In the chapter we showed (numerically) how two people (Elizabeth and Brian) could make themselves better off by specializing and trading. What holds for Elizabeth and Brian also holds for Karen and Larry.

What did eBay do that really wasn't that hard?

On any given day, 16 million items in 27,000 different categories are listed for sale on eBay.com. What does eBay do? It brings buyers and sellers together.

Consider the situation years ago when the World Wide Web did not exist. Suppose a person in London found an old Beatles' record in his attic and decided he wanted to sell it. Unbeknownst to him, a person in Los Angeles wanted to buy exactly that old Beatles' record. But alas, the record never changed hands because neither the seller nor the buyer knew how to find the other or even if the other existed. In short, the transaction costs of completing the trade were just too high.

Years later, the Web came along, and with it, eBay. What eBay actually did was use the Web to lower the transaction costs of trading. eBay basically told the world: If you're a seller and want a buyer or if you're a buyer and want a seller, come to us.

Today, the London seller of the old Beatles' record can inexpensively be matched with the Los Angeles buyer. eBay and the Web are the "matchmakers." The potential traders go online to eBay where they become actual traders. eBay charges a small fee for creating the place where buyer and seller can find each other.

chapter summary

An Economy's Production Possibilities Frontier

- An economy's production possibilities frontier (PPF) represents the possible combinations of two goods that the economy can produce in a certain period of time under the conditions of a given state of technology and fully employed resources.

Increasing and Constant Opportunity Costs

- A straight-line PPF represents constant opportunity costs: Increased production of one good comes at constant opportunity costs.
- A bowed-outward (concave-downward) PPF represents the law of increasing opportunity costs: Increased production of one good comes at increased opportunity costs.

The Production Possibilities Frontier and Various Economic Concepts

- The PPF can be used to illustrate various economic concepts. Scarcity is illustrated by the frontier itself. Choice is illustrated by our knowing that we have to locate at some particular point either on the frontier or below it. In short, of the many attainable positions, one must be chosen. Opportunity cost is illustrated by a movement from one point on the PPF to another point on the PPF. Unemployed resources and productive inefficiency are illustrated by a point below the PPF. Productive efficiency and fully employed resources are illustrated by a point on the PPF. Economic growth is illustrated by a shift outward in the PPF.

Exchange or Trade

- The three time periods relevant to the trading process are (1) the ex ante period, which is the time before the trade is made; (2) the point of trade; and (3) the ex post period, which is the time after the trade has been made.
- There is a difference between trade and the terms of trade. Trade refers to the act of giving up one thing for something else. For example, a person may trade money for a car. The terms of trade refer to *how much* of one thing is traded for *how much* of something else. For example, how much money ($25,000? $30,000?) is traded for one car.

Transaction Costs

- Transaction costs are the costs associated with the time and effort needed to search out, negotiate, and consummate a trade. Some potential exchanges are not realized because of high transaction costs. Lowering transaction costs can turn a potential exchange into an actual exchange.
- One role of an entrepreneur is to try to lower transaction costs.

Comparative Advantage and Specialization

- Individuals can make themselves better off by specializing in the production of the good in which they have a comparative advantage and then trading some of that good for other goods. A person has a comparative advantage in the production of a good if he or she can produce the good at a lower opportunity cost than another person can.
- Individuals gain by specializing and trading. Specifically, they earn a profit by specializing in the production of the goods in which they have a comparative advantage.

key terms and concepts

Production Possibilities Frontier (PPF)	Productive Efficiency	(Exchange) Trade	Terms of Trade
Law of Increasing Opportunity Costs	Productive Inefficiency	Ex Ante	Transaction Costs
	Technology	Ex Post	Comparative Advantage

questions and problems

1 Describe how each of the following would affect the U.S. production possibilities frontier: (a) an increase in the number of illegal immigrants entering the country; (b) a war; (c) the discovery of a new oil field; (d) a decrease in the unemployment rate; (e) a law that requires individuals to enter lines of work for which they are not suited.

2 Explain how the following can be represented in a PPF framework: (a) the finiteness of resources implicit in the scarcity condition; (b) choice; (c) opportunity cost; (d) productive efficiency; (e) unemployed resources.

3 What condition must hold for the production possibilities frontier to be bowed outward (concave downward)? to be a straight line?

4 Give an example to illustrate each of the following: (a) constant opportunity costs and (b) increasing opportunity costs.

5 Why are most production possibilities frontiers for goods bowed outward (concave downward)?

6 Within a PPF framework, explain each of the following: (a) a disagreement between a person who favors more domestic welfare spending and one who favors more national defense spending; (b) an increase in the population; (c) a technological change that makes resources less specialized.

7 Some people have said that during the Cold War, the Central Intelligence Agency (CIA) regularly estimated (a) the total quantity of output produced in the Soviet Union and (b) the total quantity of civilian goods produced in the Soviet Union. Of what interest would these data, or the information that might be deduced from them, be to the CIA? (Hint: Think in terms of the PPF.)

8 Suppose a nation's PPF shifts inward as its population grows. What happens, on average, to the material standard of living of the people? Explain your answer.

9 "A nation may be able to live beyond its means, but the world cannot." Do you agree or disagree? Explain your answer.

10 Use the PPF framework to explain something in your everyday life that was not mentioned in the chapter.

11 Describe the three time periods relevant to the trading process.

12 Are all exchanges or trades beneficial to both parties in the ex post position? Explain your answer.

13 A person who benefits from a trade can be disgruntled over the terms of trade. Do you agree or disagree? Explain your answer.

14 Give an example of a negative third-party effect (negative externality).

working with numbers and graphs

1 Tina can produce any of the following combinations of goods X and Y: (a) 100X and 0Y, (b) 50X and 25Y, and (c) 0X and 50Y. David can produce any of the following combinations of goods X and Y: (a) 50X and 0Y, (b) 25X and 40Y, and (c) 0X and 80Y. Who has a comparative advantage in the production of good X? of good Y? Explain your answer.

2 Using the data in Problem 1, prove that both Tina and David can be made better off through specialization and trade.

3 Exhibit 6 represents an advance in technology that made it possible to produce more of both military and civilian goods. Represent an advance in technology that makes it possible to produce more of only civilian goods. Does this indirectly make it possible to produce more military goods? Explain your answer.

4 In the following figure, which graph depicts a technological breakthrough in the production of good X only?

5 In the preceding figure, which graph depicts a change in the PPF that is a likely consequence of war?

6 If PPF$_2$ in the following graph is the relevant production possibilities frontier, then which points are unattainable? Explain your answer.

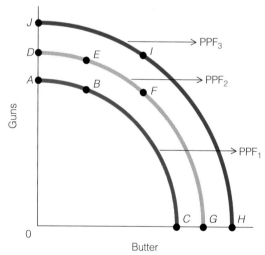

7 If PPF$_1$ in the preceding figure is the relevant production possibilities frontier, then which point(s) represent productive efficiency? Explain your answer.

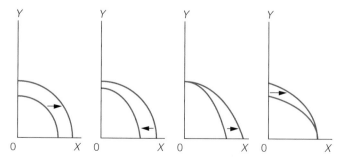

Supply and Demand: Theory

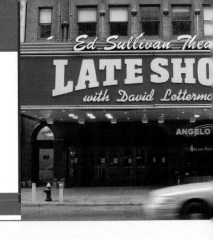

Setting the Scene

James Beider is a law student at Columbia University Law School. He lives on the Upper West Side of Manhattan, about thirty blocks from the school. The following events occurred on a day not too long ago.

9:03 A.M.

James is sitting in front of a computer in the law library at Columbia University. He's not checking on books but on the current prices of three stocks he owns (Wal-Mart, Microsoft, and Dell). He also checks on the exchange rate between the dollar and the euro. He plans to take a trip to Europe in the summer and is hoping the dollar will be stronger (against the euro) than it has been in the last few weeks. Last week, a person paid $1.10 for 1 euro; today, a person has to pay $1.28 for a euro. James mutters under his breath that if the dollar gets any weaker, he might have to cancel his trip.

1:30 P.M.

James is sitting in Tommy's Restaurant (three blocks from Columbia University), eating lunch with a few friends. His last class of the day is at 2 P.M. He picks up his cell phone and calls his apartment super-visor. No answer. James frowns as he puts his phone away. "What's wrong?" one friend asks. "I've been trying to get this

guy to fix my shower for two weeks now," James answers. "I'm just frustrated." "Ah, the joys of living in a rent-controlled apartment," his friend says.

4:55 P.M.

James and his girlfriend Kelly are in a taxi on their way to the Ed Sullivan Theater at 1697 Broadway to see the *Late Show with David Letterman*. James had wanted to see the show for two years and finally managed to get tickets. The tickets are free—but the wait time to obtain two tickets is approximately nine months.

11:02 P.M.

James is watching the 11 o'clock news as he eats a slice of cold pizza.

The TV reporter says, "The mayor said today that he is concerned that the city's burglary rate has been rising."

Cut to mayor at today's news conference.

"This city and this mayor are not going to be soft on crime. We're going to

do everything in our power to make sure that everyone knows that crime doesn't pay."

James says, "You tell 'em, mayor." Then he reaches for another slice of pizza.

? Here are some questions to keep in mind as you read this chapter:

- *At the time James checks stock prices, Wal-Mart is selling for $44.09, Microsoft for $23.75, and Dell for $21.75. Why doesn't Dell sell for more than Wal-Mart? Why does Microsoft sell for more than Dell? Why is the euro selling for $1.28 and not higher or lower?*

- *What does getting his shower fixed have to do with James living in a rent-controlled apartment?*

- *Why does it take so long (nine months) to get tickets to see the* Late Show with David Letterman?

- *Does the burglary rate have anything to do with how "hard" or "soft" a city is on crime?*

See analyzing the scene at the end of this chapter for answers to these questions.

A Note about Theories

Economists often build theories. They build **theories** to answer questions that do not have obvious answers. For example, they might build a theory to understand why interest rates rise at some times and fall at others, why the price of a car is $25,000 and not $27,000, or why some countries have higher economic growth rates than other countries. When building theories, economists omit certain variables or factors when trying to explain or understand something. To understand why, consider an analogy. Suppose you were to draw a map for a friend, showing him how to get from his house to your house. Would you draw a map that showed *every single thing* your friend would see on the trip from his house to yours, or would you simply draw the main roads and one or two landmarks? If you'd do the latter, you would be abstracting from reality; you would be omitting certain things.

You would "omit certain variables or factors" for two reasons. First, to get your friend from his house to yours, you don't need to include everything on your map. Simply noting main roads may be enough. Second, if you did note everything on your map, your friend might get confused. Giving too much detail could be as bad as giving too little. (Back in Chapter 1, you learned there is an efficient amount of almost everything. There is also an efficient amount of detail. There can be too much, too little, or just the right amount. Just the right amount is the efficient amount.)

When economists build a theory, they do the same thing you do when you draw a map. They abstract from reality; they leave out certain things. They focus on the major factors or variables that they believe will explain the phenomenon they are trying to understand.

This chapter deals with the theory of supply and demand. The objective of the theory is to try to understand why prices are what they are—for instance, why bread's price is $2 a loaf and not $20 a loaf or why a computer's price is $1,000 and not $10,000.

Theory
An abstract representation of the real world designed with the intent to better understand the world.

What Is Demand?

A **market** is any place people come together to trade. Economists often say that there are *two* sides to every market: a buying side and a selling side. The buying side of the market is usually referred to as the *demand* side; the selling side of the market is usually referred to as the *supply* side. Let's begin with a discussion of *demand*.

The word **demand** has a precise meaning in economics. It refers to:

1. the willingness and ability of buyers to purchase different quantities of a good
2. at different prices
3. during a specific time period (per day, week, etc.).[1]

For example, we can express part of John's demand for magazines by saying that he is willing and able to buy 10 magazines a month at $4 per magazine and that he is willing and able to buy 15 magazines a month at $3 per magazine.

Remember this important point about demand: Unless *both* willingness and ability to buy are present, there is no demand, and a person is not a buyer. For example, Josie may be willing to buy a computer but be unable to pay the price; Tanya may be able to buy a computer but be unwilling to do so. Neither Josie nor Tanya demands a computer, and neither is a buyer of a computer.

Market
Any place people come together to trade.

Demand
The willingness and ability of buyers to purchase different quantities of a good at different prices during a specific time period.

 If a person says that he wants a car, is this the same thing as saying that he demands a car?

No. Saying he "wants" a car does not imply that he has both the willingness and ability to buy a car. One must have both willingness and ability before one has demand.

---

[1]Demand takes into account *services* as well as goods. Goods are tangible and include such things as shirts, books, and television sets. Services are intangible and include such things as dental care, medical care, and an economics lecture. To simply the discussion, we refer only to goods.

The Law of Demand

Will people buy more units of a good at lower prices than at higher prices? For example, will people buy more computers at $1,000 per computer than at $4,000 per computer? If your answer is yes, you instinctively understand the law of demand. The **law of demand** states that as the price of a good rises, the quantity demanded of the good falls, and as the price of a good falls, the quantity demanded of the good rises, *ceteris paribus*. Simply put, the law of demand states that the price of a good and the quantity demanded of the good are inversely related, *ceteris paribus*:

$$P\uparrow Q_d\downarrow$$
$$P\downarrow Q_d\uparrow \text{ } ceteris \text{ } paribus$$

where P = price and Q_d = quantity demanded.

Quantity demanded is the number of units of a good that individuals are willing and able to buy at a particular price during some time period. For example, suppose individuals are willing and able to buy 100 TV dinners per week at a price of $4 per dinner. Therefore, 100 units is the quantity demanded of TV dinners at $4.

> **Law of Demand**
> As the price of a good rises, the quantity demanded of the good falls, and as the price of a good falls, the quantity demanded of the good rises, *ceteris paribus*.

What Does *Ceteris Paribus* Mean?

When we defined the law of demand, we used the term **ceteris paribus**. This is a Latin term that means *all other things held constant* or *nothing else changes*. For example, an economist might say: "As the price of Pepsi-Cola rises, the quantity demanded of Pepsi-Cola falls, *ceteris paribus*." Translated: If we raise the price of Pepsi-Cola, and nothing else changes—in other words, people's preferences stay the same, the recipe for Pepsi-Cola stays the same, and so on—then in response to the higher price of Pepsi-Cola, people will buy less Pepsi-Cola.

But some people ask, "Why would economists want to assume that when the price of Pepsi-Cola rises, nothing else changes? Don't other things change in the real world? Why assume things that we know are not true?"

Economists do not specify *ceteris paribus* because they want to say something false about the world. They specify it because they want to clearly define what they believe to be the real-world relationship between two variables. Look at it this way. If you drop a ball off the roof of a house, it will strike the ground *unless someone catches it*. This statement is true, and probably everyone would willingly accept it as true. But saying "unless someone catches it" is really no different than saying "assuming nothing else changes" or "*ceteris paribus*."

> **Ceteris Paribus**
> A Latin term meaning "all other things constant" or "nothing else changes."

 Please give another example to convey the meaning of why economists use the term ceteris paribus.

Wilson has eaten regular ice cream for years. Recently, he has been gaining weight. He decides to change from regular ice cream to low-fat ice cream. Now what do you expect will happen to his weight? If you think his weight will probably fall, then you are implicitly assuming "if nothing else changes." In other words, if Wilson doesn't change anything else in his life—how much ice cream he eats in total, how much he exercises each day, and so on—then his weight will decline by changing from eating regular to low-fat ice cream. Now an economist would simply put it this way: If Wilson changes from eating regular to low-fat ice cream, we can expect that he will lose weight, ceteris paribus.

Four Ways to Represent the Law of Demand

Here are four ways to represent the law of demand.

- **In Words.** We can represent the law of demand in words; we have done so already. Earlier we said that as the price of a good rises, quantity demanded falls, and as price falls, quantity demanded rises, *ceteris paribus*. That was the statement (in words) of the law of demand.

- **In Symbols.** We can also represent the law of demand in symbols, which we have also done earlier. In symbols, the law of demand is:

$$P\uparrow Q_d\downarrow$$
$$P\downarrow Q_d\uparrow \text{ } ceteris \text{ } paribus$$

- **In a Demand Schedule.** A **demand schedule** is the numerical representation of the law of demand. A demand schedule for good X is illustrated in Exhibit 1(a).

> **Demand Schedule**
> The numerical tabulation of the quantity demanded of a good at different prices. A demand schedule is the numerical representation of the law of demand.

- **As a Demand Curve.** In Exhibit 1(b), the four price-quantity combinations in part (a) are plotted and the points connected, giving us a (downward-sloping) demand curve. A **(downward-sloping) demand curve** is the graphical representation of the inverse relationship between price and quantity demanded specified by the law of demand. In short, a demand curve is a picture of the law of demand.

Two Prices: Absolute and Relative

In economics, there are absolute (or money) prices and relative prices. The **absolute price** is the price of the good in money terms. For example, the absolute price of a car might be $30,000. The **relative price** is the price of the good *in terms of another good.* For example, suppose the absolute price of a car is $30,000 and the absolute price of a computer is $2,000. The relative price of the car—that is, the price of the car *in terms of computers*—is 15 computers. A person gives up the opportunity to buy 15 computers when he or she buys a car.

$$\text{Relative price of a car (in terms of computers)} = \frac{\text{Absolute price of a car}}{\text{Absolute price of a computer}}$$
$$= \frac{\$30,000}{\$2,000}$$
$$= 15$$

Thus, the relative price of a car in this example is 15 computers.

Now let's compute the relative price of a computer—that is, the price of a computer in terms of a car:

$$\text{Relative price of a computer (in terms of cars)} = \frac{\text{Absolute price of a computer}}{\text{Absolute price of a car}}$$
$$= \frac{\$2,000}{\$30,000}$$
$$= \frac{1}{15}$$

Thus, the relative price of a computer in this example is 1/15 of a car. A person gives up the opportunity to buy 1/15 of a car when he or she buys a computer.

Now consider this question: What happens to the relative price of a good if its absolute price rises and nothing else changes? For example, if the absolute price of a car rises from $30,000 to $40,000, what happens to the relative price of a car? Obviously, it rises from 15 computers to 20 computers. In short, if the absolute price of a good rises and nothing else changes, then the relative price of the good rises too.

Why Does Quantity Demanded Go Down as Price Goes Up?

The law of demand states that price and quantity demanded are inversely related. This much you know. But do you know *why* quantity demanded moves in the opposite direction of price? We identify two reasons. The first reason is that *people substitute lower priced goods for higher priced goods.*

Often, many goods serve the same purpose. Many different goods will satisfy hunger, and many different drinks will satisfy thirst. For example, both orange juice and grapefruit juice will satisfy thirst. On Monday, the price of orange juice equals the price of grapefruit juice,

---

(Downward-Sloping) Demand Curve
The graphical representation of the law of demand.

Absolute (Money) Price
The price of a good in money terms.

Relative Price
The price of a good in terms of another good.

exhibit **1**

Demand Schedule and Demand Curve

Part (a) shows a demand schedule for good X. Part (b) shows a demand curve, obtained by plotting the different price-quantity combinations in part (a) and connecting the points. On a demand curve, the price (in dollars) represents price per unit of the good. The quantity demanded, on the horizontal axis, is always relevant for a specific time period (a week, a month, and so on).

Demand Schedule for Good X

Price (dollars)	Quantity Demanded	Point in Part (b)
4	10	A
3	20	B
2	30	C
1	40	D

(a)

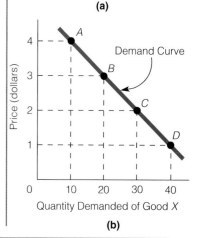

(b)

Thinking like **AN ECONOMIST**   The economist knows that it is possible for a good to go up in price at the same time as it becomes cheaper. (How can this happen?) To illustrate, suppose the absolute price of a pen is $1 and the absolute price of a pencil is 10 cents. The relative price of 1 pen, then, is 10 pencils. Now let the absolute price of a pen rise to $1.20 at the same time that the absolute price of a pencil rises to 20 cents. As a result, the relative price of 1 pen falls to 6 pencils. In other words, the absolute price of pens rises (from $1 to $1.20) at the same time as pens become relatively cheaper (in terms of how many pencils you have to give up to get a pen). Who would have thought it?

economics 24/7

TICKET PRICES AT DISNEY WORLD

The Walt Disney Company operates two major theme parks in the United States: Disneyland in California and Disney World in Florida. Every year, millions of people visit each site. The ticket price for visiting Disneyland or Disney World differs depending on how many days a person visits the theme park. For example, Disney World sells one- to ten-day tickets. On the day we checked, the price of a one-day ticket was $63 and the price of a ten-day ticket was $210.

Now if we take the price of a one-day ticket and multiply it by 10, we get $630, but oddly enough, the price of a ten-day ticket is not $630 but $210. Why does Disney World charge $420 less for a ten-day ticket rather than 10 times the one-day ticket price?

Disney World is effectively telling visitors that if they want to visit the theme park for one day, they have to pay $63. But if they want to visit the theme park for ten days, they don't

have to pay $63 for each additional day. They pay much less for additional days. But why?

An economic concept, the *law of diminishing marginal utility,* is the reason. The law of diminishing marginal utility states that as a person consumes additional units of a good, eventually, the utility from each additional unit of the good decreases. Assuming the law of diminishing marginal utility holds for Disney World, individuals will get more utility from the first day at Disney World than from, say, the second, third, or tenth day. The less utility or satisfaction a person gets from something, the lower the dollar amount he is willing to pay for it. Thus, a person would not be willing to pay as much for the second day at Disney World as the first, and he would not be willing to pay as much for the tenth day as the ninth and so on. Disney World knows this and therefore prices its ticket prices differently depending on how many days one wants to visit Disney World.

---

but on Tuesday, the price of orange juice rises. As a result, people will choose to buy less of the relatively higher priced orange juice and more of the relatively lower priced grapefruit juice. In other words, a rise in the price of orange juice will lead to a decrease in the quantity demanded of orange juice.

Law of Diminishing Marginal Utility

For a given time period, the marginal (additional) utility or satisfaction gained by consuming equal successive units of a good will decline as the amount consumed increases.

The second reason for the inverse relationship between price and quantity demanded has to do with the **law of diminishing marginal utility**, which states that for a given time period, the marginal (additional) utility or satisfaction gained by consuming equal successive units of a good will decline as the amount consumed increases. For example, you may receive more utility or satisfaction from eating your first hamburger at lunch than from eating your second and, if you continue, more utility from your second hamburger than from your third.

What does this have to do with the law of demand? Economists state that the more utility you receive from a unit of a good, the higher the price you are willing to pay for it; the less utility you receive from a unit of a good, the lower the price you are willing to pay for it. According to the law of diminishing marginal utility, individuals obtain less utility from additional units of a good. It follows that they will only buy larger quantities of a good at lower prices. And this is the law of demand.

Individual Demand Curve and Market Demand Curve

There is a difference between an individual demand curve and a market demand curve. An individual demand curve represents the price-quantity combinations of a particular

Quantity Demanded

Price	Jones		Smith		Other Buyers		All Buyers
$15	1		2		20		23
14	2		3		45		50
13	3		4		70		77
12	4	+	5	+	100	=	109
11	5	+	6	+	130	=	141
10	6		7		160		173

(a)

(b)

exhibit **2**

Deriving a Market Demand Schedule and a Market Demand Curve

Part (a) shows four demand schedules combined into one table. The market demand schedule is derived by adding the quantities demanded at each price. In (b), the data points from the demand schedule are plotted to show how a market demand curve is derived. Only two points on the market demand curve are noted.

good for a *single buyer*. For example, a demand curve could show Jones's demand for CDs. A market demand curve represents the price-quantity combinations of a particular good for *all buyers*. In this case, the demand curve would show all buyers' demand for CDs.

A market demand curve is derived by "adding up" individual demand curves, as we show in Exhibit 2. The demand schedules for Jones, Smith, and other buyers are shown in part (a). The market demand schedule is obtained by adding the quantities demanded at each price. For example, at $12, the quantities demanded are 4 units for Jones, 5 units for Smith, and 100 units for other buyers. Thus, a total of 109 units are demanded at $12. In part (b), the data points for the demand schedules are plotted and added to produce a market demand curve. The market demand curve could also be drawn directly from the market demand schedule.

A Change in Quantity Demanded Versus a Change in Demand

Economists often talk about (1) a change in quantity demanded and (2) a change in demand. Although "quantity demanded" may sound like "demand," they are not the same. In short, a "change in quantity demanded" *is not* the same as a "change in demand." (Read the last sentence at least two more times.) We use Exhibit 1 to illustrate the difference between "a change in quantity demanded" and "a change in demand."

A CHANGE IN QUANTITY DEMANDED Look at the horizontal axis in Exhibit 1, which is labeled "quantity demanded." Notice that quantity demanded is a *number*—such as 10, 20, 30, 40, and so on. More specifically, it is the number of units of a good that individuals are willing and able to buy at a particular price during some time period. In Exhibit 1, if the price is $4, then quantity demanded is 10 units of good *X*; if the price is $3, then quantity demanded is 20 units of good *X*.

> Quantity demanded = The *number* of units of a good that individuals are willing and able to buy at a particular price

Now, again looking at Exhibit 1, what can change quantity demanded from 10 (which it is at point *A*) to 20 (which it is at point *B*)? Or what has to change before quantity demanded will change? The answer is on the vertical axis of Exhibit 1. The only thing that can change the quantity demanded of a good is the price of the good, which is called **own price**.

Own Price

The price of a good. For example, if the price of oranges is $1, this is (its) own price.

> Change in quantity demanded = A *movement* from one point to another point on the same demand curve *caused* by a change in the price of the good

A CHANGE IN DEMAND Let's look again at Exhibit 1, this time focusing on the demand curve. Demand is represented by the *entire* curve. When an economist talks about a "change in demand," he or she is actually talking about a change—or shift—in the entire demand curve.

> Change in demand = Shift in demand curve

Demand can change in two ways: Demand can increase, and demand can decrease. Let's look first at an *increase* in demand. Suppose we have the following demand schedule.

Demand Schedule *A*	
Price	Quantity Demanded
$20	500
$15	600
$10	700
$ 5	800

The demand curve for this demand schedule will look like the demand curve labeled *D_A* in Exhibit 3(a).

Shifts in the Demand Curve

In part (a), the demand curve shifts rightward from *D_A* to *D_B*. This shift represents an increase in demand. At each price, the quantity demanded is greater than it was before. For example, the quantity demanded at $20 increases from 500 units to 600 units. In part (b), the demand curve shifts leftward from *D_A* to *D_C*. This shift represents a decrease in demand. At each price, the quantity demanded is less. For example, the quantity demand at $20 decreases from 500 units to 400 units.

(a)

(b)

What does an increase in demand mean? It means that individuals are willing and able to buy more units of the good at each and every price. In other words, demand schedule *A* will change as follows:

Demand Schedule *B* (increase in demand)	
Price	Quantity Demanded
$20	~~500~~ 600
$15	~~600~~ 700
$10	~~700~~ 800
$ 5	~~800~~ 900

Whereas individuals were willing and able to buy 500 units of the good at $20, now they are willing and able to buy 600 units of the good at $20; whereas individuals were willing and able to buy 600 units of the good at $15, now they are willing and able to buy 700 units of the good at $15; and so on.

As shown in Exhibit 3(a), the demand curve that represents demand schedule *B* lies to the right of the demand curve that represents demand schedule *A*. We conclude that *an increase in demand is represented by a rightward shift in the demand curve and means that individuals are willing and able to buy more of a good at each and every price.*

Increase in demand = Rightward shift in the demand curve

Now let's look at a *decrease* in demand. What does a decrease in demand mean? It means that individuals are willing and able to buy less of a good at each and every price. In this case, demand schedule *A* will change as follows:

Demand Schedule *C* (decrease in demand)	
Price	Quantity Demanded
$20	~~500~~ 400
$15	~~600~~ 500
$10	~~700~~ 600
$ 5	~~800~~ 700

As shown in Exhibit 3(b), the demand curve that represents demand schedule *C* obviously lies to the left of the demand curve that represents demand schedule *A*. We conclude that *a decrease in demand is represented by a leftward shift in the demand curve and means that individuals are willing and able to buy less of a good at each and every price.*

Decrease in demand = Leftward shift in the demand curve

What Factors Cause the Demand Curve to Shift?

We know what an increase and decrease in demand mean: An increase in demand means consumers are willing and able to buy more of a good at every price. A decrease in demand means consumers are willing and able to buy less of a good at every price. We also know that an increase in demand is graphically portrayed as a rightward shift in a demand curve and a decrease in demand is graphically portrayed as a leftward shift in a demand curve.

But what factors or variables can increase or decrease demand? What factors or variables can shift demand curves? We identify and discuss these factors or variables in this section.

INCOME As a person's income changes (increases or decreases), his or her demand for a particular good may rise, fall, or remain constant.

Normal Good

A good the demand for which rises (falls) as income rises (falls).

For example, suppose Jack's income rises. As a consequence, his demand for CDs rises. For Jack, CDs are a normal good. For a **normal good**, as income rises, demand for the good rises, and as income falls, demand for the good falls.

$$X \text{ is a normal good: If income} \uparrow \text{ then } D_X \uparrow$$
$$\text{If income} \downarrow \text{ then } D_X \downarrow$$

Inferior Good

A good the demand for which falls (rises) as income rises (falls).

Now suppose Marie's income rises. As a consequence, her demand for canned baked beans falls. For Marie, canned baked beans are an inferior good. For an **inferior good**, as income rises, demand for the good falls, and as income falls, demand for the good rises.

$$Y \text{ is an inferior good: If income} \uparrow \text{ then } D_Y \downarrow$$
$$\text{If income} \downarrow \text{ then } D_Y \uparrow$$

Neutral Good

A good the demand for which does not change as income rises or falls.

Finally, suppose when George's income rises, his demand for toothpaste neither rises nor falls. For George, toothpaste is neither a normal good nor an inferior good. Instead, it is a neutral good. For a **neutral good**, as income rises or falls, the demand for the good does not change.

PREFERENCES People's preferences affect the amount of a good they are willing to buy at a particular price. A change in preferences in favor of a good shifts the demand curve rightward. A change in preferences away from the good shifts the demand curve leftward. For example, if people begin to favor Dan Brown novels to a greater degree than previously, the demand for Brown novels increases, and the demand curve shifts rightward.

Substitutes

Two goods that satisfy similar needs or desires. If two goods are substitutes, the demand for one rises as the price of the other rises (or the demand for one falls as the price of the other falls).

PRICES OF RELATED GOODS There are two types of related goods: substitutes and complements. Two goods are **substitutes** if they satisfy similar needs or desires. For many people, Coca-Cola and Pepsi-Cola are substitutes. If two goods are substitutes, as the price of one rises (falls), the demand for the other rises (falls). For instance, higher Coca-Cola prices will increase the demand for Pepsi-Cola as people substitute Pepsi for the higher priced Coke (Exhibit 4(a)). Other examples of substitutes are coffee and tea, corn chips and potato chips, two brands of margarine, and foreign and domestic cars.

$$X \text{ and } Y \text{ are substitutes: If } P_X \uparrow \text{ then } D_Y \uparrow$$
$$\text{If } P_X \downarrow \text{ then } D_Y \downarrow$$

Complements

Two goods that are used jointly in consumption. If two goods are complements, the demand for one rises as the price of the other falls (or the demand for one falls as the price of the other rises).

Two goods are **complements** if they are consumed jointly. For example, tennis rackets and tennis balls are used together to play tennis. If two goods are complements, as the price of one rises (falls), the demand for the other falls (rises). For example, higher tennis racket prices will decrease the demand for tennis balls, as Exhibit 4(b) shows. Other examples of complements are cars and tires, light bulbs and lamps, and golf clubs and golf balls.

$$A \text{ and } B \text{ are complements: If } P_A \uparrow \text{ then } D_B \downarrow$$
$$\text{If } P_A \downarrow \text{ then } D_B \uparrow$$

NUMBER OF BUYERS The demand for a good in a particular market area is related to the number of buyers in the area: more buyers, higher demand; fewer buyers, lower demand. The number of buyers may increase owing to a higher birthrate, increased immigration, the migration of people from one region of the country to another, and so on. The number of buyers may decrease owing to a higher death rate, war, the migration of people from one region of the country to another, and so on.

EXPECTATIONS OF FUTURE PRICE Buyers who expect the price of a good to be higher next month may buy the good now—thus increasing the current (or present) demand

SUBSTITUTES

If Coca-Cola and Pepsi-Cola are substitutes, a higher price for Coca-Cola leads to . . .

. . . a rightward shift in the demand curve for Pepsi-Cola.

Price of Coca-Cola

P_2 B
P_1 A

D_{CC}

0   Q_{d_2} Q_{d_1}

Quantity Demanded of Coca-Cola

Price of Pepsi-Cola

D_{PC_2}
D_{PC_1}

0

Quantity Demanded of Pepsi-Cola

(a)

COMPLEMENTS

If tennis rackets and tennis balls are complements, a higher price for tennis rackets leads to . . .

. . . a leftward shift in the demand curve for tennis balls.

Price of Tennis Rackets

P_2 B
P_1 A

D_{TR}

0   Q_{d_2} Q_{d_1}

Quantity Demanded of Tennis Rackets

Price of Tennis Balls

D_{TB_1}
D_{TB_2}

0

Quantity Demanded of Tennis Balls

(b)

exhibit **4**

Substitutes and Complements

(a) Coca-Cola and Pepsi-Cola are substitutes: The price of one and the demand for the other are directly related. As the price of Coca-Cola rises, the demand for Pepsi-Cola increases. (b) Tennis rackets and tennis balls are complements: The price of one and the demand for the other are inversely related. As the price of tennis rackets rises, the demand for tennis balls decreases.

for the good. Buyers who expect the price of a good to be lower next month may wait until next month to buy the good—thus decreasing the current (or present) demand for the good.

For example, suppose you are planning to buy a house. One day, you hear that house prices are expected to go down in a few months. Consequently, you decide to delay your purchase of a house for a few months. Alternatively, if you hear that prices are expected to rise in a few months, you might go ahead and purchase a house now.

Movement Factors and Shift Factors

Economists often distinguish between (1) factors that can move us along curves and (2) factors that can shift curves.

The factors that move us along curves are sometimes called *movement* factors. In many economic diagrams—such as the diagram of the demand curve in Exhibit 1—the movement factor (price) is on the vertical axis.

The factors that actually shift the curves are sometimes called *shift* factors. The shift factors for the demand curve are income, preferences, the price of related goods, and so on. Often, the shift factors do not appear in the economic diagrams. For example, in Exhibit 1, the movement factor—price—is on the vertical axis, but the shift factors do not appear anywhere in the diagram. We just know what they are and that they can shift the demand curve.

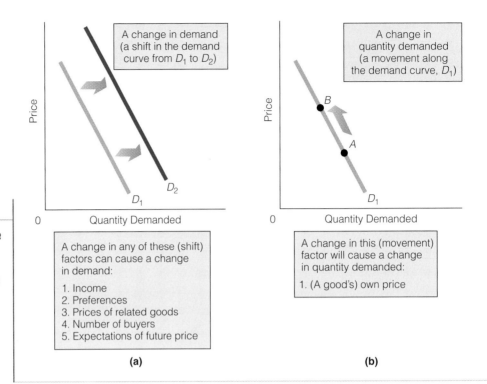

A change in demand (a shift in the demand curve from D_1 to D_2)

A change in quantity demanded (a movement along the demand curve, D_1)

D_2

D_1

B

A

D_1

Price

Price

0   Quantity Demanded

0   Quantity Demanded

A change in any of these (shift) factors can cause a change in demand:

1. Income
2. Preferences
3. Prices of related goods
4. Number of buyers
5. Expectations of future price

A change in this (movement) factor will cause a change in quantity demanded:

1. (A good's) own price

(a)

(b)

exhibit 5

A Change in Demand Versus a Change in Quantity Demanded

(a) A change in demand refers to a shift in the demand curve. A change in demand can be brought about by a number of factors (see the exhibit and text). (b) A change in quantity demanded refers to a movement along a given demand curve. A change in quantity demanded is brought about only by a change in (a good's) own price.

When you see a curve in this book, first ask what factor will move us along the curve. In other words, what is the movement factor? Second, ask what factors will shift the curve. In other words, what are the shift factors? Exhibit 5 summarizes the shift factors that can change demand and the movement factors that can change quantity demanded.

SELF-TEST

(Answers to Self-Test questions are in the Self-Test Appendix.)

1. As Sandi's income rises, her demand for popcorn rises. As Mark's income falls, his demand for prepaid telephone cards rises. What kinds of goods are popcorn and telephone cards for the people who demand each?

2. Why are demand curves downward sloping?

3. Give an example that illustrates how to derive a market demand curve.

4. What factors can change demand? What factors can change quantity demanded?

Supply

Just as the word *demand* has a specific meaning in economics, so does the word *supply*. **Supply** refers to

Supply
The willingness and ability of sellers to produce and offer to sell different quantities of a good at different prices during a specific time period.

1. the willingness and ability of sellers to produce and offer to sell different quantities of a good

2. at different prices

3. during a specific time period (per day, week, etc.).

The Law of Supply

The **law of supply** states that as the price of a good rises, the quantity supplied of the good rises, and as the price of a good falls, the quantity supplied of the good falls, *ceteris paribus*. Simply put, the price of a good and the quantity supplied of the good are directly related, *ceteris paribus*. (Quantity supplied is the number of units sellers are willing and able to produce and offer to sell at a particular price.) The **(upward-sloping) supply curve** is the graphical representation of the law of supply (see Exhibit 6). The law of supply can be summarized as follows:

$$P\uparrow Q_S\uparrow$$
$$P\downarrow Q_S\downarrow \textit{ceteris paribus}$$

where P = price and Q_S = quantity supplied.

The law of supply holds for the production of most goods. It does not hold when there is no time to produce more units of a good. For example, suppose a theater in Atlanta is sold out for tonight's play. Even if ticket prices increased from $30 to $40, there would be no additional seats in the theater. There is no time to produce more seats. The supply curve for theater seats is illustrated in Exhibit 7(a). It is fixed at the number of seats in the theater, 500.[2]

The law of supply also does not hold for goods that cannot be produced over any period of time. For example, the violinmaker Antonio Stradivari died in 1737. A rise in the price of Stradivarius violins does not affect the number of Stradivarius violins supplied, as Exhibit 7(b) illustrates.

Why Most Supply Curves Are Upward Sloping

Think back to the discussion of the *law of increasing opportunity costs* in Chapter 2. That discussion shows that if the production possibilities frontier (PPF) is bowed outward, increasing costs exist. In other words, increased production of a good comes at increased opportunity costs. An upward-sloping supply curve simply reflects the fact that costs rise when more units of a good are produced.

Law of Supply

As the price of a good rises, the quantity supplied of the good rises, and as the price of a good falls, the quantity supplied of the good falls, *ceteris paribus*.

(Upward-Sloping) Supply Curve

The graphical representation of the law of supply.

exhibit 6

A Supply Curve

The upward-sloping supply curve is the graphical representation of the law of supply, which states that price and quantity supplied are directly related, *ceteris paribus*. On a supply curve, the price (in dollars) represents price per unit of the good. The quantity supplied, on the horizontal axis, is always relevant for a specific time period (a week, a month, and so on).

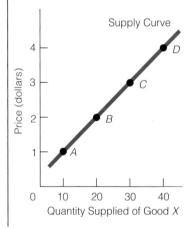

exhibit 7

Supply Curves When There Is No Time to Produce More or No More Can Be Produced

The supply curve is not upward-sloping when there is no time to produce additional units or when additional units cannot be produced. In those cases, the supply curve is vertical.

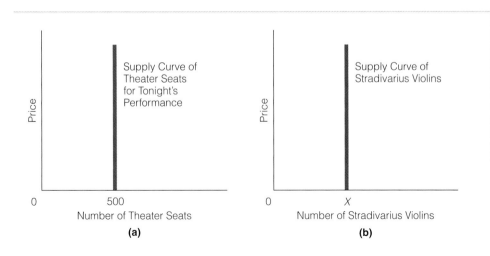

2The vertical supply curve is said to be *perfectly inelastic*.

THE MARKET SUPPLY CURVE An individual supply curve represents the price-quantity combinations for a single seller. The market supply curve represents the price-quantity combinations for all sellers of a particular good. Exhibit 8 shows how a market supply curve can be derived by "adding" individual supply curves. In part (a), a **supply schedule**, the numerical tabulation of the quantity supplied of a good at different prices, is given for Brown, Alberts, and other suppliers. The market supply schedule is obtained by adding the quantities supplied at each price, *ceteris paribus*. For example, at $11, the quantities supplied are 2 units for Brown, 3 units for Alberts, and 98 units for other suppliers. Thus, a total of 103 units are supplied at $11. In part (b), the data points for the supply schedules are plotted and added to produce a market supply curve. The market supply curve could also be drawn directly from the market supply schedule.

Supply Schedule
The numerical tabulation of the quantity supplied of a good at different prices. A supply schedule is the numerical representation of the law of supply.

Changes in Supply Mean Shifts in Supply Curves

Just as demand can change, so can supply. The supply of a good can rise or fall. What does it mean if the supply of a good increases? It means that suppliers are willing and able to produce and offer to sell more of the good at all prices. For example, suppose that in January sellers are willing and able to produce and offer for sale 600 shirts at $25 each and that in February they are willing and able to produce and sell 900 shirts at $25 each. An increase in supply shifts the entire supply curve to the right, as shown in Exhibit 9(a).

---

exhibit 8

Deriving a Market Supply Schedule and a Market Supply Curve

Part (a) shows four supply schedules combined into one table. The market supply schedule is derived by adding the quantities supplied at each price. In (b), the data points from the supply schedules are plotted to show how a market supply curve is derived. Only two points on the market supply curve are noted.

Price	Quantity Supplied			
	Brown	**Alberts**	**Other Suppliers**	**All Suppliers**
$10	1	2	96	99
11	2 +	3 +	98 =	103
12	3 +	4 +	102 =	109
13	4	5	106	115
14	5	6	108	119
15	6	7	110	123

(a)

(b)

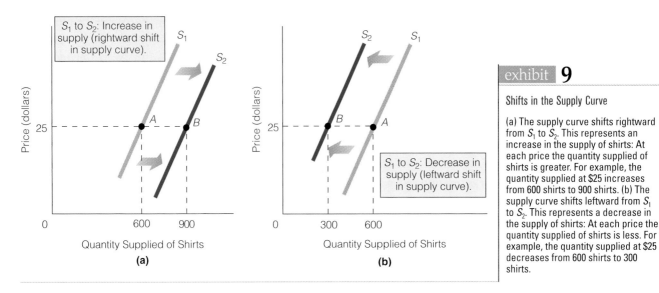

exhibit **9**

Shifts in the Supply Curve

(a) The supply curve shifts rightward from S_1 to S_2. This represents an increase in the supply of shirts: At each price the quantity supplied of shirts is greater. For example, the quantity supplied at $25 increases from 600 shirts to 900 shirts. (b) The supply curve shifts leftward from S_1 to S_2. This represents a decrease in the supply of shirts: At each price the quantity supplied of shirts is less. For example, the quantity supplied at $25 decreases from 600 shirts to 300 shirts.

The supply of a good decreases if sellers are willing and able to produce and offer to sell less of the good at all prices. For example, suppose that in January sellers are willing and able to produce and offer for sale 600 shirts at $25 each and that in February they are willing and able to produce and sell only 300 shirts at $25 each. A decrease in supply shifts the entire supply curve to the left, as shown in Exhibit 9(b).

What Factors Cause the Supply Curve to Shift?

We know the supply of any good can change. But what causes supply to change? What causes supply curves to shift? The factors that can change supply include (1) prices of relevant resources, (2) technology, (3) number of sellers, (4) expectations of future price, (5) taxes and subsidies, and (6) government restrictions.

PRICES OF RELEVANT RESOURCES Resources are needed to produce goods. For example, wood is needed to produce doors. If the price of wood falls, it becomes less costly to produce doors. How will door producers respond? Will they produce more doors, the same number of doors, or fewer doors? With lower costs and prices unchanged, the profit from producing and selling doors has increased; as a result, there is an increased (monetary) incentive to produce doors. Door producers will produce and offer to sell more doors at each and every price. Thus, the supply of doors will increase, and the supply curve of doors will shift rightward. If the price of wood rises, it becomes more costly to produce doors. Consequently, the supply of doors will decrease, and the supply curve of doors will shift leftward.

TECHNOLOGY In Chapter 2, technology is defined as the body of skills and knowledge concerning the use of resources in production. Also, an advance in technology refers to the ability to produce more output with a fixed amount of resources, thus reducing per-unit production costs. To illustrate, suppose it currently takes $100 to produce 40 units of a good. The per-unit cost is therefore $2.50. If an advance in technology makes it possible to produce 50 units at a cost of $100, then the per-unit cost falls to $2.00.

If per-unit production costs of a good decline, we expect the quantity supplied of the good at each price to increase. Why? The reason is that lower per-unit costs increase profitability and therefore provide producers with an incentive to produce more. For example, if corn growers develop a way to grow more corn using the same amount of water and other resources, it follows that per-unit production costs will fall, profitability will increase, and growers will want to grow and sell more corn at each price. The supply curve of corn will shift rightward.

NUMBER OF SELLERS If more sellers begin producing a particular good, perhaps because of high profits, the supply curve will shift rightward. If some sellers stop producing a particular good, perhaps because of losses, the supply curve will shift leftward.

EXPECTATIONS OF FUTURE PRICES If the price of a good is expected to be higher in the future, producers may hold back some of the product today (if possible, but perishables cannot be held back). Then, they will have more to sell at the higher future price. Therefore, the current supply curve will shift leftward. For example, if oil producers expect the price of oil to be higher next year, some may hold oil off the market this year to be able to sell it next year. Similarly, if they expect the price of oil to be lower next year, they might pump more oil this year than previously planned.

TAXES AND SUBSIDIES Some taxes increase per-unit costs. Suppose a shoe manufacturer must pay a $2 tax per pair of shoes produced. This tax leads to a leftward shift in the supply curve, indicating that the manufacturer wants to produce and offer to sell fewer pairs of shoes at each price. If the tax is eliminated, the supply curve shifts rightward.

Subsidy
A monetary payment by government to a producer of a good or service.

    Subsidies have the opposite effect. Suppose the government subsidizes the production of corn by paying corn farmers $2 for every bushel of corn they produce. Because of the subsidy, the quantity supplied of corn is greater at each price, and the supply curve of corn shifts rightward. Removal of the subsidy shifts the supply curve of corn leftward. A rough rule of thumb is that we get more of what we subsidize and less of what we tax.

GOVERNMENT RESTRICTIONS Sometimes, government acts to reduce supply. Consider a U.S. import quota on Japanese television sets. An import quota, or quantitative restriction on foreign goods, reduces the supply of Japanese television sets in the United States. It shifts the supply curve leftward. The elimination of the import quota allows the supply of Japanese television sets in the United States to shift rightward.

    Licensure has a similar effect. With licensure, individuals must meet certain requirements before they can legally carry out a task. For example, owner-operators of day-care centers must meet certain requirements before they are allowed to sell their services. No doubt, this reduces the number of day-care centers and shifts the supply curve of day-care centers leftward.

A Change in Supply Versus a Change in Quantity Supplied

A change in supply is not the same as a change in quantity supplied. A change in supply refers to a shift in the supply curve, as illustrated in Exhibit 10(a). For example, saying that the supply of oranges has increased is the same as saying that the supply curve for oranges has shifted rightward. The factors that can change supply (shift the supply curve) include prices of relevant resources, technology, number of sellers, expectations of future price, taxes and subsidies, and government restrictions.

    A change in quantity supplied refers to a movement along a supply curve, as in Exhibit 10(b). The only factor that can directly cause a change in the quantity supplied of a good is a change in the price of the good, or own price.

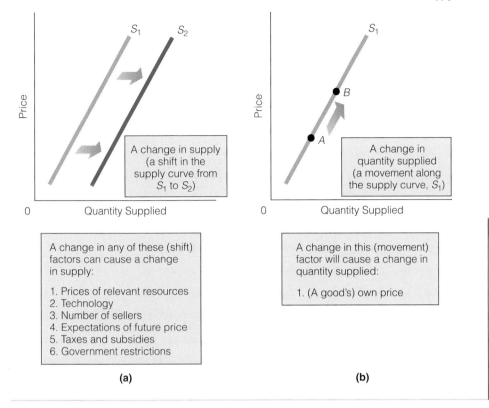

A Change in Supply Versus a Change in Quantity Supplied

(a) A change in supply refers to a shift in the supply curve. A change in supply can be brought about by a number of factors (see the exhibit and text). (b) A change in quantity supplied refers to a movement along a given supply curve. A change in quantity supplied is brought about only by a change in (a good's) own price.

SELF-TEST

1. What would the supply curve for houses (in a given city) look like for a time period of (a) the next ten hours and (b) the next three months?

2. What happens to the supply curve if each of the following occurs?
   a. There is a decrease in the number of sellers.
   b. A per-unit tax is placed on the production of a good.
   c. The price of a relevant resource falls.

3. "If the price of apples rises, the supply of apples will rise." True or false? Explain your answer.

The Market: Putting Supply and Demand Together

In this section, we put supply and demand together and discuss the market. The purpose of the discussion is to gain some understanding about how prices are determined.

Supply and Demand at Work at an Auction

Imagine you are at an auction where bushels of corn are bought and sold. At this auction, the auctioneer will adjust the corn price to sell all the corn offered for sale. The supply curve of corn is vertical, as in Exhibit 11. It intersects the horizontal axis at 40,000 bushels; that is, quantity supplied is 40,000 bushels. The demand curve for corn is downward sloping. Furthermore, suppose each potential buyer of corn is sitting in front of a computer that immediately registers the number of bushels he or she wants to buy. For example, if Nancy Bernstein wants to buy 5,000 bushels of corn, she simply keys

exhibit **11**

Supply and Demand at Work at an Auction

Q_d = quantity demanded; Q_s = quantity supplied. The auctioneer calls out different prices, and buyers record how much they are willing and able to buy. At prices of $6.00, $5.00, and $4.00, quantity supplied is greater than quantity demanded. At prices of $1.25 and $2.25, quantity demanded is greater than quantity supplied. At a price of $3.10, quantity demanded equals quantity supplied.

Surplus (Excess Supply)

A condition in which quantity supplied is greater than quantity demanded. Surpluses occur only at prices above equilibrium price.

Shortage (Excess Demand)

A condition in which quantity demanded is greater than quantity supplied. Shortages occur only at prices below equilibrium price.

Equilibrium Price (Market–Clearing Price)

The price at which quantity demanded of the good equals quantity supplied.

Equilibrium Quantity

The quantity that corresponds to equilibrium price. The quantity at which the amount of the good that buyers are willing and able to buy equals the amount that sellers are willing and able to sell, and both equal the amount actually bought and sold.

Disequilibrium Price

A price other than equilibrium price. A price at which quantity demanded does not equal quantity supplied.

Disequilibrium

A state of either surplus or shortage in a market.

Equilibrium

Equilibrium means "at rest." Equilibrium in a market is the price-quantity combination from which there is no tendency for buyers or sellers to move away. Graphically, equilibrium is the intersection point of the supply and demand curves.

"5,000" into her computer. The auction begins. (Follow along in Exhibit 11 as we relay what is happening at the auction.) The auctioneer calls out the price:

• **$6.00.** The potential buyers think for a second, and then each registers the number of bushels he or she is willing and able to buy at that price. The total is 10,000 bushels, which is the quantity demanded of corn at $6.00. The auctioneer, realizing that 30,000 bushels of corn (40,000 − 10,000 = 30,000) will go unsold at this price, decides to lower the price per bushel to:

• **$5.00.** The quantity demanded increases to 20,000 bushels, but still the quantity supplied of corn at this price is greater than the quantity demanded. The auctioneer calls out:

• **$4.00.** The quantity demanded increases to 30,000 bushels, but the quantity supplied at $4.00 is still greater than the quantity demanded. The auctioneer drops the price down to:

• **$1.25.** At this price, the quantity demanded jumps to 60,000 bushels, but that is 20,000 bushels more than the quantity supplied. The auctioneer calls out a higher price:

• **$2.25.** The quantity demanded drops to 50,000 bushels, but buyers still want to buy more corn at this price than there is corn to be sold. The auctioneer calls out:

• **$3.10.** At this price, the quantity demanded of corn is 40,000 bushels and the quantity supplied of corn is 40,000 bushels. The auction stops. The 40,000 bushels of corn are bought and sold at $3.10 per bushel.

The Language of Supply and Demand: A Few Important Terms

If quantity supplied is greater than quantity demanded, a **surplus** or **excess supply** exists. If quantity demanded is greater than quantity supplied, a **shortage** or **excess demand** exists. In Exhibit 11, a surplus exists at $6.00, $5.00, and $4.00. A shortage exists at $1.25 and $2.25. The price at which quantity demanded equals quantity supplied is the **equilibrium price** or **market-clearing price**. In our example, $3.10 is the equilibrium price. The quantity that corresponds to the equilibrium price is the **equilibrium quantity**. In our example, it is 40,000 bushels of corn. Any price at which quantity demanded is not equal to quantity supplied is a **disequilibrium price**.

   A market that exhibits either a surplus ($Q_s > Q_d$) or a shortage ($Q_d > Q_s$) is said to be in **disequilibrium**. A market in which quantity demanded equals quantity supplied ($Q_d = Q_s$) is said to be in **equilibrium** (identified by the letter E in Exhibit 11).

Moving to Equilibrium: What Happens to Price When There Is a Surplus or a Shortage?

What did the auctioneer do when the price was $6.00 and there was a surplus of corn? He lowered the price. What did the auctioneer do when the price was $2.25 and there was a shortage of corn? He raised the price. The behavior of the auctioneer can be summarized this way: If a surplus exists, lower the price; if a shortage exists, raise the price. This is how the auctioneer moved the corn market into equilibrium.

Not all markets have auctioneers. (When was the last time you saw an auctioneer in the grocery store?) But many markets act *as if* an auctioneer were calling out higher and lower prices until equilibrium price is reached. In many real-world auctioneerless markets, prices fall when there is a surplus and rise when there is a shortage. Why?

WHY DOES PRICE FALL WHEN THERE IS A SURPLUS? In Exhibit 12, there is a surplus at a price of $15: Quantity supplied (150 units) is greater than quantity demanded (50 units). Suppliers will not be able to sell all they had hoped to sell at $15. As a result, their inventories will grow beyond the level they hold in preparation for demand changes. Sellers will want to reduce their inventories. Some will lower prices to do so, some will cut back on production, others will do a little of both. As shown in the exhibit, there is a tendency for price and output to fall until equilibrium is achieved.

WHY DOES PRICE RISE WHEN THERE IS A SHORTAGE? In Exhibit 12, there is a shortage at a price of $5: Quantity demanded (150 units) is greater than quantity supplied (50 units). Buyers will not be able to buy all they had hoped to buy at $5. Some buyers will bid up the price to get sellers to sell to them instead of to other buyers. Some sellers, seeing buyers clamor for the goods, will realize that they can raise the price of the goods they have for sale. Higher prices will also call forth added output. Thus, there is a tendency for price and output to rise until equilibrium is achieved.

Take a look at Exhibit 13. It brings together much of what we have discussed about supply and demand.

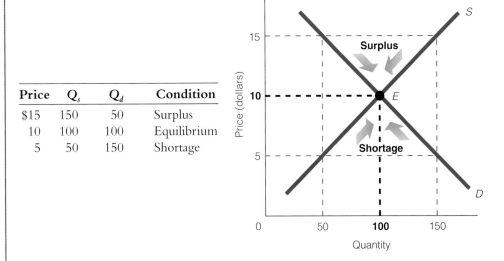

exhibit **12**

Moving to Equilibrium

If there is a surplus, sellers' inventories rise above the level they hold in preparation for demand changes. Sellers will want to reduce their inventories. As a result, price and output fall until equilibrium is achieved. If there is a shortage, some buyers will bid up price to get sellers to sell to them instead of to other buyers. Some sellers will realize they can raise the price of the goods they have for sale. Higher prices will call forth added output. Price and output rise until equilibrium is achieved. (Note: Recall that price, on the vertical axis, is price per unit of the good, and quantity, on the horizontal axis, is for a specific time period. In this text, we do not specify this on the axes themselves, but consider it to be understood.)

Price	Q_s	Q_d	Condition
$15	150	50	Surplus
10	100	100	Equilibrium
5	50	150	Shortage

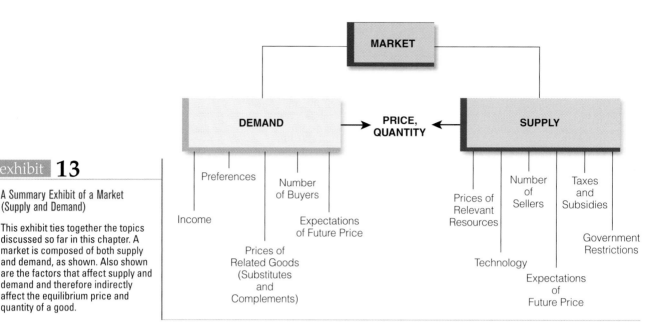

exhibit **13**

A Summary Exhibit of a Market (Supply and Demand)

This exhibit ties together the topics discussed so far in this chapter. A market is composed of both supply and demand, as shown. Also shown are the factors that affect supply and demand and therefore indirectly affect the equilibrium price and quantity of a good.

Speed of Moving to Equilibrium

On August 2, 2006, at 9:11 A.M. (Eastern time), the price of a share of IBM stock was $76.54. A few seconds later, the price had risen to $76.57. Obviously, the stock market is a market that equilibrates quickly. If demand rises, then initially there is a shortage of the stock at the current equilibrium price. The price is bid up, and there is no longer a shortage. All this happens in seconds.

Now consider a house offered for sale in any city in the United States. It is not uncommon for the sale price of a house to remain the same even though the house does not sell for months. For example, a person offers to sell her house for $400,000. One month passes, no sale; two months pass, no sale; three months pass, no sale; and so on. Ten months later, the house has still not sold, and the price is still $400,000.

Is $400,000 the equilibrium price of the house? Obviously not. At the equilibrium price, there would be a buyer for the house and a seller of the house (quantity demanded would equal quantity supplied). At a price of $400,000, there is a seller of the house but no buyer. The price of $400,000 is above equilibrium price. At $400,000, there is a surplus in the housing market; equilibrium has not been achieved.

Some people may be tempted to argue that supply and demand are at work in the stock market but not in the housing market. A better explanation, though, is that *not all markets equilibrate at the same speed.* While it may take only seconds for the stock market to go from surplus or shortage to equilibrium, it may take months for the housing market to do so.

Moving to Equilibrium: Maximum and Minimum Prices

The discussion of surpluses illustrates how a market moves to equilibrium, but there is another way to demonstrate this. Exhibit 14 shows the market for good X. Look at the first unit of good X. What is the *maximum price buyers would be willing to pay* for it? The answer is $70. This can be seen by following the dotted line up from the first unit of the good to the demand curve. What is the *minimum price sellers need to receive before they would be willing to sell* this unit of good X? It is $10. This can be seen by following the dotted

economics 24/7

OVERBOOKING AND THE AIRLINES

Airlines often overbook flights; that is, they accept more reservations than there are seats available on a flight. They do this because they know that a certain (usually small) percentage of individuals with reservations will not show up. An empty seat means that the airline's cost per actual passenger on board is higher than it would be if the seat were occupied by a paying passenger. So airlines try to make sure there are few empty seats. One way to reduce the number of empty seats is to overbook.

A while back, when an airline was confronted with more people with reservations showing up for a flight than there were seats available, it would simply "bump" passengers. In other words, the airline would tell some passengers that they could not fly on a particular flight. Obviously, the bumped passengers were disappointed and angry.

One day while shaving, economist Julian Simon (1932–1998) came up with a better way to deal with overbooking. He argued that the airline should enter into a market transaction with those persons who had reserved seats for an overbooked flight. Instead of bumping people randomly, an airline should ask passengers to sell their seats back to the airline. Passengers who absolutely had to get from X to Y would not sell their seats, but passengers who did not have to get from X to Y right away might be willing to sell their ticket for a given flight.

Simon wrote the executives of various airlines and outlined the details of his plan. He even told them that the first airline that enacted the plan would likely reap larger sales. It could, after all, guarantee its passengers that they would not get bumped. Most airline executives wrote back and told him it was a reasonably good idea but unworkable.

Simon contacted various economists asking them to support his idea publicly. Some did; some didn't. For years, Simon pushed his idea with airline executives and government officials.

Then Alfred Kahn, an economist, was appointed chairman of the Civil Aeronautics Board. Simon contacted Kahn with his plan, and Kahn liked it. According to Simon, "Kahn announced something like the scheme in his first press conference. He also had the great persuasive skill to repackage it as a 'voluntary' bumping plan, and at the same time to increase the penalties that airlines must pay to involuntary bumpees, a nice carrot-and-stick combination."[3]

The rest, as people say, is history. Simon's plan has been in operation since 1978. Simon wrote, "The volunteer system for handling airline oversales exemplifies how markets can improve life for all concerned parties. In case of an oversale, the airline agent proceeds from lowest bidder upwards until the required number of bumpees is achieved. Low bidders take the next flight, happy about it. All other passengers fly as scheduled, also happy. The airlines can overbook more, making them happy too."[4]

[3]See Julian Simon's, "Origins of the Airline Oversales Auction System," at http://www.cato.org/pubs/regulation/regv17n2/reg17n2-simon.html.
[4]Ibid.

line up from the first unit to the supply curve. Because the maximum buying price is greater than the minimum selling price, the first unit of good X will be exchanged.

What about the second unit? For the second unit, buyers are willing to pay a maximum price of $60, and sellers need to receive a minimum price of $20. The second unit of good X will be exchanged. In fact, exchange will occur as long as the maximum buying price is greater than the minimum selling price. The exhibit shows that a total of four units of good X will be exchanged. The fifth unit will not be exchanged because the maximum buying price ($30) is less than the minimum selling price ($50).

In the process just described, buyers and sellers trade money for goods as long as both benefit from the trade. The market converges on a quantity of 4 units of good X and a price of $40 per unit. This is equilibrium. In other words, mutually beneficial trade drives the market to equilibrium.

Units of Good X	Maximum Buying Price	Minimum Selling Price	Result
1st	$70	$10	Exchange
2d	60	20	Exchange
3d	50	30	Exchange
4th	40	40	Exchange
5th	30	50	No Exchange

exhibit 14

Moving to Equilibrium in Terms of Maximum and Minimum Prices

As long as the maximum buying price is greater than the minimum selling price, an exchange will occur. This condition is met for units 1−4. The market converges on equilibrium through a process of mutually beneficial exchanges.

Equilibrium in Terms of Consumers' and Producers' Surplus

Equilibrium can be viewed in terms of two important economic concepts: consumers' surplus and producers' (or sellers') surplus. **Consumers' surplus** is the difference between the maximum buying price and the price paid by the buyer.

Consumers' Surplus (CS)

The difference between the maximum price a buyer is willing and able to pay for a good or service and the price actually paid. $CS =$ Maximum buying price − Price paid

Consumers' surplus = Maximum buying price − Price paid

For example, if the highest price you would pay to see a movie is $10 and you pay $7 to see the movie, then you have received $3 consumers' surplus. Obviously, the more consumers' surplus consumers receive, the better off they are. Wouldn't you have preferred to pay, say, $4 to see the movie instead of $7? If you had paid only $4, your consumers' surplus would have been $6 instead of $3.

Producers' (Sellers') Surplus (PS)

The difference between the price sellers receive for a good and the minimum or lowest price for which they would have sold the good. $PS =$ Price received − Minimum selling price

Producers' (or sellers') surplus is the difference between the price received by the producer or seller and the minimum selling price.

Producers' (sellers') surplus = Price received − Minimum selling price

Suppose the minimum price the owner of the movie theater would have accepted for admission is $5. But she doesn't sell admission for $5; she sells it for $7. Her producers' or sellers' surplus is $2. A seller prefers a large producers' surplus to a small one. The theater owner would have preferred to sell admission to the movie for $8 instead of $7 because then she would have received $3 producers' surplus.

Total Surplus (TS)

The sum of consumers' surplus and producers' surplus. $TS = CS + PS$

Total surplus is the sum of the consumers' surplus and producers' surplus.

Total surplus = Consumers' surplus + Producers' surplus

In Exhibit 15(a), consumers' surplus is represented by the shaded triangle. This triangle includes the area under the demand curve and above the equilibrium price. According to the definition, consumers' surplus is the highest price buyers are willing to pay

(a)

Consumers' Surplus (CS)

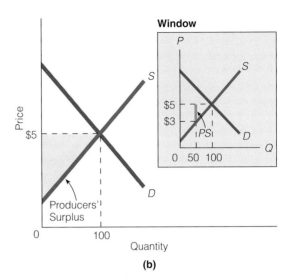

(b)

Producers' Surplus (PS)

exhibit **15**

Consumers' and Producers' Surplus

(a) Consumers' surplus. As the shaded area indicates, the difference between the maximum or highest amount buyers would be willing to pay and the price they actually pay is consumers' surplus. (b) Producers' surplus. As the shaded area indicates, the difference between the price sellers receive for the good and the minimum or lowest price they would be willing to sell the good for is producers' surplus.

(maximum buying price) minus the price they pay. For example, the window in (a) shows that buyers are willing to pay as high as $7 for the 50th unit but only pay $5. Thus, the consumers' surplus on the 50th unit of the good is $2. If we add the consumers' surplus on each unit of the good between and including the first and the 100th units (the equilibrium quantity), we obtain the shaded consumers' surplus triangle.

In Exhibit 15(b), producers' surplus is represented by the shaded triangle. This triangle includes the area above the supply curve and under the equilibrium price. Keep in mind the definition of producers' surplus—the price received by the seller minus the lowest price the seller would accept for the good. For example, the window in (b) shows that sellers would have sold the 50th unit for as low as $3 but actually sold it for $5. Thus, the producers' surplus on the 50th unit of the good is $2. If we add the producers' surplus on each unit of the good between and including the first and the 100th, we obtain the shaded producers' surplus triangle.

Now consider consumers' surplus and producers' surplus at the equilibrium quantity. Exhibit 16 shows that consumers' surplus at equilibrium is equal to areas $A + B + C + D$, and producers' surplus at equilibrium is equal to areas $E + F + G + H$. At any other exchangeable quantity, such as at 25, 50, or 75 units, both consumers' surplus and producers' surplus are less. For example, at 25 units, consumers' surplus is equal to area A, and producers' surplus is equal to area E. At 50 units, consumers' surplus is equal to areas $A + B$, and producers' surplus is equal to areas $E + F$.

Is there a special property to equilibrium? At equilibrium, both consumers' surplus and producers' surplus are maximized. In short, total surplus is maximized.

What Can Change Equilibrium Price and Quantity?

Equilibrium price and quantity are determined by supply and demand. Whenever demand changes, supply changes, or both change, equilibrium price and quantity change. Exhibit 17 illustrates eight different cases where this occurs. Cases (a)−(d) illustrate the four basic changes in supply and demand, where either supply or demand changes. Cases (e)−(h) illustrate changes in both supply and demand.

- (a) Demand rises (the demand curve shifts rightward), and supply is constant (the supply curve does not move). Equilibrium price rises, equilibrium quantity rises.

exhibit 16

Equilibrium, Consumers' Surplus, and Producers' Surplus

Consumers' surplus is greater at equilibrium quantity (100 units) than at any other exchangeable quantity. Producers' surplus is greater at equilibrium quantity than at any other exchangeable quantity. For example, consumers' surplus is areas $A + B + C$ at 75 units, but areas $A + B + C + D$ at 100 units. Producers' surplus is areas $E + F + G$ at 75 units, but areas $E + F + G + H$ at 100 units.

Quantity (units)	Consumers' Surplus	Producers' Surplus
25	A	E
50	$A + B$	$E + F$
75	$A + B + C$	$E + F + G$
100 (Equilibrium)	$A + B + C + D$	$E + F + G + H$

(a)

(b)

table 17

Equilibrium Price and Quantity Effects of Supply Curve Shifts and Demand Curve Shifts

The exhibit illustrates the effects on equilibrium price and quantity of a change in demand, a change in supply, or a change in both. Below each diagram the condition leading to the effects is noted, using the following symbols: (1) a bar over a letter means *constant* (thus, $\bar{S}$ means that supply is constant); (2) a downward-pointing arrow ($\downarrow$) indicates a fall; (3) an upward-pointing arrow ($\uparrow$) indicates a rise. A rise (fall) in demand is the same as a rightward (leftward) shift in the demand curve. A rise (fall) in supply is the same as a rightward (leftward) shift in the supply curve.

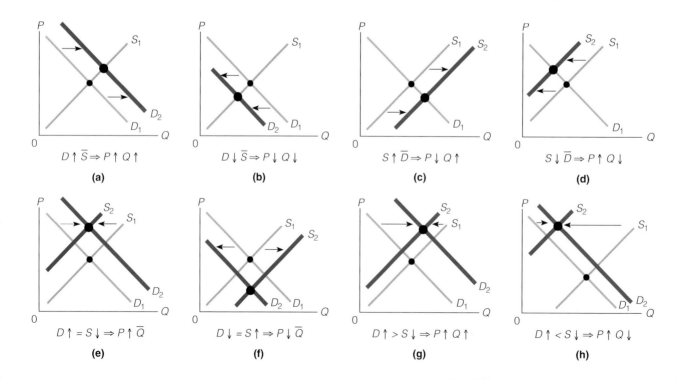

$D \uparrow \bar{S} \Rightarrow P \uparrow Q \uparrow$

(a)

$D \downarrow \bar{S} \Rightarrow P \downarrow Q \downarrow$

(b)

$S \uparrow \bar{D} \Rightarrow P \downarrow Q \uparrow$

(c)

$S \downarrow \bar{D} \Rightarrow P \uparrow Q \downarrow$

(d)

$D \uparrow = S \downarrow \Rightarrow P \uparrow \bar{Q}$

(e)

$D \downarrow = S \uparrow \Rightarrow P \downarrow \bar{Q}$

(f)

$D \uparrow > S \downarrow \Rightarrow P \uparrow Q \uparrow$

(g)

$D \uparrow < S \downarrow \Rightarrow P \uparrow Q \downarrow$

(h)

- (b) Demand falls, supply is constant. Equilibrium price falls, equilibrium quantity falls.

- (c) Supply rises, demand is constant. Equilibrium price falls, equilibrium quantity rises.

- (d) Supply falls, demand is constant. Equilibrium price rises, equilibrium quantity falls.

- (e) Demand rises and supply falls by an equal amount. Equilibrium price rises, equilibrium quantity is constant.

- (f) Demand falls and supply rises by an equal amount. Equilibrium price falls, equilibrium quantity is constant.

- (g) Demand rises by a greater amount than supply falls. Equilibrium price rises, equilibrium quantity rises.

- (h) Demand rises by a smaller amount than supply falls. Equilibrium price rises, equilibrium quantity falls.

SELF-TEST

1. When a person goes to the grocery store to buy food, there is no auctioneer calling out prices for bread, milk, and other items. Therefore, supply and demand cannot be operative. Do you agree or disagree? Explain your answer.

2. The price of a given-quality personal computer is lower today than it was five years ago. Is this necessarily the result of a lower demand for computers? Explain your answer.

3. What is the effect on equilibrium price and quantity of the following?
   a. A decrease in demand that is greater than the increase in supply
   b. An increase in supply
   c. A decrease in supply that is greater than the increase in demand
   d. A decrease in demand

4. At equilibrium quantity, what is the relationship between the maximum buying price and the minimum selling price?

5. If the price paid is $40 and the consumers' surplus is $4, then what is the maximum buying price? If the minimum selling price is $30 and producers' surplus is $4, then what is the price received by the seller?

Price Controls

Because scarcity exists, there is a need for a rationing device—such as dollar price. But price is not always permitted to be a rationing device. Sometimes, price is controlled. There are two types of price controls: price ceilings and price floors. In the discussion of price controls, the word *price* is used in the generic sense. It refers to the price of an apple, for example, the price of labor (wage), the price of credit (interest rate), and so on.

Price Ceiling: Definition and Effects

A **price ceiling** is a government-mandated maximum price above which legal trades cannot be made. For example, suppose the government mandates that the maximum price at which good X can be bought and sold is $8. It follows that $8 is a price ceiling. If $8 is below the equilibrium price of good X, as in Exhibit 18, any or all of the following effects may arise.[5]

SHORTAGES At the $12 equilibrium price in Exhibit 18, the quantity demanded of good X (150) is equal to the quantity supplied (150). At the $8 price ceiling, a shortage exists. The quantity demanded (190) is greater than the quantity supplied (100). When a

Price Ceiling

A government-mandated maximum price above which legal trades cannot be made.

---

[5]If the price ceiling is above the equilibrium price (say, $8 is the price ceiling and $4 is the equilibrium price), it has no effects. Usually, however, a price ceiling is below the equilibrium price.

Price
(dollars)

18

Equilibrium
Price   12

Price
Ceiling   8

A price ceiling
creates a shortage.

Shortage

S

D

0   100   150 190   Quantity of Good X

Equilibrium Quantity

exhibit **18**

A Price Ceiling

The price ceiling is $8 and the equilibrium price is $12. At $12, quantity demanded = quantity supplied. At $8, quantity demanded > quantity supplied. (Recall that price, on the vertical axis, always represents price per unit. Quantity, on the horizontal axis, always holds for a specific time period.)

shortage exists, there is a tendency for price and output to rise to equilibrium. But when a price ceiling exists, this tendency cannot be realized because it is unlawful to trade at the equilibrium price.

FEWER EXCHANGES At the equilibrium price of $12 in Exhibit 18, 150 units of good X are bought and sold. At the price ceiling of $8, 100 units of good X are bought and sold. (Buyers would prefer to buy 190 units, but only 100 are supplied.) We conclude that price ceilings cause fewer exchanges to be made.

Notice in Exhibit 18 that the demand curve is above the supply curve for all quantities less than 150 units. (At 150 units, the demand curve and the supply curve intersect and thus share the same point in the two-dimensional space.) This means the maximum buying price is greater than the minimum selling price for all units less than 150. In particular, the maximum buying price is greater than the minimum selling price for units 101 to 149. For example, buyers might be willing to pay $17 for the 110th unit, and sellers might be willing to sell the 110th unit for $10. But no unit after the 100th unit (not the 110th unit, not the 114th unit, not the 130th unit) will be produced and sold because of the price ceiling. In short, the price ceiling prevents mutually advantageous trades from being realized.

NONPRICE RATIONING DEVICES If the equilibrium price of $12 fully rationed good X before the price ceiling was imposed, it follows that a (lower) price of $8 can only partly ration this good. In short, price ceilings prevent price from rising to the level sufficient to ration goods fully. But if price is responsible for only part of the rationing, what accounts for the rest? The answer is some other (nonprice) rationing device, such as first come, first served (FCFS).

In Exhibit 18, 100 units of good X will be sold at $8, although buyers are willing to buy 190 units at this price. What happens? Possibly, good X will be sold on an FCFS basis for $8 per unit. In other words, to buy good X, a person must not only pay $8 per unit but also be one of the first people in line.

BUYING AND SELLING AT A PROHIBITED PRICE Buyers and sellers may regularly circumvent a price ceiling by making their exchanges "under the table." For example, some buyers may offer some sellers more than $8 per unit for good X. No doubt, some sellers will accept the offers. But why would some buyers offer more than $8 per unit when they

economics 24/7

TICKET SCALPING

I got two for Pavarotti.

—Ticket scalper

At a big rock concert, a major sports event, or a popular Broadway play, ticket scalpers are likely to be nearby trying to sell tickets. Many people do not like scalpers; they believe scalpers are taking advantage of them by charging many times more than the original supplier of the ticket charged. Some states have outlawed ticket scalping or permit it only if the scalper charges a limited amount, say, 5 to 10 percent more than the original ticket price. Scalpers who continue to practice their trade in defiance of the law are fined.

The question the economist asks is: Why does ticket scalping exist in the first place? The noneconomist may answer, "Because there is greed and selfishness in the world." But surely, greed and selfishness do not surface just for major sports events or Broadway plays. Ticket scalpers are not at all events, only some. Put the question this way: What condition is necessary before ticket scalping will exist?

If you think in terms of supply and demand, you will have the answer. Certainly, there will be no ticket scalping if the equilibrium price is initially charged for a ticket. At the equilibrium price, the quantity demanded of tickets will equal the quantity supplied.

Suppose the ticket price is above equilibrium. Will ticket scalping exist then? No, because at a price higher than equilibrium price, people will buy fewer tickets than there are tickets available. No one has ever seen a ticket scalper trying to sell a ticket that can be purchased from the ticket office.

Ticket scalping will exist only when the ticket price initially charged is lower than the equilibrium price. For example, suppose the equilibrium price to see a particular rock band is $80 a ticket, but only $50 a ticket is charged. Someone will likely buy the ticket for $50 and then turn around and sell it for $80. In other words, before ticket scalping exists, a profitable opportunity must present itself.

But why would a seller choose to sell tickets for less than equilibrium price? One answer is that the seller may not know what equilibrium price is in a particular setting. In other words, a seller may simply make a mistake and charge more or less than equilibrium price. Another answer is that the seller may be concerned about sacrificing the goodwill of her customers (many of whom she hopes will be repeat customers) if she charges the equilibrium price. For example, some Broadway theaters charge below equilibrium prices for tickets to plays. They even know they are charging below equilibrium prices because they know the prices the scalpers are getting paid. But as the president of one Broadway theater said, "Even though we could sell tickets for $100, we'd be cutting our throats because it would be a PR disaster for Broadway."

can buy good *X* for $8? The answer is because not all buyers can buy the amount of good *X* they want at $8. As Exhibit 18 shows, there is a shortage. Buyers are willing to buy 190 units at $8, but sellers are willing to sell only 100 units. In short, 90 fewer units will be sold than buyers would like to buy. Some buyers will go unsatisfied. How, then, does any one buyer make it more likely that sellers will sell to him or her instead of to someone else? The answer is by offering to pay a higher price. Because it is illegal to pay a higher price, the transaction must be made "under the table."

TIE-IN SALES In Exhibit 18, the maximum price buyers would be willing and able to pay per unit for 100 units of good *X* is $18. (This is the price on the demand curve at a quantity of 100 units.) The maximum legal price, however, is $8. This difference between two prices often prompts a **tie-in sale**, a sale whereby one good can be purchased only if another good is also purchased. For example, if Ralph's Gas Station sells gasoline to customers only if they buy a car wash, the two goods are linked together in a tie-in sale.

Tie-in Sale
A sale whereby one good can be purchased only if another good is also purchased.

Suppose that the sellers of good X in Exhibit 18 also sell good Y. They might offer to sell buyers good X at $8 only if the buyers agree to buy good Y at, say, $10. We choose $10 as the price for good Y because $10 is the difference between the maximum per-unit price buyers are willing and able to pay for 100 units of good X ($18) and the maximum legal price ($8).

In New York City and other communities with rent-control laws, tie-in sales sometimes result from rent ceilings on apartments. Occasionally, to rent an apartment, an individual must agree to buy the furniture in the apartment.

Thinking like
AN ECONOMIST   *Economists think in terms of unintended effects. For example, a price ceiling policy intended to lower prices for the poor may cause shortages, the use of nonprice rationing devices, illegal market transactions, and tie-in sales. When we consider both the price ceiling and its effects, it is not clear that the poor have been helped. The economist knows that wanting to do good (for others) is not sufficient. It is important to know how to do good too.*

Do Buyers Prefer Lower Prices to Higher Prices?

"Of course," someone might say, "buyers prefer lower prices to higher prices. What buyer would want to pay a higher price for anything?" But wait a minute. Price ceilings are often lower than equilibrium prices. Does it follow that buyers prefer price ceilings to equilibrium prices? Not necessarily. Price ceilings have effects that equilibrium prices do not: shortages, use of first come, first served as a rationing device, tie-in sales, and so on. A buyer could prefer to pay a higher price (an equilibrium price) than to pay a lower price and have to deal with the effects of a price ceiling. All we can say for certain is that buyers prefer lower prices to higher prices, *ceteris paribus*. As in many cases, the *ceteris paribus* condition makes all the difference.

Price Floor: Definition and Effects

Price Floor
A government-mandated minimum price below which legal trades cannot be made.

A **price floor** is a government-mandated minimum price below which legal trades cannot be made. For example, suppose the government mandates that the minimum price at which good X can be sold is $20. It follows that $20 is a price floor (see Exhibit 19). If the price floor is above the equilibrium price, the following two effects arise.[6]

SURPLUSES At the $15 equilibrium price in Exhibit 19, the quantity demanded of good X (130) is equal to the quantity supplied (130). At the $20 price floor, a surplus exists.

exhibit **19**

A Price Floor

The price floor is $20 and the equilibrium price is $15. At $15, quantity demanded = quantity supplied. At $20, quantity supplied > quantity demanded.

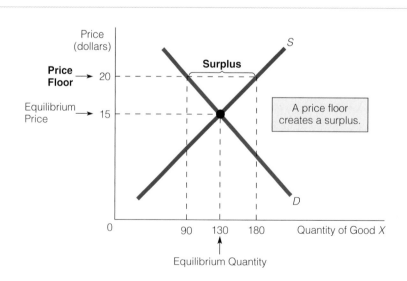

<hr />

[6]If the price floor is below the equilibrium price (say, $20 is the price floor and $25 is the equilibrium price), it has no effects. Usually, however, a price floor is above the equilibrium price.

The quantity supplied (180) is greater than the quantity demanded (90). A surplus is usually a temporary state of affairs. When a surplus exists, there is a tendency for price and output to fall to equilibrium. But when a price floor exists, this tendency cannot be realized because it is unlawful to trade at the equilibrium price.

FEWER EXCHANGES At the equilibrium price in Exhibit 19, 130 units of good *X* are bought and sold. At the price floor, 90 units are bought and sold. (Sellers want to sell 180 units, but buyers buy only 90.) We conclude that price floors cause fewer exchanges to be made.

SELF-TEST

1. Do buyers prefer lower prices to higher prices?

2. "When there are long-lasting shortages, there are long lines of people waiting to buy goods. It follows that the shortages cause the long lines." Do you agree or disagree? Explain your answer.

3. Who might argue for a price ceiling? a price floor?

A Reader Asks . . .

How Does Knowing About Supply and Demand Help Me?

Some things are interesting but not useful. Other things are useful but not interesting. For example, supply and demand are interesting but not useful. Learning how to fix a car is useful but not particularly interesting. Am I wrong? Have I missed something? Is knowledge of supply and demand useful? If it is, what can you do with it?

A knowledge of supply and demand can be used both to explain and to predict. Let's look at prediction first. Suppose you learn that the federal government is going to impose a quota on imported television sets. What will happen when the quota is imposed? With your knowledge of supply and demand, you can predict that the price of television sets will rise. In other words, you can use your knowledge of supply and demand to predict what will happen. Stated differently, you can use your knowledge of supply and demand to see into the future. Isn't the ability to see into the future useful?

Supply and demand also allows you to develop richer and fuller explanations of events. To illustrate, suppose there is a shortage of apples in country *X*. The cause of the shortage, someone says, is that apple growers in the country are simply growing too few apples. Well, of course, it's true that apple growers are growing "too few" apples compared to the number of apples consumers want to buy. But does this explanation completely account for the shortage of apples? Your knowledge of supply and demand will prompt you to ask why apple growers are growing too few apples. When you understand that quantity supplied is related to price, you understand that apple growers will grow more apples if the price of apples is higher. What is keeping the price of apples down? Could it be a price ceiling? Without a price ceiling, the price of apples would rise, and apple growers would grow (and offer to sell) more apples. The shortage of apples will vanish.

In other words, without a knowledge of supply and demand, you may have been content to explain the shortage of apples by saying that apple growers are growing too few apples. With your knowledge of supply and demand, you delve deeper into *why* apple growers are growing too few apples.

! analyzing the scene

*At the time James checks stock prices, Wal-Mart is sell-
ing for $44.09, Microsoft for $23.75, and Dell for $21.75.
Why doesn't Dell sell for more than Wal-Mart? Why
does Microsoft sell for more than Dell? Why is the euro
selling for $1.28 and not higher or lower?*

The price of each stock is determined by supply and demand.
The price of Wal-Mart stock is higher than the price of Dell
stock because the demand for Wal-Mart stock is higher than
the demand for Dell stock and/or the supply of Wal-Mart
stock is lower than the supply of Dell stock. Similar reasoning
explains why Microsoft stock sells for more than Dell stock
does.

The exchange rate between the euro and the dollar is also
determined by supply and demand. Just as there is a demand
for and supply of apples, oranges, houses, and computers,
there is a demand for and supply of various currencies (e.g.,
the dollar and the euro). The dollar price James has to pay for
a euro has to do with the demand for and supply of euros.
Thus, supply and demand may determine whether or not
James takes a trip to Europe this summer.

*What does getting his shower fixed have to do with
James living in a rent-controlled apartment?*

James has been trying for two weeks to get his apartment
supervisor to fix his shower. James's friend thinks it has taken
so long because James lives in a rent-controlled apartment.
(A rent-controlled apartment has a rent ceiling; James's
rent is lower than the equilibrium, or market-clearing, rent.)
Is James's friend right? With a rent ceiling, the quantity
demanded of apartments is greater than the quantity

supplied; that is, a shortage of apartments exists. The apartment supervisor knows there is a shortage of apartments and
realizes he could rent the apartment easily if James moved.
The supervisor is likely to be less responsive to James's request
to fix the shower than he would be if the rental market were
in equilibrium or surplus.

*Why does it take so long (nine months) to get tickets to
see the* **Late Show with David Letterman?**

We know that the price of a ticket is zero (which is not the
equilibrium or market-clearing price). At a price of zero, the
quantity demanded of tickets is much greater than the quantity supplied. How are the tickets rationed? They're rationed
on a first come, first served basis. James had to "stand in line,"
or "wait," for nine months to get tickets to see the show.
That's one long line.

*Does the burglary rate have anything to do with how
"hard" or "soft" a city is on crime?*

The law of demand holds for apples—raise the price of apples
and fewer apples will be sold. But does the law of demand
hold for burglary too? The mayor of New York City hinted
that it does in a report on the 11 o'clock news. The mayor
said, "This city and this mayor are not going to be soft on
crime. We're going to do everything in our power to make
sure that everyone knows that crime doesn't pay." He said
these words in response to the rise in the city's burglary rate.
Obviously, the mayor thinks that if the city raises the "price" a
person has to pay for committing burglary (in terms of fines
or jail time), there will be fewer burglaries.

chapter summary

Demand

- The law of demand states that as the price of a good
  rises, the quantity demanded of the good falls, and as
  the price of a good falls, the quantity demanded of the
  good rises, *ceteris paribus.* The law of demand holds that
  price and quantity demanded are inversely related.

- Quantity demanded is the total number of units of a
  good that buyers are willing and able to buy at a particular price.

- A (downward-sloping) demand curve is the graphical
  representation of the law of demand.

- Factors that can change demand and cause the demand
  curve to shift include income, preferences, prices of
  related goods (substitutes and complements), number of
  buyers, and expectations of future price.

- The only factor that can directly cause a change in the
  quantity demanded of a good is a change in the good's
  own price.

Absolute Price and Relative Price

- The absolute price of a good is the price of the good in money terms.
- The relative price of a good is the price of the good in terms of another good.

Supply

- The law of supply states that as the price of a good rises, the quantity supplied of the good rises, and as the price of a good falls, the quantity supplied of the good falls, *ceteris paribus*. The law of supply asserts that price and quantity supplied are directly related.
- The law of supply does not hold when there is no time to produce more units of a good or when goods cannot be produced at all (over any period of time).
- The upward-sloping supply curve is the graphical representation of the law of supply. More generally, a supply curve (no matter how it slopes) represents the relationship between price and quantity supplied.
- Factors that can change supply and cause the supply curve to shift include prices of relevant resources, technology, number of sellers, expectations of future price, taxes and subsidies, and government restrictions.
- The only factor that can directly cause a change in the quantity supplied of a good is a change in the good's own price.

The Market

- Demand and supply together establish equilibrium price and equilibrium quantity.
- A surplus exists in a market if, at some price, quantity supplied is greater than quantity demanded. A shortage exists if, at some price, quantity demanded is greater than quantity supplied.
- Mutually beneficial trade between buyers and sellers drives the market to equilibrium.

Consumers' Surplus, Producers' Surplus, and Total Surplus

- Consumers' surplus is the difference between the maximum buying price and price paid by the buyer.

  Consumers' surplus = Maximum buying price − Price paid

- Producers' (or sellers') surplus is the difference between the price the seller receives and minimum selling price.

  Producers' surplus = Price received − Minimum selling price

- The more consumers' surplus that buyers receive, the better off they are. The more producers' surplus that sellers receive, the better off they are.
- Total surplus is the sum of consumers' surplus and producers' surplus.
- Total surplus (the sum of consumers' surplus and producers' surplus) is maximized at equilibrium.

Price Ceilings

- A price ceiling is a government-mandated maximum price. If a price ceiling is below the equilibrium price, some or all of the following effects arise: shortages, fewer exchanges, nonprice rationing devices, buying and selling at prohibited prices, and tie-in sales.
- Consumers do not necessarily prefer (lower) price ceilings to (higher) equilibrium prices. They may prefer higher prices and none of the effects of price ceilings to lower prices and some of the effects of price ceilings. All we can say for sure is that consumers prefer lower prices to higher prices, *ceteris paribus.*

Price Floors

- A price floor is a government-mandated minimum price. If a price floor is above the equilibrium price, the following effects arise: surpluses and fewer exchanges.

key terms and concepts

Theory	Demand Curve	Normal Good	Law of Supply
Market	Absolute (Money) Price	Inferior Good	Supply Curve
Demand	Relative Price	Neutral Good	Supply Schedule
Law of Demand	Law of Diminishing	Substitutes	Subsidy
Ceteris Paribus	Marginal Utility	Complements	Surplus (Excess Supply)
Demand Schedule	Own Price	Supply	

Shortage (Excess Demand)

Equilibrium Price (Market-Clearing Price)

Equilibrium Quantity

Disequilibrium Price

Disequilibrium

Equilibrium

Consumers' Surplus

Producers' (Sellers') Surplus

Total Surplus

Price Ceiling

Tie-in Sale

Price Floor

questions and problems

1 True or false? As the price of oranges rises, the demand for oranges falls, *ceteris paribus*. Explain your answer.

2 "The price of a bushel of wheat, which was $3.00 last month, is $3.70 today. The demand curve for wheat must have shifted rightward between last month and today." Discuss.

3 "Some goods are bought largely because they have 'snob appeal.' For example, the residents of Beverly Hills gain prestige by buying expensive items. In fact, they won't buy some items unless they are expensive. The law of demand, which holds that people buy more at lower prices than higher prices, obviously doesn't hold for the residents of Beverly Hills. The following rules apply in Beverly Hills: "high prices, buy; low prices, don't buy." Discuss.

4 "The price of T-shirts keeps rising and rising, and people keep buying more and more. T-shirts must have an upward-sloping demand curve." Identify the error.

5 Predict what would happen to the equilibrium price of marijuana if it were legalized.

6 Compare the ratings for television shows with prices for goods. How are ratings like prices? How are ratings different from prices? (Hint: How does rising demand for a particular television show manifest itself?)

7 Must consumers' surplus equal producers' surplus at equilibrium price? Explain your answer.

8 Many movie theaters charge a lower admission price for the first show on weekday afternoons than they do for a weeknight or weekend show. Explain why.

9 A Dell computer is a substitute for a Hewlett-Packard computer. What happens to the demand for Hewlett-Packard computers and the quantity demanded of Dell computers as the price of a Dell falls?

10 Describe how each of the following will affect the demand for personal computers: (a) a rise in incomes (assuming computers are a normal good); (b) a lower expected price for computers; (c) cheaper software; (d) computers become simpler to operate.

11 Describe how each of the following will affect the supply of personal computers: (a) a rise in wage rates; (b) an increase in the number of sellers of computers; (c) a tax placed on the production of computers; (d) a subsidy placed on the production of computers.

12 The law of demand specifies an inverse relationship between price and quantity demanded, *ceteris paribus*. Is the "price" in the law of demand absolute price or relative price? Explain your answer.

13 Use the law of diminishing marginal utility to explain why demand curves slope downward.

14 Explain how the market moves to equilibrium in terms of shortages and surpluses and in terms of maximum buying prices and minimum selling prices.

15 Identify what happens to equilibrium price and quantity in each of the following cases:
   a   Demand rises and supply is constant
   b   Demand falls and supply is constant
   c   Supply rises and demand is constant
   d   Supply falls and demand is constant
   e   Demand rises by the same amount that supply falls
   f   Demand falls by the same amount that supply rises
   g   Demand falls by less than supply rises
   h   Demand rises by more than supply rises
   i   Demand rises by less than supply rises
   j   Demand falls by more than supply falls
   k   Demand falls by less than supply falls

16 Many of the proponents of price ceilings argue that government-mandated maximum prices simply reduce producers' profits and do not affect the quantity supplied of a good on the market. What must the supply curve look like before a price ceiling does not affect quantity supplied?

working with numbers and graphs

1 If the absolute price of good X is $10 and the absolute price of good Y is $14, then what is (a) the relative price of good X in terms of good Y and (b) the relative price of good Y in terms of good X?

2 Price is $10, quantity supplied is 50 units, and quantity demanded is 100 units. For every $1 rise in price, quantity supplied rises by 5 units and quantity demanded falls by 5 units. What is the equilibrium price and quantity?

3 Draw a diagram that shows a larger increase in demand than the decrease in supply.

4 Draw a diagram that shows a smaller increase in supply than the increase in demand.

5 At equilibrium in the following figure, what area(s) does consumers' surplus equal? producers' surplus?

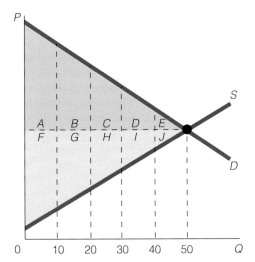

6 At what quantity in the preceding figure is the maximum buying price equal to the minimum selling price?

7 In the following figure, can the movement from point 1 to point 2 be explained by a combination of an increase in the price of a substitute and a decrease in the price of nonlabor resources? Explain your answer.

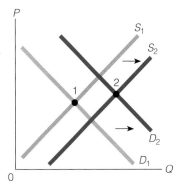

8 The demand curve is downward sloping, the supply curve is upward sloping, and the equilibrium quantity is 50 units. Show on a graph that the difference between the maximum buying price and minimum selling price is greater at 25 units than at 33 units.

9 Diagrammatically show and explain why a price ceiling that is above the equilibrium price will not prompt a tie-in sale.

4 Supply and Demand: Practice

Setting the Scene

The following events occurred on a day in April.

3:15 P.M.

Bob Mason, 18 years old, walks to the mailbox in front of his house. He reaches inside the mailbox, pulls out the mail, and nervously looks through the letters. It's there. He's been anxiously waiting for the mail every day just for this letter. In the next few seconds, he'll learn whether or not he's been accepted by the college he so desperately wants to attend.

3:43 P.M.

Carl and Karen Jenkins, married one year, are in their real estate agent's car driving to the next house they'll look at today. Carl wonders out loud why houses are so expensive in their area. "A person can get twice the house for almost half the money in other parts of the country," he says.

5:15 P.M.

Carlos is on the freeway driving home from work. Traffic is heavy, as usual, and Carlos is driving about 30 mph at the moment. As he half listens to a talk show on the radio, Carlos picks up his cell phone and makes a call. Just as he ends his call, traffic slows down to 5 mph. "I'm not sure how much longer I can take these commutes," Carlos thinks. "This traffic is really getting ridiculous."

5:35 P.M.

Samantha Wilson is standing at the counter of American Airlines in the Dallas-Fort Worth Airport. She asks for an aisle seat for her flight. The response: "I'm afraid the only seats I have left are center seats."

? Here are some questions to keep in mind as you read this chapter:

- *What is the relationship between the probability of Bob Mason being admitted to the college of his choice and the tuition the college charges?*

- *Why are house prices higher in some parts of the country than in other parts of the country?*

- *What do supply, demand, and price have to do with Carlos driving 5 mph on a freeway on his way home from work?*

- *Why aren't any aisle seats left?*

See analyzing the scene at the end of this chapter for answers to these questions.

In this chapter we apply what we learned in the last chapter. In short, we take what we know about the law of demand, the law of supply, equilibrium price, price ceilings, consumers' surplus, etc., and then apply that knowledge to the real world.

Application 1: Why Do Colleges Use GPAs, ACTs, and SATs for Purposes of Admission?

At many colleges and universities, a student pays part of the price of his or her education (by way of tuition payments), and taxpayers and private donors pay part (by way of tax payments and charitable donations, respectively). Thus, the tuition that students pay to attend colleges and universities is usually less than the equilibrium tuition. To illustrate, suppose a student pays tuition T_1 at a given college or university. As shown in Exhibit 1, T_1 is below the equilibrium tuition, T_E. At T_1, the number of students who want to attend the university (N_1) is greater than the number of openings at the university (N_2); that is, quantity demanded is greater than quantity supplied. The university receives more applications for admission than there are places available. Something has to be done. But what?

The college or university is likely to ration its available space by a combination of money price and some other nonprice rationing devices. The student must pay the tuition, T_1, *and* meet the standards of the nonprice rationing devices. Colleges and universities usually use such things as GPAs (grade point averages), ACT scores, and SAT scores as rationing devices.

Thinking like **AN ECONOMIST**   *The layperson sees a university that requires a GPA of 3.8 and an SAT score of 1900 or better for admission. An economist sees a rationing device. The economist then goes on to ask why this particular nonprice rationing device is used. He reasons that there would be no need for a nonprice rationing device if (dollar) price were fully rationing the good or service.*

SELF-TEST

(Answers to Self-Test questions are in the Self-Test Appendix).

1. Suppose the demand rises for admission to a university but both the tuition and the number of openings in the entering class remain the same. Will this affect the admission standards of the university? Explain your answer.

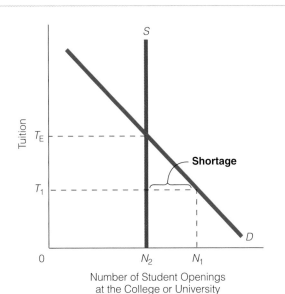

2. Administrators and faculty at state colleges and universities often say that their standards of admission are independent of whether there is a shortage or surplus of openings at the university. Do you think this is true? Do you think that faculty and administrators ignore surpluses and shortages of openings when setting admission standards? Explain your answer.

Application 2: What Will Happen to the Price of Marijuana If the Purchase and Sale of Marijuana Are Legalized?

In the United States, the purchase or sale of marijuana is unlawful. However, there is still a demand for and supply of marijuana. There is also an equilibrium price of marijuana. Let's say that price is P_1.

Suppose that beginning tomorrow, the purchase and sale of marijuana become legal. Will P_1 rise, fall, or remain the same?

The answer, of course, depends on what we think will happen to the demand for and supply of marijuana. If the purchase and sale of marijuana are legal, then some people currently producing corn and wheat will likely choose instead to produce and sell marijuana. So, the supply of marijuana will rise. If nothing else changes, the price of marijuana will fall.

But something else is likely to change. If marijuana consumption is no longer illegal, then the number of people who want to buy and consume marijuana will likely rise. In other words, there will be more buyers of marijuana. This will increase the demand for marijuana.

Thus, decriminalizing the purchase and sale of marijuana is likely to shift both the marijuana demand and supply curves to the right. What happens to the price of marijuana depends on how much the curves shift. Three possibilities exist:

1. The demand curve shifts to the right by the same amount as the supply curve shifts to the right. In this case, the price of marijuana will not change. (Try to visualize the demand and supply curves shifting.)

2. The demand curve shifts to the right by more than the supply curve shifts to the right. In this case, the price of marijuana will rise. (Try to visualize the demand curve shifting to the right by more than the supply curve shifts to the right. Can you see the higher price on the vertical axis?)

3. The supply curve shifts to the right by more than the demand curve shifts to the right. In this case, the price of marijuana will fall.

If you can't visualize the shifts of the demand and supply curves for the three possibilities, draw the original demand and supply curves, then draw the shift in each curve, and finally, identify the new equilibrium price.

SELF-TEST

1. What will happen to the price of marijuana if the supply of marijuana increases by more than the demand for it?

2. What will happen to the quantity of marijuana (purchased and sold) if the demand for marijuana rises by more than the supply of marijuana falls?

Application 3: Where Did You Get That Music?

In recent years, the recording industry feels it has suffered some reduced sales because of music piracy. People download music (or transfer files) from the Internet instead of buying the music on CDs sold by recording companies.

The recording industry, we expect, would like to reduce the amount of downloading and file transferring to zero. If zero piracy is not possible, the industry at least wants less than currently exists. In other words, if 100,000 songs are downloaded on an average day, the recording industry wants that number reduced to 50,000 or, even better, to 25,000. The fewer, the better. How can the recording industry get what it wants?

We can use a supply-and-demand framework to find out how to get less of something. Let's consider how to reduce the amount of apples purchased each day. Suppose buyers are currently buying 30,000 apples a day. What has to happen for fewer apples to be purchased each day? One of three things:

1. A higher price will cause apple buyers to move up their demand curves (change in quantity demanded) and purchase fewer apples.

2. A lower demand (shift leftward in the demand curve) will result in buyers purchasing fewer apples.

3. A lower supply (shift leftward in the supply curve) will result in buyers purchasing fewer apples.

The recording industry has tried all three—higher price, lower demand, and lower supply—in its attempt to reduce the amount of pirated music.

To try to lower supply, the recording industry brought a legal suit against certain companies, such as Napster, that made downloading possible. The recording industry charged Napster with "willful contributory and vicarious copyright infringement." By getting rid of the "middlemen" that made music trading (some would say music pirating) possible, the recording industry would lower the supply of music available on the Internet.

The recording industry also stated that it would sue scores of people who download music. This statement by the recording industry was intended to raise the price of downloading music. The message to downloaders was: You thought the cost of downloading music was zero, but it is not. We may sue you and force you to pay damages. This attempt to reduce the amount of downloaded music worked. Soon after the announcement, the number of Internet users who said they downloaded music fell from about 35 million to 18 million.

Not long ago, the recording industry ran TV commercials to try to lower the demand for downloading music. One commercial showed many of the people who work in the recording industry. The ad showed the artists, of course, but it also showed the technicians behind the scenes and the scores of other people who depend on the recording industry for their livelihood. The message was that there are hundreds of everyday people working behind the scenes, and when you download music instead of buying it, you hurt these people—you jeopardize their jobs and their families. The recording industry hoped to affect a person's preferences in a way that would lead to a decline in the demand for downloading music. The industry wanted a person to think, "I didn't know that I might put someone out of a job by downloading music. Maybe I shouldn't download anymore, or at least do less of it."

SELF-TEST

1.   On January 21, 2004, the recording industry filed lawsuits against 532 people it accused of illegally swapping copyrighted music on the Internet. What does this have to do with supply, demand, or price?

2.   Suppose the recording industry runs only a few TV commercials trying to lower demand for downloading music. Instead, it continually takes legal action against either the people who download the music or the companies that make downloading (and file transferring) possible. What might explain these actions?

Application 4: Television Shows During the Olympics

For two weeks in February 2006, NBC broadcast the Winter Olympics from Turin, Italy. During the two Olympic weeks, many of the other television networks chose to not broadcast new episodes of some of their regular prime-time shows. For example, for the person who usually watches *CSI* on Thursday night on CBS, the network ran a rerun of *CSI* instead of a new episode. Other networks chose to run old movies instead of their regular prime-time shows.

In Chapter 3, we learned that "expectations of future price" can affect the supply of a good. Can expectations of future price also affect the supply of a television show? What was CBS thinking when it decided to show a rerun of *CSI* during the Olympics

© JERRY LAMPEN/REUTERS/LANDOV

instead of a new episode? It probably was thinking that the demand to watch *CSI* would be less during the Olympics than during other weeks. And if the demand for *CSI* is lower during the Olympics, how much an advertiser would pay for a half-minute commercial during that week is lower as well. In other words, CBS believed that the future price of a half-minute commercial in a non-Olympic week would be higher than in an Olympic week, so it reduced its supply of new *CSI* episodes in an Olympic week to zero and transferred what supply of new *CSI* episodes it had to non-Olympic weeks—when it could fetch a higher price for a half-minute commercial.

SELF-TEST

1.   How might the expectation of a higher price for houses affect the (current) demand for houses?

2.   How might the expectation of a lower price for cars affect the (current) demand for cars?

Application 5: Who Feeds Cleveland?

Rarely does anyone ask who feeds Cleveland or who feeds (the people in) any other city in the world for that matter. Most of us take it for granted that we somehow get fed. We go to the grocery store, we select certain items off the shelves, we pay for those items, and then we go home and eat the food. What more do we need to think about?

To understand just how much is involved, suppose you had the job of feeding Cleveland: You need to tell farmers how much corn, wheat, and soybeans to grow. You need to decide what the right price is for Cheerios and ketchup and milk. (How do you figure out these prices?) You need to send so many cartons of orange juice to various grocery stores. (We wonder whether you might send too much orange juice to one grocery store and not enough to another.)

To get the right amount of food to your local grocery store, literally hundreds of decisions have to be made along the way. Yet, no giant computer decides how much corn and wheat will be grown and how much orange juice will be sent to the grocery store at the corner of 13th Street and Main. No government bureaucracy in Washington, D.C., decides such things. As far as we know, we cannot point to a single person in the world and say: "She feeds Cleveland."

Well, if no one feeds Cleveland, then how does Cleveland get fed? The answer is "supply and demand feeds Cleveland." That's right, supply and demand, or what we have come to know as "the market." If the demand for Cheerios rises, the price rises, which prompts the manufacturer to produce more Cheerios. If the demand for corn rises, the price rises, which prompts corn farmers to plant and harvest more corn. If the demand for fat-free ice cream falls, then fat-free ice cream stays in the grocery freezer longer, and soon the price drops, which signals to ice cream manufacturers that they shouldn't produce as much fat-free ice cream.

A famous economist once said that if "supply and demand" or "the market" didn't naturally exist, it would have to be invented—and then it would be hailed as the greatest invention the world had ever seen. Of course, the market was not invented; it just is.

Who feeds Cleveland, New York, Chicago, New Orleans, London, Buenos Aires, and Paris?

And who feeds you?

Application 6: The Minimum Wage Law

Recall that a price floor is a legislated minimum price below which trades cannot legally be made. The *minimum wage* is a price floor—a government-mandated minimum price for labor. It affects the market for unskilled labor. In Exhibit 2, we assume the minimum

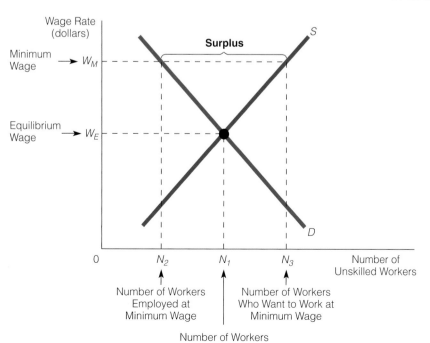

exhibit **2**

Effects of the Minimum Wage

At a minimum wage of W_M an hour, there is a surplus of workers and fewer workers are employed than would be at the equilibrium wage W_E.

wage is W_M and the equilibrium wage is W_E. At the equilibrium wage, N_1 workers are employed. At the higher minimum wage, N_3 workers want to work but only N_2 actually do work. There is a surplus of workers equal to $N_3 - N_2$ in this unskilled labor market. In addition, fewer workers are working at the minimum wage (N_2) than at the equilibrium wage (N_1). Overall, the effects of the minimum wage are (1) a surplus of unskilled workers and (2) fewer workers employed.

Suppose two economists decide to test the theory that as the minimum wage rises, some unskilled workers will lose their jobs. They look at the number of unskilled workers before and after the minimum wage is raised, and surprisingly, they find that the number of unskilled workers is the same. Is this sufficient evidence to conclude that an increase in the minimum wage does not cause some workers to lose their jobs?

We'll leave that question hanging while we consider whether or not the economists have adequately tested their theory. Instead of focusing on the number of people who lose their jobs, suppose they look at the people who keep their jobs but have their hours reduced as a result of the higher minimum wage.

Let's look at an example. Suppose a local hardware store currently employs David and Francesca to work after school cleaning up and stocking shelves. The owner of the store pays each of them the minimum wage of, say, $5.15 an hour. Then, the minimum wage is raised to $6.75 an hour. Will either David or Francesca lose their jobs as a result? Not necessarily. Instead, the owner of the store could reduce the number of hours he employs the two workers. For example, instead of having each of them work 20 hours a week, he might ask each to work only 14 hours a week.[1]

Now, let's reconsider our original question: Has the higher minimum wage eliminated jobs? In a way, no. It has, however, reduced the number of hours a person works in a job. (Of course, if we define a job as including both a particular task and a certain number of hours completing that task, then the minimum wage increase has eliminated "part" of the job.) This discussion argues for changing the label on the horizontal axis in Exhibit 2 from "Number of Unskilled Workers" to "Number of Unskilled Labor Hours."

Thinking like AN ECONOMIST

In economics, some questions relate to "direction" and some to "magnitude." For example, suppose someone asks, "If the demand for labor is downward sloping and the labor market is competitive, how will a minimum wage (above the equilibrium wage) affect employment?" This person is asking a question that relates to the direction of the change in employment. Usually, these types of questions can be answered by applying a theory. Applying the theory of demand, an economist might say, "At higher wages, the quantity demanded of labor, or the employment level, will be lower than at lower wages." The word **lower** *speaks to the directional change in employment.*

Now suppose someone asks, "How much will employment decline?" This person is asking a question that relates to magnitude. Usually, questions that deal with magnitude can be answered only through some kind of empirical (data-collecting and analyzing) work. In other words, we would have to collect employment figures at the equilibrium wage and at the minimum wage and then find the difference.

SELF-TEST

1. When the labor supply curve is upward sloping, a minimum wage law that sets the wage rate above its equilibrium level creates a surplus of labor. If the labor supply curve is vertical, does a surplus of labor still occur? Explain your answer.

2. Someone says that an increase in the minimum wage will not cause firms to hire fewer workers. What is this person assuming?

Application 7: Loud Talking at a Restaurant

We discussed the concept of equilibrium at length in the last chapter. Equilibrium in a competitive market comes at the point at which the quantity demanded of a good equals the quantity supplied of a good. Another way to describe equilibrium is as a state of affairs that exists after all adjustments have been made. To illustrate, consider a shortage

---

[1]Our two economists need to find data that relate not only to how many, if any, people lose their jobs as a result of the higher minimum wage but also to how many people who keep their jobs end up working fewer hours.

in a market. Here quantity demanded of a good is greater than quantity supplied. Is this consistent with all adjustments having been made? Absolutely not. Buyers will still find it in their interest to bid up prices.

Or consider a surplus in a market. Is this consistent with all adjustments having been made? No. Sellers will still find it in their interest to lower prices.

It is only at equilibrium where neither buyers nor sellers will have any incentive to do anything different. Buyers won't bid up prices and sellers won't lower prices. Both sides of the market—the buying side and the selling side—are content with things just the way they are.

Now economists often ask themselves if what they see in front of them at the current moment is or is not consistent with equilibrium. If there are no more adjustments to come, then equilibrium exists; if there are more adjustments to come, then equilibrium does not exist.

With this in mind, suppose you are at a restaurant with some friends. Over time, you notice that the volume of the people talking in the restaurant is getting louder. If volume can be measured on a scale from 1 to 10, the volume was at 4 when you entered the restaurant, but it has now risen to 7.

You ask yourself two questions. First, what caused the increase in volume; second, is the current volume at equilibrium?

The answer to the first question is that as more people were seated in the restaurant, the volume naturally went up. But then, as the volume naturally went up (because of more people talking), each person had an incentive to raise his own volume of speaking. In other words, you are at a table talking to your friends. Then you notice that it is getting louder in the restaurant. To be heard by your friends, you raise your volume of speech. But because you raise your volume of speech, the overall volume of speech in the restaurant goes up, and then somebody else, noticing that the volume has just increased, raises her volume of speech to be heard by her friends at her table.

Where does it all end? It ends at equilibrium, at the point at which no one has any incentive either to raise or lower his or her voice. It ends when all adjustments to one's own volume of speech are complete. This comes when everyone sees the additional benefits of raising his voice as equal to the additional costs of raising his voice. When this state of affairs exists, equilibrium has been achieved. Or in supply-and-demand terms, it comes when, for each person in the restaurant, the quantity demanded of a higher volume of speech is equal to the quantity supplied of a higher volume of speech that each person is willing to provide.

> **Thinking like AN ECONOMIST**
>
> *Economists will often identify equilibrium in a competitive market as a desirable state of affairs. After all, it is at equilibrium that the sum of consumers' and producers' surplus is maximized and all "gains from trade" have been realized. But the economist knows that equilibrium is not necessarily descriptive of a desirable state of affairs. Think of the loud talking in a restaurant. Things may get so loud that everyone in the restaurant realizes that he or she would be better off if everyone spoke less loudly, but still, no one has an incentive to be the first person to speak less loudly. In other words, equilibrium is consistent with loud talking, a condition that no one is particularly fond of.*

Application 8: Price Ceiling in the Kidney Market

Just as there are people who want to buy houses, computers, and books, there are people who want to buy kidneys. These people have kidney failure and either will die without a new kidney or will have to endure years of costly and painful dialysis. This demand for kidneys is shown as D_K in Exhibit 3.

The supply of kidneys is shown as S_K in Exhibit 3. Notice that at \$0 price, the quantity supplied of kidneys is 350. These kidneys are from people who donate their kidneys to others, asking nothing in return. They may donate their kidneys upon their death or may donate one of their two kidneys while living. We have drawn the supply curve as upward sloping because we assume that some people who today are unwilling to donate a kidney for \$0 might be willing to do so for some positive dollar amount.

The Market for Kidneys

We have identified the demand for kidneys as D_K and the supply of kidneys as S_K. Given the demand for and supply of kidneys, the equilibrium price of a kidney is P_1. It does not follow, though, that simply because there is an equilibrium price, people will be allowed to trade at this price. Today, it is unlawful to buy and sell kidneys at any positive price. In short, there is a price ceiling in the kidney market and the ceiling is $0. At the price ceiling, there is a shortage of kidneys, a nonprice rationing device for kidneys (first-come-first-served), fewer kidney transplants (than there would be at P_1), and illegal purchases and sales of kidneys.

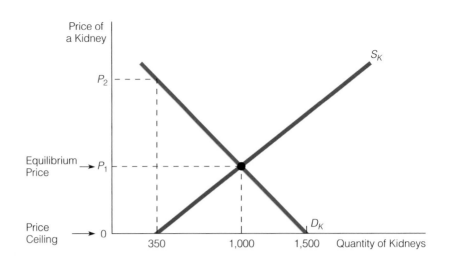

Specifically, we assume that as the price of a kidney rises, the quantity supplied of kidneys will rise.

If there were a free market in kidneys, the price of a kidney would be P_1 in Exhibit 3. At this price, 1,000 kidneys would be purchased and sold—1,000 kidney transplants would occur.

Today, there is no free market in kidneys. Buying or selling kidneys is illegal at any dollar amount. In essence, then, there is a price ceiling in the kidney market, and the ceiling is set at $0. What is the effect of this price ceiling?

If the demand curve for kidneys and the supply curve of kidneys intersected at $0, there would be neither a surplus nor a shortage of kidneys. But there is evidence that the demand and supply curves do not intersect at $0; they look more like those shown in Exhibit 3. In other words, there is a shortage of kidneys at $0: The quantity supplied of kidneys is 350 and the quantity demanded is 1,500. (Although these are not the actual numbers of kidneys demanded and supplied at $0, they are representative of the current situation in the kidney market.)

The last chapter described the possible effects of a price ceiling set below equilibrium price: shortages, nonprice rationing devices, fewer exchanges, tie-in sales, and buying and selling at prohibited prices (in other words, illegal trades). Are any of these effects occurring in the kidney market?

First, there is evidence of a shortage. In almost every country in the world, there are more people on national lists who want a kidney than there are kidneys available. Some of these people die waiting for a kidney.

Second, as just indicated, the nonprice rationing device used in the kidney market is (largely) first come, first served. A person who wants a kidney registers on a national waiting list. How long one waits is a function of how far down the list one's name appears.

Third, there are fewer exchanges; not everyone who needs a kidney gets a kidney. With a price ceiling of $0, only 350 kidneys are supplied. All these kidneys are from people who freely donate their kidneys. If P_1 were permitted, some people who are unwilling to supply a kidney (at $0) would be willing to do so. In short, monetary payment would provide the incentive for some people to supply a kidney. At P_1, 1,000 kidneys are demanded and supplied, so more people would get kidney transplants when the price of a kidney is P_1 (1,000 in total) than when the price of a kidney is $0 (350 in total). More transplants, of course, means fewer people die waiting for a kidney.

Fourth, kidneys are bought and sold at prohibited prices. People buy and sell kidneys today; they just do so illegally. There are stories of people paying between $25,000 and $200,000 for a kidney.

Some people argue that a free market in kidneys would be wrong. Such a system would place the poor at a disadvantage. Think of it: A rich person who needed a kidney could buy the kidney, but a poor person could not. The rich person would get a second chance at life, whereas the poor person would not. No one particularly enjoys contemplating this stark reality.

But consider another stark reality. If it is unlawful to pay someone for a kidney, fewer kidneys will be forthcoming. In other words, the quantity supplied of kidneys is less at $0 than at, say, $20,000. Fewer kidneys supplied mean fewer kidney transplants. And fewer kidney transplants mean more people will die from kidney failure.

SELF-TEST

1. A shortage of kidneys for transplants is a consequence of the price of a kidney being below equilibrium price. Do you agree or disagree? Explain your answer.

2. Assume the price ceiling in the kidney market is $0. Will there be a shortage of kidneys? Explain your answer.

Application 9: Healthcare and the Right to Sue Your HMO

A discussion of renters, landlords, and eviction notices is relevant to the right to sue an HMO. So we begin with an analysis of two laws related to eviction of a renter. Under law 1, a renter has 30 days to vacate an apartment after being served with an eviction notice. Under law 2, the renter has 90 days to vacate.

Landlords will find it less expensive to rent apartments under law 1 than under law 2. Under law 1, the most money a landlord can lose after serving an eviction notice is 30 days' rent. Under law 2, a landlord can lose 90 days' rent. Obviously, losing 90 days' rent is more costly than losing 30 days' rent.

A different supply curve of apartments exists under each law. The supply curve under law 1 (S_1 in Exhibit 4) lies to the right of the supply curve under law 2 (S_2 in the

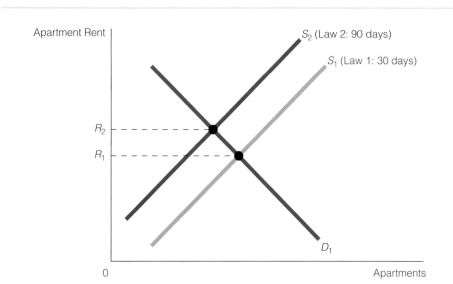

exhibit 4

Apartment Rent and the Law

Under law 1, a renter has 30 days to leave an apartment after receiving an eviction notice from his or her landlord. Under law 2, a renter has 90 days to leave an apartment after receiving an eviction notice from his or her landlord. The cost to the landlord of renting an apartment is higher under law 2 than law 1, and so the supply curve of apartments under law 1 lies to the right of the supply curve of apartments under law 2. Different supply curves mean different rents. Apartment rent is higher under law 2 (R_2) than under law 1 (R_1).

exhibit). Again, that's because it is less expensive to supply apartments under law 1 than under law 2.

If the supply curve is different under the two laws, the equilibrium rent will be different too. As shown in Exhibit 4, the equilibrium rent will be lower under law 1 (R_1) than under law 2 (R_2).

In conclusion, under law 1, a renter pays lower rent (good) and has fewer days to vacate the apartment (bad). Under law 2, a renter pays a higher rent (bad) and has more days to vacate the apartment (good). Who pays for the additional days to vacate the apartment under law 2? The renter pays for these additional days by paying higher rent.

Now let's turn from apartments to healthcare. You may frequently hear people complain about their health maintenance organizations (HMOs). The complaints are diverse and wide-ranging. One common complaint is that patients cannot sue their HMOs in state courts for denial of benefits and poor-quality care. Some people argue that patients should have the right to sue their HMOs.

Let's consider two settings: one in which patients cannot sue their HMOs and one in which patients can sue. If patients cannot sue, an HMO's liability cost is lower than if patients can sue. A difference in liability costs will be reflected in different supply curves.

To illustrate, recall that any single point on a supply curve is the minimum price sellers need to receive for them to be willing and able to sell that particular unit of a good. Suppose when patients cannot sue, an HMO is willing and able to provide healthcare to John for $300 a month. If patients can sue, is the HMO still willing and able to provide healthcare to John for $300 a month? Not likely. Because of the higher liability cost due to the patient's ability to sue, the HMO is no longer willing and able to provide healthcare to John for $300 month. It will, however, be willing and able to provide healthcare to John for, say, $350 a month.

Saying a seller's minimum price for providing a good or service rises is the same as saying the seller's supply curve has shifted upward and to the left. In other words, the supply curve of HMO-provided healthcare will shift upward and to the left if patients have the right to sue. This is the same way the supply curve of apartments moved in Exhibit 4.

Will a difference in supply curves affect the price patients pay for their HMO-provided healthcare coverage? Yes. One effect of moving from a setting where patients do not have the right to sue to one where patients do have the right to sue is that patients will have to pay more for their HMO-provided healthcare coverage.

Economists don't determine whether patients having the right to sue is good or bad or right or wrong. Economists use their tools (in this instance, supply and demand) to point out that things people want, such as the right to sue their HMOs, often come with price tags. Individuals must decide whether the price they pay is worth what they receive in return.

SELF-TEST

1.   Economists often say, "There is no such thing as a free lunch." How is this saying related to patients moving from a system where they cannot sue their HMOs to one where they can?

2.   A professor tells her students that they can have an extra week to complete their research papers. Under what condition are the students better off with the extra week? Can you think of a case where the students would actually be worse off with the extra week?

Application 10: Being Late to Class

We usually think of the demand for goods and services that are traded in a market—goods such as oranges, computers, television sets, and cars and services such as hair-cutting services, attorney services, and so on. For goods and services that are traded in markets, the demand curve is downward sloping: The lower the price of the good or service, the more units of these goods and services buyers will want to buy; the higher the price of the good or service, the fewer units of these goods and services buyers will want to buy.

But we wonder if there is a demand for goods that are not traded in markets. For example, consider something like "being late to class." Does it makes sense to talk about the demand for being late to class? It makes sense if, in fact, being late to class is subject to the law of demand.

Are students more likely to be late to some classes than others? If so, might they be more likely to be late to classes where the instructor does not charge them a "price" for being late than to classes where the instructor does?

Consider a thought experiment. Two professors, Smith and Jones, each teach economics. Professor Smith tells students that for each time they are late to class, he will deduct one point from their final course grade. Professor Jones tells students that they should be on time to class but does not penalize them in any way if they are late. In which class would we expect students to more likely be late to class? If you answered "Professor Jones's class," then you are telling us that you believe there is a downward-sloping demand curve for being late to class.

To support the idea of a downward-sloping demand curve for being late to class, some professors point out that students are much less likely to be late to class on an exam day. Why? Because the price of being late to class on an exam day is higher than it is on most other days. Lateness on an exam day means the student has less time to complete the exam, which can adversely affect his or her grade.

Thinking like
AN ECONOMIST   *The economist knows that the law of demand does not only hold for goods and services that are traded in a market. The law of demand sometimes holds for things that are not traded at all.*

SELF-TEST

1.   What has to hold for there to be a downward-sloping demand curve for using foul language?

2.   Do you think there is a downward-sloping demand curve for sneezing? Explain your answer.

Application 11: If Gold Prices Are the Same Everywhere, Then Why Aren't House Prices?

The price of an ounce of gold is the same everywhere in the world. For example, the price of an ounce of gold is the same in London as it is in New York City. House prices are not the same everywhere, though. For example, the median price of a house in Los Angeles, California, is higher than the median price of a house in Dubuque, Iowa. Why are gold prices the same everywhere while house prices are different?

To answer the question, let's look at what would happen if gold prices were not the same everywhere in the world. Let's assume the price of an ounce of gold is $250 in London and $300 in New York City. What happens? Obviously, this difference in prices for the same good presents a profit opportunity. People will buy gold in London for $250 an ounce, ship it to New York City, and sell it for $300 an ounce. If we ignore the costs of transporting the gold, a $50 profit per ounce is earned. When an opportunity exists for profit—by buying low and selling high—individuals are quick to try to capture the profit.

As gold is moved from London to New York City in search of profit, the supply of gold in London will fall, and the supply of gold in New York City will rise. A falling gold supply in London will push up the price of gold (from $250), and a rising gold supply in New York City will push down the price of gold (from $300). As the London gold price rises and the New York City gold price falls, a point will eventually be reached where the two prices are the same. When the London price and New York City price for gold are the same, profit cannot be earned by moving gold from London to New York City. In short, any difference in the price of gold in various locations will quickly be eliminated by changes in the supply of gold in the various locations.

Can the same hold for houses? If the price of a house in Los Angeles is higher than the price of a house in Dubuque, is it possible to move houses and land from Dubuque to Los Angeles? Of course not. We can't pick up a house and its lot in Dubuque and move them to Los Angeles, in the process reducing the supply of houses and land in Dubuque and increasing the supply of houses and land in Los Angeles. Because the supply of houses and land cannot be reshuffled the way the supply of gold can be, we expect differences in house prices in various locations but not differences in gold prices.

SELF-TEST

1.   What causes the price of gold to be the same in New York City and London?

2.   The price of a Honda Pilot is nearly the same in Miami as it is in Dallas. Why?

Application 12: Do You Pay for Good Weather?

Some places in the country are considered to have better weather than other places. For example, most people would say the weather in San Diego, California, is better than the weather in Fargo, North Dakota. Often, a person in San Diego will say, "You can't beat the weather today. And the good thing about it is that you don't have to pay a thing for it. It's free."

In one sense, the San Diegan is correct: There is no weather market. Specifically, no one comes around and asks San Diegans to pay a certain dollar amount for the weather on a given day.

But in another sense, the San Diegan is incorrect. The fact is that San Diegans indirectly pay for their good weather. How do they pay? To enjoy the weather in San Diego on a regular basis, you have to live in San Diego—you need to have housing. There is a demand for housing in San Diego just as there is a demand for housing in other places. Is the demand for housing in San Diego higher than it would be if the weather were not so good? Without the good weather, living in San Diego would not be as pleasurable, and therefore, the demand to live there would be lower. In short, the demand for housing in San Diego is higher because San Diego enjoys good weather. It follows that the price of housing is higher too. Thus, San Diegans indirectly pay for their good weather because they pay higher housing prices than they would if San Diego had bad weather.

Was our representative San Diegan right when he said the good weather was free?

SELF-TEST

1.   Give an example to illustrate that someone may "pay" for clean air in much the same way that she "pays" for good weather.

2.   If people pay for good weather, who ultimately receives the "good-weather payment"?

Application 13: Paying All Professors the Same Salary

In college, you take various courses. You may take courses in accounting, economics, English, and history. From your perspective, the professors in the courses may do much the same work. Each professor regularly comes to class, lectures and leads discussions, holds office hours, gives tests and exams, grades those tests and exams, and so on. Does it follow, then, that all professors of equal experience should be paid the same salary? In other words, if a professor in computer science with 10 years of experience earns $100,000 a year, should a professor in history with 10 years of experience earn $100,000 a year too? If your answer is yes, then what might the effects of such a policy be?

Let's again turn to supply and demand for an answer. Exhibit 5(a) shows the market for accounting professors; Exhibit 5(b) shows the market for history professors. In each market, there is a demand for and supply of professors. However, the equilibrium wage in the accounting market (W_A) is higher than the equilibrium wage in the history market (W_H).

If accounting and history professors are each paid their respective equilibrium wage, neither market will be in shortage or surplus. But pay both professors the same wage when their equilibrium wages are different, and shortages or surpluses will appear.

For example, suppose both accounting and history professors are paid the higher wage, W_A. The accounting market remains in equilibrium, but a surplus appears in the history market. There will be more historians who want to work at colleges (N_2) than colleges will hire (N_3).

Or suppose both accounting and history professors are paid the lower wage, W_H. The history market remains in equilibrium, but a shortage appears in the accounting market. Colleges will want to hire more accountants (N_2) than will be willing to work at the colleges (N_3).

Sitting in class, you may think that while the supply-and-demand analysis of the accounting and history markets is interesting, it does not affect you. What does it matter if your professors are paid the same or not?

But look at the number of professors hired in each market at the equilibrium wage and at the disequilibrium wage. In the accounting market, when the wage is W_A, N_1 accounting professors are hired. At W_H, only N_3 are hired because N_3 is the number of accounting professors who are willing and able to work at W_H. N_3 is less than N_1.

In the history market, when the wage is W_H, N_1 history professors are hired. At W_A, N_3 are hired because N_3 is the number of history professors colleges are willing and able to hire at W_A. N_3 is less than N_1.

Paying Professors the Same Salary

Suppose the market supply and demand conditions are as shown in (a) for accounting professors and as shown in (b) for history professors. Consequently, the equilibrium wage in the two markets would be different. As shown, the equilibrium wage for accounting professors (W_A) is higher than the equilibrium wage for history professors (W_H). What happens if both accounting and history professors are paid W_A? A surplus of history professors appears. What happens if both accounting and history professors are paid W_H? A shortage of accounting professors appears. Paying all college professors the same salary when there are differences in demand and supply creates shortages and surpluses.

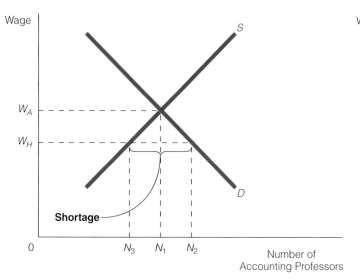

(a) Market for
Accounting Professors

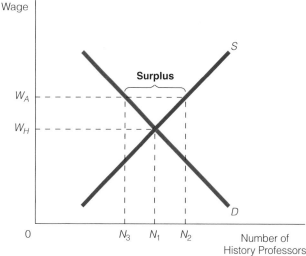

(b) Market for
History Professors

In short, more professors are working at colleges teaching students when professors are paid equilibrium wages than when they are paid disequilibrium wages. So, how professors are paid affects the student-to-faculty ratio. Instead of 40 students per faculty member at disequilibrium wages, we might have 30 students per faculty member at equilibrium wages.

SELF-TEST

1.   Suppose the supply of biology and computer science professors is the same but the demand for computer scientists is greater than the demand for biologists. Furthermore, suppose both biologists and computer scientists are paid the same wage. If a shortage exists in both fields, in which field is the shortage greater? Explain your answer.

2.   Under what condition might an economist propose that all college professors (irrespective of their field) be paid the same?

Application 14: Price Floors and Winners and Losers

Exhibit 6 shows the demand for and supply of an agricultural foodstuff (corn, wheat, soybeans, etc.). If the market is allowed to move to equilibrium, the equilibrium price will be P_1, and the equilibrium quantity will be Q_1. Consumers' surplus will equal the area under the demand curve and above the equilibrium price: areas $1 + 2 + 3$. Producers' surplus will equal the area under the equilibrium price and above the supply curve: areas $4 + 5$. Total surplus, of course, is the sum of consumers' surplus and producers' surplus: areas $1 + 2 + 3 + 4 + 5$.

Now suppose that the suppliers of the foodstuff argue for (and receive) a price floor, P_F. At this higher price, consumers do not buy as much as they once did. They now buy Q_2, whereas they used to buy Q_1. In addition, consumers' surplus is now only area 1, and producers' surplus is areas $2 + 4$.

Obviously, consumers have been hurt by the new higher (government-mandated) price of P_F; specifically, they have lost consumers' surplus equal to areas $2 + 3$.

Agricultural Price Floors

The demand for and supply of an agricultural foodstuff are shown in this exhibit. The equilibrium price is P_1; consumers' surplus (CS) is areas $1 + 2 + 3$; producers' surplus is areas $4 + 5$. A price floor of P_F effectively transfers some of the consumers' surplus to producers in the form of a gain in producers' surplus. Specifically, at P_F, consumers' surplus is area 1 and producers' surplus is areas $2 + 4$. Consumers are net losers because consumers' surplus has decreased by areas $2 + 3$. Producers are net gainers because producers' surplus has increased from areas $4 + 5$ to areas $2 + 4$ and area 2 is larger than area 5. Overall, the economic pie of $CS + PS$ has decreased from areas $1 + 2 + 3 + 4 + 5$ to areas $1 + 2 + 4$.

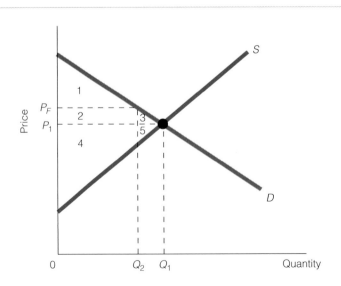

How have suppliers fared? Whereas their producers' surplus was equal to areas 4 + 5 at P_1, it is now equal to areas 2 + 4. (Area 2, which used to be part of consumers' surplus, has been transferred to producers and is now part of producers' surplus.) Whether or not producers are better off depends on whether or not area 2 (what they gain from P_F) is larger than area 5 (what they lose from P_F). Visually, we can tell that area 2 is larger than area 5, so producers are better off.

What is the overall effect of the price floor? Have producers gained more than consumers have lost, or have consumers lost more than producers have gained? To answer this question, we note that consumers lose areas 2 + 3 in consumers' surplus; producers gain area 2 in producers' surplus and lose area 5 in producers' surplus. So, the gains and losses are:

Losses to consumers: areas 2 + 3
Gains to producers: area 2
Losses to producers: area 5

Part of the loss to consumers is offset by the gain to producers (area 2), so net losses amount to areas 3 + 5. In other words, total surplus—the sum of consumers' surplus and producers' surplus—is lower than it was. Whereas it used to be areas 1 + 2 + 3 + 4 + 5, it now is areas 1 + 2 + 4. The total surplus lost is areas 3 + 5.

In short, (1) consumers lose, (2) producers gain, and (3) society (which is the sum of consumers and producers) loses.

You can think of this example in terms of a pie. Initially, the pie was made up of areas 1 + 2 + 3 + 4 + 5. This rather large pie registered all the gains of consumers and producers. After the price floor of P_F was imposed, the pie shrank to areas 1 + 2 + 4; in other words, the pie was smaller by areas 3 + 5.

A loss in total surplus—in our example, areas 3 + 5—is sometimes called a **deadweight loss**. It is the loss to society of not producing the competitive, or supply-and-demand-determined, level of output. In terms of Exhibit 6, it is the loss to society of producing Q_2 instead of producing Q_1.

Deadweight loss
The loss to society of not producing the competitive, or supply-and-demand-determined, level of output.

SELF-TEST

1. Look at the area equal to areas 3 + 5 in Exhibit 6. If there is a price floor, this area ends up being a deadweight loss. It is the loss to society of not producing Q_1. Are there mutually beneficial trades that exist between Q_2 and Q_1, and if so, how do you know this?

2. Why might producers argue for a price floor if it ends up making society worse off?

Application 15: College Superathletes

Let's consider a young man, 17 years old, who is one of the best high school football players in the country. As a superathlete, the young man will be recruited by many college and university football coaches. Every one of those colleges and universities will likely want its coach to be successful at getting the young athlete; after all, at many universities, athletics is a moneymaker.

Our superathlete decides to attend college A, where he receives a "full ride"—a full scholarship. How should this full scholarship be viewed? One way is to say the superathlete is charged zero tuition to attend the college. (In other words, whereas some students pay a price of $10,000 a year to attend the college, the superathlete pays nothing.)

Another way to view the full scholarship involves a two-step process. First, the college pays the superathlete a dollar amount equal to the full tuition. Second, it then charges the superathlete the full tuition. (In other words, the college gives the athlete $10,000 with one hand and then collects the $10,000 with the other hand.)

Although it ends up being the same for the athlete regardless of which way we view the full scholarship, for purposes of our analysis, let's view the full scholarship the second way: as a payment to the athlete combined with full price being charged. This way of viewing the scholarship leads to two important questions:

1. Can the college pay the athlete more than the full tuition of the college? In other words, if the full tuition is $10,000 a year, can the college pay the athlete, say, $15,000 a year?

2. Is the superathlete being paid what he is worth?

Because of NCAA rules, the answer to the first question is essentially no. The NCAA states that a college or university cannot pay a student to attend, and for all practical purposes, the NCAA views payment as anything more than a full scholarship. The NCAA takes the position that college athletes are amateurs, and amateurs cannot be paid to play their sport.

How does the NCAA rule affect our second question? What if the athlete's worth to the college or university is greater than the dollar amount of the full tuition? For example, suppose the athlete will increase the revenues of the college by $50,000 a year, and the full tuition is only $10,000 a year. In this case, the NCAA rule sets a price ceiling for the college. It sets a ceiling on what the college can pay an athlete. What is the effect of this price ceiling?

Let's consider the demand (on the part of various colleges) for a single superathlete and the supply of this single superathlete (see Exhibit 7). We assume that the supply curve is vertical at 1 "athletic services."

Now suppose the representative college charges tuition of $10,000. Because of the NCAA rule, this dollar amount is the effective price ceiling (or wage ceiling). Furthermore, let's suppose that the single college athlete's market equilibrium wage is $15,000. So, if the NCAA rule did not exist, the athlete's wage would rise to $15,000. This dollar amount is equal to areas $B + C$ in Exhibit 7. What is the consumers' surplus for the college that buys the athlete's services for $15,000? Obviously, it is equal to area A.

However, the NCAA rule stipulates that the college cannot pay the athlete more than $10,000 (full tuition). So, the athlete's payment falls from $15,000 to $10,000, or from areas $B + C$ to simply area C. The college's consumers' surplus increases to areas A

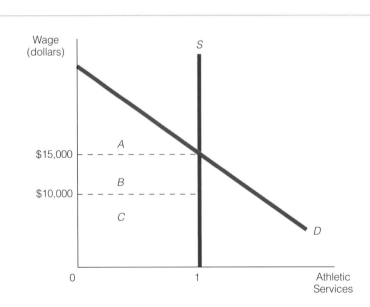

exhibit 7

The College Athlete

The exhibit shows the demand for and supply of a college athlete. If the market wage for the college athlete is **$15,000**, then the buyer of the athlete—in this case, the college—receives consumers' surplus equal to area *A*. If the wage can be held down to the tuition cost of attending the college—**$10,000** in this example—then the college receives consumers' surplus of areas *B + C*.

+ *B*. Essentially, the NCAA rule transfers part of the athlete's income—area *B*—to the college in the form of greater consumers' surplus.

Just as the price floor in Application 14 leads to a transfer (from consumers to producers), a price ceiling leads to a transfer. The price ceiling set by the NCAA rule results in a transfer from the athlete to the college. In short, the athlete loses and the college gains. Moreover, in this case, the college gain in consumers' surplus equals the income loss for the athlete.

SELF-TEST

1.   University *X* is a large university with a major football team. A new field house and track were just added to the university. How is this related to the discussion in this application?

2.   Sometimes it is argued that if colleges paid student athletes, the demand for college sports would decline. In other words, the demand for college sports is as high as it is because student athletes are not paid (the way athletes in professional sports are paid). How would the analysis in this application change if we assume this argument is true?

Application 16: Supply and Demand on a Freeway

What does a traffic jam on a busy freeway in any large city have to do with supply and demand? Actually, it has quite a bit to do with supply and demand. Look at it this way: There is a demand for driving on the freeway and a supply of freeway space. The supply of freeway space is fixed (freeways do not expand and contract over a day, week, or month). The demand, however, fluctuates. It is higher at some times than at other times. For example, we would expect the demand for driving on the freeway to be higher at 8 A.M. (rush hour) than at 11 P.M. But even though the demand may vary, the money price for driving on the freeway is always the same—zero. A zero money price means that motorists do not pay tolls to drive on the freeway.

Exhibit 8 shows two demand curves for driving on the freeway: $D_{8 \text{ A.M.}}$ and $D_{11 \text{ P.M.}}$. We have assumed the demand at 8 A.M. is greater than at 11 P.M. We have also assumed that at $D_{11 \text{ P.M.}}$ and zero money price the freeway market clears: Quantity demanded of freeway space equals quantity supplied of freeway space. At the higher demand, $D_{8 \text{ A.M.}}$, however, this is not the case. At zero money price, a shortage of freeway space exists: Quantity demanded of freeway space is greater than quantity supplied of freeway space. The shortage appears in the form of freeway congestion and bumper-to-bumper traffic.

One way to eliminate the shortage is through an increase in the money price of driving on the freeway at 8 A.M. For example, as Exhibit 8 shows, a toll of 70 cents would clear the freeway market at 8 A.M.

If charging different prices (tolls) at different times of the day on freeways sounds like an unusual idea, consider how Miami Beach hotels price their rooms. They charge different prices for their rooms at different times of the year. During the winter months when the demand for vacationing in Miami Beach is high, the hotels charge higher prices than when the demand is (relatively) low. If different prices were charged for freeway space at different times of the day, freeway space would be rationed the same way Miami Beach hotel rooms are rationed.

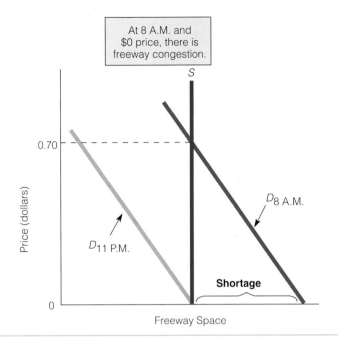

At 8 A.M. and $0 price, there is freeway congestion.

exhibit **8**

Freeway Congestion and Supply and Demand

The demand for driving on the freeway is higher at 8 A.M. than at 11 P.M. At zero money price and $D_{11\ P.M.}$, the freeway market clears. At zero money price and $D_{8\ A.M.}$, there is a shortage of freeway space, which shows up as freeway congestion. At a price (toll) of 70 cents, the shortage is eliminated and freeway congestion disappears.

Before we leave this topic, let's consider the three alternatives usually proposed for freeway congestion. Some people propose tolls, some propose building more freeways, and others propose encouraging carpooling. Tolls deal with the congestion problem by adjusting price to its equilibrium level, as shown in Exhibit 8. Building more freeways deals with the problem by increasing supply. In Exhibit 8, it would be necessary to shift the supply curve of freeway space to the right so there is no longer any shortage of space at 8 A.M. More carpooling deals with the problem by decreasing demand. Two people in one car take up less space on a freeway than two people in two cars. In Exhibit 8, if through carpooling the demand at 8 A.M. begins to look like the demand at 11 P.M., then there is no longer a shortage of freeway space at 8 A.M.

A final note: A fee to drive in the Central London area was introduced in 2003. Anyone going into or out of the Central London area between 7:00 A.M. and 6:30 P.M., Monday through Friday, must pay a fee of approximately $14. (Not everyone has to pay the fee. For example, taxi drivers, ambulance drivers, police vehicles, motorcycle drivers, and bicyclists do not have to pay the fee. The residents who live in the area receive a 90 percent discount.) Many people have claimed the fee a success because it has cut down on traffic and travel times and reduced pollution in the area.

> *Thinking like*
> **AN ECONOMIST**
>
> *The economist knows that when there are buyers and sellers of anything (bread, cars, or freeway space), only three conditions are possible—equilibrium, shortage, or surplus. When the economist sees traffic congestion, the first thing that comes to mind is that there is a shortage of road space. Buy why is there a shortage? The economist knows that shortages occur at prices below equilibrium price. In other words, price is too low.*

Some people have urged New York City to institute a similar fee program to drive on certain streets in the city. On any given day in New York City, there are approximately 800,000 cars on the streets south of 60th Street in Manhattan. According to many, the city is "choking in traffic." We will have to wait to see if New York City goes the way of London.

SELF-TEST

1.   In Exhibit 8, at what price is there a surplus of freeway space at 8 A.M.?

2.   If the driving population increases in an area and the supply of freeway space remains constant, what will happen to freeway congestion? Explain your answer.

Application 17: What Does Price Have to Do with Getting to Class on Time?

Class starts at 10 o'clock in the morning. At 10:09, Pam Ferrario walks in late. She apologizes to the instructor, saying, "I've been on campus for 20 minutes, but I couldn't find a parking space." Her classmates nod, knowing full well what she is talking about. At Pam's university, especially between the hours of 8 A.M. and 2 P.M., parking spaces are hard to find.

This scene is replayed every day at many universities and colleges across the country. Students are late for class because on many days there isn't a parking space to be found. Why can't students find parking spaces? The immediate answer is because there is a shortage of parking spaces. But why is there a shortage of parking spaces? There is a shortage of parking spaces for the same reason there is any shortage: The equilibrium price is not being charged.

Who pays for the shortage of parking spaces? The students pay—not in money, but in time. Because students know parking spaces on campus are hard to find, they often leave home or work sooner than they would if there were no shortages. Or like Pam Ferrario, they pay by being late to class.

Are there alternatives to the *pay-in-time* and *pay-in-being-late-to-class* schemes for rationing campus parking spots? Some economists have suggested a *pay-in-price* scheme. For example, the university could install meters in the parking lot and raise the fee high enough so that between the hours of 8 A.M. and 2 P.M., the quantity demanded for parking spaces equals the quantity supplied.

Such suggestions are sometimes criticized on the basis that students must pay the parking fee, no matter how high, to attend classes. But that's not exactly true. Parking off campus and using public transportation are sometimes alternatives. But this is not really the main point. The issue isn't paying or not paying but choosing *how* to pay—in dollar price, time, or being late for class.

Some economists have taken the pay-in-price scheme further and have argued that parking spots should be auctioned on a yearly basis. In other words, a student would rent a parking spot for a year. This way, the student would always know that a parking spot would be open when he or she arrived at the campus. People who parked in someone else's spot would be ticketed by campus police.

Additionally, under this scheme, a student who rented a parking spot and chose not to use it between certain hours of the day could rent it to someone else during this period. So we would expect to see notices like this on campus billboards:

Thinking like **AN ECONOMIST** *The economist knows that just because someone doesn't pay a price in money terms, it doesn't mean there is no price to pay. People can pay for something in time. In fact, when money prices are below equilibrium levels, individuals usually pay in terms of something else (e.g., time).*

PARKING SPOT FOR RENT
Near Arts Building and Student Union. Ideal for liberal arts students. Available on a 2–12 hour basis between 12 noon and 12 midnight. Rate: $1 per hour. Call Jenny at 867-5309.

SELF-TEST

1. If a person pays for something in terms of time, he or she is really paying in terms of money. Do you agree or disagree? Explain your answer.

2. Suppose at the price of $1 a day for parking, quantity supplied is equal to quantity demanded. What happens if the demand for parking rises more than the supply of parking and the price of parking is kept constant at $1 a day?

Application 18: The Space Within Space

According to the law of supply, a rise in the price of housing will lead to an increase in the quantity supplied of housing. But can this happen if the number of houses, apartments, condos, and duplexes cannot increase?

Consider the following thought experiment. Suppose there are 100 houses in an area and that a law has been passed stating that no one can build another house in the area.

Now suppose the demand for housing in this particular area rises. We would expect the price of housing to rise. But will the quantity supplied rise as well? Perhaps your first answer is no; after all, a law has been passed stating that no one can build another house in the area.

But this doesn't necessarily mean that more housing can't become available. The higher the price of housing, the greater the incentive will be for people who already own houses to make some part of their houses available to others. For example, a couple living in a three-bedroom house might decide to rent one of the three rooms. A person living in a one-room house might be willing to share the house with a roommate.

This phenomenon is not unheard of, especially in large cities that have witnessed recent large increases in housing prices. For example, if you go online to Craigslist New York (http://newyork.craigslist.org/), you will find people who own houses, apartments, and condominiums advertising rooms, or even parts of rooms, for rent. (Craigslist is a centralized network of online urban communities featuring free classified advertisements.)

Application 19: 10 a.m. Classes in College

Suppose an economics class is offered in the same classroom at 10 A.M. in the morning and at 8 P.M. at night. Most students would prefer the 10 A.M. class to the 8 P.M. class. Notice in Exhibit 9 that the supply of seats in the class is the same at each time, but the demand to occupy those seats is not. Because the demand is greater for the 10 A.M. class than for the 8 P.M. class, the equilibrium price for the 10 A.M. class is higher than the equilibrium price for the 8 P.M. class.

But the university or college charges the same tuition no matter what time students choose to take the class. The university doesn't charge students a higher tuition if they enroll in 10 A.M. classes than if they enroll in 8 P.M. classes.

Suppose tuition of T_1 is charged for all classes, and T_1 is the equilibrium tuition for 8 P.M. classes (see Exhibit 9). It follows that T_1 is below the equilibrium tuition for 10 A.M.

Thinking like
AN ECONOMIST   The layperson sees students clamoring to get 10 A.M. classes and concludes that the demand is high for classes at this time. He then wonders why the university doesn't schedule more 10 A.M. classes. The economist knows that what the layperson sees is as much an effect of price as of demand. The demand for 10 A.M. classes may be high, but the quantity demanded may not be if the price is high enough. In fact, even though the demand for various classes at various times may be different, there is some set of prices that will make the quantity demanded of each class the same.

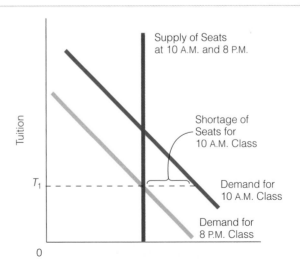

classes. At T_1, the quantity demanded of seats for 10 o'clock classes will be greater than the quantity supplied; more students will want the 10 o'clock class than there is space available.

How will the university allocate the available seats? It may do it the same way that airlines ration aisle seats—that is, on a first come, first served basis. Students who are first to register get the 10 A.M. class; the latecomers have to take the 8 P.M. class. Or the university could ration these "high-demand classes" by giving their upper-class students (seniors) first priority.

SELF-TEST

1. Suppose college students are given two options. With option *A*, the price a student pays for a class is always the equilibrium price. For example, if the equilibrium price to take Economics 101 is $600 at 10 A.M. and is $400 at 4 P.M., then students pay more for the 10 A.M. class than they do for the 4 P.M. class. With option *B*, the price a student pays for a class is the same regardless of the time the class is taken. When given the choice between options *A* and *B*, many students would say they prefer option *B* to option *A*. Is this the case for you? If so, why would this be your choice?

2. How is the analysis of the 10 A.M. class similar to the analysis of a price ceiling in the kidney market?

Application 20: Who Pays the Tax?

Supply-and-demand analysis can be used to clear up one of the main myths of economics. Many people mistakenly believe that the placement of a tax determines the payment of a tax. In other words, if a tax is placed on the seller of a good, then it is the seller of the good that pays the full tax. But this need not be the case, as supply and demand help us to understand.

To illustrate, suppose the government imposes a tax on sellers of DVDs. They are taxed $1 for every DVD they sell. DVD sellers are told: "Sell a DVD and send $1 to the government." This government action changes equilibrium in the DVD market. To illustrate, in Exhibit 10, before the tax is imposed, the equilibrium price and quantity of DVDs is $15 and Q_1, respectively. The tax per DVD shifts the supply curve leftward from S_1 to S_2. The vertical distance between the two supply curves represents the $1 per DVD tax.

Why does the vertical distance between the two curves represent the $1 per DVD tax? That's because it matters to sellers how much they keep for each DVD sold, not

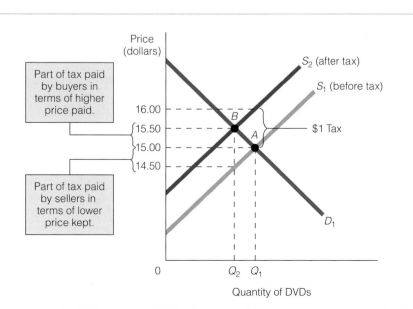

Who Pays the Tax?

A tax placed on the sellers of DVDs shifts the supply curve from S_1 to S_2 and raises the equilibrium price from $15.00 to $15.50. Part of the tax is paid by buyers through a higher price paid ($15.50 instead of $15.00), and part of the tax is paid by sellers through a lower price kept ($14.50 instead of $15.00).

how much buyers pay. If sellers are keeping $15 per DVD for Q_1 DVDs before the tax is imposed, then they want to keep $15 per DVD for Q_1 DVDs after the tax is imposed. But if the tax is $1, the only way they can keep $15 per DVD for Q_1 DVDs is to receive $16 per DVD. They receive $16 per DVD from buyers, turn over $1 to the government, and keep $15. In other words, each quantity on the new supply curve, S_2, corresponds to a $1 higher price than it did on the old supply curve, S_1. *It does not follow, though—and this is critically important—that the new equilibrium price will be $1 higher than the old equilibrium price.*

The new equilibrium is at a price of $15.50 and a quantity of Q_2. Buyers pay $15.50 per DVD (after the tax is imposed) as opposed to $15.00 (before the tax was imposed). The difference between the new price and the old price is the amount of the $1.00 tax that buyers pay per DVD. In this example, buyers pay 50 cents, or one-half of the $1.00 tax per DVD.

Before the tax: Buyers pay $15.00.
After the tax: Buyers pay $15.50.

The sellers receive $15.50 per DVD from buyers (after the tax is imposed) as opposed to $15.00 per DVD (before the tax was imposed), but they do not get to keep $15.50 per DVD. One dollar has to be turned over to the government, leaving the sellers with $14.50. Before the tax was imposed, however, sellers received and kept $15.00 per DVD. As we noted, the relevant price to sellers is the price they get to keep. The difference between $15.00 and $14.50 is the amount of the tax per DVD that sellers pay. In this example, the sellers pay 50 cents, or one-half of the $1.00 tax per DVD.

Before the tax: Sellers receive $15.00 and keep $15.00.
After the tax: Sellers receive $15.50 and keep $14.50.

We conclude that the full tax was *placed* on the sellers, but they *paid* only one-half of the tax, whereas none of the tax was placed on buyers, but they paid one-half of the tax too. What is the lesson we learn through our supply-and-demand analysis? Government can place a tax on whomever it wants, but the laws of supply and demand determine who actually ends up paying the tax.

SELF-TEST

1.   Is it necessarily the case that if government places a tax on the seller of a good, the seller of the good will end up paying the full tax?

2.   In Application 20, explain why the vertical distance between the two supply curves is the (per-unit) tax.

𝒜 𝑅𝑒𝑎𝑑𝑒𝑟 𝒜𝑠𝑘𝑠...

How Do I Find My Own Supply-and-Demand Applications?

I can understand an economist's applications of supply and demand, but I don't know how to apply supply and demand myself. How do I find my own supply-and-demand applications?

You can proceed in several ways, two of which we discuss here. First, you can heed the words of Robert Solow: "I am a supply-and-demand economist. When I come across something, I ask myself what is being transferred here and where does the supply come from and where does the demand come from."[2]

We can reformulate what Solow has said into a single question: *Is trade involved?* This is the relevant supply-and-demand question because supply and demand are about trade. In other words, when you observe something, simply ask: Is this about trade? If you are driving on a freeway, ask: Is driving on a freeway about trade? Specifically, is something being "bought" and "sold"? If so, what? If you are applying to college, ask: Is this about trade? What is being bought and sold?

A second way to proceed is to look for surpluses and shortages around you. Surpluses and shortages are manifestations of market disequilibrium. If you find them, you can be fairly sure that supply and demand are relevant. If you are sitting in a classroom with empty seats, ask: Is there a surplus or shortage here? In this case, of course, there is a surplus, which should lead you to think about price. Surpluses exist when prices are too high. Why is the price too high? If you observe more people applying to a particular college than the college will admit, ask: Is there a surplus or shortage here? In this case, there is a shortage, which again should lead you to think about price. Shortages exist when prices are too low. Why is price too low?

The key to finding your own supply-and-demand applications is to (1) observe things around you and then (2) ask questions about the things you observe. If you are sitting in a restaurant eating a meal, ask questions about what you observe. Is trade involved here? Yes. Is the restaurant filled to capacity, and is there a line of people waiting to get in? Yes. Are there more people who want to eat at this restaurant than there are spaces to accommodate them? Yes. Is there a shortage here? Yes. Why do shortages exist? Prices are too low. Why doesn't the restaurant raise its prices and eliminate the shortage?

The process isn't that hard, is it?

---

[2]Interview with Robert Solow. The entire interview is in *Economics* by Roger A. Arnold (St. Paul, Minn.: West Publishing Company, 1992).

! analyzing the scene

What is the relationship between the probability of Bob Mason being admitted to the college of his choice and the tuition the college charges?

Bob Mason is about to open the letter from the college he wants to attend. We don't know what the letter says, but we do know that the higher Bob's GPA and the smaller the gap between the equilibrium tuition and the tuition charged, the better Bob's chances of being accepted.

Why are house prices higher in some parts of the country than in other parts of the country?

Supply and demand explain the difference in house prices. In some parts of the country, the demand for houses (relative to the supply of houses) is high, perhaps because of good weather, excellent job opportunities, or a wide variety of fine entertainment. In other parts of the country, the demand for houses is low. Land (unlike gold) can't be moved to increase supply where demand is high, so house prices are higher in desirable locations than they are in less desirable locations, *ceteris paribus*.

What do supply, demand, and price have to do with Carlos driving 5 mph on a freeway on his way home from work?

Carlos is frustrated because congestion has caused traffic to slow to 5 mph on the freeway. Application 16 discusses how supply, demand, and price affect freeway traffic. If the price of driving on a freeway is below the equilibrium price, quantity demanded of freeway space is greater than quantity supplied. The result is a shortage of freeway space, and Carlos and other drivers having to drive more slowly than perhaps they would like.

Why aren't any aisle seats left?

When Samantha Wilson asks for an aisle seat, she's told that only center seats are left. Why are aisle seats taken before center seats? The short answer is because most people prefer aisle seats to center seats. Let's look a little further. A greater preference for aisle seats indicates a higher demand for aisle seats than for center seats. If the airlines charge the same price for both aisle and center seats and that price equals the equilibrium price for center seats, then there will likely be a shortage of aisle seats. The seats will be rationed partly by price and partly by first come, first served. Samantha doesn't get an aisle seat partly because of the airlines' pricing policy.

chapter summary

Why do Colleges Use GPAs, ACTs, and SATs for Purposes of Admission?

- Colleges and universities charging students less than the equilibrium tuition for admission create a shortage of spaces at the colleges or universities. Consequently, colleges and universities have to impose some nonprice rationing device, such as GPAs or ACT or SAT scores.

Legalization of Marijuana

- If the purchase and sale of marijuana are legalized, the price of marijuana may rise, fall, or remain the same. The price will depend on whether the rise in the demand for marijuana is more than, less than, or equal to the rise in the supply of marijuana.

Where Did You Get That Music?

- The recording industry can do, and has done, three things to reduce the amount of music piracy. (1) Raise the price of downloading music. The industry has done this by pursuing legal suits against some individuals. (2) Reduce the supply of music that can be downloaded. The industry has done this by bringing suit against companies such as Napster. (3) Reduce the demand for downloadable music. The industry has done this by running TV commercials that send the message that if you download music you are affecting everyday workers in the recording industry in a negative way.

Television Shows During the Olympics

- If a television network expects that demand for a time-specific slot (e.g., its 8 P.M. time slot) is likely to be low, it is more likely to run a rerun than a new episode of a program.

The Minimum Wage

- A minimum wage (above equilibrium wage) reduces the number of unskilled workers working or reduces the number of unskilled labor hours purchased by employers.

Equilibrium (Loud Talking in a Restaurant)

- Equilibrium is a state of affairs that exists when no further adjustments will be made. Although equilibrium is a desirable state in a competitive market (at which quantity demanded equals quantity supplied), it does not necessarily follow that all equilibrium states are desirable. The example of loud talking in a restaurant makes our point.

Price Ceiling in the Kidney Market

- Currently, there is a price ceiling in the kidney market, and the price is set at $0. Many of the effects of a price ceiling (shortages, fewer exchanges, etc.) are seen in the kidney market.

Healthcare and the Right to Sue Your HMO

- The supply curve of HMO-provided healthcare will shift upward and to the left if patients have the right to sue. As a result, patients will pay more for their HMO-provided healthcare coverage when they have the right to sue than when they do not have the right to sue.

Being Late to Class

- There is a downward-sloping demand curve for some things that are not traded in markets. For example, there probably exists a downward-sloping demand curve for being late to class: The higher the price of being late to class, the less lateness students will consume; the lower the price of being late to class, the more lateness students will consume.

Gold Prices and House Prices

- Gold prices are the same everywhere in the world, but house prices are not. When the price of a good is higher in one location than in another location and that good can be moved from the lower priced location to the higher priced location, then the price of the good will end up being the same in both locations. Obviously, if the good cannot be moved from the lower priced location to the higher priced location, then the price of the good will not end up being the same in both locations.

Do You Pay for Good Weather?

- If good weather gives people utility, then the demand for and the price of housing will be higher in a city with good weather than in a city with bad weather. Conclusion: People who buy houses in good-weather locations indirectly pay for the good weather.

Paying All Professors the Same Salary

- Suppose the equilibrium wage rate as determined by supply and demand conditions is higher, say, for a biology professor than for a history professor. If both professors are paid the equilibrium wage in biology, then there will be a surplus of history professors. If both professors are paid the equilibrium wage in history, then there will be a shortage of biology professors.

Price Floors and Winners and Losers

- A price floor placed on an agricultural foodstuff ends up lowering consumers' surplus, raising producers' surplus, and creating a deadweight loss. In short, a price floor can transfer "surplus" from consumers to producers and leave society (as a whole) worse off too.

College Superathletes

- If a college superathlete receives a full scholarship to play a sport at a university and if the full scholarship is less than the equilibrium wage for the superathlete (because of a prohibition mandating that the athlete cannot be paid the difference between his higher equilibrium wage and the dollar amount of his full scholarship), then the university gains at the expense of the athlete.

Supply and Demand on a Freeway

- The effect of a disequilibrium price for driving on a freeway is a traffic jam. If the price to drive on a freeway is $0 and at this price the quantity demanded of freeway space is greater than the quantity supplied, then there will be a shortage of freeway space that will manifest itself as freeway congestion.

What Does Price Have to Do with Getting to Class on Time?

- If price doesn't fully ration campus parking spots, something will. The rationing device may be first-come-first-served, which often prompts students to leave for campus at earlier times than they would if price rationed parking spots.

10 A.M. Classes in College

- Colleges usually charge the same tuition for a class no matter when the class is taken. The supply of seats in the class may be the same at each time, but the demand for the class may be different at different times. At least for some classes, the quantity demanded of seats (in the class) will be greater than the quantity supplied. Thus, some nonprice rationing device will have to be used to achieve equilibrium.

Who Pays the Tax?

- The placement of a tax and the payment of a tax are two different things. For example, a tax placed on the seller of a good may be paid by both the seller and the buyer.
- In this chapter, we discuss a per-unit tax that was placed on the seller of a specific good (DVDs). This tax shifted the supply curve of DVDs leftward. The vertical distance between the old supply curve (before the tax) and the new supply curve (after the tax) was equal to the per-unit tax.

key terms and concepts

Deadweight Loss

questions and problems

1 Harvard, Yale, and Princeton all charge relatively high tuition. Still, each uses ACT and SAT scores as admission criteria. Are charging a relatively high tuition and using standardized test scores (as admission criteria) inconsistent? Explain your answer.

2 Suppose the purchase and sale of marijuana are legalized and the price of marijuana falls. What explains the lower price of marijuana?

3 The minimum wage in year 1 is $1 higher than the equilibrium wage. In year 2, the minimum wage is increased so that it is $2 above the equilibrium wage. We observe that the same number of people are working at the minimum wage in year 2 as in year 1. Does it

follow that an increase in the minimum wage does not cause some workers to lose their jobs? Explain your answer.

4 Using supply-and-demand analysis, explain the recording industry's efforts to reduce the amount of pirated music.

5 In our discussion of the kidney market, we represent the demand curve for kidneys as downward sloping and the supply curve of kidneys as upward sloping. At the end of the discussion, we state, "If it is unlawful to pay someone for a kidney, fewer kidneys will be forthcoming. In other words, the quantity supplied of kidneys is less at $0 than at, say, $20,000. Fewer kidneys supplied

mean fewer kidney transplants." Would there be fewer kidney transplants if the supply curve of kidneys is vertical? Explain your answer.

6 What do the applications about freeway congestion, campus parking, and 10 A.M. classes have in common?

7 Economics has been called the "dismal science" because it sometimes "tells us" that things are true when we would prefer they were false. For example, although there are no free lunches, might we prefer that there were? Was there anything in this chapter that you learned was true that you would have preferred to be false? If so, identify it. Then explain why you would have preferred it to be false.

8 In the discussion of healthcare and the right to sue your HMO, we state, "Saying a seller's minimum price for providing a good or service rises is the same as saying the seller's supply curve has shifted upward and to the left." Does it follow that if a seller's minimum price falls, the supply curve shifts downward and to the right? Explain your answer.

9 Application 12 explains that even though no one directly and explicitly pays for good weather ("Here is $100 for the good weather"), it is still possible to pay for good weather indirectly, such as through housing prices. Identify three other things (besides good weather) that you believe people pay for indirectly.

10 If the equilibrium wage for economics professors is higher than the equilibrium wage for history professors, which professors (do you think) are more likely to argue that all professors should be paid the same? Explain your answer.

11 Suppose there exists a costless way to charge drivers on the freeway. Under this costless system, tolls on the freeway would be adjusted according to traffic conditions. For example, when traffic is usually heavy, such as from 6:30 A.M. to 9:00 A.M. on a weekday, the toll to drive on the freeway would be higher than the toll would be when traffic is light. In other words, freeway tolls would be used to equate the demand for freeway space and

the supply of freeway space. Would you be in favor of such a system to replace our current (largely, zero-price) system? Explain your answer.

12 Wilson walks into his Economics class ten minutes late because he couldn't find a place to park. Because of his tardiness, he doesn't hear the professor tell the class there will be a quiz at the next class session. At the next class session, Wilson is unprepared for the quiz and ends up failing it.
  a Might Wilson's failing the quiz have anything to do with the price of parking? Explain your answer.
  b Suppose Wilson says to his professor: "If this university had set equilibrium prices for parking, I wouldn't have been late to class, and therefore, I would have heard about the upcoming quiz, studied for it, and probably passed it. It's not my fault I failed the quiz. It's the university's fault for not setting the equilibrium price for parking." What would you say if you were the professor?

13 University A charges more for a class for which there is high demand than for a class for which there is low demand. University B charges the same for all classes. All other things being equal between the two universities, which university would you prefer to attend? Explain your answer.

14 Explain and diagrammatically represent how a price floor can bring about a transfer from consumers to producers.

15 Suppose the equilibrium wage for a college athlete is $40,000, but because of NCAA rules, the university can offer him only $22,000 (full tuition). How might the university administrators, coaches, or university alumni lure the college athlete to choose their school over others?

16 Consider the theater in which a Broadway play is performed. If tickets for all seats are the same price (say, $70), what economic effect might arise?

17 How does a grocery store know how much cereal, butter, and candy it should stock on its shelves?

working with numbers and graphs

1 The price to drive on a freeway is $0 at all times of the day. This price establishes equilibrium at 3 A.M. but is too low to establish equilibrium at 5 P.M. There is a shortage of freeway space at 5 P.M.
  a Graphically show and explain how carpooling may eliminate the shortage.
  b Graphically show and explain how building more freeways may eliminate the shortage.

2 Diagrammatically show and explain why there is a shortage of classroom space for some college classes and a surplus for others.

3 Smith has been trying to sell his house for six months, but so far, there are no buyers. Draw the market for Smith's house.

4 Explain and diagrammatically represent why the placement of a tax may be different than the payment of a tax.

Elasticity 5

Setting the Scene George McClintock, 45 years old, lives in Bridgeport, Connecticut. He works for a pharmaceutical company. The following events happened one day in May.

8:04 A.M.

As he's driving to work, George is listening to a news report on the radio. The reporter says that some group (George didn't catch the name of the group) is urging people to trade in their SUVs for smaller cars. The group argues that smaller, more gas-efficient cars will reduce the amount of air pollution and make for a more healthful environment. George wonders if he should trade in his SUV and "do his part."

3:33 P.M.

George is in a meeting that has been called to discuss the prices of the company's new products. Some of his coworkers think the company should raise the price of one of its products by 5 percent; others are arguing against a price rise. One person at the meeting says, "How can we lose by raising the price? Currently, we sell 2,000 units a day at $40 a unit. If we raise the price $2, we can bring in $4,000 more every day."

4:56 P.M.

Driving home after work, George is listening to a report on the radio about an earthquake in Los Angeles. In one area of LA, the earthquake destroyed many of the apartment buildings. A news reporter says, "If anything, the earthquake will drive up the price of water and apartment rents."

? Here are some questions to keep in mind as you read this chapter:

- *If everyone with an SUV trades it in for a smaller, more efficient car, will air pollution be reduced?*

- *If the pharmaceutical company raises the price of one of its products by 5 percent, will its total revenue rise?*

- *If the LA earthquake does result in higher apartment rents, does it follow that apartment landlords will have greater total revenue?*

See analyzing the scene at the end of this chapter for answers to these questions.

How to Approach the Study of Microeconomics

Before we begin our discussion of microeconomics, we need to take some time to discuss what microeconomics is about and how best to approach the study of microeconomics. Microeconomics is the branch of economics that deals with human behavior and choices as they relate to relatively small units: an individual, a firm, an industry, a single market.

There are some key players in microeconomics—players we will discuss time and again. The key microeconomic players are:

1. consumers
2. business firms
3. factor (or resource) owners

Each of these three microeconomic players will have an objective (or goal), face some constraints, and have to make choices. In a way, all of microeconomics is really about three things:

1. objectives
2. constraints
3. choices

Let's discuss each of the three players in terms of its objectives, constraints, and choices.

Consumers

Consumers buy goods and services produced by firms. This advances their *objective* of trying to maximize their utility or satisfaction. Yet very few people can buy all the goods they might like to consume. Consumers' purchases are *constrained* by their limited incomes and by the positive prices for each good. Each purchase subtracts from the consumer's available income and eventually nothing remains. Given limited purchasing ability, the consumer will attempt to gain as much utility as possible from each dollar spent. In practice, this is done by *choosing* to use *marginal analysis* in making consumption decisions—by comparing the additional (or marginal) benefits and additional (or marginal) costs of each purchase.

Firms

Firms *hire* productive factors or resources, combine them in a certain way to *produce* a final good, and then *sell* that good to consumers. In short, firms play two roles in the economy: They are the buyers of factors and the sellers of goods.

FIRMS AS BUYERS When they hire workers and other productive factors, the *objective* of firms is to maximize profit. Among other things, this implies that they will hire a mix of factors that will minimize their costs of producing the desired amount of output. Their hiring decisions are *constrained* by the positive price of factors and by the need to cover opportunity costs. Firms achieve their objectives by *choosing* to hire only factors that contribute more at the margin to the firm's output and sales receipts than the additional cost of employing them.

FIRMS AS SELLERS The *objective* here is to maximize profit. In their attempt to maximize profit, firms (as sellers) will have to *choose* what quantity of the good or service they will produce and *choose* what price to charge. The *constraints* placed on sellers comes from consumers, who search for lower prices and higher quality, and from competitors, who attempt to undercut prices charged by other sellers or produce a more desirable good or service.

Factor Owners

Factor owners (or resource owners) sell the factors or resources to firms that firms use to produce goods and services. The *objective* of factor owners is to maximize the income they earn from selling their factors. Since factors are not infinite, factor owners are *constrained* by the prices paid for their services in the marketplace and by the finite amount of factors they have to sell. For example, you, as the owner of your labor, can sell only as much labor as you have in a 24-hour day (where approximately 8 hours each day are needed for sleep). Factor owners achieve their objective by *choosing* to sell those units (of the factor) for which the additional (marginal) benefits, in terms of price offered for the resource, are greater than or equal to the additional (marginal) cost. For example, how much of your labor you choose to sell will depend on the value you place on what you could be doing if you didn't work (your opportunity costs) in relation to the price you are offered for one hour's worth of your labor.

Choices Are Made in Market Settings

The choices of consumers, firms, and factor owners are not made in a vacuum; instead, they are made in market settings. Not all market settings are alike. In other words, the setting (or environment) in which consumers, firms, and factor owners make choices may differ from one time to the next. To illustrate, consumers might make choices in one market setting that has many buyers and many sellers and later make choices in a market setting that has many buyers and only a few sellers. Much of our discussion of microeconomics will focus on the various market settings in which choices are made.

Recap

What should you look for as you begin your study of microeconomics?

1. You should look for the different players—consumers, firms, and factor owners.
2. You should identify the objective of each.
3. You should identify the constraint(s) that each faces.
4. You should focus on the way the economic player chooses within those constraints.
5. You should keep in mind the environment—or the market setting—in which all this takes place.

Elasticity: Part 1

The law of demand states that price and quantity demanded are inversely related, *ceteris paribus*. But it doesn't tell us by what percentage quantity demanded changes as price changes. Suppose price rises by 10 percent. As a result, quantity demanded falls. But by what percentage does it fall? The notion of price elasticity of demand can help answer this question. The general concept of elasticity provides a technique for estimating the response of one variable to changes in some other variable. It has numerous applications in economics.

Price Elasticity of Demand

Have you ever watched any of the TV shopping networks, such as QVC or the Home Shopping Network? Every now and then, the people on these networks will offer computers for sale. For example, QVC will often advertise Dell computers for sale. You may hear the following: "Today, we're offering this Dell computer, along with a printer, digital camera, flat-panel monitor, and scanner all for the unbelievable price of $1,700."

No matter how many computers QVC sells with its offer, one question almost always pops into the minds of the top managers of both QVC and Dell. It is, "How many more computers could we have sold if the price had been, say, $100 lower?" A similar question is, "How many fewer computers would we have sold if the price had been, say, $100 higher?"

Specifically, QVC and Dell managers want to know the *price elasticity of demand* for the computer being offered for sale. **Price elasticity of demand** is a measure of the responsiveness of quantity demanded to changes in price. More specifically, it addresses the "percentage change in quantity demanded for a given percentage change in price."

Price Elasticity of Demand

A measure of the responsiveness of quantity demanded to changes in price.

Let's say that QVC raises the price of the computer by 10 percent, and as a result, quantity demanded for the computer falls by 20 percent. The percentage change in quantity demanded—20 percent—divided by the percentage change in price—10 percent—is called the *coefficient of price elasticity of demand* (E_d).

$$E_d = \frac{\text{Percentage change in quantity demanded}}{\text{Percentage change in price}} = \frac{\%\Delta Q_d}{\%\Delta P}$$

In the formula, E_d = coefficient of price elasticity of demand, or simply elasticity coefficient; % = percentage; and Δ stands for "change in."

If we carry out the calculation in our simple example—where quantity demanded changes by 20 percent and price changes by 10 percent—we get the number 2. An economist would say either, "The coefficient of price elasticity of demand is 2" or, more simply, "Price elasticity of demand is 2."

Q&A

What does "price elasticity of demand is 2" mean?

A price elasticity of demand equal to 2 means that the percentage change in quantity demanded will be 2 times any percentage change in price.[1] If price changes 5 percent, quantity demanded will change 10 percent; if price changes 10 percent, quantity demanded will change 20 percent.

WHERE IS THE MISSING MINUS SIGN? You know that price and quantity demanded move in opposite directions: When price rises, quantity demanded falls; when price falls, quantity demanded rises. In our previous example, when price rises by 10 percent, quantity demanded falls by 20 percent. Now, when you divide a *minus 20 percent* by a *positive 10 percent,* you don't get 2; you get –2. Instead of saying that the price elasticity of demand is 2, you might think the price elasticity of demand is –2. However, by convention, economists usually simplify things by speaking of the absolute value of the price elasticity of demand; thus, they drop the minus sign.

FORMULA FOR CALCULATING PRICE ELASTICITY OF DEMAND Using percentage changes to calculate price elasticity of demand can lead to conflicting results depending on whether price rises or falls. Therefore, economists use the following formula to calculate price elasticity of demand.[2]

$$E_d = \frac{\dfrac{\Delta Q_d}{Q_{d\,\text{Average}}}}{\dfrac{\Delta P}{P_{\text{Average}}}}$$

In the formula, ΔQ_d stands for the absolute change in Q_d. For example, if Q_d changes from 50 units to 100 units, then ΔQ_d is 50 units. ΔP stands for the absolute change in price. For example, if price changes from $12 to $10, then ΔP is $2. $Q_{d\,\text{Average}}$ stands for the average of the two quantities demanded, and P_{Average} stands for the average of the two prices.

---

[1] This assumes we are changing price from its current level.
[2] This formula is sometimes called the midpoint formula for calculating price elasticity of demand.

For the price and quantity demanded data in Exhibit 1, the calculation is

$$E_d = \dfrac{\dfrac{50}{75}}{\dfrac{2}{11}} = 3.67$$

Because we use the "average price" and "average quantity demanded" in our price elasticity of demand equation, 3.67 may be considered the price elasticity of demand at a point *midway between the two points identified on the demand curve.* For example, in Exhibit 1, 3.67 is the price elasticity of demand between points *A* and *B* on the demand curve.

Elasticity Is Not Slope

There is a tendency to think that slope and price elasticity of demand are the same, but they are not. Suppose we identify a third point on the demand curve in Exhibit 1. The following table shows the price and quantity demanded for our three points.

Point	Price	Quantity Demanded
A	$12	50
B	10	100
C	8	150

To calculate the *price elasticity of demand* between points *A* and *B,* we divide the percentage change in quantity demanded (between the two points) by the percentage change in price (between the two points). Using the price elasticity of demand formula, we get 3.67.

The *slope of the demand curve* between points *A* and *B* is the ratio of the change in the variable on the vertical axis to the change in the variable on the horizontal axis.

$$\text{Slope} = \dfrac{\Delta \text{Variable on vertical axis}}{\Delta \text{Variable on horizontal axis}} = \dfrac{-2}{50} = -0.04$$

Now let's calculate the price elasticity of demand and the slope between points *B* and *C.* The price elasticity of demand is 1.80; the slope is still −0.04.

From Perfectly Elastic to Perfectly Inelastic Demand

Look back at the equation for the elasticity coefficient and think of it as

$$E_d = \dfrac{\text{Percentage change in quantity demanded}}{\text{Percentage change in price}} = \dfrac{\text{Numerator}}{\text{Denominator}}$$

Focusing on the numerator and denominator, we realize that (1) the numerator can be greater than the denominator, (2) the numerator can be less than the denominator, or (3) the numerator can be equal to the denominator. These three cases, along with two peripherally related cases, are discussed in the following paragraphs. Exhibits 2 and 3 provide summaries of the discussion.

Elasticity Coefficient	Responsiveness of Quantity Demanded to a Change in Price	Terminology
$E_d > 1$	Quantity demanded changes proportionately more than price changes: $\%\Delta Q_d > \%\Delta P$.	Elastic
$E_d < 1$	Quantity demanded changes proportionately less than price changes: $\%\Delta Q_d < \%\Delta P$.	Inelastic
$E_d = 1$	Quantity demanded changes proportionately to price change: $\%\Delta Q_d = \%\Delta P$.	Unit elastic
$E_d = \infty$	Quantity demanded is extremely responsive to even very small changes in price.	Perfectly elastic
$E_d = 0$	Quantity demanded does not change as price changes.	Perfectly inelastic

exhibit 3

Graphical Representation of Price Elasticity of Demand

(a) The percentage change in quantity demanded is greater than the percentage change in price: $E_d > 1$ and demand is elastic. (b) The percentage change in quantity demanded is less than the percentage change in price: $E_d < 1$ and demand is inelastic. (c) The percentage change in quantity demand is equal to percentage change in price: $E_d = 1$ and demand is unit elastic. (d) A small change in price reduces quantity demanded to zero: $E_d = \infty$ and demand is perfectly elastic. (e) A change in price does not change quantity demanded: $E_d = 0$ and demand is perfectly inelastic.

Elastic Demand

The percentage change in quantity demanded is greater than the percentage change in price. Quantity demanded changes proportionately more than price changes.

Inelastic Demand

The percentage change in quantity demanded is less than the percentage change in price. Quantity demanded changes proportionately less than price changes.

Unit Elastic Demand

The percentage change in quantity demanded is equal to the percentage change in price. Quantity demanded changes proportionately to price changes.

ELASTIC DEMAND ($E_d > 1$) If the numerator (percentage change in quantity demanded) is greater than the denominator (percentage change in price), the elasticity coefficient is greater than 1 and demand is **elastic**. This means, of course, that quantity demanded changes proportionately more than price changes. A 10 percent increase in price causes, say, a 20 percent reduction in quantity demanded ($E_d = 2$).

Percentage change in quantity demanded > Percentage change in price →
$E_d > 1 \rightarrow$ Demand is elastic

INELASTIC DEMAND ($E_d < 1$) If the numerator (percentage change in quantity demanded) is less than the denominator (percentage change in price), the elasticity coefficient is less than 1 and demand is **inelastic**. This means that quantity demanded changes proportionately less than price changes. A 10 percent increase in price causes, say, a 4 percent reduction in quantity demanded ($E_d = 0.4$).

Percentage change in quantity demanded < Percentage change in price →
$E_d < 1 \rightarrow$ Demand is inelastic

UNIT ELASTIC DEMAND ($E_d = 1$) If the numerator (percentage change in quantity demanded) equals the denominator (percentage change in price), the elasticity coefficient is 1. This means quantity demanded changes proportionately to price changes. For example, a 10 percent increase in price causes a 10 percent decrease in quantity demanded ($E_d = 1$). In this case, demand exhibits unitary elasticity or is **unit elastic**.

Percentage change in quantity demanded = Percentage change in price →
$E_d = 1 \rightarrow$ Demand is unit elastic

PERFECTLY ELASTIC DEMAND ($E_d = \infty$) If quantity demanded is extremely responsive to changes in price, demand is **perfectly elastic**. For example, buyers are willing to buy all units of a seller's good at $5 per unit but nothing at $5.10. A small percentage change in price causes an extremely large percentage change in quantity demanded (from buying all to buying nothing). The percentage is so large, in fact, that economists say it is "infinitely large."

PERFECTLY INELASTIC DEMAND ($E_d = 0$) If quantity demanded is completely unresponsive to changes in price, demand is **perfectly inelastic**. A change in price causes no change in quantity demanded. For example, suppose the price of Dogs Love It dog food rises 10 percent (from $10 to $11), and Jeremy doesn't buy any less of it per week for his dog. It follows that Jeremy's demand for Dogs Love It dog food is perfectly inelastic between a price of $10 and $11.

PERFECTLY ELASTIC AND PERFECTLY INELASTIC DEMAND CURVES You are used to seeing downward-sloping demand curves. Now, Exhibit 3 shows two demand curves that are not downward sloping. You may be thinking: Aren't all demand curves supposed to be downward sloping because according to the law of demand, an inverse relationship exists between price and quantity demanded? The answer is that in the real world, no demand curves are perfectly elastic (horizontal) or perfectly inelastic (vertical) at all prices. Thus, the perfectly elastic and perfectly inelastic demand curves in Exhibit 3 should be viewed as representations of the extreme limits between which all real-world demand curves fall.

However, a few real-world demand curves do *approximate* the perfectly elastic and inelastic demand curves in (d) and (e) of Exhibit 3. In other words, they come very close. For example, the demand for a particular farmer's wheat approximates the perfectly elastic demand curve in (d). A later chapter discusses the perfectly elastic demand curve for firms in perfectly competitive markets.

Price Elasticity of Demand and Total Revenue (Total Expenditure)

Total revenue (*TR*) of a seller equals the price of a good times the quantity of the good sold.[3] For example, if the hamburger stand down the street sells 100 hamburgers today at $1.50 each, its total revenue is $150.

Suppose the hamburger vendor raises the price of hamburgers to $2 each. What do you predict will happen to total revenue? Most people say it will increase; there is a widespread belief that higher prices bring higher total revenue. But total revenue may increase, decrease, or remain constant.

Suppose price rises to $2, but because of the higher price, the quantity of hamburgers sold falls to 50. Total revenue is now $100 (whereas it was $150). Whether total revenue rises, falls, or remains constant after a price change depends on whether the percentage change in quantity demanded is less than, greater than, or equal to the percentage change in price. Thus, price elasticity of demand influences total revenue.

ELASTIC DEMAND AND TOTAL REVENUE If demand is elastic, the percentage change in quantity demanded is greater than the percentage change in price. Given a price rise of, say, 5 percent, quantity demanded falls by more than 5 percent—say, 8 percent. What happens

---

Perfectly Elastic Demand
A small percentage change in price causes an extremely large percentage change in quantity demanded (from buying all to buying nothing).

Perfectly Inelastic Demand
Quantity demanded does not change as price changes.

Total Revenue (*TR*)
Price times quantity sold.

Q&A
Are we saying here that as the price of a good rises, the total revenue a firm receives for selling the good may go down? Isn't this counterintuitive?

Whether or not it is counterintuitive is not the main issue. What matters is whether or not it is right. In what we plan to show next, as price goes up, total revenue can go up, down, or stay the same—depending on elasticity of demand.

---

[3]In this discussion, *total revenue* and *total expenditure* are equivalent terms. Total revenue equals price times the quantity sold. Total expenditure equals price times the quantity purchased. If something is sold, it must be purchased, making total revenue equal to total expenditure. The term *total revenue* is used when looking at things from the point of view of the sellers in a market. The term *total expenditure* is used when looking at things from the point of view of the buyers in a market. Buyers make expenditures; sellers receive revenues.

How, again, do we know that if demand is elastic, it follows that total revenue falls as price rises?

First, keep in mind what elastic demand means. It means that the percentage change in quantity demanded changes more than the percentage change in price. Now let's say that price rises by 5 percent. We know that quantity demanded will change by more than 5 percent; let's say quantity demanded changes by 10 percent. So now we have price going up by 5 percent and quantity demanded going down by 10 percent. What happens to total revenue? The 5 percent higher price is pushing total revenue up, but the 10 percent lower quantity demanded is pushing total revenue down by more. On net, then, total revenue falls. We conclude that if demand is elastic, a rise in price will bring about a decrease in total revenue.

to total revenue? Because quantity demanded falls, or sales fall off, by a greater percentage than the percentage rise in price, total revenue decreases. In short, if demand is elastic, a price rise decreases total revenue.

Demand is elastic: $P\uparrow \rightarrow TR\downarrow$

What happens to total revenue if demand is elastic and price falls? In this case, quantity demanded rises (price and quantity demanded are inversely related) by a greater percentage than the percentage fall in price, causing total revenue to increase. In short, if demand is elastic, a price fall increases total revenue.

Demand is elastic: $P\downarrow \rightarrow TR\uparrow$

Exhibit 4(a) may help you see the relationship between a change in price and total revenue if demand is elastic. The exhibit shows elastic demand between points A and B on the demand curve. At point A, price is P_1 and quantity demanded is Q_1. Total revenue is equal to the rectangle $0P_1AQ_1$. Now suppose we lower price to P_2. Total revenue is now the rectangle $0P_2BQ_2$. You can see that the rectangle $0P_2BQ_2$ (after the price decline) is larger than rectangle $0P_1AQ_1$. In other words, if demand is elastic and price declines, total revenue will rise.

Of course, when price moves in the opposite direction, rising from P_2 to P_1, then the total revenue rectangle becomes smaller. In other words, if demand is elastic and price rises, total revenue will fall.

INELASTIC DEMAND AND TOTAL REVENUE If demand is inelastic, the percentage change in quantity demanded is less than the percentage change in price. If price rises, quantity demanded falls but by a smaller percentage than the percentage rise in price. As a result, total revenue increases. So if demand is inelastic, a price rise increases total revenue. However, if price falls, quantity demanded rises by a smaller percentage than the percentage fall in price and total revenue decreases. If demand is inelastic, a price fall decreases total revenue. If demand is inelastic, price and total revenue are directly related.

Demand is inelastic: $P\uparrow \rightarrow TR\uparrow$
Demand is inelastic: $P\downarrow \rightarrow TR\downarrow$

exhibit **4**

Price Elasticity of Demand and Total Revenue

In (a) demand is elastic between points *A* and *B*. A fall in price, from P_1 to P_2, will increase the size of the total revenue rectangle from $0P_1AQ_1$ to $0P_2BQ_2$. A rise in price, from P_2 to P_1, will decrease the size of the total revenue rectangle from $0P_2BQ_2$ to $0P_1AQ_1$. In other words, when demand is elastic, price and total revenue are inversely related. In (b) demand is inelastic between points *A* and *B*. A fall in price, from P_1 to P_2, will decrease the size of the total revenue rectangle from $0P_1AQ_1$ to $0P_2BQ_2$. A rise in price, from P_2 to P_1, will increase the size of the total revenue rectangle from $0P_2BQ_2$ to $0P_1AQ_1$. In other words, when demand is inelastic, price and total revenue are directly related.

(a)

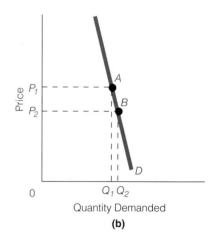

(b)

economics 24/7

DRUG BUSTS AND CRIME

Most people believe the sale or possession of drugs such as cocaine and heroin should be illegal. But sometimes, laws may have unintended effects. Do drug laws have unintended effects? Let's analyze the enforcement of drug laws in terms of supply, demand, and price elasticity of demand.

Suppose for every $100 of illegal drug sales, 60 percent of the $100 paid is obtained by illegal means. That is, buyers of $100 worth of illegal drugs obtain $60 of the purchase price from criminal activities such as burglaries, muggings, and so on.

We assume the demand for and supply of cocaine in a particular city are represented by D_1 and S_1 in Exhibit 5. The equilibrium price of $50 an ounce and the equilibrium quantity of 1,000 ounces give cocaine dealers a total revenue of $50,000. If 60 percent of this total revenue is obtained by the criminal activities of cocaine buyers, then $30,000 worth of crime has been committed to purchase the $50,000 worth of cocaine.

Now suppose there is a drug bust in the city. As a result, the drug enforcement authorities reduce the supply of cocaine. The supply curve shifts leftward from S_1 to S_2. The equilibrium price rises to $120 an ounce, and the equilibrium quantity falls to 600 ounces. The demand for cocaine is inelastic between the two prices, at 0.607. When demand is inelastic, an increase in price will raise total revenue. The total revenue received by cocaine dealers is now $72,000. If, again, we assume that 60 percent of the total revenue paid comes from criminal activity, then $43,200 worth of crime has been committed to purchase the $72,000 worth of cocaine.

Our conclusion: If the demand for cocaine is inelastic and people commit crimes to buy drugs, then a drug bust can actually increase the amount of drug-related crime. Obviously, this is an unintended effect of the enforcement of drug laws.

exhibit 5

Drug Busts and Drug-Related Crime

In the exhibit, P = price of cocaine, Q = quantity of cocaine, and TR = total revenue from selling cocaine. At a price of $50 for an ounce of cocaine, equilibrium quantity is 1,000 ounces and total revenue is $50,000. If $60 of every $100 cocaine purchase is obtained through crime, then $30,000 worth of crime is committed to purchase $50,000 worth of cocaine. As a result of a drug bust, the supply of cocaine shifts leftward; the price rises and the quantity falls. Because we have assumed the demand for cocaine is inelastic, total revenue rises to $72,000. Sixty percent of this comes from criminal activities, or $43,200.

	P	Q	TR	Dollar Amount of TR Obtained Through Crime
Before Drug Bust	$50	1,000	$50,000	$30,000
After Drug Bust	120	600	72,000	43,200

economics 24/7

WILL HIGH TAXES ON CIGARETTES REDUCE SMOKING?

In recent years, there have been attempts to raise the taxes on cigarettes. The stated purpose of the increase in taxes is to make smoking more expensive in the hope that people will quit smoking, reduce the amount they smoke, or never start smoking.

But will higher taxes on cigarettes cause millions of smokers to stop or cut back on smoking? Will it prevent many teenagers from starting to smoke and reduce the number of teenagers who are smoking? If the demand curve for cigarettes is downward sloping, higher cigarette prices (brought about by higher taxes) will decrease the quantity demanded of cigarettes. But the question is: How much? Thus, price elasticity of demand is needed for the analysis.

To take an extreme case, suppose the demand curve for cigarettes is perfectly inelastic between the current price and the new higher price brought about through higher taxes. In this case, the quantity demanded of cigarettes will not change. If the demand curve is inelastic (but not perfectly inelastic), the percentage decline in the quantity demanded of cigarettes will be less than the percentage increase in the price of cigarettes.

The anti-tobacco lobby would prefer that the demand curve for cigarettes be highly elastic. In this case, the percentage change in the quantity demanded of cigarettes will be greater than the percentage change in price. Many more people will stop smoking if cigarette demand is elastic than if it is inelastic.

Another consideration is that the elasticity of demand for cigarettes may be different for adults than it is for teenagers. In fact, some studies show that teenagers are much more sensitive to cigarette price than adults are. In other words, the elasticity of demand for cigarettes is greater for teenagers than for adults.

One study found the elasticity of demand for cigarettes to be 0.35 (in the long run). This study did not separate adult smoking and teenage smoking. Another study looked at only teenage smoking and concluded that for every 10 percent rise in price, quantity demanded would decline by 12 percent. In other words, demand for cigarettes by teenagers is elastic. For those who want to use higher cigarette taxes as a means of curtailing teenage smoking, that is encouraging news.

You can see the relationship between inelastic demand and total revenue in Exhibit 4(b), where demand is inelastic between points A and B on the demand curve. If we start at P_1 and lower price to P_2, the total revenue rectangle goes from $0P_1AQ_1$ to the smaller total revenue rectangle $0P_2BQ_2$. In other words, if demand is inelastic and price falls, total revenue will fall.

Moving from the lower price, P_2, to the higher price, P_1, does just the opposite. If demand is inelastic and price rises, the total revenue rectangle becomes larger; that is, total revenue rises.

UNIT ELASTIC DEMAND AND TOTAL REVENUE If demand is unit elastic, the percentage change in quantity demanded equals the percentage change in price. If price rises, quantity demanded falls by the same percentage as the percentage rise in price. Total revenue does not change. If price falls, quantity demanded rises by the same percentage as the percentage fall in price. Again, total revenue does not change. If demand is unit elastic, a rise or fall in price leaves total revenue unchanged.

Thinking like AN ECONOMIST

The layperson asks what happens to total revenue as price rises. The economist says, "It depends." But what does it depend on? The answer is price elasticity of demand. If demand is elastic, total revenue will fall; if demand is inelastic, total revenue will rise; and if demand is unit elastic, total revenue will not change. Often, the layperson seeks "one definitive answer" to his or her question. But often, what the economist gives is a "conditional answer": Given a particular condition, the answer is X, but given another condition, the answer is Y.

$$\text{Demand is unit elastic: } P\uparrow \rightarrow \overline{TR}$$
$$\text{Demand is unit elastic: } P\downarrow \rightarrow \overline{TR}$$

For a review of the relationship between price elasticity of demand and total revenue, see Exhibit 6.

SELF-TEST

(Answers to Self-Test questions are in the Self-Test Appendix.)

1. On Tuesday, price and quantity demanded are $7 and 120 units, respectively. Ten days later, price and quantity demanded are $6 and 150 units, respectively. What is the price elasticity of demand between the price of $7 and the price of $6?

2. What does a price elasticity of demand of 0.39 mean?

3. Identify what happens to total revenue as a result of each of the following: (a) price rises and demand is elastic; (b) price falls and demand is inelastic; (c) price rises and demand is unit elastic; (d) price rises and demand is inelastic; (e) price falls and demand is elastic.

4. Alexi says, "When a seller raises his price, his total revenue rises." What is Alexi implicitly assuming?

Elasticity: Part 2

This section discusses the elasticity ranges of a straight-line downward-sloping demand curve and the determinants of price elasticity of demand.

Price Elasticity of Demand Along a Straight-Line Demand Curve

The price elasticity of demand for a straight-line downward-sloping demand curve varies from highly elastic to highly inelastic. To illustrate, consider the price elasticity of demand at the upper range of the demand curve in Exhibit 7(a). No matter whether the price falls from $9 to $8 or rises from $8 to $9, using the price elasticity of demand formula (identified earlier in the chapter), we calculate price elasticity of demand as 5.66.[4]

Now consider the price elasticity of demand at the lower range of the demand curve in Exhibit 7(a). Whether the price falls from $3 to $2 or rises from $2 to $3, we calculate the price elasticity of demand as 0.33.

In other words, along the range of the demand curve we have identified, price elasticity goes from being greater than 1 (5.66) to being less than 1 (0.33). Obviously, on its way from being greater than 1 to being less than 1, price elasticity of demand must be equal to 1. In Exhibit 7(a), we have identified price elasticity of demand as equal to 1 at the *midpoint* of the demand curve.[5]

What do the elastic and inelastic ranges along the straight-line downward-sloping demand curve mean in terms of total revenue? If we start in the elastic range of the demand curve in Exhibit 7(a) and lower price, total revenue rises. This is shown in Exhibit 7(b). That is, as price is coming down within the elastic range of the demand curve in (a), total revenue is rising in (b).

When price has fallen enough such that we move into the inelastic range of the demand curve in (a), further price declines simply lower total revenue, as shown in (b). It

exhibit **6**

Elasticities, Price Changes, and Total Revenue

If demand is elastic, a price rise leads to a decrease in total revenue (*TR*), and a price fall leads to an increase in total revenue. If demand is inelastic, a price rise leads to an increase in total revenue and a price fall leads to a decrease in total revenue. If demand is unit elastic, a rise or fall in price does not change total revenue.

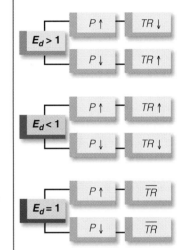

<hr>

[4]Keep in mind that our formula uses the average of the two prices and the average of the two quantities demanded. You may want to look back at the formula to refresh your memory.

[5]For any straight-line downward-sloping demand curve, price elasticity of demand equals 1 at the midpoint of the curve.

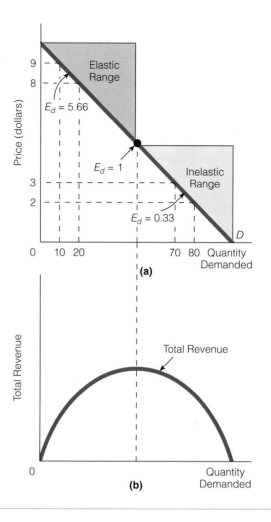

Price Elasticity of Demand Along a Straight-Line Demand Curve

In (a), the price elasticity of demand varies along the straight-line downward-sloping demand curve. There is an elastic range to the curve (where $E_d > 1$) and an inelastic range (where $E_d < 1$). At the midpoint of any straight-line downward-sloping demand curve, price elasticity of demand is equal to 1 ($E_d = 1$).

Part (b) shows that in the elastic range of the demand curve, total revenue rises as price is lowered. In the inelastic range of the demand curve, further price declines result in declining total revenue. Total revenue reaches its peak when price elasticity of demand equals 1.

holds, then, that total revenue is at its highest—its peak—when price elasticity of demand equals 1.

Determinants of Price Elasticity of Demand

The following four factors are relevant to the determination of price elasticity of demand:

1. Number of substitutes
2. Necessities versus luxuries
3. Percentage of one's budget spent on the good
4. Time

Because all four factors interact, we hold all other things constant as we discuss each.

NUMBER OF SUBSTITUTES Suppose good A has 2 substitutes and good B has 15 substitutes. Assume that each of the 2 substitutes for good A is as good (or close) a substitute for that good as each of the 15 substitutes is for good B.

Let the price of each good rise by 10 percent. The quantity demanded of each good decreases. Will the percentage change in quantity demanded of good A be greater or less than the percentage change in quantity demanded of good B? That is, will quantity demanded be more responsive to the 10 percent price rise for the good that has 2 sub-

economics 24/7

WHY DO COMPANIES HIRE CELEBRITIES?

Many companies hire celebrities to advertise their products. In the past, Shaquille O'Neal was hired to advertise Burger King, Shakira was hired to advertise Pepsi, Jerry Seinfeld to advertise American Express, Celine Dion to advertise Chrysler, Tim McGraw to advertise Anheuser-Busch, and Michael Jordan to advertise products such as Gatorade and Nike.

Why do companies hire celebrities to pitch their wares? The obvious answer is to get the attention of consumers. When people see a sports star, television star, model, or movie star talking about a product, they are likely to take notice.

But there are other ways companies can get the attention of consumers, so maybe another factor is involved. Some economists have hypothesized that this other factor is related to price elasticity of demand and total revenue.

Consider the case of basketball star Shaquille O'Neal, who has advertised Burger King in the past. What message was Burger King trying to convey with its ads showing Shaq ordering a Whopper? The message may have been this: For Shaq, there is only one hamburger—no substitutes.

If the buying public accepts this message—if buyers believe there are no substitutes for a Whopper or if they want to do

what Shaq does—then the price elasticity of a Whopper declines. The fewer substitutes, the lower the price elasticity of demand.

And if it is possible to get the demand for Whoppers to become inelastic (at least for a short range of the demand curve above current price), then Burger King can raise both price and total revenue. Remember, if demand is inelastic, an increase in price leads to higher total revenue.

Does Burger King want to increase its total revenue? Under the conditions stated here, it certainly does.

It's true that, at a higher price, fewer Whoppers will be sold. But profit is the objective, not number of Whoppers sold. Profit is the difference between total revenue and total cost. If the demand for a Whopper is inelastic, a price increase will raise total revenue. It will also mean fewer Whoppers sold, which will lower costs. If revenues rise and costs decline, profits rise.

Our concluding point is a simple one: The discussion of price elasticity of demand in this chapter isn't as far removed from the discussions in the offices of major companies and advertising firms as you may have thought.

stitutes (good *A*) or for the good that has 15 substitutes (good *B*)? The answer is the good with 15 substitutes, good *B*. This occurs because the greater the opportunities for substitution (there is more chance of substituting a good for *B* than of substituting a good for *A*), the greater the cutback in the quantity of the good purchased as its price rises. When the price of good *A* rises 10 percent, people can turn to 2 substitutes. Quantity demanded of good *A* falls, but not by as much as if 15 substitutes had been available, as there were for good *B*.

The relationship between the availability of substitutes and price elasticity is clear: *The more substitutes for a good, the higher the price elasticity of demand; the fewer substitutes for a good, the lower the price elasticity of demand.*

For example, the price elasticity of demand for Chevrolets is higher than the price elasticity of demand for all cars. This is because there are more substitutes for Chevrolets than there are for cars. Everything that is a substitute for a car (bus, train, walking, bicycle, etc.) is also a substitute for a specific type of car, such as a Chevrolet; but some things that are substitutes for a Chevrolet (Ford, Toyota, Chrysler, Mercedes-Benz, etc.) are not substitutes for a car. Instead, they are simply types of cars.

Thus, the relationship above can be stated as: *The more broadly defined the good, the fewer the substitutes; the more narrowly defined the good, the greater the substitutes.* There are

> **Q&A**   *Is price elasticity of demand greater for computers or for Sony computers?*
>
> *Ask yourself which good—computers or Sony computers—has more substitutes. The answer is Sony computers. Thus, it follows that the elasticity of demand is greater for Sony computers than it is for computers.*

> **Q&A**   *Are we saying that the demand for, say, gasoline is elastic and the demand for, say, paper, is inelastic because one usually spends a larger percentage of his budget on gasoline (for the car) than on paper?*
>
> *First, we are not saying that the demand for gasoline is elastic and the demand for paper is inelastic. The words* elastic *and* inelastic *come with precise definitions. Elastic means that the percentage change in quantity demanded is greater than the percentage change in price so that $E_d > 1$. We do not know if gasoline has $E_d > 1$. Similarly, we do not know if the demand for paper is inelastic so that $E_d < 1$.*
>
> *What we are saying is that if gasoline consumption is a larger percentage of the budget than paper consumption, it follows that the elasticity of demand for gasoline is greater than the elasticity of demand for paper. In other words, E_d is a larger number for gasoline than it is for paper. Whether it is greater than 1 or less than 1, we cannot say without actual data.*

> **Q&A**   *Would the elasticity of demand for gasoline be greater in the short run or in the long run?*
>
> *In the long run. If the price of gasoline rises, the consumption of gasoline does not fall dramatically in the short run. For example, motorists don't immediately stop driving big gas-guzzling cars. As time passes, however, many car owners trade in their big cars for compact cars. Car buyers become more concerned with the miles a car can travel per gallon of gas. People begin to form carpools. As a result, gasoline consumption ends up falling more in the long run.*

more substitutes for this economics textbook than there are for textbooks. There are more substitutes for Coca-Cola than there are for soft drinks.

NECESSITIES VERSUS LUXURIES Generally, *the more that a good is considered a luxury (a good that we can do without) rather than a necessity (a good that we can't do without), the higher the price elasticity of demand.* For example, consider two goods—jewelry and a medicine for controlling high blood pressure. If the price of jewelry rises, it is easy to cut back on jewelry purchases. No one really needs jewelry to live. However, if the price of the medicine for controlling one's high blood pressure rises, it is not so easy to cut back on it. We expect the price elasticity of demand for jewelry to be higher than the price elasticity of demand for medicine used to control high blood pressure.

PERCENTAGE OF ONE'S BUDGET SPENT ON THE GOOD Claire Rossi has a monthly budget of $3,000. Of this monthly budget, she spends $3 per month on pens and $400 per month on dinners at restaurants. In percentage terms, she spends 0.1 percent of her monthly budget on pens and 13 percent of her monthly budget on dinners at restaurants. Suppose both the price of pens and the price of dinners at restaurants double. Would Claire be more responsive to the change in the price of pens or the change in the price of dinners at restaurants? The answer is the change in the price of dinners at restaurants. The reason is that a doubling in price of a good on which Claire spends 0.1 percent of her budget is not felt as strongly as a doubling in price of a good on which she spends 13 percent. Claire is more likely to ignore the doubling in the price of pens than she is to ignore the doubling in the price of dinners at restaurants. Buyers are (and thus quantity demanded is) more responsive to price the larger the percentage of their budget that goes for the purchase of the good. *The greater the percentage of one's budget that goes to purchase a good, the higher the price elasticity of demand; the smaller the percentage of one's budget that goes to purchase a good, the lower the price elasticity of demand.*

TIME As time passes, buyers have greater opportunities to be responsive to a price change. If the price of electricity went up today, and you knew about it, you probably would not change your consumption of electricity today as much as you would 3 months from today. As time passes, you have more chances to change your consumption by finding substitutes (natural gas), changing your lifestyle (buying more blankets and turning down the thermostat at night), and so on. We conclude: *The more time that passes (since the price change), the higher the price elasticity of demand for the good; the less time that passes, the lower the price elasticity of demand for the good.*[6] In other words, price elasticity of demand for a good is higher in the long run than in the short run.

---

[6]If we say, "The more time that passes (since the price change), the higher the price elasticity of demand," wouldn't it follow that price elasticity of demand gets steadily larger? For example, might it be that on Tuesday the price of good X rises, and 5 days later, $E_d = 0.70$, 10 days later it is 0.76, and so on toward infinity? This is not exactly the case. Obviously, there comes a time when quantity demanded is no longer adjusting to a change in price (just as there comes a time when there are no longer any ripples in the lake from the passing motorboat). Our conditional statement ("the more time that passes . . .") implies this condition

SELF-TEST

1. If there are 7 substitutes for good X and demand is inelastic, does it follow that if there are 9 substitutes for good X, demand will be elastic? Explain your answer.

2. Price elasticity of demand is predicted to be higher for which good of the following combinations of goods: (a) Dell computers or computers; (b) Heinz ketchup or ketchup; (c) Perrier water or water? Explain your answers.

Other Elasticity Concepts

This section looks at three other elasticities: cross elasticity of demand, income elasticity of demand, and price elasticity of supply.

Cross Elasticity of Demand

Cross elasticity of demand measures the responsiveness in the quantity demanded of one good to changes in the price of another good. It is calculated by dividing the percentage change in the quantity demanded of one good by the percentage change in the price of another good.

> **Cross Elasticity of Demand**
> Measures the responsiveness in quantity demanded of one good to changes in the price of another good.

$$E_c = \frac{\text{Percentage change in quantity demanded of one good}}{\text{Percentage change in price of another good}}$$

where E_c stands for the coefficient of cross elasticity of demand, or elasticity coefficient.[7]

This concept is often used to determine whether two goods are substitutes or complements and the degree to which one good is a substitute for or complement to another. Consider two goods: Skippy peanut butter and Jif peanut butter. Suppose that when the price of Jif increases by 10 percent, the quantity demanded of Skippy increases by 45 percent. The cross elasticity of demand for Skippy with respect to the price of Jif is written

$$E_c = \frac{\text{Percentage change in quantity demanded of Skippy}}{\text{Percentage change in price of Jif}}$$

In this case, the cross elasticity of demand is a positive 4.5. When the cross elasticity of demand is positive, the percentage change in the quantity demanded of one good (numerator) moves in the same direction as the percentage change in the price of another good (denominator). This is representative of goods that are substitutes. As the price of Jif rises, the demand curve for Skippy shifts rightward, causing the quantity demanded of Skippy to increase at every price.[8] We conclude that if $E_c > 0$, the two goods are substitutes.

$$E_c > 0 \rightarrow \text{Goods are substitutes}$$

If the elasticity coefficient is negative, $E_c < 0$, then the two goods are complements.

$$E_c < 0 \rightarrow \text{Goods are complements}$$

A negative cross elasticity of demand occurs when the percentage change in the quantity demanded of one good (numerator) and the percentage change in the price of another good (denominator) move in opposite directions. Consider an example. Suppose

---

[7] A question normally arises: How can E_d and E_c both be the elasticity coefficient? It is a matter of convenience. When speaking about price elasticity of demand, the coefficient of price elasticity of demand is referred to as the "elasticity coefficient." When speaking about cross elasticity of demand, the coefficient of cross elasticity of demand is referred to as the "elasticity coefficient." The practice holds for other elasticities as well.

[8] Recall that if two goods are substitutes, a rise in the price of one good causes the demand for the other good to increase.

economics 24/7

ARE CHILDREN SUBSTITUTES OR COMPLEMENTS?

Not all parents are alike. Some parents spend a lot of time with their children; others do not. Some parents (with similar incomes) spend a lot of money on their children; others do not. Some parents are strict disciplinarians; others are not. Which parental behavioral differences are significant? For example, if parents A and parents B spend different amounts of time reading to their children at bedtime, is this difference significant? Are children who are read to a lot different from children who are read to very little or not at all? If not, then perhaps this parental difference does not matter.

One difference in parental behavior that may be significant is whether parents treat their children as substitutes or as complements. To illustrate, suppose Bob is the father of two boys, Zack, 4 years old, and Dylan, 6 years old. Bob spends time with each of his boys, and the amount of time he spends with each boy often depends on the "price" the son "charges" his father to be with him. For example, Zack is a little harder to be around than Dylan (he asks for more things from his father, he doesn't seem to be as happy doing certain things, etc.), so the "price" Bob has to pay to be around Zack is higher than the price he has to pay to be around Dylan.

How will a change in the price each son charges his father influence the time the father spends with the other son? This question involves cross elasticity of demand, where

$$E_c = \frac{\text{Percentage change in quantity demanded of time spent with Dylan}}{\text{Percentage change in price Zack charges his father to be with him}}$$

Suppose Zack increases the price he charges his father to be with him. He demands more of his father, he seems less content when his father suggests certain activities, and so

on. How will Bob react? If an increase in the price he has to pay to be with Zack increases the amount of time he wants to spend with Dylan, then as far as Bob is concerned, Dylan and Zack are substitutes ($E_c > 0$). But if an increase in the price he has to pay to be with Zack causes Bob to decrease the time he spends with Dylan, then Dylan and Zack are complements ($E_c < 0$).

In the first case, where the two boys are substitutes, the father may be saying, "I like to be with both my boys, but if one makes it harder for me to be with him, I'll spend less time with him and I'll spend more time with the other." In the second case, where the two boys are complements, the father may be saying, "I like to be with both my boys, but if one makes it harder for me to be with him, I'll spend less time with him and less time with the other too."

Does it matter to the two boys whether they are viewed by their father as substitutes or complements? Consider things from Dylan's perspective. Suppose he wants his father to spend more time with him. If Zack raises the price to his father of being with him (Zack) and Dylan and Zack are substitutes, then Dylan will benefit from Zack's raising the price. His father will spend less time with Zack and more with him. But if Zack and Dylan are complements, an increase in the price Zack charges his father to be with him (Zack) will cause his father to spend less time with Dylan.

Will Dylan act differently to Zack depending on whether he perceives himself as a substitute or as a complement? If he perceives himself as a substitute, he may urge Zack to act up with Dad, knowing that this means Dad will spend more time with him, Dylan. But if he perceives himself as a complement, he may urge Zack to be good with Dad, knowing that if Zack charges his father a lower price to be around him (Zack), this will increase the amount of time the father will spend with Dylan.

the price of cars increases by 5 percent, and the quantity demanded of car tires decreases by 10 percent. Calculating the cross elasticity of demand, we have −10 percent/5 percent = −2. Cars and car tires are complements.

The concept of cross elasticity of demand can be very useful. Suppose a company sells cheese. A natural question might be: What goods are substitutes for cheese? The answer would help identify the company's competitors. The company could find out which goods are substitutes for cheese by calculating the cross elasticity of demand between cheese and other goods. A positive cross elasticity of demand would indicate the two goods were substitutes, and the higher the cross elasticity of demand, the greater the degree of substitution.

Income Elasticity of Demand

Income elasticity of demand measures the responsiveness of quantity demanded to changes in income. It is calculated by dividing the percentage change in quantity demanded of a good by the percentage change in income.

$$E_y = \frac{\text{Percentage change in quantity demanded}}{\text{Percentage change in income}}$$

where E_y = coefficient of income elasticity of demand, or elasticity coefficient.

Income elasticity of demand is positive, $E_y > 0$, for a *normal good*. Recall that a normal good is one whose demand, and thus quantity demanded, increases, given an increase in income. Thus, the variables in the numerator and denominator in the income elasticity of demand formula move in the same direction for a normal good.

$$E_y > 0 \rightarrow \text{Normal good}$$

In contrast to a normal good, the demand for an *inferior good* decreases as income increases. Income elasticity of demand for an inferior good is negative, $E_y < 0$.

$$E_y < \rightarrow \text{Inferior good}$$

To calculate the income elasticity of demand for a good, we use the same approach that we used to calculate price elasticity of demand.

$$E_y = \frac{\dfrac{\Delta Q_d}{Q_{d \text{ Average}}}}{\dfrac{\Delta Y}{Y_{\text{Average}}}}$$

where $Q_{d \text{ Average}}$ is the average quantity demanded and Y_{Average} is the average income.

Suppose income increases from \$500 to \$600 per month, and as a result, quantity demanded of good X increases from 20 units to 30 units per month. We have

$$E_y = \frac{\dfrac{10}{25}}{\dfrac{100}{550}} = 2.2$$

E_y is a positive number, so good X is a normal good. Also, because $E_y > 1$, demand for good X is said to be **income elastic**. This means the percentage change in quantity demanded of the good is greater than the percentage change in income. If $E_y < 1$, the demand for the good is said to be **income inelastic**. If $E_y = 1$, then the demand for the good is **income unit elastic**.

Price Elasticity of Supply

Price elasticity of supply measures the responsiveness of quantity supplied to changes in price. It is calculated by dividing the percentage change in quantity supplied of a good by the percentage change in the price of the good.

$$E_s = \frac{\text{Percentage change in quantity supplied}}{\text{Percentage change in price}}$$

where E_s stands for the coefficient of price elasticity of supply, or elasticity coefficient. We use the same approach to calculate price elasticity of supply that we used to calculate price elasticity of demand.

Income Elasticity of Demand
Measures the responsiveness of quantity demanded to changes in income.

Income Elastic
The percentage change in quantity demanded of a good is greater than the percentage change in income.

Income Inelastic
The percentage change in quantity demanded of a good is less than the percentage change in income.

Income Unit Elastic
The percentage change in quantity demanded of a good is equal to the percentage change in income.

Price Elasticity of Supply
Measures the responsiveness of quantity supplied to changes in price.

In addition, supply can be classified as elastic, inelastic, unit elastic, perfectly elastic, or perfectly inelastic (Exhibit 8). Elastic supply ($E_s > 1$) refers to a percentage change in quantity supplied that is greater than the percentage change in price.

Percentage change in quantity supplied > Percentage change in price →
$E_s > 1$ → Elastic supply

Inelastic supply ($E_s < 1$) refers to a percentage change in quantity supplied that is less than the percentage change in price.

Percentage change in quantity supplied < Percentage change in price →
$E_s < 1$ → Inelastic supply

Unit elastic supply ($E_s = 1$) refers to a percentage change in quantity supplied that is equal to the percentage change in price.

Percentage change in quantity supplied = Percentage change in price →
$E_s = 1$ → Unit elastic supply

Perfectly elastic supply ($E_s = \infty$) represents the case where a small change in price changes quantity supplied by an infinitely large amount (and thus, the supply curve, or a portion of the overall supply curve, is horizontal). Perfectly inelastic supply ($E_s = 0$) represents the case where a change in price brings no change in quantity supplied (and thus, the supply curve, or a portion of the overall supply curve, is vertical).

See Exhibit 9 for a summary of the elasticity concepts.

exhibit **8**

Price Elasticity of Supply

(a) The percentage change in quantity supplied is greater than the percentage change in price: $E_s > 1$ and supply is elastic. (b) The percentage change in quantity supplied is less than the percentage change in price: $E_s < 1$ and supply is inelastic. (c) The percentage change in quantity supplied is equal to the percentage change in price: $E_s = 1$ and supply is unit elastic. (d) A small change in price changes quantity supplied by an infinite amount: $E_s = \infty$ and supply is perfectly elastic. (e) A change in price does not change quantity supplied: $E_s = 0$ and supply is perfectly inelastic.

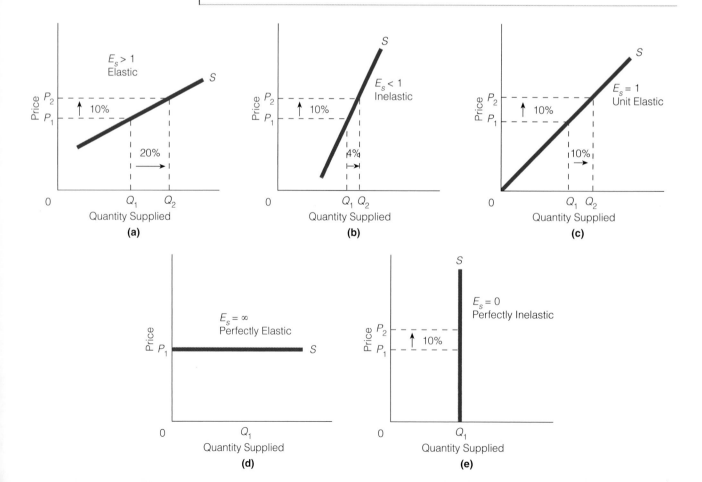

Type	Calculation	Possibilities	Terminology
Price elasticity of demand	$$\frac{\text{Percentage change in quantity demanded}}{\text{Percentage change in price}}$$	$E_d > 1$ $E_d < 1$ $E_d = 1$ $E_d = \infty$ $E_d = 0$	Elastic Inelastic Unit elastic Perfectly elastic Perfectly inelastic
Cross elasticity of demand	$$\frac{\text{Percentage change in quantity demanded of one good}}{\text{Percentage change in price of another good}}$$	$E_c < 0$ $E_c > 0$	Complements Substitutes
Income elasticity of demand	$$\frac{\text{Percentage change in quantity demanded}}{\text{Percentage change in income}}$$	$E_y > 0$ $E_y < 0$ $E_y > 1$ $E_y < 1$ $E_y = 1$	Normal good Inferior good Income elastic Income inelastic Income unit elastic
Price elasticity of supply	$$\frac{\text{Percentage change in quantity supplied}}{\text{Percentage change in price}}$$	$E_s > 1$ $E_s < 1$ $E_s = 1$ $E_s = \infty$ $E_s = 0$	Elastic Inelastic Unit elastic Perfectly elastic Perfectly inelastic

exhibit **9**

Summary of the Four Elasticity Concepts

Price Elasticity of Supply and Time

The longer the period of adjustment to a change in price, the higher the price elasticity of supply. (We are referring to goods whose quantity supplied can increase with time. This covers most goods. It does not, however, cover original Picasso paintings.) There is an obvious reason for this: Additional production takes time.

For example, suppose the demand for new housing increases in your city. Further, suppose this increase in demand occurs all at once on Tuesday. This places upward pressure on the price of housing. Will the number of houses supplied be much different on Saturday than it was on Tuesday? No, it won't. It will take time for suppliers to determine whether the increase in demand is permanent. If they decide it is a temporary state, not much will be done. If contractors decide it is permanent, they need time to move resources from the production of other things into the production of additional new housing. Simply put, the change in quantity supplied of housing is likely to be different in the long run than in the short run, given a change in price. This translates into a higher price elasticity of supply in the long run than in the short run.

SELF-TEST

1. What does an income elasticity of demand of 1.33 mean?

2. If supply is perfectly inelastic, what does this signify?

Thinking like
AN ECONOMIST   *In a way, this chapter is about ratios. Ratios describe how one thing changes (the numerator) relative to a change in something else (the denominator). For example, when we discuss price elasticity of demand, we investigate how quantity demanded changes as price changes; when we discuss income elasticity of demand, we explore how quantity demanded changes as income changes. Economists often think in terms of ratios because they are often comparing the change in one variable to the change in another variable.*

A Reader Asks...

Is the Type of Thinking Inherent in Elasticity Useful?

The elasticity concepts in this chapter are interesting, and I'm sure they're useful to business firms. But I don't really see how thinking about elasticities helps me in any fundamental way. Any comments?

Elasticity (price, income, supply, cross) relates to a change in one thing relative to a change in something else. Thinking in terms of these types of relationships can help you gain insight into certain phenomena. For example, consider this question: If a company is forced to pay its employees higher wage rates ($20 an hour instead of $18 an hour), will the higher wage rate result in the company paying a larger total amount in wages (say, $500,000 a month instead of $400,000)?

Now the answer most people will give is yes. They reason this way: Multiplying a given number of hours worked by $20 results in a greater total dollar amount than multiplying the number of hours by $18.

Thinking elastically, we know that changing one thing can lead to a change in something else. Specifically, we know that an increase in wage rates can affect the number of hours worked. Companies may not hire as many employees or may not have their employees work as many hours if the wage rate is $20 an hour than if it is $18 an hour. In short, hours worked are likely to fall as wage rates rise. Whether the total amount the firm pays in wages rises, falls, or remains constant depends on the percentage rise in wage rates relative to the percentage fall in hours worked. For example, if the percentage increase in wage rates is less than the percentage decline in hours worked, the total amount paid in wages will decline. We could not have easily come up with this conclusion had we not looked at the percentage change in one thing relative to the percentage change in something else. This type of thinking, of course, is inherent in the elasticity concepts discussed in this chapter.

! analyzing the scene

If everyone with an SUV trades it in for a smaller, more efficient car, will air pollution be reduced? If the pharmaceutical company raises the price of one of its products by 5 percent, will its total revenue rise? If the LA earthquake does result in higher apartment rents, does it follow that apartment landlords will have greater total revenue?

The theme in all of these questions is the same: One thing actually changes or a change is proposed, and you are asked to wonder what the effect of the change might be. Let's consider each question separately.

If people trade in their SUVs for small, gas-efficient cars, will air pollution be reduced? The answer is not necessarily. When people have small cars, they may increase the amount they drive because the cost per mile is less for a small car than for an SUV. For example, suppose it takes $2 worth of gas to drive 15 miles in an SUV and $2 worth of gas to drive 25 miles in a Honda Civic. On a per mile basis, the cost would

be 13 cents a mile in an SUV and 8 cents a mile in a Honda Civic. If the demand curve for driving is downward sloping, people will drive more at 8 cents a mile than at 13 cents a mile. The question is: How much more will they drive? Certainly, the possibility exists that drivers will drive so much more (in their small cars as opposed to their big SUVs) that the amount of air pollution (due to driving more) increases instead of decreases. In other words, the small cars might emit less pollution than SUVs per mile traveled, but if drivers travel significantly more miles in their smaller cars than in their SUVs, we might end up with more instead of less air pollution.

Now let's turn to the pharmaceutical company and prices. Will the company take in more total revenue if it raises the price of a particular product? Yes, if the demand for the product is inelastic between the old (lower) price and the new (higher) price. No, if the demand for the product is elastic between the old (lower) price and the new (higher) price.

Finally, will the LA earthquake cause a rise in apartment rents? Yes, because as the supply of apartments falls (due to the earthquake), the demand for apartments intersects the supply of apartments higher up the demand curve and brings about a higher dollar rent. But it doesn't necessarily follow that higher apartment rents will increase total revenue for apartment owners—in much the same way that it did not neces-

sarily follow that a higher product price will increase total revenue for the pharmaceutical company. It all depends on price elasticity of demand. If the demand for apartments is inelastic between the old (lower, pre-earthquake) rents and the new (higher, post-earthquake) rents, total apartment revenue will rise. If the demand for apartments is elastic, total revenue will fall.

chapter summary

Price Elasticity of Demand

- Price elasticity of demand is a measure of the responsiveness of quantity demanded to changes in price:

$$E_d = \frac{\text{Percentage change in quantity demanded}}{\text{Percentage change in price}}$$

- If the percentage change in quantity demanded is greater than the percentage change in price, demand is elastic. If the percentage change in quantity demanded is less than the percentage change in price, demand is inelastic. If the percentage change in quantity demanded is equal to the percentage change in price, demand is unit elastic. If a small change in price causes an infinitely large change in quantity demanded, demand is perfectly elastic. If a change in price causes no change in quantity demanded, demand is perfectly inelastic.

- The coefficient of price elasticity of demand (E_d) is negative, signifying the inverse relationship between price and quantity demanded. For convenience, however, the absolute value of the elasticity coefficient is used.

Total Revenue and Price Elasticity of Demand

- Total revenue equals price times quantity sold. Total expenditure equals price times quantity purchased. Total revenue equals total expenditure.

- If demand is elastic, price and total revenue are inversely related: As price rises (falls), total revenue falls (rises).

- If demand is inelastic, price and total revenue are directly related: As price rises (falls), total revenue rises (falls).

- If demand is unit elastic, total revenue is independent of price: As price rises (falls), total revenue remains constant.

Determinants of Price Elasticity of Demand

- The more substitutes for a good, the higher the price elasticity of demand; the fewer substitutes for a good, the lower the price elasticity of demand.

- The more that a good is considered a luxury instead of a necessity, the higher the price elasticity of demand.

- The greater the percentage of one's budget that goes to purchase a good, the higher the price elasticity of demand; the smaller the percentage of one's budget that goes to purchase a good, the lower the price elasticity of demand.

- The more time that passes (since a price change), the higher the price elasticity of demand; the less time that passes, the lower the price elasticity of demand.

Cross Elasticity of Demand

- Cross elasticity of demand measures the responsiveness in the quantity demanded of one good to changes in the price of another good:

$$E_c = \frac{\text{Percentage change in quantity demanded of one good}}{\text{Percentage change in price of another good}}$$

- If $E_c > 0$, two goods are substitutes. If $E_c < 0$, two goods are complements.

Income Elasticity of Demand

- Income elasticity of demand measures the responsiveness of quantity demanded to changes in income:

$$E_y = \frac{\text{Percentage change in quantity demanded}}{\text{Percentage change in income}}$$

- If $E_y > 0$, the good is a normal good. If $E_y < 0$, the good is an inferior good.

- If $E_y > 1$, demand is income elastic. If $E_y < 1$, demand is income inelastic. If $E_y = 1$, demand is income unit elastic.

Price Elasticity of Supply

- Price elasticity of supply measures the responsiveness of quantity supplied to changes in price:

$$E_s = \frac{\text{Percentage change in quantity supplied}}{\text{Percentage change in price}}$$

- If the percentage change in quantity supplied is greater than the percentage change in price, supply is elastic. If the percentage change in quantity supplied is less than the percentage change in price, supply is inelastic. If the percentage change in quantity supplied is equal to the percentage change in price, supply is unit elastic.

- Price elasticity of supply is higher in the long run than in the short run.

key terms and concepts

Price Elasticity of
  Demand

Elastic Demand

Inelastic Demand

Unit Elastic Demand

Perfectly Elastic Demand

Perfectly Inelastic
  Demand

Total Revenue (*TR*)

Cross Elasticity of
  Demand

Income Elasticity of
  Demand

Income Elastic

Income Inelastic

Income Unit Elastic

Price Elasticity of Supply

questions and problems

1   Explain how a seller can determine whether the demand for his or her good is inelastic, elastic, or unit elastic between two prices.

2   Suppose the current price of gasoline at the pump is $1 per gallon and that 1 million gallons are sold per month. A politician proposes to add a 10-cent tax to the price of a gallon of gasoline. She says the tax will generate $100,000 tax revenues per month (1 million gallons × $0.10 = $100,000). What assumption is she making?

3   Suppose a straight-line downward-sloping demand curve shifts rightward. Is the price elasticity of demand higher, lower, or the same between any two prices on the new (higher) demand curve than on the old (lower) demand curve?

4   Suppose Austin, Texas, is hit by a tornado that destroys 25 percent of the housing in the area. Would you expect the total expenditure on housing after the tornado to be greater than, less than, or equal to what it was before the tornado?

5   Which good in each of the following pairs of goods has the higher price elasticity of demand? (a) airline travel in the short run or airline travel in the long run; (b) television sets or Sony television sets; (c) cars or Toyotas; (d) telephones or AT&T telephones; (e) popcorn or Orville Redenbacher's popcorn?

6   How might you determine whether toothpaste and mouthwash manufacturers are competitors?

7   Assume the demand for product *A* is perfectly inelastic. Further, assume that the buyers of *A* get the funds to pay for it by stealing. If the supply of *A* decreases, what happens to its price? What happens to the amount of crime committed by the buyers of *A?*

8   Suppose you learned that the price elasticity of demand for wheat is 0.7 between the current price for wheat and a price $2 higher per bushel. Do you think farmers collectively would try to reduce the supply of wheat and drive the price up $2 higher per bushel? Why? Assuming that they would try to reduce supply, what problems might they have in actually doing so?

9   In 1947, the U.S. Department of Justice brought a suit against the DuPont Company (which at the time sold 75 percent of all the cellophane in the United States) for monopolizing the production and sale of cellophane. In court, the DuPont Company tried to show that cellophane was only one of several goods in the market in which it was sold. It argued that its market was not the cellophane market but the "flexible packaging materials" market, which included (besides cellophane) waxed paper, aluminum foil, and so forth. DuPont pointed out that it had only 20 percent of all sales in this more broadly defined market. Using this information, discuss how the concept of cross elasticity of demand would help establish whether DuPont should have been viewed as a firm in the cellophane market or as a firm in the "flexible packaging materials" market.

working with numbers and graphs

1   A college raises its annual tuition from $2,000 to $2,500, and its student enrollment falls from 4,877 to 4,705. Compute the price elasticity of demand. Is demand elastic or inelastic?

2   As the price of good X rises from $10 to $12, the quantity demanded of good Y rises from 100 units to 114 units. Are X and Y substitutes or complements? What is the cross elasticity of demand?

3   The quantity demanded of good X rises from 130 to 145 units as income rises from $2,000 to $2,500 a month. What is the income elasticity of demand?

4   The quantity supplied of a good rises from 120 to 140 as price rises from $4 to $5.50. What is the price elasticity of supply?

5   In the following figure, what is the price elasticity of demand between the two prices on D_1? on D_2?

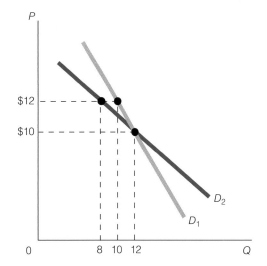

6

Consumer Choice: Maximizing Utility and Behavioral Economics

Setting the Scene

Zach and Viv Harris have been married for 6 years and have 2 children, 4-year-old Adrian and 2-year-old Michael. Zach and Viv are looking to the future, when their children begin school. Both parents think that the school district in which they reside leaves something to be desired. They would like to move to the east side of town where there are better schools.

Zach:
I think the kids would be better off if we just went ahead and moved.

Viv:
But house prices are so much higher on the east side. Do you think we can afford to move there?

Zach:
I don't think we can afford not to move there. You know the schools are better on the other side of town.

Viv:
That's what I've heard. The kids seem to get higher scores on standardized tests.

Zach:
I suppose the kids will miss their friends, but they're probably young enough that they'll adjust.

Viv:
What do you think about staying here and sending the kids to a private school?

Zach:
Private schools are getting pretty expensive. I really don't want to pay for a private school.

Viv:
I don't want to either. I just think we should look at all our options.

BARBARA AND STEVE OBERLIN ARE LOOKING FOR A HOUSE TO BUY. THEY'RE CONSIDERING TWO HOUSES FOR SALE ON THE SAME STREET. ONE OF THE HOUSES HAS AN OCEAN VIEW; THE OTHER DOES NOT.

Barbara:
I like that ocean view.

Steve:
Who wouldn't? But the house is pricey. The one down the street is essentially the same house.

Barbara:
But without the view.

Steve:
Yeah, I know. Maybe we should think about it some more.

Barbara:
I guess it comes down to how much we're willing to pay for the view.

Steve:
What's the most you think we should pay?

Barbara:
I'm not sure. What do you think?

Steve:
I'm not sure either.

? Here are some questions to keep in mind as you read this chapter:

- *How is buying a house in a good school district like sending children to a private school?*

- *What is the price of an ocean view?*

See analyzing the scene at the end of this chapter for answers to these questions.

Utility Theory

Water is cheap and diamonds are expensive. But water is necessary to life and diamonds are not. Isn't it odd—paradoxical?—that what is necessary to life is cheap and what is not necessary is expensive? Eighteenth-century economist Adam Smith wondered about this question. He observed that often things that have the greatest value in use, or are the most useful, have a relatively low price, and things that have little or no value in use have a high price. Smith's observation came to be known as the **diamond–water paradox**, or the paradox of value. The paradox challenged economists, and they sought a solution to it. This section begins to develop parts of the solution they found.

Utility: Total and Marginal

Saying that a good gives you **utility** is the same as saying that it has the power to satisfy your wants or that it gives you satisfaction. For example, suppose you buy your first unit of good X. You obtain a certain amount of utility, say, 10 **utils** from it. (Utils are an artificial construct used to "measure" utility; we realize you have never seen a util—no one has.)

You buy a second unit of good X. Once again, you get a certain amount of utility from this second unit, say, 8 utils. You purchase a third unit and receive 7 utils. The sum of the amount of utility you obtain from each of the 3 units is the *total utility* you receive from purchasing good X—which is 25 utils. **Total utility** is the total satisfaction one receives from consuming a particular quantity of a good (in this example, 3 units of good X).

Total utility is different from marginal utility. **Marginal utility** is the *additional* utility gained from consuming an additional unit of good X. Marginal utility is the change in total utility divided by the change in the quantity consumed of a good:

$$MU = \frac{\Delta TU}{\Delta Q}$$

where the change in the quantity consumed of a good is usually equal to 1 unit.

To illustrate, suppose you receive 10 utils of total utility from consuming 1 apple and 19 utils of total utility from consuming 2 apples. What is the marginal utility of the second apple, or what is the additional utility of consuming an additional apple? It is 9 utils.

Notice that as a person consumes more apples, total utility rises (column 2); however, at the same time total utility is rising, marginal utility (additional utility received from the additional apple) is falling (column 3). In other words, the numbers in column 2 rise as the numbers in column 3 fall.

Law of Diminishing Marginal Utility

Do you think the marginal utility of the second unit is greater than, less than, or equal to the marginal utility of the first unit? Before answering, consider the difference in marginal utility between the third unit and the second unit or between the fifth unit and the fourth unit (had we extended the number of units consumed). In general, we are asking whether the marginal utility of the unit that comes next is greater than, less than, or equal to the marginal utility of the unit that comes before.

Economists have generally answered "less than." The **law of diminishing marginal utility** states that for a given time period, the marginal utility gained by consuming equal successive units of a good will decline as the amount consumed increases. In terms of our artificial units, utils, this means that the number of utils gained by consuming the

Diamond-Water Paradox

The observation that things that have the greatest value in use sometimes have little value in exchange and things that have little value in use sometimes have the greatest value in exchange.

Utility

A measure of the satisfaction, happiness, or benefit that results from the consumption of a good.

Util

An artificial construct used to measure utility.

Total Utility

The total satisfaction a person receives from consuming a particular quantity of a good.

Marginal Utility

The additional utility a person receives from consuming an additional unit of a particular good.

Thinking like **AN ECONOMIST**   *The economist knows that the total utility of something can be rising as the marginal utility of that something is falling. In fact, this is often the case. To illustrate, look at the table that follows:*

(1) Number of apples consumed	(2) Total Utility (utils)	(3) Marginal Utility (utils)
1	10	10
2	19	9
3	27	8

Law of Diminishing Marginal Utility

The marginal utility gained by consuming equal successive units of a good will decline as the amount consumed increases.

first unit of a good is greater than the number of utils gained by consuming the second unit (which is greater than the number gained by the third, which is greater than the number gained by the fourth, etc.).

The law of diminishing marginal utility is illustrated in Exhibit 1. The table in part (a) shows both the total utility of consuming a certain number of units of a good and the marginal utility of consuming additional units. The graph in part (b) shows the total utility curve for the data in part (a), and the graph in part (c) shows the marginal utility curve for the data in part (a). Notice how the graphs in (b) and (c) show that total utility can increase as marginal utility decreases. This relationship between total utility and marginal utility is important in unraveling the diamond-water paradox.

The law of diminishing marginal utility is based on the idea that if a good has a variety of uses but only 1 unit of the good is available, then the consumer will use the first unit to satisfy his or her most urgent want. If 2 units are available, the consumer will use the second unit to satisfy a less urgent want.

To illustrate, suppose that good X can be used to satisfy wants A through E, with A being the most urgent want and E being the least urgent want. Also, B is more urgent than C, C is more urgent than D, and D is more urgent than E. We can chart the wants as follows:

WANTS				
A	B	C	D	E
Most Urgent				Least Urgent

exhibit **1**

Total Utility, Marginal Utility, and the Law of Diminishing Marginal Utility

TU = total utility and MU = marginal utility. (a) Both total utility and marginal utility are expressed in utils. Marginal utility is the change in total utility divided by the change in the quantity consumed of the good, $MU = \Delta TU/\Delta Q$. (b) Total utility curve. (c) Marginal utility curve. Together, (b) and (c) demonstrate that total utility can increase (b) as marginal utility decreases (c).

(1) **Units of Good X**	(2) **Total Utility (utils)**	(3) **Marginal Utility (utils)**
0	0	–
1	10	10
2	19	9
3	27	8
4	34	7
5	40	6

(a)

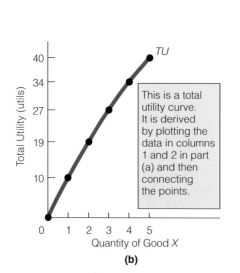

This is a total utility curve. It is derived by plotting the data in columns 1 and 2 in part (a) and then connecting the points.

(b)

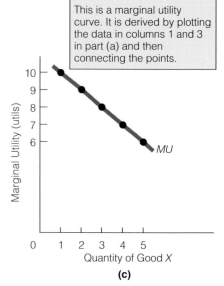

This is a marginal utility curve. It is derived by plotting the data in columns 1 and 3 in part (a) and then connecting the points.

(c)

economics 24/7

CUBAN CIGARS, CHILEAN GRAPES

The law of diminishing marginal utility explains why people trade. To illustrate, consider two people, Smith and Jones. Smith has 100 apples and Jones has 100 oranges. As Smith consumes her apples, marginal utility declines. Her tenth apple doesn't give her as much utility as her ninth and so on. The same is true for Jones with respect to oranges. In other words, as Smith and Jones consume successive units of what they have, marginal utility falls.

At some point, Smith's marginal utility of consuming another apple is likely less than her marginal utility of consuming something different—say, an orange. And at some point, Jones's marginal utility of consuming another orange is likely less than his marginal utility of consuming something different—say, an apple. When this point comes, Smith and Jones will trade. For Smith, the marginal utility of an apple will be less than the marginal utility of an orange, and she will gladly trade an apple for an orange. For Jones, the marginal utility of an orange will be less than the marginal utility of an apple, and he will gladly trade an orange for an apple.

Suppose the law of diminishing marginal utility did not exist. Smith would have the same marginal utility when she consumed her first and her one-hundredth apple, and this marginal utility would always be greater than her marginal utility of an orange. The same would be true for Jones with respect to oranges. In this case, Smith and Jones would not trade with each other. It is the law of diminishing marginal utility, at work on both apples and oranges, that gets Smith and Jones to eventually trade with each other.

What holds for individuals in the same country holds for individuals from different countries. Cubans may like cigars, but at some point, the marginal utility of a cigar is less than the marginal utility of some good produced in another country, and Cubans are happy to trade cigars for other goods. Chileans might like grapes, but at some point, the marginal utility of a grape is less than the marginal utility of some good produced in another country, and Chileans are then happy to trade grapes for other goods.

Suppose the first unit of good X can satisfy any one—but only one—of wants A through E. Which want will an individual choose to satisfy? The answer is the most urgent want—A. The individual chooses to satisfy A instead of B, C, D, or E because people will ordinarily satisfy their most urgent want before all others. If you were dying of thirst in a desert (having gone without water for 3 days)

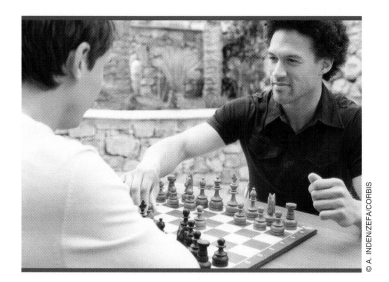

© A. INDEN/ZEFA/CORBIS

Q&A

When I first started playing chess, I received less utility (per game) than I do now as an accomplished chess player. Doesn't this observation invalidate the law of diminishing marginal utility?

Some economists think not. They argue that a person's first game of chess may not be the same good as his one-hundredth game. Although to an onlooker the first and the one-hundredth games may appear much alike (they use the same board and so forth), from the viewpoint of the chess player, there may be a large difference between the first game of chess and the one-hundredth game (in terms of how well he knows the game). In fact, the difference may be so large that we are dealing with two different goods.

and came across a quart of water, would you drink it or use it to wash your hands? You would drink it, of course. You would satisfy your most urgent want first. Washing your hands in the water would give you less utility than drinking the water.

THE MILLIONAIRE AND THE PAUPER: WHAT THE LAW SAYS AND DOESN'T SAY Who gets more utility from one more dollar, a poor man or a millionaire? Most people would say that a poor man gets more utility from one more dollar because the poor man has so many fewer dollars than the millionaire. "What's an extra dollar to a millionaire?" they ask. Then they answer, "Nothing. A millionaire has so many dollars, one more doesn't mean a thing."

Some people think the law of diminishing marginal utility substantiates the claim that a millionaire gets less utility from one more dollar than a poor man does. Unfortunately, though, this is a misreading of the law. In terms of this example, the law says that for the millionaire, an additional dollar is worth less than the dollar that preceded it; and for the poor man, an additional dollar is worth less than the dollar that preceded it. Let's say the millionaire has $2 million, and the poor man has $1,000. We now give each of them one more dollar. The law of diminishing marginal utility says (1) the additional dollar is worth less to the millionaire than her two-millionth dollar, and (2) the additional dollar is worth less to the poor man than his one-thousandth dollar. That is all the law says. We do not and cannot know whether the additional dollar is worth more or less to the millionaire than it is to the poor man. In summary, the law says something about the millionaire and about the poor man (both persons value the last dollar less than the next-to-last dollar), but it does not say anything about the millionaire's utility compared to the poor man's utility.

To compare the utility the millionaire gets from the additional dollar with the utility the poor man gets from it is to fall into the trap of making an **interpersonal utility comparison**. The utility obtained by one person cannot be scientifically or objectively compared with the utility obtained from the same thing by another person because utility is subjective. Who knows for certain how much satisfaction (utility) the millionaire gets from the additional dollar compared with that of the poor man? The poor man may care little for money; he may shun it, consider the love of it the root of all evil, and prefer to consume the things in life that do not require money. On the other hand, the millionaire may be interested only in amassing more money. We should not be so careless as to "guess" at the utility one person obtains from consuming a certain item, compare it to our "guess" of the utility another person obtains from consuming the same item, and then call these "guesses" scientific facts.

> *Thinking like*
> **AN ECONOMIST**
>
> *The economist knows that what "looks true" or "seems true" may not "be true." It may seem only reasonable to believe that the millionaire receives less utility from an additional dollar than a pauper. But this does not make it so. At one time, it only seemed reasonable to believe that the world was flat, but we know that the world is not flat.*

Interpersonal Utility Comparison

Comparing the utility one person receives from a good, service, or activity with the utility another person receives from the same good, service, or activity.

The Solution to the Diamond-Water Paradox

Goods have both total utility and marginal utility. Take water, for example. Water is extremely useful; we cannot live without it. We would expect its total utility (its total usefulness) to be high. But we would expect its marginal utility to be low because water is relatively plentiful. As the law of diminishing marginal utility states, the utility of successive units of a good diminishes as consumption of the good increases. In short, water is immensely useful, but there is so much of it that individuals place relatively little value on another unit of it.

In contrast, diamonds are not as useful as water. We would expect the total utility of diamonds to be lower than the total utility of water. However, we would expect the marginal utility of diamonds to be high. Why? There are relatively few diamonds in the world, so the consumption of diamonds (in contrast to the consumption of water) takes place at relatively high marginal utility. Diamonds, which are rare, get used only for their few valuable uses. Water, which is plentiful, gets used for its many valuable uses and for its not-so-valuable uses (e.g., spraying the car with the hose for 2 more minutes even though you are 99 percent sure that the soap is fully rinsed off).

In conclusion, the total utility of water is high because water is extremely useful. The total utility of diamonds is low in comparison because diamonds are not as useful as water. The marginal utility of water is low because water is so plentiful that people end up consuming it at low marginal utility. The marginal utility of diamonds is high because diamonds are so scarce that people end up consuming them at high marginal utility.

Do prices reflect total or marginal utility? Marginal utility.

SELF-TEST

(Answers to Self-Test questions are in the Self-Test Appendix.)

1. State and solve the diamond-water paradox.

2. If total utility is falling, what does this imply for marginal utility? Give an arithmetical example to illustrate your answer.

3. When would the total utility of a good and the marginal utility of a good be the same?

Consumer Equilibrium and Demand

This section identifies the condition necessary for consumer equilibrium and then discusses the relationship between equilibrium and the law of demand. The analysis is based on the assumption that individuals seek to maximize utility.

Equating Marginal Utilities per Dollar

Suppose there are only two goods in the world: apples and oranges. At present, a consumer is spending his entire income consuming 10 apples and 10 oranges a week. We assume that for a particular week, the marginal utility and price of each are as follows:[1]

$$MU_{oranges} = 30 \text{ utils}$$
$$MU_{apples} = 20 \text{ utils}$$
$$P_{oranges} = \$1$$
$$P_{apples} = \$1$$

So the consumer's marginal (last) dollar spent on apples returns 20 utils per dollar, and his marginal (last) dollar spent on oranges returns 30 utils per dollar. The ratio MU_O/P_O (O = oranges) is greater than the ratio MU_A/P_A (A = apples): $MU_O/P_O > MU_A/P_A$.

If the consumer found himself in this situation one week, he would redirect his purchases of apples and oranges the next week. He would think: If I buy an orange, I receive more utility (30 utils) than if I buy an apple (20 utils). It's better to buy 1 more orange with $1 and 1 less apple. I gain 30 utils from buying the orange, which is 10 utils more than if I buy the apple.

 Q&A   *Can you give a numerical example that illustrates the solution to the diamond-water paradox?*

Look at the two tables below.

Units of water	MU (utils)	Units of diamonds	MU (utils)
1	100	1	60
2	99	2	59
–			
–			
100	1		

In the first two columns, we show the marginal utility of different units of water. In the second two columns, we show the marginal utility of different units of diamonds.

Notice that the first unit of water brings greater marginal utility (100 utils) than the first unit of diamonds (60 utils). If there were no more than 1 unit of each good in the world, water would likely be more expensive than diamonds. But there is more than 1 unit of each good in the world. We have assumed that there are 100 units of water and 2 units of diamonds.

Because there is so much more water than diamonds, we end up consuming water around the one-hundredth unit (where marginal utility is low) and consuming diamonds around the second unit (where marginal utility is high).

---

[1] You may wonder where we get these marginal utility figures. They are points on hypothetical marginal utility curves such as the one in Exhibit 1. The important point is that one number is greater than the other. We could easily have picked other numbers, such as 300 and 200.

What happens as the consumer buys 1 more orange and 1 less apple? The marginal utility of oranges falls (recall what the law of diminishing marginal utility says happens as a person consumes additional units of a good), and the marginal utility of apples rises (the consumer is consuming fewer apples). Because the consumer has bought 1 more orange and 1 less apple, he now has 11 oranges and 9 apples. At this new combination of goods,

$$MU_{oranges} = 25 \text{ utils}$$
$$MU_{apples} = 25 \text{ utils}$$
$$P_{oranges} = \$1$$
$$P_{apples} = \$1$$

Now, the ratio MU_O/P_O equals the ratio MU_A/P_A. The consumer is getting exactly the same amount of utility (25 utils) per dollar from each of the 2 goods. There is no way for the consumer to redirect his purchases (buy more of 1 good and less of another good) and have more utility. Thus, the consumer is in equilibrium. In short, a consumer is in equilibrium when he or she derives the same marginal utility per dollar for all goods. The condition for **consumer equilibrium** is

$$\frac{MU_A}{P_A} = \frac{MU_B}{P_B} = \frac{MU_C}{P_C} = \ldots = \frac{MU_Z}{P_Z}$$

where the letters A–Z represent all the goods a person buys.[2]

A person in consumer equilibrium has *maximized his total utility*. By spending his dollars on goods that give him the greatest marginal utility and in the process bringing about the consumer equilibrium condition, he is adding as much to his total utility as he can possibly add.

> **Consumer Equilibrium**
>
> Occurs when the consumer has spent all income and the marginal utilities per dollar spent on each good purchased are equal: $MU_A/P_A = MU_B/P_B = \ldots = MU_Z/P_Z$, where the letters A–Z represent all the goods a person buys.

Maximizing Utility and the Law of Demand

Suppose a consumer is currently in equilibrium; that is,

$$\frac{MU_O}{P_O} = \frac{MU_A}{P_A}$$

When the consumer is in equilibrium, he or she is maximizing utility.

Now suppose the price of oranges falls. The situation now becomes this:

$$\frac{MU_O}{P_O} > \frac{MU_A}{P_A}$$

The consumer will attempt to restore equilibrium by buying more oranges. This behavior—buying more oranges when the price of oranges falls—is consistent with the law of demand.

We conclude: The consumer's attempt to reach equilibrium—which is simply another way of saying that the consumer is seeking to maximize utility—is consistent with the law of demand. In short, utility maximization is consistent with the law of demand.

Should the Government Provide the Necessities of Life for Free?

Sometimes, you will hear people say, "Food and water are necessities of life. No one can live without them. It is wrong to charge for these goods. The government should provide them free to everyone."

Or you might hear, "Medical care is a necessity to those who are sick. Without it, people will either experience an extremely low quality

Thinking like **AN ECONOMIST** *The economist knows that if certain things are true, then certain other things follow. To illustrate, if people seek to maximize utility, then the law of demand follows. How so? Start in consumer equilibrium where the marginal utility-price ratio (MU/P) for good A equals the marginal utility-price ratio for good B: $MU_A/P_A = MU_B/P_B$. Now let the price of good A fall. We now get $MU_A/P_A > MU_B/P_B$. To increase his utility, the person in this position buys more A (and less B). In other words, to increase his utility (maximize utility), the person buys more of a good when the price of the good falls.*

---

[2] We are assuming here that the consumer exhausts his or her income and that saving is treated as a good.

economics 24/7

HOW YOU PAY FOR GOOD WEATHER

Suppose there are two cities that are alike in every way except one—the weather. We'll call one city Good-Weather City (*GWC*) and the other Bad-Weather City (*BWC*). In *GWC*, temperatures are moderate all year (75 degrees) and the sky is always blue. In *BWC*, the winter brings snow and freezing rain, and the summer brings high humidity and high temperatures. *BWC* has all the forms of weather that people dislike. We assume people get more utility from living in good weather than from living in bad weather. We also assume the median price of a home in the two cities is the same—$200,000.

In terms of marginal utility and housing prices,

$$\frac{MU_{GWC}}{P_{H,GWC}} > \frac{MU_{BWC}}{P_{H,BWC}}$$

That is, the marginal utility of living in *GWC* (MU_{GWC}) divided by the price of a house in *GWC* ($P_{H,GWC}$) is greater than the marginal utility of living in *BWC* (MU_{BWC}) divided by the price of a house in *BWC* ($P_{H,BWC}$). In other words, there is greater utility per dollar in *GWC* than in *BWC*.

What will people do? At least some people will move from *BWC* to *GWC*. The people in *BWC* who want to move will put their houses up for sale. This will increase the supply of houses for sale and lower the price. As these people move to *GWC*, they increase the demand for houses, and house prices in *GWC* begin to rise.

This process will continue until the price of a house in *GWC* has risen high enough, and the price of a house in *BWC* has fallen low enough, so that the *MU/P* ratios in the two cities are the same. In other words, the process continues until this condition is reached:

$$\frac{MU_{GWC}}{P_{H,GWC}} = \frac{MU_{BWC}}{P_{H,BWC}}$$

When this has occurred, one receives the same utility per dollar in the two cities. In other words, the two cities are the same.

Now let's consider a young couple that has to choose between living in the two cities. Is it clear that the young couple will choose *GWC* instead of *BWC* because *GWC* has a better climate? Not at all. *GWC* has a better climate than *BWC*, but *BWC* has lower housing prices. One partner says, "Let's live in *GWC*. Think of all that great weather we'll enjoy. We can go outside every day." The other partner says, "But if we live in *BWC*, we can have either a much bigger and better house for the money or more money to spend on things other than housing. Think of the better cars and clothes we'll be able to buy or the vacations we'll be able to take because we won't have to spend as much money to buy a house."

What has happened is that the initial greater satisfaction of living in *GWC* (the higher utility per dollar) has been eroded by people moving to *GWC* and raising housing prices. *GWC* doesn't look as good as it once did.

On the other hand, *BWC* doesn't look as (relatively) bad as it once did. It still doesn't have the good climate that *GWC* has, but it has lower housing prices now. The utility per dollar of living in *BWC* has risen as a consequence of housing prices falling.

As long as one city is better (in some way) than another, people will move to the relatively better city. In the process, they will change things just enough so that it is no longer relatively better. In the end, you have to pay for paradise.

of life (you can't experience a high quality of life when you're sick) or die. Making people pay for medical care is wrong. The government should provide it free to the people who need it."

Each of these statements labels something as a necessity of life (food and water, medical care) and then makes the policy proposal that government should provide the necessity for free.

Suppose government did give food, water, and medical care to everyone for free—at zero price (although not at zero taxes). At zero price, people would want to consume these goods up to the point of zero marginal utility for each good. They would do so because if the marginal utility of the good (expressed in dollars) is greater than its price, one could derive more utility from purchasing the good than one would lose in parting with the dollar price of the good. That is, if the price of a good is $5, an individual will continue consuming it as long as the marginal utility she derives from it is greater than $5. If the price is $0, she will continue to consume the good as long as the marginal utility she derives from it is greater than $0.

Resources must be used to produce every unit of a good consumed. If the government uses scarce resources to provide goods that have low marginal utility (which food, water, and medical care would have at zero price), then fewer resources are available to produce other goods. However, if some resources are withdrawn from producing these low-utility goods, total utility would fall very little. The resources could then be redirected to producing goods with a higher marginal utility, thereby raising total utility.

The people who argue that certain goods should be provided free implicitly assume that the not-so-valuable uses of food, water, and medical care are valuable enough to warrant a system of taxes to pay for the complete provision of these goods at zero price. It is questionable, however, if the least valuable uses of food, water, and medical care are worth the sacrifices of other goods that would necessarily be forfeited if more of these goods were produced.

Think about this: Currently, water is relatively cheap, and people use it to satisfy its more valuable uses and its not-so-valuable uses too. But suppose water was cheaper than it is. Suppose it had a zero price. Would it be used to satisfy its more valuable uses, its not-so-valuable uses, and its absolutely least valuable use? If food had a zero price, would it be used to satisfy its more valuable uses, its not-so-valuable uses, and its absolutely least valuable use (food fights perhaps)?

SELF-TEST

1.   Alesandro purchases two goods, *X* and *Y*, and the utility gained for the last unit purchased of each is 16 utils and 23 utils, respectively. The prices of *X* and *Y* are $1 and $1.75, respectively. Is Alesandro in consumer equilibrium? Explain your answer.

2.   In a two-good world, in which the goods are *A* and *B*, what does it mean to be in consumer disequilibrium?

Behavioral Economics

Economists are interested in how people behave. This chapter has shown how economists predict people will behave when the MU/P ratio for one good is greater than it is for another good. In this situation, economic theory predicts that individuals will buy more of the good with the higher MU/P ratio and less of the good with the lower MU/P ratio. In other words, individuals, seeking to maximize their utility, buy more of one good and less of another good until the MU/P ratio for all goods is the same.

In traditional economic theories and models, individuals are assumed to be rational, self-interested, and consistent. For about the last 30 years, behavioral economists have challenged the traditional economic models. Behavioral economists argue that some human behavior does not fit neatly—at a minimum, easily—into the traditional economic framework. In this section, we describe some of the findings of behavioral economists.

Are People Willing to Reduce Others' Incomes?

Two economists, Daniel Zizzo and Andrew Oswald, set up a series of experiments with 4 groups, each with 4 people. Each person was given the same amount of money and asked to gamble with the new money. At the end of each act of gambling, 2 of the 4 persons in each group had won money and 2 had lost money. Then each of the 4 people in each group was given the opportunity to pay some amount of money to reduce the take of the others in the group. To illustrate, suppose in the group consisting of Smith, Jones, Brown, and Adams, Smith and Adams had more money after gambling, and Jones and Brown had less money. All four were given the opportunity to reduce the amount of money held by the others in the group. For example, Brown could pay to reduce Smith's money, Jones could pay to reduce Adams's, and so on.

At this point, some people argue that no one will spend his money to hurt someone else if it means leaving himself poorer. However, Zizzo and Oswald found that 62 percent of the participants did just that: They made themselves worse off to make someone else worse off.

Why might people behave this way? One explanation is that individuals are concerned with relative rank and status more than with absolute well-being. Thus, the poorer of the two individuals doesn't mind paying, say, 25 cents if it means he can reduce the richer person's take by, say, $1. After the 25 cents is spent by the poorer person, the gap between him and the richer person is smaller.

Some economists argue that such behavior is irrational and inconsistent with utility maximization. Other economists say it is no such thing. They argue that if people get utility from relative rank, then, in effect, what is happening is that people are buying a move up the relative rank ladder by reducing the size of the gap between themselves and others.

Is $1 Always $1?

Do people treat money differently depending on where it comes from? Traditional economics argues that they should not—after all, a dollar is a dollar is a dollar. Specifically, $1 that someone gives to you as a gift is no different from $1 you earn or $1 you find on the street. When people treat some dollars differently from other dollars, they are *compartmentalizing.* They are saying that dollars in some compartments (of their minds) are valued differently from dollars in other compartments.

Let's consider the following situation. Suppose you plan to see a Broadway play, the ticket for which costs $100. You buy the $100 ticket on Monday to see the play on Friday night. When Friday night arrives, you realize you have lost the ticket. *Do you spend another $100 to buy another ticket (assuming another ticket can be purchased)?*[3]

Now let's change the circumstances slightly. Suppose instead of buying the ticket on Monday, you plan to buy the ticket at the ticket window on Friday night. At the ticket window on Friday night, you realize you have lost $100 somewhere between home and the theater. *Assuming you still have enough money to buy a $100 ticket to the play, do you buy it?*

Now, regardless of how you answer each question, some economists argue that your answers should be consistent. If you say no to the first question, you should say no to the second question. If you say yes to the first question, you should say yes to the second question. That's because the two questions, based on two slightly different settings, essentially present you with the same choice.

However, many people, when asked the two questions, say that they will not pay an additional $100 to buy a second ticket (having lost the first $100 ticket) but will spend an additional $100 to buy a first ticket (having lost $100 in cash between home and the theater). Why? Some people argue that spending an additional $100 on an additional

Could you give an example of a person who benefits in absolute terms but finds himself declining in relative terms?

Look at the table that follows.

Person	Dollar Income
A	$100,000
B	80,000
C	60,000
D	40,000
E	20,000

Person B has a dollar income of $80,000, and his income is the second highest of the five persons. Now suppose everyone's income rises by $100,000—except for B's income. His income rises by $20,000. In absolute dollar terms, B is better off. But in relative terms, his income is now the lowest of the five persons. His income rises in absolute terms (going from $80,000 to $100,000) but falls in relative terms (going from second highest to lowest).

---

[3]The example comes from Gary Belsky and Thomas Gilovich, *Why Smart People Make Big Money Mistakes and How to Correct Them* (New York: Simon & Schuster, 1999).

ticket is the same as paying $200 to see the play—and that is just too much to pay. However, they don't see themselves as spending $200 to see the play when they lose $100 and pay $100 for a ticket. In either case, though, $200 is gone.

Behavioral economists argue that people who answer the two questions differently (yes to one and no to the other) are compartmentalizing. They are treating two $100 amounts in two different ways—as if they come from two different compartments. For example, the person who says she will not buy a second $100 ticket (having lost the first $100 ticket) but will buy a first ticket (having lost $100 cash) is effectively saying by her behavior that $100 lost on a ticket is different from $100 lost in cash.

Let's consider another situation. Suppose you earn $1,000 by working hard at a job and also win $1,000 at the roulette table in Las Vegas. Would you feel freer to spend the $1,000 won in Las Vegas than to spend the $1,000 you worked hard to earn? If the answer is yes, then you are treating money differently depending on where it came from and what you had to do to get it. Nothing is necessarily wrong or immoral about that, but still, it is interesting because $1,000 is $1,000 is $1,000—no matter where it came from and no matter what you had to do to get it.

Finally, let's look at an experiment conducted by two marketing professors. Drazen Prelec and Duncan Simester once organized a sealed-bid auction to a Boston Celtics basketball game. Half the participants in the auction were told that if they had the winning bid, they had to pay in cash. The other half of the participants were told that if they had the winning bid, they had to pay with a credit card.

One would think that the average bid from the people who had to pay cash would be the same as the average bid from the people who had to pay with a credit card—assuming that the two groups were divided randomly and that no group showed a stronger or weaker preference for seeing the Celtics game. But this didn't happen. The average bid of the people who had to pay with a credit card was higher than the average bid of the people who had to pay with cash. Using a credit card somehow caused people to bid higher dollar amounts than they would have bid had they known they were going to pay cash. Money from the credit card compartment seemed to be more quickly or easily spent than money from the cash compartment.

Coffee Mugs and the Endowment Effect

In one economic experiment, coffee mugs were allocated randomly to half the people in a group. Each person with a mug was asked to state a price at which he would be willing to sell his mug. Each person without a mug was asked to state a price at which he would be willing to buy a mug.

It turns out that, even though the mugs were allocated randomly (dispelling the idea that somehow the people who received a mug valued it more than the people who did not receive one), the lowest price at which the owner would sell the mug was, on average, higher than the highest price at which a buyer would pay to buy a mug. It is as if sellers said they wouldn't sell mugs for less than $15, and buyers said they wouldn't buy mugs for more than $10.

This outcome—which is called the *endowment effect*—is odd. It's odd because even though there is absolutely no reason to believe that the people who received the mugs valued them more than the people who didn't receive them, it turns out that people place a higher value on something (like a mug) simply because they own it. In other words, people seem to show an inclination to hold on to what they have.

If this applies to you, think of what it means. When you go into a store to buy a sweater, you say the sweater is worth no more to you than, say, $40, and you are not willing to pay more than $40 for it. But if someone gave you the sweater as a gift and you were asked to sell it, you wouldn't be willing to sell it for less than, say, $50. Simply owning the sweater makes it more valuable to you.

Economist David Friedman says that such behavior is not limited to humans.[4] He points out that some species of animals exhibit territorial behavior—that is, they are more likely to fight to keep what they have than fight to get what they don't have. As Friedman notes, "It is a familiar observation that a dog will fight harder to keep his own bone than to take another dog's bone."

Friedman argues that this type of behavior in humans makes perfect sense in a hunter-gatherer society. Here is what Friedman has to say:

> Now consider the same logic [found in the fact that a dog will fight harder to keep the bone he has than to take a bone from another dog] in a hunter-gatherer society—in which there are no external institutions to enforce property rights. Imagine that each individual considers every object in sight, decides how much each is worth to him, and then tries to appropriate it, with the outcome of the resulting Hobbesian struggle determined by some combination of how much each wants things and how strong each individual is. It does not look like a formula for a successful society, even on the scale of a hunter-gatherer band.
>
> There is an alternative solution, assuming that humans are at least as smart as dogs, robins, and fish. Some method, possibly as simple as physical possession, is used to define what "belongs to" whom. Each individual then commits himself to fight very hard to protect his "property"—much harder than he would be willing to fight in order to appropriate a similar object from someone else's possession—with the commitment made via some psychological mechanism presumably hardwired into humans. The result is both a considerably lower level of (risky) violence and a considerably more prosperous society.
>
> The fact that the result is attractive does not, of course, guarantee that it will occur—evolution selects for the reproductive interest of the individual, not the group. But in this case they are the same. To see that, imagine a population in which some individuals have adopted the commitment strategy [outlined above—that is, fighting for what you physically possess], and some have adopted different commitment strategies—for example, a strategy of fighting to the death for whatever they see as valuable. It should be fairly easy to see that individuals in the first group will, on average, do better for themselves—hence have (among other things) greater reproductive success—than those in the second group.
>
> How do I commit myself to fight very hard for something? One obvious way is some psychological quirk that makes that something appear very valuable to me. Hence the same behavior pattern that shows up as territorial behavior in fish and ferocious defense of bones in dogs shows up in Cornell students [who were given the coffee mugs] as an endowment effect. Just as in the earlier cases, behavior that was functional in the environment in which we evolved continues to be observed, even in an environment in which its function has largely disappeared.[5]

We value X more highly if we have it than if we do not have it because such behavior at one point in our evolution made possible a system of property rights in a world where the alternative was the Hobbesian jungle.

Does the Endowment Effect Hold Only for New Traders?

The endowment effect has not gone untested. John List, an economist at the University of Maryland, wanted to know if new traders were more likely to experience the endowment effect than experienced traders were. He went to a sports-card exchange where people trade regularly. In one experiment, he took aside a group of card fans and gave them such things as sports autographs and sports badges. He then gave them the opportunity to trade. It turned out that the more experience the trader had (at trading such items), the less prone he or she was to the endowment effect.

One criticism of this experiment was that novice traders were less likely to trade than were experienced traders because novices were not sure what the sports autographs

[4]See his "Economics and Evolutionary Psychology" at his Web site, http://www.daviddfriedman.com/JLE/jie.htm.
[5]Ibid., p. 10.

were worth. To meet this criticism, List conducted another experiment with chocolate and coffee mugs where he was sure everyone did know the values of the items. Once again, there was some endowment effect, but it was not as strong as in the sports memorabilia case, and—more important—it was only present with newer traders. In other words, experience as a trader seems to make one less prone to the endowment effect.

SELF-TEST

1. Brandon's grandmother is very cautious about spending money. Yesterday, she gave Brandon a gift of $100 for his birthday. Brandon also received a gift of $100 from his father, who isn't nearly as cautious about spending money as Brandon's grandmother is. Brandon believes that it would somehow be wrong to spend his grandmother's gift on frivolous things, but it wouldn't be wrong to spend his father's gift on such things. Is Brandon compartmentalizing? Explain your answer.

2. Summarize David Friedman's explanation of the endowment effect.

A Reader Asks . . .

Do People Really Equate Marginal Utility-Price Ratios?

Am I expected to believe that real people actually go around with marginal utility-price ratios in their heads and that they behave according to how these ratios change? After all, most people don't even know what marginal utility is.

We could answer that most people may not know the laws of physics, but this doesn't prevent their behavior from being consistent with the laws of physics. But we present a different argument. First, let's review how a person who equates MU/P ratios behaves in accordance with the law of demand. When the MU/P ratio for good A is equal to the MU/P ratio for good B, the person is in consumer equilibrium. Suppose the price of good A falls so that the MU/P ratio for good A is now greater than the MU/P ratio for B. What does the individual do? To maximize utility, we predict that the person will buy more of good A because he receives more utility per dollar buying A than he does buying B. Buying more A when the price of good A declines—to maximize utility—is consistent with the law of demand, which states that price and quantity demanded are inversely related, *ceteris paribus*. In other words, to act in accordance with the law of demand is consistent with equating MU/P ratios.

Now our real question is, "Is it possible that people act in a manner consistent with the law of demand, even though they don't know what the law of demand says?" If the answer is yes, then they are acting *as if* they are equating MU/P ratios in their heads.

But let's not talk about people for a minute. Let's talk about rats. Certainly, rats do not understand what marginal utility is. They will not be able to define it, compute it, or do anything else with it. But do they act *as if* they equate MU/P ratios? Do they observe the law of demand?

With these questions in mind, consider an experiment conducted by economists at Texas A&M University, who undertook to study the "buying" behavior of two white rats. Each rat was put in a laboratory cage with two levers. By pushing one lever, a rat obtained root beer; by pushing the other lever, it obtained non-alcoholic collins mix. Every day, each rat was given a "fixed income" of 300 pushes. (When the combined total of pushes on the two levers reached 300, the levers could not be pushed down until the next day.) The prices of root beer and collins mix were both 20 pushes per milliliter of beverage. Given this income and the price of root beer and collins mix, one rat settled in to consuming 11 milliliters of root beer and 4 milliliters of collins mix. The other rat settled in to consuming almost all root beer.

Then the prices of the two beverages were changed. The price of collins mix was halved while the price of root beer was doubled.[6] Using economic theory, we would predict that with these new prices, the consumption of collins mix would increase and the consumption of root beer would decrease. This is exactly what happened. Both rats began to consume more collins mix and less root beer. In short, both rats had

downward-sloping demand curves for collins mix and root beer.

The point? If the behavior of rats is consistent with the law of demand and the law of demand is consistent with equating *MU/P* ratios, then do you really have to know you are equating *MU/P* ratios before you can be doing it? Obviously not.

[6] The researchers raised the price of root beer by reducing the quantity of root beer dispensed per push. This is the same as increasing the number of pushes necessary to obtain the original quantity of root beer.

! analyzing the scene

How is buying a house in a good school district like sending children to a private school?

Zach and Viv are thinking of moving to the east side of town to be in a better school district. Better-than-average public schools come with a price tag, though. The price tag is generally attached to the houses located in the better-than-average school district. In short, houses in better-than-average school districts have a higher price than houses in average or below-average school districts, *ceteris paribus*. Zach doesn't want to stay in the current house and send their children to a private school because he doesn't want to pay for a private school. But he will have to pay for better schooling one way or another: Either buy the higher priced house in the better-than-average school district or stay in the old house and pay for a private school.

What is the price of an ocean view?

In the feature "How You Pay for Good Weather," we explain how a house located in a city with good weather will be priced higher than a house located in a city with bad weather. We pay a premium for things that are "above average" (like the house in the good-weather city), and we receive a discount for things that are "below average" (like the house in the bad-weather city). A house located in a good school district is similar to a house in a good-weather city.

Now, let's consider the price of an ocean view. Barbara and Steve are looking at two houses on the same street. The houses are similar except that one has an ocean view and the other doesn't. The price of the ocean view is the dollar difference between the prices of the two houses. If, for example, the house with the view is priced at $750,000 and the house without the view is priced at $500,000, then the price of the ocean view is $250,000.

chapter summary

The Law of Diminishing Marginal Utility

- The law of diminishing marginal utility holds that as the amount of a good consumed increases, the marginal utility of the good decreases.
- The law of diminishing marginal utility should not be used to make interpersonal utility comparisons. For example, the law does not say that a millionaire receives less (or more) utility from an additional dollar than a poor man receives. Instead, it says that for both the

millionaire and the poor man, the last dollar has less value for both the millionaire and the poor man than the next-to-last dollar has.

The Diamond-Water Paradox

- The diamond-water paradox states that what has great value in use sometimes has little value in exchange, and what has little value in use sometimes has great value in exchange. A knowledge of the difference between total utility and marginal utility is necessary to unravel the diamond-water paradox.

- A good can have high total utility and low marginal utility. For example, water's total utility is high, but because water is so plentiful, its marginal utility is low. In short, water is immensely useful, but it is so plentiful that individuals place relatively low value on another unit of it. In contrast, diamonds are not as useful as water, but because there are few diamonds in the world, the marginal utility of diamonds is high. In summary, a good can be extremely useful and have a low price if the good is in plentiful supply (high value in use, low value in exchange). On the other hand, a good can be of little use and have a high price if the good is in short supply (low value in use, high value in exchange).

Consumer Equilibrium

- Individuals seek to equate marginal utilities per dollar. For example, if a person receives more utility per dollar spent on good A than on good B, she will reorder her purchases and buy more A and less B. There is a tendency to move away from the condition $MU_A/P_A > MU_B/P_B$ to the condition $MU_A/P_A = MU_B/P_B$. The latter condition represents consumer equilibrium (in a two-good world).

Marginal Utility Analysis and the Law of Demand

- Marginal utility analysis can be used to illustrate the law of demand. The law of demand states that price and quantity demanded are inversely related, *ceteris paribus.* Starting from consumer equilibrium in a world in which there are only two goods, A and B, a fall in the price of A will cause MU_A/P_A to be greater than MU_B/P_B. As a result, the consumer will purchase more of good A to restore herself to equilibrium.

Behavioral Economics

- Behavioral economists argue that some human behavior does not fit neatly—at a minimum, easily—into the traditional economic framework.

- Behavioral economists believe they have identified human behaviors that are inconsistent with the model of men and women as rational, self-interested, and consistent. These behaviors include the following: (1) Individuals are willing to spend some money to lower the incomes of others even if it means their incomes will be lowered. (2) Individuals don't always treat $1 as $1; some dollars seem to be treated differently from other dollars. (3) Individuals sometimes value X more if it is theirs than if it isn't theirs and they are seeking to acquire it.

key terms and concepts

Diamond-Water Paradox	Util	Marginal Utility	Interpersonal Utility Comparison
Utility	Total Utility	Law of Diminishing Marginal Utility	Consumer Equilibrium

questions and problems

1 "If we take $1 away from a rich person and give it to a poor person, the rich person loses less utility than the poor person gains." Comment.

2 Is it possible to get so much of a good that it turns into a bad? If so, give an example.

3 If a person consumes fewer units of a good, will marginal utility of the good increase as total utility decreases? Why or why not?

4 Assume the marginal utility of good A is 4 utils and its price is $2, and the marginal utility of good B is 6 utils

and its price is $1. Is the individual consumer maximizing (total) utility if she spends a total of $3 by buying one unit of each good? If not, how can more utility be obtained?

5 Individuals who buy second homes usually spend less for them than they do for their first homes. Why is this the case?

6 Describe five everyday examples of you or someone else making an interpersonal utility comparison.

7 Is there a logical link between the law of demand and the assumption that individuals seek to maximize utility? (Hint: Think of how the condition for consumer equilibrium can be used to express the inverse relationship between price and quantity demanded.)

8 List five sets of two goods (each set is composed of two goods; e.g., diamonds and water are one set) where the good with the greater value in use has a lower value in exchange than does the good with the lower value in use.

9 Do you think people with high IQs are in consumer equilibrium (equate marginal utilities per dollar) more often than people with low IQs? Why or why not?

10 What is the endowment effect?

11 After each toss of the coin, one person has more money and one person has less. If the person with less money cares about relative rank and status, will he be willing to pay, say, $1 to reduce the other person's winnings by, say, 50 cents? Will he be willing to pay 25 cents to reduce the other person's winnings by $1? Explain your answers.

working with numbers and graphs

1 The marginal utility for the third unit of X is 60 utils, and the marginal utility for the fourth unit of X is 45 utils. If the law of diminishing marginal utility holds, what is the minimum total utility?

2 Fill in blanks A–D in the following table.

Units of Good Consumed	Total Utility (utils)	Marginal Utility (utils)
1	10	10
2	19	A
3	B	8
4	33	C
5	35	D

3 The total utilities of the first 5 units of good X are 10, 19, 26, 33, and 40 utils, respectively. In other words, the total utility of 1 unit is 10 utils, the total utility of 2 units is 19 utils, and so on. What is the marginal utility of the third unit?

Use the following table to answer Questions 4 and 5.

Units of Good X	TU of Good X (utils)	Units of Good Y	TU of Good Y (utils)
1	20	1	19
2	35	2	32
3	48	3	40
4	58	4	45
5	66	5	49

4 If George spends $5 (total) a week on good X and good Y, and if the price of each good is $1 per unit, then how many units of each good does he purchase to maximize utility?

5 Given the number of units of each good George purchased in Question 4, what is his total utility?

6 Draw the marginal utility curve for a good that has constant marginal utility.

7 The marginal utility curve for units 3–5 of good X is below the horizontal axis. Draw the corresponding part of the total utility curve for good X.

C

Budget Constraint and Indifference Curve Analysis

This chapter uses marginal utility theory to discuss consumer choice. Sometimes budget constraint and indifference curve analysis is used instead, especially in upper-division economics courses. We examine this important topic in this appendix.

The Budget Constraint

Budget Constraint

All the combinations or bundles of two goods a person can purchase given a certain money income and prices for the two goods.

Societies have production possibilities frontiers, and individuals have **budget constraints**. The budget constraint is built on two prices and the individual's income. To illustrate, consider O'Brien, who has a monthly income of $1,200. In a world of two goods, X and Y, O'Brien can spend his total income on X, he can spend his total income on Y, or he can spend part of his income on X and part on Y. Suppose the price of X is $100 and the price of Y is $80. Given this, if O'Brien spends his total income on X, he can purchase a maximum of 12 units; if he spends his total income on Y, he can purchase a maximum of 15 units. Locating these two points on a two-dimensional diagram and then drawing a line between them, as shown in Exhibit 1, gives us O'Brien's budget constraint. Any point on the budget constraint, as well as any point below it, represents a possible combination (bundle) of the two goods available to O'Brien.

Slope of the Budget Constraint

The slope of the budget constraint has special significance. The absolute value of the slope represents the relative prices of the two goods, X and Y. In Exhibit 1, the slope, or

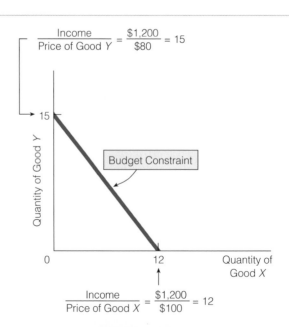

$$\frac{\text{Income}}{\text{Price of Good } Y} = \frac{\$1,200}{\$80} = 15$$

$$\frac{\text{Income}}{\text{Price of Good } X} = \frac{\$1,200}{\$100} = 12$$

P_X / P_Y, is equal to 1.25, indicating that the relative price of 1 unit of X is 1.25 units of Y.

What Will Change the Budget Constraint?

The budget constraint is built on two prices and the individual's income. This means that if any of the three variables changes (either of the prices or the individual's income), the budget constraint changes. Not all changes are alike, however. Consider a fall in the price of good X from \$100 to \$60. With this change, the maximum number of units of good X purchasable with an income of \$1,200 rises from 12 to 20. The budget constraint revolves away from the origin, as shown in Exhibit 2(a). Notice that the number of O'Brien's possible combinations of the two goods increases; there are more bundles of the two goods available after the price decrease than before.

Consider what happens to the budget constraint if the price of good X rises. If it goes from \$100 to \$150, the maximum number of units of good X falls from 12 to 8. The budget constraint revolves toward the origin. As a consequence, the number of bundles available to O'Brien decreases. We conclude that a change in the price of either good changes the slope of the budget constraint, with the result that relative prices and the number of bundles available to the individual also change.

We turn now to a change in income. If O'Brien's income rises to \$1,600, the maximum number of units of X rises to 16 and the maximum number of units of Y rises to 20. The budget constraint shifts rightward (away from the origin) and is parallel to the old budget constraint. As a consequence, the number of bundles available to O'Brien increases (Exhibit 2(b)). If O'Brien's income falls from \$1,200 to \$800, the extreme end points on the budget constraint become 8 and 10 for X and Y, respectively. The budget constraint shifts leftward (toward the origin) and is parallel to the old budget constraint. As a consequence, the number of bundles available to O'Brien falls (Exhibit 2(b)).

Indifference Curves

An individual can, of course, choose any bundle of the two goods on or below the budget constraint. We assume that she spends her total income and therefore chooses a point on the budget constraint. This raises two important questions: (1) Which bundle of the many bundles of the two goods does the individual choose? (2) How does the individual's chosen combination of goods change given a change in prices or income? Both

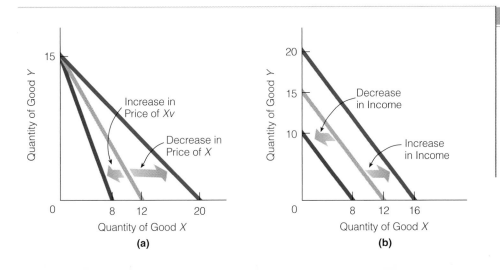

exhibit **2**

Changes in the Budget Constraint

(a) A change in the price of good X or good Y will change the slope of the budget constraint. (b) A change in income will change the position of the budget constraint while the slope remains constant. Whenever a budget constraint changes, the number of combinations (bundles) of the two goods available to the individual changes too.

questions can be answered by combining the budget constraint with the graphical expression of the individual's preferences—that is, indifference curves.

Constructing an Indifference Curve

Is it possible to be indifferent between two bundles of goods? Yes, it is. Suppose bundle *A* consists of 2 pairs of shoes and 6 shirts and bundle *B* consists of 3 pairs of shoes and 4 shirts. A person who is indifferent between these two bundles is implicitly saying that it doesn't matter which bundle he has; one is as good as the other. He is likely to say this, though, only if he receives equal total utility from the two bundles. If this were not the case, he would prefer one bundle to the other.

If we tabulate all the different bundles from which the individual receives equal utility, we have an **indifference set**. We can then plot the data in the indifference set and draw an **indifference curve**. Consider the indifference set illustrated in Exhibit 3(a). There are four bundles of goods, *A–D*; each bundle gives the same total utility as every other bundle. These equal-utility bundles are plotted in Exhibit 3(b). Connecting these bundles in a two-dimensional space gives us an indifference curve.

Characteristics of Indifference Curves

Indifference curves for goods have certain characteristics that are consistent with reasonable assumptions about consumer behavior.

1. **Indifference curves are downward-sloping (from left to right).** The assumption that consumers always prefer more of a good to less requires that indifference curves slope downward left to right. Consider the alternatives to downward-sloping: vertical, horizontal, and upward-sloping (left to right). A horizontal or vertical curve would combine bundles of goods some of which had more of one good and no less of another good than other bundles (Exhibit 4(a–b)). (If bundle *B* contains more of one good and no less of another good than bundle *A,* would an individual be *indifferent* between the two bundles? No, he or she wouldn't. Individuals prefer more to less.) An upward-sloping curve would combine bundles of goods some of which had more of *both* goods than other bundles (Exhibit 4(c)). A simpler way of putting

Indifference Set

Group of bundles of two goods that give an individual equal total utility.

Indifference Curve

Represents an indifference set. A curve that shows all the bundles of two goods that give an individual equal total utility.

---

exhibit **3**

An Indifference Set and an Indifference Curve

An indifference set is a number of bundles of two goods in which each bundle yields the same total utility. An indifference curve represents an indifference set. In this exhibit, data from the indifference set (a) are used to derive an indifference curve (b).

An Indifference Set		
Bundle	**Milk (units)**	**Orange Juice (units)**
A	8	3
B	5	4
C	3	5
D	2	6

(a)

(b)

Indifference Curves for Goods Do Not Look Like This

(a) Bundle *B* has more milk and no less orange juice than bundle *A*, so an individual would prefer *B* to *A* and not be indifferent between them.
(b) Bundle *B* has more orange juice and no less milk than bundle *A*, so an individual would prefer *B* to *A* and not be indifferent between them.
(c) Bundle *B* has more milk and more orange juice than bundle *A*, so an individual would prefer *B* to *A* and not be indifferent between them.

it is to say that indifference curves are downward-sloping because a person has to get more of one good in order to maintain his or her level of satisfaction (utility) when giving up some of another good.

2. **Indifference curves are convex to the origin.** This implies that the slope of the indifference curve becomes flatter as we move down and to the right along the indifference curve. For example, at 8 units of milk (point *A* in Exhibit 3(b)), the individual is willing to give up 3 units of milk to get an additional unit of orange juice (and thus move to point *B*). At point *B*, where she has 5 units of milk, she is willing to give up only 2 units of milk to get an additional unit of orange juice (and thus move to point *C*). Finally, at point *C*, with 3 units of milk, she is now willing to give up only 1 unit of milk to get an additional unit of orange juice. We conclude that the more of one good that an individual has, the more units he or she will give up to get an additional unit of another good; the less of one good that an individual has, the fewer units he or she will give up to get an additional unit of another good. Is this reasonable? The answer is yes. Our observation is a reflection of diminishing marginal utility at work. As the quantity of a good consumed increases, the marginal utility of that good decreases; therefore we reason that the more of one good an individual has, the more units he or she can (and will) sacrifice to get an additional unit of another good and still maintain total utility. Stated differently, if the law of diminishing marginal utility did not exist then it would not make sense to say that indifference curves of goods are convex to the origin.

An important peripheral point about marginal utilities is that *the absolute value of the slope of the indifference curve*—which is called the **marginal rate of substitution**—*represents the ratio of the marginal utility of the good on the horizontal axis to the marginal utility of the good on the vertical axis:*

$$\frac{MU_{\text{good on horizontal axis}}}{MU_{\text{good on vertical axis}}}$$

Let's look carefully at the words in italics. First, we said that the absolute value of the slope of the indifference curve is the marginal rate of substitution. The marginal rate of substitution (*MRS*) is the amount of one good an individual is willing to give up to obtain an additional unit of another good and maintain equal total utility. For example, in Exhibit 3(b), we see that moving from point *A* to point *B*, the individual is willing to give up 3 units of milk to get an additional unit of

Marginal Rate of Substitution

The amount of one good an individual is willing to give up to obtain an additional unit of another good and maintain equal total utility.

orange juice, with total utility remaining constant (between points A and B). The marginal rate of substitution is therefore 3 units of milk for 1 unit of orange juice in the area between points A and B. And as we said, the absolute value of the slope of the indifference curve, the marginal rate of substitution, is equal to the ratio of the MU of the good on the horizontal axis to the MU of the good on the vertical axis. How can this be? Well, if it is true that an individual giving up 3 units of milk and receiving 1 unit of orange juice maintains her total utility, it follows that (in the area under consideration) the marginal utility of orange juice is approximately three times the marginal utility of milk. In general terms

$$\text{Absolute value of the slope of the indifference curve} = \text{Marginal rate of substitution}$$
$$= \frac{MU_{\text{good on horizontal axis}}}{MU_{\text{good on vertical axis}}}$$

3. **Indifference curves that are farther from the origin are preferable because they represent larger bundles of goods.** Exhibit 3(b) shows only one indifference curve. However, different bundles of the two goods exist and have indifference curves passing through them. These bundles have less of both goods or more of both goods than those in Exhibit 3(b). Illustrating a number of indifference curves on the same diagram gives us an **indifference curve map**. Strictly speaking, an indifference curve map represents a number of indifference curves for a given individual with reference to two goods. A "mapping" is illustrated in Exhibit 5.

    Notice that although only five indifference curves have been drawn, many more could have been added. For example, there are many indifference curves between I_1 and I_2.

    Also notice that the farther away from the origin an indifference curve is, the higher total utility it represents. You can see this by comparing point A on I_1 and point B on I_2. At point B, there is the same amount of orange juice as at point A but more milk. Point B is therefore preferable to point A, and because B is on I_2 and A is on I_1, I_2 is preferable to I_1. The reason for this is simple: An individual receives more utility at any point on I_2 (because more goods are available) than at any point on I_1.

Indifference Curve Map

Represents a number of indifference curves for a given individual with reference to two goods.

---

exhibit **5**

An Indifference Map

A few of the many possible indifference curves are shown. Any point in the two-dimensional space is on an indifference curve. Indifference curves farther away from the origin represent greater total utility than those closer to the origin.

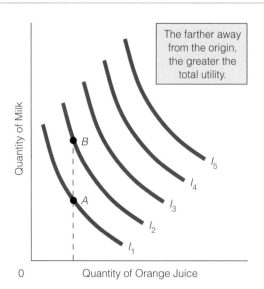

The farther away from the origin, the greater the total utility.

4. **Indifference curves do not cross (intersect).** Indifference curves do not cross because individuals' preferences are **transitive**. Consider the following example. If Kristin prefers Coca-Cola to Pepsi-Cola and she also prefers Pepsi-Cola to root beer, then it follows that she prefers Coca-Cola to root beer. If she preferred root beer to Coca-Cola, she would be contradicting her earlier preferences. To say that an individual has transitive preferences means that he or she maintains a logical order of preferences during a given time period. Consider what indifference curves that crossed would represent. In Exhibit 6, indifference curves I_1 and I_2 intersect at point A. Notice that point A lies on both I_1 and I_2. Comparing A and B, we hold that the individual must be indifferent between them because they lie on the same indifference curve. The same holds for A and C. But if the individual is indifferent between A and B and between A and C, it follows that she must be indifferent between B and C. But C has more of both goods than B, and thus the individual will not be indifferent between B and C; she will prefer C to B. We cannot have transitive preferences and make sense of crossing indifference curves. We can, however, have transitive preferences and make sense of non-crossing indifference curves. We go with the latter.

The Indifference Map and the Budget Constraint Come Together

At this point, we bring the indifference map and the budget constraint together to illustrate consumer equilibrium. We have the following facts: (1) The individual has a budget constraint. (2) The absolute value of the slope of the budget constraint is the relative prices of the two goods under consideration, say, P_X/P_Y. (3) The individual has an indifference map. (4) The absolute value of the slope of the indifference curve at any point is the marginal rate of substitution, which is equal to the marginal utility of one good divided by the marginal utility of another good; for example, MU_X/MU_Y.

With this information, what is the necessary condition for consumer equilibrium? Obviously, the individual will try to reach a point on the highest indifference curve she can reach. This point will be where the slope of the budget constraint is equal to the slope of an indifference curve (or where the budget constraint is tangent to an indifference curve). At this point, consumer equilibrium is established and the following condition holds:

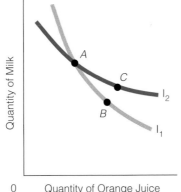

Slope of budget constraint = slope of indifference curve

$$\frac{P_X}{P_Y} = \frac{MU_X}{MU_Y}$$

This condition is met in Exhibit 7 at point E. Note that this condition looks similar to the condition for consumer equilibrium earlier in this chapter. By rearranging the terms in the condition, we get[1]

$$\frac{MU_X}{P_X} = \frac{MU_Y}{P_Y}$$

From Indifference Curves to a Demand Curve

We can now derive a demand curve within a budget constraint–indifference curve framework. Exhibit 8(a) shows two budget constraints, one reflecting a $10 price for good X and the other reflecting a $5 price for good X. Notice that as the price of X falls, the consumer moves from point A to point B. At B, 35 units of X are consumed; at A, 30 units of X were consumed. We conclude that a lower price for X results in greater consumption of X. By plotting the relevant price and quantity data, we derive a demand curve for good X in Exhibit 8(b).

Consumer Equilibrium

Consumer equilibrium exists at the point where the slope of the budget constraint is equal to the slope of an indifference curve, or where the budget constraint is tangent to an indifference curve. In the exhibit, this point is E. Here $P_X/P_Y = MU_X/MU_Y$; or rearranging, $MU_X/P_X = MU_Y/P_Y$.

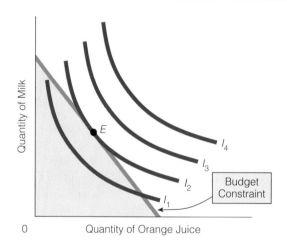

---

[1]Start with $P_X/P_Y = MU_X/MU_Y$ and cross multiply. This gives $P_X MU_Y = P_Y MU_X$. Next divide both sides by P_X. This gives $MU_Y = P_Y MU_X/P_X$. Finally, divide both sides by P_Y. This gives $MU_Y/P_Y = MU_X/P_X$.

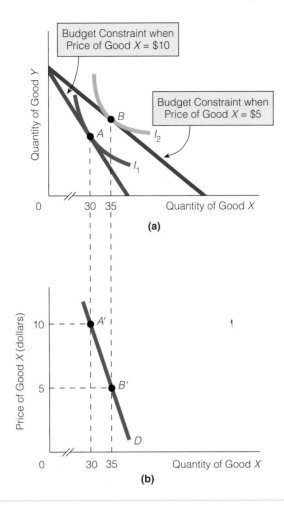

From Indifference Curves to a Demand Curve

(a) At a price of $10 for good *X*, consumer equilibrium is at point *A* with the individual consuming 30 units of *X*. As the price falls to $5, the budget constraint moves outward (away from the origin), and the consumer moves to point *B* and consumes 35 units of *X*. Plotting the price-quantity data for *X* gives a demand curve for *X* in (b).

appendix summary

- A budget constraint represents all combinations of bundles of two goods a person can purchase given a certain money income and prices for the two goods.

- An indifference curve shows all the combinations or bundles of two goods that give an individual equal total utility.

- Indifference curves are downward-sloping, convex to the origin, and do not cross. The farther away from the origin an indifference curve is, the greater total utility it represents for the individual.

- Consumer equilibrium is at the point where the slope of the budget constraint equals the slope of the indifference curve.

- A demand curve can be derived within a budget constraint-indifference curve framework.

questions and problems

1   Diagram the following budget constraints:

   a   Income = $4,000; P_X = $50; P_Y = $100
   b   Income = $3,000; P_X = $25; P_Y = $200
   c   Income = $2,000; P_X = $40; P_Y = $150

2   Explain why indifference curves (a) are downward-sloping, (b) are convex to the origin, and (c) do not cross.

3   Explain why consumer equilibrium is equivalent whether using marginal utility analysis or using indifference curve analysis.

4   Derive a demand curve using indifference curve analysis.

Production and Costs

Setting the Scene

The following events occurred one day recently.

8:45 A.M.

Olaf, who owns a small chair company, has incurred $76 in costs in producing a particular type of chair. Initially, he priced the chair at $150, but no one wanted to buy the chair at that price. Last week, he put the chair on sale for $109; still no one purchased it. Today, he's wondering if he should sell the chair for less than his cost to produce it.

10:19 A.M.

Lisa, a junior at a large public university in the South, is majoring in computer science. In a little over a year, she will graduate with a degree in computer science. She just has one problem: She doesn't like computer science. People keep telling her to stick with it. After all, they say, you can't quit now after investing nearly four years in computer science. Besides, they add, computer scientists usually earn more in their first jobs than individuals who have selected other majors. Lisa feels torn; she isn't sure what she should do.

2:56 P.M.

Ursula is in her chemistry class taking a multiple-choice test. She realizes that she doesn't know the answers to most of the questions on the test. Ian and Charles sit next to her. She could easily look over and check her answers against theirs. But she doesn't. It's not because Ursula feels particularly guilty about cheating . . . it's something else.

5:05 P.M.

Quentin Hammersmith is driving home after work, thinking about his job. He's worked for Smithies and Brown, an accounting firm, for 10 years. He finds the work rewarding—but lately he's thought about quitting his job and doing what he's always wanted to do. He's always wanted to own and operate a sports bar. But every time he's about ready to quit, he reminds himself of his $150,000 salary at the accounting firm.

> **?** Here are some questions to keep in mind as you read this chapter:
>
> - *Should Olaf sell the chair for a price below his cost?*
>
> - *What would you do if you were Lisa?*
>
> - *What keeps Ursula from cheating?*
>
> - *Would Quentin be more likely to quit his accounting job to own a sports bar if he earned a salary of $60,000 a year instead of $150,000 a year?*
>
> See analyzing the scene at the end of this chapter for answers to these questions.

Why Firms Exist

Business Firm
An entity that employs factors of production (resources) to produce goods and services to be sold to consumers, other firms, or the government.

A **business firm** is an entity that employs resources, or factors of production, to produce goods and services to be sold to consumers, other firms, or the government. This section explores a basic question: Why do firms exist? The answer to this question leads to discussions of worker behavior, markets, and questions a firm must answer.

The Market and the Firm: Invisible Hand Versus Visible Hand

In our discussion of supply and demand, the market guides and coordinates individuals' actions. Moreover, the market does this in an impersonal manner. No one orders buyers to reduce quantity demanded when price increases; they just do it. No one orders sellers to increase quantity supplied when price increases; they just do it. No one orders more resources to be moved into the production of personal computers when the demand and price for personal computers increase. The market guides individuals from the production of one good into the production of another good. It coordinates individuals' actions so that suppliers and demanders find mutual satisfaction at equilibrium. As economist Adam Smith observed, individuals in a market setting are "led by an invisible hand to promote an end which was no part of their intention."

Contrast the invisible hand of the market with the visible hand of a manager in a firm. Who tells the employee on the assembly line to make more computer chips? The manager does. Who tells the employee to design a new engine, to paint the lamps green, to put steak and lobster on the menu? The manager does. Thus, both the invisible hand of the market and the visible hand of the manager of a firm guide and coordinate individuals' actions. There is, in other words, both **market** and **managerial coordination**.

Market Coordination
The process in which individuals perform tasks, such as producing certain quantities of goods, based on changes in market forces, such as supply, demand, and price.

Managerial Coordination
The process in which managers direct employees to perform certain tasks.

If the market is capable of guiding and coordinating individuals' actions, why did firms (and managers) arise in the first place? Thus, we return to our original question: Why do firms exist?

The Alchian and Demsetz Answer

Economists Armen Alchian and Harold Demsetz suggest that firms are formed when benefits can be obtained from individuals working as a team.[1] Sometimes, the sum of what individuals can produce as a team is greater than the sum of what they can produce alone:

$$\text{Sum of team production} > \text{Sum of individual production}$$

Consider 11 individuals, all making shoe boxes. Each working alone produces 10 shoe boxes per day, for a total daily output of 110 shoe boxes. If they work as a team, however, the same 11 individuals can produce 140 shoe boxes. The added output (30 shoe boxes) may be reason enough for them to work together as a team and form a firm.

Shirking in a Team

Shirking
The behavior of a worker who is putting forth less than the agreed-to effort.

Although forming a firm can increase output, team production can have problems that do not occur in individual production. One problem of team production is **shirking**, which occurs when workers put forth less than the agreed-to effort. The amount of shirking increases in teams because the costs of shirking to individual team members are lower than when they work alone.

[1]Armen Alchian and Harold Demsetz, "Production, Information Costs, and Economic Organization," *American Economic Review* 62 (December 1972): 777–795.

Consider five individuals, Alice, Bob, Carl, Denise, and Elizabeth, who form a team to produce light bulbs because they realize that the sum of their team production will be more than the sum of their individual production. They agree to team-produce light bulbs, sell the light bulbs, and split the proceeds five equal ways. On an average day, they produce 140 light bulbs and sell each one for $2. Total revenue per day is $280, with each of the five team members receiving $56. Then Carl begins to shirk. Owing to his shirking, production falls to 135 light bulbs per day and total revenue falls to $270 per day. Each person now receives $54. Notice that while Carl did all the shirking, Carl's reduction in pay was only $2, one-fifth of the $10 drop in total revenue.

In situations (such as team production) where one person receives all the benefits from shirking and pays only a part of the costs, economists predict there will be more shirking than in the situation where the person who shirks bears the full cost of his or her shirking.

THE MONITOR (MANAGER): TAKING CARE OF SHIRKING The **monitor** (or manager) plays an important role in the firm. The monitor reduces the amount of shirking by firing shirkers and rewarding the productive members of the firm. In doing this, the monitor can preserve the benefits that often come with team production (increased output) and reduce, if not eliminate, the costs associated with team production (increased shirking). But this raises a question: *Who or what monitors the monitor?* That is, *how can the monitor be kept from shirking?*

One possibility is to give the monitor an incentive not to shirk by making him or her a **residual claimant** of the firm. A residual claimant receives the excess of revenues over costs (profits) as income. If the monitor shirks, then profits are likely to be lower (or even zero or negative), and therefore, the monitor will receive less income.

Monitor
Person in a business firm who coordinates team production and reduces shirking.

Residual Claimants
Persons who share in the profits of a business firm.

Ronald Coase on Why Firms Exist

Ronald Coase, winner of the 1991 Nobel Prize in Economics, argued that "the main reason why it is profitable to establish a firm would seem to be that there is a cost of using the price mechanism."[2] Stated differently, firms exist to economize on buying and selling everything, or they exist to reduce transaction costs.

Consider an example. Suppose it takes 20 different operations to produce good X. One way to produce good X, then, is to enter into a separate contract with everyone necessary to complete the 20 different operations. If we assume that one person completes one and only one operation, then we have 20 different contracts. Obviously, there are costs associated with preparing and monitoring these various contracts. A firm is a recipe for reducing these costs. It effectively replaces many contracts with one.

Here is what Coase had to say:

> The costs of negotiating and concluding a separate contract for each exchange transaction which takes place on a market must also be taken into account. . . . It is true that contracts are not eliminated when there is a firm, but they are greatly reduced. A factor of production (or the owner thereof) does not have to make a series of contracts as would be necessary, of course, if this co-operation were a direct result of the working of the price mechanism. For this series of contracts is substituted one. At this state, it is important to note the character of the contract into which a factor enters that is employed within a firm. The contract is one whereby the factor [the employee], for a certain remuneration (which may be fixed or fluctuating), agrees to obey the directions of an entrepreneur within certain limits.[3]

---

[2]Ronald Coase, "The Nature of the Firm," *Economica* (November 1937).
[3]Ibid.

Markets: Outside and Inside the Firm

What do we see when we put the firm under the microeconomic microscope? Basically, we see a market of sorts at work. Economics is largely about trades or exchanges; it is about market transactions. In supply-and-demand analysis, the exchanges are between buyers of goods and services and sellers of goods and services. In the theory of the firm, the exchanges take place at two levels: (1) at the level of individuals coming together to form a team and (2) at the level of workers "choosing" a monitor.

Let's look at the theory of the firm in the context of exchange. Individuals initially come together because they realize that the sum of what they can produce as a team is greater than the sum of what they can produce as individuals. In essence, each individual "trades" working alone for working in a team. Later, after the team has been formed, the team members learn that shirking reduces the amount of the added output they came together to capture in the first place. Now the team members enter into another trade or market transaction. They trade some control over their daily behavior—specifically, they trade an environment in which the cost of shirking is low for an environment in which the cost of shirking is high—to receive a larger absolute amount of the potential benefits that drew them together. It is in this trade that the monitor appears: Some individuals "buy" the monitoring services that other individuals "sell."

As you continue your study of microeconomics, look for the "markets" that appear at different levels of analysis.

The Firm's Objective: Maximizing Profit

Profit
The difference between total revenue and total cost.

Firms produce goods to sell the goods. Economists assume that a firm's objective in producing and selling goods is to maximize profit. **Profit** is the difference between total revenue and total cost.

$$\text{Profit} = \text{Total revenue} - \text{Total cost}$$

Recall that *total revenue* is equal to the price of a good multiplied by the quantity of the good sold. For example, if a business firm sells 100 units of X at $10 per unit, its total revenue is $1,000.

Almost everyone defines total revenue the same way, but a disagreement sometimes arises as to what total cost should include. To illustrate, suppose Jill currently works as an attorney earning $80,000 a year. One day, dissatisfied with her career, Jill quits her job as an attorney and opens a pizzeria. After one year of operating the pizzeria, Jill sits down to compute her profit. She sold 20,000 pizzas at a price of $10 per pizza, so her total revenue (for the year) is $200,000. Jill computes her total costs by adding the dollar amounts she spent for everything she bought or rented to run the pizzeria. She spent

Explicit Cost
A cost incurred when an actual (monetary) payment is made.

$2,000 on plates, $3,000 on cheese, $4,000 on soda, $20,000 for rent in the mall where the pizzeria is located, $2,000 for electricity, and so on. The dollar payments Jill made for everything she bought or rented are called her *explicit costs*. An **explicit cost** is a cost that is incurred when an actual (monetary) payment is made. So Jill sums her explicit costs, which turn out to be $90,000. Then she computes her profit by subtracting $90,000 from $200,000. This gives her a profit of $110,000.

A few days pass before Jill tells her friend Marian that she earned a $110,000 profit her first year of running the pizzeria. Marian asks: "Are you sure your profit is $110,000?" Jill assures her that it is. "Did you count the salary you earned as an attorney as a cost?" Marian asks. Jill tells Marian that she did not count the $80,000 salary as a cost of running the pizzeria because the $80,000 is not something

Thinking like **AN ECONOMIST**   *The economist wants to know what a person "gives up" when she goes into business for herself. What she gives up isn't only the money she pays for resources (to run the business), but she also gives up the job she would have had (and the income she would have been earning) had she not gone into business for herself.*

economics 24/7

DO SECRETARIES WHO WORK FOR INVESTMENT BANKS EARN MORE THAN SECRETARIES WHO WORK FOR HOTELS?[4]

A person who lives in Des Moines, Iowa, pays the same price for a Snickers candy bar as a person who lives in Tucson, Arizona; a person who lives in Billings, Montana, pays the same price for a soft drink as a person who lives in Orlando, Florida. Many goods fetch the same price no matter where they are bought and sold.

If many of the same goods fetch the same price, do many of the people who do the same work earn the same wage? For example, will secretaries at different types of businesses earn the same wage? Probably not. There is some evidence that not all firms pay workers doing identical jobs the same wage. Industries where profits are higher tend to pay workers higher wages. For example, secretaries in investment banks tend to earn more than secretaries in hotels. Cleaners in law firms earn more than cleaners in hotels. Mexican truck drivers who deliver oil earn more than drivers who deliver corn. British clerical workers earn more in the computer industry than in the textile industry.

One explanation of this difference in wage rates is that secretaries working in high-profit industries are paid more than secretaries working in low-profit industries because they do more or harder work. But there is not much evidence that this is true.

Another explanation of the difference is that the higher wage rate in some industries compensates for the relative unpleasantness of work in that industry. Although wages do adjust for the degree of risk on the job, the amount of unpleasantness, and so on, there seems to be no evidence

that this is the case in the examples mentioned. A secretary who works in an investment bank doesn't seem to have a more pleasant or less pleasant work environment than a secretary who works in a hotel.

Then, what does explain the difference in wage rates? Some efficiency wage theorists have hypothesized that above-equilibrium wages are paid by many high-profit industries because the managerial cost of monitoring employees in these industries is higher. They argue that in a high-profit industry, a manager's time is more valuable. In this setting, it is particularly costly for managers to monitor employees—that is, to make sure they do not shirk. Managers know that if they pay workers above-equilibrium wages, the workers will be less likely to shirk. Workers don't want to take the chance of losing jobs that pay them more than they can earn elsewhere. Therefore, to a large degree, the higher wage acts as an incentive for workers to monitor themselves. Managers in high-profit industries find it less costly to pay the higher wages that ensure employees will monitor themselves than to spend their valuable time monitoring employees. In short, if an investment banker doesn't want to waste her time monitoring her secretary's output, the easiest and least costly way to do this is to pay him more than he could earn in another job.

---

[4] This feature is based on "When Paying More Costs Less," *The Economist* (May 30–June 5, 1998), and Shailendra Raj Mehta, "The Law of One Price and a Theory of the Firm: A Ricardian Perspective on Interindustry Wages," *Rand Journal of Economics* (Spring 1998).

---

she "paid out" to run the pizzeria. "I wrote a check to my suppliers for the pizza ingredients, soda, dishes, and so on," Jill says, "but I didn't write a check to anyone for the $80,000."

Marian says that although Jill did not "pay out" $80,000 in salary to run the pizzeria, still she forfeited $80,000 to run the pizzeria. "What you could have earned but didn't is a cost to you of running the pizzeria," says Marian.

Jill's $80,000 salary is what economists call an *implicit cost*. An **implicit cost** is a cost that represents the value of resources used in production for which no actual (monetary) payment is made. It is a cost incurred as a result of a firm using resources that it owns or that the owners of the firm contribute to it.

Implicit Cost

A cost that represents the value of resources used in production for which no actual (monetary) payment is made.

If total cost is computed as explicit costs plus implicit costs, then Jill's total cost of running the pizzeria is $90,000 plus $80,000, or $170,000. Subtracting $170,000 from a total revenue of $200,000 leaves a profit of $30,000.

> ### *micro* Theme
>
> In an earlier chapter, we mentioned that economic actors (e.g., firms, consumers, resource owners, etc.) have objectives. The objective of the business firm is to maximize profit.

Accounting Profit Versus Economic Profit

Accounting Profit

The difference between total revenue and explicit costs.

Economic Profit

The difference between total revenue and total cost, including both explicit and implicit costs.

Economists refer to the first profit that Jill calculated ($110,000) as *accounting profit*. **Accounting profit** is the difference between total revenue and total cost, where total cost equals explicit costs (see Exhibit 1(a)).

Accounting profit = Total revenue − Total cost (Explicit costs)

Economists refer to the second profit calculated ($30,000) as *economic profit*. **Economic profit** is the difference between total revenue and total cost, where total cost equals the sum of explicit and implicit costs (see Exhibit 1(b)).

Economic profit = Total revenue − Total cost (Explicit costs + Implicit costs)

Let's consider another example that explains the difference between explicit and implicit costs. Suppose a person has $100,000 in the bank, earning an interest rate of 5 percent a year. This amounts to $5,000 in interest a year. Now suppose this person takes the $100,000 out of the bank to start a business. The $5,000 in *lost interest* is included in the implicit costs of owning and operating the firm. To see why, let's change the example somewhat. Assume the person does not use her $100,000 in the bank to start a business. Suppose she leaves her $100,000 in the bank and instead takes out a $100,000 loan at an interest rate of 5 percent. The interest she has to pay on the loan— $5,000 a year—certainly would be an explicit cost and would take away from overall profit. It just makes sense, then, to count the $5,000 interest the owner doesn't earn if she uses her own $100,000 to start the business (instead of taking out a loan) as a cost, albeit an implicit cost.

exhibit 1

Accounting and Economic Profit

Accounting profit equals total revenue minus explicit costs. Economic profit equals total revenue minus both explicit and implicit costs.

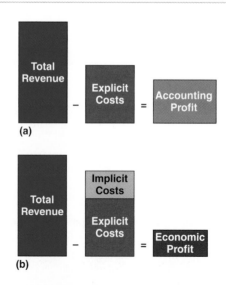

Zero Economic Profit Is Not as Bad as It Sounds

Economic profit is usually lower (never higher) than accounting profit because economic profit is the difference between total revenue and total cost, where total cost is the sum of explicit and implicit costs, whereas accounting profit is the difference between total revenue and only explicit costs. Thus, it is possible for a firm to earn both a positive accounting profit and a zero economic profit. In economics, a firm that makes a zero economic profit is said to be earning a **normal profit**.

Normal profit = Zero economic profit

Should the owner of a firm be worried if he has made zero economic profit for the year just ending? The answer is no. A zero economic profit—as bad as it may sound—means the owner has generated total revenue sufficient to cover total cost—that is, *both explicit and implicit costs*. If, for example, the owner's implicit cost is a (forfeited) $100,000 salary working for someone else, then earning a zero economic profit means he has done as well as he could have done in his next best (alternative) line of employment.

When we realize that zero economic profit (or normal profit) means "doing as well as could have been done," we understand that it isn't bad to make zero economic profit. Zero accounting profit, however, is altogether different; it implies that some part of total cost has not been covered by total revenue.

Normal Profit
Zero economic profit. A firm that earns normal profit is earning revenue equal to its total costs (explicit plus implicit costs). This is the level of profit necessary to keep resources employed in that particular firm.

When most people use the word profit, *do they mean accounting profit or economic profit?*

They probably mean accounting profit. Still, in this text, when we use the term profit, *we are referring to economic profit.*

SELF-TEST

(Answers to Self-Test questions are in the Self-Test Appendix.)

1. Will individuals form teams or firms in all settings?
2. Suppose everything about two people is the same except that one person currently earns a high salary and the other person currently earns a low salary. Which is more likely to start his or her own business and why?
3. Is accounting or economic profit larger? Why?
4. When can a business owner be earning a profit but not covering his costs?

Production

Production is a transformation of resources or inputs into goods and services. You may think of production the way you might think of making a cake. It takes certain ingredients to make a cake—sugar, flour, and so on. Similarly, it takes certain resources, or inputs, to produce a computer, a haircut, a piece of furniture, or a house.

Economists often talk about two types of inputs in the production process: fixed and variable. A **fixed input** is an input whose quantity cannot be changed as output changes. To illustrate, suppose the McMahon and McGee Bookshelf Company has rented a factory under a six-month lease: McMahon and McGee, the owners of the company, have contracted to pay the $2,500 monthly rent for six months—no matter what. Whether McMahon and McGee produce 1 bookshelf or 7,000 bookshelves, the $2,500 rent for the factory must be paid. The factory is an input in the production process of bookshelves; specifically, it is a fixed input.

A **variable input** is an input whose quantity can be changed as output changes. Examples of variable inputs for the McMahon and McGee Bookshelf Company include wood, paint, nails, and so on. These inputs can (and most likely will) change as the production of bookshelves changes. As more bookshelves are produced, more of

Fixed Input
An input whose quantity cannot be changed as output changes.

Variable Input
An input whose quantity can be changed as output changes.

these inputs will be purchased by McMahon and McGee; as fewer bookshelves are produced, fewer of these inputs will be purchased. Labor might also be a variable input for McMahon and McGee. As they produce more bookshelves, they might hire more employees; as they produce fewer bookshelves, they might lay off some employees.

If any of the inputs of a firm are fixed inputs, then it is said to be producing in the *short run*. In other words, the **short run** is a period of time in which some inputs are fixed.

If none of the inputs of a firm are fixed inputs—if all inputs are variable—then the firm is said to be producing in the *long run*. In other words, the **long run** is a period of time in which all inputs can be varied (no inputs are fixed).

When firms produce goods and services and then sell them, they necessarily incur costs. In this section, we discuss the production activities of the firm in the short run, a discussion that leads to the law of diminishing marginal returns and marginal costs. In the next section, we tie the production of the firm to all the costs of production in the short run. We then turn to an analysis of production in the long run.

Short Run
A period of time in which some inputs in the production process are fixed.

Long Run
A period of time in which all inputs in the production process can be varied (no inputs are fixed).

Q&A

What is the best way to understand the difference between the short run and the long run? Is the long run longer than the short run? For example, if the short run is 6 months, is the long run something longer than 6 months?

This is not the right way to differentiate the short run from the long run. Think of each as a period of time during which some condition exists. The short run is that period of time during which at least one input is fixed. This could be a period of 6 months, 2 years, and so on. The long run is not necessarily longer in months and years than the short run. It is simply that period of time during which all inputs are variable (i.e., no input is fixed). In terms of days, weeks, and months, the short run could be a longer period of time than the long run.

Production in the Short Run

Suppose two inputs (or resources), labor and capital, are used to produce some good. Furthermore, suppose one of those inputs—capital—is fixed. Obviously, because an input is fixed, the firm is producing in the short run.

Column 1 of Exhibit 2 shows the units of the fixed input, capital. Notice that capital is fixed at 1 unit. Column 2 shows different units of the variable input, labor. Notice that we go from 0 units of labor through 10 units of labor (10 workers). Column 3 shows the quantities of output produced with 1 unit of capital and different amounts of labor. (The quantity of output is sometimes referred to as the *total physical product*, or *TPP.*) For example, 1 unit of capital and 0 units of labor produce 0 output; 1 unit of capital and 1 unit of labor produce 18 units of output; 1 unit of capital and 2 units of labor produce 37 units of output; 1 unit of capital and 3 units of labor produce 57 units of output; and so on.

exhibit 2

Production in the Short Run and the Law of Diminishing Marginal Returns

In the short run, as additional units of a variable input are added to a fixed input, the marginal physical product of the variable input may increase at first. Eventually, the marginal physical product of the variable input decreases. The point at which marginal physical product decreases is the point at which diminishing marginal returns have set in.

(1) Fixed Input, Capital (units)	(2) Variable Input, Labor (workers)	(3) Quantity of Output, Q (units)	(4) Marginal Physical Product of Variable Input (units) Δ(3)/Δ(2)
1	0	0	
1	1	18	18
1	2	37	19
1	3	57	20
1	4	76	19
1	5	94	18
1	6	111	17
1	7	127	16
1	8	137	10
1	9	133	-4
1	10	125	-8

Column 4 shows the marginal physical product of the variable input. The **marginal physical product (MPP)** of a variable input is equal to the change in output that results from changing the variable input by one unit, *holding all other inputs fixed.* In our example, the variable input is labor, so here we are talking about the *MPP* of labor. Specifically, the *MPP* of labor is equal to the change in output, *Q*, that results from changing labor, *L*, by one unit, *holding all other inputs fixed.*

$$MPP = \frac{\Delta Q}{\Delta L}$$

Notice that the marginal physical product of labor first rises (from 18 to 19 to 20), then falls (from 20 to 19 to 18 to 17 to 16 to 10), and then becomes negative (–4 and –8). When the *MPP* is rising, we say there is increasing *MPP*, when it is falling, there is diminishing *MPP*, and when it is negative, there is negative *MPP*.

Focus on the point at which the *MPP* first begins to decline—with the addition of the fourth worker. The point at which the marginal physical product of labor first declines is the point at which diminishing marginal returns are said to have "set in." Diminishing marginal returns are common in production—so common, in fact, that economists refer to the **law of diminishing marginal returns** (or the law of diminishing marginal product). The law of diminishing marginal returns states that *as ever-larger amounts of a variable input are combined with fixed inputs, eventually, the marginal physical product of the variable input will decline.*

Some persons ask, "But why does the *MPP* of the variable input eventually decline?" To answer this question, think of adding agricultural workers (variable input) to 10 acres of land (fixed input). The workers must clear the land, plant the crop, and then harvest the crop. In the early stages of adding labor to the land, perhaps the *MPP* rises or remains constant. But eventually, as we continue to add more workers to the land, there comes a point when the land is overcrowded with workers. Workers are stepping around each other, stepping on the crops, and so on. Because of these problems, output growth begins to slow.

You may be wondering why the firm in Exhibit 2 would ever hire beyond the third worker. After all, the *MPP* of labor is at its highest (20) with the third worker. Why hire the fourth worker if the *MPP* of labor falls to 19? The reason the firm may hire the fourth worker is because this worker adds output. It would be one thing if the quantity of output was 57 units with three workers and fell to 55 units with the addition of the fourth worker. But this isn't the case here. With the addition of the fourth worker, output rises from 57 units to 76 units. The firm has to ask and answer two questions: (1) What can the additional 19 units of output be sold for? (2) What does it cost to hire the fourth worker? Suppose the additional 19 units can be sold for $100, and it costs the firm $70 to hire the fourth worker. Will the firm hire the fourth worker? Yes.

Marginal Physical Product (MPP)

The change in output that results from changing the variable input by one unit, holding all other inputs fixed.

Law of Diminishing Marginal Returns

As ever-larger amounts of a variable input are combined with fixed inputs, eventually, the marginal physical product of the variable input will decline.

Thinking like **AN ECONOMIST**
In economics, when making decisions, it is usually the case that you compare one thing to something else. To illustrate, suppose you need to decide how much time to devote to studying. Would you consider only the additional benefits of spending more time studying, or would you consider the additional benefits and costs of spending more time studying? You would want to consider both the additional benefits and costs of spending more time studying.

The same idea comes into play when a firm has to decide how many workers to hire. It wouldn't want to consider only the additional benefits of hiring more workers (let's say as measured by the additional output they produce times the price the additional output could be sold for). Instead, it would want to consider the additional benefits of hiring more workers against the additional costs of hiring more workers.

micro **Theme**
In an earlier chapter, we mentioned that economic actors (firms, consumers, resource owners) have to make choices. Often, economic actors make their choices by comparing one thing with another. More formally, they usually are comparing the "additional benefits" of an action with the "additional costs" of an action.

Marginal Physical Product and Marginal Cost

A firm's costs are tied to its production. Specifically, the *marginal cost (MC)* of producing a good is a reflection of the marginal physical product (*MPP*) of the variable input. Our objective in this section is to prove that this last statement is true. But before we can do this, we need to define and discuss some economic cost concepts.

SOME ECONOMIC COST CONCEPTS Recall our earlier discussion of fixed inputs and variable inputs. Certainly, a cost is incurred whenever a fixed input or variable input is employed in the production process. The costs associated with fixed inputs are called **fixed costs**. The costs associated with variable inputs are called **variable costs**.

Because the quantity of a fixed input does not change as output changes, fixed costs do not change as output changes. Payments for such things as fire insurance (the same amount every month), liability insurance, and the rental of a factory and machinery are usually considered fixed costs. Whether the business produces 1, 10, 100, or 1,000 units of output, it is likely that the rent for its factory will not change. It will be whatever amount was agreed to with the owner of the factory for the duration of the rental agreement.

Because the quantity of a variable input changes with output, so do variable costs. For example, it takes labor, wood, and glue to produce wooden bookshelves. It is likely that the quantity of all these inputs (labor, wood, and glue) will change as the number of wooden bookshelves produced changes.

Fixed Costs

Costs that do not vary with output; the costs associated with fixed inputs.

Variable Costs

Costs that vary with output; the costs associated with variable inputs.

exhibit 3

Marginal Physical Product and Marginal Cost

(a) The marginal physical product of labor curve. The curve is derived by plotting the data from columns 2 and 4 in the exhibit. (b) The marginal cost curve. The curve is derived by plotting the data from columns 3 and 8 in the exhibit. Notice that as the *MPP* curve rises, the *MC* curve falls; and as the *MPP* curve falls, the *MC* curve rises.

(1) Fixed Input, Capital (units)	(2) Variable Input, Labor (workers)	(3) Quantity of Output, Q (units)	(4) Marginal Physical Product of Variable Input (units) Δ(3)/Δ(2)	(5) Total Fixed Cost (dollars)	(6) Total Variable Cost (dollars)	(7) Total Cost (dollars) (5) + (6)	(8) Marginal cost (dollars) Δ(7)/Δ(3)
1	0	0		$40	$ 0	$ 40	
			18				$1.11
1	1	18		40	20	60	
			19				$1.05
1	2	37		40	40	80	
			20				$1.00
1	3	57		40	60	100	
			19				$1.05
1	4	76		40	80	120	
			18				$1.11
1	5	94		40	100	140	
			17				$1.17
1	6	111		40	120	160	
			16				$1.25
1	7	127		40	140	180	

(a)

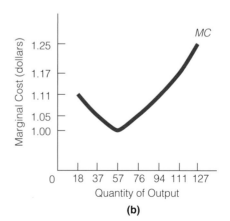

(b)

The sum of fixed costs and variable costs is **total cost (TC)**. If total fixed costs (TFC) are \$100 and total variable costs (TVC) are \$300, then total cost (TC) is \$400.

$$TC = TFC + TVC$$

Now that we know what total cost is, we can formally define marginal cost. **Marginal cost (MC)** is the change in total cost, TC, that results from a change in output, Q.

$$MC = \frac{\Delta TC}{\Delta Q}$$

Total Cost (TC)
The sum of fixed costs and variable costs.

Marginal Cost (MC)
The change in total cost that results from a change in output: $MC = \Delta TC/\Delta Q$.

THE LINK BETWEEN MPP AND MC In Exhibit 3, we establish the link between the marginal physical product of a variable input and marginal cost. The first four columns present much of the same data first presented in Exhibit 2. Essentially, column 3 shows the different quantities of output produced by 1 unit of capital (fixed input) and various amounts of labor (variable input), and column 4 shows the MPP of labor. Exhibit 3(a) shows the MPP curve, which is based on the data in column 4. Notice that the MPP curve first rises and then falls.

In column 5, we have identified the total fixed cost (TFC) of production as \$40. (Recall that fixed costs do not change as output changes.) For column 6, we have assumed that each worker is hired for \$20, so when there is only 1 worker, total variable cost (TVC) is \$20; when there are 2 workers, total variable cost is \$40; and so on. Column 7 shows total cost at various output levels; the total cost figures in this column are simply the sum of the fixed costs in column 5 and the variable costs in column 6. Finally, in column 8, we compute marginal cost. Exhibit 3(b) shows the MC curve, which is based on the data in column 8.

Let's focus on columns 4 and 8 in Exhibit 3, which show the MPP and MC, respectively. Notice that when the MPP is rising (from 18 to 19 to 20), marginal cost is decreasing (from \$1.11 to \$1.05 to \$1.00), and when the MPP is falling (from 20 to 19 etc.), marginal cost is increasing (from \$1.00 to \$1.05 etc.). In other words, the MPP and MC move in opposite directions. You can also see this by comparing the MPP curve with the MC curve. When the MPP curve is going up, the MC curve is moving down, and when the MPP curve is going down, the MC curve is going up. Of course, all this is common sense: As marginal physical product rises, or to put it differently, as the productivity of the variable input rises, we would expect costs to decline. And as the productivity of the variable input declines, we would expect costs to rise.

In conclusion, then, what the MC curve looks like depends on what the MPP curve looks like. Recall that the MPP curve must have a declining portion because of the law of diminishing marginal returns. So if the MPP curve first rises and then (when diminishing marginal returns set in) falls, it follows that the MC curve must first fall and then rise.

 Suppose an MPP curve is entirely horizontal. What would the corresponding MC curve look like?

The MC curve would be horizontal too. Look at it this way: (1) If the MPP curve is entirely horizontal, it means that MPP is constant—it neither rises nor falls. (2) We know that the MC curve declines as the MPP curve rises and the MC curve rises as the MPP curve falls. Well, then, if the MPP curve neither rises nor falls, it follows that the MC curve neither falls nor rises.

ANOTHER WAY TO LOOK AT THE RELATIONSHIP BETWEEN MPP AND MC An easy way to see that marginal physical product and marginal cost move in *opposite directions* involves reexamining the definition of marginal cost. Recall that marginal cost is defined as the change in total cost divided by the change in output. The change in total cost is the additional cost of an additional unit of the variable input (see Exhibit 3). The change in output is the marginal physical product of the variable input. Thus, marginal cost is equal to the additional cost of an additional unit of the variable input divided by the input's marginal physical product. In Exhibit 3, the variable input is labor, so $MC = W/MPP$, where MC = marginal cost, W = wage, and MPP = marginal physical product of labor. The following table reproduces column 4 from Exhibit 3, notes the wage, and computes MC using the equation $MC = W/MPP$.

MPP	Variable Cost (W)	W/MPP = MC
18 units	$20	$20/18 = $1.11
19	20	20/19 = 1.05
20	20	20/20 = 1.00
19	20	20/19 = 1.05
18	20	20/18 = 1.11
17	20	20/17 = 1.17
16	20	20/16 = 1.25

Now, compare the marginal cost figures in the last column in the table above with the marginal cost figures in column 8 of Exhibit 3. Whether marginal cost is defined as equal to $\Delta TC/\Delta Q$ or as equal to W/MPP, the result is the same. The latter way of defining marginal cost, however, explicitly shows that as MPP rises, MC falls, and as MPP falls, MC rises.

$$\frac{W}{MPP \uparrow} = MC \downarrow$$

$$\frac{W}{MPP \downarrow} = MC \uparrow$$

Average Productivity

When the word *productivity* is used in the press or by the layperson, what is usually referred to is *average physical product* instead of *marginal physical product*. To illustrate the difference, suppose 1 worker can produce 10 units of output a day and 2 workers can produce 18 units of output a day. Marginal physical product is 8 units (MPP of labor $= \Delta Q/\Delta L$). Average physical product, which is output divided by the quantity of labor, is equal to 9 units.

$$AP \text{ of labor} = Q/L$$

Usually, when the term *labor productivity* is used in the newspaper and in government documents, it refers to the average (physical) productivity of labor on an hourly basis. By computing the average productivity of labor for different countries and noting the annual percentage changes, we can compare labor productivity between and within countries. Government statisticians have chosen 1992 as a benchmark year (a year against which we measure other years). They have also set a productivity index, which is a measure of productivity, for 1992 equal to 100. By computing a productivity index for other years and noting whether each index is above, below, or equal to 100, they know whether productivity is rising, falling, or remaining constant, respectively. Finally, by computing the percentage change in productivity indexes from one year to the next, they know the rate at which productivity is changing.

Suppose the productivity index for the United States is 120 in year 1 and 125 in year 2. The productivity index is higher in year 2 than in year 1, so labor productivity increased over the year; that is, output produced increased per hour of labor expended.

SELF-TEST

1.   If the short run is 6 months, does it follow that the long run is longer than 6 months? Explain your answer.

2.   "As we add more capital to more labor, eventually the law of diminishing marginal returns will set in." What is wrong with this statement?

3.   Suppose a marginal cost (*MC*) curve falls when output is in the range of 1 unit to 10 units, flattens out and remains constant over an output range of 10 units to 20 units, and then rises over a range of 20 units to 30 units. What does this have to say about the marginal physical product (*MPP*) of the variable input?

economics 24/7

HIGH SCHOOL STUDENTS, STAYING OUT LATE, AND MORE

Can marginal cost affect a person's behavior? Let's analyze two different situations in which it might.

High School Students and Staying Out Late

A 16-year-old high school student asks her parents if she can have the car tonight. She says she plans to go with some friends to a concert. Her parents ask what time she will get home. She says that she plans to be back by midnight.

The girl's parents tell her that she can have the car and that they expect her home by midnight. If she's late, she will lose her driving privileges for a week.

Now suppose it is later that night. In fact, it is midnight and the 16-year-old is 15 minutes away from home. When she realizes she can't get home until 12:15 A.M., will she continue on home? She may not. The marginal cost of staying out later is now zero. In short, whether she arrives home at 12:15, 1:15, or 2:25, the punishment is the same: She will lose her driving privileges for a week. There is no additional cost for staying out an additional minute or an additional hour. There may, however, be additional benefits. Her "punishment" places a zero marginal cost on staying out after midnight. Once midnight has come and gone, the additional cost of staying out later is zero.

No doubt her parents would prefer her to get home at, say, 12:01 rather than at 1:01 or even later. If this is the case, then they should not have made the marginal cost of staying out after midnight zero. What they should have done is increased the marginal cost of staying out late for every minute (or 15-minute period) the 16-year-old was late. In other words, one of the parents might have said, "For the first 15 minutes you're late, you'll lose 1 hour of driving

privileges, for the second 15 minutes you're late, you'll lose 2 hours of driving privileges, and so on." This would have presented our teen with a rising marginal cost of staying out late. With a rising marginal cost, it is more likely she will get home close to midnight.

Crime

Suppose the sentence for murder in the first degree is life imprisonment and the sentence for burglary is 10 years. In a given city, the burglary rate has skyrocketed in the past few months. Many of the residents have become alarmed. They have called on the police and other local and state officials to do something about the rising burglary rate.

Someone proposes that the way to lower the burglary rate is to increase the punishment for burglary. Instead of only 10 years in prison, make the punishment stiffer. In his zeal to reduce the burglary rate, a state legislator proposes that burglary carry the same punishment as first-degree murder: life in prison. That will certainly get the burglary rate down, he argues. After all, who will take the chance of committing a burglary if he knows that if he gets caught and convicted, he will spend the rest of his days in prison?

Unfortunately, by making the punishment for burglary and murder the same, the marginal cost of murdering someone that a person is burglarizing falls to zero. To illustrate, suppose Smith is burglarizing a home and the residents walk in on him. Smith realizes the residents can identify him as the burglar, so he shoots and kills them. What does it matter? If he gets apprehended for burglary, the penalty will be the same as it is for murder. Raising the cost of burglary from 10 years to life imprisonment may reduce the number of burglaries, but it may have the unintended effect of raising the murder rate.

Costs of Production: Total, Average, Marginal

In this section, we continue our discussion of the costs of production. The easiest way to see the relationships among the various costs is with the example in Exhibit 4.

Column 1 of Exhibit 4 shows the various quantities of output, ranging from 0 units to 10 units.

Column 2 shows the total fixed costs of production. We have set *TFC* at $100. Recall that fixed costs do not change as output changes. Therefore, *TFC* is $100 when output is 0 units, 1 unit, or 2 units, and so on. Because *TFC* does not change as *Q* changes, the *TFC* curve in the exhibit is a horizontal line at $100.

(1) Quantity of Output, Q (units)	(2) Total Fixed Cost (TFC)	(3) Average Fixed Cost (AFC) $AFC = TFC/Q$ $= (2)/(1)$	(4) Total Variable Cost (TVC)	(5) Average Variable Cost (AVC) $AVC = TVC/Q$ $= (4)/(1)$
0	$100	—	$ 0	—
1	100	$100.00	50	$50.00
2	100	50.00	80	40.00
3	100	33.33	100	33.33
4	100	25.00	110	27.50
5	100	20.00	130	26.00
6	100	16.67	160	26.67
7	100	14.28	200	28.57
8	100	12.50	250	31.25
9	100	11.11	310	34.44
10	100	10.00	380	38.00

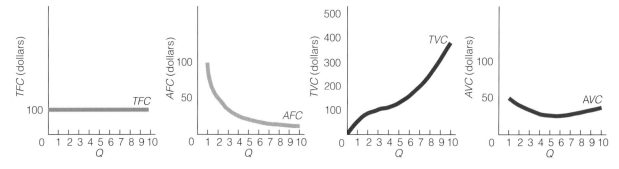

Total, Average, and Marginal Costs

TFC equals $100 (column 2) and TVC is as noted in column 4. From the data, we calculate AFC, AVC, TC, ATC, and MC. The curves associated with TFC, AFC, TVC, AVC, TC, ATC, and MC are shown in diagrams at the bottom of the corresponding columns. (Note: Scale is not the same for all diagrams.)

Average Fixed Cost (AFC)

Total fixed cost divided by quantity of output: $AFC = TFC / Q$.

Average Variable Cost (AVC)

Total variable cost divided by quantity of output: $AVC = TVC / Q$.

Average Total Cost (ATC), or Unit Cost

Total cost divided by quantity of output: $ATC = TC / Q$.

In column 3, we have computed *average fixed cost*. **Average fixed cost (AFC)** is total fixed cost divided by quantity of output.

$$AFC = TFC/Q$$

For example, look at the fourth entry in column 3. How did we get a dollar amount of $33.33? We simply took *TFC* at 3 units of output, which is $100, and divided by 3. Notice that the *AFC* curve in the exhibit continually declines.

In column 4, we have simply entered some hypothetical data for total variable cost (*TVC*). The *TVC* curve in the exhibit rises because it is likely that variable costs will increase as output increases.

In column 5, we have computed average variable cost. **Average variable cost (AVC)** is total variable cost divided by quantity of output.

$$AVC = TVC/Q$$

For example, look at the third entry in column 5. How did we get a dollar amount of $40.00? We simply took *TVC* at 2 units of output, which is $80, and divided by 2. Notice that the *AVC* curve declines and then rises.

Column 6 shows total cost (*TC*). Total cost is the sum of total variable cost and total fixed cost. Notice that the *TC* curve does not start at zero. Why not? Because even when output is zero, there are some fixed costs. In this example, total fixed cost (*TFC*) at zero output is $100. It follows, then, that the total cost (*TC*) curve starts at $100 instead of at $0.

Column 7 shows *average total cost*. **Average total cost (ATC)** is total cost divided by quantity of output. Average total cost is sometimes called *unit cost*.

$$ATC = TC/Q$$

exhibit **4**

Continued

(6) Total Cost (TC) TC = TFC + TVC = (2) + (4)	(7) Average Total Cost (ATC) ATC = TC/Q = (6)/(1)	(8) Marginal Cost (MC) MC = ΔTC/ΔQ = Δ(6)/Δ(1)
$100.00	—	—
150.00	$150.00	$50.00
180.00	90.00	30.00
200.00	66.67	20.00
210.00	52.50	10.00
230.00	46.00	20.00
260.00	43.33	30.00
300.00	42.86	40.00
350.00	43.75	50.00
410.00	45.56	60.00
480.00	48.00	70.00

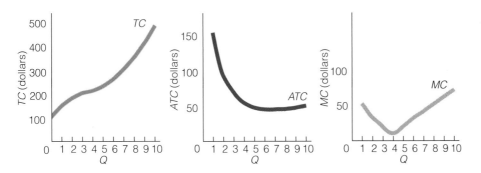

Alternatively, we can say that *ATC* equals the sum of *AFC* and *AVC*.

$$ATC = AFC + AVC$$

To understand why this makes sense, remember that $TC = TFC + TVC$. Thus, if we divide all total magnitudes by quantity of output (Q), we necessarily get $ATC = AFC + AVC$. Notice that the *ATC* curve falls and then rises.

Column 8 shows marginal cost (*MC*). Recall that marginal cost is the change in total cost divided by the change in output.

$$MC = ΔTC/ΔQ$$

The *MC* curve has a declining portion and a rising portion. What is happening to the *MPP* of the variable input when *MC* is declining? The *MPP* is rising. What is happening to the *MPP* of the variable input when *MC* is rising? *MPP* is falling. Obviously, the low point on the *MC* curve is when diminishing marginal returns set in.

Thinking like **AN ECONOMIST** *Economists often deduce things from what they know. We just did this when discussing* MPP *and* MC. *Here is what we know: (1)* MPP *and* MC *are inversely related; as* MPP *rises,* MC *falls, and as* MPP *falls,* MC *rises. (2) When diminishing marginal returns "kick in,"* MPP *begins to decline. We deduce then that (3) when diminishing marginal returns kick in,* MC *begins to rise.*

The *AVC* and *ATC* Curves in Relation to the *MC* Curve

What do the average total and average variable cost curves look like in relation to the marginal cost curve? To explain, we need to discuss the **average-marginal rule**, which is best defined with an example.

Suppose there are 20 persons in a room and each person weighs 170 pounds. Your task is to calculate the average weight. This is accomplished by adding the individual

Average–Marginal Rule
When the marginal magnitude is above the average magnitude, the average magnitude rises; when the marginal magnitude is below the average magnitude, the average magnitude falls.

weights and dividing by 20. Obviously, this average weight will be 170 pounds. Now let an additional person enter the room. We shall refer to this additional person as the marginal (additional) person and the additional weight he brings to the room as the marginal weight.

Let's suppose the weight of the marginal person is 275 pounds. The average weight based on the 21 persons now in the room is 175 pounds. The new average weight is greater than the old average weight. The average weight was pulled up by the weight of the additional person. In short, *when the marginal magnitude is above the average magnitude, the average magnitude rises.* This is one part of the average-marginal rule.

Suppose the weight of the marginal person is less than the average weight of 170 pounds, for example, 65 pounds. Then the new average is 165 pounds. In this case, the average weight was pulled down by the weight of the additional person. Thus, *when the marginal magnitude is below the average magnitude, the average magnitude falls.* This is the other part of the average-marginal rule.

$$\text{Marginal} < \text{Average} \rightarrow \text{Average} \downarrow$$
$$\text{Marginal} > \text{Average} \rightarrow \text{Average} \uparrow$$

We can apply the average-marginal rule to find out what the average total and average variable cost curves look like in relation to the marginal cost curve. The following analysis holds for both the average total cost curve and the average variable cost curve.

We reason that

1. if marginal cost is below (less than) average variable cost, average variable cost is falling;

2. if marginal cost is above (greater than) average variable cost, average variable cost is rising.

This reasoning implies that the relationship between the average variable cost curve and the marginal cost curve must look like that in Exhibit 5(a). In Region 1 of (a), marginal cost is below average variable cost, and consistent with the average-marginal rule, average variable cost is falling. In Region 2 of (a), marginal cost is above average variable cost, and average variable cost is rising. In summary, the relationship between the average

MC curve cuts both *AVC* and *ATC* curves at their respective low points.

economics 24/7

WHAT MATTERS TO GLOBAL COMPETITIVENESS?

What does a country need to do to be competitive in the global marketplace? The usual answer is that it needs to produce goods that people in other countries want to buy at prices they want to pay. For example, for the United States to be competitive in the global car and computer markets, U.S. firms must produce cars and computers at prices that people all over the world are willing and able to pay.

Price is a major factor in the race to be competitive in the global market. If U.S. firms charge higher prices for their cars than German and Japanese firms charge for their similar-quality cars, then it is unlikely that U.S. firms will be competitive in the global car market. We conclude: If U.S. firms are to be competitive in the global market, they must keep their prices down, all other things equal.

But how do firms keep their prices down? One way is to keep their unit cost, or average total cost, down. Look at it this way:

Profit per unit = Price per unit − Unit cost (or *ATC*)

The lower unit cost is, the lower price can go and still earn the producer/seller an acceptable profit per unit. That is, to be competitive on price, firms must be competitive on unit cost; they need to find ways to lower unit cost. This chapter shows how unit cost will decline when marginal cost (*MC*) is below unit cost (*ATC*). In other words, to lower *ATC*, marginal cost must fall and go below (current) average total cost. But how do firms get *MC* to fall and eventually go below current *ATC*? This chapter also explains that before *MC* can decline, marginal physical product (*MPP*) must rise.

Let's summarize our analysis so far: To be competitive in the global marketplace, U.S. firms must be competitive on price. To be competitive on price, firms must be competitive on unit cost (*ATC*). This requires that firms get their *MC* to decline and, ultimately, go below their current *ATC*. And the way to get *MC* to decline and go below current *ATC* is to raise the marginal productivity (*MPP*) of the inputs the firms use. To a large degree, the key to becoming or staying globally competitive is to find and implement ways to increase factor productivity.

How do you fit into the picture? Your education may affect the marginal physical product (*MPP*) of labor. As you learn more things and become more skilled (more productive)—and as many others do too—the *MPP* of labor in the United States rises. This, in turn, lowers firms' marginal cost, which ideally will decline enough to pull both average variable and average total costs down. As this happens, U.S. firms can become more competitive on price and still earn a profit.

---

variable cost curve and the marginal cost curve in Exhibit 5(a) is consistent with the average-marginal rule.

In addition, because average variable cost is pulled down when marginal cost is below it and pulled up when marginal cost is above it, it follows that the marginal cost curve must intersect the average variable cost curve at the latter's lowest point. This lowest point is point *L* in Exhibit 5(a).

The same relationship that exists between the *MC* and *AVC* curves also exists between the *MC* and *ATC* curves, as shown in Exhibit 5(b). In Region 1 of (b), marginal cost is below average total cost, and consistent with the average-marginal rule, average total cost is falling. In Region 2 of (b), marginal cost is above average total cost, and average total cost is rising. It follows that the marginal cost curve must intersect the average total cost curve at the latter's lowest point.

What about the average fixed cost curve? Is there any relationship between it and the marginal cost curve? The answer is no. We can indirectly see why by recalling that average fixed cost is simply total fixed cost (which is constant over output) divided by output ($AFC = TFC/Q$). As output (Q) increases and total fixed cost (TFC) remains constant, it follows that average fixed cost (TFC/Q) must decrease continuously (see Exhibit 5(c)).

Tying Short-Run Production to Costs

As we have said before, costs are tied to production. To see this explicitly, let's summarize some of our earlier discussions (see Exhibit 6).

We assume production takes place in the short run, so there is at least one fixed input. Suppose we initially add units of a variable input to the fixed input, and the marginal physical product of the variable input (e.g., labor) rises. As a result of MPP rising, marginal cost (MC) falls. When MC has fallen enough to be below average variable cost (AVC), we know from the average-marginal rule that AVC will begin to decline. Also, when MC has fallen enough to be below average total cost (ATC), ATC will begin to decline.

Eventually, though, the law of diminishing marginal returns will set in. When this happens, the MPP of the variable input declines. As a result, MC rises. When MC has risen enough to be above AVC, AVC will rise. Also, when MC has risen enough to be above ATC, ATC will rise.

We conclude: What happens in terms of production (Is MPP rising or falling?) affects MC, which in turn eventually affects AVC and ATC. In short, the cost of a good is tied to the production of that good.

One More Cost Concept: Sunk Cost

Sunk Cost

A cost incurred in the past that cannot be changed by current decisions and therefore cannot be recovered.

Sunk cost is a cost incurred in the past that cannot be changed by current decisions and therefore cannot be recovered. For example, suppose a firm must purchase a $10,000 government license before it can legally produce and sell lamp poles. Furthermore, suppose the government will not buy back the license or allow it to be resold. The $10,000

---

exhibit **6**

Tying Production to Costs

What happens in terms of production (*MPP* rising or falling) affects *MC*, which in turn eventually affects *AVC* and *ATC*.

the firm spends to purchase the license is a sunk cost. It is a cost that, after it has been incurred (the $10,000 was spent), cannot be changed by a current decision (the firm cannot go back into the past and undo what was done) and cannot be recovered (the government will neither buy back the license nor allow it to be resold).

Let's consider another example of a sunk cost. Suppose Jeremy buys a movie ticket, walks into the theater, and settles down to watch the movie. Thirty minutes into the movie, he realizes that he hates it. The money he paid for the ticket is a sunk cost. The cost was incurred in the past, it cannot be changed, and it cannot be recovered. (We are assuming that movie theaters do not give your money back if you dislike the movie.)

ECONOMISTS' ADVICE: IGNORE SUNK COSTS Economists advise individuals to ignore sunk costs. To illustrate, consider the case of Jeremy who bought the movie ticket but dislikes the movie. Given the constraints in this case, the movie ticket is a sunk cost. Now suppose Jeremy says the following to himself as he is watching the movie:

> I paid to watch this movie, but I really hate it. Should I get up and walk out or should I stay and watch the movie? I think I'll stay and watch the movie because if I leave, I'll lose the money I paid for the ticket.

Can you see the error Jeremy is making? He believes that if he walks out of the theater, he will lose the money he paid for the ticket. But he has already lost the money he paid for the ticket. Whether he stays and watches the movie or leaves, the money he paid for the ticket is gone forever. It is a sunk cost.

An economist would advise Jeremy to ignore what has happened in the past and can't be undone. In other words, ignore sunk costs. Instead, Jeremy should simply ask and answer these questions: What do I gain (what are my benefits) if I stay and watch the movie? What do I lose (what are my costs) if I stay and watch the movie? (Not: What have I already lost? Nothing can be done about what has already been lost.)

If what Jeremy expects to gain by staying and watching the movie is greater than what he expects to lose, he should stay and watch the movie. However, if what he expects to lose by staying and watching the movie is greater than what he expects to gain, he should leave.

To see this more clearly, suppose again that Jeremy has decided to stay and watch the movie *because he doesn't want to lose the price of the movie ticket*. Two minutes after he has made this decision, you walk up to Jeremy and offer him $200 to leave the theater. What do you think Jeremy will do now? Do you think he will say, "I can't leave the movie theater because if I do, I will lose the price of the movie ticket"? Or do you think he is more likely to say, "Sure, I'll take the $200 and leave the movie theater"?

Most people will say that Jeremy will take the $200 and leave the movie theater. Why? The simple reason is because if he doesn't leave, he loses the opportunity to receive $200.

Well, wouldn't he have forfeited something—albeit not $200—if he stayed at the movie theater before the $200 was offered? (Might he have given up at least $1 in benefits doing something else?) In short, didn't he have some opportunity cost of staying at the movie theater before the $200 was offered? Surely he did. The problem is that somehow, by letting sunk cost influence his decision, Jeremy was willing to ignore this opportunity cost of staying at the theater. All the $200 did was to make this opportunity cost of staying at the movie theater obvious.

Thinking like
AN ECONOMIST

In economics, it is important to learn what comes before a particular event. To illustrate, suppose ATC is rising at this moment. Can you see the process that brought this particular event (ATC rising) at this particular moment?

Let's take one step back at a time. ATC is rising because (one step back) MC rose to a level above ATC. But why did MC rise to a level above ATC or why is MC rising at all? MC is rising because MPP (one step back) is declining. But why is MPP declining? MPP is declining because (one step back) the law of diminishing marginal returns set in.

When you look at a tree, you see a tree with branches and leaves. If you "look back" though, you can see the seed that was planted that grew into the tree. It is the same in economics. When you look at rising ATC, most of us simply see "rising ATC." But if you look far enough back, you can see the law of diminishing marginal returns "growing" into "rising ATC."

economics 24/7

"I HAVE TO BECOME AN ACCOUNTANT"

Don: I don't like accounting, but I have to become an accountant.

Mike: Why?

Don: Because I've spent four years in college studying accounting. I spent all that money and time on accounting; I have to get some benefits from it.

Mike: The money and time you spent on accounting are sunk costs. You can't get those back.

Don: Sure I can. All I have to do is work as an accountant. I'll be earning a good income and getting my "college investment" to pay off.

Mike: It sounds to me as if you're letting your four years in college studying accounting determine what you will do for the rest of your work life. Why do that?

Don: Because accounting is all I know how to do.

Mike: If you could do it over, what would you study and do?

Don: I'd study English literature and then I'd become a high school teacher.

Mike: Can't you still do that? You're only 24 years old.

Don: Sure, but that would mean my last 4 years in college were completely wasted. I'm not going to waste them.

Mike: Again, you're letting your past determine what you do now and in the future.

Don: It sounds like you're telling me to get out of accounting.

Mike: I'm not advising you to stay in or to get out of accounting. I'm simply saying that the time and money you spent getting a degree in accounting are sunk costs and that you shouldn't let sunk costs determine what you will do with your life.

Don: It still seems as if you're advising me to get out of accounting.

Mike: But that's not true. I'm simply saying that you should look at the benefits and costs of being an accountant—starting at this moment in time. You shouldn't look over your shoulder and say that because you "invested" four years in accounting that you now have to become an accountant. Those four years are gone; you can never get them back. And you shouldn't try.

Don: In other words, starting from this moment in time, I should ask myself what the costs and benefits are of becoming an accountant. If the costs are greater than the benefits, I should not become one, but if the benefits are greater than the costs, I should become one.

Mike: That's right. Let me put it to you this way. Suppose tomorrow the bottom fell out of the accounting market. Accountants couldn't earn even $100 a month. Would you still want to be an accountant?

Now consider the following situation: Suppose Alicia purchases a pair of shoes, wears them for a few days, and then realizes they are uncomfortable. Furthermore, suppose she can't return the shoes for a refund. Are the shoes a sunk cost? Would an economist recommend that Alicia simply not wear the shoes? An economist would consider the shoes a sunk cost because the purchase of the shoes represents a cost (1) incurred in the past that (2) cannot be changed by a current decision and (3) cannot be recovered. An economist would recommend that Alicia not base her current decision to wear or not wear the shoes on what has happened and cannot be changed. If Alicia lets what she has done, and can't undo, influence her present decision, she runs the risk of compounding her mistake.

To illustrate, if Alicia decides to wear the uncomfortable shoes because she thinks it is a waste of money not to, then she may end up with an even bigger loss: certainly less comfort and possibly a trip to the podiatrist later. The relevant question she must ask herself is, "What will I give up by wearing the uncomfortable shoes?" and not, "What did I give up by buying the shoes?"

The message here is that only the future can be affected by a present decision, never the past. Bygones are bygones; sunk costs are sunk costs.

Don: No way. It wouldn't make any sense. I couldn't earn enough income.

Mike: Well, if you wouldn't become an accountant because the benefits ($100 a month) are too low relative to the costs, doesn't it make sense not to become an accountant if the costs are too high relative to the benefits?

Don: What do you mean?

Mike: Well, suppose the bottom does not fall out of the accounting market, and you can earn $4,000 a month working as an accountant. The question now is: How much do you have to give up, say, in terms of less utility, to get this $4,000 a month? If you would be happy as an English literature teacher, although earning less than you would earn as an accountant, and unhappy as an accountant, then the cost of becoming an accountant and not a teacher may be more than $4,000 a month.

Don: I agree that if I become an accountant, I will have to give up some happiness. But if I don't become an accountant and become a high school teacher instead, I will have to give up some income because I probably would earn less as a teacher than as an accountant. And by the way, income gives me some happiness.

Mike: I agree. But now you're at least looking at the choice you have to make without considering something in the past that you can't change—that is, studying accounting in college.

Don: How so?

Mike: You're asking yourself what the benefits will be of becoming an accountant, and your answer seems to be the happiness or utility you'll receive from $4,000 a month. You're then asking yourself what the costs will be of becoming an accountant, and you seem to be saying that you'll have to forfeit some happiness. The question then becomes: Will the $4,000 a month provide you with enough utility to overcome the disutility you will feel because you're unhappy working as an accountant?

Don: But by doing this, how am I ignoring sunk cost? All this seems to tell me is that economics is about utility, not money.

Mike: You're ignoring the sunk cost of obtaining an accounting degree because when you consider the costs of becoming an accountant, you are considering only what you will (in the future) give up if you become one. You're not considering what you already have (in the past) given up and that cannot be changed.

Don: And are you suggesting that this is what I should do—only consider future costs and not sunk costs?

Mike: Yes, because you're better off not trying to change something that cannot be changed. It would be a little like your trying to change the weather. You can't do it, and you shouldn't waste your time and energy trying. If you do try, you're simply forfeiting other things that you could be accomplishing.

Don: In other words, I shouldn't try to get back the sunk costs I incurred getting an accounting degree because trying to do this means that I'll be forfeiting the opportunity to do other things. I'd be compounding an error. I'd be trying to get back something I can't get back and, in the process, losing some important time, energy, and perhaps money that I could be using in a more "utility productive" way.

Mike: That's right.

BEHAVIORAL ECONOMICS AND SUNK COST In one real-life experiment, two researchers randomly distributed discounts to buyers of subscriptions to Ohio University's 1982–1983 theater season.[5] One group of ticket buyers paid the normal ticket price of $15 per ticket, a second group received $2 off per ticket, and a third group received $7 off per ticket. In short, some buyers paid lower ticket prices than other buyers did.

The researchers found that people who paid more for their tickets attended the theater performances more often than those who paid less for their tickets. Now some people argue that this is because the people who paid more for their tickets somehow wanted to attend the theater more than those who paid less. But this isn't likely because the discounts to buyers were distributed randomly.

Thinking like
AN ECONOMIST
The economist knows that an understanding of sunk cost helps us to see the truth of the old saying, "Don't cry over spilled milk." Milk that has been spilled cannot be unspilled, so crying over it doesn't change a thing. If it did—if, by crying, you could unspill the milk—then by all means go ahead and cry

---

[5]Hal Arkes and Catherine Blumer, "The Psychology of Sunk Cost," *Organizational Behavior and Human Decision Processes* 124 (1985).

Microeconomics emphasizes that all economic actors deal with objectives, constraints, and choices. Let's focus briefly on constraints. All economic actors would prefer to have fewer rather than more constraints and to have constraints that offer more rather than less latitude. For example, a firm would probably prefer to be constrained in having to buy its resources from five suppliers rather than from only one supplier. A consumer would rather have a budget constraint of $4,000 a month instead of $2,000 a month.

Think of two persons, A and B. Person A considers sunk cost when she makes a decision, and person B ignores it when she makes a decision. Does one person face fewer constraints, ceteris paribus? The answer is that the person who ignores sunk cost when making a decision, person B, faces fewer constraints. What person A does, in fact, is act as if a constraint is there— the constraint of sunk cost, the constraint of having to rectify a past decision—when it really exists only because person A thinks it does.

In this sense, the "constraint" of sunk cost is very different from the constraint of, say, scarcity. Whether a person believes it or not, scarcity exists. People are constrained by scarcity, as they are by the force of gravity, whether they know it or not. But people are not constrained by sunk cost if they choose not to be constrained by it. If you choose to let bygones be bygones, if you realize that sunk cost is a cost that has been incurred and cannot be changed, then you will not be constrained by it when making a current decision.

Economists look at things this way: There are already enough constraints in the world. You are not made better off by behaving as if there is one more than there actually is.

Instead, what seems to be the case here is that the more someone paid for the ticket (and everyone paid for his or her ticket before the night of the theater performance), the greater the sunk cost. And the greater the sunk cost, the more likely individuals were to attend the theater performance. In other words, (at least some) people were not ignoring sunk cost.

SELF-TEST

1. Identify two ways to compute average total cost (*ATC*).

2. Would a business ever sell its product for less than cost? Explain your answer.

3. What happens to unit costs as marginal costs rise? Explain your answer.

4. Do changes in marginal physical product influence unit costs? Explain your answer.

Production and Costs in the Long Run

This section discusses production and long-run costs. As noted previously, in the long run, there are no fixed inputs and no fixed costs. Consequently, the firm has *greater flexibility* in the long run than in the short run.

Long-Run Average Total Cost Curve

In the short run, there are fixed costs and variable costs; therefore, total cost is the sum of the two. But in the long run, there are no fixed costs, so variable costs *are* total costs. This section focuses on (1) what the long-run average total cost (*LRATC*) curve is and (2) what it looks like.

Consider the manager of a firm that produces bedroom furniture. When all inputs are variable, the manager must decide what the situation of the firm should be in the (upcoming) short-run period. For example, suppose he needs to determine the size of the plant; that is, he must decide whether the plant will be small, medium, or large. After this decision is made, he is locked into a specific plant size; he is locked in for the short run.

Associated with each of the three different plant sizes is a short-run average total cost (*SRATC*) curve. (We discuss both short-run and long-run average total cost curves here, so we distinguish between the two with prefixes: *SR* for short run and *LR* for long run.) The three short-run average total cost curves, representing the different plant sizes, are illustrated in Exhibit 7(a).

Suppose the manager of the firm wants to produce output level Q_1. Which plant size will he choose? Obviously, he will choose the plant size represented by $SRATC_1$ because this gives a lower unit cost of producing Q_1 than the plant size represented by $SRATC_2$. The latter plant size has a higher unit cost of producing Q_1 ($6 as opposed to $5).

Suppose, though, the manager chooses to produce Q_2. Which plant size will he choose now? He will choose the plant size represented by $SRATC_3$ because the unit cost of producing Q_2 is lower with the plant size represented by $SRATC_3$ than it is with the plant size represented by $SRATC_2$.

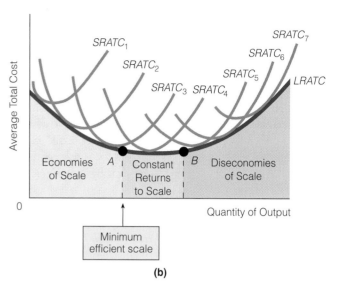

(a)

(b)

exhibit **7**

Long-Run Average Total Cost Curve (*LRATC*)

(a) There are three short-run average total cost curves for three different plant sizes. If these are the only plant sizes, the long-run average total cost curve is the heavily shaded, blue scalloped curve. (b) The long-run average total cost curve is the heavily shaded, blue smooth curve. The *LRATC* curve in (b) is not scalloped because it is assumed that there are so many plant sizes that the *LRATC* curve touches each *SRATC* curve at only one point.

If we were to ask the same question for every (possible) output level, we would derive the **long-run average total cost (*LRATC*)** curve. The *LRATC* curve shows the lowest unit cost at which the firm can produce any given level of output. In Exhibit 7(a), it is those portions of the three *SRATC* curves that are tangential to the blue curve. The *LRATC* curve is the scalloped blue curve.

Exhibit 7(b) shows a host of *SRATC* curves and one *LRATC* curve. In this case, the *LRATC* curve is not scalloped, as it is in part (a). The *LRATC* curve is smooth in part (b) because we assume there are many plant sizes in addition to the three represented in (a). In other words, although they have not been drawn, short-run average total cost curves representing different plant sizes exist in (b) between $SRATC_1$ and $SRATC_2$ and between $SRATC_2$ and $SRATC_3$ and so on. In this case, the *LRATC* curve is smooth and touches each *SRATC* curve at one point.

Economies of Scale, Diseconomies of Scale, and Constant Returns to Scale

Suppose two inputs, labor and capital, are used together to produce a particular good. If inputs are increased by some percentage (say, 100 percent) and output increases by a greater percentage (more than 100 percent), then unit costs fall and **economies of scale** are said to exist.

For example, suppose good X is made with two inputs, Y and Z, and it takes $20Y$ and $10Z$ to produce 5 units of X. The cost of each unit of input Y is $1, and the cost of each unit of input Z is $1. Thus, a total cost of $30 is required to produce 5 units of X. The unit cost (average total cost) of good X is $6 ($ATC = TC/Q$). Now consider a doubling of inputs Y and Z to $40Y$ and $20Z$ and a more than doubling in output, say, to 15 units of X. This means a total cost of $60 is required to produce 15 units of X, and the unit cost (average total cost) of good X is $4.

An increase in inputs can have two other results. If inputs are increased by some percentage and output increases by an equal percentage, then unit costs remain constant and **constant returns to scale** are said to exist. If inputs are increased by some percentage and output increases by a smaller percentage, then unit costs rise and **diseconomies of scale** are said to exist.

The three conditions can easily be seen in the *LRATC* curve in Exhibit 7(b). If economies of scale are present, the *LRATC* curve is falling, if constant returns to scale are present, the curve is flat, and if diseconomies of scale are present, the curve is rising.

Long-Run Average Total Cost (*LRATC*) Curve
A curve that shows the lowest (unit) cost at which the firm can produce any given level of output.

Economies of Scale
Exist when inputs are increased by some percentage and output increases by a greater percentage, causing unit costs to fall.

Constant Returns to Scale
Exist when inputs are increased by some percentage and output increases by an equal percentage, causing unit costs to remain constant.

Diseconomies of Scale
Exist when inputs are increased by some percentage and output increases by a smaller percentage, causing unit costs to rise.

Economies of scale → LRATC is falling
Constant returns to scale → LRATC is constant
Diseconomies of scale → LRATC is rising

Minimum Efficient Scale
The lowest output level at which average total costs are minimized.

If, in the production of a good, economies of scale give way to constant returns to scale or diseconomies of scale, as in Exhibit 7(b), the point at which this occurs is referred to as the minimum efficient scale. The **minimum efficient scale** is the lowest output level at which average total costs are minimized. Point *A* represents the minimum efficient scale in Exhibit 7(b).

What is the significance of the minimum efficient scale of output? Its significance can be seen by looking at the long-run average total cost curve between points *A* and *B* in
Exhibit 7(b). Between points *A* and *B,* there are constant returns to scale; the average total cost is the same over the various output levels between the two points. This means that larger firms (firms producing greater output levels) within this range do not have a cost advantage over smaller firms that operate at the minimum efficient scale.

Keep in mind that economies of scale, diseconomies of scale, and constant returns to scale are only relevant in the long run. Implicit in the definition of the terms, and explicit in the example of economies of scale, all inputs necessary to the production of a good are changeable. Because no input is fixed, economies of scale, diseconomies of scale, and constant returns to scale must be relevant only in the long run.

Q&A

What is the difference between diminishing marginal returns and diseconomies of scale?

Diminishing marginal returns are the result of using, say, a given plant size more intensively (adding more labor to a fixed amount of capital). Diseconomies of scale result from changes in the size of the plant.

Why Economies of Scale?

Up to a certain point, long-run unit costs of production fall as a firm grows. There are two main reasons for this: (1) Growing firms offer greater opportunities for employees to specialize. Individual workers can become highly proficient at more narrowly defined tasks, often producing more output at lower unit costs. (2) Growing firms (especially large, growing firms) can take advantage of highly efficient mass production techniques and equipment that ordinarily require large setup costs and thus are economical only if they can be spread over a large number of units. For example, assembly line techniques are usually "cheap" when millions of units of a good are produced but are "expensive" when only a few thousand units are produced.

Why Diseconomies of Scale?

Diseconomies of scale usually arise at the point where a firm's size causes coordination, communication, and monitoring problems. In very large firms, managers often find it difficult to coordinate work activities, communicate their directives to the right persons in satisfactory time, and monitor personnel effectively. The business operation simply gets "too big." There is, of course, a monetary incentive not to pass the point of operation where diseconomies of scale exist. Firms will usually find ways to avoid diseconomies of scale. They will reorganize, divide operations, hire new managers, and so on.

Minimum Efficient Scale and Number of Firms in an Industry

Some industries are composed of a smaller number of firms than other industries are. Or we can say there is a different degree of concentration in different industries.

The minimum efficient scale (*MES*) as a percentage of U.S. consumption or total sales is not the same for all industries. For example, in industry *X, MES* as a percentage of total sales might be 6.6, and in industry *Y,* it might be 2.3. This means the firms in industry *X* reach the minimum efficient scale of plant, and thus exhaust economies of scale, at an output level of 6.6 percent of total industry sales, whereas the firms in industry *Y* experience economies of scale only up to an output level of 2.3 percent of total industry sales. Ask yourself in which industry you would expect to find fewer firms? The answer is in industry X. By dividing the *MES* as a percentage of total sales into 100, we can estimate the number of efficient firms it takes to satisfy total consumption for a particular product. For the product produced by industry X, it takes 15 firms ($100/6.6 = 15$). For the product produced by industry Y, it takes 43 firms.

Shifts in Cost Curves

In discussing the shape of short-run and long-run cost curves, we assumed that certain factors remained constant. We discuss a few of these factors here and describe how changes in them can shift cost curves.

Taxes

Consider a tax on each unit of a good produced. Suppose company X has to pay a tax of $3 for each unit of X it produces. What effects will this have on the firm's cost curves? Will the tax affect the firm's fixed costs? No, it won't. The tax is paid only when output is produced, and fixed costs are present even if output is zero. (Note that if the tax is a lump-sum tax, requiring the company to pay a lump sum no matter how many units of X it produces, the tax will affect fixed costs.) We conclude that the tax does not affect fixed costs and therefore cannot affect average fixed cost.

Will the tax affect variable costs? Yes, it will. As a consequence of the tax, the firm has to pay more for each unit of X it produces. Because variable costs rise, so does total cost. This means that average variable cost and average total cost rise, and the representative cost curves shift upward. Finally, because marginal cost is the change in total cost divided by the change in output, marginal cost rises and the marginal cost curve shifts upward.

Input Prices

A rise or fall in variable input prices causes a corresponding change in the firm's average total, average variable, and marginal cost curves. For example, if the price of steel rises, the variable costs of building skyscrapers rise, and so must average variable cost, average total cost, and marginal cost. The cost curves shift upward. If the price of steel falls, the opposite effects occur.

Technology

Technological changes often bring either (1) the capability of using fewer inputs to produce a good (e.g., the introduction of the personal computer reduced the hours necessary to key and edit a manuscript) or (2) lower input prices (e.g., technological improvements in transistors have led to price reductions in the transistor components of calculators). In either case, technological changes of this variety lower variable costs and, consequently, lower average variable cost, average total cost, and marginal cost. The cost curves shift downward.

SELF-TEST

1. Give an arithmetical example to illustrate economies of scale.

2. What would the *LRATC* curve look like if there were always constant returns to scale? Explain your answer.

3. Firm A charged $4 per unit when it produced 100 units of good X, and it charged $3 per unit when it produced 200 units. Furthermore, the firm earned the same profit per unit in both cases. How can this happen?

A Reader Asks . . .

Will a Knowledge of Sunk Cost Help Prevent Me from Making a Mistake in the Stock Market?

I have a friend who bought some stock at $40 a share. Soon after she bought the stock, it fell to $30 a share. I asked my friend if she planned to sell the stock. She said that she couldn't because if she did, she would take a $10 loss per share of stock. Is she looking at things correctly?

No. Your friend is letting a past decision (the purchase of stock at $40 a share) influence a present decision (whether or not to sell the stock).

Let's go back in time to when your friend was thinking about whether or not to buy the stock. Before she made the purchase, she must have asked herself this question: "Do I think the price of the stock will rise or fall?" She must have thought the price of the stock would rise or else she wouldn't have purchased it.

Why, then, doesn't she ask herself the same question now that the price of the stock has fallen? Why not ask, "Do I think the price of the stock will rise or fall?" Isn't this the best question she can ask herself? If she thinks the price of the stock will rise, then she should not sell the stock. But if she thinks the price will fall, then she should sell the stock before it falls further in price.

Instead, she lets her present be influenced by her past. She cannot change the past; she cannot change the fact that the price of her stock has fallen $10 per share. The $10 per share fall in price is a sunk cost. It is something that happened in the past and cannot be changed by a current decision. If she doesn't ignore sunk cost, she risks losing even more than she already has lost.

! analyzing the scene

Should Olaf sell the chair for a price below his cost? What would you do if you were Lisa?

Are both Olaf and Lisa looking at a sunk cost? Let's consider Olaf's situation. When someone says that he's going to sell something for below cost, usually we wonder what's wrong with him. How can Olaf make any profit if he sells the chair below his cost? Well, sometimes things don't turn out the way people would like. Profit is not guaranteed. The two options Olaf might have now are (1) don't sell the chair for less than cost and therefore don't sell the chair or (2) sell the chair below cost. If the choice is between not receiving any money for the chair and receiving some money for the chair, it is better to receive some money than no money. The $76 Olaf spent on producing the chair is a sunk cost. He cannot get back the $76. Now the choice is between selling the chair—at whatever price he can get—and ending up with some money or refusing to sell the chair and ending up with no money.

Now let's consider Lisa, a computer science major who doesn't like computer science. People tell her to stay with computer science because it pays well and because she has already invested so many years in the major. However, Lisa cannot change the past, and she should not let something she cannot change affect her future. She needs to ignore the past because the past is a sunk cost. Instead, she must ask herself what her future will be like if she continues in computer science and what her future will be like if she chooses to give up computer science and do something she likes better. For a feature that directly touches on this subject, read "I Have to Become an Accountant."

What keeps Ursula from cheating?

If Ursula doesn't feel any guilt from cheating, then why doesn't she cheat? The first and obvious answer is that she is afraid of being caught. But suppose there is no chance of her being caught. Will she cheat then? The answer is "not necessarily."

Whether she cheats or not actually has something to do with the average-marginal rule. People usually cheat by copying the work of someone they believe is smarter than they are. Suppose Ursula believes that her grade on the test will be 65 and that Ian and Charles will each receive a grade of 60 on the test. Her 65 can be viewed as the "average grade" and the grade of Ian and Charles as the "marginal grade." Because the marginal is less than the average, the marginal will pull the average down. There's no need to cheat if copying someone else's work will lower your grade. Ursula is likely to cheat only if she believes her grade will rise by cheating. But this will only occur if Ian and Charles are better students than she is. If a teacher wants to minimize cheating on a test, he or she should sit people with similar grades together.

Would Quentin be more likely to quit his accounting job to own a sports bar if he earned a salary of $60,000 a year instead of $150,000 a year?

The less Quentin gives up if he leaves his job as an accountant, the more likely he will leave his job as an accountant. Forfeiting $60,000 is easier than forfeiting $150,000, so the answer to the question is yes. There are benefits (to Quentin) of owning and operating a sports bar, but there are costs too. Some of those costs are explicit (rent for the bar, pretzels, TV sets, beer, etc.), and some of those costs are implicit (specifically, his salary as an accountant). Quentin is likely to consider both explicit and implicit costs in deciding whether or not to quit his job to own and operate a sports bar.

chapter summary

The Firm

- Alchian and Demsetz argue that firms are formed when there are benefits from individuals working as a team—specifically, when the sum of what individuals can produce as a team is greater than the sum of what individuals can produce alone: sum of team production > sum of individual production.

- There are both advantages and disadvantages to team production. The chief advantage (in many cases) is the positive difference between the output produced by the team and the sum of the output produced by individuals working alone. The chief disadvantage is the increased shirking in teams. The role of the monitor (manager) in the firm is to preserve the increased output and reduce or eliminate the increased shirking. The monitors have a monetary incentive not to shirk their monitoring duties when they are residual claimants.

- Ronald Coase argued that firms exist to reduce the "costs of negotiating and concluding a separate contract for each exchange transaction which takes place on a market." In short, firms exist to reduce transaction costs.

Explicit Cost and Implicit Cost

- An explicit cost is incurred when an actual (monetary) payment is made. An implicit cost represents the value of resources used in production for which no actual (monetary) payment is made.

Economic Profit and Accounting Profit

- Economic profit is the difference between total revenue and total cost, including both explicit and implicit costs. Accounting profit is the difference between total revenue

and explicit costs. Economic profit is usually lower (never higher) than accounting profit. Economic profit (not accounting profit) motivates economic behavior.

Production and Costs in the Short Run

- The short run is a period in which some inputs are fixed. The long run is a period in which all inputs can be varied. The costs associated with fixed and variable inputs are referred to as fixed costs and variable costs, respectively.

- Marginal cost is the change in total cost that results from a change in output.

- The law of diminishing marginal returns states that as ever-larger amounts of a variable input are combined with fixed inputs, eventually, the marginal physical product of the variable input will decline. As this happens, marginal cost rises.

- The average-marginal rule states that if the marginal magnitude is above (below) the average magnitude, the average magnitude rises (falls).

- The marginal cost curve intersects the average variable cost curve at its lowest point. The marginal cost curve intersects the average total cost curve at its lowest point. There is no relationship between marginal cost and average fixed cost.

Production and Costs in the Long Run

- In the long run, there are no fixed costs, so variable costs equal total costs.

- The long-run average total cost curve is the envelope of the short-run average total cost curves. It shows the lowest unit cost at which the firm can produce any given level of output.

- If inputs are increased by some percentage and output increases by a greater percentage, then unit costs fall and economies of scale exist. If inputs are increased by some percentage and output increases by an equal percentage, then unit costs remain constant and constant returns to scale exist. If inputs are increased by some percentage and output increases by a smaller percentage, then unit costs rise and diseconomies of scale exist.

- The minimum efficient scale is the lowest output level at which average total costs are minimized.

Sunk Cost

- Sunk cost is a cost incurred in the past that cannot be changed by current decisions and therefore cannot be recovered. A person or firm that wants to minimize losses will hold sunk costs to be irrelevant to present decisions.

Shifts in Cost Curves

- A firm's cost curves will shift if there is a change in taxes, input prices, or technology.

key terms and concepts

Business Firm	Accounting Profit	Law of Diminishing Marginal Returns	Average Total Cost (ATC), or Unit Cost
Market Coordination	Economic Profit	Fixed Costs	Average-Marginal Rule
Managerial Coordination	Normal Profit	Variable Costs	Sunk Cost
Shirking	Fixed Input	Total Cost (TC)	Long-Run Average Total Cost (LRATC) Curve
Monitor	Variable Input	Marginal Cost (MC)	
Residual Claimant	Short Run	Average Fixed Cost (AFC)	Economies of Scale
Profit	Long Run		Constant Returns to Scale
Explicit Cost	Marginal Physical Product (MPP)	Average Variable Cost (AVC)	Diseconomies of Scale
Implicit Cost			Minimum Efficient Scale

questions and problems

1   Explain the difference between managerial coordination and market coordination.

2   Is the managerial coordination that goes on inside a business firm independent of market forces? Explain your answer.

3   Explain why even conscientious workers will shirk more when the cost of shirking falls.

4   Illustrate the average-marginal rule in a noncost setting.

5   "A firm that earns only normal profit is not covering all its costs." Do you agree or disagree? Explain your answer.

6   The average variable cost curve and the average total cost curve get closer to each other as output increases. What explains this?

7   When would total costs equal fixed costs?

8   Is studying for an economics exam subject to the law of diminishing marginal returns? If so, what is the fixed input? What is the variable input?

9   Some individuals decry the decline of the small family farm and its replacement with the huge corporate megafarm. Discuss the possibility that this is a consequence of economies of scale.

10   We know there is a link between productivity and costs. For example, recall the link between the marginal physical product of the variable input and marginal cost. With this in mind, what link might there be between productivity and prices?

11   Some people's everyday behavior suggests that they do not hold sunk costs irrelevant to present decisions. Give some examples different from those discussed in this chapter.

12   Explain why a firm might want to produce its good even after diminishing marginal returns have set in and marginal cost is rising.

13   People often believe that large firms in an industry have cost advantages over small firms in the same industry.

For example, they might think a big oil company has a cost advantage over a small oil company. For this to be true, what condition must exist? Explain your answer.

14 The government says that firm X must pay $1,000 in taxes simply because it is in the business of producing a good. What cost curves, if any, does this tax affect?

15 Based on your answer to question 14, does MC change if TC changes?

16 Under what condition would Bill Gates be the richest person in the United States and earn zero economic profit?

working with numbers and graphs

1 Determine the appropriate dollar amount for each lettered space.

(1) Quantity of Output, Q (units)	(2) Total Fixed Cost (dollars)	(3) Average Fixed Cost (AFC)	(4) Total Variable Cost (TVC)	(5) Average Variable Cost (AVC)	(6) Total Cost (TC)	(7) Average Total Cost (ATC)	(8) Marginal cost (MC)
0	$200	_A_	$0		_V_		
1	200	_B_	30	_L_	_W_	_GG_	_QQ_
2	200	_C_	50	_M_	_X_	_HH_	_RR_
3	200	_D_	60	_N_	_Y_	_I_	_SS_
4	200	_E_	65	_O_	_Z_	_JJ_	_TT_
5	200	_F_	75	_P_	_AA_	_KK_	_UU_
6	200	_G_	95	_Q_	_BB_	_LL_	_VV_
7	200	_H_	125	_R_	_CC_	_MM_	_WW_
8	200	_I_	165	_S_	_DD_	_NN_	_XX_
9	200	_J_	215	_T_	_EE_	_OO_	_YY_
10	200	_K_	275	_U_	_FF_	_PP_	_ZZ_

2 Give a numerical example to show that as marginal physical product (MPP) rises, marginal cost (MC) falls.

3 Price = $20, quantity = 400 units, unit cost = $15, implicit costs = $4,000. What does economic profit equal?

4 If economic profit equals accounting profit, what do implicit costs equal?

5 If accounting profit is $400,000 greater than economic profit, what do implicit costs equal?

6 If marginal physical product is continually declining, what does marginal cost look like? Explain your answer.

7 If the ATC curve is continually declining, what does this imply about the MC curve? Explain your answer.

Setting the Scene

The following events occurred on a day in July.

11:12 A.M.

Pam Weatherspoon owns 2,000 shares of Wal-Mart stock. She has been thinking about selling 500 shares of the stock. Today, she goes online to find the current selling price of Wal-Mart stock; it's $58.68 a share. She decides to sell the 500 shares at this per-share price.

2:30 P.M.

Ricky Amador started his company, Amador Electronics, 10 years ago. Last year, he took a loss—his first loss in 10 years. He's thinking it might be a good idea to go out of business.

2:54 P.M.

A U.S. senator is speaking on a newly proposed tax bill. Some members of the Senate are walking about, some are at their desks reading, and a few are listening to the U.S. senator speak.

The senator says, "Certain companies in our country have been reaping huge windfall profits over the past year. I am not against profits—not when people

work for them. But when huge profits are handed to certain firms not because the firms did anything to make their product a better product, not because they served the buying public better, and not because they built a better mousetrap, well then I have to say that something is wrong with those profits. In the America of today, certain companies are reaping huge windfall profits simply because the demand for their product increased. Unearned profits must be taxed at a higher rate than earned profits—or else we do not live in a fair and just society."

3:08 P.M.

Steven Pickering manufactures and sells small fans—the type a person might buy for an office. As he walks out of his factory to his car, Steven is wondering how many fans he should produce in the upcoming six-month period.

3:23 P.M.

A TV executive is in her office, looking out the window. She's thinking about one

of the networks hottest TV shows. Last year, the show was the network's biggest profit maker. This year, the stars of the show are asking for huge salary increases. The TV executive wonders if the show would be as successful without two of the six major cast members. She also wonders if the stars are worth the salaries they want.

? Here are some questions to keep in mind as you read this chapter:

- *If Pam had decided to sell 400 shares of Wal-Mart stock instead of 500 shares, could she have sold each share for more than $58.68?*

- *Should a company shut down if it is incurring a loss?*

- *What will happen if taxes are imposed on companies because demand for their products has increased?*

- *How does a business owner decide how much of his or her product to produce?*

- *Why do profits sometimes get turned into salaries?*

See analyzing the scene at the end of this chapter for answers to these questions.

Market Structures

Every firm shares two things with all other firms. First, every firm has to answer certain questions. These questions are:

1. What price should the firm charge for the good it produces and sells?

2. How many units of the good should the firm produce?

3. How much of the various resources that the firm needs to produce its good should it buy?

In short, regardless of whether a firm sells shirts or cars, whether it is large or small, whether it is located in Georgia or Maine, it must answer all three of these questions, period.

Second, every firm is like all other firms in that every firm finds itself operating within a certain *market structure*. A **market structure** is a firm's particular environment or setting, the characteristics of which influence the firm's pricing and output decisions.

Economists often discuss four different market structures: perfect competition, monopoly, monopolistic competition, and oligopoly. This chapter focuses on perfect competition; the next chapter, on monopoly; and the following chapter, on monopolistic competition and oligopoly. Essentially, in these three chapters, we outline the various theories that relate to each of the four market structures. Within these theories, you will see how firms go about answering the first two questions that all firms must answer. We begin to explain how the last question is answered when we discuss factor markets (later in the text).

Market Structure

The particular environment of a firm, the characteristics of which influence the firm's pricing and output decisions.

Perfect Competition

A theory of market structure based on four assumptions: There are many sellers and buyers, sellers sell a homogeneous good, buyers and sellers have all relevant information, and there is easy entry into and exit from the market.

The Theory of Perfect Competition

In this section, we begin our discussion of the theory of **perfect competition**, which is built on four assumptions:

1. **There are many sellers and many buyers, none of which is large in relation to total sales or purchases.** This assumption speaks to both demand (number of buyers) and supply (number of sellers). Because there are many buyers and sellers, it is reasonably assumed that each buyer and each seller acts independently of other buyers and sellers, respectively, and each is so small a part of the market that he or she has no influence on price.

2. **Each firm produces and sells a homogeneous product.** This means each firm sells a product that is indistinguishable from all other firms' products in a given industry. (For example, a buyer of wheat cannot distinguish between Farmer Stone's wheat and Farmer Gray's wheat.) As a consequence, buyers are indifferent to the sellers of the product.

3. **Buyers and sellers have all relevant information about prices, product quality, sources of supply, and so forth.** Buyers and sellers know who is selling what, at what prices, at what quality, and on what terms. In short, they know everything that relates to buying, producing, and selling the product.

4. **Firms have easy entry and exit.** New firms can enter the market easily, and existing firms can exit the market easily. There are no barriers to entry or exit.

When we were discussing supply and demand (in Chapter 3), we briefly discussed what a theory is and why economists build theories. We are beginning to build a theory in this chapter—the theory of perfect competition. In every theory, assumptions are made. Do the assumptions of a theory have to be perfectly descriptive, or else are they useless? Most economists think not. Economists do not judge the worthiness of theories by how realistic the assumptions of the theory are. They judge the worthiness of the theory by how well it predicts real-world events. For example, the third assumption we made in the theory of perfect competition—buyers and sellers have all relevant information about prices, product quality, sources of supply, and so forth—may seem unrealistic. After all, can buyers and sellers really have all relevant information? The answer is they may not. But they may have enough of the relevant information (90 percent instead of 100 percent) so that things "turn out" the way they would if they had all relevant information.

What is our main point? Simply this: Even though a theory's assumptions may not be 100 percent accurate, they may be, as economist Milton Friedman has noted, "sufficiently good approximations for the purpose at hand."

economics 24/7

AMAZON: THERE MAY NOT BE ANY CAPPUCCINO, BUT THERE ARE MILLIONS OF BOOKS

Book superstores seem to be springing up everywhere in recent years. Usually, these superstores are about 25,000 square feet and have comfortable chairs and a coffee area. You can relax with a hot cup of cappuccino as you browse through a book you pulled off the seemingly endless rows of shelves. Companies such as Borders, Crown, Books-a-Million, and Barnes & Noble have been opening book superstores all over the country.

So far, superstores have been profitable ventures for Barnes & Noble. On average, a book superstore costs about $2 million to create and generates more than $6 million in total revenues in its first year.

When there are positive economic profits such as these, firms outside the market will enter to compete for a share of the positive profits earned by existing firms. In the book-selling market, the Internet has made this easier to do. Now, instead of building a $2 million physical superstore, it is possible to "build" a book superstore in cyberspace. In other words, it is possible to compete with Barnes & Noble, Crown, and Borders—firms that have physical superstores—by selling books via the Internet.

Amazon entered the book superstore market because the brick-and-mortar superstores had proved there were profits in the market. But Amazon entered the market in a way that had never been done before—through cyberspace. In April 1997, CEO Jeff Bezos said that a list of Amazon's 2.5 million titles would fill 14 New York City phone books. In other words, in the world of book superstores, Amazon is the super book superstore.

So what have we learned? First, when there are positive economic profits in a competitive market, new firms will enter the market. This is what Amazon did. Second, it is possible to enter a market today—as opposed to only a few years ago—through cyberspace. The Internet has given potential competitors another road they can travel to enter new markets.

Before discussing the perfectly competitive firm in the short run and in the long run, we discuss some of the characteristics of the perfectly competitive firm that result from these four assumptions.

A Perfectly Competitive Firm Is a Price Taker

A perfectly competitive firm is a **price taker**. A price taker is a seller that does not have the ability to control the price of the product it sells; it takes the price determined in the market. For example, if Farmer Stone is a price taker, it follows that he can increase or decrease his output without significantly affecting the price of the product he sells.

Why is a perfectly competitive firm a price taker? A firm is restrained from being anything but a price taker if it finds itself one among many firms where its supply is small relative to the total market supply (assumption 1 in the theory of perfect competition), and it sells a homogeneous product (assumption 2) in an environment where buyers and sellers have all relevant information (assumption 3).

Some people might suggest that the assumptions of the theory of perfect competition give economists what they want. Economists want the perfectly competitive firm to be a price taker, and so they choose the assumptions that will make this so. But this isn't the case. Economists start out with certain assumptions and then logically conclude that the firm for which these assumptions hold, or that behaves as if these assumptions hold, is a price taker; that is, it has no control over price. Afterward, economists test the theory by observing whether it accurately predicts and explains the real-world behavior of some firms.

Price Taker

A seller that does not have the ability to control the price of the product it sells; it takes the price determined in the market.

Q&A

An earlier chapter notes that demand curves are downward sloping. Now it appears that the demand curve for a perfectly competitive firm is not downward sloping but horizontal. How can this happen?

To answer this question, we emphasize the distinction between the market demand curve and a single firm's demand curve.

The market demand curve *in Exhibit 1(a) is downward sloping, positing an inverse relationship between price and quantity demanded, ceteris paribus. The* single perfectly competitive firm's demand curve *does not contradict this relationship; it simply represents the pricing situation in which the* single *perfectly competitive firm finds itself. Recall from an earlier chapter that the more substitutes for a good, the higher the price elasticity of demand. In the perfectly competitive market setting, there are many substitutes for the firm's product—so many, in fact, that the firm's demand curve is perfectly elastic.*

A single perfectly competitive firm's supply is such a small percentage of the total market supply *that the firm cannot perceptibly influence price by changing its quantity of output. To put it differently, the firm's supply is so small compared with the total market supply that the inverse relationship between price and quantity demanded, although present, cannot be observed on the firm's level, although it is observable on the market level.*

The Demand Curve for a Perfectly Competitive Firm Is Horizontal

In the perfectly competitive setting, there are many sellers and many buyers. Together, all buyers make up the market demand curve; together, all sellers make up the market supply curve. An equilibrium price is established at the intersection of the market demand and market supply curves (Exhibit 1(a)).

When the equilibrium price has been established, a single perfectly competitive firm faces a horizontal (flat, perfectly elastic) demand curve at the equilibrium price (Exhibit 1(b)). In short, the firm "takes" the equilibrium price as given—hence, the firm is a price taker—and sells all quantities of output at this price.[1]

WHY DOES A PERFECTLY COMPETITIVE FIRM SELL AT EQUILIBRIUM PRICE? If a perfectly competitive firm tries to charge a price higher than the market-established equilibrium price, it won't sell any of its product. This is because the firm sells a homogeneous product, its supply is small relative to the total market supply, and all buyers are informed about where they can obtain the product at the lower price.

---

exhibit **1**

Market Demand Curve and Firm Demand Curve in Perfect Competition

(a) The market, composed of all buyers and sellers, establishes the equilibrium price. (b) A single perfectly competitive firm then faces a horizontal (flat, perfectly elastic) demand curve. We conclude that the firm is a price taker; it "takes" the equilibrium price established by the market and sells any and all quantities of output at this price. (The capital *D* represents the market demand curve; the lowercase *d* represents the single firm's demand curve.)

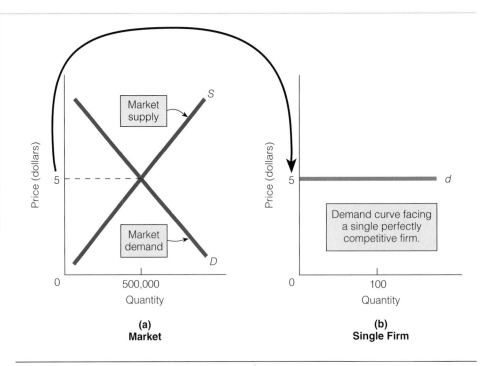

(a)
Market

(b)
Single Firm

---

[1]The horizontal demand curve does not mean that the firm can sell an infinite amount at the equilibrium price; rather, it means that price will be virtually unaffected by the variations in output that the firm may find it practicable to make.

© ASSOCIATED PRESS, AP

economics 24/7

DO CHURCHES COMPETE?

This chapter discusses the competition between business firms for customers. Do religions compete in the same way business firms do? Some economists think so; they go on to say that problems often arise when one religion tries to use government to prevent other religions from competing with it.

To illustrate, the United States has a rather open and free religious environment. The First Amendment of the U.S. Constitution states, "Congress shall make no law respecting an establishment of religion, or prohibiting the free exercise thereof." It would be unconstitutional, for example, for the U.S. government to say that only Christianity could be practiced in the United States. That would be similar to saying that only Microsoft could sell software in the United States, that only NBC could broadcast television programs, or that only Harvard University could grant degrees of higher education.

When the Founding Fathers made it unconstitutional for government to favor one religion over another, they essentially made it impossible for any one religion to have a competition-free environment. Although Christianity is the major religion in the United States, one can "purchase" spirituality, codes of conduct, moral guides, and so on from other religions.

Because religions in the United States have to compete with other religions—for believers or, if we are to take the market analogy further, for "customers"—they serve people better. A religion that has to compete provides a higher quality product than a religion that doesn't have to compete. Even within Christianity, different denominations compete. The Southern Baptist Church has to compete with the Methodist Church, and the Methodist Church competes with the Southern Baptists. Today, the competition between denominations and between religions has provided the United States with a wide variety of religious experiences and institutions.

Contrast the United States with some Islamic countries. In some Islamic countries, especially those where the Islamic clergy occupy high positions of state, it is unlawful to openly practice other religions or even to conduct oneself in a way that is contrary to the cleric's interpretation of Islam. In such countries, government has effectively established one religion. Is that one religion and the people in that country better off because of it? To economists, a single producer in a market, whether it's a software producer or a producer of religious doctrine, doesn't serve its customers or believers well. Competition drives producers to try and do better.

If the firm wants to maximize profits, it will not offer to sell its good at a lower price than the equilibrium price. Why should it? It can sell all it wants at the market-established equilibrium price.

The equilibrium price is the only relevant price for the perfectly competitive firm.

The Marginal Revenue Curve of a Perfectly Competitive Firm Is the Same as Its Demand Curve

Recall that total revenue is the price of a good multiplied by the quantity sold. If the equilibrium price is $5, as in Exhibit 2(a), and the perfectly competitive firm sells 3 units of its good, its total revenue is $15. Now suppose the firm sells an additional unit, bringing the total number of units sold to 4. Its total revenue is now $20.

A firm's **marginal revenue (MR)** is the change in total revenue (TR) that results from selling one additional unit of output (Q); that is,

$$MR = \Delta TR / \Delta Q$$

Marginal Revenue (MR)

The change in total revenue that results from selling one additional unit of output.

(1) Price	(2) Quantity	(3) Total Revenue = (1) × (2)	(4) Marginal Revenue = $\Delta TR/\Delta Q$ = $\Delta(3)/\Delta(2)$
$5	1	$ 5	$5
5	2	10	5
5	3	15	5
5	4	20	5

(a)

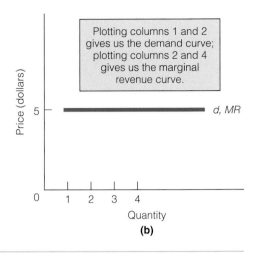

(b)

exhibit 2

The Demand Curve and the Marginal Revenue Curve for a Perfectly Competitive Firm

(a) By computing marginal revenue, we find that it is equal to price. (b) By plotting columns 1 and 2, we obtain the firm's demand curve; by plotting columns 2 and 4, we obtain the firm's marginal revenue curve. The two curves are the same.

Column 4 in Exhibit 2(a) shows that the firm's marginal revenue ($5) at any output level is always equal to the equilibrium price ($5). We conclude that for a perfectly competitive firm, price is equal to marginal revenue ($P = MR$).

For a Perfectly Competitive Firm, $P = MR$

If price is equal to marginal revenue, it follows that *the marginal revenue curve for the perfectly competitive firm is the same as its demand curve.*

A demand curve plots price against quantity, whereas a marginal revenue curve plots marginal revenue against quantity. If price equals marginal revenue, then the demand curve and marginal revenue curve are the same (Exhibit 2(b)).

For a Perfectly Competitive Firm, Demand Curve = Marginal Revenue Curve

Theory and Real-World Markets

The theory of perfect competition describes how firms act in a market structure where (1) there are many buyers and sellers, none of which is large in relation to total sales or purchases; (2) sellers sell a homogeneous product; (3) buyers and sellers have all relevant information; and (4) there is easy entry and exit. These assumptions are closely met in some real-world markets. Examples include some agricultural markets and a small subset of the retail trade. The stock market, where there are hundreds of thousands of buyers and sellers of stock, is also sometimes cited as an example of perfect competition.

The four assumptions of the theory of perfect competition are also *approximated* in some real-world markets. In such markets, the number of sellers may not be large enough for every firm to be a price taker, but the firm's control over price may be negligible. The amount of control may be so negligible, in fact, that the firm acts *as if* it were a perfectly competitive firm.

Similarly, buyers may not have all relevant information concerning price and quality, but they may still have a great deal of information, and the information they do not have may not matter. The products that the firms in the industry sell may not be homogeneous, but the differences may be inconsequential.

In short, a market that does not *exactly* meet the assumptions of perfect competition may nonetheless *approximate* those assumptions to such a degree that it behaves *as if* it were a perfectly competitive market. If so, the theory of perfect competition can be used to predict the market's behavior.

SELF-TEST

(Answers to Self-Test questions are in the Self-Test Appendix.)

1. If a firm is a price taker, it does not have the ability to control the price of the product it sells. What does this mean?

2. Why is a perfectly competitive firm a price taker?

3. The horizontal demand curve for the perfectly competitive firm signifies that it cannot sell any of its product for a price higher than the market equilibrium price. Why can't it?

4. Suppose the firms in a real-world market do not sell a homogeneous product. Does it necessarily follow that the market is not perfectly competitive?

Perfect Competition in the Short Run

The perfectly competitive firm is a price taker. So for a perfectly competitive firm, price is equal to marginal revenue, $P = MR$, and therefore, the firm's demand curve is the same as its marginal revenue curve. This section discusses the amount of output the firm will produce in the short run.

micro Theme   If you want to predict economic behavior, ask yourself what the objective is for the economic actor (whose behavior you want to predict). In the last chapter, we stated that the firm's objective is to maximize profit. Because we know what the firm's objective is, we have an insight into what its behavior will be. Simply stated, there are certain behaviors consistent with trying to maximize profit and certain behaviors that are inconsistent with trying to maximize profit. Much of the material we discuss in this section can be viewed as "actions that are consistent with a firm attempting to maximize profit."

What Level of Output Does the Profit-Maximizing Firm Produce?

Consider the situation in Exhibit 3. The perfectly competitive firm's demand curve and marginal revenue curve (which are the same) are drawn at the equilibrium price of $5. The firm's marginal cost curve is also shown. On the basis of these curves, what quantity of output will the firm produce?

exhibit **3**

The Quantity of Output the Perfectly Competitive Firm Will Produce

The firm's demand curve is horizontal at the equilibrium price. Its demand curve is its marginal revenue curve. The firm produces that quantity of output at which $MR = MC$.

The firm will continue to increase its quantity of output as long as marginal revenue is greater than marginal cost. It will not produce units of output for which marginal revenue is less than marginal cost. We conclude that the firm will stop increasing its quantity of output when marginal revenue and marginal cost are equal. The **profit-maximization rule** for a firm says: *Produce the quantity of output at which MR = MC.*[2] In Exhibit 3, *MR = MC* at 125 units of output.

Profit-Maximization Rule

Profit is maximized by producing the quantity of output at which *MR = MC*.

For the perfectly competitive firm, the profit-maximization rule can be written as *P = MC* because for the perfectly competitive firm, *P = MR*. In perfect competition, profit is maximized when

$$P = MR = MC$$

micro
Theme   Firms have objectives, face constraints, and have to make choices. The perfectly competitive firm's objective is to maximize profit. It faces the constraint of having to sell its output at the market-determined price—and only at that price. It chooses to produce the quantity of output at which *MR = MC*.

Q&A   *Why doesn't the firm in Exhibit 3 stop producing at 50 units of output?*

This is where the largest difference between marginal revenue and marginal cost occurs. Why does the firm continue to produce until marginal revenue equals marginal cost?

If the firm had stopped producing with unit 50, it wouldn't have produced unit 51, which comes with a marginal revenue that is greater than marginal cost. Nor would it have produced unit 52, for which marginal revenue is also greater than marginal cost. In short, the firm would not have produced some units of output for which a marginal (additional) profit could have been earned; thus, it would not have been maximizing profit. What matters is whether MR *is greater than* MC, *not how much greater* MR *is than* MC.

The Perfectly Competitive Firm and Resource Allocative Efficiency

Resources (or inputs) are used to produce goods and services; for example, wood may be used to produce a chair. The resources used in the production of goods have a certain exchange value to the buyers of the goods. This exchange value is approximated by the price that people pay for the good. When Smith buys a chair for $100, we know that Smith values the resources used to produce the chair by at least $100.

Wood that is used to produce chairs can't be used to produce desks. Hence, there is an opportunity cost of producing chairs that is best measured by its marginal cost.

Now suppose 100 chairs are produced, and at this quantity, price is greater than marginal cost; for example, price is $100 and marginal cost is $75. What does this mean? Obviously, it means that buyers place a higher value on wood when it is used to produce chairs than when it is used to produce some alternative good.

Producing a good—any good—until price equals marginal cost ensures that all units of the good are produced that are of greater value to buyers than the alternative goods that might have been produced. Stated differently, a firm that produces the quantity of output at which price equals marginal cost (*P = MC*) is said to exhibit **resource allocative efficiency**.

Resource Allocative Efficiency

The situation that exists when firms produce the quantity of output at which price equals marginal cost: *P = MC*.

Does the perfectly competitive firm exhibit resource allocative efficiency? We know two things about this firm so far. First, it produces the quantity of output at which *MR = MC*. Second, for the perfectly competitive firm, *P = MR*. Well, if the perfectly competitive firm produces the output at which *MR = MC* and for this firm, *P = MR,* then it naturally follows that it produces the output at which *P = MC*. In short, the perfectly competitive firm is resource allocative efficient.

An important point to note is that for a perfectly competitive firm, profit maximization and resource allocative efficiency are not at odds. (Might they be for other market

---

[2]The profit-maximization rule is the same as the loss-minimization rule because it is impossible to maximize profits without minimizing losses. The profit-maximization rule holds for *all firms,* not just perfectly competitive firms.

structures? See the next two chapters.) The perfectly competitive firm seeks to maximize profit by producing the quantity of output at which $MR = MC$, and because for the firm, $P = MR$, it automatically accomplishes resource allocative efficiency ($P = MC$) when it maximizes profit ($MR = MC$).

To Produce or Not to Produce: That Is the Question

The following cases illustrate three applications of the profit-maximization (loss-minimization) rule by a perfectly competitive firm.

CASE 1: PRICE IS ABOVE AVERAGE TOTAL COST Exhibit 4(a) illustrates the perfectly competitive firm's demand and marginal revenue curves. If the firm follows the profit-maximization rule and produces the quantity of output at which marginal revenue equals marginal cost, it will produce 100 units of output. This will be the profit-maximizing quantity of output. Notice that at this quantity of output, price is above average total cost. Using the information in the exhibit, we can make the following calculations:

Case 1	
Equilibrium price (P)	= $15
Quantity of output produced (Q)	= 100 units
Total revenue ($P \times Q = \$15 \times 100$)	= $1,500
Total cost ($ATC \times Q = \$11 \times 100$)	= $1,100
Total variable cost ($AVC \times Q = \$7 \times 100$)	= $700
Total fixed cost ($TC - TVC = \$1,100 - \$700$)	= $400
Profits ($TR - TC = \$1,500 - \$1,100$)	= $400

Think of good X. With good X, as with all other goods, there is a right and a wrong quantity to produce. From the perspective of consumers, the right quantity is the efficient quantity. The consumer says to the manufacturers of X: "Keep producing X as long as the price of X is greater than its marginal cost. Stop when P = MC." Let say that P = MC when the quantity of X is 10,000 a month.

Now let's ask ourselves if 10,000 units of X a month is what the manufacturers of X want to produce. The right quantity of X for manufacturers is the quantity at which MR = MC. In other words, manufacturers of X will continue making units of X as long as MR is greater than MC, and they will stop when MR = MC.

For a perfectly competitive firm, we know that P = MR, so it follows that what consumers want (produce until P = MC) is really the same thing that manufacturers want (produce until MR = MC). Simply put, when manufacturers do what is in their best interest—produce until MR = MC—they are automatically producing the efficient amount of the good, which is what consumers want. Who would have thought it?

We conclude that if price is above average total cost for the perfectly competitive firm, the firm maximizes profits by producing the quantity of output at which $MR = MC$.

CASE 2: PRICE IS BELOW AVERAGE VARIABLE COST Exhibit 4(b) illustrates the case in which price is below average variable cost. The equilibrium price at which the perfectly competitive firm sells its good is $4. At this price, total revenue is less than both total cost and total variable cost, as the following calculations indicate. To minimize its loss, the firm should shut down.

Case 2	
Equilibrium price (P)	= $4
Quantity of output produced (Q)	= 50 units
Total revenue ($P \times Q = \$4 \times 50$)	= $200
Total cost ($ATC \times Q = \$13 \times 50$)	= $650
Total variable cost ($AVC \times Q = \$5 \times 50$)	= $250
Total fixed cost ($TC - TVC = \$650 - \$250$)	= $400
Profits ($TR - TC = \$200 - \$650$)	= -$450

If the firm produces in the short run, it will take a loss of $450. If it shuts down, its loss will be less. It will lose its fixed costs, which amount to the difference between total cost and variable cost ($TFC + TVC = TC$, so $TC - TVC = TFC$). This is $400 ($650 − $250). So between the two options of producing in the short run or shutting down, the firm minimizes its losses by choosing to shut down ($Q = 0$). It will lose $400 by shutting down, whereas it will lose $450 by producing in the short run.

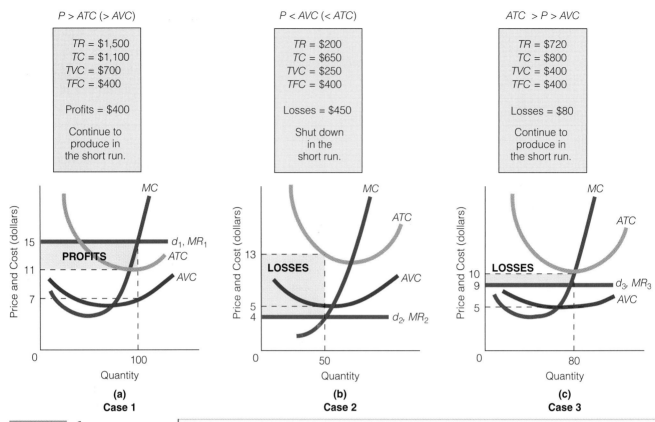

exhibit 4

Profit Maximization and Loss Minimization for the Perfectly Competitive Firm: Three Cases

(a) In Case 1, TR > TC and the firm earns profits. It continues to produce in the short run. (b) In Case 2, TR < TC and the firm takes a loss. It shuts down in the short run because it minimizes its losses by doing so; it is better to lose $400 in fixed costs than to take a loss of $450. (c) In Case 3, TR < TC and the firm takes a loss. It continues to produce in the short run because it minimizes its losses by doing so; it is better to lose $80 by producing than to lose $400 in fixed costs.

We conclude that if price is below average variable cost, the perfectly competitive firm minimizes losses by choosing to shut down—that is, by not producing.

CASE 3: PRICE IS BELOW AVERAGE TOTAL COST BUT ABOVE AVERAGE VARIABLE COST Exhibit 4(c) illustrates the case in which price is below average total cost but above average variable cost. Here the equilibrium price at which the perfectly competitive firm sells its good is $9. If the firm follows the profit-maximization rule, it will produce 80 units of output. At this price and quantity of output, total revenue is less than total cost (hence, there will be a loss), but total revenue is greater than total variable cost. The calculations are as follows:

Case 3	
Equilibrium price (P)	= $9
Quantity of output produced (Q)	= 80 units
Total revenue ($P \times Q = \$9 \times 80$)	= $720
Total cost ($ATC \times Q = \$10 \times 80$)	= $800
Total variable cost ($AVC \times Q = \$5 \times 80$)	= $400
Total fixed cost ($TC - TVC = \$800 - \$400$)	= $400
Profits ($TR - TC = \$720 - \$800$)	= −$80

If the firm decides to produce in the short run, it will take a loss of $80. Should it shut down instead? If it does, it will lose its fixed costs, which, in this case, are $400 ($TC - TVC = \$800 - \$400$). It is better to continue to produce in the short run than to shut down. Losses are minimized by producing.

We conclude that if price is below average total cost but above average variable cost, the perfectly competitive firm minimizes its losses by continuing to produce in the short run instead of shutting down.

SUMMARY OF CASES 1–3 We conclude: *A perfectly competitive firm produces in the short run as long as price is above average variable cost (Cases 1 and 3). A perfectly competitive firm shuts down in the short run if price is less than average variable cost (Case 2).*

$$P > AVC \rightarrow \text{Firm produces}$$
$$P < AVC \rightarrow \text{Firm shuts down}$$

We can summarize the same information in terms of total revenue and total variable costs. *A perfectly competitive firm produces in the short run as long as total revenue is greater than total variable costs (Cases 1 and 3). A perfectly competitive firm shuts down in the short run if total revenue is less than total variable costs (Case 2).*

$$TR > TVC \rightarrow \text{Firm produces}$$
$$TR < TVC \rightarrow \text{Firm shuts down}$$

Exhibit 5 reviews some of the material discussed in this section.

The Perfectly Competitive Firm's Short-Run Supply Curve

The perfectly competitive firm produces (supplies output) in the short run if price is above average variable cost. It shuts down (does not supply output) if price is below average variable cost. It follows that the **short-run supply curve** of the firm is that portion of its marginal cost curve that lies above the average variable cost curve. Only a price above average variable cost will induce the firm to supply output. The short-run supply curve of the perfectly competitive firm is illustrated in Exhibit 6.

From Firm to Market (Industry) Supply Curve

After we know that the perfectly competitive firm's short-run supply curve is the part of its marginal cost curve above its average variable cost curve, it is a simple matter to derive the **short-run market (industry) supply curve**.[3] We horizontally "add" the short-run supply curves for all firms in the perfectly competitive market or industry.

Short-Run (Firm) Supply Curve
The portion of the firm's marginal cost curve that lies above the average variable cost curve.

Q&A

*I thought the entire **MC** curve would have been the firm's supply curve. But it isn't, is it?*

No it isn't. Only that part of the firm's MC curve that lies above the firm's AVC curve turns out to be the firm's supply curve.

Short-Run Market (Industry) Supply Curve
The horizontal "addition" of all existing firms' short-run supply curves.

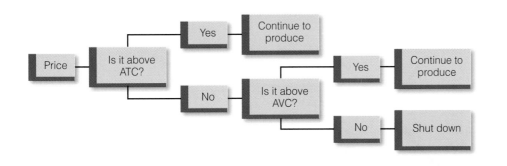

A CLOSER LOOK

exhibit **5**

What Should a Perfectly Competitive Firm Do in the Short Run?

The firm should produce in the short run as long as price (*P*) is above average variable cost (*AVC*). It should shut down in the short run if price is below average variable cost.

---

[3]In discussing market structures, the words *industry* and *market* are often used interchangeably when a single-product industry is under consideration, which is the case here.

exhibit **6**

The Perfectly Competitive Firm's Short-Run Supply Curve

The short-run supply curve is that portion of the firm's marginal cost curve that lies above the average variable cost curve.

Consider, for simplicity, an industry made up of three firms, *A, B,* and *C* (see Exhibit 7(a)). At a price of P_1, firm *A* supplies 10 units, firm *B* supplies 8 units, and firm *C* supplies 18 units. One point on the market supply curve thus corresponds to P_1 on the price axis and 36 units $(10 + 8 + 18 = 36)$ on the quantity axis.[4] If we follow this procedure for all prices, we have the short-run market supply curve. This market supply curve is shown in the market setting in part (b) of the exhibit.

This market supply curve is used along with the market demand curve (derived in Chapter 3) to determine equilibrium price and quantity.

Why Is the Market Supply Curve Upward Sloping?

Recall that in Chapter 3, when the demand and supply curves were introduced, the supply curve was drawn upward sloping. The supply curve is upward sloping because of the law of diminishing marginal returns. To see this, consider the following questions and answers.

Question 1: Why do we draw market supply curves upward sloping?
Answer: Because market supply curves are the horizontal "addition" of firms' supply curves, and firms' supply curves are upward sloping.

Question 2: But why are firms' supply curves upward sloping?
Answer: Because the supply curve for each firm is that portion of its marginal cost (*MC*) curve that is above its average variable cost (*AVC*) curve—and this portion of the *MC* curve is upward sloping.

---

[4]We add one qualification: Each firm's supply curve is drawn on the assumption that the prices of the variable inputs are constant.

exhibit **7**

Deriving the Market (Industry) Supply Curve for a Perfectly Competitive Market

In (a) we "add" (horizontally) the quantity supplied by each firm to derive the market supply curve. The market supply curve and the market demand curve are shown in (b). Together, they determine equilibrium price and quantity.

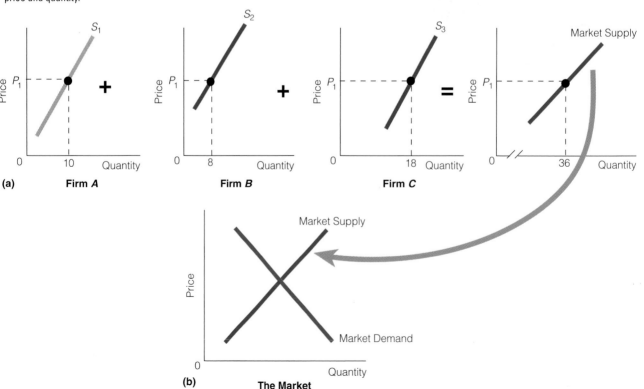

economics 24/7

WHAT DO AUDREY HEPBURN, LUCILLE BALL, AND BUGS BUNNY HAVE IN COMMON?

The U.S. Postal Service has issued certain special, collectors' stamps in the past. These stamps have had likenesses of Audrey Hepburn, Harry Houdini, James Dean, Lucille Ball, The Beatles, Niagara Falls, Alfred Hitchcock, Daffy Duck, and Bugs Bunny.

Why does the U.S. Postal Service issue these special, collectors' stamps? To find out, let's analyze stamps from the point of view of the Postal Service.

Most people buy stamps to send letters or other items through the mail. When a stamp is placed on a letter, the Postal Service is required to deliver the letter to the address on the envelope. Suppose the unit variable cost (AVC) of producing a stamp is 7 cents, regardless of the likeness on the front, and the unit variable cost of delivering a letter with a stamp on it is 19 cents. The sum of the unit variable costs of producing the stamp and delivering the letter is 26 cents.

$$AVC \text{ stamp} =$$
$$AVC \text{ producing the stamp} + AVC \text{ delivering the letter}$$

For purposes of simplicity, we assume $AFC = 0$; so $AVC = ATC$. In other words, the per-unit cost of the stamp is 26 cents. It follows, then, that if the price of a stamp is 39 cents, the U.S. Postal Service earns a per-unit profit of 13 cents per stamp issued and used.

Now suppose the U.S. Postal Service wants to increase its per-unit profit. How might it do this? One way is to issue stamps that people wouldn't put on items to be mailed. That is, issue stamps that people want to collect.

This brings us to the special, collectors' stamps the U.S. Postal Service issues and sells. Many people buy these stamps but do not use them to mail letters. They buy the stamps to collect them. But if people buy these stamps to collect them and not to use them, the U.S. Postal Service doesn't incur the unit variable cost of delivering mail for these special stamps. This means the average total cost of the collectors' stamp falls by the AVC of delivering the letter, which in turn means the ATC of the stamp falls to 7 cents (the AVC of producing the stamp). Consequently, the profit per unit for issuing collectors' stamps rises to 32 cents for a 39-cent stamp.

Question 3: But why do MC curves have an upward-sloping portion?

Answer: Because of the law of diminishing marginal returns. Remember that according to the law of diminishing marginal returns, the marginal physical product (MPP) of a variable input eventually declines. When this happens, the MC curve begins to rise. We conclude that because of the law of diminishing marginal returns, MC curves are upward-sloping, and because MC curves are upward sloping, so are market supply curves.

> ### Q&A
> *We saw an upward-sloping supply curve back in Chapter 3 when we learned about supply and demand. Are you saying that the upward-sloping supply curve in Chapter 3 was derived by (1) summing the individual supply curves for the firms in the market and (2) those individual supply curves for the firms were simply that part of their MC curves above their AVC curves?*
>
> *That is exactly what we are saying.*

SELF-TEST

1. If a firm produces the quantity of output at which $MR = MC$, does it follow that it earns profits?

2. In the short run, if a firm finds that its price (P) is less than its average total cost (ATC), should it shut down its operation?

3. The layperson says that a firm maximizes profits when total revenue (*TR*) minus total cost (*TC*) is as large as possible and positive. The economist says that a firm maximizes profits when it produces the level of output at which *MR* = *MC*. Explain how the two ways of looking at profit maximization are consistent.

4. Why are market supply curves upward sloping?

Perfect Competition in the Long Run

The number of firms in a perfectly competitive market may not be the same in the short run as in the long run. For example, if the typical firm is making economic profits in the short run, new firms will be attracted to the industry, and the number of firms will increase. If the typical firm is sustaining losses, some existing firms will exit the industry, and the number of firms will decrease. This process is explained in greater detail later in this section. We begin by outlining the conditions of long-run competitive equilibrium.

The Conditions of Long-Run Competitive Equilibrium

Long-Run Competitive Equilibrium

The condition where *P* = *MC* = *SRATC* = *LRATC*. There are zero economic profits, firms are producing the quantity of output at which price is equal to marginal cost, and no firm has an incentive to change its plant size.

The following conditions characterize **long-run competitive equilibrium**:

1. **Economic profit is zero: Price (*P*) is equal to short-run average total cost (*SRATC*).**

$$P = SRATC$$

The logic of this condition is clear when we analyze what will happen if price is above or below short-run average total cost. If it is above, positive economic profits will attract firms to the industry to obtain the profits. If price is below, losses will result and some firms will want to exit the industry. Long-run competitive equilibrium cannot exist if firms have an incentive to enter or exit the industry in response to positive economic profits or losses, respectively. For long-run equilibrium to exist, there can be no incentive for firms to enter or exit the industry. This condition is brought about by zero economic profit (normal profit), which is a consequence of the equilibrium price being equal to short-run average total cost.

2. **Firms are producing the quantity of output at which price (*P*) is equal to marginal cost (*MC*).**

$$P = MC$$

As previously noted, perfectly competitive firms naturally move toward the output level at which marginal revenue, or price because *MR* = *P* for a perfectly competitive firm, equals marginal cost.

3. **No firm has an incentive to change its plant size to produce its current output; that is, *SRATC* = *LRATC* at the quantity of output at which *P* = *MC*.**

To understand this condition, suppose *SRATC* > *LRATC* at the quantity of output established in condition 2. If this is the case,

Thinking like
AN ECONOMIST
Perhaps as you have noticed by now, the concept of equilibrium is an important one in economics. But why? Because equilibrium is where things are headed; in a way, it is the destination point. To illustrate, suppose that firms in a perfectly competitive market are currently earning positive economic profit. At this point, there are, say, 100 firms in the market. Are things likely to stay this way? Is the number of firms likely to remain at 100? The answer is no. Because firms are earning positive profits, firms not currently in the market will join the market, pushing the number of firms upward from 100. Only when all firms are earning normal profit (zero economic profit) will things remain the way they are. Only then will the market be in equilibrium.[5]

When you get on a train in, say, Los Angeles that is headed for New York City, you are fairly sure the trip is not over until you reach New York City. It is not as easy to know when the "trip" is over in economics. Theoretically, we know the trip is over when equilibrium has been reached. But then it is incumbent upon the economist to define the conditions that specify equilibrium.

---

[5]We are assuming here that our other long-run equilibrium conditions hold, such as no firms want to change plant size and there is no incentive for any firm to produce any more or any less output.

the firm has an incentive to change plant size in the long run because it wants to produce its product with the plant size that will give it the lowest average total cost (unit cost). It will have no incentive to change plant size when it is producing the quantity of output at which price equals marginal cost and *SRATC* equals *LRATC*.

$$SRATC = LRATC$$

The three conditions necessary for long-run competitive equilibrium can be stated as: Long-run competitive equilibrium exists when $P = MC = SRATC = LRATC$ (Exhibit 8).

In conclusion, long-run competitive equilibrium exists when firms have no incentive to make any changes. Specifically, long-run competitive equilibrium exists when:

1. There is no incentive for firms to enter or exit the industry.
2. There is no incentive for firms to produce more or less output.
3. There is no incentive for firms to change plant size.

The Perfectly Competitive Firm and Productive Efficiency

A firm that produces its output at the lowest possible per-unit cost (lowest *ATC*) is said to exhibit **productive efficiency**. The perfectly competitive firm does this in long-run equilibrium, as shown in Exhibit 8. Productive efficiency is desirable from society's standpoint because it means that perfectly competitive firms are economizing on society's scarce resources and therefore not wasting them.

To illustrate, suppose the lowest unit cost at which good X can be produced is $3— this is the minimum *ATC*. If a firm produces 1,000 units of good X at this unit cost, its total cost is $3,000. Now suppose the firm produces good X not at its lowest unit cost of $3 but at a slightly higher unit cost of $3.50. Total cost now equals $3,500. This means resources worth $500 were employed producing good X that could have been used to produce other goods had the firm exhibited productive efficiency. Society could have been "richer" in goods and services, but now it is not.

> **Productive Efficiency**
> The situation that exists when a firm produces its output at the lowest possible per-unit cost (lowest *ATC*).

Industry Adjustment to an Increase in Demand

An increase in market demand for a product can throw an industry out of long-run competitive equilibrium. Suppose we start at long-run competitive equilibrium, where

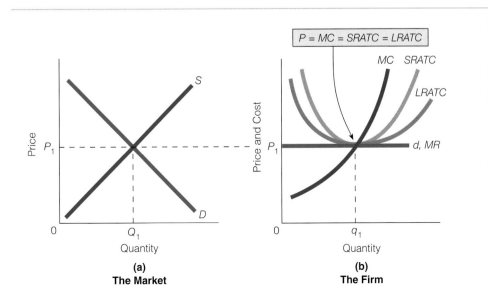

exhibit 8

Long-Run Competitive Equilibrium

(a) Equilibrium in the market. (b) Equilibrium for the firm. In (b), $P = MC$ (the firm has no incentive to move away from the quantity of output at which this occurs, q_1); $P = SRATC$ (there is no incentive for firms to enter or exit the industry); and $SRATC = LRATC$ (there is no incentive for the firm to change its plant size).

$P = MC = SRATC = LRATC$ (see Exhibit 9). Then market demand rises for the product produced by the firms in the industry. What happens? Equilibrium price rises. As a consequence, the demand curve faced by an individual firm (which is its marginal revenue curve) shifts upward.

A CLOSER LOOK

exhibit **9**

The Process of Moving from One Long-Run Competitive Equilibrium Position to Another

This exhibit describes what happens on both the market level and the firm level when demand rises and throws an industry out of long-run competitive equilibrium.

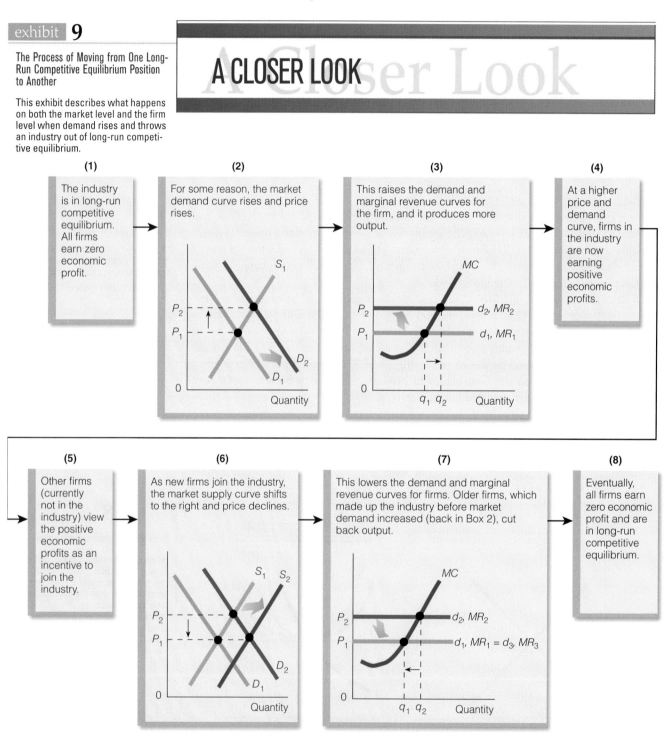

(1) The industry is in long-run competitive equilibrium. All firms earn zero economic profit.

(2) For some reason, the market demand curve rises and price rises.

(3) This raises the demand and marginal revenue curves for the firm, and it produces more output.

(4) At a higher price and demand curve, firms in the industry are now earning positive economic profits.

(5) Other firms (currently not in the industry) view the positive economic profits as an incentive to join the industry.

(6) As new firms join the industry, the market supply curve shifts to the right and price declines.

(7) This lowers the demand and marginal revenue curves for firms. Older firms, which made up the industry before market demand increased (back in Box 2), cut back output.

(8) Eventually, all firms earn zero economic profit and are in long-run competitive equilibrium.

Next, *existing firms* in the industry increase quantity of output because marginal revenue now intersects marginal cost at a higher quantity of output. In the long run, new firms begin to enter the industry because price is currently above average total cost, and there are positive economic profits.

As new firms enter the industry, the market (industry) supply curve shifts rightward. As a consequence, equilibrium price falls. It falls until long-run competitive equilibrium is reestablished—that is, until there is, once again, zero economic profit.

If you look at the process again, from the initial increase in market demand to the reestablishment of long-run competitive equilibrium, you will notice that price increased in the short run (owing to the increase in demand) and then decreased in the long run (owing to the increase in supply). Also, profits increased (owing to the increase in demand and consequent increase in price) and then decreased (owing to the increase in supply and consequent decrease in price). They went from zero to some positive amount and then back to zero.

The *up-and-down* movements in both price and profits in response to an increase in demand are important to note. Why? Because too often people see only the primary upward movements in both price and profits and ignore or forget the secondary downward movements. The secondary effects in price and profits are as important as the primary effects.

The process of adjustment to an increase in demand brings up an important question. If price first rises owing to an increase in market demand and later falls owing to an increase in market supply, will the new equilibrium price be greater than, less than, or equal to the *original* equilibrium price? (In Exhibit 9, it is shown as equal to the original equilibrium price, but this need not be the case.)

For example, if the equilibrium price is $10 before the increase in market demand, will the new equilibrium price (after market and firm adjustments have taken place) be greater than, less than, or equal to $10? The answer depends on whether increasing cost, decreasing cost, or constant cost, respectively, describes the industry in which the increase in demand has taken place.

CONSTANT-COST INDUSTRY In a **constant-cost industry**, average total costs (unit costs) do not change as output increases or decreases when firms enter or exit the market or industry. If market demand increases for a good produced by firms in a constant-cost industry, price will initially rise and then will finally fall to its original level. This is illustrated in Exhibit 10(a).

We start from a position of long-run competitive equilibrium where there are zero economic profits. This is at point 1. Then, demand increases and price rises from P_1 to P_2. At P_2, there are positive economic profits, which cause the firms currently in the industry to increase output. We move up the supply curve, S_1, from point 1 to point 2. Next, new firms, drawn by the profits, enter the industry, causing the supply curve to shift rightward.

For a constant-cost industry, output is increased without a change in the price of inputs. Because of this, the firms' cost curves do not shift. But if costs do not rise to reduce the profits in the industry, then price must fall. (Profits can be reduced in two ways: through a rise in costs or a fall in price.) Price must fall to its original level (P_1) before profits can be zero. This implies that the supply curve shifts rightward by the same amount that the demand curve shifts rightward. In the exhibit, this is a shift from S_1 to S_2. The two long-run equilibrium points (1 and 3), where economic profits are zero, define the **long-run (industry) supply (LRS) curve**. A constant-cost industry is characterized by a horizontal long-run supply curve.

Constant-Cost Industry
An industry in which average total costs do not change as (industry) output increases or decreases when firms enter or exit the industry, respectively.

Long-Run (Industry) Supply (LRS) Curve
Graphic representation of the quantities of output that the industry is prepared to supply at different prices after the entry and exit of firms are completed.

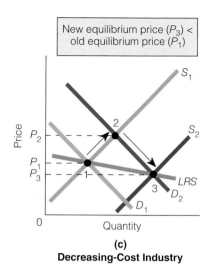

(a)
Constant-Cost Industry

(b)
Increasing-Cost Industry

(c)
Decreasing-Cost Industry

exhibit **10**

Long-Run Industry Supply Curves

LRS = long-run industry supply. Each part illustrates the same scenario, but with different results depending on whether the industry has (a) constant costs, (b) increasing costs, or (c) decreasing costs. In each part, we start at long-run competitive equilibrium (point 1). Demand increases, price rises from P_1 to P_2, and there are positive economic profits. Consequently, existing firms increase output and new firms are attracted to the industry. In (a), input costs remain constant as output increases, so the firms' cost curves do not shift. Profits fall to zero through a decline in price. This implies that in a constant-cost industry, the supply curve shifts rightward by the same amount as the demand curve shifts rightward. In (b), input costs increase as output increases. Profits are squeezed by a combination of rising costs and falling prices. The new equilibrium price (P_3) for an increasing-cost industry is higher than the old equilibrium price (P_1). In (c), input costs decrease as output increases. The new equilibrium price (P_3) for a decreasing-cost industry is lower than the old equilibrium price (P_1).

Increasing-Cost Industry

An industry in which average total costs increase as output increases and decrease as output decreases when firms enter and exit the industry, respectively.

Decreasing-Cost Industry

An industry in which average total costs decrease as output increases and increase as output decreases when firms enter and exit the industry, respectively.

INCREASING-COST INDUSTRY In an **increasing-cost industry**, average total costs (unit costs) increase as output increases and decrease as output decreases when firms enter and exit the industry, respectively. If market demand increases for a good produced by firms in an increasing-cost industry, price will initially rise and then will finally fall to a level above its original level.

Consider the situation in Exhibit 10(b). We start, as before, in long-run competitive equilibrium at point 1. Demand increases and price rises from P_1 to P_2. This brings about positive economic profits, which cause firms in the industry to increase output and new firms to enter the industry. So far, this is the same process as for a constant-cost industry. However, in an increasing-cost industry, as firms purchase more inputs to produce more output, some input prices rise and cost curves shift. In short, as industry output increases, profits are caught in a two-way squeeze: Price is coming down, and costs are rising. If costs are rising as price is falling, then it is not necessary for price to fall to its original level before zero economic profits rule once again. Price will not have to fall so far to restore long-run competitive equilibrium in an increasing-cost industry as in a constant-cost industry. We would expect, then, that when an increasing-cost industry experiences an increase in demand, the new equilibrium price will be higher than the old equilibrium price. This means the supply curve shifts rightward by less than the demand curve shifts rightward. An increasing-cost industry is characterized by an upward-sloping long-run supply curve.

DECREASING-COST INDUSTRY In a **decreasing-cost industry**, average total costs (unit costs) decrease as output increases and increase as output decreases when firms enter and exit the industry, respectively. If market demand increases for a good produced by firms in a decreasing-cost industry, price will initially rise and then will finally fall to a level below its original level. In Exhibit 10(c), price moves from P_1 to P_2 and then to P_3. In such an industry, average total costs decrease as new firms enter the industry, so price must fall below its original level to eliminate profits. A decreasing-cost industry is characterized by a downward-sloping long-run supply curve.

What Happens as Firms Enter an Industry in Search of Profits?

In 1969, the first handheld calculator was introduced in the United States; it sold for $395. In 1975, Sony sold the first videocassette recorder (VCR) for a price of $1,400. In 1977, Apple Computer Corporation sold the first personal computer—it had only 4K random access memory (RAM)—for just under $1,300. In 2007, the prices of all three goods were much lower in both nominal and real (inflation-adjusted) terms, and the quality was generally much higher than when the goods were introduced. Handheld calculators of higher quality than the one introduced in 1969 were selling for approximately $10. Videocassette recorders of higher quality than those in 1975 were selling for approximately $109. Personal home computers of much higher quality than those in 1977 were selling for approximately $499.

What brought about this sharp decrease in price and increase in quality? The entry of new firms into the calculator, VCR, and personal computer industries was partly responsible. Positive economic profits, realized by the first companies in the different industries, attracted new firms, the supply of the goods increased, and prices fell.[6] These examples illustrate how easy entry into a market can affect price and profits. They also suggest the potential benefits that incumbent firms can enjoy if they can successfully limit entry into the industry.

> ### *Thinking like* AN ECONOMIST
>
> *Members of the public often see "profit" as something left over after all costs have been incurred. Economists see it as this, but they also see it as something more. Profit is a signal; specifically, it is a signal to firms not earning it. To illustrate, suppose there are 25 firms in a market, all of which are earning profit. That profit is essentially saying to firms that are not in the market: "Hey, come over here and get me." Firms (not in the market) then proceed to enter the market in which profit can be earned. As a result, the supply of the good (connected to the profit) rises and price begins to fall.*

Industry Adjustment to a Decrease in Demand

Demand can decrease as well as increase. The analysis outlined for an increase in demand can be reversed to explain industry adjustment to a decrease in demand. Starting at long-run competitive equilibrium, market demand decreases. As a consequence, in the short run, the equilibrium price falls, effectively shifting the firm's demand curve (marginal revenue curve) downward. Following this, some firms in the industry will decrease production because marginal revenue intersects marginal cost at a lower level of output, and some firms will shut down.

In the long run, some firms will leave the industry because price is below average total cost, and they are suffering continual losses. As firms leave the industry, the market supply curve shifts leftward. As a consequence, the equilibrium price rises. It will rise until long-run competitive equilibrium is reestablished—that is, until there are, once again, zero economic profits (instead of negative economic profits). Whether the new equilibrium price is greater than, less than, or equal to the original equilibrium price depends on whether decreasing cost, increasing cost, or constant cost, respectively, describes the industry in which demand decreased.

Differences in Costs, Differences in Profits: Now You See It, Now You Don't

Suppose two farmers, Hancock and Cordero, produce wheat. Farmer Cordero grows his wheat on fertile land; Farmer Hancock grows her wheat on poor soil. Both farmers sell their wheat for the same price, but because of the difference in the quality of their land, Cordero has lower average total costs than Hancock, as shown in Exhibit 11.

If we compare the initial situations for the two farmers (each farmer's ATC_1), we notice that Cordero is earning profits and Hancock is not. Cordero is earning profits because he pays lower average total costs than Hancock as a consequence of farming higher quality land. But is this situation likely to continue? Is Cordero likely to continue earning profits? The answer is no.

Individuals will bid up the price of the fertile land that Cordero farms vis-à-vis the poor-quality land that Hancock farms. In other words, if Cordero is renting his farmland, the rent he pays will increase to reflect the superior quality of the land. The rent will increase by an amount equal to the profits per time period—that is, an amount

---

[6]Changes in technology also occurred at about this time.

exhibit **11**

Differences in Costs, Differences in Profits: Now You See It, Now It's Gone

At ATC_1 for both farmers, Cordero earns profits and Hancock does not. Cordero earns profits because the land he farms is of higher quality (more productive) than Hancock's land. Eventually, this fact is taken into account, by Cordero either paying higher rent for the land or incurring implicit costs for it. This moves Cordero's ATC curve upward to the same level as Hancock's, and Cordero earns zero economic profits. The profits have gone as payment (implicit or explicit) for the higher quality, more productive land.

(a)
Farmer Hancock

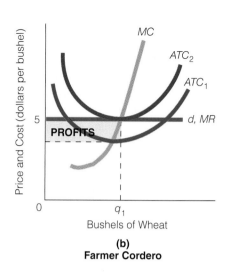

(b)
Farmer Cordero

equal to the shaded portion in Exhibit 11(b). If Cordero owns the land, the superior quality of the land will have a higher implicit cost attached to it (Cordero can rent it for more than Hancock can rent her land, assuming Hancock owns her land). This fact will be reflected in the average total cost curve.

In Exhibit 11(b), ATC_2 reflects either the higher rent Cordero must pay for the superior land or the full implicit cost he incurs by farming land he owns. In either case, when the average total cost curve reflects all costs, Cordero will be in the same situation as Hancock; he, too, will be earning zero economic profits.

Where has the profit gone? It has gone as payment for the higher quality, more productive resource responsible for the lower average total costs in the first place. Consequently, average total costs are no longer relatively lower for the person or firm that employs the higher quality, more productive resource or input.

Profit and Discrimination

A firm's discriminatory behavior can affect its profits in the context of the model of perfect competition. Let's start at the position of long-run competitive equilibrium where firms are earning zero economic profits. Consider the owner of a firm who chooses not to hire an excellent worker (a worker who is above average, let's say) simply because of that worker's race, religion, or gender.

If the owner of the firm discriminates in any way, what happens to his profits? If he chooses not to employ high-quality employees because of their race, religion, or gender, then his costs will rise above the costs of his competitors who hire the best employees—irrespective of race, religion, or gender. Because he is initially earning zero profit, where $TR = TC$, this act of discrimination will raise TC and push him into taking economic losses.

If the owner in the example is instead a manager, he may lose his job. Owners may decide to replace managers of firms earning subnormal profits. Thus, profit maximization by shareholders works to reduce discrimination.

Our conclusion is that if a firm is in a perfectly competitive market structure, it will pay penalties if it chooses to discriminate. This is not to say that discrimination will disappear. It only says that discrimination comes with a price tag. And according to economic theory, the more something costs, the less of it there will be, *ceteris paribus*.

SELF-TEST

1. If firms in a perfectly competitive market are earning positive economic profits, what will happen?

2. If firms in a perfectly competitive market want to produce more output, is the market in long-run equilibrium?

3. If a perfectly competitive market in long-run equilibrium witnesses an increase in demand, what will happen to price?

4. Suppose two firms produce computer software. Firm *A* employs a software genius at the same salary that firm *B* employs a mediocre software engineer. Will the firm that employs the software genius earn higher profits than the other firm, *ceteris paribus*?

Topics for Analysis Within the Theory of Perfect Competition

This section briefly analyzes three topics within the theory of perfect competition: higher costs and higher prices, advertising, and setting prices.

Do Higher Costs Mean Higher Prices?

Suppose there are 600 firms in an industry. Each firm sells the identical product at the same price. Suppose one of these firms experiences a rise in its marginal costs of production. Someone immediately comments, "Higher costs for the firm today, higher prices for the consumer tomorrow." Her assumption is that firms that experience a rise in costs simply pass on these higher costs to consumers in the form of higher prices.

Will this occur in a perfectly competitive market structure? Remember that each firm in the industry is a price taker; furthermore, only one firm has experienced a rise in marginal costs. Because this firm supplies only a tiny percentage of the total market supply, it is unlikely that the market supply curve will undergo more than a negligible change. And if the market supply curve does not change, neither will equilibrium price. In short, a rise in costs incurred by one of many firms does not mean consumers will pay higher prices. The situation would have been different, of course, if many of the firms in the industry had experienced a rise in costs. In this case, the market supply curve would have been affected, along with price.

Will the Perfectly Competitive Firm Advertise?

Do individual farmers advertise? Have you ever seen an advertisement for, say, Farmer Johnson's milk? We think not. First, Farmer Johnson sells a homogeneous product, so advertising his milk is the same as advertising every dairy farmer's milk. Second, Farmer Johnson is in a perfectly competitive market, so he can sell all the milk he wants at the going price. Why should he advertise? From his viewpoint, advertising has costs and no benefits.

Will a perfectly competitive industry advertise? For example, if Farmer Johnson won't advertise his milk, will the milk industry advertise milk? It may. The industry as a whole may advertise milk in the hope of shifting the market demand curve for milk to the right. This is actually what the milk industry hopes to do with its commercial message, "Got milk?"

Thinking like AN ECONOMIST

Sometimes, two or more explanations may seem equally reasonable. For example, observing that all firms within an industry sell their products for the same price, both the explanation that the firms collude on price and the explanation that the firms are price takers seem equally reasonable. But for the economist, a reasonable explanation is not sufficient; she wants the correct explanation. The economist is skeptical of any explanation that simply sounds reasonable. She needs evidence that supports the explanation.

Supplier-Set Price Versus Market-Determined Price: Collusion or Competition?

Suppose the only thing you know about a particular industry is that all firms within it sell their products at the same price. To explain this, some people argue that the firms are colluding—that is, the firms come together, pick a price, and stick to it.

This, of course, is one way all firms can arrive at the same price for their products. But it is not the only way. Another way has been described in this chapter. It could be that all firms are price takers; that is, the firms are in a perfectly competitive market structure. In this case, there is no collusion.

SELF-TEST

1.   In a perfectly competitive market, do higher costs mean higher prices?

2.   Suppose you see a product advertised on television. Does it follow that the product cannot be produced in a perfectly competitive market?

A Reader Asks...

Does Job Security Have Anything to Do with Fixed and Variable Costs?

What is the relationship among fixed, variable, and total costs, the firm's shut-down decision, and employee job security?

Consider the total fixed cost–total cost ratio (*TFC/TC*) for firms. The greater the ratio—that is, the larger *TFC* is relative to *TC*—the more likely the firm will operate in the short run; the smaller the ratio, the less likely the firm will operate in the short run. It follows that the more likely the firm will operate in the short run, the greater the job security for the employees of the firm; the less likely the firm will operate in the short run, the less job security for the employees of the firm.

To illustrate, suppose two firms, *X* and *Y*, have the following costs and ratios:

Notice that the two firms have the same total cost ($600) but that the fixed and variable costs are different percentages of total cost for the two firms. Firm *X* has a lower *TVC/TC* ratio and a higher *TFC/TC* ratio than firm *Y* has. If total revenue falls to, say, $499, firm *Y* will shut down because its total revenue will be less than its total variable cost (*TVC*). However, firm *X* will continue to operate. For firm *X*, total revenue will have to fall below $400 before it will shut down. In other words, the firm with the higher *TFC/TC* ratio (firm *X*) stays operational longer than the firm with the lower *TFC/TC* ratio (firm *Y*). It follows, then, that if everything else is equal between the two firms, an employee working for firm *X* is less likely to be laid off due to declining total revenue than is an employee working for firm *Y*.

Firm X	Firm Y
$TC = \$600$	$TC = \$600$
$TVC = \$400$	$TVC = \$500$
$TFC = \$200$	$TFC = \$100$
$TVC/TC = \$400/\$600 = 0.66$	$TVC/TC = \$500/\$600 = 0.83$
$TFC/TC = \$200/\$600 = 0.33$	$TFC/TC = \$100/\$600 = 0.17$

! analyzing the scene

If Pam had decided to sell 400 shares of Wal-Mart stock instead of 500 shares, could she have sold each share for more than $58.68?

Could Pam have received a higher per-share price if she had decided to sell fewer shares? In other words, is the market price "somewhat" under Pam's control? The answer is no. Her shares are such a small percentage of the total shares of Wal-Mart stock that if she holds back 100 shares (sells 400 shares instead of 500 shares), it is unlikely that she can affect the market price of Wal-Mart stock. In short, Pam is a price taker: She takes the market price as given.

Should a company shut down if it is incurring a loss?

Ricky Amador's company incurred a loss last year, and he wonders if he should shut down the company. However, a loss does not necessarily mean that shutting down is the best option. A loss occurs any time a firm sells its good for less than its unit costs (or ATC). But if price is above AVC (even though it is below ATC), it will still be better for the company to continue to operate in the short run than to shut down. Ricky Amador should look at the price he charges for his good in relation to his AVC. If price is above AVC, continue to operate; if price is below AVC, shut down.

What will happen if taxes are imposed on companies because demand for their products has increased?

A U.S. senator argues for a higher tax on "unearned profits" than on earned profits. According to the senator, unearned profits are profits that a company acquired because the demand for its product increased; they are not profits that the company earned because it produced a better good and so on. The senator is looking at profits as a dollar amount (which is the way many people look at profits). What he doesn't see (or if he sees, he doesn't indicate) is that profits direct resources.

To illustrate, suppose government taxes away all the profits of a company whose profits are the result of increasing demand. For example, the demand for good X rises, and in the short run, price and profits rise, and the government taxes away all these profits.

However, by increasing demand, the buying public was sending a signal to producers to produce more of good X. If current firms are permitted to keep the higher profits, then other firms will enter the industry and start to compete with them. In the process of the new firms competing with the old existing firms, more of good X will be produced, which the buying public was saying it wanted.

By taxing the profits away, government will prevent new firms from joining the industry and producing more of good X. And without the supply response from new firms, government will prevent price from falling. In terms of Exhibit 9, the process will stop at Step 4 and will not be able to go to Step 6 (more output and price back to its original level).

How does a business owner decide how much of his or her product to produce?

Steven Pickering, who manufactures and sells small fans, wonders how many fans he should produce in the upcoming 6-month period. What would we advise? The answer is consistent with good common sense: Keep producing as long as the additional revenue (or marginal revenue) of producing and selling an additional fan is greater than the additional cost (or marginal cost) of producing and selling an additional fan. He should produce the number of fans at which $MR = MC$.

Why do profits sometimes get turned into salaries?

This scene is similar to the situation for farmers Cordero and Hancock. Recall that Cordero earned profits, and Hancock did not. But Cordero earned profits because he was farming higher quality land than Hancock was farming. In time, Cordero's profits were turned into higher land payments—that is, payments for the higher quality, more productive resource responsible for the original profits.

Just as land is a resource for a farmer, the stars of the TV show are a resource for the network. If the network's profits are the result of the actors' superior acting, then the actors' superior acting is much like the higher quality land in the Cordero and Hancock example. In the end, it is likely that the higher profits for the network will go as payments for the higher quality, more productive resource responsible for the profits. Thus, the profits will be turned into higher salaries for the actors.

chapter summary

The Theory of Perfect Competition

- The theory of perfect competition is built on four assumptions: (1) There are many sellers and many buyers, none of which is large in relation to total sales or purchases. (2) Each firm produces and sells a homogeneous product. (3) Buyers and sellers have all relevant information with respect to prices, product quality, sources of supply, and so on. (4) There is easy entry into and exit from the industry.

- The theory of perfect competition predicts the following: (1) Economic profits will be squeezed out of the industry in the long run by the entry of new firms; that is, zero economic profit exists in the long run. (2) In equilibrium, firms produce the quantity of output at which price equals marginal cost. (3) In the short run, firms will stay in business as long as price covers average variable costs. (4) In the long run, firms will stay in business as long as price covers average total costs. (5) In the short run, an increase in demand will lead to a rise in price; whether the price in the long run will be higher than, lower than, or equal to its original level depends on whether the firm is in an increasing-, decreasing-, or constant-cost industry.

The Perfectly Competitive Firm

- A perfectly competitive firm is a price taker. It sells its product only at the market-established equilibrium price.

- The perfectly competitive firm faces a horizontal (flat, perfectly elastic) demand curve. Its demand curve and its marginal revenue curve are the same.

- The perfectly competitive firm (as well as all other firms) maximizes profits (or minimizes losses) by producing the quantity of output at which $MR = MC$.

- For the perfectly competitive firm, price equals marginal revenue.

- A perfectly competitive firm is resource allocative efficient because it produces the quantity of output at which $P = MC$.

Production in the Short Run

- If $P > ATC (> AVC)$, the firm earns economic profits and will continue to operate in the short run.

- If $P < AVC (< ATC)$, the firm takes losses. It will shut down because the alternative (continuing to produce) increases the losses.

- If $ATC > P > AVC$, the firm takes losses. Nevertheless, it will continue to operate in the short run because the alternative (shutting down) increases the losses.

- The firm produces in the short run only when price is greater than average variable cost. Therefore, the portion of its marginal cost curve that lies above the average variable cost curve is the firm's short-run supply curve.

Conditions of Long-Run Competitive Equilibrium

- Long-run competitive equilibrium exists when (1) there is no incentive for firms to enter or exit the industry, (2) there is no incentive for firms to produce more or less output, and (3) there is no incentive for firms to change plant size. We formalize these conditions as follows: (1) Economic profits are zero. (This is the same as saying there is no incentive for firms to enter or exit the industry.) (2) Firms are producing the quantity of output at which price is equal to marginal cost. (This is the same as saying there is no incentive for firms to produce more or less output. After all, when $P = MC$, it follows that $MR = MC$ for the perfectly competitive firm, and thus, the firm is maximizing profits.) (3) $SRATC = LRATC$ at the quantity of output at which $P = MC$. (This is the same as saying firms do not have an incentive to change plant size.)

- A perfectly competitive firm exhibits productive efficiency because it produces its output in the long run at the lowest possible per-unit cost (lowest ATC).

Industry Adjustment to a Change in Demand

- In a constant-cost industry, an increase in demand will result in a new equilibrium price equal to the original equilibrium price (before demand increased). In an increasing-cost industry, an increase in demand will result in a new equilibrium price higher than the original equilibrium price. In a decreasing-cost industry, an increase in demand will result in a new equilibrium price lower than the original equilibrium price.

- The long-run supply curve for a constant-cost industry is horizontal (flat, perfectly elastic). The long-run supply curve for an increasing-cost industry is upward sloping. The long-run supply curve for a decreasing-cost industry is downward sloping.

key terms and concepts

Market Structure

Perfect Competition

Price Taker

Marginal Revenue (*MR*)

Profit-Maximization Rule

Resource Allocative
Efficiency

Short-Run (Firm) Supply
Curve

Short-Run Market
(Industry) Supply Curve

Long-Run Competitive
Equilibrium

Productive Efficiency

Constant-Cost Industry

Long-Run (Industry)
Supply (*LRS*) Curve

Increasing-Cost Industry

Decreasing-Cost Industry

questions and problems

1 True or false: The firm's entire marginal cost curve is its short-run supply curve. Explain your answer.

2 True or false: In a perfectly competitive market, firms always operate at the lowest per-unit cost. Explain your answer.

3 "Firm *A,* one firm in a competitive industry, faces higher costs of production. As a result, consumers end up paying higher prices." Discuss.

4 Suppose all firms in a perfectly competitive market structure are in long-run equilibrium. Then demand for the firms' product increases. Initially, price and economic profits rise. Soon afterward, the government decides to tax most (but not all) of the economic profits, arguing that the firms in the industry did not earn the profits. They were simply the result of an increase in demand. What effect, if any, will the tax have on market adjustment?

5 Explain why one firm sometimes appears to be earning higher profits than another but in reality is not.

6 For a perfectly competitive firm, profit maximization does not conflict with resource allocative efficiency. Do you agree? Explain your answer.

7 The perfectly competitive firm does not increase its quantity of output without limit even though it can sell all it wants at the going price. Why not?

8 Suppose you read in a business magazine that computer firms are reaping high profits. With the theory of perfect competition in mind, what do you expect to happen over time to the following: computer prices, the profits of computer firms, the number of computers on the market, the number of computer firms?

9 In your own words, explain resource allocative efficiency.

10 The term *price taker* can apply to buyers as well as sellers. A price-taking buyer is one who cannot influence price by changing the amount she buys. What goods do you buy for which you are a price taker? What goods do you buy for which you are not a price taker?

11 Why study the theory of perfect competition if no real-world market completely satisfies all of the theory's assumptions?

12 Explain why a perfectly competitive firm will shut down in the short run if price is lower than average variable cost but will continue to produce if price is below average total cost but above average variable cost.

13 In long-run competitive equilibrium, $P = MC = SRATC = LRATC$. Because $P = MR$, we can write the condition as $P = MR = MC = SRATC = LRATC$. Now let's look at the condition as consisting of four parts: (a) $P = MR$, (b) $MR = MC$, (c) $P = SRATC$, and (d) $SRATC = LRATC$. To explain (b), why $MR = MC$, we say that this condition exists because the perfectly competitive firm attempts to maximize profits and this is how it does it. What are the explanations for (a), (c), and (d)?

14 Suppose the government imposes a production tax on one perfectly competitive firm in an industry. For each unit the firm produces, it must pay $1 to the government. Will consumers in this market end up paying higher prices because of the tax? Why or why not?

15 Why is the marginal revenue curve for a perfectly competitive firm the same as its demand curve?

16 Many plumbers charge the same price for coming to your house to fix a kitchen sink. Is this because plumbers are colluding together on price?

17 Do firms in a perfectly competitive market exhibit productive efficiency? Why or why not?

working with numbers and graphs

1   Given the following information, state whether the perfectly competitive firm should shut down or continue to operate in the short run.

a $Q = 100; P = \$10; AFC = \$3; AVC = \$4$
b $Q = 70; P = \$5; AFC = \$2; AVC = \$7$
c $Q = 150; P = \$7; AFC = \$5; AVC = \$6$

2   If total revenue increases at a constant rate, what does this imply about marginal revenue?

3   Using the following table, what quantity of output should the firm produce? Explain your answer.

Q	TR	TC
0	$0	$0
1	100	50
2	200	110
3	300	180
4	400	260
5	500	360
6	600	480

4   Is the firm in Question 3 a perfectly competitive firm? Explain your answer.

5   Explain how a market supply curve is derived.

6   Draw the following:

a   A perfectly competitive firm that earns profits
b   A perfectly competitive firm that incurs losses but will continue operating in the short run
c   A perfectly competitive firm that incurs losses and will shut down in the short run

7   Why is the perfectly competitive firm's supply curve that portion of its marginal cost curve that is above its average variable cost curve?

8   In the following figure, what area(s) represent(s) the following at Q_1?

a   Total cost
b   Total variable cost
c   Total revenue
d   Loss (negative profit)

9   Why does the MC curve cut the ATC curve at the latter's lowest point?

10 Suppose all firms in a perfectly competitive market are in long-run equilibrium. Illustrate what a perfectly competitive firm will do if market demand rises.

Setting the Scene

The following events occurred on a day in April.

10:01 A.M.

Jackson is looking at cars at a Toyota dealership. A car salesman walks over and asks him what car he likes. Jackson tells him. Then the salesman asks Jackson what he does for a living. Jackson wonders what that question has to do with anything, but still he answers. He tells the salesman that he is "an attorney, here in town." "What kind of law do you practice?" the salesman asks.

12:33 P.M.

A musical artist is in the office of one of BT Productions' executives. She is arguing about the price the company wants to charge for her latest CD. "I think the price should be at least $2 lower," she says. "We don't," says the executive. "Don't forget," he adds, "your royalties are tied to our revenues."

9:44 P.M.

Two years ago, Carl Wilson opened the only restaurant in a rather large town that provided its customers with "mud wrestling while you eat." Granted, it was a novel idea, and it was written up in the local newspaper. One columnist wrote, "Mr. Wilson is an entrepreneur. He has come up with a new kind of restaurant. I could even say that, as things stand right now, he is a monopolist; after all, he is the only restaurateur within a 100-mile radius that offers his patrons mud wrestling while they eat."

Tonight, Carl Wilson is sitting in his living room watching television. He has just decided to close his restaurant. It seems that very few people want to eat at a restaurant that provides mud wrestling as entertainment.

? Here are some questions to keep in mind as you read this chapter:

- *Is the car salesman simply making small talk by asking Jackson what he does for a living?*

- *Why does the musical artist want to price her CD lower than the BT Productions executive wants to price it?*

- *Did Carl Wilson think his one-of-a-kind restaurant bestowed monopoly status on him—and therefore, he just couldn't fail?*

See analyzing the scene at the end of this chapter for answers to these questions.

The Theory of Monopoly

The last chapter discussed one market structure theory—the theory of perfect competition. At the opposite end of the market structure spectrum is the theory of **monopoly**. The theory of monopoly is built on three assumptions:

Monopoly
A theory of market structure based on three assumptions: There is one seller, it sells a product for which no close substitutes exist, and there are extremely high barriers to entry.

1. **There is one seller.** This means that the firm is the industry. Contrast this situation with perfect competition, where many firms make up the industry.

2. **The single seller sells a product for which there are no close substitutes.** Because there are no close substitutes for its product, the single seller—the monopolist or monopoly firm—faces little, if any, competition.

3. **There are extremely high barriers to entry.** In the theory of perfect competition, we assume it is easy for a firm to enter the industry. In the theory of monopoly, we assume it is very hard (if not impossible) for a firm to enter the industry. Extremely high barriers keep out new firms.

Examples of monopoly include many public utilities (local public utilities such as electricity, water, and gas companies) and the U.S. Postal Service (in the delivery of first-class mail).

Barriers to Entry: A Key to Understanding Monopoly

If a firm is a single seller of a product, why don't other firms enter the market and produce the same product? Legal barriers, economies of scale, or one firm's exclusive ownership of a scarce resource may make it difficult or impossible for new firms to enter the market.

Public Franchise
A right granted to a firm by government that permits the firm to provide a particular good or service and excludes all others from doing the same.

LEGAL BARRIERS Legal barriers include public franchises, patents, and government licenses. A **public franchise** is a right granted to a firm by government that permits the firm to provide a particular good or service and excludes all others from doing the same (thus eliminating potential competition by law). For example, the U.S. Postal Service has been granted the exclusive franchise to deliver first-class mail. Many public utilities operate under state and local franchises, as do food and gas suppliers along many state turnpikes.

© LAWRENCE MIGDALE/STONE/GETTY IMAGES

In the United States, patents are granted to inventors of a product or process for a period of 20 years. During this time, the patent holder is shielded from competitors; no one else can legally produce and sell the patented product or process. The rationale behind patents is that they encourage innovation in an economy. It is argued that few people will waste their time and money trying to invent a new product if their competitors can immediately copy the product and sell it.

Entry into some industries and occupations requires a government-granted license. For example, radio and television stations cannot operate without a license from the Federal Communications Commission (FCC). In most states, a person needs to be licensed to join the ranks of physicians, dentists, architects, nurses, embalmers, barbers, veterinarians, and lawyers, among others.

Some cities also use licensing as a form of legal barrier. For example, the Taxi & Limousine Commission requires a person to have a taxi license, called a *taxi medallion,* to own and operate a taxi in New York City. A taxi medallion is similar to a business license; a person needs it to lawfully operate a taxicab business.

© BETTMANN/CORBIS

economics 24/7

MONOPOLY AND THE BOSTON TEA PARTY

The original meaning of the word *monopoly* was "an exclusive right to sell something." At one time, kings and queens granted monopolies to people in their favor. The monopoly entitled the person to be the sole producer or seller of a particular good. If anyone dared to compete with him, then the king or queen could have that person fined or imprisoned.

The issue of monopoly comes up in the early history of the United States. In 1767, the British Parliament passed the Townsend Acts. These acts imposed taxes (or duties) on various products that were imported into the American colonies. The taxes were so hated in the colonies that they prompted protest and noncompliance. The taxes were repealed in 1770, except for one—the tax on tea. Some historians state that the British Parliament left the tax on tea to

show the colonists that it had the right to raise tax revenue without seeking colonial approval. To get around the tax, the colonists started to buy tea from Dutch traders.

Then, in 1773, the British East India Company was in financial trouble. To help solve its financial problems, it sought a special privilege—a monopoly—from the British Parliament. In response, Parliament passed the Tea Act, which granted the British East India Company the sole right—the monopoly right—to export tea to the colonies. The combination of the tax and the monopoly right given to the British East India Company angered the colonists and is said to have led to the Boston Tea Party on December 16, 1773. The colonists who took part in the Boston Tea Party threw overboard 342 chests of tea owned by the monopoly-wielding British East India Company.

The number of taxi medallions (licenses) has been fixed at about 12,000 for many years. The price of a medallion changes according to changes in the demand for medallions. In 1976, a medallion was about $45,000; in 1988, it was $125,000; and in January 2004, it was $242,000. Obviously, many people find $242,000 a barrier to entering the taxi business. Thus, many economists believe that taxi medallions in New York City are a form of legal barrier.

ECONOMIES OF SCALE In some industries, low average total costs (low unit costs) are obtained only through large-scale production. Thus, if new entrants are to compete in the industry, they must enter it on a large scale. But having to produce on this scale is risky and costly and therefore acts as a barrier to entry. If economies of scale are so pronounced that only one firm can survive in the industry, this firm is called a **natural monopoly**. Often-cited examples of natural monopoly include public utilities that provide gas, water, and electricity. A later chapter discusses government regulation of a natural monopoly.

Natural Monopoly
The condition where economies of scale are so pronounced that only one firm can survive.

EXCLUSIVE OWNERSHIP OF A NECESSARY RESOURCE Existing firms may be protected from the entry of new firms by the exclusive or near-exclusive ownership of a resource needed to enter the industry. The classic example is the Aluminum Company of America (Alcoa), which for a time controlled almost all sources of bauxite in the United States. Alcoa was the sole producer of aluminum in the country from the late 19th century until the 1940s. Many people today view the De Beers Company of South Africa as a monopoly because it controls a large percentage of diamond production and sales. Strictly speaking, De Beers is more of a marketing cartel than a monopolist, although, as discussed in the next chapter, a successful cartel acts much like a monopolist.

What Is the Difference Between a Government Monopoly and a Market Monopoly?

Sometimes, high barriers to entry exist because competition is legally prohibited; sometimes, they exist independently. When high barriers take the form of public franchises, patents, or government licenses, competition is *legally* prohibited. When high barriers take the form of economies of scale or exclusive ownership of a resource, competition is not legally prohibited. In these latter cases, nothing legally prohibits rival firms from entering the market and competing, even though they may choose not to do so. The high barrier to entry does not have a sign attached to it that reads: "No competition allowed."

Some economists use the term *government monopoly* to refer to a monopoly that is legally protected from competition and the term *market monopoly* to refer to a monopoly that is not legally protected from competition. But these terms do not imply that one type is better or worse than the other.

SELF-TEST

(Answers to Self-Test questions are in the Self-Test Appendix.)

1.   John states that there are always some close substitutes for the product any firm sells; therefore, the theory of monopoly (which assumes no close substitutes) cannot be useful. Comment.

2.   How do economies of scale act as a barrier to entry?

3.   How is a movie superstar like a monopolist?

Monopoly Pricing and Output Decisions

Price Searcher

A seller that has the ability to control to some degree the price of the product it sells.

A monopolist is a **price searcher**; that is, it is a seller that has the ability to control to some degree the price of the product it sells. In contrast to a price taker, a price searcher can raise its price and still sell its product—although not as many units as it could sell at the lower price. The pricing and output decisions of the price-searching monopolist are discussed in this section.

> *Theme* **micro**
>
> In an earlier chapter, we mentioned that microeconomics has a lot to do with (1) objectives, (2) constraints, and (3) choices. Think of both a perfectly competitive firm and a monopoly firm in terms of constraints. The perfectly competitive firm is constrained in that it cannot raise its price (above the market-equilibrium price) and still sell some of its good. The monopoly firm, though, is not constrained this way. It can raise its price and still sell some of its good.

The Monopolist's Demand and Marginal Revenue

In the theory of monopoly, the monopoly firm is the industry, and the industry is the monopoly firm—they are the same. It follows that the demand curve for the monopoly firm *is* the market demand curve, which is downward sloping. A downward-sloping demand curve posits an inverse relationship between price and quantity demanded: More is sold at lower prices than at higher prices, *ceteris paribus*. Unlike the perfectly competitive firm, the monopolist can raise its price and still sell its product (though not as much).

Suppose a monopolist wants to sell an additional unit of its product. What must it do? Because it faces a downward-sloping demand curve, it must necessarily lower price.

For example, let's assume the monopoly seller originally planned to sell 2 units of X a day at \$10 each and now wishes to sell 3 units a day. To sell more units, it must lower price, say, to \$9.75. It sells the 3 units at \$9.75 each.[1]

So to sell an additional unit, a monopoly firm must lower price on all previous units. Note that *previous* and *additional* don't refer to an actual sequence of events. A firm doesn't sell 100 units of a good and then decide to sell one more unit. The firm is in an either–or situation. Either the firm sells 100 units over some period of time, or it sells 101 units over the same period of time. If the firm wants to sell 101 units, the price per unit must be lower than if it wants to sell 100 units.

A monopoly seller both gains and loses by lowering price. As Exhibit 1 shows, the monopolist in our example gains \$9.75, the price of the additional unit sold, because price was lowered. It loses 50 cents—25 cents on the first unit it used to sell at \$10 plus 25 cents on the second unit it used to sell at \$10.

Gains are greater than losses; the monopolist's net gain from selling the additional unit of output is \$9.25 (\$9.75 − \$0.50 = \$9.25). This is the monopolist's *marginal revenue:* the change in total revenue that results from selling one additional unit of output. (Total revenue is \$20 when 2 units are sold at \$10 each. Total revenue is \$29.25 when 3 units are sold at \$9.75 each. The change in total revenue that results from selling one additional unit of output is \$9.25.)

Notice that the price of the good (\$9.75) is greater than the marginal revenue (\$9.25), $P > MR$. This is the case for a monopoly seller or any price searcher. (Recall that for the firm in perfect competition, $P = MR$.)

For a monopolist, $P > MR$

The Monopolist's Demand and Marginal Revenue Curves Are Not the Same: Why Not?

In perfect competition, the firm's demand curve *is* the same as its marginal revenue curve. In monopoly, the firm's demand curve is not the same as its marginal revenue curve. The monopolist's demand curve lies above its marginal revenue curve.

(1) P	(2) Q	(3) TR	(4) MR
\$10.00	2	\$20.00	$\underline{}$ \$9.25
9.75	3	29.25	

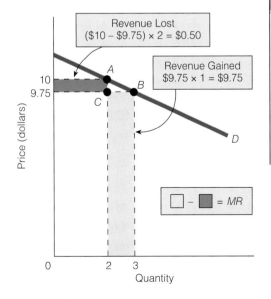

exhibit 1

The Dual Effects of a Price Reduction on Total Revenue

To sell an additional unit of its good, a monopolist needs to lower price. This price reduction both gains revenue and loses revenue for the monopolist. In the exhibit, the revenue gained and revenue lost are shaded and labeled. Marginal revenue is equal to the larger shaded area minus the smaller shaded area.

[1]This discussion is about how a single-price monopolist behaves. This is a monopolist that sells all units of its product for the same price. Later, we discuss a price-discriminating monopolist.

exhibit **2**

Demand and Marginal Revenue Curves

The demand curve plots price and quantity. The marginal revenue curve plots marginal revenue and quantity. For a monopolist, $P > MR$, so the marginal revenue curve must lie below the demand curve. (Note that when a demand curve is a straight line, the marginal revenue curve bisects the horizontal axis halfway between the origin and the point where the demand curve intersects the horizontal axis.)

For a monopolist, the marginal revenue curve lies below the demand curve.

The demand curve plots price and quantity (P and Q); the marginal revenue curve plots marginal revenue and quantity (MR and Q). Because price is greater than marginal revenue for a monopolist, its demand curve necessarily lies *above* its marginal revenue curve. (Note that price and marginal revenue are the same for the first unit of output, so the demand curve and the marginal revenue curve will share one point in common.) The relationship between a monopolist's demand and marginal revenue curves is illustrated in Exhibit 2.

Price and Output for a Profit-Maximizing Monopolist

The monopolist that seeks to maximize profit produces the quantity of output at which $MR = MC$ (as did the profit-maximizing perfectly competitive firm) and *charges the highest price per unit at which this quantity of output can be sold.*

In Exhibit 3, the highest price at which Q_1, the quantity at which $MR = MC$, can be sold is P_1. Notice that at Q_1, the monopolist charges a price that is greater than marginal cost, $P > MC$. Therefore, the monopolist is *not* resource allocative efficient.

Whether profits are earned depends on whether P_1 is greater or less than average total cost at Q_1. In short, the profit-maximizing price may be the loss-minimizing price. Monopoly profits and monopoly losses are illustrated in Exhibit 4.

Some people argue that it is unrealistic to suggest that a monopolist can take a loss. They say that if the monopolist is the only seller in the industry, then it is guaranteed a profit. But just because a firm is the only seller of a particular product does not guarantee it will earn profits. Remember, a monopolist cannot charge any price it wants for its good; it charges the highest price that the demand curve allows it to charge. In some instances, the highest price may be lower than the firm's average total costs (unit costs). If so, the monopolist incurs a loss, as shown in Exhibit 4(b).

If a Firm Maximizes Revenue, Does It Automatically Maximize Profit Too?

We assume that all firms, whether price searchers or price takers, seek to maximize profit. Many people easily fall into the trap of thinking that the price that maximizes total revenue is necessarily the price that maximizes profit. In other words, the higher

exhibit **3**

The Monopolist's Profit-Maximizing Price and Quantity of Output

The monopolist produces the quantity of output (Q_1) at which $MR = MC$, and charges the highest price per unit at which this quantity of output can be sold (P_1). Notice that at the profit-maximizing quantity of output, price is greater than marginal cost, $P > MC$.

Profit-maximizing price (highest price per unit at which Q_1 can be sold).

At Q_1, $P > MC$

$MR = MC$

Profit-maximizing quantity of output

(a)
Monopoly Profits

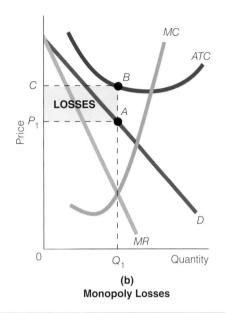

(b)
Monopoly Losses

exhibit **4**

Monopoly Profits and Losses

A monopoly seller is not guaranteed any profits. In (a), price at above average total cost at Q_1, the quantity of output at which $MR = MC$. Therefore, TR (the area $0P_1BQ_1$) is greater than TC (the area $0CAQ_1$), and profits equal the area CP_1BA. In (b), price is below average total cost at Q_1. Therefore, TR (the area $0P_1AQ_1$) is less than TC (the area $0CBQ_1$) and losses equal the area P_1CBA.

the firm's total revenue (TR), the higher the firm's profit. But this is not necessarily the case. To illustrate, suppose $TR =$ $100, $TFC =$ $40, and $TVC =$ $20. Because $TC = TFC + TVC$, it follows that $TC =$ $60. The firm's profit, which is TR minus TC, is $40.

Now suppose the firm can sell one more unit of a good and raise its TR to $105. Should it sell one more unit of the good? The answer is that it depends; specifically, it depends on how much more it costs to produce one more unit. Suppose producing one more unit raises the firm's TVC to $30. Again, $TC = TFC + TVC$, and because TVC has risen to $30, TC rises to $70. The difference between TR and TC is now $35 ($105 − $70). Thus, selling one more unit of the good raises TR from $100 to $105, but it lowers profit from $40 to $35. A firm seeks to maximize profit, not total revenue.

Under one condition, maximizing revenue will be the same as maximizing profit. Can you guess the condition? It is when TC is constant. Of course, the only time TC is constant is when it is composed of only TFC; that is, variable costs are zero. To illustrate, suppose $TR =$ $100, $TFC =$ $40, and $TVC =$ $0. Because $TVC =$ $0, it follows that $TC = TFC =$ $40.

Now again suppose that if the firm sells one more unit of a good, its TR will rise to $105. Should it sell one more unit? The answer is obviously yes. That's because, in this case, $TC = TFC$ (and TFC is constant), so TC remains at $40. The firm increases its total revenue and its profit by $5 if it sells an additional unit of the good.

We conclude that maximizing profit is not consistent with maximizing revenue when variable costs exist. But when variable costs do not exist (i.e., variable costs are zero), then maximizing profit is consistent with maximizing revenue.

Q&A *In the last chapter, we learned that a perfectly competitive firm produces the quantity of output at which* **MR = MC.** *The monopoly firm does the same thing, correct? I would have thought that a perfectly competitive firm and monopoly firm would have acted differently in this regard.*

First, you are correct that both the monopoly firm and the perfectly competitive firm choose to produce the quantity of output for which MR = MC. *Think about why this happens. Each firm would want to produce as long as its additional revenue (MR) is greater than its additional cost (MC), and it wouldn't want to produce where its additional cost (MC) was greater than its additional revenue (MR). That only leaves producing the quantity of output at which* MR = MC.

Q&A *Can you give an example of when it might be bad for a firm to try to maximize its total revenue?*

Suppose the firm's total revenue is currently $100 and its total cost is $99. It follows that it is earning a $1 profit. Now suppose the firm can sell one more unit of its good and increase its total revenue to $102, but at the same time, it raises its total cost to $106. Although $102 of revenue is greater than $100, if the firm seeks to increase its total revenue by $2 (make its total revenue as large as possible), it will end up incurring a loss of $4.

Perfect Competition and Monopoly

We discussed perfect competition in the last chapter and monopoly in this chapter. Perfect competition and monopoly are at opposite ends of the (market structure) spectrum. This means there are major differences between them. In this section, we discuss those differences.

Price, Marginal Revenue, and Marginal Cost

Here are two key differences between perfect competition and monopoly:

1.   For the perfectly competitive firm, $P = MR$; for the monopolist, $P > MR$. The perfectly competitive firm's demand curve *is* its marginal revenue curve; the monopolist's demand curve *lies above* its marginal revenue curve.

2.   The perfectly competitive firm charges a price equal to marginal cost; the monopolist charges a price greater than marginal cost.

$$\text{Perfect competition: } P = MR \text{ and } P = MC$$
$$\text{Monopoly: } P > MR \text{ and } P > MC$$

Monopoly, Perfect Competition, and Consumers' Surplus

A monopoly firm differs from a perfectly competitive firm in terms of how much consumers' surplus buyers receive. To illustrate, consider Exhibit 5, which shows a downward-sloping market demand curve, a downward-sloping marginal revenue curve, and a horizontal marginal cost (MC) curve. Although you are used to seeing upward-sloping marginal cost curves, there is nothing to prevent marginal cost from being constant over some range of output. A horizontal MC curve simply means that marginal cost is constant. If the market in Exhibit 5 is perfectly competitive, the demand curve *is* the marginal revenue curve. Therefore, the profit-maximizing output is Q_{PC}.[2] The buyer will pay P_{PC} per

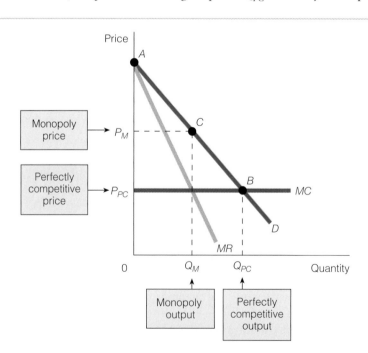

exhibit **5**

Monopoly, Perfect Competition, and Consumers' Surplus

If the market in the exhibit is perfectly competitive, the demand curve is the marginal revenue curve. The profit-maximizing output is Q_{PC} and price is P_{PC}. Consumers' surplus is the area $P_{PC}AB$. If the market is a monopoly market, the profit-maximizing output is Q_M and price is P_M. In this case, consumers' surplus is the area P_MAC. Consumers' surplus is greater in perfect competition than in monopoly; it is greater by the area $P_{PC}P_MCB$.

[2]Keep in mind that we are looking at the market demand curve, not the firm's demand curve. This is why the demand curve is downward sloping. All market demand curves are downward sloping.

unit of the good. Recall that consumers' surplus is the area under the demand curve and above the price. For the perfectly competitive firm, consumers' surplus is the area $P_{PC}AB$.

Now suppose the market is a monopoly market. In this case, the demand curve and the marginal revenue curve are different. The profit-maximizing output is where the MR curve intersects the MC curve; thus, the profit-maximizing output is Q_M. The price the buyer pays is P_M. Consumers' surplus in the monopoly case is P_MAC.

Obviously, consumers' surplus is greater in the perfectly competitive case than in the monopoly case. How much greater? It is greater by the area $P_{PC}P_MCB$. Stated differently, this is the loss in consumers' surplus due to monopolization.

Monopoly or Nothing?

Suppose you could push one of two buttons to determine the conditions under which a particular good is produced. If you push the first button, the good is produced under the conditions of perfect competition. If you push the second button, the good is produced under the conditions of monopoly. Which button would you push?

From a consumer's perspective, pushing the first button and producing the good under the conditions of perfect competition would seem to be the better choice. After all, perfect competition provides more output than monopoly and a lower price. In short, there is more consumers' surplus. Perfect competition would seem to be superior to monopoly.

But life doesn't always present a choice between perfect competition and monopoly. Sometimes, it presents a choice between monopoly and nothing. To illustrate, consider Exhibit 6, which shows the demand curve for a good along with the relevant marginal revenue curve. The exhibit also shows two sets of MC and ATC curves. Let's assume that MC_1 and ATC_1 are the relevant cost curves. Notice that because the MC_1 curve is so far above the MR curve, there is no intersection point. In other words, there is no profit-maximizing quantity of output for a firm to produce. Simply put, although there is demand for the particular good, the costs of producing the good are so high that no firm would produce it. Given this situation, consumers receive no consumers' surplus from the purchase and consumption of the good.

Now suppose a firm—one single firm—is able to lower costs to MC_2 and ATC_2. Now marginal cost is low enough for the firm to produce the good. The firm produces Q_M and charges a price of P_M. The area $P_M AB$ is equal to consumers' surplus.

exhibit **6**

Monopoly or Nothing?

We start with the demand and marginal revenue curves and with MC_1 $= ATC_1$. Because cost is "so high," no firm produces the good. Later, a single firm figures out how to lower cost to $MC_2 = ATC_2$. This firm produces Q_M and charges the monopoly price of P_M per unit. Is monopoly preferable to no firm producing the good? From a consumer's perspective, the answer is yes. Consumers' surplus is zero when no firm produces the good, and consumers' surplus is area $P_M AB$ when the monopoly firm produces the good.

No doubt the firm producing this good and charging a price of P_M is a monopoly firm. But are consumers better off having a monopoly firm produce the good than having no firm produce it? If no firm produces the good (because costs are just too high), consumers' surplus is zero. But when the monopoly firm produces the good, consumers' surplus is positive.

So under certain conditions, a monopoly may be created in a market because a firm figures out a way to lower the cost of producing a good to a level that makes it worthwhile to produce. Of course, once the monopoly firm exists, consumers would prefer that the good be produced under perfect competition than under monopoly conditions. But that is not always the relevant choice. Sometimes, the choice is between monopoly and nothing, and when this is the choice, the consumers' surplus is greater with monopoly than it is with nothing.

SELF-TEST

1. Why does the monopolist's demand curve lie above its marginal revenue curve?

2. Is a monopolist guaranteed to earn profits?

3. Is a monopolist resource allocative efficient? Why or why not?

4. A monopolist is a price searcher. Why do you think it is called a price searcher? What is it searching for?

The Case Against Monopoly

Monopoly is often said to be inefficient in comparison with perfect competition. This section examines some of the shortcomings associated with monopoly.

The Deadweight Loss of Monopoly

Exhibit 7 shows demand, marginal revenue, marginal cost, and average total cost curves. We have made the simplifying assumption that the product is produced under constant-cost conditions; as a consequence, marginal cost equals long-run average total cost.

exhibit **7**

Deadweight Loss and Rent Seeking as Costs of Monopoly

The monopolist produces Q_M, and the perfectly competitive firm produces the higher output level Q_{PC}. The deadweight loss of monopoly is the triangle (*DCB*) between these two levels of output. Rent-seeking activity is directed to obtaining the monopoly profits, represented by the area $P_{PC}P_M CD$. Rent seeking is a socially wasteful activity because resources are expended to transfer income rather than to produce goods and services.

If the product is produced under perfect competition, output Q_{PC} is produced and is sold at a price of P_{PC}. At the competitive equilibrium output level, $P = MC$.

If the product is produced under monopoly, output Q_M is produced and is sold at a price of P_M. At the monopoly equilibrium, $P > MC$.

Greater output is produced under perfect competition than under monopoly. The net value of the difference in these two output levels is said to be the **deadweight loss of monopoly**. In Exhibit 7, the value to buyers of increasing output from Q_M to Q_{PC} is equal to the maximum amount they would pay for this increase in output. This amount is designated by the area $Q_M CBQ_{PC}$. The costs that would have to be incurred to produce this additional output are designated by the area $Q_M DBQ_{PC}$. The difference between the two is the triangle DCB. *This is the amount buyers value the additional output over and above the costs of producing the additional output.* It is the loss attached to not producing the competitive quantity of output. The triangle DCB is referred to as the *deadweight loss triangle.*

We conclude that monopoly produces a quantity of output that is "too small" in comparison to the quantity of output produced in perfect competition. This difference in output results in a welfare loss to society.

Arnold Harberger was the first economist who tried to determine the actual size of the deadweight loss cost of monopoly in the manufacturing sector of the U.S. economy. He estimated the deadweight loss to be a small percentage of the economy's total output. Additional empirical work by other economists puts the figure at approximately 1 percent of total output.

Rent Seeking

Sometimes, individuals and groups try to influence public policy in the hope of redistributing (transferring) income from others to themselves. To illustrate, look again at the perfectly competitive outcome in Exhibit 7. The market produces Q_{PC} output and charges a price of P_{PC}.

Suppose one of the many firms that is currently producing some of Q_{PC} asks the government to grant it a monopoly. For example, of the 100 firms currently producing Q_{PC}, one firm, firm A, asks the government to prevent the 99 remaining firms from competing with it. Let's consider the benefits for firm A of becoming a monopolist (single seller). Currently, it is earning zero economic profit because it is selling at a price that equals ATC. If it becomes a monopolist, though, it will earn profits equal to the area $P_{PC}P_M CD$ in Exhibit 7. These profits are the result of a *transfer* from buyers to the monopolist.

To see this, let's go back to our discussion of consumers' surplus. If the market in Exhibit 7 is perfectly competitive, consumers' surplus is equal to the area $P_{PC}AB$; if the market is monopolized, consumers' surplus is equal to the area $P_M AC$. The difference is the area $P_{PC}P_M CB$, the area that represents the loss in consumers' surplus if the market is monopolized. Part of this area—$P_{PC}P_M CD$—is transferred to the monopolist in terms of profits. *In other words, if the market is monopolized, part of the consumers' surplus that is lost to buyers becomes profits for the monopolist.* (The other part is the deadweight loss of monopoly, identified by the deadweight loss triangle.)

If firm A tries to get the government to transfer "income" or consumers' surplus from buyers to itself, it is undertaking a *transfer-seeking activity*. In economics, these transfer-seeking activities are usually called **rent seeking**. In other words, firm A is rent seeking.[3]

Deadweight Loss of Monopoly

The net value (value to buyers over and above costs to suppliers) of the difference between the monopoly quantity of output (where $P > MC$) and the competitive quantity of output (where $P = MC$). The loss of not producing the competitive quantity of output.

Rent Seeking

Actions of individuals and groups who spend resources to influence public policy in the hope of redistributing (transferring) income to themselves from others.

---

[3]The word *rent* (used in this context) often confuses people. In everyday life, *rent* refers to the payment for an apartment. In economics, rent, or more formally, economic rent, is a payment in excess of opportunity cost. The term *rent* was introduced by economist Anne Krueger in her article "The Political Economy of the Rent-Seeking Society," *American Economic Review* 64 (June 1974): 291–303.

Here is an economics joke: Two economists are walking down the street. One sees a $10 bill lying on the sidewalk and asks, "Isn't that a $10 bill?" "Obviously not," says the other. "If it were, someone would have already picked it up."

This joke tells us something about how economists think. Specifically, economists believe that if the opportunity for gain exists, it won't last long because someone will grab it—quickly. By the time you come along, it's gone.

Think of this in terms of what Gordon Tullock has said about monopoly. As a seller, being a monopolist is better than being a competitive firm. Like a $10 bill lying on the sidewalk, a monopoly position is "worth something." Just as people will pick up a $10 bill on the sidewalk, they'll try to become monopolists.

This brings up the whole topic of rent seeking, to which Tullock first called our attention. Just as people will bend down to pick up the $10 bill, so will they invest resources in an attempt to capture the monopoly rents. In other words, no opportunity for gain is likely to be ignored.

Economist Gordon Tullock has made the point that rent-seeking behavior is individually rational but socially wasteful. To see why, let's say the profits in Exhibit 7 are equal to $10 million. That is, the area $P_{PC}P_{M}CD$ is equal to $10 million. Firm A wants the $10 million in profits, so it asks the government for a monopoly favor because it wants the government to prevent 99 firms from competing with it.

Firm A will not get its monopoly privilege simply by asking for it. The firm will have to spend money and time to convince government officials that it should be given this monopoly privilege. It will have to hire lobbyists, take politicians and other government officials to dinner, and perhaps give donations to certain politicians. Firm A will have to spend resources to get what it wants, and all the resources firm A uses to try to bring about a transfer from buyers to itself are wasted, says Tullock. How so? Well, resources used to bring about a transfer can't be used to produce shoes, computers, television sets, and many other things that people would like to buy. The resources are used to try to transfer income from one party to another. They aren't used to produce more goods and services.

Ask yourself what society would look like if no one produced anything but only invested time and money in rent seeking. Jones would try to get what is Smith's, Smith would try to get what is Brown's, and Brown would try to get what is Thompson's. No one would produce anything; everyone would simply spend time and money trying to get what currently belongs to someone else. In this world, who would produce the food, the computers, and the cars? The answer is no one.

Tullock makes the point that the resource cost of rent seeking should be added to the deadweight loss of monopoly. This addition, according to Tullock, makes the overall cost of monopoly to society higher than anyone initially thought.

X-Inefficiency

Economist Harvey Leibenstein maintains that the monopolist is not under pressure to produce its product at the lowest possible cost. The monopolist can produce its product above the lowest possible unit cost and still survive. Certainly, the monopolist benefits if it can and does lower its costs, but the point is that it doesn't have to in order to survive (with the proviso that average total costs cannot rise so high as to be higher than price). Leibenstein refers to a monopolist operating at higher than the lowest possible cost, and to the organizational slack that is directly tied to this, as **X-inefficiency**.

It is hard to obtain accurate estimates of X-inefficiency, but whatever its magnitude, there are forces working to mitigate it. For example, if a market monopoly is being run inefficiently, other people realizing this may attempt to buy the monopoly and, if successful, lower costs to make higher profits.

X-Inefficiency

The increase in costs and organizational slack in a monopoly resulting from the lack of competitive pressure to push costs down to their lowest possible level.

Price Discrimination

Price Discrimination

Occurs when the seller charges different prices for the product it sells and the price differences do not reflect cost differences.

In our discussions about monopoly, we have assumed that the monopoly seller sells all units of its product for the same price (it is a single-price monopolist). However, this is not always the case. Under certain conditions, a monopolist could practice **price discrimination**. This occurs when the seller charges different prices for the product it sells, and the price differences do not reflect cost differences.

Types of Price Discrimination

There are three types of price discrimination: perfect price discrimination, second-degree price discrimination, and third-degree price discrimination.

Suppose a monopolist produces and sells 1,000 units of good X. If it sells each unit separately and charges the highest price each consumer would be willing to pay for the product rather than go without it, the monopolist is said to practice **perfect price discrimination**. This is sometimes called *discrimination among units*.

If it charges a uniform price per unit for one specific quantity, a lower price for an additional quantity, and so on, the monopolist practices **second-degree price discrimination**. This is sometimes called *discrimination among quantities*. For example, the monopolist might sell the first 10 units for $10 each, the next 20 units for $9 each, and so on.

If it charges a different price in different markets or charges a different price to different segments of the buying population, the monopolist practices **third-degree price discrimination**. This is sometimes called *discrimination among buyers*. For example, if your local pharmacy charges senior citizens lower prices for medicine than it charges nonsenior citizens, it practices third-degree price discrimination.

Why a Monopolist Wants to Price Discriminate

Suppose these are the maximum prices at which the following units of a product can be sold: first unit, $10; second unit, $9; third unit, $8; fourth unit, $7. If the monopolist wants to sell 4 units, and it charges the same price for each unit (it is a single-price monopolist), its total revenue is $28 ($7 × 4).

Now suppose the monopolist can and does practice perfect price discrimination. It charges $10 for the first unit, $9 for the second unit, $8 for the third unit, and $7 for the fourth unit. Its total revenue is $34 ($10 + $9 + $8 + $7). A comparison of total revenue when the monopolist does and does not price discriminate explains why the monopolist would want to price discriminate. A perfectly price-discriminating monopolist receives the maximum price for each unit of the good it sells; a single-price monopolist does not.

For the monopolist who practices perfect price discrimination, price equals marginal revenue, $P = MR$. To illustrate, when the monopolist sells its second unit for $9 (having sold the first unit for $10), its total revenue is $19—or its marginal revenue is $9, which is equal to price.

Conditions of Price Discrimination

It is obvious why the monopolist would want to price discriminate. But what conditions must exist before it can? To price discriminate, the following conditions must hold:

1. The seller must exercise some control over price; that is, it must be a price searcher.
2. The seller must be able to distinguish among buyers who would be willing to pay different prices.
3. It must be impossible or too costly for one buyer to resell the good to other buyers. The possibility of **arbitrage**, or "buying low and selling high," must not exist.

If the seller is not a price searcher (if it is a price taker), it has no control over price and therefore cannot sell a good at different prices to different buyers. Also, unless the seller can distinguish among buyers who would pay different prices, it cannot price discriminate. After all, how would it know whom to charge the higher (lower) prices? Finally, if a buyer can resell the good, there can be no price discrimination because buyers who buy the good at a lower price will simply turn around and sell the good to other buyers for a price lower than the seller's higher price. In time, no one will pay the higher price.

Perfect Price Discrimination
Occurs when the seller charges the highest price each consumer would be willing to pay for the product rather than go without it.

Second-Degree Price Discrimination
Occurs when the seller charges a uniform price per unit for one specific quantity, a lower price for an additional quantity, and so on.

Third-Degree Price Discrimination
Occurs when the seller charges different prices in different markets or charges a different price to different segments of the buying population.

Arbitrage
Buying a good at a low price and selling the good for a higher price.

Q&A

When a firm price discriminates, doesn't one consumer end up paying a higher price because some other consumer pays a lower price?

Some people argue that if a firm charges one person $40 for its product and charges another person only $33, the first person is paying a higher price so the second person can pay a lower price. But this is not the case. Suppose there are two persons, O'Neill and Stevens. The maximum price O'Neill will pay for good X is $40; the maximum price Stevens will pay for good X is $33. If a monopolist can and does perfectly price discriminate, it charges O'Neill $40 and charges Stevens $33.

Is O'Neill somehow paying the higher price so that Stevens can pay the lower price? It is easy to see that O'Neill is not by considering whether the monopolist would have charged O'Neill a price under $40 if Stevens's maximum price had been $39 instead of $33. Probably it wouldn't. Why should it when it could have received O'Neill's maximum price of $40?

Our point is that the perfectly price-discriminating monopolist tries to get the highest price *from each customer,* irrespective of what other customers pay. *In short, the price O'Neill is charged is independent of the price Stevens is charged.*

---

exhibit 8

Comparison of a Perfectly Competitive Firm, Single-Price Monopolist, and Perfectly Price-Discriminating Monopolist

For both the perfectly competitive firm and the perfectly price-discriminating monopolist, $P = MR$ and the demand curve is the marginal revenue curve. Both produce where $P = MC$. The single-price monopolist, however, produces where $P > MC$ because for it, $P > MR$ and its demand curve lies above its marginal revenue curve. One different between the perfectly competitive firm and the perfectly price-discriminating monopolist is that the former charges the same price for each unit of the good it sells and the latter charges a different price for each unit of the good it sells.

Moving to $P = MC$ Through Price Discrimination

We learned in the last chapter that the perfectly competitive firm exhibits resource allocative efficiency; it produces the quantity of output at which $P = MC$. We learned earlier in this chapter that the single-price monopolist produces the quantity of output at which $P > MC$. The single-price monopolist produces an inefficient level of output. But what about the monopolist that can and does practice perfect price discrimination? Does it also produce an inefficient level of output?

The answer is no. A perfectly price-discriminating monopolist does not lower price on all previous units to sell an additional unit of its product. For it, $P = MR$ (as is the case for the perfectly competitive firm). Naturally, when the perfectly price-discriminating monopolist produces the quantity of output at which $MR = MC$, it automatically produces the quantity where $P = MC$. In short, the perfectly price-discriminating monopolist and the perfectly competitive firm both exhibit resource allocative efficiency.

Some important points are reviewed in Exhibit 8. In part (a), the perfectly competitive firm produces where $P = MC$. In part (b), the single-price monopolist produces where $P > MC$. In part (c), the perfectly price-discriminating monopolist produces where

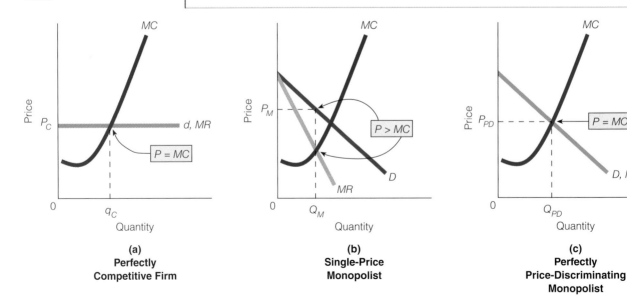

(a)
Perfectly Competitive Firm

(b)
Single-Price Monopolist

(c)
Perfectly Price-Discriminating Monopolist

economics 24/7

AMAZON AND PRICE DISCRIMINATION[4]

Not too long ago, Amazon, the online retailer charged different customers different prices for DVDs. For example, it charged some customers $74.99 for the movie *Planet of the Apes,* while it charged other customers $64.99 for the same movie. Who was charged the higher price? In this case, Amazon charged the higher price to persons who used Internet Explorer as a browser, and it charged the lower price to persons who used Netscape Navigator as a browser. At other times, Amazon charged different customers different prices depending on whether they were repeat buyers or first-time buyers and depending on what Internet service provider they used.

How does Amazon know which customers are willing to pay a higher price for a DVD and which customers are not? An Amazon spokesperson said that the price differences on certain DVDs were the result of tests that the company performs to reevaluate various aspects of its Web site, such as the navigation system, what the home page looks like, overall site design, and product pricing. Some economists speculated that it had much to do with maximizing profits.

As stated in this chapter, one condition of price discrimination is that sellers must be able to distinguish among buyers who would be willing to pay different prices. For example, book publishers do this through their sales of hardcover and paperback books. Most books are first offered in hardcover, and the people who are least price sensitive buy the hardcover book. Later, the book is released as a paperback. Then the persons who are most price sensitive buy the book in paperback form.

The Internet makes such market segmentation as that used by book publishers seem rather crude. Online sellers often ask for (and receive) market information from their customers. This information can be analyzed and categorized to give the seller some idea of the likelihood of a particular customer paying a higher price for a particular good. For example, customers who live in a certain zip code area or in a particular state (a high-income state as opposed to a low-income state) may be more likely to pay a higher price for a good than customers who live in a different zip code area or state.

[4]This feature is based on "Reckonings: What Price Fairness?" by Paul Krugman, *New York Times,* October 4, 2000.

$P = MC$. Notice one important difference between the perfectly competitive firm and the perfectly price-discriminating monopolist. Although both produce where $P = MC$, the perfectly competitive firm charges the same price for each unit of the good it sells, and the perfectly price-discriminating monopolist charges a different price for each unit of the good it sells.

You Can Have the Comics, Just Give Me the Coupons

Third-degree price discrimination, or discrimination among buyers, is sometimes employed through the use of cents-off coupons. (Remember that third-degree price discrimination exists if a seller sells the same product at different prices to different segments of the population.)

One of the conditions of price discrimination is that the seller has to be able to distinguish among customers who would be willing to pay different prices. Would people who value their time highly be

Thinking like AN ECONOMIST

Looks can be deceiving. It certainly looks like the perfectly price-discriminating monopolist charges one customer a higher price because some other customer is paying a lower price. But it is only when we note that the monopolist would want to charge the "highest price to each customer" that we see the error in our thinking. The seller may be selling his goods at a low price to one customer and at a high price to another, but we can be sure he wants to sell at the "highest low price" he can sell at.

economics 24/7

WHY DO DISTRICT ATTORNEYS PLEA-BARGAIN?

On the television series *Law & Order,* the assistant district attorney often offers the accused a chance to plead to a lesser charge in return for providing information about a crime or for agreeing to testify against someone. In short, the assistant district attorneys on *Law & Order* are willing to plea-bargain.

To some people, a district attorney who plea-bargains is similar to a seller who price discriminates. Let's analyze plea bargaining to see whether or not this is true. Suppose two people, Smith and Jones, have committed the same crime. The district attorney has the same type and amount of evidence against each person, and the chance of a successful prosecution is approximately the same for each case. A successful prosecution will end in each person going to prison for 25 years.

Now suppose the district attorney offers Smith a plea bargain. In exchange for Smith's testimony against Brown, who is someone the DA's office has been after for a long time, Smith will be charged with a lesser crime and will have to serve only 5 years in prison. Thus, Smith can pay a smaller price for his crime than Jones must pay. In other words, each person commits the same crime and each has an equal chance of being successfully prosecuted for that crime, but Smith (if he accepts the plea bargain) will serve 5 years in prison and Jones will serve 25 years.

Do district attorneys want to plea-bargain for a reason analogous to why sellers want to price discriminate?[5] A seller wants to price discriminate because it raises her total revenue without affecting her costs. Recall the example in the text: $10 is the highest price at which the first unit of a good can be sold, $9 is the highest price for the second unit, $8 is the highest price for the third unit, and $7 is the highest price for the fourth unit. A single-price monopolist that wants to sell 4 units of the good charges a price of $7 per unit and earns total revenue of $28. But a perfectly price-discriminating monopolist charges the highest price per unit and gains total revenue of $34. In other words, price discrimination leads to higher total revenue.

District attorneys do not want to maximize total revenue, but they may want to maximize the number of successfully prosecuted crimes given certain budget constraints. Just as price discrimination leads to higher total revenue, plea bargaining may lead to more successfully prosecuted crimes. Let's consider Smith and Jones again. Each has committed the same crime. Without a plea bargain, each person goes to prison for 25 years. But if the DA offers Smith 5 years, and in return, Smith helps the DA send Brown to prison, then because of the plea bargain, three crimes are successfully prosecuted—the crimes committed by Smith, Jones, and Brown.

Finally, just as certain conditions have to be met before a seller can price discriminate, certain conditions have to be satisfied before district attorneys can plea-bargain successfully.

To price discriminate, a seller must exercise some control over the price of the product she sells. To plea-bargain, a district attorney has to exercise some control over the sentence for the accused. In reality, district attorneys do exercise some control over sentences because they largely control the charges against the accused. If they reduce the charges (say, from murder to manslaughter), they automatically affect the sentence.

A seller who price discriminates has to be able to distinguish among customers who would be willing to pay different prices for the good she sells. Similarly, a district attorney has to be able to distinguish between accused persons who do and do not have something to "sell" to the authorities. District attorneys seem to be able to do this. In many cases, the accused person who has something to "sell" will say so.

Finally, for price discrimination to exist, arbitrage has to be impossible or too costly. Obviously, it is impossible to resell a plea bargain.

---

[5]Be careful here. We are not saying that a plea bargain is an act of price discrimination, broadly defined. We are saying that there are similarities between why sellers want to price discriminate and why district attorneys want to plea-bargain. Later in the feature, we explain that, just as certain conditions need to be met to price discriminate, certain conditions need to be met for district attorneys to offer plea bargains—and there seems to be a rough similarity between the two sets of conditions.

willing to pay a higher price for a product than people who do not? Some sellers think so. They argue that people who place a high value on their time want to economize on the shopping time connected with the purchase of the product. If sellers want to price discriminate between these two types of customers—charging more to customers who value time more and charging less to customers who value time less—they must determine the category into which each of their customers falls.

How would you go about this if you were a seller? What many real-world sellers do is place cents-off coupons in newspapers and magazines. They hypothesize that people who place a relatively low value on their time are willing to spend it clipping and sorting coupons. People who place a relatively high value on their time are not.

In effect, things work much like the following in, say, a grocery store:

1. The posted price for all products is the same for all customers.

2. Both Linda and Josh put product X in their shopping carts.

3. When Linda gets to the checkout counter, the clerk asks, "Do you have any coupons today?" Linda says no. She is therefore charged the posted price for all products, including X.

4. When Josh gets to the checkout counter, the clerk asks, "Do you have any coupons today?" Josh says yes and gives the clerk a coupon for product X. Josh pays a lower price for product X than Linda pays.

Thus, one of the uses of the cents-off coupon is to make it possible for the seller to charge a higher price to one group of customers than to another group. (We say one of the uses because cents-off coupons are also used to induce customers to try a product.)

micro Theme

In an earlier chapter, we mentioned that microeconomics is about objectives, constraints, and choices. We have talked about three types of firms so far. In the last chapter, we discussed a perfectly competitive firm. In this chapter, we discussed both the single-price and perfectly price-discriminating monopolist.

All three firms have the same objective: to maximize profit. All three firms face constraints, although not always the same constraints. For example, the single-price monopolist is constrained to selling its good for the same price to each customer, whereas the price-discriminating monopolist is not.

Finally, all three firms make choices such as choosing what quantity of output to produce, what price to charge, and so on.

SELF-TEST

1. What are some of the "costs," or shortcomings, of monopoly?

2. What is the deadweight loss of monopoly?

3. Why must a seller be a price searcher (among other things) before he can price discriminate?

A Reader Asks...

Do Colleges and Universities Price Discriminate?

At the university I attend, scholarships are given to students with low incomes, excellent grades, or athletic ability. Are these scholarships a form of price discrimination?

Let's ask this question: Do scholarships to these types of students (low income, high academic ability, high athletic ability) satisfy the definition of price discrimination? The low-income student might not come to the university unless he or she receives a lower tuition price (than other students pay). The university price discriminates because the scholarship, in effect, reduces the tuition the low-income student has to pay. The excellent student and the athlete have numerous universities competing for them. In other words, both have a high elasticity of demand for education at a given university because they have so many substitutes (other universities) from which to choose. Consequently, a university will have to offer them a lower tuition price to secure them as students. The university price discriminates through an academic scholarship

for the excellent student and an athletic scholarship for the athlete.

Now, let's consider whether or not the university meets the conditions of a price discriminator. First, it is a price searcher. Not all universities are alike, nor do they sell a homogeneous good as they would in the case of perfect competition (price taker).

Second, the university can distinguish among students (customers) who would be willing to pay different prices. For example, the student with few universities seeking him would probably be willing to pay more than the student with many options.

Third, the service being purchased cannot be resold to someone else. For example, it is difficult to resell an economics lecture. You could, of course, tell someone what was covered in the lecture, perhaps for a small payment or a promise to do the same for you at a later time, but this would be similar to telling someone about a movie instead of the person seeing the movie herself. It is often difficult or impossible to resell something that is consumed on the premises.

! analyzing the scene

Is the car salesman simply making small talk by asking Jackson what he does for a living?

One of the conditions for price discrimination is that the seller "must be able to distinguish among buyers who would be willing to pay different prices." "Willingness to pay" is, of course, not the same as "ability to pay," but that might not prevent the car salesmen from thinking that the two are strongly correlated. Why does the salesman ask Jackson a question that relates to his income? The salesman may simply be trying to get some idea of what Jackson can afford to pay. What he thinks Jackson can afford to pay may influence future price negotiations between Jackson and the salesman.

All this is reminiscent of an old episode of *The Cosby Show* on television. Dr. Huxtable (played by Bill Cosby) was

thinking of buying a new car. He went to the new car showroom with a friend. Dr. Huxtable made sure to "dress down" because he didn't want the car salesman to think he earned a high income. Dr. Huxtable is standing there negotiating the price with the salesman when all of a sudden his friend, who is on the other side of the showroom, yells out to him, "Dr. Huxtable . . ." Cosby grimaces as he now knows the cat is out of the bag.

Why does the musical artist want to price her CD lower than the BT Productions executive wants to price it?

The BT Productions executive wants to maximize the company's profit, which is the difference between the company's total revenue and its total cost. The musical artist receives a percentage of total revenue, not a percentage of profit, so she wants to maximize total revenue. She wants the total revenue to be as large as possible because a 10 percent royalty rate of, say, $10 million is larger than a 10 percent royalty rate of $7 million. The price that will maximize profit is not the same as the price that will maximize total revenue, and so the company executive and musical artist have different opinions on the best price to charge for the CD.

Let's look at Exhibit 9, which shows a demand curve and a marginal revenue curve for the CD. Note that there are two marginal cost curves. The one for the music company is positive and (we have assumed) constant. The other marginal cost curve is for the musical artist and is zero at all levels of output because we assume the artist does not have any costs of actually producing and selling the CD (this is the music company's job). In all, the exhibit shows one demand curve, one marginal revenue curve, and two marginal cost curves. (Most artists receive a fixed percentage of total receipts from the sale of their CDs, so the music company's demand and marginal revenue curves are relevant for the artist.) The artist wants to sell the quantity of CDs at which marginal revenue equals her marginal cost. This is at Q_A. The highest price per CD at which this quantity of CDs can be sold is P_A. This is the artist's best price. Because the artist is paid a fixed percentage of total sales revenues, she wants to maximize revenues. This occurs where $MR = 0$. (How so? If the artist has maximized total revenue, this means there is no *additional revenue* to be obtained. In other words, marginal revenue is zero.)

Assuming the music company wants to maximize profits, it will want to sell that quantity of CDs at which marginal revenue equals its marginal cost. This is at Q_{BT}. The highest price per CD at which this quantity of CDs can be sold is

P_{BT}. Notice that P_{BT} is higher than P_A—the best price for the music company is higher than the best price for the artist.

Did Carl Wilson think his one-of-a-kind restaurant bestowed monopoly status on him—and therefore, he just couldn't fail?

A firm can be the single seller of a good for which there are no close substitutes—that is, it can be a monopoly—and still fail. Monopoly is no guarantee of success. Success—that is, earning a profit—means that the firm sells its good for a price that is greater than its average total cost (*ATC*). The highest price a firm can charge is determined by the demand curve it faces. If demand is low, the price it can charge is likely to be low, *ceteris paribus*. In fact, the price may be so low that the firm's *ATC* is higher. Obviously, the demand for restaurants that offer mud wrestling while you eat is fairly low.

exhibit **9**

The Music Company and the Musical Artist Opt for Different Prices

The artist faces zero costs of producing and selling the CD; BT Productions, the music company, faces positive (and we assume) constant marginal costs. Both the artist and the music company may want to equate marginal revenue and marginal cost, but they do not have the same marginal cost. The artist wants Q_A CDs produced and sold at a price of P_A; the music company wants Q_{BT} CDs produced and sold at a price of P_{BT}.

chapter summary

The Theory of Monopoly

- The theory of monopoly is built on three assumptions: (1) There is one seller. (2) The single seller sells a product for which there are no close substitutes. (3) There are extremely high barriers to entry into the industry.

- High barriers to entry may take the form of legal barriers (public franchise, patent, government license), economies of scale, or exclusive ownership of a scarce resource.

Monopoly Pricing and Output

- The profit-maximizing monopolist produces the quantity of output at which $MR = MC$ and charges the highest price per unit at which this quantity of output can be sold.

- For the single-price monopolist, $P > MR$; therefore, its demand curve lies above its marginal revenue curve.

- The single-price monopolist sells its output at a price higher than its marginal cost, $P > MC$, and therefore is *not* resource allocative efficient.

- Consider a perfectly competitive market and a monopoly market, each with the same demand and marginal cost curves. Consumers' surplus is greater in the perfectly competitive market.

Rent Seeking

- Activity directed at competing for and obtaining transfers is referred to as rent seeking. From society's perspective, rent seeking is a socially wasteful activity. People use resources to bring about a transfer of income from others to themselves instead of producing goods and services.

Price Discrimination

- Price discrimination occurs when a seller charges different prices for its product and the price differences are not due to cost differences.

- Before a seller can price discriminate, certain conditions must hold: (1) The seller must be a price searcher. (2) The seller must be able to distinguish among customers who would be willing to pay different prices. (3) It must be impossible or too costly for a buyer to resell the good to others.

- A seller that practices perfect price discrimination (charges the maximum price for each unit of product sold) sells the quantity of output at which $P = MC$. It exhibits resource allocative efficiency.

- The single-price monopolist is said to produce too little output because it produces less than would be produced under perfect competition. This is not the case for a perfectly price-discriminating monopolist.

key terms and concepts

Monopoly

Public Franchise

Natural Monopoly

Price Searcher

Deadweight Loss of Monopoly

Rent Seeking

X-Inefficiency

Price Discrimination

Perfect Price Discrimination

Second-Degree Price Discrimination

Third-Degree Price Discrimination

Arbitrage

questions and problems

1 The perfectly competitive firm exhibits resource allocative efficiency ($P = MC$), but the single-price monopolist does not. What is the reason for this difference?

2 Because the monopolist is a single seller of a product with no close substitutes, is it able to obtain any price for its good that it wants? Why or why not?

3 When a single-price monopolist maximizes profits, price is greater than marginal cost. This means that buyers would be willing to pay more for additional units of output than the units cost to produce. Given this, why doesn't the monopolist produce more?

4 Is there a deadweight loss if a firm produces the quantity of output at which price equals marginal cost? Explain.

5 It has been noted that rent seeking is individually rational but socially wasteful. Explain.

6   Occasionally, students accuse their instructors, rightly or wrongly, of practicing grade discrimination. These students claim that the instructor "charges" some students a higher price for a given grade than he or she "charges" other students (by requiring some students to do more or better work). Unlike price discrimination, grade discrimination involves no money. Discuss the similarities and differences between the two types of discrimination. Which do you prefer less or perhaps dislike more? Why?

7   Make a list of real-world price discrimination practices. Do they meet the conditions posited for price discrimination?

8   For many years in California, car washes would advertise "Ladies' Day." On one day during the week, a woman could have her car washed for a price lower than a man could have his car washed. Some people argued that this was a form of sexual discrimination. A California court accepted the argument and ruled that car washes could no longer have a Ladies' Day. Do you think this was a case of sexual discrimination or price discrimination? Explain your answer.

9   Make a list of market monopolies and a list of government monopolies. Which list is longer? Why do you think this is so?

10 Fast-food stores often charge higher prices for their products in high-crime areas than they charge in low-crime areas. Is this an act of price discrimination? Why or why not?

11 In general, coupons are more common on small-ticket items than they are on big-ticket items. Explain why.

12 A firm maximizes its total revenue. Does it follow that it has automatically maximized its profit too? Why or why not?

working with numbers and graphs

1   Draw a graph that shows a monopoly firm incurring losses.

2   A monopoly firm is currently earning positive economic profit. The owner of the firm decides to sell it. He asks for a price that takes into account the economic profit. Explain and diagrammatically show what this does to the average total cost (ATC) curve of the firm.

3   Suppose a single-price monopolist sells its output (Q_1) at P_1. Then it raises its price to P_2 and its output falls to Q_2. In terms of Ps and Qs, what does marginal revenue equal?

4   If the market is perfectly competitive, what does profit equal?

5   If the market is a monopoly market, what does profit equal?

6   Redraw the figure and label consumers' surplus when the market is perfectly competitive and when it is monopolized.

Use the following figure to answer Questions 4–6.

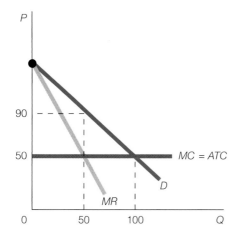

10

Monopolistic Competition, Oligopoly, and Game Theory

Setting the Scene

Carl and Amanda, two professors at a nearby college, were discussing grades one day recently.

AMANDA:

The grading distribution is becoming increasingly skewed toward the top end—toward the A end of the spectrum. At Harvard in 1966, 22 percent of all grades were As, but in 2002, the percentage of As was about 46 percent. It's the same at other colleges and universities, including right here where we teach.

CARL:

I know. I'm fairly sure that I give out more high grades today than I did years ago when I first started teaching. Students who receive a B from me today would have received a C or lower 15 years ago.

AMANDA:

What do you think explains the changes in the grading distribution? Could students be getting smarter or professors getting better at teaching?

CARL:

It's somewhat hard for me to believe that the average student at Harvard in 1966 wasn't as smart, or as hardworking, as the average student at Harvard in 2002. Or that somehow Harvard professors in 1966 were less talented instructors than Harvard professors in 2002. I think it must be grade inflation. It appears to me that professors are giving higher grades today for

work that in the past would have earned a lower grade. In other words, C work in 1966 now becomes B+ or A− work.

AMANDA:

I think I agree with you. But how can we get away from the current distribution? If I do away with grade inflation in my class and you and others do not, then I just place my students at a disadvantage relative to your students.

CARL:

I know. In a way, we seem to be trapped.

? Here is a question to keep in mind as you read this chapter:

• *If Carl and Amanda both want to end grade inflation, why don't they just do it?*

See analyzing the scene at the end of this chapter for an answer to this question.

The Theory of Monopolistic Competition

The theory of **monopolistic competition** is built on three assumptions:

Monopolistic Competition

A theory of market structure based on three assumptions: many sellers and buyers, firms producing and selling slightly differentiated products, and easy entry and exit.

1. **There are many sellers and buyers.** This assumption holds for perfect competition too. For this reason, you might think the monopolistic competitor should be a price taker, but this is not the case. It is a price searcher, basically because of the next assumption.

2. **Each firm (in the industry) produces and sells a slightly differentiated product.** Differences among the products may be due to brand names, packaging, location, credit terms connected with the sale of the product, friendliness of the salespeople, and so forth. Product differentiation may be real or imagined. For example, aspirin may be aspirin, but if some people view a name-brand aspirin (such as Bayer) as better than a generic brand, product differentiation exists.

3. **There is easy entry and exit.** Monopolistic competition resembles perfect competition in this respect. There are no barriers to entry and exit, legal or otherwise.

Examples of monopolistic competition include retail clothing, computer software, restaurants, and service stations.

The Monopolistic Competitor's Demand Curve

The perfectly competitive firm has many rivals, all producing the same good, and so there are an endless number of substitutes for the good it produces. The elasticity of demand for its product is extremely high—so high, in fact, that the demand curve it faces is horizontal (for all practical purposes).

The monopoly firm has practically no rivals, and it produces a good for which there are no substitutes. The elasticity of demand for its product is low, and its downward-sloping demand curve reflects this fact.

What is the situation for the monopolistic competitor? Like the perfectly competitive firm, it has many rivals. But unlike the perfectly competitive firm, its rivals don't sell exactly the same product the monopolistic competitor sells. There are substitutes for its product, but not perfect substitutes. Because of this, the elasticity of demand for its product is not as great as that of the perfectly competitive firm. Nor does its demand curve look like the demand curve faced by the perfectly competitive firm. The monopolistic competitor's demand curve is not horizontal; it is downward sloping.

> **Q&A**
>
> *It seems that one way to differentiate between firms in different market structures is in terms of the number and quality of substitutes each faces. Is this correct?*
>
> *Yes. As we have just said, the perfectly competitive firm has a lot of perfect substitutes for the good it sells; the monopoly firm has no good substitutes for the good it sells; and the monopolistic competitive firm has substitutes for the good it sells, but not perfect substitutes.*

The Relationship Between Price and Marginal Revenue for a Monopolistic Competitor

Because a monopolistic competitor faces a downward-sloping demand curve, it has to lower price to sell an additional unit of the good it produces. (It is a price searcher.) For example, let's say that it can sell 3 units at $10 each but that it has to lower its price to $9 to sell 4 units. It follows that its marginal revenue is $6 (total revenue at 3 units is $30 and total revenue at 4 units is $36), which is below its price of $9. Thus, for the monopolistic competitor $P > MR$.

Output, Price, and Marginal Cost for the Monopolistic Competitor

The monopolistic competitive firm is the same as both the perfectly competitive firm and the monopoly firm in one regard. It produces the quantity of output at which

All firms, no matter what market setting they find themselves in, seem to produce the quantity of output at which MR = MC. Is this correct?

Yes, it is correct.

$MR = MC$. We see this in Exhibit 1, where the firm produces q_1. What price does the monopolistic competitor charge for this quantity? Answer: The highest price it can charge. This is P_1 in the exhibit.

For the monopolistic competitor, $P > MR$. Because the monopolistic competitor produces the quantity of output at which $MR = MC$, it follows that it must produce a level of output at which price is greater than marginal cost, $P > MC$. This is obvious in Exhibit 1.

Will There Be Profits in the Long Run?

Suppose the firms in a monopolistic competitive market are currently earning profits, such as the firm in Exhibit 1. Will they continue to earn profits in the long run? Most likely, they won't. The assumption of easy entry and exit precludes this. If firms in the industry are earning profits, new firms will enter the industry and reduce the demand that each firm faces. In other words, the demand curve for each firm may shift to the left. Eventually, competition will reduce economic profits to zero in the long run, as shown for the monopolistic competitive firm in Exhibit 2.

Notice that the answer to the question of whether firms will continue to earn profits in the long run was, "Most likely, they won't" instead of, "no." In monopolistic competition, new firms usually produce a *close substitute* for the product produced by existing firms rather than the *identical* product produced in perfect competition. Is this enough of a difference to upset the zero economic profit condition in the long run? In some instances, it may be. An existing firm may differentiate its product sufficiently in the minds of buyers such that it continues to earn profits, even though new firms enter the industry and compete with it.

Firms that try to differentiate their products from those of other sellers in ways other than price are said to be engaged in *nonprice competition*. This may take the form of advertising or of trying to establish a well-respected brand name, among other things. For example, soft drink companies' advertising often tries to stress the uniqueness of their product. In the past, Dr. Pepper has been advertised as "the unusual one," 7-Up as "the uncola." Apple has a well-respected name in personal computers, Bayer in aspirin,

---

The Monopolistic Competitive Firm's Output and Price

The monopolistic competitor produces that quantity of output for which $MR = MC$. This is q_1 in the exhibit. It charges the highest price consistent with this quantity, which is P_1.

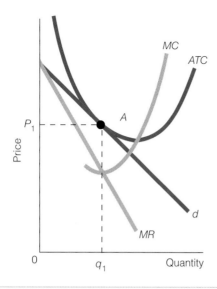

exhibit **2**

Monopolistic Competition in the Long Run

Because of easy entry into the industry, there are likely to be zero economic profits in the long run for a monopolistic competitor. In other words, $P = ATC$.

Marriott in hotels. Such well-respected names sometimes sufficiently differentiate products in the minds of buyers so that short-run profits are not easily, or completely, eliminated by the entry of new firms into the industry.

> ### micro Theme
>
> We have studied various firms over the past three chapters. We have learned, so far, that a firm either faces (1) a horizontal demand curve or (2) a downward-sloping demand curve. Another way of putting this is to say that a firm is either (1) a price taker or a (2) price searcher. If it faces a horizontal demand curve (which means it can only sell its good at the market-equilibrium price), then it is a price taker. If it faces a downward-sloping demand curve (which means it can sell some of its good at different prices, albeit less at higher prices), then it is a price searcher. In other words, the firms you encounter in the real world are either price takers or price searchers.

Excess Capacity: What Is It, and Is It "Good" or "Bad"?

The theory of monopolistic competition makes one major prediction, which is generally referred to as the **excess capacity theorem**. The theorem states that in equilibrium, a monopolistic competitor will produce an output smaller than the one that would minimize its unit costs of production.

To illustrate, look at point A in Exhibit 3(a). At this point, the monopolistic competitor is in long-run equilibrium because profits are zero ($P = ATC$). Notice that point A *is not* the lowest point on the average total cost curve. The lowest point on the ATC curve is point L. We conclude that in long-run equilibrium, when the monopolistic competitor earns zero economic profits, it is not producing the quantity of output at which average total costs (unit costs) are minimized for the given scale of plant. Exhibit 3 contrasts the perfectly competitive firm and the monopolistic competitor in long-run equilibrium. In part (b), the perfectly competitive firm is earning zero economic profits, and price (P_{C1}) equals average total cost (ATC). Furthermore, the point at which price equals average total cost (point L) is the lowest point on the ATC curve. In long-run equilibrium, the perfectly competitive firm produces the quantity of output at which unit costs are minimized.

Excess Capacity Theorem
States that a monopolistic competitor in equilibrium produces an output smaller than the one that would minimize its costs of production.

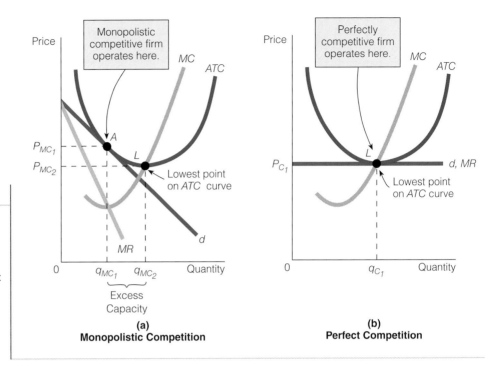

exhibit **3**

A Comparison of Perfect Competition and Monopolistic Competition: The Issue of Excess Capacity

The perfectly competitive firm produces a quantity of output consistent with lowest unit costs. The monopolistic competitor does not. If it did, it would produce instead q_{MC2} of q_{MC1}. The monopolistic competitor is said to underutilize its plant size or to have excess capacity.

Now look back at part (a). The monopolistic competitor is earning zero economic profits, and price (P_{MC1}) equals average total cost. As previously noted, the monopolistic competitor does not produce the quantity of output at which unit costs are minimized. If it did, it would produce q_{MC2}. For this reason, it has been argued that the monopolistic competitor produces "too little" output (q_{MC1} instead of q_{MC2}) and charges "too high" a price (P_{MC1} instead of P_{MC2}). With respect to the former, "too little" output translates into the monopolistic competitor underutilizing its present plant size. It is said to have *excess capacity.* In part (a), the excess capacity is equal to the difference between q_{MC2} and q_{MC1}.

It is sometimes argued that the monopolistic competitor operates at excess capacity because it faces a downward-sloping demand curve. Look once again at Exhibit 3(a). The only way the firm would not operate at excess capacity is if its demand curve were tangent to the *ATC* curve at point *L*—the lowest point on the *ATC* curve. But for this to occur, the demand curve *would have to be horizontal*, which would require homogeneous products. It is impossible for a downward-sloping demand curve to be tangent to the *ATC* curve at point *L*.

In short, *the monopolistic competitor operates at excess capacity as a consequence of its downward-sloping demand curve,* and its downward-sloping demand curve is a consequence of differentiated products. We leave you with a question many economists ask but do not always answer the same way: *If excess capacity is the price we pay for differentiated products (more choice), is it too high a price?*

Theme micro

One way economists differentiate one firm from another is in terms of the outcomes that flow from its choices. For example, we saw (in an earlier chapter) that a perfectly competitive firm is both resource allocative efficient (which means it produces the quantity of output at which $P = MC$) and productive efficient (which means it produces the quantity of output at which *ATC* is minimized). In contrast, the monopolistic competitive firm is neither resource allocative efficient nor productive efficient, as we discuss next.

The Monopolistic Competitor and Two Types of Efficiency

An earlier chapter explains that a firm is resource allocative efficient if it charges a price that is equal to marginal cost, $P = MC$. Because the monopolistic competitive firm charges a price that is greater than marginal cost ($P > MC$), it is not resource allocative efficient.

An earlier chapter also explains that a firm is productive efficient if it charges a price that is equal to its lowest ATC. Because the monopolistic competitor operates at excess capacity, it is not productive efficient.

Advertising and Designer Labels

Suppose you own a business that is considered a monopolistic competitive firm. Your business is one of many sellers, you sell a product slightly differentiated from the products of your competitors, and there is easy entry into and exit from the industry. Would you rather your business were a monopoly firm instead? Wouldn't it be better for you to be the only seller of a product than to be one of many sellers? Most business owners would say that it is better to be a monopoly firm than a monopolistic competitive firm. This being the case, we consider how monopolistic competitors may try to become monopolists.

One possibility is through advertising. If a monopolistic competitor can, through advertising, persuade the buying public that her product is *more than just slightly differentiated* from those of her competitors, she stands a better chance of becoming a monopolist. (Remember, a monopolist produces a good for which there are no close substitutes.)

Consider an example. Many firms produce men's and women's jeans. To many people, the jeans produced by these firms look very much alike. How, then, does any one firm differentiate its product from the pack? It could add a "designer label" to the jeans to suggest that the jeans are unique—that they are the only Levi's jeans, for example. Or through advertising, it could try to persuade the buying public that its jeans are "the" jeans worn by the most famous, best-looking people living and vacationing in the most exciting places in the world.

We are not concerned here with whether or not the advertising is successful in meeting its objective. Our point is that firms sometimes use advertising to try to differentiate their products from their competitors' products.

Q&A

One thing seems odd to me. Both the perfectly competitive firm and the monopolistic competitive firm produce the quantity of output at which **MR** *=* **MC**. *And both charge the highest price (per unit) they can charge. In other words, they make the same choices with respect to "how much to produce" and "what price to charge." But even though they make the same choices, the outcomes of their choices are different. The perfectly competitive firm is resource allocative efficient and productive efficient, whereas the monopolistic competitive firm is neither. How can you make the same choices and get different outcomes?*

The different outcomes are a result of the perfectly competitive firm facing a horizontal demand curve and the monopolistic competitive firm facing a downward-sloping demand curve. The demand curve difference (between the two firms) is enough of a difference to make the same choices result in different outcomes.

SELF-TEST

(Answers to Self-Test questions are in the Self-Test Appendix.)

1. How is a monopolistic competitor like a monopolist? How is it like a perfect competitor?

2. Why do monopolistic competitors operate at excess capacity?

Oligopoly: Assumptions and Real-World Behavior

Unlike perfect competition, monopoly, and monopolistic competition, there is no one theory of **oligopoly**. However, the different theories of oligopoly do have the following common assumptions:

Oligopoly

A theory of market structure based on three assumptions: few sellers and many buyers, firms producing either homogeneous or differentiated products, and significant barriers to entry.

1. **There are few sellers and many buyers.** It is usually assumed that the few firms of an oligopoly are interdependent; each one is aware that its actions influence the other firms and that the actions of the other firms affect it. This interdependence among firms is a key characteristic of oligopoly.

2. **Firms produce and sell either homogeneous or differentiated products.** Aluminum is a homogeneous product produced in an oligopolistic market; cars are a differentiated product produced in an oligopolistic market.

3. **There are significant barriers to entry.** Economies of scale are perhaps the most significant barrier to entry in oligopoly theory, but patent rights, exclusive control of an essential resource, and legal barriers also act as barriers to entry.

The oligopolist is a price searcher. Like all other firms, it produces the quantity of output at which $MR = MC$.

Which industries today are dominated by a small number of firms; that is, which industries are oligopolistic? Economists have developed the *concentration ratio* to help answer this question. The **concentration ratio** is the percentage of industry sales (or assets, output, labor force, or some other factor) accounted for by x number of firms in the industry. The "x number" in the definition is usually four or eight, but it can be any number (although it is usually small).

> *Four-Firm Concentration Ratio:* CR_4 = Percentage of industry sales accounted for by four largest firms
>
> *Eight-Firm Concentration Ratio:* CR_8 = Percentage of industry sales accounted for by eight largest firms

Concentration Ratio

The percentage of industry sales (or assets, output, labor force, or some other factor) accounted for by x number of firms in the industry.

A high concentration ratio implies that few sellers make up the industry; a low concentration ratio implies that more than a few sellers make up the industry.

Suppose we calculate a four-firm concentration ratio for industry Z. Total industry sales for a given year are $5 million, and the four largest firms in the industry account for $4.5 million in sales. The four-firm concentration ratio would be 0.90, or 90 percent ($4.5 million is 0.90 of $5 million). Industries with high four- and eight-firm concentration ratios in recent years include cigarettes, cars, tires, cereal breakfast foods, farm machinery, and soap and other detergents, to name a few.

Although concentration ratios are often used to determine the extent (or degree) of oligopoly, they are not perfect guides to industry concentration. Most important, they do not take into account foreign competition and competition from substitute domestic goods. For example, the U.S. automobile industry is concentrated, but it still faces stiff competition from abroad. A more relevant concentration ratio for this particular industry might be one computed on a worldwide basis.

Price and Output Under Three Oligopoly Theories

There is not just one theory of oligopoly; there are many. We present three in this section: the cartel theory, the kinked demand curve theory, and the price leadership theory.

The Cartel Theory

Cartel Theory

In this theory of oligopoly, oligopolistic firms act as if there were only one firm in the industry.

Cartel

An organization of firms that reduces output and increases price in an effort to increase joint profits.

The key behavioral assumption of the **cartel theory** is that oligopolists in an industry act as if there were only one firm in the industry. In short, they form a cartel to capture the benefits that would exist for a monopolist. A **cartel** is an organization of firms that reduces output and increases price in an effort to increase joint profits.

Let's consider the benefits that may arise from forming and maintaining a cartel. Exhibit 4 shows an industry in long-run competitive equilibrium. Price is P_1 and quantity of output is Q_1. The industry is producing the output at which price equals marginal cost, and there are zero economic profits. Now suppose the firms that make up the industry form a cartel and reduce output to Q_C. The new price is P_C (cartel price), and there are profits equal to the area $CP_C AB$, which can be shared among the members of the cartel. With no cartel, there are no profits; with a cartel, profits are earned. Thus, the firms have an incentive to form a cartel and to behave cooperatively rather than competitively.

However, firms may not be able to form a cartel, even though they have a profit incentive to do so. Also, even if they are able to form the cartel, the firms may not be able to maintain it successfully. Firms that wish to form and maintain a cartel will encounter several problems, in addition to the fact that legislation prohibits certain types of cartels in the United States. Organizing and forming a cartel involves costs as well as benefits.[1]

THE PROBLEM OF FORMING THE CARTEL Even if it were legal, getting the sellers of an industry together to form a cartel can be costly, even when the number of sellers is small. Each potential cartel member may resist incurring the costs of forming the cartel because it stands to benefit more if another firm does the work. In other words, each potential member has an incentive to be a free rider—that is, to stand by and take a free ride on the actions of others.

THE PROBLEM OF FORMULATING CARTEL POLICY Suppose the first problem is solved, and potential cartel members form a cartel. Now comes the problem of formulating policy. For example, firm A might propose that each cartel member reduce output by 10 percent, while firm B advocates that all bigger cartel members reduce output by 15 percent and all smaller members reduce output by 5 percent. There may be as many policy proposals as there are cartel members. Reaching agreement may be difficult. Such disagreements are harder to resolve the greater the differences among cartel members in costs, size, and so forth.

exhibit **4**

The Benefits of a Cartel (to Cartel Members)

We assume the industry is in long-run competitive equilibrium, producing Q_1 and charging P_1. There are no profits. A reduction in output to Q_C through the formation of a cartel raises prices to P_C and brings profits of CP_CAB. (Note: In an earlier chapter, a horizontal demand curve faces the *firm*. Here a downward-sloping demand curve faces the *industry*. Don't be misled by this difference. No matter what type of demand curve we use, long-run competitive equilibrium is where $P = MC = SRATC = LRATC$.)

[1]Sometimes, economists discuss the benefits and costs of organizing a cartel without specifying the market structure. We have followed suit here by broadening our discussion of cartel theory to include market structures other than oligopoly. This will be noticeable in places. For example, even though there are few sellers in oligopoly, we discuss cartel theory in the context of both few and many sellers.

economics 24/7

HOW IS A NEW YEAR'S RESOLUTION LIKE A CARTEL AGREEMENT?

In a cartel, one firm makes an agreement with another firm or firms. In a New Year's resolution, you essentially make an agreement with yourself. So both cases—the cartel and the resolution—involve an agreement.

Both cases also raise the possibility of cheating on the agreement. Suppose your New Year's resolution is to exercise more, take better notes in class, and read one "good" book a month. You might set such objectives for yourself because you know you will be better off in the long run if you do these things. But then, the short run interjects itself into the picture. You have to decide between exercising today or plopping down in your favorite chair and watching some television. You have to decide between starting to read *Moby Dick* or catching up on the latest entertainment news in *People* magazine. The part of you that wants to hold to the resolution is at odds with the part of you that wants to watch television or read *People*. Often, the television-watching, *People*-reading part wins out. It is just too easy to break a New Year's resolution—as you probably already know.

Similarly, it is easy to break a cartel agreement. For the firm that has entered into the agreement, the lure of higher

profits is often too strong to resist. In addition, the firm is concerned that if it doesn't break the agreement (and cheat), some other firm might, and then it will have lost out completely.

In short, both resolutions and cartel agreements take a lot of willpower to hold them together. And willpower, it seems, is in particularly short supply.

What, if anything, can take the place of willpower? What do both a resolution and a cartel agreement need to sustain long life? The answer is something or someone who will exact some penalty from the party that breaks the resolution or cartel agreement. Government sometimes plays this role for firms. Family members and friends occasionally play this role for individuals by reminding or reprimanding them if they fail to live up to their resolutions. (Usually, though, family members and friends are not successful.)

We conclude the following: First, an agreement is at the heart of both a New Year's resolution and a cartel. Second, both the resolution and the cartel are subject to cheating behavior. Third, if the resolution and the cartel are to sustain long life, they often need someone or something to prevent each party from breaking the agreement.

THE PROBLEM OF ENTRY INTO THE INDUSTRY Even if the cartel members manage to agree on a policy that generates high profits, those high profits will provide an incentive for firms outside the industry to join the industry. If current cartel members cannot keep new suppliers from entering, the cartel is likely to break up.

THE PROBLEM OF CHEATING As paradoxical as it first appears, after the cartel agreement is made, cartel members have an incentive to cheat on the agreement. Consider Exhibit 5, which shows a *representative firm* of the cartel. We compare three situations for this firm: (1) the situation before the cartel is formed; (2) the situation after the cartel is formed when all members adhere to the cartel price; and (3) the situation if the firm cheats on the cartel agreement, but the other cartel members do not.

Before the cartel is formed, the firm is in long-run competitive equilibrium; it produces output q_1 and charges price P_1. It earns zero economic profits. Next, it reduces its output to q_C as directed by the cartel (the cartel has set a quota for each member), and it charges the cartel price of P_C. Now the firm earns profits equal to the area CP_CAB.

What happens if the firm cheats on the cartel agreement and produces q_{CC} instead of the stipulated q_C? As long as other firms do not cheat, this firm views its demand curve as horizontal at the cartel price (P_C). The reason is simple: It is one of a number of

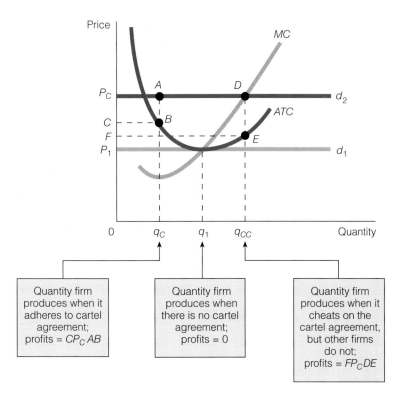

Quantity firm produces when it adheres to cartel agreement; profits = $CP_C AB$

Quantity firm produces when there is no cartel agreement; profits = 0

Quantity firm produces when it cheats on the cartel agreement, but other firms do not; profits = $FP_C DE$

firms, so it cannot affect price by changing output. Therefore, it can produce and sell additional units of output without lowering price. We conclude that if the firm cheats on the cartel agreement and other firms do not, then the cheating firm can increase its profits from the smaller amount $CP_C AB$ to the larger amount $FP_C DE$. Of course, if all firms cheat, the cartel members are back where they started—with no cartel agreement and at price P_1.

This analysis illustrates a major theme of cartels: Firms have an incentive to form a cartel, but once it is formed, they have an incentive to cheat. As a result, some economists have concluded that even if cartels are formed successfully, it is unlikely that they will be effective for long.

The Kinked Demand Curve Theory

The behavioral assumption in the **kinked demand curve theory** is that if a single firm lowers price, other firms will do likewise, but if a single firm raises price, other firms will not follow suit. Suppose there are five firms in an industry, A, B, C, D, and E. If firm A raises its price, the other firms maintain their prices. If firm A cuts its price, the other firms match the price cut.

The kinked demand curve theory was developed in the 1930s by Paul Sweezy. We explain the theory using the example in Exhibit 6. The current price charged by the firm is $25. If the firm raises its price to $27, other firms will not match it, and therefore, the firm's sales will drop (from 20 to 10). In short, the demand curve for the firm above $25 is highly elastic. However, if the firm lowers its price to, say, $23, other firms will match the price cut, and therefore, the firm's sales will not increase by much (only from 20 to 22). Demand is much less elastic below $25 than above it. We conclude that

Thinking like **AN ECONOMIST**

In economics, there are moving targets. Consider the target of higher profits for the firms in an oligopolistic industry. After the firms form a cartel to capture the higher profits, the target of higher profits moves—to where a cartel member must cheat on the cartel to "hit" it. But if all cartel members take aim at the target's new position, the target moves back to its original position—to where cartel members must agree to stop cheating.

The layperson may think that an economic objective, or economic target, is stationary. All that an economic actor has to do to hit it is take careful aim. But the economist knows that sometimes the target moves, and careful aim is not always enough.

Kinked Demand Curve Theory

A theory of oligopoly that assumes that if a single firm in the industry cuts prices, other firms will do likewise, but if it raises price, other firms will not follow suit. The theory predicts price stickiness or rigidity.

there is a kink in the firm's demand curve at the current price (point K in Exhibit 6). The kink signifies that other firms respond radically differently to a single firm's price hikes than to its price cuts.

Actually, there are two demand curves and two marginal revenue curves in the kinked demand curve theory, as shown in the window in Exhibit 6. Only the thicker portions of the curves in the window are relevant, however, and thus appear in the main diagram. To illustrate, starting at a price of $25, the firm believes price cuts will be matched but price hikes will not. So when considering a price cut, the firm believes it faces the more inelastic of the two demand curves, d_2, and the corresponding marginal revenue curve, MR_2. But when considering a price hike, the firm believes it faces the more elastic of the two demand curves, d_1, and the corresponding marginal revenue curve, MR_1. It follows that the firm's demand curve includes part of d_1 and part of d_2; the firm's marginal revenue curve includes part of MR_1 and part of MR_2. This occurs because the theory assumes the market reacts one way to a price cut and a different way to a price hike.

PRICE RIGIDITY Look at the marginal revenue curve for the oligopolist in the main diagram of Exhibit 6. Directly below the kink, it drops sharply. In fact, the marginal revenue curve can be viewed as three segments: a line from point A to point B, which corresponds to the upper part of the demand curve; a gap between points B and C directly below the kink in the demand curve; and a line from point C onward, which corresponds to the lower part of the demand curve (from point K onward).

The gap between points B and C represents the sharp change in marginal revenue that occurs when price is lowered below the kink on the demand curve. The gap helps explain why prices might be less flexible (more rigid) in oligopoly than in other market structures.

Recall that the oligopolistic firm produces the output at which $MR = MC$. For the firm in Exhibit 6, though, marginal cost (MC) can change between points B and C, and the firm will continue to produce the same quantity of output and charge the same price. For example, an increase in marginal cost from MC_1 to MC_2 will not lead to a change in production levels or price.

To put it differently, prices are "sticky" if oligopolistic firms face kinked demand curves. Costs can change within certain limits, and such firms will not change their prices because they expect that none of their competitors will follow their price hikes, but all will match their price cuts.

exhibit 6

Kinked Demand Curve Theory

The key behavioral assumption of the theory is that rival firms will not match a price hike but will match a price cut. The theory predicts that changes in marginal costs between B and C will not cause changes in price or output. The window in the exhibit shows two demand curves and two marginal revenue curves. The firm believes it faces d_2, the more inelastic demand curve, if it cuts price; the firm believes it faces d_1, the more elastic demand curve, when it raises price. The relevant portions of each demand curve are indicated by heavy lines. Only the relevant parts of the demand and marginal revenue curves are shown in the main diagram.

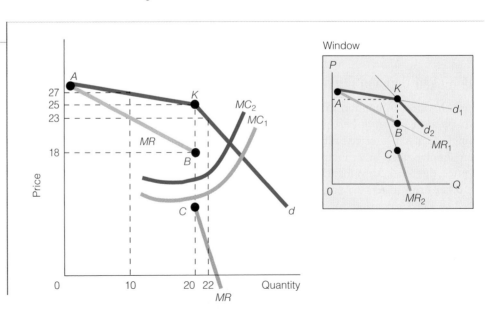

All firms have to make choices—how much to produce, how much to charge, and so on. When the perfectly competitive firm makes such choices, it does not strategize. It doesn't say: I will do W if my competitors do X, but I will do Y if my competitors do Z. However, when it comes to oligopoly, there is strategizing. For example, one oligopolistic firm in a given market might lower price if other oligopolistic firms in the market lower price, but it won't raise price if other firms raise price. In other words, in an oligopolistic market (compared with a perfectly competitive market), one firm's behavior depends to a greater degree on the behavior of other firms.

CRITICISMS OF THE KINKED DEMAND CURVE THEORY The kinked demand curve (and resulting MR curve) posits that prices in oligopoly will be less flexible (or more rigid) than in other market structures. The theory has been criticized on both theoretical and empirical grounds.

On a theoretical level, looking at Exhibit 6, the theory fails to explain how the original price of $25 came about. In other words, why does the kink come at $25? The theory is better at explaining things after the kink (the current price) has been identified than in explaining the placement of the kink. On empirical grounds, the theory has been challenged as a general theory of oligopoly. For example, economist George Stigler found no evidence that the oligopolists he examined were more reluctant to match price increases than price cuts, which calls into question the behavioral assumption behind the kinked demand curve theory.

The Price Leadership Theory

The key behavioral assumption in the **price leadership theory** is that one firm in the industry—called the dominant firm—determines price, and all other firms take this price as given. Suppose there are 10 firms in an industry, A–J, and that firm A is the dominant firm; also suppose firm A is much larger than its rival firms. (The dominant firm need not be the largest firm in the industry; it could be the low-cost firm.) The dominant firm sets the price that maximizes its profits, and all other firms take this price as given. All other firms, then, are seen as price takers; thus, they will equate price with their respective marginal costs.

This explanation suggests that the dominant firm acts without regard to the other firms in the industry and simply forces the other firms to adapt. This is not quite correct. The dominant firm sets the price based on information it has about the other firms in the industry, as shown in Exhibit 7.

Part (a) shows the market demand curve and the horizontal sum of the marginal cost curves of the fringe firms (all firms other than the dominant firm). Because these fringe firms are price takers, the marginal cost curve in (a) is their supply curve. The dominant firm observes that at a price of P_1, the fringe firms alone can supply the entire market. They will supply Q_1. In short, P_1 and Q_1 define the situation in the industry or market that excludes the dominant firm.

Now add the dominant firm. It derives its demand curve, D_{DN}, by noting how much is left for it to supply at each given price. For example, at a price of P_1, the fringe firms would supply the entire market, and nothing would be left for the dominant firm to supply. So a price of P_1 and an output of zero is one point on the dominant firm's demand curve, as shown in part (b). (Sometimes, the dominant firm's demand curve is

Price Leadership Theory

In this theory of oligopoly, the dominant firm in the industry determines price, and all other firms take their price as given.

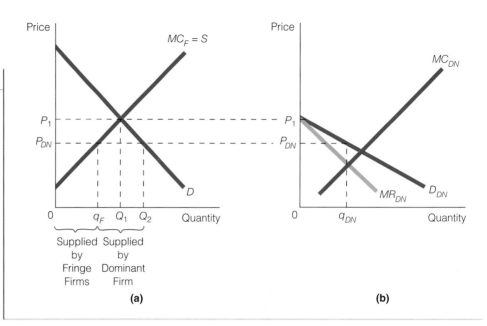

Price Leadership Theory

There is one dominant firm and a number of fringe firms. (a) The horizontal sum of the marginal cost curves of the fringe firms is their supply curve. At P_1, the fringe firms supply the entire market. (b) The dominant firm derives its demand curve by computing the difference between market demand, D, and MC_F at each price below P_1. It then produces q_{DN} (where $MR_{DN} = MC_{DN}$) and charges P_{DN}. P_{DN} becomes the price that the fringe firms take. They equate price and marginal cost and produce q_F in (a). The remainder of the output—the difference between Q_2 and q_F—is produced by the dominant firm.

referred to as the *residual demand curve* for obvious reasons.) The dominant firm continues to locate other points on its demand curve by noting the difference between the market demand curve (D) and MC_F at each price below P_1.

After the dominant firm calculates its residual demand curve, it produces the quantity of output at which its marginal revenue equals its marginal cost. This level is q_{DN} in Exhibit 7(b). It charges the highest price for this quantity of output, which is P_{DN}. This is the price that the dominant firm sets and the fringe firms take. Because they act as price takers, the fringe firms equate P_{DN} with marginal cost and produce q_F, as shown in part (a). The remainder of the total output produced by the industry—the difference between Q_2 and q_F—is produced by the dominant firm. This means that the distance from the origin to q_{DN} in (b) is equal to the difference between Q_2 and q_F in (a).

At one time or another, the following firms have been price leaders in their industries: R. J. Reynolds (cigarettes), General Motors (autos), Kellogg's (breakfast cereals), and Goodyear Tire and Rubber (tires).

SELF-TEST

1.   The text states, "Firms have an incentive to form a cartel, but once it is formed, they have an incentive to cheat." What, specifically, is the incentive to form the cartel, and what is the incentive to cheat on the cartel?

2.   What explains the kink in the kinked demand curve theory of oligopoly?

3.   According to the price leadership theory of oligopoly, how does the dominant firm determine what price to charge?

Game Theory, Oligopoly, and Contestable Markets

Of the four market structures (perfect competition, monopoly, monopolistic competition, and oligopoly), oligopoly is often described as the most difficult to analyze. Analysis is difficult because of the interdependence among firms in an oligopolistic market. Economists often use game theory to get a workable understanding of this interdependence of oligopoly firms. **Game theory** is a mathematical technique used to analyze the behavior of decision makers who (1) try to reach an optimal position through game playing or the use of strategic behavior, (2) are fully aware of the interactive nature of the process at hand, and (3) anticipate the moves of other decision makers.

In this section, we describe a famous game in game theory and then use it to discuss oligopoly behavior. We also discuss the issue of contestable markets.

Prisoner's Dilemma

A well-known game in game theory, called *prisoner's dilemma,* illustrates a case where individually rational behavior leads to a jointly inefficient outcome. It has been described this way: "You do what is best for you, I'll do what is best for me, and somehow we end up in a situation that is not best for either of us." The mechanics of the prisoner's dilemma game are explained in this section.

THE FACTS Two men, Bob and Nathan, are arrested and charged with jointly committing a crime. They are put in separate cells so that they cannot communicate with each other. The district attorney goes to each man separately and says the following:

- If you confess to the crime and agree to turn state's evidence and your accomplice does not confess, I will let you off with a $500 fine.

- If your accomplice confesses to the crime and agrees to turn state's evidence and you do not confess, I will fine you $5,000.

- If both you and your accomplice remain silent and refuse to confess to the crime, I will charge you with a lesser crime, which I can prove you committed, and both you and your accomplice will pay fines of $2,000.

- If both you and your accomplice confess, I will fine each of you $3,000.

THE OPTIONS AND CONSEQUENCES Each man has two choices: confess or not confess. These choices are shown in the grid in Exhibit 8. According to the possibilities laid out by the district attorney, if both men do not confess, each pays a fine of $2,000. This is shown in box 1 in the exhibit.

If Nathan confesses and Bob does not, then Nathan gets off with the light fine of $500 and Bob pays the stiff penalty of $5,000. This is shown in box 2.

If Nathan does not confess and Bob confesses, then Nathan pays the stiff penalty of $5,000 and Bob pays the light fine of $500. This is shown in box 3.

Finally, if both men confess, each pays $3,000. This is shown in box 4.

Game Theory

A mathematical technique used to analyze the behavior of decision makers who try to reach an optimal position for themselves through game playing or the use of strategic behavior, are fully aware of the interactive nature of the process at hand, and anticipate the moves of other decision makers.

Nathan's Choices

		Not Confess	Confess
Bob's Choices	Not Confess	1 — Nathan pays $2,000. Bob pays $2,000.	2 — Nathan pays $500. Bob pays $5,000.
	Confess	3 — Nathan pays $5,000. Bob pays $500.	4 — Nathan pays $3,000. Bob pays $3,000.

exhibit **8**

Prisoner's Dilemma

Nathan and Bob each have two choices: confess or not confess. No matter what Bob does, it is always better for Nathan to confess. No matter what Nathan does, it is always better for Bob to confess. Both Nathan and Bob confess and end up in box 4 where each pays a $3,000 fine. Both men would have been better off had they not confessed. That way they would have ended up in box 1 paying a $2,000 fine.

WHAT NATHAN THINKS Nathan considers his choices and their possible outcomes. He reasons to himself, "I have two options, confess or not confess, and Bob has the same two options. Let me ask myself two questions:

- *"If Bob chooses not to confess, what is the best thing for me to do?* The answer is confess because if I do not confess, I will end up in box 1 paying $2,000, but if I confess I will end up in box 2 paying only $500. No doubt about it, if Bob chooses not to confess, I should confess.

- *"If Bob chooses to confess, what is the best thing for me to do?* The answer is confess because if I do not confess, I will end up in box 3 paying $5,000, but if I confess I will pay $3,000. No doubt about it, if Bob chooses to confess, I should confess."

NATHAN'S CONCLUSION Nathan concludes that no matter what Bob chooses to do, not confess or confess, he is always better off if he confesses. Nathan decides to confess to the crime.

THE SITUATION IS THE SAME FOR BOB Bob goes through the same mental process that Nathan does. Asking himself the same two questions Nathan asked himself, Bob gets the same answers and draws the same conclusion. Bob decides to confess to the crime.

THE OUTCOME The DA goes to each man and asks what he has decided. Nathan says, "I confess." Bob says, "I confess." The outcome is shown in box 4 with each man paying a fine of $3,000.

LOOK WHERE THEY COULD BE Is there an outcome, represented by one of the four boxes, that is better for both Nathan and Bob than the outcome where each pays $3,000? Yes, there is; it is box 1. In box 1, both Nathan and Bob pay $2,000. To get to box 1, all the two men had to do was keep silent and not confess.

CHANGING THE GAME What would happen if the DA gave Nathan and Bob another chance? Suppose she tells them that she will not accept their confessions. Instead, she wants them to talk it over together for 10 minutes, after which time she will come back, place each man in a separate room, and ask for his decision. The second time, she will accept each man's decision, no matter what.

Will this change the outcome? Most people will say yes, arguing that Nathan and Bob will now see that their better choice is to remain silent so that each ends up with a $2,000 fine instead of a $3,000 fine. Let's assume this happens, and Nathan and Bob enter into an agreement to remain silent.

NATHAN'S THOUGHTS ON THE WAY TO HIS ROOM The DA returns and takes Nathan to a separate room. On the way, Nathan thinks to himself, "I'm not sure I can trust Bob. Suppose he goes back on our agreement and confesses. If I hold to the agreement and he doesn't, he'll end up with a $500 fine and I'll end up paying $5,000. Of course, if I break the agreement and confess and he holds to the agreement, then I'll reduce my fine to $500. Maybe the best thing for me to do is break the agreement and confess, hoping that he doesn't and I'll pay only $500. If I'm not so lucky, at least I'll protect myself from paying $5,000."

Once in the room, the DA asks Nathan what his decision is. He says, "I confess."

THE SITUATION IS THE SAME FOR BOB Bob sees the situation the same way Nathan does and again chooses to confess.

THE OUTCOME AGAIN Both men end up confessing a second time. Each pays $3,000, realizing that if they had been silent and kept to their agreement, their fine would be only $2,000 each.

Oligopoly Firms' Cartels and the Prisoner's Dilemma

Think back to our discussion of the cartel theory of oligopoly. Were the oligopoly firms that entered into a cartel agreement in a prisoner's dilemma? Most economists answer yes. To illustrate, suppose there are two firms, *A* and *B,* that produce and sell the same product and are in stiff competition with each other. Currently, the competition between them is so stiff that each earns only $10,000 profits. Soon, the two firms decide to enter into a cartel agreement in which each agrees to raise prices and, after prices are raised, not to undercut the other. If they hold to the agreement, each firm will earn profits of $50,000. But if one firm holds to the cartel agreement and the other does not, the one that does not will earn profits of $100,000 and the one that does will earn $5,000 profits. Of course, if neither holds to the agreement, then both will be back where they started—earning $10,000 profits. The choices for the two firms and the possible outcomes are outlined in Exhibit 9.

Each firm is likely to behave the way the two prisoners did in our prisoner's dilemma. Each firm will see the chance to earn $100,000 by breaking the agreement (instead of $50,000 by holding to it); each will also realize that if it does not break the agreement and the other firm does, it will be in a worse situation than when it was in stiff competition with the other firm. Most economists predict that the two firms will end up in box 4 in Exhibit 9, earning the profits they did before they entered into the agreement. In summary, they will cheat on the cartel agreement and again be in competition—the very situation they wanted to escape.

Is there any way out of the prisoner's dilemma for the two firms? The only way out is to have some entity actually enforce the cartel agreement so that the two firms do not cheat. As odd as it may sound, sometimes government has played this role. We say this "sounds odd" because normally we think of government as trying to break up cartel agreements. After all, cartel agreements are illegal. Nevertheless, sometimes government acts as the enforcer, and not the eliminator, of the cartel agreement.

Consider the Civil Aeronautics Board (CAB) in the days of airline regulation. The CAB was created to protect the airlines from "cutthroat competition." It had the power to set airfares, allocate air routes, and prevent the entry of new carriers into the airline industry. In the days before deregulation, the federal government's General Accounting Office estimated that airline fares would have been, on average, as much as 52 percent

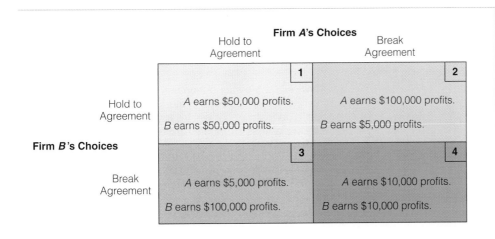

exhibit **9**

Cartels and Prisoner's Dilemma

Many economists suggest that firms trying to form a cartel are in a prisoner's dilemma situation. Both firms *A* and *B* earn higher profits holding to a (cartel) agreement than not, but each will earn even higher profits it it breaks the agreement while the other firm holds to it. If cartel formation is a prisoner's dilemma situation, we predict that cartels will be short-lived.

Firm *A*'s Choices

	Hold to Agreement	Break Agreement
Hold to Agreement	**1** A earns $50,000 profits. B earns $50,000 profits.	**2** A earns $100,000 profits. B earns $5,000 profits.
Break Agreement	**3** A earns $5,000 profits. B earns $100,000 profits.	**4** A earns $10,000 profits. B earns $10,000 profits.

Firm *B*'s Choices

economics 24/7

AN ECONOMIC THEORY OF THE MAFIA

The U.S. government prohibits its residents from engaging in certain activities. With only a few exceptions, it forbids residents from being either buyers or sellers of illegal drugs, prostitution services, or gambling services. Because government is willing to punish anyone who goes against its prohibitions, there is a high barrier to entering the illegal drug, prostitution, and gambling markets.

Of course, not everyone has abided by the government's prohibitions; there are both buyers and sellers of illegal goods and services in spite of the high barrier. One of the historically biggest sellers in these markets is the Mafia. (The term Mafia has been adopted internationally to refer to an organized crime unit that sells illegal goods and services and is willing to use extreme force [violence] to protect what it perceives as its business interests.) In reality, numerous Mafia firms (sometimes referred to as families) benefit from the high barrier to entry established by the government. Each Mafia firm faces a higher demand curve than it would if there were no legal barriers to entry. Consequently, prices and profits are higher for the few Mafia firms that supply the market.[2]

The question each Mafia firm has to ask itself is: Could its profits be even higher without the other Mafia firms? In economic terms, the question becomes: Are there benefits from moving from being one of a few oligopoly firms to being the sole monopoly firm? Or stated differently, are there benefits from facing the entire market demand curve instead of only some fraction of it?

There are benefits, of course, but there are also costs in trying to obtain the benefits. How can a Mafia firm obtain the benefits of a monopoly? It can try to put other Mafia firms out of business by offering higher quality goods and services, lower prices, better credit terms, better delivery, and so on. Or it can try to eliminate (literally, kill) the members of the other Mafia firms. What will be the costs of using these methods?

If any one Mafia firm tries to kill its competitors, then the other Mafia firms will likely band together against it. To understand why, consider five Mafia firms, *A–E*. Firm *A* tries to eliminate firm *B* by killing the members of the firm. Firms *C–E* know that if firm *A* is successful, it will probably try to eliminate them next. They will then band together with firm

B to try to eliminate firm *A*. In short, each firm will soon realize that trying to kill its competition is not likely to be a successful strategy.

Now consider the option of trying to outcompete rivals by offering lower prices, higher quality, and so on. Will the Mafia firms proceed this way? Perhaps not. They may recognize that stiff competition among them may simply reduce their profits.

The Mafia firms may choose a third option: They may agree to form a cartel. Often in the past, Mafia cartel agreements have taken the form of dividing up the market. Each Mafia firm gets a certain geographic area in which it can exclusively supply all illegal goods and services.

But economists know that cartel agreements are notoriously unstable because there are often huge benefits from breaking the cartel agreement when others do not. Once the Mafia firms form a cartel agreement, each firm is in a prisoner's dilemma. In the end, the firms soon learn that cheating behavior puts everyone in a worse position. How then do Mafia firms make sure that each cooperates and holds to the cartel agreement? Who or what will enforce the Mafia cartel agreements?

Economist Robert Axelrod reports that the only strategy that seemingly solves the (repeated) prisoner's dilemma game and gets participants to cooperate with each other instead of cheating on each other is tit for tat. The tit-for-tat strategy is simple: You give to others what you get from them. When individuals know that they will get what they give, they will want to give (to others) what they want to receive from them. And what they want is cooperation—that is, holding to the cartel agreement. They want to make sure they are in box 1 of the prisoner's dilemma payoff matrix, not box 4 (see Exhibit 8).

Applied to Mafia firms, tit for tat works this way: If one Mafia family kills a member of another family, then the second family must kill someone in the first family. The message has to be that you get whatever you give. There is evidence that Mafia firms are rather efficient practitioners of tit for tat.

---

[2]We assume throughout our discussion that each Mafia firm faces constant marginal cost and therefore constant unit cost.

lower if the CAB had not been regulating them. Clearly, the CAB was doing for the airlines what an airline cartel would have done—prevent price competition, allocate routes, and prevent new entries into the industry.

In a similar vein, Judge Richard Posner has observed that "the railroads supported the enactment of the first Interstate Commerce Act, which was designed to prevent railroads from price discrimination, because discrimination was undermining the railroad's cartels."[3]

Are Markets Contestable?

The discussion of market structures, from perfect competition to oligopoly, has focused on the *number of sellers* in each market structure. In perfect competition, there are many sellers; in monopoly, there is only one; in monopolistic competition, there are many; in oligopoly, there are few. The message is that the number of sellers in a market influences the behavior of the sellers within the market. For example, the monopoly seller is more likely to restrict output and charge higher prices than is the perfect competitor.

Some economists have shifted the emphasis from the number of sellers in a market to the issue of *entry into and exit from an industry*. This focus is a result of the work of William Baumol and other economists who have put forth the idea of contestable markets.

A **contestable market** is one in which the following conditions are met:

1. **There is easy entry into the market and costless exit from the market.**

2. **New firms entering the market can produce the product at the same cost as current firms.**

3. **Firms exiting the market can easily dispose of their fixed assets by selling them elsewhere** (less depreciation; thus, fixed costs are not sunk but recoverable).

Contestable Market
A market in which entry is easy and exit is costless, new firms can produce the product at the same cost as current firms, and exiting firms can easily dispose of their fixed assets by selling them.

To illustrate, suppose there are currently eight firms in an industry, all of which are earning profits. Firms outside the industry notice this and decide to enter the industry (nothing prevents entry). They acquire the necessary equipment and produce the product at the same cost as current producers do. Time passes, and the firms that entered the industry decide to exit it. They can either switch their machinery into another line of production or sell their equipment for what they paid for it, less depreciation.

Perhaps the most important element of a contestable market is "hit-and-run" entry and exit. New entrants can enter—hit—produce the product and take profits from current firms and then exit costlessly—run.

The theory of contestable markets has been criticized because of its assumptions—in particular, the assumption that there is extremely free entry into and costless exit from the industry. However, although this theory, like most theories, does not perfectly describe the real world, this does not of itself destroy the theory's usefulness.

At a minimum, contestable markets theory has rattled orthodox market structure theory. Here are a few of its conclusions:

1. Even if an industry is composed of a small number of firms, or simply one firm, this is not evidence that the firms perform in a noncompetitive way. They might be extremely competitive if the market they are in is contestable.

2. Profits can be zero in an industry even if the number of sellers in the industry is small.

3. If a market is contestable, inefficient producers cannot survive. Cost inefficiencies invite lower cost producers into the market, driving price down to minimum *ATC* and forcing inefficient firms to change their ways or exit the industry.

---

[3]Richard A. Posner, "Theories of Regulation," *Bell Journal of Economics and Management Science* 5 (Autumn): 337.

4. If, as conclusion 3 suggests, a contestable market encourages firms to produce at their lowest possible average total cost and charge $P = ATC$, it follows that they will also sell at a price equal to marginal cost. (Recall that the marginal cost curve intersects the average total cost curve at its minimum point.)

The theory of contestable markets has also led to a shift in policy perspectives. To some (but certainly not all) economists, the theory suggests a new way to encourage firms to act as perfect competitors. Rather than direct interference in the behavioral patterns of firms, efforts should perhaps be directed at lowering entry and exit costs.

A Review of Market Structures

With the discussion of oligopoly, examination of the four different market structures—perfect competition, monopoly, monopolistic competition, and oligopoly—comes to an end. Exhibit 10 reviews some of the characteristics and consequences of the different market structures.

The first four columns of the exhibit simply summarize the characteristics of the different market structures. The last column notes the long-run market tendency of price and average total cost in the different market structures. The relationship between price and ATC indicates whether long-run profits are possible. Note that three of the four market structures (monopoly, monopolistic competition, and oligopoly) have superscript letters beside the possible profits. These letters refer to notes that describe alternative market tendencies given different conditions. For example, the market tendency in oligopoly is $P > ATC$ and for profits to exist in the long run. The reason is that there are significant barriers to entry in oligopoly, so short-run profits cannot be reduced by competition from new firms entering the industry. However, the market tendency of price and average total cost may be different if the particular oligopolistic market is contestable.

Applications of Game Theory

Game theory, especially prisoner's dilemma, is applicable in a number of real-world situations. In this section, we discuss a few of these applications.

Grades and Partying

Your economics professor announces in class one day that on the next test, she will give the top 10 percent of the students in the class As, the next 15 percent Bs, and so on. You realize it takes less time studying to get, say, a 60 than a 90 on the test, so you hope everyone studies only a little. That way, you can study only a little and earn a high letter grade. But of course, everyone in the class is thinking the same thing.

exhibit **10**

Characteristics and Consequences
of Market Structures

Market Structure	Number of Sellers	Type of Product	Barriers to Entry	Long-Run Market Tendency of Price and ATC
Perfect competition	Many	Homogeneous	No	$P = ATC$ (zero economic profits)
Monopoly	One	Unique	Yes	$P > ATC$ (positive economic profits)[a, c]
Monopolistic competition	Many	Slightly differentiated	No	$P = ATC$ (zero economic profits)[b]
Oligopoly	Few	Homogeneous or differentiated	Yes	$P > ATC$ (positive economic profits)[a, c]

a. It is possible for positive profits to turn to zero profits through the capitalization of profits or rent-seeking activities.
b. It is possible for the firm to earn positive profits in the long run if it can differentiate its product sufficiently in the minds of the buying public.
c. It is possible for positive profits to turn to zero profits if the market is contestable.

Envision yourself entering into an agreement with your fellow students. You say the following to them one day:

> *There are 30 students in our class. Each of us can choose to study either 2 hours or 4 hours for the test. Our relative standing in the class will be the same whether we all study for 2 hours or all study for 4 hours. So why don't we all agree to study for only 2 hours. That way, we have 2 extra hours to do other things. I'd rather receive my B by studying only 2 hours instead of by having to study 4 hours.*

Suppose everyone agrees with the logic of the argument and agrees to study only 2 hours. Of course, once everyone has agreed to this, there is an incentive to cheat on the agreement and study more. If everyone else in your class agrees to study 2 hours and you study 4 hours, you increase your relative standing in the class. You go from, say, a B to an A.

You and the other students in your class are in a prisoner's dilemma. Look at Exhibit 11, which shows the payoffs for you and for Jill, a representative other student. If both you and Jill study 4 hours, each receives an 85, which is a B (box 4). With your professor's new relative grading plan, if you study 2 hours and Jill studies 2 hours, the grade for each of you falls to 65, but now 65 is a B (box 1). In other words, comparing box 4 with box 1, box 1 is better because you receive the same letter grade (B) in both cases but spend less time studying.

Of course, once you and Jill agree to lower your study time from 4 hours to 2 hours, each of you has an incentive to cheat on the agreement. If you study 4 hours and Jill studies 2 hours, then you raise your grade to an 85, which is now an A, while Jill's grade is 65, which now becomes a C (box 2). Of course, if Jill studies 4 hours and you study 2 hours, then Jill raises her grade to an 85, which is now an A, while your grade is 65, which is now a C (box 3).

No matter what you think Jill is going to do, the best thing for you to do is study 4 hours.[4] The same holds for Jill with respect to whatever you choose to do. The outcome then is box 4, where both of you study 4 hours.

Ideally, what you need (and Jill needs too) is a way to enforce your agreement not to study more than 2 hours. How might students do this? One way is to party. That's right—party. If you can get all the students in your class together and party, you can be fairly sure that no one is studying too much.

Think about this: Students in the same class understand that (1) some professors set aside some percentage of As for the top students in the class (no matter how low the top

exhibit **11**

Studying and Grades

Suppose your letter grade in class depends on how well you do relative to others. In this setting, you and the other students are in a prisoner's dilemma, which is shown here. If both you and Jill (a representative other student) each study 4 hours, each of you earns a point grade of 85, which is a B (box 4). If each of study 2 hours, each of you earn a point grade of 65, which is a B (box 1). Box 1 is preferred over box 4 because you get the same letter grade in each box, but you study less in box 1 than in box 4.

If you study 4 hours while Jill studies 2 hours, your point grade rises to 85 and Jill's point grade remains at 65. In this case, 85 is an A and 65 is a C (box 2). You are better off and Jill is worse off.

If you study 2 hours while Jill studies 4 hours, Jill's point grade rises to 85 and your point grade remains at 65. Jill earns a letter grade of A, and you earn a letter grade of C.

No matter what Jill decides to do—study 2 or 4 hours—it is always better for you to study 4 hours (assuming the costs of studying additional hours are less than the benefits of studying additional hours). The same holds for Jill. Our outcome, then, is box 4, where both you and Jill study 4 hours.

	You Study 2 Hours	Study 4 Hours
Jill Study 2 Hours	**1** You: 65, B Jill: 65, B	**2** You: 85, A Jill: 65, C
Study 4 Hours	**3** You: 65, C Jill: 85, A	**4** You: 85, B Jill: 85, B

[4]We are assuming that the cost of studying 2 additional hours is lower than the benefits you receive by raising your grade one letter.

is) and (2) they are in a prisoner's dilemma. They realize it would be better for them to cooperate and study less than to compete and study more. Instead of actually entering into an agreement to study less (sign on the dotted line), they "think up" ways to keep the studying time down. One way to keep the studying time down—one way to enforce the implicit and unspoken agreement not to study too much—is to do things with others that do not entail studying. One "institution" that satisfies all requirements is partying—everyone is together not studying.

The Arms Race

During much of the Cold War, the United States and the Soviet Union engaged in an arms race. Both countries were producing armaments that were directed at the other. Occasionally, representatives of the two countries would meet and try to slow down the arms race. The United States would agree to cut armaments production if the Soviet Union did, and vice versa. Many arms analysts generally agreed that the arms agreements between the United States and the Soviet Union were unsuccessful. In other words, representatives of the two countries would meet and enter into an agreement not to compete so heavily in arms production. But then, the countries would end up competing on arms production.

Were the two countries in a prisoner's dilemma? Look at Exhibit 12. When both the United States and the Soviet Union were competing on arms production, they were in box 4, each receiving a utility level of 7. Their collective objective was to move from box 4 to box 1, where each cooperated with the other and reduced its armaments production. In box 1, each country received a utility level of 10. The arms agreements that the United States and the Soviet Union entered into were an attempt to get to box 1.

Of course, after the agreement was signed, each country had an incentive to cheat on the agreement. Certainly, the United States would be better off if it increased its armaments production while the Soviet Union cut back its production. Then, the United States could establish clear military superiority over the Soviet Union. The same held for the Soviet Union with respect to the United States.

Looking at the payoff matrix in Exhibit 12, it is easy to see that the best strategy for the United States was to compete; the same holds for the Soviet Union. And so the two countries ended up in box 4, racing to outproduce the other in arms.

Speed Limit Laws

Envision a world with no law against speeding. In this world, you and everyone else speeds. With everyone speeding, a good number of accidents occur each day, some of which may involve you. In time, everyone decides that something has to be done

exhibit **12**

An Arms Race

In the days of the Cold War, the United States and the Soviet Union were said to be in an arms race. Actually, the arms race was a result of the two countries being in a prisoner's dilemma. Start with each country racing to produce more military goods than the other country; that is, each country is in box 4. In their attempt to move to box 1, they enter into an arms agreement (to reduce the rate at which they produce arms). But no matter what the Soviet Union does (hold to the arms agreement or break it), it is always better for the United States o break the agreement. The same holds for the Soviet Union with respect to the United States. The two countries end up in box 4. (Note: In the exhibit, the higher the number, the better the position for the country.)

	United States Hold to Arms Agreement	**United States** Break Arms Agreement
Soviet Union Hold to Arms Agreement	**1** United States, 10 Soviet Union, 10	**2** United States, 15 Soviet Union, 5
Soviet Union Break Arms Agreement	**3** United States, 5 Soviet Union, 15	**4** United States, 7 Soviet Union, 7

about the speeding. It is just too dangerous, everyone admits, to let the speeding continue.

Someone offers a proposal: "Let's agree that we will post signs on the road that state the maximum speed. Furthermore, let's agree here and now that we will all obey the speed limits." The proposal sounds like a good one, and so everyone agrees to follow it.

Of course, as we know by now, once the agreement not to speed is made, we have a prisoner's dilemma. Each person will be better off if he (and he alone) speeds while everyone else obeys the speed limit. In the beginning, everyone agrees to the speed limit; in the end, however, everyone breaks it.

What is missing, of course, is an effective enforcement mechanism. To move the speeders out of the classic prisoner's dilemma box (box 4 in our earlier examples) to box 1, someone or something has to punish people who do not cooperate with others. A law against speeding—backed up by the police and court system—solves the prisoner's dilemma. The law, the police, and the court system change the payoff for cheating on the agreement.

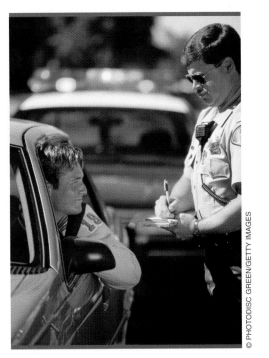

The Fear of Guilt as an Enforcement Mechanism

Might there be a social purpose for guilt? Might there be a good reason for feeling guilty? With these two questions in mind, consider the following. John and Mary decide to get married. As part of their wedding vows, they promise to remain faithful to each other. In other words, each promises the other that he or she will not cheat.

Of course, once an agreement is made between two parties, often each party will be better off if one party cheats and the other does not. In the case of John and Mary, John may think, "I can gain utility by cheating on Mary." Of course, Mary can think the same thing with respect to John. Their utility payoffs are shown in Exhibit 13.

Notice in part (a) that both Mary and John receive a utility level of 15 when one cheats but the other does not. Possibly, if each person felt some guilt over cheating on his or her partner, the utility level would be something lower than 15. In some sense, both Mary and John might prefer to feel guilty when cheating. After all, both would prefer to be in box 1, where neither is cheating, than in box 4, where both are cheating. In short, given that box 1 is better than box 4 for both Mary and John, we would expect that both would opt for some enforcement mechanism that prevented them from moving away from box 1. Think back to the speeding example. Don't the speeders actually want a law against speeding that is enforced by the police and courts?

Of course, there is no outside enforcement mechanism for John and Mary. But an internal sense of guilt over cheating might be a good substitute for an external enforcement mechanism. Instead of the police and the court system putting John and Mary in prison for cheating, each one's sense of guilt will put him or her in a personal jail. (Isn't this what someone is implying by saying, "There is no way I can do that; I would feel too guilty." In other words, many people want to prevent themselves from suffering the pangs of guilt in much the same way they don't want to suffer the pain of prison. Both guilt pangs and prison are *bads*. Both come with disutility.)

Suppose, as shown in Exhibit 13(b), a sense of guilt would change Mary's utility level in box 2 from 15 to 4 and would change John's utility level in box 3 from 15 to 4. Then, neither Mary nor John would find it advantageous to cheat on the other if his or her spouse did not cheat.[5]

---

[5]Of course, the way we have structured the payoff matrix, each finds it advantageous to cheat on the other if the other cheats. If Mary does not cheat on John, then John is better off not cheating than cheating, but if Mary cheats on John, and John knows that Mary is cheating on him, then he is better off cheating than not cheating.

exhibit 13

Cheating and Guilt

Does guilt sometimes serve a useful social purpose? John and Mary are married and may be in a prisoner's dilemma. If Mary cheats on John, but John doesn't cheat on Mary, Mary may be better off and therefore moves from box 1 to box 2 in part (a). If John cheats on Mary, but Mary doesn't cheat on John, John may be better off and therefore moves from box 1 to box 3 in (a). Of course, if both cheat, they both end up in box 4, which is inferior for both to box 1. A sense of guilt for each person may change the payoffs in part (a). If each person feels guilty about cheating, then the payoff from cheating is lowered. Look at the new payoffs for each person in part (b). The payoff for cheating goes from 15 to 4 for both Mary and John. With the new, lower payoffs (resulting from a sense of guilt over cheating), both Mary and John remove themselves from a prisoner's dilemma and therefore are more likely to end up in box 1, a box that is better for both.

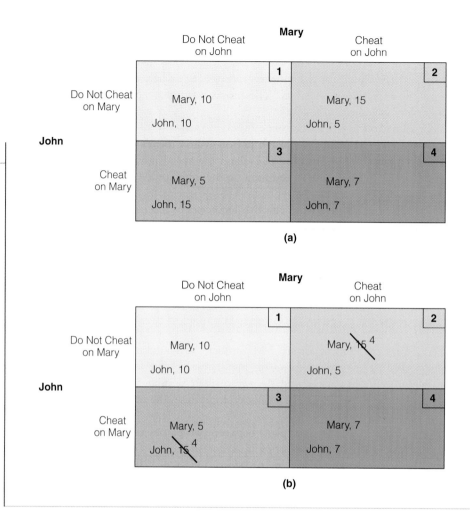

(a)

(b)

We end with a question: When is guilt good? One answer is that when the fear of guilt allows two people to remove themselves from a setting they would prefer not to be in to a better setting. If the fear of guilt moves Mary and John from box 4 to box 1 (which is what they want), then the fear of guilt is good.

A Reader Asks . . .

Are Some Prisoner's Dilemmas Good and Others Bad?

Are there times when we're glad that people are in a prisoner's dilemma and times when we're not glad? In other words, are there some settings in which we actually want people to end up in box 4 instead of box 1 and other settings in which we want people to end up in box 1 instead of box 4?

Let's look again at two of the prisoner's dilemma settings in the chapter. In one of our settings, two competing sellers enter into a cartel agreement to reduce or eliminate the competition between them. If the cartel agreement is successful, sellers are better off and consumers are worse off. If the cartel agreement is unsuccessful (if the cartel agreement is broken by one or both of the sellers), then sellers are worse off and consumers are better off.

The sellers, as you know, are in a prisoner's dilemma. Each seller agrees to cooperate with the other (to reduce or eliminate cooperation) but also has an incentive to cheat on the agreement. The incentive to cheat (and make oneself better off at the other's expense) is what gets each seller to break the cartel agreement. Outcome: Competition between sellers means benefits for consumers.

Consumers should be glad that sellers are in a prisoner's dilemma and therefore end up in box 4 competing with each other for consumers' business. In other words, if the sellers weren't in a prisoner's dilemma, consumers would want to put them in one.

Now consider our discussion about the arms race between the United States and the Soviet Union. Just like our two sellers, the two countries are in a prisoner's dilemma. Each country agrees to cooperate with the other (to reduce the arms race between them) but also has an incentive to cheat on any arms agreement. The incentive to cheat (and clearly establish military superiority over the other country) is what gets each country to break the arms agreement. Outcome: Arms race.

It is not clear in this case that there are any obvious beneficiaries (other than perhaps armament producers) to the two countries being stuck in a prisoner's dilemma and ending up in box 4, engaged in an arms race. So this might be an example of a prisoner's dilemma that almost everyone would have preferred did not exist.

! analyzing the scene

If Carl and Amanda both want to end grade inflation, why don't they just do it?

Carl and Amanda are stuck in a prisoner's dilemma game. Think of how you might model the game. Each professor enters into an agreement with every other professor to stop inflating grades. Each professor now has the choice of holding to the agreement or breaking it (continuing to inflate grades). If a professor wants to raise the relative grading standard of his students relative to other students, he may choose to inflate grades—thinking that other professors are not inflating grades. The result? All (or almost all) professors will end up inflating grades.

---

chapter summary

Monopolistic Competition

- The theory of monopolistic competition is built on three assumptions: (1) There are many sellers and buyers. (2) Each firm in the industry produces and sells a slightly differentiated product. (3) There is easy entry and exit.
- The monopolistic competitor is a price searcher.
- For the monopolistic competitor, $P > MR$, and the marginal revenue curve lies below the demand curve.
- The monopolistic competitor produces the quantity of output at which $MR = MC$. It charges the highest price per unit for this output.

- Unlike the perfectly competitive firm, the monopolistic competitor does not exhibit resource allocative efficiency.
- The monopolistic competitive firm does not earn profits in the long run (because of easy entry into the industry) unless it can successfully differentiate its product (e.g., by brand name) in the minds of buyers.

Excess Capacity Theorem

- The excess capacity theorem states that a monopolistic competitor will, in equilibrium, produce an output smaller than the one at which average total costs (unit costs) are minimized. Thus, the monopolistic competitor is not productive efficient.

Oligopoly Assumptions

- There are many different oligopoly theories. All are built on the following assumptions: (1) There are few sellers and many buyers. (2) Firms produce and sell either homogeneous or differentiated products. (3) There are significant barriers to entry.
- One of the key characteristics of oligopolistic firms is their interdependence.

Oligopoly Theories

- The cartel theory assumes that firms in an oligopolistic industry act in a manner consistent with there being only one firm in the industry.
- Four problems are associated with cartels: (1) the problem of forming the cartel, (2) the problem of formulating policy, (3) the problem of entry into the industry, and (4) the problem of cheating.
- Firms that enter into a cartel agreement are in a prisoner's dilemma situation where individually rational behavior leads to a jointly inefficient outcome.
- The kinked demand curve theory assumes that if a single firm lowers price, other firms will do likewise, but if a single firm raises price, other firms will not follow suit.
- The kinked demand curve theory predicts that an oligopolistic firm will experience price stickiness or rigidity. This is because there is a gap in its marginal revenue curve in which the firm's marginal cost can rise or fall and the firm will still produce the same quantity of output and charge the same price. The evidence in some empirical tests rejects the theory.
- The price leadership theory assumes that the dominant firm in the industry determines price and all other firms take this price as given.

The Theory of Contestable Markets

- A contestable market is one in which the following conditions are met: (1) There is easy entry into the market and costless exit from it. (2) New firms entering the market can produce the product at the same cost as current firms. (3) Firms exiting the market can easily dispose of their fixed assets by selling them elsewhere (less depreciation).
- Compared to orthodox market structure theories, the theory of contestable markets places more emphasis on the issue of entry into and exit from an industry and less emphasis on the number of sellers in an industry.

Game Theory

- Game theory is a mathematical technique used to analyze the behavior of decision makers who (1) try to reach an optimal position through game playing or the use of strategic behavior, (2) are fully aware of the interactive nature of the process at hand, and (3) anticipate the moves of other decision makers.
- The prisoner's dilemma game illustrates a case where individually rational behavior leads to a jointly inefficient outcome.

key terms and concepts

Monopolistic
  Competition
Excess Capacity Theorem

Oligopoly
Concentration Ratio
Cartel Theory

Cartel
Kinked Demand Curve
  Theory

Price Leadership Theory
Game Theory
Contestable Market

questions and problems

1   What, if anything, do all firms in all four market structures have in common?

2   What causes the unusual appearance of the marginal revenue curve in the kinked demand curve theory?

3   Would you expect cartel formation to be more likely in industries comprised of a few firms or in those that include many firms? Explain your answer.

4   Does the theory of contestable markets shed any light on oligopoly pricing theories? Explain your answer.

5   There are 60 types or varieties of product X on the market. Is product X made in a monopolistic competitive market? Explain your answer.

6   Why does interdependence of firms play a major role in oligopoly but not in perfect competition or monopolistic competition?

7 Airline companies sometimes fly airplanes that are one-quarter full between cities. Some people point to this as evidence of economic waste. What do you think? Would it be better to have fewer airline companies and more full planes?

8 Concentration ratios have often been used to note the tightness of an oligopoly market. A high concentration ratio indicates a tight oligopoly market, and a low concentration ratio indicates a loose oligopoly market. Would you expect firms in tight markets to reap higher profits, on average, than firms in loose markets? Would

it matter if the markets were contestable? Explain your answers.

9 Market theories are said to have the happy consequence of getting individuals to think in more focused and analytical ways. Has this happened to you? Give examples to illustrate.

10 Give an example of a prisoner's dilemma situation other than the ones mentioned in this chapter.

11 How are oligopoly and monopolistic competition alike? How are they different?

working with numbers and graphs

1 Diagrammatically identify the quantity of output a monopolistic competitor produces and the price it charges.

2 Diagrammatically identify a monopolistic competitor that is incurring losses.

3 In Exhibit 6, what is the highest dollar amount to which marginal cost can rise without changing price?

4 Total industry sales are $105 million. The top four firms account for sales of $10 million, $9 million, $8 million, and $5 million, respectively. What is the four-firm concentration ratio?

5 According to the kinked demand curve theory, if the firm is considering a price hike, which demand curve in the following figure does it believe it faces and why?

6 Refer to the following figure. Because of a cartel agreement, the firm has been assigned a production quota of q_2 units. The cartel price is P_2. What do the firm's profits equal if it adheres to the cartel agreement? What do the firm's profits equal if it breaks the cartel agreement and produces q_3?

Government and Product Markets: Antitrust and Regulation

Setting the Scene

The following conversations took place on a day in December.

9:55 A.M. GOVERNMENT OFFICE, KUALA LUMPUR, MALAYSIA

First person:
    The AIDS problem is getting worse. People are dying because they can't afford treatment. I think we should issue a compulsory license.

Second person:
    To Cipla?

First person:
    Yes.

10:43 A.M. OFFICE OF THE ATTORNEY GENERAL OF TENNESSEE

First person:
    That company is violating antitrust laws, and the Justice Department hasn't filed any action against it. If the federal government isn't going to do its job, then maybe we should.

Second person:
    I think you may be right.

1:00 P.M. A PUB IN ENNIS, IRELAND

First person:
    Remember the days when you could smoke in a pub?

Second person:
    I miss those days.

3:07 P.M. AN APARTMENT IN MANHATTAN

First person:
    Excessive regulation is killing businesses.

Second person:
    I'm not sure you're right. I think that sometimes businesses want to be regulated. Some regulation can keep competition out.

First person:
    At every business club meeting I've ever attended, businesspeople were talking about how government overburdened them with regulations and red tape. They always say that they'd be better off—and the economy would be better off—with fewer regulations.

Second person:
    Well, I think some regulation can stifle business, and perhaps regulation is excessive in some cases. But I remember hearing once that sometimes a business asks government to regulate it. For instance, firms in a particular industry might ask government to set prices so that firms don't continue to compete on price. If one firm lowers price, then another firm has to follow, and so on.

First person:
    You may have a point. Maybe there are different types of regulation—some that hurt businesses and others that help.

> **?** Here are some questions to keep in mind as you read this chapter:
>
> *What does AIDS have to do with antitrust?*
>
> *At what level of government are antitrust and regulatory issues best addressed?*
>
> *What are the arguments for and against outlawing smoking in Irish pubs?*
>
> *Would businesses ever ask for government regulation?*
>
> See analyzing the scene at the end of this chapter for answers to these questions.

Antitrust

A monopoly (1) produces a smaller output than is produced by a perfectly competitive firm with the same revenue and cost considerations, (2) charges a higher price, and (3) causes a deadweight loss. Some economists argue that based on these facts, government should place certain restrictions on monopolies. In addition, government should restrict the activities of cartels because the objective of a cartel is to behave as if it were a monopoly.

Other economists argue that monopolies do not have as much market power as some people think—witness the competition some monopolies face from broadly defined substitutes and imports. As for cartels, they usually contain the seeds of their own destruction. Therefore, it is only a matter of time (usually short) before they crumble naturally.

We are not concerned here with the debate about whether or not to restrict monopoly power. Instead, we examine the ways government deals with it. Two of the ways include antitrust laws and regulation. We examine antitrust law in this section and regulation in the next.

Antitrust law is legislation passed for the stated purpose of controlling monopoly power and preserving and promoting competition. Let's look at how a few of the major antitrust acts have been used and the effects they have had.

Antitrust Law
Legislation passed for the stated purpose of controlling monopoly power and preserving and promoting competition.

Antitrust Acts

A few key acts that constitute U.S. antitrust policy are the Sherman Act (1890), the Clayton Act (1914), the Federal Trade Commission Act (1914), the Robinson-Patman Act (1936), the Wheeler-Lea Act (1938), and the Celler-Kefauver Antimerger Act (1950).

THE SHERMAN ACT (1890) The Sherman Act was passed when mergers of companies were common. (A merger occurs when two companies combine under single ownership of control.) At that time, the organization that companies formed by combining was called a **trust**; this in turn gave us the word *antitrust*.

Trust
A combination of firms that come together to act as a monopolist.

The Sherman Act contains two major provisions:

1. "Every contract, combination in the form of trust or otherwise, or conspiracy, in restraint of trade or commerce among the several states, or with foreign nations, is hereby declared to be illegal."

2. "Every person who shall monopolize, or attempt to monopolize, or combine or conspire with any other person or persons to monopolize any part of the trade or commerce . . . shall be guilty of a misdemeanor."

Some people have argued that the provisions of the Sherman Act are vague. For example, the act never explains which specific acts constitute "restraint of trade," although it declares such acts illegal.

THE CLAYTON ACT (1914) The Clayton Act makes the following business practices illegal when their effects "may be to substantially lessen competition or tend to create a monopoly":

1. Price discrimination—charging different customers different prices for the same product where the price differences are not related to cost differences.

2. Exclusive dealing—selling to a retailer on the condition that the retailer not carry any rival products.

3. Tying contracts—arrangements whereby the sale of one product is dependent on the purchase of some other product(s).

4. The acquisition of competing companies' stock if the acquisition reduces competition. (Some say a major loophole of the act is that it does not ban the acquisition of competing companies' physical assets and therefore does not prevent anticompetitive mergers as it was designed to do.)

5. Interlocking directorates—an arrangement whereby the directors of one company sit on the board of directors of another company in the same industry. These were made illegal, irrespective of their effects (i.e., interlocking directorates are illegal at all times, not just when their effects "may be to substantially lessen competition . . .").

THE FEDERAL TRADE COMMISSION ACT (1914) The Federal Trade Commission Act contains the broadest and most general language of any antitrust act. It declares illegal "unfair methods of competition in commerce." In essence, this amounts to declaring illegal acts that are judged to be "too aggressive" in competition. The problem is how to decide what is fair and what is unfair, what is aggressive but not too aggressive. This act also set up the Federal Trade Commission (FTC) to deal with "unfair methods of competition."

THE ROBINSON-PATMAN ACT (1936) The Robinson-Patman Act was passed in an attempt to decrease the failure rate of small businesses by protecting them from the competition of large and growing chain stores. The large chain stores were receiving price discounts from suppliers and, in turn, were passing the discounts on to their customers. As a result, small businesses had a difficult time competing, and many of them failed. The Robinson-Patman Act prohibits suppliers from offering special discounts to large chain stores unless they also offer the discounts to everyone else. Many economists believe that, rather than preserving and strengthening competition, the Robinson-Patman Act limits it. The act seems to be more concerned about a certain group of competitors than about the process of competition and the buying public as a whole.

THE WHEELER-LEA ACT (1938) The Wheeler-Lea Act empowers the Federal Trade Commission to deal with false and deceptive acts or practices. Major moves in this area have been against advertising that the FTC has deemed false and deceptive.

THE CELLER-KEFAUVER ANTIMERGER ACT (1950) The Celler-Kefauver Act was designed to close the merger loophole in the Clayton Act (see point 4 of the Clayton Act). It bans anticompetitive mergers that occur as a result of one company acquiring the physical assets of another company.

Unsettled Points in Antitrust Policy

It is not always clear where lines should be drawn in implementing antitrust policy. Which firms should be allowed to enter into a merger, and which firms should be prohibited? What constitutes restraint of trade? Which firms should be termed "monopolists" and broken into smaller firms, and which firms should be left alone?

As you might guess, not everyone answers these questions the same way. In short, some points of antitrust policy are still unsettled. A few of the more important unsettled points are noted here.

DOES THE DEFINITION OF THE MARKET MATTER? Should a market be defined broadly or narrowly? The way the market is defined helps determine whether or not a particular firm is considered a monopoly. For example, in an important antitrust suit in 1945, a court ruled that Alcoa (Aluminum Company of America) was a monopoly because it had 90 percent of the virgin aluminum ingot market. If Alcoa's market had been broadened to include stainless steel, copper, tin, nickel, and zinc (some of the goods competing with aluminum), it is unlikely that Alcoa would have been ruled a monopoly.

Later court rulings have tended to define markets broadly rather than narrowly. For instance, in the DuPont case in 1956, the market relevant to DuPont was ruled to be the flexible wrapping materials market rather than the narrower cellophane market.

CONCENTRATION RATIOS Concentration ratios have often been used to gauge the amount of competition in an industry, but as pointed out in the last chapter, their use presents two major problems. First, concentration ratios do not address the issue of foreign competition. For example, the four-firm concentration ratio may be very high, but the four firms that make up the concentration ratio may still face stiff competition from abroad. Second, a four-firm concentration ratio can remain stable over time even though there is competition among the four major firms in the industry.

In 1982, the Justice Department replaced the four- and eight-firm concentration ratios with the Herfindahl index, although it too is subject to some of the same criticisms as the concentration ratios. The **Herfindahl index** measures the degree of concentration in an industry. It is equal to the sum of the squares of the market shares of each firm in the industry:

$$\text{Herfindahl index} = (S_1)^2 + (S_2)^2 + \ldots + (S_n)^2$$

where S_1 through S_n are the market shares of firms 1 through n. For example, if there are 10 firms in an industry, and each firm has a 10 percent market share, the Herfindahl index is 1,000 ($10^2 + 10^2 + 10^2 + 10^2 + 10^2 + 10^2 + 10^2 + 10^2 + 10^2 + 10^2 = 1,000$).

Exhibit 1 compares the Herfindahl index and the four-firm concentration ratio. When the four-firm concentration ratio is used, the top four firms, *A–D*, have a 48 percent market share, which generally is thought to describe a concentrated industry. A merger between any of the top four firms and any other firm (e.g., between firm *B* and firm *G* in Exhibit 1) would give the newly merged firm a greater market share than any existing firm and usually would incur frowns from the Justice Department.

The Herfindahl index for the industry is 932, however, and the Justice Department generally considers any number less than 1,000 representative of an unconcentrated (or competitive) industry. An index between 1,000 and 1,800 is considered representative of a moderately concentrated industry, and an index greater than 1,800 is representative of a concentrated industry.

Antitrust actions are usually brought by the Justice Department if (1) the index rises by 100 points or more and the (premerger) index is initially in the 1,000 to 1,800 category

Herfindahl Index
Measures the degree of concentration in an industry. It is equal to the sum of the squares of the market shares of each firm in the industry.

Firms	Market Share
A	15%
B	12
C	11
D	10
E	8
F	7
G	7
H	6
I	6
J	6
K	6
L	6

OLD METHOD: FOUR-FIRM CONCENTRATION RATIO
15% + 12% + 11% + 10% = 48%

NEW METHOD: HERFINDAHL INDEX
Square the market share of each firm and then add:
$(15)^2 + (12)^2 + (11)^2 + (10)^2 + (8)^2 + (7)^2 + (7)^2 + (6)^2 + (6)^2 + (6)^2 + (6)^2 + (6)^2 = 932$

economics 24/7

HOLLYWOOD

THOMAS EDISON AND HOLLYWOOD

Thomas Alva Edison was born in 1847 and died in 1931. In his 84 years of life, Edison was granted 1,093 patents. Almost everyone knows the role Edison played in the development of electric light and power, but not everyone knows the role he played in indirectly and unwittingly making Hollywood the film capital of the world.

Our story begins with an Edison invention—a machine called the kinetophonograph. The kinetophonograph showed a moving picture that was synchronized with a phonograph record. Later, Edison invented the kinetoscope, which was a device that allowed users to deposit a coin and watch a short motion picture through a small hole.

After inventing the kinetophonograph and kinetoscope, Edison went on to construct the first building that was used solely to make movies. A hole in the ceiling of the building allowed the sun to shine through and illuminate the stage. The entire building was on a set of tracks so that it could be moved around to follow the sun. The first film that Edison produced was a 15-minute movie called *The Great Train Robbery*. Over the years, he produced more than 2,000 short films.

There is some evidence that Edison and a few other people tried to gain complete control over the movie industry in its early days. Edison played a critical role in putting together

the Movie Trust, sometimes called the Edison Trust, a group of ten film producers and distributors. The Movie Trust reportedly tried to eliminate its competition. First, the Movie Trust entered into a contract with Eastman Kodak Company, which manufactured film, to sell film only to it. Second, the Movie Trust refused to lease or sell equipment to certain filmmakers and theater owners.

One of the independent movie producers whom the Movie Trust tried to run out of the industry was Carl Laemmie. Laemmie and some other movie producers decided to leave the East Coast where the Movie Trust had the greatest control over the industry. They went to the West Coast, specifically to southern California, to get away from the stranglehold the Movie Trust had over the industry on the East Coast. Others soon followed. The rush of independent filmmakers to southern California set the stage for the development of Hollywood as the film capital of the world. In 1917, the Movie Trust was dissolved by court order, but by then, the movie industry had a new home. Laemmie, for example, founded Universal Studios in Hollywood in 1912.

Would Hollywood be the film capital of the world had it not been for the Movie Trust? It is doubtful. Without the exclusionary and anticompetitive tactics of the Movie Trust, the film capital of the world would probably be on the East Coast of the United States, very likely in or near New York City.

or (2) the index rises by 50 points or more and the (premerger) index is initially in the greater than 1,800 category.

To illustrate, suppose 2 firms, *A* and *B,* want to merge. The market share of firm *A* is 20 percent, and the market share of firm *B* is 10 percent; together, these firms account for 30 percent of the market. We assume there are 7 other firms in the industry, and each has a 10 percent market share. The Herfindahl index in this industry is 1,200 ($20^2 + 10^2 + 10^2 + 10^2 + 10^2 + 10^2 + 10^2 + 10^2 + 10^2 = 1,200$).

If the merger is approved, there will be 8, not 9, firms. Moreover, the market share of the merged firm (*A* and *B* now form one firm) will be 30 percent. The Herfindahl index after the merger will be 1,600. In other words, there will be an increase of 400 points if the firms merge. With this substantial increase in the index, it is likely the proposed merger would be blocked.

INNOVATION AND CONCENTRATION RATIOS According to the 1999 *Economic Report of the President,* more than half of all productivity gains in the U.S. economy in the previous 50 years, as measured by output per labor hour, came from innovation and technical change. Because innovation and technical change are so important to our economic well-being, some economists argue that concentration ratios should not play so large a role in determining a merger's approval. The merger's effect on innovation should also be taken into account. There is some evidence that antitrust authorities are beginning to accept this line of thinking.

It used to be thought that small firms in highly competitive markets with many rivals had a stronger incentive to innovate than firms in markets where only a few firms existed and each firm had sizable market power. Increasingly, however, it is thought that these small competitive firms often face a greater risk of innovation than firms with substantial market power. And therefore, they innovate less.

To illustrate, consider a market with 100 firms, each of which supplies one-hundredth of the market. Suppose one of these firms invests heavily in research and develops a new product or process. It has to worry about any of its 99 rivals soon developing a similar innovation and therefore reducing the value of its innovation. On the other hand, if a firm is 1 of 4 firms and has substantial market power, it doesn't face as much "innovative risk." It has only 3, not 99, rivals to worry about. And of course, the less likely that competitors can make one's own innovations less valuable, the higher the expected return from innovating.

Today, antitrust authorities say that they consider the benefits of both competition and innovation when ruling on proposed mergers. On the one hand, increased competition lowers prices for consumers. On the other hand, monopoly power may yield more innovation. If it does, then the lower prices brought about through increased competition have to be weighed against the increased innovation that may come about through greater market concentration and monopoly power.

Antitrust and Mergers

There are three basic types of mergers.

1. A **horizontal merger** is a merger between firms that are selling similar products in the same market. For example, suppose both companies *A* and *B* produce cars. If the two companies combined under single ownership of control, it would be a horizontal merger.

2. A **vertical merger** is a merger between companies in the same industry but at different stages of the production process. Stated differently, a vertical merger occurs between companies where one buys (or sells) something from (to) the other. For example, suppose company *C*, which produces cars, buys tires from company *D*. If the two companies combined under single ownership of control, it would be a vertical merger.

3. A **conglomerate merger** is a merger between companies in different industries. For example, if company *E*, in the car industry, and company *F*, in the pharmaceutical industry, combined under single ownership of control, it would be a conglomerate merger.

Of the three types of mergers—vertical, horizontal, and conglomerate—the federal government looks most carefully at proposed horizontal mergers. The reason is that horizontal mergers are more likely (than vertical or conglomerate mergers) to change the degree of concentration, or competition, in an industry. For example, if General Motors

 Q&A *Does the Herfindahl index have an advantage over the four- and eight-firm concentration ratios?*

Yes. It provides information about the dispersion of firm size in an industry. For example, the Herfindahl index will distinguish between these two situations: (1) 4 firms together have a 50 percent market share and there are only 4 other firms in the industry and (2) 4 firms together have a 50 percent market share and there are 150 other firms in the industry.

Of course, both the Herfindahl index and the four- and eight-firm concentration ratios have been criticized for implicitly arguing from firm size to market power. Both assume firms that have large market shares have market power that they are likely to be abusing. But of course, size could be a function of efficiency, and a firm with a large market share could be serving the buying public well.

Thinking like AN ECONOMIST *Suppose we observe that a firm has a large share of the market. The economist will ask, "Is there only one possible explanation for this, or are there many?" If there are many, then the economist will try to find out which one is the correct explanation. Think of an analogy. Suppose someone gets the highest grade in three of three courses. Is there more than one explanation for this? Yes, there is. The person could be studying more than anyone else. Or the person could be innately smarter than anyone else. Or the person could be cheating. The economist knows that there are usually different roads that end up at the same destination. Trying to figure out which road was taken to the destination is part of the task economists set for themselves.*

Horizontal Merger

A merger between firms that are selling similar products in the same market.

Vertical Merger

A merger between companies in the same industry but at different stages of the production process.

Conglomerate Merger

A merger between companies in different industries.

(cars) and Ford Motor Company (cars) horizontally merge, competition in the car industry is likely to decrease by more than if General Motors (cars) and BF Goodrich (tires) vertically merge. In the latter case, it is even possible that the competition among car companies, and among tire companies, will be the same after the merger as it was before. This is not necessarily the case, however, and the government does not always approve vertical mergers; in some notable examples, it has not.

Seven Antitrust Cases and Actions

Most people agree that the stated purpose of the antitrust laws—promoting and strengthening competition—is a worthwhile goal. Often, however, the stated purpose or objective of a policy and its effects turn out to be quite different. Some economists have argued that the antitrust laws have not, in all instances, accomplished their stated objective. The following cases and actions illustrate some of the ways that courts and government policymakers have approached antitrust cases over the years.

CASE 1: VON'S GROCERY In 1966, the U.S. Supreme Court ruled on the legality of a merger between Von's Grocery Co. and Shopping Bag Food Stores, both of Los Angeles. Together, the two grocery chains had a little more than 7 percent of the grocery market in the Los Angeles area. However, the Supreme Court ruled that a merger between the two companies violated the Clayton Act. The Court based its ruling largely on the fact that between 1950 and the early 1960s, the number of small grocery stores in Los Angeles had declined sharply. The Court took this as an indication of increased concentration in the industry.

Economists are quick to point out that the number of firms in an industry might be falling due to technological changes, and when this happens, the average size of an existing firm rises. Justice Potter Stewart, in a dissenting opinion to the 1966 decision, argued that the Court had erroneously assumed that the "degree of competition is invariably proportional to the number of competitors."

CASE 2: UTAH PIE In 1967, the Utah Pie Company, which was based in Salt Lake City, charged that three of its competitors in Los Angeles were practicing price discrimination. Utah Pie charged that these companies were selling pies in Salt Lake City for lower prices than they were selling pies near their plants of operation. The Supreme Court ruled in favor of Utah Pie.

Some economists note, though, that Utah Pie charged lower prices for its pies than did its competitors and that it continued to increase its sales volume and make a profit during the time its competitors were supposedly exhibiting anticompetitive behavior. They suggest that Utah Pie was using the antitrust laws to hinder its competition.

CASE 3: CONTINENTAL AIRLINES In 1978, Continental Airlines set out to acquire National Airlines. The Justice Department opposed the merger of the two companies on the grounds that the merged company would dominate the New Orleans air-traffic market. The Civil Aeronautics Board (CAB) did not oppose the merger because it believed the market under consideration was contestable. Recall that firms in a contestable market that operate inefficiently or that consistently earn positive economic profits will be joined by competing firms. By refusing to oppose the merger, the CAB implied that it believed that statistical measures, such as concentration ratios, mean less than whether the market is contestable.

CASE 4: IBM In 1969, the Justice Department filed antitrust charges against IBM, saying that it had monopolized the "general-purpose computer and peripheral-equipment" industry. IBM argued that the antitrust authorities had interpreted its market too narrowly.

economics 24/7

HIGH-PRICED INK CARTRIDGES AND EXPENSIVE MINI-BARS

You want to buy a printer for your computer. You see one priced at $69. That's a good price you say, so you buy it. Later, you learn that you have to pay $33 for an ink cartridge. The printer wasn't so well-priced after all, you think.

You spend the night at a hotel. Once in your room, you open the mini-bar and look around. You decide to eat a small bag of almonds. You learn later, after looking at your bill, that the small bag of almonds came with the big price of $6.

You sign up with a cell phone company. You decide on a plan; you get a cell phone for free. Later, you learn that for every minute you go over your allotted monthly number of minutes, you pay 33 cents.

Because of these everyday occurrences, some economists today are talking about the "hidden fee" economy—an economy in which many main items for sale (printer, hotel room, cell phone service) have attached to them certain hidden (high) fees—fees you did not expect when you purchased the main item.

So, why the hidden fees? According to two economists, David Laibson and Xavier Gabaix, it is because there are certain benefits (firms reap) through hidden fees. There are certain costs, too, but sometimes the benefits are greater than the costs.

To illustrate why a seller may use hidden fees, consider the following example.[1] Suppose there are two similar hotels, X and Y. Hotel X rents its rooms for $80 a night. It also has some hidden fees: $12 for parking, $6 for a small bag of almonds from the mini-bar, and $3 for a local call.

Hotel Y rents its rooms for $95 a night and it has no hidden high fees. It does not charge for parking nor for a local call and the small bag of almonds comes at the same price one could buy it at a grocery store.

What are the major differences between the two hotels? When it comes to the price of a room, Hotel X is cheaper than Hotel Y. When it comes to hidden and unexpectedly high fees, Hotel X is a culprit and Hotel Y is not.

The natural question that arises is: Why doesn't Hotel Y simply advertise the fact that its competitor, Hotel X, is trying to "dupe its customers" by charging high hidden fees? (The ad might read: "Sure, Hotel X has cheaper rooms, but what about all the hidden fees?") According to Laibon and

Gabaix, it's because that strategy could backfire. It backfires because of one of the two types of customers that frequent Hotel X.

One type of customer is somewhat clueless to the hidden fees and initially responds to the lower room rate of Hotel X. With this customer, the ad campaign by Hotel Y (pointing out the hidden fees of Hotel X) will be successful. But another type of customer is sophisticated when it comes to sellers' tactics. The sophisticated customer realizes that if she doesn't park at Hotel X, doesn't purchase anything from the mini-bar in her room, and makes calls on her cell phone instead of on the hotel telephone, she can then get a lower-priced room at Hotel X than Y. The ad by Hotel Y simply notifies the sophisticated customer that she can get a good deal at the hotel with the hidden fees—assuming she doesn't purchase the goods or services that come with the high hidden fees.

Simply put, Hotel Y gains and loses with its ad pointing out the high hidden fees of Hotel X. It gains the clueless customers ("thanks for telling me about those hidden fees") but it may end up losing some sophisticated customers ("thanks for telling me about the lower-priced rooms your competitor is offering"). If it thinks it will lose more sophisticated customers than it will gain clueless customers, it will not run the ad. Instead, it may simply join the ranks of hotels like Hotel X and lower its room rate and increase the use of high hidden fees.

But there is something else to consider. Barry Nalebuff, a professor of business strategy, has noted that there is a cost to a firm that charges hidden fees. That cost comes in the form of customers getting angry at the hidden fees. And angry customers, Nalebuff says, often turn their backs on sellers they are angry with. In other words, they seek out other (perhaps more up front and straightforward) sellers to buy from.

In the end, it becomes a matter of a seller having to consider both the benefits and the costs of a hidden fees strategy. Perhaps initially the benefits outweigh the costs, but there is no guarantee that in time the costs won't rise above the benefits.

---

[1] The source of the material in this feature (and the example) is "The Hidden Economy" by Christopher Shea, *The Boston Globe,* June 27, 2006.

© KEVIN FLEMING/CORBIS

After 13 years of litigation against IBM, the government decided to drop the suit. During the years of litigation, the computer market had changed. New competitors had entered the broadly defined computer market. Although IBM might have once dominated the mainframe computer industry, there was little evidence that it dominated the minicomputer, word processor, or computer-services markets.

CASE 5: UNIVERSITIES For many years, the upper level administrators of some of the country's top universities—Brown, Columbia, Cornell, Dartmouth, Harvard, MIT, Princeton, the University of Pennsylvania, and Yale—met to discuss such things as tuition, faculty salaries, and financial aid. There seemed to be evidence that these meetings occurred because the universities were trying to align tuition, faculty raises, and financial need. For example, one of the universities once wanted to raise faculty salaries by more than the others wanted and was persuaded not to do so. At these meetings, the administrators also compared lists of applicants to find the names of students who had applied to more than one of their schools (e.g., someone might have applied to Harvard, Yale, and MIT). Then, the administrators adjusted their financial aid packages for that student so that no university was offering more than another.

The Justice Department charged the universities with a conspiracy to fix prices. Eight of the universities settled the case by agreeing to sign a consent decree to cease colluding on tuition, salaries, and financial aid. MIT did not agree to sign the consent decree and pursued the case to the Supreme Court. In 1992, the Supreme Court ruled against MIT, saying that it had violated antitrust laws.

CASE 6: LOCKHEED MARTIN AND NORTHROP GRUMMAN In 1997, Lockheed Martin Corporation proposed to acquire Northrop Grumman Corporation. Both Lockheed and Northrop were leading suppliers of aircraft and electronics systems to the U.S. military. The Justice Department challenged the acquisition, saying that it would give Lockheed a monopoly in fiberoptic-towed decoys and in systems for airborne early warning radar. In this case, the issue of innovation played a major role. The Justice Department noted that both Lockheed and Northrop had invested heavily in the research and development of advanced airborne early warning radar systems. If the two companies merged, research and development activities would decline, and innovation would be hampered. The Justice Department blocked the acquisition of Northrop by Lockheed.

CASE 7: BOEING AND MCDONNELL DOUGLAS In 1997, the Federal Trade Commission approved the merger of Boeing Co. and McDonnell Douglas Corp., the two largest commercial aircraft manufacturers in the United States. Innovation was an issue in the Boeing–McDonnell Douglas case, just as it was in the Lockheed Martin–Northrop Grumman case. However, innovation played a different role in this case. The FTC approved the merger to *increase* innovation. The FTC's analysis showed that McDonnell Douglas had fallen behind technologically and was no longer applying competitive innovative pressure on Boeing. The FTC felt that because McDonnell Douglas was not stimulating innovation in the aircraft manufacturing market, nothing would be lost from the standpoint of innovation in allowing the two firms to merge. In fact, something might be gained. McDonnell Douglas's assets might be put to better use by a technologically advanced company like Boeing.

Network Monopolies

A network connects things. For example, a telephone network connects telephones, the Internet (which is a network of networks) connects computers, and a bank network may connect automated teller machines (ATMs). A **network good** is a good whose value increases as the expected number of units sold increases. A telephone is a network good. You buy a telephone to network with other people. It has little value to you if you expect only 100 people to buy telephones. Its value increases if you expect thousands of people to buy telephones.

Software is also a network good in the sense that if Smith buys software X and Jones also buys software X, they can then easily exchange documents with each other. As new buyers buy a network good, present owners of the good receive greater benefits because the network connects them to more people. For example, if Brown and Thompson also buy software X, Smith and Jones will receive greater benefits because they can exchange documents with two more people.

Let's see how the production and sales of a network good can lead to monopoly. Suppose three companies, A, B, and C, make some version of network good X. Company A makes the most popular version of good X, or has the greatest "network worthiness" linked to its good. Consequently, people who are thinking of buying good X buy it from company A. As more people purchase good X from company A, the "network worthiness" increases even more. This prompts even more people to buy good X from company A rather than to buy it from the other two companies. Eventually, the customers of companies B and C may switch to company A, and at some point, almost everyone buys good X from company A. Company A is a network monopoly.

ANTITRUST POLICY FOR NETWORK MONOPOLIES Currently, the antitrust authorities move against a network monopoly based on how it behaves, not because of what it is. For example, the authorities would not issue a complaint against company A in our example unless it undertook predatory or exclusionary practices to *maintain* its monopoly position.

INNOVATION IN NETWORK MONOPOLIES Recall that economists are still undecided as to whether market share assists or detracts from innovation. For example, it was argued that 1 firm among 4 firms may have less "innovative risk" than 1 firm among 100 firms. Therefore, the firm with a larger market share would innovate more, *ceteris paribus*. Presumably, a network monopoly will have a large market share and therefore should be a major innovator. But actually, the situation may be different for network monopolies because high switching costs sometimes accompany a network monopoly.

To illustrate, suppose firm A produces network good A. Network good A begins to sell quite well. Because it is a network good, its robust sales increase the value of the good to potential customers. Potential customers turn into actual customers, and before long, good A has set the market, or industry, standard.

Because network good A is now the industry standard and because network goods (especially those related to the high-tech industries) are sometimes difficult to learn, it may have a "lock" on the market. Specifically, there is a **lock-in effect** that increases the costs of switching from good A to another good. Because of the (relatively) high switching costs, good A has some staying power in the market. Firm A, the producer of good A, thus has staying power too. This may cause firm A to rest on its laurels, so to speak. Instead of innovating, instead of trying to outcompete its existing and future rivals with better production processes or better products, it may do very little. Firm A will realize that the high switching costs keep customers from changing to a different network good. Some economists suggest that in this environment, the network monopoly may have little reason to innovate.

Network Good
A good whose value increases as the expected number of units sold increases.

Lock-In Effect
Descriptive of the situation where a particular product or technology becomes settled upon as the standard and is difficult or impossible to dislodge as the standard.

Civil Action No. 98-1232

On May 18, 1998, the U.S. Department of Justice joined with 20 states and issued a civil action complaint against Microsoft, Inc. The action claimed basis in Sections 1 and 2 of the Sherman Act. The complaint claimed that Microsoft possessed monopoly power in the market for personal computer operating systems. It stated that (1) Microsoft Windows is used on more than 80 percent of Intel-based PCs, and (2) there are high barriers to entry in the market for PC operating systems essentially because Microsoft Windows is a network good that is the industry standard.

The Justice Department claimed that Microsoft was using its dominance in the personal computer operating systems market not only to maintain monopoly power but also to gain dominance in the Internet browser market. The Justice Department claimed that Microsoft, which packaged its Internet browser with Windows, required computer manufacturers to agree, as a condition for receiving licenses to install Windows on their products, not to remove Microsoft's browser and not to allow a more prominent display of a rival browser. The Justice Department also claimed that Microsoft refused to display the icons of Internet service providers (ISPs) on the main Windows screen unless the ISPs would first agree to withhold information from their customers about non-Microsoft browsers.

In the antitrust case, Microsoft argued that it did not have a monopoly in the operating systems market. It stated that it was part of a cutthroat software industry where today's industry leaders could go out of business tomorrow. It essentially argued that none of its business practices hurt any consumers and that all were necessary to its survival. Microsoft claimed that if it was guilty of anything, it was guilty of charging prices that were too low. It charged nothing, for example, for its Internet browser. Furthermore, Microsoft said that the addition of its browser to Windows was not an attempt to monopolize anything; it was an attempt to provide the buying public with a better product. In short, the browser was simply a new feature of Windows and not an illegal tie-in that violated a consent degree that Microsoft had signed in 1995.

Some economists contended that Microsoft's low pricing strategy made sense. They argued that it approximated marginal cost pricing. After all, software, once written, costs very little for each additional copy. Also, low prices are simply a way to sell a lot of copies. And what is wrong with that?

Critics contended that the low prices to gain customers worked to Microsoft's advantage because its operating system was a network good. Low prices mean more customers, and more customers mean Microsoft would eventually become the industry standard. Once there, it would wield its market power to maintain its current position and would try to establish itself as a monopolist in other markets (such as the browser market).

On Friday, November 4, 1999, Judge Thomas Penfield Jackson, the judge who heard the case against Microsoft, issued his findings of fact. Findings of fact simply present the facts of the case as the judge sees them; it does not constitute a ruling in the case. (The ruling was to come later.) In his findings of fact, Judge Jackson essentially agreed with the case the Justice Department made against Microsoft. He said that Microsoft is not only a monopolist in the operating systems market but also that it used its monopoly power to thwart competition. Specifically, it tied its operating system (Windows) together with its browser (Internet Explorer) not for purposes of efficiency and not to satisfy consumers but to establish a monopoly position in the browser market and to preserve its monopoly position in the operating systems market.

Before issuing his final judgment in the case, Judge Jackson appointed Judge Richard Posner, chief of the 7th U.S. Circuit of Appeals, to try to mediate a settlement between the government and Microsoft. After a few months, mediation talks broke down. There was to be no settlement between the two parties.

On Monday, April 3, 2000, Judge Jackson issued a ruling in the case. He ruled that Microsoft had violated the Sherman Act. The judge wrote that Microsoft was guilty of "unlawfully tying its Web browser" to Windows. He continued by saying that "Microsoft's anticompetitive actions trammeled the competitive process through which the computer software industry generally stimulates innovation."

On July 7, 2000, Judge Jackson issued his final ruling in the case. He ordered that Microsoft be split into two companies: one for operating systems and one for applications. Bill Gates said that Microsoft would appeal the ruling to a higher court.

The U.S. Court of Appeals heard the case months later. On June 28, 2001, the U.S. Court of Appeals reversed Judge Jackson's order to break up Microsoft, but it agreed with some of the judge's findings—specifically, that Microsoft had broken federal antitrust law. The appeals court sent the Microsoft case back to a lower court but this time to a different judge.

The new judge, U.S. District Judge Colleen Kollar-Kotelly, ordered both Microsoft and the Justice Department to set out the key issues in the case and determine how it might proceed. Before Judge Kollar-Kotelly issued a decision in the case, Microsoft and the Justice Department announced on November 2, 2001, that they had reached a settlement that would end the case. Under the settlement, Microsoft would make portions of its Windows software code available to competitors and Microsoft would allow computer manufacturers to choose the products they would load onto their machines without the threat of any retaliation from Microsoft. As of this writing, the plaintiffs in the case and the defendant (Microsoft) periodically file joint status reports on Microsoft's compliance with the final judgment. These reports can be found at the U.S. Department of Justice Web site (http://www.usdoj.gov).

SELF-TEST

(Answers to Self-Test questions are in the Self-Test Appendix.)

1. Why does it matter whether a market is defined broadly or narrowly for purposes of antitrust policy?

2. Suppose there are 20 firms in an industry and each firm has a 5 percent market share. What is the four-firm concentration ratio for this industry? What is the Herfindahl index?

3. What is the advantage of the Herfindahl index over the four- and eight-firm concentration ratios? Explain your answer.

Regulation

This section examines the types of regulation, theories of regulation, the stated objectives of regulatory agencies, and the effects of regulation on natural and other monopolies.

The Case of Natural Monopoly

In an earlier chapter, we noted that if economies of scale are so pronounced or large in an industry that only one firm can survive, that firm is a *natural monopoly*. Firms that supply local electricity, gas, and water service are usually considered natural monopolies.

Let's consider the situation in Exhibit 2. There is one firm in the market, and it produces Q_1 units of output at an average total cost of ATC_1. (Q_1 is the output at which $MR = MC$; to simplify the diagram, the MR curve is not shown.) At Q_1, there is an inefficient allocation of resources. Resource allocative efficiency exists when the marginal benefit to demanders of the resources used in the goods they buy equals the marginal cost to suppliers of the resources used in the production of the goods they sell. In Exhibit 2, resource allocative efficiency exists at Q_2, corresponding to the point where the demand curve intersects the MC curve.

exhibit **2**

The Natural Monopoly Situation

The only existing firm produces Q_1 at an average total cost of ATC_1. (Q_1 is the output at which $MR = MC$; to simplify the diagram, the MR curve is not shown.) Resource allocative efficiency exists at Q_2. There are two ways to obtain this output level: (1) The only existing firm can increase its production to Q_2, or (2) a new firm can enter the market and produce Q_3, which is the difference between Q_2 and Q_1. The first way minimizes total cost; the second way does not. This, then, is a natural monopoly situation: One firm can supply the entire output demanded at a lower cost than two or more firms can.

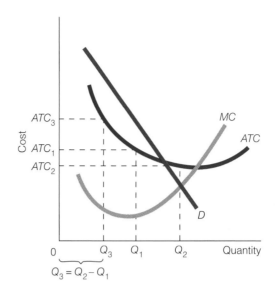

![Q&A] **In many towns, the local gas company is considered a natural monopoly; local government officials argue that no other firm can successfully compete with it (it can produce gas at a lower average total cost than all other firms, therefore outcompeting them). Furthermore, the government officials prohibit other firms from even trying to compete with the gas company.**

But why does the government need to prohibit other firms from competing with the local gas company? If the gas company really is a natural monopolist, it can outcompete all newcomers. Why does it need government protection from the competitors it can outcompete?

One answer is that government isn't so much protecting the natural monopolist from competition as it is protecting the public from inefficient entry into the natural monopoly setting. According to this argument, if new firms are permitted to enter a natural monopoly setting to compete against the natural monopolist, they will be outcompeted, leave the industry, and the resources they used to enter the industry will have been wasted. The situation is analogous to preventing a 135-pound weakling from getting into the boxing ring with a 250-pound professional boxer. If you know the 135-pound weakling is going to lose anyway, it may be better (some say) to prevent him from wasting his time trying to do something he can't possibly do.

Other economists do not accept this argument. They point out that we don't protect the public from "inefficient entry" in other market structures, and therefore, we should not do so here. In addition, they sometimes note, it is difficult to know for certain if a particular firm's entry into an industry will turn out to waste resources or not.

There are two ways to reach the higher, efficient quantity of output, Q_2: (1) The firm currently producing Q_1 could increase its output to Q_2. (2) Another firm could enter the market and produce Q_3—the difference between Q_2 and Q_1.

Different costs are associated with each way. If the firm currently in the market increases its production to Q_2, it incurs average total costs of ATC_2. If, instead, a new firm enters the market and produces Q_3, it incurs an average total cost of ATC_3. In this way, both firms together produce Q_2, but the new firm incurs average total costs of ATC_3, while the existing firm incurs average total costs of ATC_1.

As long as the objective is to increase output to the level of resource allocative efficiency, it is cheaper (lower total costs) to have the firm currently in the market increase its output to Q_2 than to have two firms together produce Q_2. So the situation in Exhibit 2 describes a natural monopoly situation. *Natural monopoly* exists when one firm can supply the entire output demanded at lower cost than two or more firms can. It is a natural monopoly because a monopoly situation will naturally evolve over time as the low-cost producer undercuts its competitors.

Will the natural monopolist charge the monopoly price? Some economists say yes. See Exhibit 3, where the natural monopoly firm produces Q_1, at which marginal revenue equals marginal cost, and charges price P_1, which is the highest price per unit consistent with the output it produces.

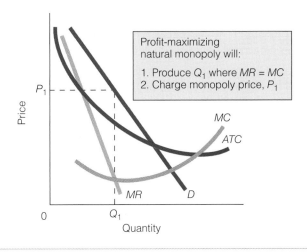

Because it charges the monopoly price, some people argue that the natural monopoly firm should be regulated. What form should the regulation take? This question is addressed in the next section.

Regulating the Natural Monopoly

The natural monopoly may be regulated through price, profit, or output regulation.

1. **Price regulation.** Marginal cost pricing is one form of price regulation. The objective is to set a price for the natural monopoly firm that equals its marginal cost at the quantity of output at which demand intersects marginal cost. In Exhibit 4, this price is P_1. At this price, the natural monopoly takes a loss. At Q_1, average total

cost is greater than price, and thus, total cost is greater than total revenue.[2] Obviously, the natural monopoly would rather go out of business than be subject to this type of regulation unless it receives a subsidy for its operation.

2. **Profit regulation.** Government may want the natural monopoly to earn only zero economic profits. If so, government will require the natural monopoly to charge a price of P_2 (because $P_2 = ATC$) and to supply the quantity demanded at that price (Q_2). This form of regulation is often called *average cost pricing*. Theoretically, this may seem like a good way to proceed, but in practice, it often turns out differently. The problem is that if the natural monopoly is always held to zero economic profits—and is not allowed to fall below or rise above this level—then it has an incentive to let costs rise. Higher costs—in the form of higher salaries or more luxurious offices—simply mean higher prices to cover the higher costs. In this case, it is unlikely that average cost pricing is an efficient way to proceed.

3. **Output regulation.** Government can mandate a quantity of output it wants the natural monopoly to produce. Suppose this is Q_3 in Exhibit 4. Here, there are positive economic profits because price is above average total cost at Q_3. It is possible, however, that the natural monopoly would want even higher profits. At a fixed quantity of output, this can be obtained by lowering costs. The natural monopolist might lower costs by reducing the quality of the good or service it sells, knowing that it faces no direct competition and that it is protected (by government) from competitors.

Regulation of a natural monopoly does not always turn out the way it was intended. Government regulation of a natural monopoly—whether it takes the form of price, profit, or output regulation—can distort the incentives of those who operate the natural monopoly. For example, if profit is regulated to the extent that zero economic profits are guaranteed, then the natural monopoly has little incentive to hold costs down. Furthermore, the owners of the natural monopoly have an incentive to try to influence the government officials or other persons who are regulating the natural monopoly.

In addition, each of the three types of regulation requires information. For example, if the government wishes to set price equal to marginal cost or average total cost for the natural monopoly, it must know the cost conditions of the firm.

Three problems arise in gathering information: (1) The cost information is not easy to determine, even for the natural monopoly itself. (2) The cost information can be rigged (to a degree) by the natural monopoly, and therefore, the regulators will not get a true picture of the firm. (3) The regulators have little incentive to obtain accurate information because they are likely to keep their jobs and prestige even if they work with less-than-accurate information. (This raises a question: Who will ensure that the regulators do a good job?)

Finally, there is the issue of *regulatory lag,* which is indirectly related to information. **Regulatory lag** refers to the time period between when a natural monopoly's costs change and when the regulatory agency adjusts prices for the natural monopoly. For example, suppose the rates your local gas company charges customers are regulated. The gas company's costs rise, and it seeks a rate hike through the local regulatory body. The rate hike is not likely to be approved quickly. The gas company will probably have to submit an application for a rate hike, document its case, have a date set for a hearing, argue its case at the hearing, and then wait for the regulatory agency to decide on the merits of the application. Many months may pass between the beginning of the process and the end. During that time, the regulated firm is operating in ways and under conditions that both the firm and the regulatory body might not have desired.

Regulatory Lag

The time period between when a natural monopoly's costs change and when the regulatory agency adjusts prices for the natural monopoly.

---

[2]Remember that $TC = ATC \times Q$ and $TR = P \times Q$. Here $ATC > P$, so it follows that $TC > TR$.

Regulating Industries That Are Not Natural Monopolies

Some firms are regulated even though they are not natural monopolies. For instance, in the past, government has regulated both the airline and trucking industries. In the trucking industry, the Interstate Commerce Commission (ICC) fixed routes, set minimum freight rates, and erected barriers to entry. In the airline industry, the Civil Aeronautics Board (CAB) did much the same thing. Some economists view the regulation of competitive industries as unnecessary. They see it as evidence that the firms being regulated are controlling the regulation to reduce their competition. We discuss this in greater detail next.

Theories of Regulation

The **capture theory of regulation** holds that no matter what the motive is for the initial regulation and the establishment of the regulatory agency, eventually, the agency will be "captured" (controlled) by the special interests of the industry being regulated. The following are a few of the interrelated points that have been put forth to support this theory:

1. In many cases, persons who have been in the industry are asked to regulate the industry because they know the most about it. Such regulators are likely to feel a bond with people in the industry, see their side of the story more often than not, and thus be inclined to cater to them.

2. At regulatory hearings, members of the industry attend in greater force than do taxpayers and consumers. The industry turns out in force because the regulatory hearing can affect it substantially and directly. In contrast, the effect on individual taxpayers and consumers is usually small and indirect (the effect is spread over millions of people). Thus, regulators are much more likely to hear and respond to the industry's side of the story.

3. Members of the regulated industry make a point of getting to know the members of the regulatory agency. They may talk frequently about business matters; perhaps they socialize. The bond between the two groups grows stronger over time. This may have an impact on regulatory measures.

4. After they either retire or quit their jobs, regulators often go to work for the industries they once regulated.

The capture theory is markedly different from what has come to be called the **public interest theory of regulation**. This theory holds that regulators are seeking to do, and will do through regulation, what is in the best interest of the public or society at large.

An alternative to both theories is the **public choice theory of regulation**. This theory suggests that to understand the decisions of regulatory bodies, we must first understand how the decisions affect the regulators themselves. For example, a regulation that increases the power of the regulators and the size and budget of the regulatory agency should not be viewed the same way as a regulation that decreases the agency's power and size. The theory predicts that the outcomes of the regulatory process will tend to favor the regulators instead of either business interests or the public.

Here, then, are three interesting, different, and at first sight, believable theories of regulation. Economists have directed much effort to testing the three theories. There is no clear consensus yet, but in the area of business regulation, the adherents of the capture and public choice theories have been increasing.

Thinking like
AN ECONOMIST

The public is perhaps naturally inclined to think that a solution (e.g., regulation) to a problem (e.g., monopoly) is better than no solution at all—that something is better than nothing. The economist has learned, though, that a "solution" can do one of three things: (1) solve a problem, (2) not solve a problem but do no damage, or (3) make the problem worse. Thinking in terms of the entire range of possibilities is natural for an economist, who, after all, understands that solutions come with both costs and benefits.

Capture Theory of Regulation

Holds that no matter what the motive is for the initial regulation and the establishment of the regulatory agency, eventually, the agency will be "captured" (controlled) by the special interests of the industry being regulated.

Public Interest Theory of Regulation

Holds that regulators are seeking to do, and will do through regulation, what is in the best interest of the public or society at large.

Public Choice Theory of Regulation

Holds that regulators are seeking to do, and will do through regulation, what is in their best interest (specifically to enhance their power and the size and budget of their regulatory agencies).

The Costs and Benefits of Regulation

Suppose a business firm is polluting the air with smoke from its factories. The government passes an environmental regulation requiring such firms to purchase antipollution devices that reduce the smoke emitted into the air.

What are the benefits of this kind of regulation? The obvious benefit is cleaner air. But cleaner air can lead to other benefits. For example, people may have fewer medical problems in the future. In some parts of the country, pollution from cars and factories causes people to cough, feel tired, and experience eye discomfort. More important, some people have chronic medical problems from constantly breathing dirty air. Government regulation that reduces the amount of pollution in the air clearly helps these people.

But regulation usually doesn't come with benefits only. It comes with costs too. For example, when a business firm incurs the cost of antipollution devices, its overall costs of production rise. Simply put, it is costlier for the business firm to produce its product after the regulation is imposed. As a result, the business firm may produce fewer units of its product, raising its product price and causing some workers to lose their jobs.

If you are the worker who loses your job, you may view the government's insistence that businesses install antipollution devices differently than if, say, you are the person suffering from chronic lung disease. If you have asthma, less pollution may be the difference between feeling well and feeling sick. If you are a worker for the business firm, less pollution may end up costing you your job. Ideally, you prefer a little less pollution in your neighborhood, but perhaps not at the cost of losing your job.

Are economists for or against government regulation of the type described? The answer is neither. The job of the economist is to make the point that regulation involves both benefits and costs. To the person who sees only the costs, the economist asks: But what about the benefits? And to the person who sees only the benefits, the economist asks: But what about the costs? Then, the economist goes on to outline the benefits and the costs as best she can.

Some Effects of Regulation Are Unintended

Besides outlining the benefits and costs of regulation, the economist tries to point out the unintended effects that can occur with regulation. To illustrate, consider the example concerning fuel standards. Suppose the government requires new cars to get an average of 40 miles per gallon of gasoline instead of, say, 30 miles per gallon. Many people will say that this is a good thing. They will reason that if car companies are made to produce cars that get better mileage, people will not need to buy and burn as much gasoline. When less gasoline is burned, less air pollution will be produced.

There is no guarantee the regulation will have this effect, though. The effects could be quite different. If cars are more fuel efficient, people will buy less gasoline to drive from one place to another—say, from home to college. This means that the (dollar) cost per mile of driving will fall. As a result of lower costs, people might begin to drive more. Leisure driving on the weekend might become more common, people might begin to drive farther on vacations, and so on. If people begin to drive more, then the gasoline saving that resulted from the higher fuel economy standards might be offset or even outweighed. And more gasoline consumption due to more driving will mean more gasoline will be burned and more pollutants will end up in the air.

Thus, a regulation requiring automakers to produce cars that get better fuel mileage may have an unintended effect. The net result might be that people purchase and burn more gasoline and thus produce more air pollution, not less as the government intended.

economics 24/7

"WHY AM I ALWAYS FLYING TO DALLAS?"

The shortest distance between two points is a straight line. Some say that the airline industry doesn't care much about straight lines (or obviously, about short distances). It cares about hubs and spokes.

Suppose you want to go from Phoenix to New York City. The shortest route is the direct route: Phoenix directly to New York. Very likely, however, you won't be able to get a direct flight. Often (but not always), you will be routed through Dallas or Chicago. In other words, you will get on the plane in Phoenix, get off the plane in Dallas, get on another plane in Dallas, fly to New York, and finally get off the plane in New York. This is referred to as the hub-and-spoke delivery system. The hub represents the center of an airline network; the spokes (much like the spokes on a bicycle wheel) represent origin and destination cities and are always linked through the hub.

The hub-and-spoke system has been used more often since airline deregulation. In several instances, airline departures from major hubs (e.g., Dallas and Chicago) have doubled. Most economists believe the increased use of the hub-and-spoke system, which makes average travel time longer, is the result of increased price competition brought on by deregulation.

After deregulation, airlines were under greater pressure to compete on price; thus, it became more important to cut costs. One way to cut costs is to use bigger planes because bigger planes cost less to operate per seat mile. But it takes more people to fill the bigger planes. To accomplish both objectives—flying bigger planes that are more fully occupied—the airlines began to gather passengers at one spot. Then at the hub, they could put more passengers on one plane and fly them to the same destination. For example, instead of flying people in Phoenix and people in Albuquerque directly but separately to New York, both groups of people are flown first to Dallas, and then the combined group is flown to New York.

This system may have benefits that offset the costs of inconvenience and longer travel time. Some people think it is better to pay lower airline ticket prices and reach one's destination a little later than to pay higher prices and get there sooner. They also maintain that increased use of the hub-and-spoke system has given passengers more options to travel on different airlines (in Dallas, numerous airlines can fly you to New York) at more convenient times (numerous flights leave Dallas every hour).

Deregulation

In the early 1970s, many economists, basing their arguments on the capture and public choice theories of regulation, argued that regulation was actually promoting and protecting market power instead of reducing it. They argued for deregulation. And since the late 1970s, many industries have been deregulated, including airlines, trucking, long-distance telephone service, and more.

Consider a few details that relate to the deregulation of the airline industry. The Civil Aeronautics Act, which was passed in 1938, gave the Civil Aeronautics Authority (CAA) the authority to regulate airfares, the number of carriers on interstate routes, and the pattern of routes. The CAA's successor, the Civil Aeronautics Board (CAB), regulated fares in such a way that major air carriers could meet their average costs. An effect of this policy was that fares were raised so high-cost, inefficient air carriers could survive. In addition, the CAB did not allow price competition between air carriers. As a result, air carriers usually competed in a nonprice dimension: They offered more scheduled flights, better meals, more popular in-flight movies, and so forth.

In 1978, under CAB Chairman Alfred Kahn, an economist, the airline industry was deregulated. With deregulation, airlines can compete on fares, initiate service along a new route, or discontinue a route. Empirical research after deregulation showed that passenger miles increased and fares decreased. For example, in 1978, fares fell 20 percent, and between 1979 and 1984, fares fell approximately 14 percent.

Deregulation has also led to a decline in costs in various industries. For example, a recent study by Clifford Winston of the Brookings Institution shows that since deregulation, costs in the airline industry have fallen 24 percent (per unit of output); in trucking, operating costs have fallen 30–35 percent per mile; in railroads, there has been a 50 percent decline in costs per ton-mile and a 141 percent increase in productivity; and in natural gas, there has been a 35 percent decline in operating and maintenance expenses.

SELF-TEST

1. What is a criticism of average cost pricing?

2. State the essence of the capture theory of regulation.

3. What is the difference between the capture theory and the public choice theory of regulation?

4. Are economists for or against regulation?

𝒜 𝑅𝑒𝑎𝑑𝑒𝑟 𝒜𝑠𝑘𝑠 . . .

Do Auction Houses Engage in Price Fixing?

Not too long ago, I read that the two major auction houses, Sotheby's and Christie's, were engaged in price fixing. What were the details?

Sotheby's (founded in 1744) and Christie's (founded in 1766) are the two biggest auction houses in the world. In 1983, A. Alfred Taubman, a Michigan shopping-mall magnate, bought Sotheby's (some say for his wife as a wedding present). In 1994, Taubman appointed Diana Brooks president and CEO of Sotheby's. In 1997, the U.S. Justice Department began investigating possible collusion between Sotheby's and Christie's to fix the prices people paid to have their items auctioned.

Under American law, accused conspirators are encouraged to confess and to name others involved in the conspiracy. In fact, the first party to do this is given leniency. Christopher Davidge, the president and CEO of Christie's, came forth and turned over papers describing the price-fixing arrangement with Sotheby's.

According to Diana Brooks, who pleaded guilty to the charge, she had been ordered by Taubman to enter into the illegal collusive agreement with Christie's. Taubman claimed that Brooks was lying. Taubman's spokesman declared, "We believe that Mrs. Brooks is lying to save her skin and that she has a clear motivation for doing so."

On April 23, 2002, A. Alfred Taubman was sentenced to a year and a day in prison and fined $7.5 million for leading a 6-year price-fixing scheme with Sotheby's chief competitor, Christie's, that is said to have swindled more than $100 million from their customers. In handing down the sentence, the judge said, "Price fixing is a crime whether it's committed in the grocery store or the halls of a great auction house."

! analyzing the scene

What does AIDS have to do with antitrust?

Differences of opinion often surface in antitrust issues. To illustrate, some people argue that patent laws are necessary to stimulate innovation. Someone might argue that a pharmaceutical company will not spend millions of dollars in research on a new drug unless it will be the only company (for a period of years) permitted to sell the drug. Why spend the money to develop the drug if once it is developed and marketed, another company can copy the drug and sell it?

Now consider that AIDS is a major medical problem in some countries. Many of these are relatively poor countries. This means that many of the individuals in the poor countries who have AIDS will not be able to purchase the best AIDS treatment that exists—which costs approximately $12,000 a year today in the United States. Along comes Cipla, an Indian pharmaceutical company. Cipla has developed a generic for the best AIDS treatment possible, and the company sells its generic for approximately $300 a year. The Malaysian government recently issued a compulsory license to Cipla, which means Cipla can sell its generic AIDS treatment in Malaysia. Some argue that this situation constitutes an antitrust issue. If the original manufacturers of the AIDS treatment (U.S. firms) are not protected from "copycats," then they will no longer have so strong an incentive to spend the money necessary to develop effective drugs—for AIDS or anything else. On the other hand, without the "copycat drugs" (without the generics), no doubt some people will die. One alternative, which is sometimes adopted, is for the country that issues the compulsory license to pay the original manufacturers some royalty rate.

At what level of government are antitrust and regulatory issues best addressed?

In December 2003, the Ford Motor Company paid $52 million to resolve claims that it had misled consumers about the safety of its sports utility vehicles. Instead of settling with federal authorities, it settled with 50 state attorneys general. When Household International paid out $484 million to settle allegations of predatory mortgage lending, it settled with the states. In recent years, the question has been asked: Should antitrust and regulatory issues be dealt with at (1) only the federal level, (2) only the state level, or (3) both the federal

and state levels? State attorneys general often comment that they move in when the federal authorities are negligent. They argue that they fill a void left by federal regulators and politicians who are too often swayed by big business. Critics point out that if both federal and state authorities can launch antitrust and regulatory actions against companies, then the cost of doing business will unnecessarily escalate.

What are the arguments for and against outlawing smoking in Irish pubs?

When issues of regulation are raised, the discussion often turns to who has the right to regulate what. Not long ago, an Irish law was passed that banned smoking in public places, such as restaurants and pubs. Critics of the law often remarked that the restaurant or pub owner is the right person to decide on regulations within his or her environment. If the pub owner wants a smoking pub, then so be it; if he wants a non-smoking pub, so be that too. In the end, customers will go to the pubs they most want to frequent. Others argue differently, saying that no one should have to breathe in cigarette or cigar smoke if he or she doesn't want to. In other words, it is fine to smoke, as long as I am not harmed by your smoke.

Would businesses ever ask for government regulation?

According to the capture theory of regulation, businesses seek to control government regulatory agencies. That is, a business seeks to "pull the strings" of its regulatory agency so that the agency advances the policies that the business wants. Think back to the discussion of cartels in the last chapter. Business firms may want to form a cartel and raise prices, but cheating among them prevents them from doing so. Now suppose the business firms can get a government regulatory agency to do for them what they can't do for themselves. A government regulatory agency has the power to prevent business firms from competing on prices. For example, when airlines in the United States were regulated, the price of an airline ticket from Los Angeles to New York was the same no matter what airline you traveled on. At that time, the airlines were effectively prevented (by government) from competing on price. When the airlines were deregulated, they began to compete on price—and ticket prices fell.

chapter summary

Dealing with Monopoly Power

- A monopoly produces less than a perfectly competitive firm produces (assuming the same revenue and cost conditions), charges a higher price, and causes a deadweight loss. This is the monopoly power problem, and solving it is usually put forth as a reason for antitrust laws and/or government regulatory actions. Some economists note, though, that government antitrust and regulatory actions do not always have the intended effect. In addition, they are sometimes implemented when there is no monopoly power problem to solve.

Antitrust Laws

- Two major criticisms have been directed at the antitrust acts. First, some argue that the language in the laws is vague; for example, even though the words "restraint of trade" are used in the Sherman Act, the act does not clearly explain what actions constitute a restraint of trade. Second, it has been argued that some antitrust acts appear to hinder, rather than promote, competition; an example is the Robinson-Patman Act.

- There are a few unsettled points in antitrust policy. One centers on the proper definition of a market. Should a market be defined narrowly or broadly? How this question is answered will have an impact on which firms are considered monopolies. In addition, the use of concentration ratios for identifying monopolies or deciding whether to allow two firms to enter into a merger has been called into question. Recently, concentration ratios have been largely replaced (for purposes of implementing antitrust policy) with the Herfindahl index. This index is subject to some of the same criticisms as the concentration ratios. Antitrust authorities are also beginning to consider the benefits of innovation in ruling on proposed mergers.

Regulation

- Even if we assume that the intent of regulation is to serve the public interest, it does not follow that this will be accomplished. To work as desired, regulation must be based on complete information (e.g., the regulatory body must know the cost conditions of the regulated firm), and it must not distort incentives (e.g., to keep costs down). Many economists are quick to point out that neither condition is likely to be fully met. In itself, this does not mean that regulation should not be implemented but only that regulation may not have the expected effects.

- Government uses three basic types of regulation to regulate natural monopolies: price, profit, or output regulation. Price regulation usually means marginal cost price regulation—that is, setting $P = MC$. Profit regulation usually means zero economic profits. Output regulation specifies a particular quantity of output that the natural monopoly must produce.

- The capture theory of regulation holds that no matter what the motive is for the initial regulation and the establishment of the regulatory agency, eventually, the agency will be "captured" (controlled) by the special interests of the industry being regulated. The public interest theory holds that regulators are seeking to do, and will do through regulation, what is in the best interest of the public or society at large. The public choice theory holds that regulators are seeking to do, and will do through regulation, what is in their best interest (specifically, to enhance their power and the size and budget of their regulatory agencies).

key terms and concepts

Antitrust Law

Trust

Herfindahl Index

Horizontal Merger

Vertical Merger

Conglomerate Merger

Network Good

Lock-In Effect

Regulatory Lag

Capture Theory
   of Regulation

Public Interest Theory
   of Regulation

Public Choice Theory
   of Regulation

questions and problems

1 Why was the Robinson-Patman Act passed? the Wheeler-Lea Act? the Celler-Kefauver Antimerger Act?

2 Explain why defining a market narrowly or broadly can make a difference in how antitrust policy is implemented.

3 What is one difference between the four-firm concentration ratio and the Herfindahl index?

4 How does a vertical merger differ from a horizontal merger? Why would the government look more carefully at one than at the other?

5 What is the implication of saying that regulation is likely to affect incentives?

6 Explain price regulation, profit regulation, and output regulation.

7 Why might profit regulation lead to rising costs for the regulated firm?

8 What is the major difference between the capture theory of regulation and the public interest theory of regulation?

9 George Stigler and Claire Friedland studied both unregulated and regulated electric utilities and found no difference in the rates they charged. One could draw the conclusion that regulation is ineffective when it comes to utility rates. What ideas or hypotheses presented in this chapter might have predicted this result?

10 The courts have ruled that it is a reasonable restraint of trade (and therefore permissible) for the owner of a business to sell his business and sign a contract with the new owner saying he will not compete with her within a vicinity of, say, 100 miles, for a period of, say, 5 years. If this is a reasonable restraint of trade, can you give an example of what you would consider an unreasonable restraint of trade? Explain how you decide what is a reasonable restraint of trade and what isn't.

11 In your opinion, what is the best way to deal with the monopoly power problem? Do you advocate antitrust laws, regulation, or something not discussed in the chapter? Give reasons for your answer.

12 It is usually asserted that public utilities such as electric companies and gas companies are natural monopolies. But an assertion is not proof. How would you go about trying to prove (disprove) that electric companies and the like are (are not) natural monopolies? (Hint: You might consider comparing the average total cost of a public utility that serves many customers with the average total cost of a public utility that serves relatively few customers.)

13 Discuss the advantages and disadvantages of regulation (as you see it).

working with numbers and graphs

1 Calculate the Herfindahl index and the four-firm concentration ratio for the following industry:

Firms	Market Share
A	17%
B	15
C	14
D	14
E	12
F	10
G	9
H	9

Use the following figure to answer Questions 2–4.

2 Is the firm in the figure a natural monopoly? Explain your answer.

3 Will the firm in the figure earn profits if it produces Q_3 and charges P_3? Explain your answer.

4 Which quantity in the figure is consistent with profit regulation? with price regulation? Explain your answers.

Factor Markets: With Emphasis on the Labor Market

Setting the Scene

The following events occurred one day in May.

9:07 A.M.

Marion Smithies owns a small company that produces fans. Currently, she has 35 employees. She is thinking of hiring a few more workers but is unsure of the right number to hire. Are three too few? Are six too many? What is the right number?

1:03 P.M.

Jesse and Sid are having lunch together. Jesse comments, "I don't see how this country can compete any longer. Wages are so much lower in other countries."

"I know," agrees Sid. "What company is going to pay an employee $20 an hour when it can pay $3 an hour?"

Jesse sighs and shakes his head. "I think it's just a matter of time," he says, "until it's impossible to get a decent job here."

3:01 P.M.

Harry Masterson is reading a government report. It states that higher wages are likely to increase the number of hours workers want to work. A thought runs through Harry's mind: This has got to be wrong. I'd want to work fewer at higher wages. After all, at higher wages, I wouldn't need to work as much.

5:45 P.M.

Aaron Lawrence and his 13-year-old son, Damon, are at Yankee Stadium in New York watching the New York Yankees play the Boston Red Sox. The Yankees have two men on base and two outs. Alex Rodriguez, who bats next, is walking up to the plate. Aaron turns to his son and asks, "Do you know how much money Rodriguez is paid to play baseball?" His son says no. Aaron says, "$25 million a year." Then he adds, "That seems like a lot of money just to play baseball, doesn't it?" Damon nods in agreement.

? Here are some questions to keep in mind as you read this chapter:

- *What is the right number of employees to hire?*

- *Will jobs always flow to where wages are the lowest?*

- *Would you work more or less at higher wages?*

- *Is Alex Rodriguez paid too much?*

See analyzing the scene at the end of this chapter for answers to these questions.

Factor Markets

Just as there is a demand for and supply of a product, there is a demand for and a supply of a factor, or resource, such as the demand for and supply of labor.

The Demand for a Factor

Why do firms purchase factors? The answer is obvious: to produce products to sell. This is true for all firms, whether they are perfectly competitive firms, oligopolistic firms, or whatever. For example, farmers buy tractors and fertilizer to produce crops to sell. General Motors buys steel to build cars to sell.

Derived Demand

Demand that is the result of some other demand. For example, factor demand is the result of the demand for the products that the factors go to produce.

The demand for factors is a **derived demand**. It is derived from and directly related to the demand for the product that the resources go to produce. If the demand for the product rises, the demand for the factors used to produce the product rises. If the demand for the product falls, the demand for the factors used to produce the product falls. For example, if the demand for a university education falls, so does the demand for university professors. If the demand for computers rises, so does the demand for skilled computer workers.

When the demand for a seller's product rises, the seller needs to decide how much more of a factor it should buy. The concepts of marginal revenue product and marginal factor cost are relevant to this decision.

Theme **micro**

In an earlier chapter, we discussed a few questions that every business firm has to answer. One of those questions was, "How many units of a resource (or factor) should a firm buy?" That is the question we explicitly address in this chapter.

Marginal Revenue Product: Two Ways to Calculate It

Marginal Revenue Product (MRP)

The additional revenue generated by employing an additional factor unit.

Marginal revenue product (*MRP*) is the additional revenue generated by employing an additional factor unit. For example, if a firm employs one more unit of a factor and its total revenue rises by \$20, the *MRP* of the factor equals \$20. Marginal revenue product can be calculated in two ways:

$$MRP = \Delta TR/\Delta \text{Quantity of the factor}$$

or

$$MRP = MR \times MPP$$

where TR = total revenue, MR = marginal revenue, and MPP = marginal physical product. In Exhibit 1, we use data for a hypothetical firm to show the two methods for calculating *MRP*.

METHOD 1: *MRP* = $\Delta TR/\Delta$QUANTITY OF THE FACTOR Look at Exhibit 1(a). Column 1 shows the different quantities of factor X. Column 2 shows the quantity of output produced at the different quantities of factor X.

Column 3 lists the price and the marginal revenue of the product that the factor goes to produce. Notice that we have assumed the price of the product (P) equals the product's marginal revenue (MR). So we have assumed the seller in Exhibit 1 is a perfectly competitive firm. Recall that for a perfectly competitive firm, $P = MR$.

In column 4, we calculate the total revenue, or price multiplied by quantity. In column 5, we calculate the marginal revenue product (*MRP*) by dividing the change in total revenue (from column 4) by the change in the quantity of the factor.

(1) Quantity of Factor X	(2) Quantity of Output, Q	(3) Product Price, Marginal Revenue (P = MR)	(4) Total Revenue TR = P × Q = (3) × (2)	(5) Marginal Revenue Product of Factor X MRP = ΔTR/ΔQuantity of factor X = Δ(4)/Δ(1)
0	10★	$5	$ 50	—
1	19	5	95	$45
2	27	5	135	40
3	34	5	170	35
4	40	5	200	30
5	45	5	225	25

(a)

(1) Quantity of Factor X	(2) Quantity of Output, Q	(3) Marginal Physical Product MPP = Δ(2)/Δ(1)	(4) Product Price, Marginal Revenue (P = MR)	(5) Marginal Revenue Product of Factor X MRP = MR × MPP = (4) × (3)
0	10★	—	$5	—
1	19	9	5	$45
2	27	8	5	40
3	34	7	5	35
4	40	6	5	30
5	45	5	5	25

(b)

★Because the quantity of output is 10 at 0 units of factor X, other factors (not shown in the exhibit) must also be used to product the good.

exhibit **1**

Calculating Marginal Revenue Product (*MRP*)

There are two methods of calculating *MRP*. Part (a) shows one method (*MRP* = Δ*TR*/ΔQuantity of the factor), and (b) shows the other (*MRP* = *MR* × *MPP*).

METHOD 2: *MRP* = *MR* × *MPP* Now look at Exhibit 1(b). Columns 1 and 2 are the same as in Exhibit 1(a).

In column 3, we calculate the marginal physical product (*MPP*) of factor X. Recall (from an earlier chapter) that *MPP* is the change in the quantity of output divided by the change in the quantity of the factor.

Column 4 lists the price and marginal revenue of the product. Column 4 is the same as column 3 in part (a).

In column 5, we calculate the *MRP* by multiplying the marginal revenue (in column 4) by *MPP* (in column 3). The *MRP* figures in column 5 of (b) are the same as the *MRP* figures in column 5 of (a), showing that *MRP* can be calculated in two ways.

The *MRP* Curve Is the Firm's Factor Demand Curve

Look again at column 5 in Exhibit 1, which shows the *MRP* for factor X. By plotting the data in column 5 against the quantity of the factor (shown in column 1), we derive the *MRP* curve for factor X. This curve is the same as the firm's demand curve for factor X (or simply, the firm's factor demand curve) (see Exhibit 2).

MRP curve = Factor demand curve

Notice that the *MRP* curve in Exhibit 2 is downward sloping. You can understand why when you recall that *MRP* can be calculated as *MRP* = *MR* × *MPP*. What do you know about *MPP*, the marginal physical product of a factor? According to the law of

Value Marginal Product (VMP)

The price of the good multiplied by the marginal physical product of the factor: $VMP = P \times MPP$.

exhibit **2**

The MRP Curve Is the Firm's Factor Demand Curve

The data in columns (1) and (5) in Exhibit 1 are plotted to derive the MRP curve. The MRP curve shows the various quantities of the factor the firm is willing to buy at different prices, which is what a demand curve shows. The MRP curve is the firm's factor demand curve.

Thinking like **AN ECONOMIST** *As we have stated before, when decisions need to be made, it is customary to compare one thing to another. The decision before the firm is: How much of a factor or resource should it buy or hire? When making this decision, the firm will want to look at the additional benefits of hiring or buying one more unit of the factor against the additional costs of hiring or buying one more unit of the factor.*

Marginal Factor Cost (MFC)

The additional cost incurred by employing an additional factor unit.

Factor Price Taker

A firm that can buy all of a factor it wants at the equilibrium price. It faces a horizontal (flat, perfectly elastic) supply curve of factors.

diminishing marginal returns, eventually, the *MPP* of a factor will diminish. Because *MRP* is equal to *MR* × *MPP* and *MPP* will eventually decline, it follows that *MRP* will eventually decline too.

Value Marginal Product

Value marginal product (VMP) is equal to the price of the product multiplied by the marginal physical product of the factor:

$$VMP = P \times MPP$$

For example, if $P = \$10$ and $MPP = 9$ units, then $VMP = \$90$. Think of *VMP* as a measure of the value that each factor unit adds to the firm's product. Or you can think of it simply as "*MPP* measured in dollars."

A firm wants to know the *VMP* of a factor because it helps the firm decide how many units of the factor to hire. To illustrate, put yourself in the shoes of the owner of a firm that produces computers. Suppose one of the factors you need to produce computers is labor. Currently, you are thinking of hiring an additional worker. Whether or not you actually hire the additional worker will depend on (1) how much better off you are—in dollars and cents—with the additional worker than without him or her and (2) what you have to pay to hire the worker. Simply put, you want to know what the worker will do for you and what you will have to pay for the worker. The *VMP* of a factor is a dollar measure of how much an additional unit of the factor will do for you.

An Important Question: Is *MRP* = *VMP*?

In the computations of *MRP* shown in Exhibit 1, price (*P*) was equal to marginal revenue (*MR*) because we assumed the firm was perfectly competitive. Because $P = MR$ for a perfectly competitive firm, does it follow that for a perfectly competitive firm *MRP* = *VMP*? The answer is yes. Given that

$$MRP = MR \times MPP$$

and

$$VMP = P \times MPP$$

then because $P = MR$ for a perfectly competitive firm, it follows that

$$MRP = VMP \text{ for a perfectly competitive firm}$$

See Exhibit 3(a).

Although $MRP = VMP$ for perfectly competitive firms, this is not the case for firms that are price searchers: monopoly, monopolistic competitive, and oligopolistic firms. All these firms face downward-sloping demand curves for their products. For all of these firms, $P > MR$, and so *VMP* (which is $P \times MPP$) is greater than *MRP* (which is $MR \times MPP$).[1] See Exhibit 3(b).

Marginal Factor Cost: The Firm's Factor Supply Curve

Marginal factor cost (MFC) is the additional cost incurred by employing an additional factor unit. It is calculated as

$$MFC = \Delta TC / \Delta \text{Quantity of the factor}$$

where $TC = $ total costs.

Let's suppose a firm is a **factor price taker**. This means it can buy all it wants of a factor at the equilibrium price. For example, suppose the equilibrium price for factor *X*

---

[1]An exception is the perfectly price-discriminating monopoly firm. For this firm, $P = MR$.

This is the case for a perfectly competitive firm.

$MRP = MR \times MPP$
$VMP = P \times MPP$

MRP (= factor demand curve)
VMP

(a)

This is the case for a monopolist, a monopolistic competitor, and an oligopolist.

$MRP = MR \times MPP$

$VMP = P \times MPP$

VMP

MRP (= factor demand curve)

(b)

is $5. If a firm is a factor price taker, it can buy any quantity of factor X at $5 per factor unit (see Exhibit 4(a)).

What would the marginal factor cost (MFC) curve (the firm's factor supply curve) look like for this kind of firm? It would be horizontal (flat, or perfectly elastic), as shown in Exhibit 4(b).[2]

How Many Units of a Factor Should a Firm Buy?

Suppose you graduate with a B.A. in economics and go to work for a business firm. The first day on the job, you are involved in a discussion about factor X. Your employer asks you, "How many units of this factor should we buy?" What would you say?

[2]Although the MFC, or factor supply curve, for the single factor price taker is horizontal, the market supply curve is upward sloping. This is similar to the situation for the perfectly competitive firm where the firm's demand curve is horizontal but the market (or industry) demand curve is downward sloping. In factor markets, we are simply talking about the supply side of the market instead of the demand side. The firm's supply curve is flat because it can buy additional factor units without driving up the price of the factor; it buys a relatively small portion of the factor. For the industry, however, higher factor prices must be offered to entice factors (e.g., workers) from other industries. The difference in the two supply curves—the firm's and the industry's—is basically a reflection of the different sizes of the firm and the industry.

exhibit **3**

MRP and VMP Curves

$MRP = MR \times MPP$ and $VMP = P \times MPP$. (a) The MRP (factor demand) curve and VMP curve. These are the same for a price taker, or perfectly competitive firm, because $P = MR$. (b) The MRP (factor demand) curve and VMP curve for a firm that is a price searcher (monopolist, monopolistic competitor, oligopolist). The MRP curve lies below the VMP curve because for these firms, $P > MR$.

exhibit **4**

Calculating MFC and Deriving the MFC Curve (the Firm's Factor Supply Curve)

In (a), MFC is calculated in column 4. Notice that the firm is a factor price taker because it can buy a quantity of factor X at a given price ($5, as shown in column 2). In (b), the data from columns (1) and (4) are plotted to derive the MFC curve, which is the firm's factor supply curve.

(1) Quantity of Factor X	(2) Price of Factor X	(3) Total cost $TC = (2) \times (1)$	(4) $MFC = \Delta TC/\Delta quantity$ of the factor $= \Delta(3)/\Delta(1)$
0	$5	$ 0	—
1	5	5	$5
2	5	10	5
3	5	15	5
4	5	20	5
5	5	25	5
6	5	30	5

(a)

MFC Curve = Factor Supply Curve

(b)

In the product market, a firm produces that quantity of output at which marginal revenue equals marginal cost, MR = MC. In the factor market, a firm buys the factor quantity at which marginal revenue product equals marginal factor cost, MRP = MFC. The economic principle of equating additional benefits with additional costs holds in both markets.

Recall that economists often make use of marginal analysis. An economist is likely to answer this question by saying, "Continue buying additional units of the factor until the additional revenue generated by employing an additional factor unit is equal to the additional cost incurred by employing an additional factor unit." Simply stated, keep buying additional units of the factor until $MRP = MFC$. In Exhibit 5, MRP equals MFC at a factor quantity of Q_1.

When There Is More Than One Factor, How Much of Each Factor Should the Firm Buy?

Until now, we have only discussed the purchase of one factor. Suppose we have two factors. For example, suppose a firm requires two factors, labor (L) and capital (K), to produce its product. How does it combine these two factors to minimize costs? Does it combine, say, 20 units of labor with 5 units of capital or perhaps 15 units of labor with 8 units of capital?

The firm purchases the two factors until the ratio of MPP to price for one factor equals the ratio of MPP to price for the other factor. In other words,

$$\frac{MPP_L}{P_L} = \frac{MPP_K}{P_K}$$

Least-Cost Rule

Specifies the combination of factors that minimizes costs. This requires that the following condition be met: $MPP_1/P_1 = MPP_2/P_2 = \ldots = MPP_N/P_N$, where the numbers stand for the different factors.

This is the **least-cost rule**. To understand the logic behind it, let's consider an example. Suppose for a firm, (1) the price of labor is $5, (2) the price of capital is $10, (3) an extra unit of labor results in an increase in output of 25 units, and (4) an extra unit of capital results in an increase in output of 25 units.

Notice that MPP_L/P_L is greater than MPP_K/P_K: 25/$5 > 25/$10. Thus, for this firm, $1 spent on labor is more effective at raising output than $1 spent on capital. In fact, it is twice as effective.

Now suppose the firm currently spends an extra $5 on labor and an extra $10 on capital. With this purchase of the two factors, the firm *is not* minimizing costs. It spends an additional $15 ($5 on labor and $10 on capital) and produces 50 additional units of output. If, instead, it spends an additional $10 on labor and spends $0 on capital, it can still produce the 50 additional units of output and will save $5.

To minimize costs, the firm will rearrange its purchases of factors until the least-cost rule is met. To illustrate, if $MPP_L/P_L > MPP_K/P_K$, the firm buys more labor and less capital. As this happens, the MPP of labor falls and the MPP of capital rises, bringing the two ratios closer in line. The firm continues to buy more of the factor whose MPP-to-price ratio is larger. It stops when the two ratios are equal.

exhibit **5**

Equating *MRP* and *MFC*

The firm continues to purchase a factor as long as the factor's *MRP* exceeds its *MFC*. In the exhibit, the firm purchases Q_1.

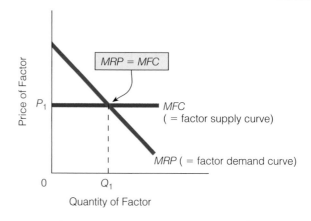

> *Thinking like*
> **AN ECONOMIST**   *We can compare a firm's least-cost rule with the way buyers allocate their consumption dollars. A buyer of goods in the product market chooses combinations of goods so that the marginal utility of good A divided by the price of good A is equal to the marginal utility of good B divided by the price of good B; that is, $\mathrm{MU_A/P_A = MU_B/P_B}$.*
>
> *A firm buying factors in the factor market chooses combinations of factors so that the marginal physical product of, say, labor divided by the price of labor (the wage rate) is equal to the marginal physical product of capital divided by the price of capital; that is, $\mathrm{MPP_L/P_L = MPP_K/P_K}$.*
>
> *Consumers buy goods the same way firms buy factors. This points out something that you may have already sensed. Economic principles are few, but they sometimes seem numerous because we find them in so many different settings.*
>
> *The same economic principle lies behind equating the MU/P ratio for different goods in the product market and equating the MPP/P ratio for different resources in the resource market. In short, there are not two different economic principles at work—one in the product market and another in the factor market—but only one economic principle at work in two markets. That principle simply says that economic actors will, in their attempt to meet their objectives, arrange their purchases in such a way that they receive equal additional benefits per dollar of expenditure.*
>
> *Seeing how a few economic principles operate in many different settings is part of the economic way of thinking.*

SELF-TEST

(Answers to Self-Test questions are in the Self-Test Appendix.)

1. When a perfectly competitive firm employs one worker, it produces 20 units of output, and when it employs two workers, it produces 39 units of output. The firm sells its product for $10 per unit. What is the marginal revenue product connected with hiring the second worker?

2. What is the difference between marginal revenue product (*MRP*) and value marginal product (*VMP*)?

3. What is the distinguishing characteristic of a factor price taker?

4. How much labor should a firm purchase?

The Labor Market

Labor is a factor of special interest because at one time or another, most people find themselves in the labor market. This section first discusses the demand for labor, then the supply of labor, and finally the two together. The discussion focuses on the firm that is a price taker in the product market (i.e., a perfectly competitive firm) and also is a price taker in the factor market.[3] In this setting, the demand for and supply of labor are the forces that determine wage rates.

Shifts in a Firm's *MRP*, or Factor Demand, Curve

As mentioned earlier, a firm's *MRP* curve is its factor demand curve, and marginal revenue product equals marginal revenue multiplied by marginal physical product:

$$MRP = MR \times MPP \qquad (1)$$

---

[3]It is important to keep in mind that the labor market we discuss here is a labor market in which neither buyers nor sellers have any control over wage rates. Because of this, supply and demand are our analytical tools. In the next chapter, we modify this analysis.

economics 24/7

WHY JOBS DON'T ALWAYS MOVE TO THE LOW-WAGE COUNTRY

Are tariffs needed to protect U.S. workers? Some people think so. They argue that without tariffs, U.S. companies will relocate to countries where wages are lower. They will produce their products there and then transport the products to the United States to sell them. Tariffs will make this scenario less likely because the gains the companies receive in lower wages will be offset by the tariffs imposed on their goods.

What this argument overlooks is that U.S. companies are not only interested in what they pay workers; they are also interested in the marginal productivity of the workers.

For example, suppose a U.S. worker earns $10 an hour and a Mexican worker earns $4 an hour. Also suppose the marginal physical product (*MPP*) of the U.S. worker is 10 units of good X and the *MPP* of the Mexican worker is 2 units of good X. Thus, we have lower wages in Mexico and higher productivity in the United States. Where will the company produce?

To answer this question, we need to compare the output produced per $1 of cost in the two countries.

$$\text{Output produced per \$1 of cost} = \frac{MPP \text{ of the factor}}{\text{Cost of the factor}}$$

In the United States, at an *MPP* of 10 units of good X and a wage rate of $10, workers produce 1 unit of good X for every $1 they are paid:

$$\frac{MPP \text{ of U.S. labor}}{\text{Wage rate of U.S. labor}} = \frac{10 \text{ units of good } X}{\$10}$$
$$= 1 \text{ unit of good } X \text{ per \$1}$$

In Mexico, at an *MPP* of 2 units and a wage rate of $4, workers produce 1/2 unit of good X for every $1 they are paid:

$$\frac{MPP \text{ of Mexican labor}}{\text{Wage rate of Mexican labor}} = \frac{2 \text{ units of good } X}{\$4}$$
$$= 1/2 \text{ unit of good } X \text{ per \$1}$$

Thus, the company gets more output per $1 of cost by using U.S. labor and will produce good X in the United States. It is cheaper to produce the good in the United States than it is in Mexico—even though wages are lower in Mexico.

In other words, U.S. companies look at the following ratios:

(1)	(2)
$\dfrac{MPP \text{ of labor in U.S.}}{\text{Wage rate in U.S.}}$	$\dfrac{MPP \text{ of labor in country } X}{\text{Wage rate in country } X}$

If ratio (1) is greater than ratio (2), U.S. companies will hire labor in the United States. As they do this, the *MPP* of labor in the United States will decline. (Remember the law of diminishing marginal returns?) Companies will continue to hire labor in the United States until ratio (1) is equal to ratio (2).

For a perfectly competitive firm, where $P = MR$, we can write equation (1) as

$$MRP = P \times MPP \tag{2}$$

Now consider the demand for a specific factor input, labor. What will happen to the factor demand (*MRP*) curve for labor as the price of the product that the labor produces changes?

In Exhibit 6, we start with a product price of $10 and factor demand curve MRP_1. At the wage rate of W_1, the firm hires Q_1 labor.

Suppose product price rises to $12. As we can see from equation (2), *MRP* rises. At each wage rate, the firm wants to hire more labor. For example, at W_1, it wants to hire Q_2 labor instead of Q_1. In short, a rise in product price shifts the firm's *MRP*, or factor demand, curve rightward.

If product price falls from $10 to $8, *MRP* falls. At each wage rate, the firm wants to hire less labor. For example, at W_1, it wants to hire Q_3 labor instead of Q_1. In short, a fall in product price shifts the firm's *MRP*, or factor demand, curve leftward.

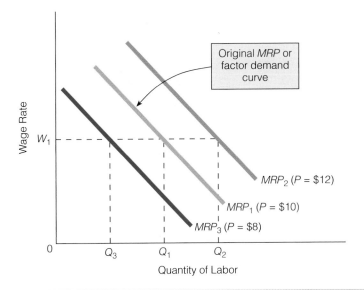

exhibit **6**

Shifts in the Firm's *MRP*, or Factor Demand, Curve

It is always the case that *MRP* = *MR* × *MPP*. For a perfectly competitive firm, where *P* = *MR*, it follows that *MRP* = *P* × *MPP*. If *P* changes, *MRP* will change. For example, if product price rises, *MRP* rises, and the firm's *MRP* curve (factor demand curve) shifts rightward. If product price falls, *MRP* falls, and the firm's *MRP* curve (factor demand curve) shifts leftward. If *MPP* rises (reflected in a shift in the *MPP* curve), *MRP* rises and the firm's *MRP* curve shifts rightward. If *MPP* falls, *MRP* falls and the firm's *MRP* curve shifts leftward.

Changes in the *MPP* of the factor—reflected in a shift in the *MPP* curve—also change the firm's *MRP* curve. As we can see from equation (2), an increase in, say, the *MPP* of labor will increase *MRP* and shift the *MRP*, or factor demand, curve rightward. A decrease in *MPP* will decrease *MRP* and shift the *MRP*, or factor demand, curve leftward.[4]

micro *Theme*   One of the themes that gets played over and again in microeconomics is this one: (1) Derive a particular curve and then (2) explain what factors will shift it. We first encountered this theme back in Chapter 3 when discussing supply and demand. We derived a demand curve (from a demand schedule) and then discussed the factors that could shift the curve. We are playing that theme again here. We have just derived the firm's demand curve for a factor. Then we identified factors (e.g., a change in the price of the good the factor goes to produce and a change in MPP) that could shift the curve.

Market Demand for Labor

We would expect the market demand curve for labor to be the horizontal "addition" of the firms' demand curves (*MRP* curves) for labor. However, this is not the case, as Exhibit 7 illustrates.

Assume two firms, *A* and *B*, make up the buying side of the factor market. Also assume that the product price for both firms is P_1. Parts (a) and (b) in the exhibit show the *MRP* curves for the two firms based on this product price.

At a wage rate of W_1, firm *A* purchases 100 units of labor. This is the amount of labor at which its marginal revenue product equals marginal factor cost (or the wage). At this same wage rate, firm *B* purchases 150 units of labor. If we horizontally "add" the *MRP* curves of firms *A* and *B*, we get the *MRP* curve in (c) where the two firms together purchase 250 units of labor at W_1.

---

[4]Notice here that we are talking about a change in *MPP* that is reflected in a *shift* in the *MPP* curve; we are not talking about a *movement* along a given *MPP* curve.

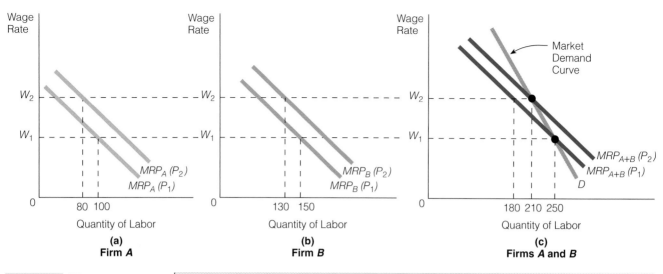

The Derivation of the Market Demand Curve for Labor Units

Two firms, A and B, make up the buying side of the market for labor. At a wage rate of W_1, firm A purchases 100 units of labor and firm B purchases 150 units. Together, they purchase 250 units, as illustrated in (c). The wage rate rises to W_2, and the amount of labor purchased by both firms initially falls to 180 units, as shown in (c). Higher wage rates translate into higher costs, a fall in product supply, and a rise in product price initially falls from P_1 to P_2. Finally, an increased price raises MRP and each firm has a new MRP curve. The horizontal "addition" of the new MRP curves shows they purchase 210 units of labor. Connecting the units of labor purchased by both firms at W_1 and W_2 gives the market demand curve.

Now assume the wage rate increases to W_2. In (c), firms A and B move up the given MRP_{A+B} curve and purchase 180 units of labor. This may seem to be the end of the process, but of course, it is not. But why not? It's because a higher wage rate increases each firm's costs and thus shifts its supply curve leftward. This leads to an increase in product price to P_2.

Recall that the firm's marginal revenue product is equal to marginal revenue (or price, when the firm is perfectly competitive) times marginal physical product: $MRP = MR \times MPP = P \times MPP$. So if price rises (which it has), so does MRP, and therefore, each firm faces a new MRP curve at the wage rate W_2. Parts (a) and (b) in Exhibit 7 illustrate these new MRP curves for firms A and B, and (c) shows the horizontal "addition" of the *new* MRP curves. The firms together now purchase 210 units of labor at W_2.

After all adjustments have been made, connecting the units of labor purchased by both firms at W_1 and W_2 gives the market demand curve in (c).

micro
Theme

One of the themes in microeconomics is that if one thing changes, this leads to something else changing, which in turn leads to something else changing, and so on. You have just seen that theme in action. The wage rate increased, which raised the firm's costs, which caused the firm's supply curve (for the good it produces) to shift leftward. But then, a leftward shift in the supply curve ended up raising the price of the good the firm produces and sells, which resulted in the firm's demand for factors rising.

Think of a pebble you throw into a lake. The pebble causes ripples in the lake. It is much the same in economics. If you throw the "pebble" of a "higher wage rate" into a market setting, certain ripples will materialize.

The Elasticity of Demand for Labor

Elasticity of Demand for Labor

The percentage change in the quantity demanded of labor divided by the percentage change in the wage rate.

If the wage rate rises, firms will cut back on the labor they hire. But how much they cut back depends on the elasticity of demand for labor. The **elasticity of demand for labor** is the percentage change in the quantity demanded of labor divided by the percentage change in the price of labor (the wage rate).

$$E_L = \frac{\text{Percentage change in quantity demanded of labor}}{\text{Percentage change in wage rate}}$$

where E_L = coefficient of elasticity of demand for labor, or simply elasticity coefficient.

For example, suppose when the wage rate changes by 20 percent, the quantity demanded of a particular type of labor changes by 40 percent. Then the elasticity of demand for this type of labor is 2 (40 percent/20 percent), and the demand between the old wage rate and the new wage rate is elastic. There are three main determinants of elasticity of demand for labor.

ELASTICITY OF DEMAND FOR THE PRODUCT THAT LABOR PRODUCES If the demand for the product that labor produces is highly elastic, a small percentage increase in price (e.g., owing to a wage increase that shifts the supply curve for the product leftward) will decrease quantity demanded of the product by a relatively large percentage. In turn, this will greatly reduce the quantity of labor needed to produce the product, implying the demand for labor is highly elastic too.

The relationship between the elasticity of demand for the product and the elasticity of demand for labor is as follows:

The higher the elasticity of demand for the product, the higher the elasticity of demand for the labor that produces the product; the lower the elasticity of demand for the product, the lower the elasticity of demand for the labor that produces the product.

RATIO OF LABOR COSTS TO TOTAL COSTS Labor costs are a part of total costs. Consider two situations. In one, labor costs are 90 percent of total costs, and in the other, labor costs are only 5 percent of total costs. Now suppose wages increase by $2 per hour. Total costs are affected more when labor costs are 90 percent of total costs (the $2-per-hour wage increase is being applied to 90 percent of all costs) than when labor costs are only 5 percent of total costs. Thus, price rises by more when labor costs are a larger percentage of total costs. And of course, the more price rises, the more quantity demanded of the product falls. It follows that labor, being a derived demand, is affected more. In short, the decline in the quantity demanded of labor is greater for a $2-per-hour wage increase when labor costs are 90 percent of total costs than when labor costs are 5 percent of total costs.

The relationship between the labor cost–total cost ratio and the elasticity of demand for labor is as follows:

The higher the labor cost–total cost ratio, the higher the elasticity of demand for labor (the greater the cutback in labor for any given wage increase); the lower the labor cost–total cost ratio, the lower the elasticity of demand for labor (the less the cutback in labor for any given wage increase).

NUMBER OF SUBSTITUTE FACTORS The more substitutes there are for labor, the more sensitive buyers of labor will be to a change in the price of labor. This principle was established in the discussion of price elasticity of demand. The more possibilities for substituting other factors for labor, the more likely firms will cut back on their use of labor if the price of labor rises.

The more substitutes for labor, the higher the elasticity of demand for labor; the fewer substitutes for labor, the lower the elasticity of demand for labor.

Market Supply of Labor

As the wage rate rises, the quantity supplied of labor rises, *ceteris paribus*. The upward-sloping labor supply curve in Exhibit 8 illustrates this.

economics 24/7

HOW MAY CRIME, OUTSOURCING, AND MULTITASKING BE RELATED?

Consider three seemingly unrelated images of life in the United States in recent years:

- A lower crime rate. For example, violent crime, property crime, and homicides were all down in the late 1990s and early 2000s.

- More people choosing to multitask—that is, to work on more than one task at a time. For example, if you drive a car at the same time as you talk to your office on your cell phone, you are multitasking.

- Increasingly more professional people outsourcing their routine tasks. They are hiring people to run errands, buy groceries, plan parties, drop off dry cleaning, take pets to the vet, and so on.

Could all three images be the result of the same thing— higher real wages?[5] How might higher real wages affect crime, multitasking, and outsourcing? Let's consider crime first. There are both costs and benefits to committing a crime. As long as the benefits are greater than the costs, crimes will be committed; increase the costs of crime relative to the benefits, and the crime rate will decline. Suppose part of the cost of crime is equal to the probability of being sentenced to jail multiplied by the real wage that would be earned if the person were not in jail.

Part of the cost of crime = Probability of jail sentence
× Real wage

If this is the case, then as the real wage rises, the overall cost of crime rises and fewer crimes will be committed.

How does the real wage relate to individuals outsourcing their routine tasks? To illustrate, suppose John and Mary are married and have two daughters. Currently, Mary works as a physician and John works part time as an accountant. Because John has chosen to work part time, he takes care of many of the routine household tasks. He buys the groceries, runs the errands, and so on. If the real wage rises

for accountants, John may rethink his part-time work. An increase in the real wage is the same as an increase in the reward from working, and so John may choose to work more. In fact, it may be cheaper for him to work full time and pay someone else to run the errands, buy the groceries, and so on.

Finally, what about multitasking? As the real wage rises, one's time becomes more valuable. And as time becomes more valuable, people will want to economize on it. One way to economize on time is to do several things at the same time. Instead of spending 20 minutes driving to work and another 10 minutes talking on the phone, why not "kill two birds with one stone" and talk on the phone while driving to work? Ten minutes are saved this way. Of course, there is a downside to this. (Economists are quick to point out that most activities come with both benefits and costs.) Talking on a cell phone while driving is not only illegal in some states, but it probably makes you and others around you less safe while driving.

If higher real wages can affect the crime rate, the amount of outsourcing, and the degree to which people multitask, it is important to know what can cause real wages to rise. One way real wages can rise is through a technological advance that increases the quality of the capital goods used by labor. To illustrate, consider a technological advance that makes it possible for computers to complete more tasks in less time. As a result, the productivity of labor rises and the demand curve for labor shifts to the right. Higher demand for labor increases the nominal wage rate and, as long as the price level doesn't rise by more than the nominal wage rate, the real wage rises too.

Can a technological advance indirectly lead to a lower crime rate, more outsourcing, and greater multitasking? We think so.

---

[5]Nominal wages are dollar wages—such as $30 an hour. Real wages are nominal wages adjusted for price changes. Stated differently, real wages measure what nominal wages can actually buy in terms of goods and services. So when real wages rise, people can buy more goods and services.

At a wage rate of W_1, individuals are willing to supply 100 labor units. At the higher wage rate of W_2, individuals are willing to supply 200 labor units. Some individuals who were not willing to work at a wage rate of W_1 are willing to work at a wage rate of W_2, and some individuals who were working at W_1 will be willing to supply more labor units at W_2. At the even higher wage rate of W_3, individuals are willing to supply 280 labor units.

An Individual's Supply of Labor

Exhibit 8 shows an upward-sloping *market* supply curve of labor. Let's consider an individual's supply curve of labor—say, John's supply curve of labor. Is it upward sloping? The answer to this question depends on the relative strengths of the substitution and income effects.

To illustrate, suppose John currently earns $10 an hour and works 40 hours a week. If John's wage rate rises to, say, $15 an hour, he will feel two effects, each pulling him in opposite directions.

One effect, the *substitution effect,* works as follows: As his wage rate rises, John recognizes that the monetary reward from working has increased. As a result, John will want to work more—say, 45 hours a week instead of 40 hours (+5 hours).

The other effect, the *income effect,* works this way: As his wage rate rises, John knows that he can earn $600 a week (40 hours at $15 an hour) instead of $400 a week (40 hours at $10 an hour). If leisure is a normal good (the demand for which increases as income increases), then John will want to consume more leisure as his income rises. But the only way to consume more leisure is to work fewer hours. Let's say John wants to decrease his work hours per week from 40 to 37 hours (−3 hours).

The substitution effect pulls John in one direction (toward working 5 more hours), and the income effect pulls John in the opposite direction (toward working 3 fewer hours). Which effect is stronger? In our numerical example, the substitution effect is stronger, so on net, John wants to work 2 more hours a week as his wage rate rises. This means John's supply curve of labor is upward sloping between a wage rate of $10 and $15.

Shifts in the Labor Supply Curve

Changes in the wage rate change the quantity supplied of labor units; that is, they cause a *movement* along a given supply curve. But what *shifts* the entire labor supply curve? Two factors of major importance are wage rates in other labor markets and the non-money, or nonpecuniary, aspects of a job.

WAGE RATES IN OTHER LABOR MARKETS Deborah currently works as a technician in a television manufacturing plant. She has skills suitable for a number of jobs. One day, she learns that the computer manufacturing plant on the other side of town is offering 33 percent more pay per hour. Deborah is also trained to work as a computer operator, so she decides to leave her current job and apply for work at the computer manufacturing plant. In short, the wage rate offered in other labor markets can bring about a shift of the supply curve in a particular labor market.

NONMONEY, OR NONPECUNIARY, ASPECTS OF A JOB Other things held constant, people prefer to avoid dirty, heavy, dangerous work in cold climates. An increase in the overall "unpleasantness" of a job (e.g., an increased probability of contracting lung cancer working in a coal mine) will cause a decrease in the supply of labor to that firm or industry and a leftward shift in its labor supply curve. An increase in the overall "pleasantness" of a job (e.g., employees are now entitled to a longer lunch break and use of the company gym) will cause an increase in the supply of labor to that firm or industry and a rightward shift in its labor supply curve.

Putting Supply and Demand Together

Exhibit 9 illustrates a particular labor market. The equilibrium wage rate and quantity of labor are established by the forces of supply and demand. At a wage rate of W_2, there is a surplus of labor. Some people who want to work at this wage rate will not be able to find jobs. A subset of this group will begin to offer their services for a lower wage rate. The wage rate will move down until it reaches W_1.

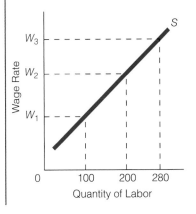

The Market Supply of Labor

A direct relationship exists between the wage rate and the quantity of labor supplied.

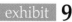

exhibit **9**

Equilibrium in a Particular Labor Market

The forces of supply and demand bring about the equilibrium wage rate and quantity of labor. At the equilibrium wage rate, the quantity demanded of labor equals the quantity supplied. At any other wage rate, there is either a surplus or a shortage of labor.

At a wage rate of W_3, there is a shortage of labor. Some demanders of labor will begin to bid up the wage rate until it reaches W_1. At the equilibrium wage rate, W_1, the quantity supplied of labor equals the quantity demanded of labor.

Why Do Wage Rates Differ?

To discover why wage rates differ, we must determine what conditions would be necessary for everyone to receive the same pay. Assume the following conditions hold:

1. The demand for every type of labor is the same. (Throughout our analysis, any wage differentials caused by demand are short-run differentials.)

2. There are no special nonpecuniary aspects to any job.

3. All labor is ultimately homogeneous and can costlessly be trained for different types of employment.

4. All labor is mobile at zero cost.

Given these conditions, there would be no difference in wage rates in the long run. To illustrate, consider Exhibit 10, where two labor markets, A and B, are shown. Initially, the supply conditions are different, with a greater supply of workers in labor market B (represented by S_B) than in labor market A (represented by S_A). Because of the different supply conditions, more labor is employed in labor market B (Q_B) than in labor market A (Q_A), and the equilibrium wage rate in labor market B ($10) is lower than the equilibrium wage rate in labor market A ($30).

The differences in the wage rates between the two labor markets will not last. We have assumed (1) labor can move costlessly from one labor market to another (so why not move from the lower paying job to the higher paying job?), (2) there are no special nonpecuniary aspects to any job (there is no nonpecuniary reason for not moving), (3) labor is ultimately homogeneous (workers who work in labor market B can work in labor market A), and (4) if workers need training to make a move from one labor market to another, they not only are capable of being trained but also can acquire the training costlessly.

As a result, some workers in labor market B will relocate to labor market A, decreasing the supply of workers to S'_B in labor market B and increasing the supply of workers to S'_A in labor market A. The relocation of workers ends when the equilibrium wage rate in both markets is the same—$20. We conclude that wage rates will not differ in the long run if our four conditions hold.

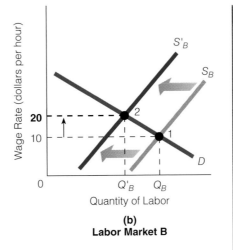

exhibit 10

Wage Rate Equalization Across Labor Markets

Given the four necessary conditions (noted in the text), there will be no wage rate differences across labor markets. We start with a wage rate of $30 in labor market *A* and a wage rate of $10 in labor market *B*. Soon some individuals in *B* relocate to *A*. This increases the supply in one market (*A*), driving down the wage rate, and decreases the supply in the other market (*B*), driving up the wage rate. Equilibrium comes when the same wage rate is paid in both labor markets. This outcome critically depends on the necessary conditions holding.

Because we know the conditions under which wage rates will not differ, we now know why wage rates do differ. Obviously, they differ because demand conditions are not the same in all labor markets (important to explain short-run wage differentials only) and because supply conditions are not the same in all markets: There are nonpecuniary aspects to different jobs, labor is not homogeneous, labor cannot be retrained without cost, and labor is not costlessly mobile.

Why Demand and Supply Differ in Different Labor Markets

Saying that wage rates differ because demand and supply conditions in different labor markets differ raises the question of why this is the case. Let's consider what factors affect the demand for and supply of labor.

DEMAND FOR LABOR The market demand curve for labor is based on the *MRP* curves for labor of the individual firms in the market. So we need to look at what affects the components of *MRP,* namely, *MR* and *MPP.*

Marginal revenue is indirectly affected by product supply and demand conditions because these conditions determine price ($MR = \Delta TR/\Delta Q$ and $TR = P \times Q$). Thus, product demand and supply conditions affect factor demand. In short, because the supply and demand conditions in different product markets are different, it follows that the demand for labor in different labor markets will be different too.

The second factor, the marginal physical product of labor, is affected by individual workers' *own abilities and skills* (both innate and learned), the *degree of effort* they put forth on the job, and the *other factors of production* available to them. With respect to the latter, American workers are more productive than workers in many other countries because they work with many more capital goods and much more technical know-how. If all individuals had the same innate and learned skills and abilities, applied the same degree of effort on the job, and worked with the same amount and quality of other factors of production, wages would differ less than they currently do.

SUPPLY OF LABOR As noted earlier, the supply conditions in different labor markets are different. First, jobs have *different nonpecuniary qualities.* Working as a coal miner in West Virginia is not as attractive a job as working as a tour guide at a lush resort in Hawaii. We would expect this fact to be reflected in the supply of coal miners and tour guides.

economics 24/7

WHAT IS THE WAGE RATE FOR A STREET-LEVEL PUSHER IN A DRUG GANG?

Gangs that deal drugs exist in almost every large city in the United States. It is not uncommon to see a 16- or 17-year-old gang member selling or delivering drugs in Los Angeles, New York, Chicago, Houston, or elsewhere. Often, in a public debate about drugs in one of these cities, someone will say, "No wonder these kids sell drugs; it's the best job they can get. When your alternatives are working at McDonald's earning the minimum wage or selling drugs for big money, you sell drugs. If we want to get kids off the streets and out of gangs and if we want to stop them from selling drugs, we need to have something better for them than the minimum wage."

But we wonder: Do the young gang members who sell and deliver drugs really earn "big money"? Economics would predict that they wouldn't. After all, one would think that the supply of people who can sell or deliver drugs is rather large. In fact, a recent study found that low-level foot soldiers in a drug gang actually earned very low wages.

Steven Levitt, an economist, and Sudhir Venkatesh, a sociologist, analyzed the data set of a drug-selling street gang.[6] They estimated that the average hourly wage rate in the gang was $6 at the time they started the study and $11 at the time they finished.[7] They also noted that the distribution of wages was extremely skewed. Actual street-level dealers (foot soldiers) appeared to earn less than the minimum wage. According to Levitt and Venkatesh, "While these wages are almost too low to be believable, there are both theoretical arguments and corroborating empirical evidence in support of these numbers. From a theoretical perspective, it is hardly surprising that foot-soldier wages would be low given the minimal skill requirements for the job and the presence of a 'reserve army' of potential replacements among the rank and file."

---

[6]Steven Levitt and Sudhir Venkatesh, *An Economic Analysis of a Drug-Selling Gang's Finances*, NBER Working Paper No. W6592 (Cambridge, MA: National Bureau of Economic Research, 1998).
[7]Wage rates are in 1995 dollars.

Second, supply is also a reflection of the *number of persons who can actually do a job.* Williamson may want to be a nuclear physicist but may not have the ability in science and mathematics to become one. Johnson may want to be a basketball player but may not have the ability to become one.

Third, even if individuals have the ability to work at a certain job, they may perceive the *training costs as too high* (relative to the perceived benefits) to train for it. Tyler may have the ability to be a brain surgeon but views the years of schooling required to become one too high a price to pay.

Fourth, sometimes supply in different labor markets reflects a difference in the *cost of moving* across markets. Wage rates might be higher in Alaska than in Alabama for comparable labor because the workers in Alabama find the cost of relocating to Alaska too high relative to the benefits of receiving a higher wage.

In conclusion, because the wage rate is determined by supply-and-demand forces, the factors that affect these forces indirectly affect wage rates. Exhibit 11 summarizes these factors.

Why Did You Choose the Major That You Chose?

Our lives are sometimes influenced by what happens in labor markets. Consider a college student who is trying to decide whether to major in accounting or English. The student believes that English is more fun and interesting but that accounting, on average, will earn her enough additional income to compensate for the lack of fun in accounting. Specif-

exhibit **11**

The Wage Rate

A step-by-step framework that describes the factors that affect the wage rate.

A CLOSER LOOK

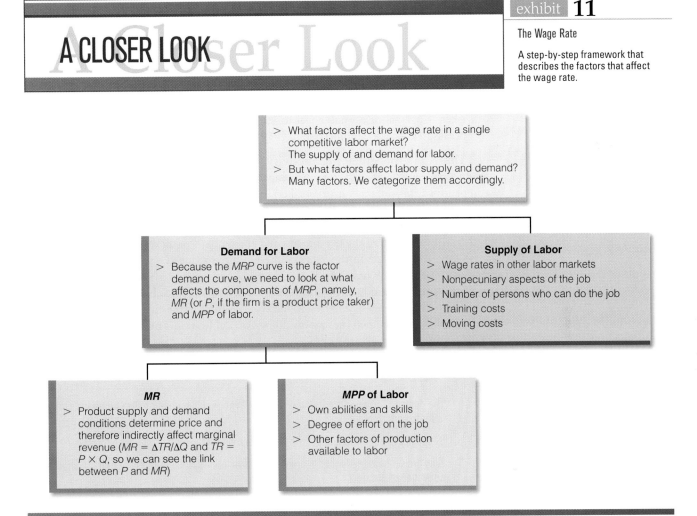

> What factors affect the wage rate in a single competitive labor market?
> The supply of and demand for labor.
> But what factors affect labor supply and demand? Many factors. We categorize them accordingly.

Demand for Labor
> Because the *MRP* curve is the factor demand curve, we need to look at what affects the components of *MRP*, namely, *MR* (or *P*, if the firm is a product price taker) and *MPP* of labor.

Supply of Labor
> Wage rates in other labor markets
> Nonpecuniary aspects of the job
> Number of persons who can do the job
> Training costs
> Moving costs

MR
> Product supply and demand conditions determine price and therefore indirectly affect marginal revenue ($MR = \Delta TR/\Delta Q$ and $TR = P \times Q$, so we can see the link between P and MR)

***MPP* of Labor**
> Own abilities and skills
> Degree of effort on the job
> Other factors of production available to labor

ically, at a \$55,000 annual salary for accounting and a \$39,000 annual salary for English, the student is indifferent between accounting and English. But at a \$56,000 annual salary for accounting and a \$39,000 annual salary for English, accounting moves ahead.

Of course, what accounting "pays" is determined by the demand for and supply of accountants. When we realize this, we realize that other people influenced the person's decision to become an accountant. To illustrate, suppose Congress passes more intricate tax laws that require more accountants to figure them out. This increases the demand for accountants, which in turn raises the wage rate for accountants. And an increase in the wage rate that accountants receive increases the probability that more people—perhaps you—will major in accounting and not in English, philosophy, or history.

As you can see, economics—in which markets play a major role—helps explain why part of your life is the way it is.

Marginal Productivity Theory

Let's see where an analysis of some of the things we know from this chapter leads us:

1. If a firm is a factor price taker, marginal factor cost is constant and equal to factor price, $MFC = P$. Suppose the factor price taker hires labor. For the firm, $MFC = W$, where W is the wage rate.

2. Firms hire the factor quantity at which $MRP = MFC$.

3. Taking points 1 and 2 together, a factor price taker pays labor a wage equal to its marginal revenue product: $W = MRP$. That is, because $MFC = W$ (point 1) and $MRP = MFC$ (point 2), it follows that $W = MRP$.

4. If a firm is perfectly competitive, $MRP = VMP$.

5. If a firm is both perfectly competitive (a product price taker) and a factor price taker, it pays labor a wage equal to its value marginal product: $W = VMP$. That is, because $W = MRP$ (point 3) and $MRP = VMP$ (point 4), it follows that $W = VMP$.

Marginal Productivity Theory

States that firms in competitive or perfect product and factor markets pay factors their marginal revenue products.

This is the **marginal productivity theory**, which states that if a firm sells its product and purchases its factors in competitive or perfect markets (i.e., it is a perfectly competitive firm and a factor price taker), it pays its factors their MRP or VMP (the two are equal for a product price taker).

The theory holds that under the competitive conditions specified, if a factor unit is withdrawn from the productive process and the amount of all other factors remains the same, then the decrease in the value of the product produced equals the factor payment received by the factor unit. To illustrate, suppose Wilson works for a perfectly competitive firm (firm X) producing good X. One day, he quits his job (but nothing else relevant to the firm changes). As a result, the total revenue of the firm falls by $100. If Wilson was paid $100, then he received his MRP. He was paid a wage equal to his contribution to the productive process.[8]

SELF-TEST

1. The demand for labor is a derived demand. What could cause the firm's demand curve for labor to shift rightward?

2. Suppose the coefficient of elasticity of demand for labor is 3. What does this mean?

3. Why are wage rates higher in one competitive labor market than in another? In short, why do wage rates differ?

4. Workers in labor market X do the same work as workers in labor market Y, but they earn $10 less per hour. Why?

Labor Markets and Information

This section looks at job hiring, employment practices, employment discrimination, and how information, or the lack of it, affects these processes.

Screening Potential Employees

Employers typically do not know exactly how productive a potential employee will be. What the employer wants, but lacks, is complete information about the potential employee's future job performance.

This raises two questions: Why would an employer want complete information about a potential employee's future job performance? What does the employer do because he or she lacks complete information?

The answer to the first question is obvious. Employers have a strong monetary incentive to hire good, stable, quick-learning, responsible, hardworking, punctual

---

[8]Recall that there are two ways to calculate MRP: $MRP = \Delta TR/\Delta$quantity of the factor, and $MRP = MR \times MPP$. In this example, we use the first method. When Wilson quits his job, the change in the denominator is 1 factor unit. If, as a result, TR falls by $100, then the change in the numerator must be $100.

employees. One study found that corporate spending on training employees reached $40 billion annually. Obviously, corporations want to see the highest return possible for their training expenditures, so they try to hire employees who will make the training worthwhile. This is where screening comes in.

Screening is the process used by employers to increase the probability of choosing "good" employees based on certain criteria. For example, an employer might ask a young college graduate searching for a job what his or her GPA was in college. This is a screening mechanism. The employer might know from past experience that persons with high GPAs turn out to be better employees, on average, than persons with low GPAs. Screening is one thing an employer does because he or she lacks complete information.

Screening
The process used by employers to increase the probability of choosing "good" employees based on certain criteria.

Promoting from Within

Sometimes, employers promote from within the company because they have more information about company employees than about potential employees.

Suppose the executive vice president in charge of sales is retiring from Trideck, Inc. The president of the company could hire an outsider to replace the vice president, but often, she will select an insider about whom she has some knowledge. What may look like discrimination to outsiders—"That company discriminates against persons not working for it"—may simply be a reflection of the difference in costs to the employer of acquiring relevant information about employees inside and outside the company.

Is It Discrimination or Is It an Information Problem?

Suppose the world is made up of just two kinds of people: those with characteristic X and those with characteristic Y. We call them X people and Y people, respectively. Over time, we observe that most employers are X people and that they tend to hire and promote proportionally more X than Y people. Are the Y people being discriminated against?

They could be. Nothing we have said so far rules this out. But then, it may be that X people rarely hire or promote Y people because over time X employers have learned that Y people, on average, do not perform as well as X people.

So in this example, we simply state that X people are not discriminating against Y people. Instead, Y people are not being hired and promoted as often as X people because, for whatever reason, Y people, on average, are not as productive as X people.

Suppose in this environment, an extremely productive Y person applies for a job with an X employer. The problem is that the X employer does not know—she lacks complete information—about the full abilities of the Y person. Furthermore, acquiring complete information is costly. She bases her decision to reject the Y person's job application on what she knows about Y people, which is that, on average, they are not as productive as X people. She doesn't do this because she has something against Y people but because it is simply too costly for her to acquire complete information on every potential employee—X or Y.

We do not mean to imply that everything that looks like discrimination is really a problem of the high cost of information. Nonetheless, sometimes, what looks like discrimination ("he doesn't like me; I'm a Y person") is a consequence of living in a world where acquiring complete information is "too costly."

Legislation mandating equal employment opportunities requires employers to absorb some information costs to open labor markets to all. All but the smallest of firms are required to search for qualified Y persons who can perform the job even if the employer believes that the average Y person cannot. Requiring employers to forgo the use of a screening mechanism will likely increase firm costs and raise prices to consumers, but the premise of the legislation is that those costs are more than outweighed by the social benefits of having more Y persons in the mainstream of society.

A Reader Asks...

Does Education Matter to Income?

The greater the demand for my labor and the smaller the supply, the higher the wage I'll be paid. One of the things that can shift the factor demand curve for my labor to the right (and thus bring me a higher wage) is a rise in "my *MPP*." Is this where education plays a role? Does more education lead to a higher *MPP* and higher wages?

Certainly, there are people with little education who earn high salaries, but generally speaking, more education does seem to raise one's productivity. And as a result, it tends to raise one's pay. For example, in 2001, a person with only a high school diploma had average annual earnings of $26,795; a person with a bachelor's degree, $50,623; and a person with a master's degree, $63,592.

Let's also consider Charles, who is 22 years old and has just completed his associate's degree. He is trying to decide whether or not to continue his education. In 2001, a person with an associate's degree (as the highest degree) had average annual earnings of $34,744. Let's look at Charles's lifetime earnings in two cases.

If Charles stops his education with an associate's degree and works until he is 65 years old, he will earn $34,744 each year for 43 years.[9] That is a total of $1,493,992. If, however, Charles goes on to get a master's degree and we assume it takes him 6 more years of schooling to do so, then he will earn $63,592 each year for the next 37 years. That is a total of $2,352,904. The difference in lifetime earnings for a person with an associate's degree and a person with a master's degree is $858,912. Stated differently, Charles's lifetime earnings will be approximately 57 percent higher with a master's degree than with an associate's degree (as the highest degree).

The difference in lifetime earnings is even greater for a person with a doctorate. (In 2001, a person with a doctorate had average annual earnings of $85,675.) If we assume a doctorate requires 2 years of additional schooling beyond a master's degree, then the total lifetime earnings with a doctorate will be $2,998,625. It follows, then, that the difference in lifetime earnings (between an associate's degree and a doctorate) is $1,504,633. This is more than 100 percent more lifetime earnings.

Or we can think of it this way. If going from an associate's degree to a doctorate more than doubles Charles's lifetime earnings, it is as if he produces a clone of his associate-degree self during his 8 more years of schooling. (What do you produce in school? Nothing is the wrong answer. You produce clones of yourself.)

[9]We are not adjusting in our example for annual percentage increases in earnings.

! analyzing the scene

What is the right number of employees to hire?

Marion Smithies, the owner of a small company, is undecided as to how many additional employees to hire. The right number of employees is the number at which the *MRP* of an additional employee equals the *MFC* of the additional employee. As long as the additional benefits the employee brings to the firm are greater than the additional costs incurred by hiring the employee, it is best to hire the employee. She should stop hiring when additional benefits equal additional costs.

Will jobs always flow to where wages are the lowest?

People often believe that jobs will flow to where wages are the lowest. But if this is true, then why is there a single job in the United States, a relatively high-wage country? Obviously, wages aren't the only thing considered by firms. Firms also look at the productivity of workers—the marginal physical product of the labor that they hire. For example, suppose John is paid $4 an hour and can produce 1 unit of *X* an hour, and Stephanie is paid $10 an hour and can produce 5 units of X an hour. John receives the relatively lower wage, and Stephanie receives the relatively higher wage, but is John really "cheaper" than Stephanie? The feature "Why Jobs Don't Always Move to the Low-Wage Country" discusses this topic in detail.

Would you work more or less at higher wages?

Whether you would work more or less at higher wages depends on how strong your substitution effect is relative to your income effect. If your substitution effect is stronger than your income effect, you will work more at higher wages. If your income effect is stronger than your substitution effect, you will work less at higher wages. If your substitution effect is equal in strength to your income effect, you will work no more and no less at higher wages than at lower wages.

Keep in mind that at some range of wage rates—say, $10 to $40 an hour—your substitution effect might be stronger than your income effect and at another range of wage rates—say, anything over $40 an hour—your income effect might be stronger than your substitution effect. In other words, as wages rise from $10 to $40, you work more, but then if wages rise over $40, you begin to cut back on how much you work. What would your supply curve of labor look like under these conditions?

Is Alex Rodriguez paid too much?

Before we can accurately answer this question, we need to determine what it means to say a person is worth a certain salary—whether the salary is $25 million or $25,000.

Consider this example. Suppose if a firm hires a person, she will generate $90,000 a year in additional revenue for the firm, but the firm will have to pay her only $75,000 a year. Is she worth $75,000? The obvious answer is yes. The additional benefits of hiring her ($90,000) are greater than the additional costs of hiring her ($75,000). Another way of saying this is that her marginal revenue product (MRP) is greater than her marginal factor cost (MFC). In this setting, a person is worth hiring at a particular salary as long as the person's (annual) MRP is greater than her (annual) salary.

So is Alex Rodriguez worth $25 million a year? There is no way to know for sure without knowing his MRP. If his MRP is greater than $25 million a year, then he is worth $25 million. He might be worth even more. If his MRP is less than $25 million, then he isn't worth $25 million. We can say one thing, though: Certainly, the owner of the New York Yankees expected Alex Rodriguez's MRP to be greater than $25 million a year, or he wouldn't have paid him that amount.

chapter summary

Derived Demand

- The demand for a factor is derived; hence, it is called a *derived demand*. Specifically, it is derived from and directly related to the demand for the product that the factor goes to produce; for example, the demand for auto workers is derived from the demand for autos.

MRP, MFC, VMP

- Marginal revenue product (MRP) is the additional revenue generated by employing an additional factor unit. Marginal factor cost (MFC) is the additional cost incurred by employing an additional factor unit. The profit-maximizing firm buys the factor quantity at which $MRP = MFC$.
- The MRP curve is the firm's factor demand curve; it shows how much of a factor the firm buys at different prices.
- Value marginal product (VMP) is a measure of the value that each factor unit adds to the firm's product. Whereas $MRP = MR \times MPP$, $VMP = P \times MPP$. For a perfectly competitive firm, $P = MR$, so $MRP = VMP$. For a monopolist, a monopolistic competitor, or an oligopolist, $P > MR$, so $VMP > MRP$.

The Least-Cost Rule

- A firm minimizes costs by buying factors in the combination at which the MPP-to-price ratio for each factor is the same. For example, if there are two factors, labor (L) and capital (K), the least-cost rule reads $MPP_L/P_L = MPP_K/P_K$.

Labor and Wages

- A change in the price of the product labor produces or a change in the marginal physical product of labor (reflected in a shift in the MPP curve) will shift the demand curve for labor.
- The higher (lower) the elasticity of demand for the product labor produces, the higher (lower) the elasticity of demand for labor. The higher (lower) the labor cost–total cost ratio, the higher (lower) the elasticity of demand for labor. The more (fewer) substitutes for labor, the higher (lower) the elasticity of demand for labor.
- As the wage rate rises, the quantity supplied of labor rises, *ceteris paribus*.
- At the equilibrium wage rate, the quantity supplied of labor equals the quantity demanded of labor.

Demand for and Supply of Labor

- The demand for labor is affected by (1) marginal revenue and (2) marginal physical product. The supply of labor is affected by (1) wage rates in other labor markets, (2) nonpecuniary aspects of the job, (3) number of persons who can do the job, (4) training costs, and (5) moving costs.

Marginal Productivity Theory

- Marginal productivity theory states that firms in competitive or perfect product and factor markets pay their factors their marginal revenue products.

key terms and concepts

Derived Demand

Marginal Revenue
  Product (*MRP*)

Value Marginal Product
  (*VMP*)

Marginal Factor Cost
  (*MFC*)

Factor Price Taker

Least-Cost Rule

Elasticity of Demand for
  Labor

Marginal Productivity
  Theory

Screening

questions and problems

1   The supply curve is horizontal for a factor price taker; however, the industry supply curve is upward sloping. Explain why this occurs.

2   What forces and factors determine the wage rate for a particular type of labor?

3   What is the relationship between labor productivity and wage rates?

4   What might be one effect of government legislating wage rates?

5   Using the theory developed in this chapter, explain the following: (a) why a worker in Ethiopia is likely to earn much less than a worker in Japan; (b) why the army expects recruitment to rise during economic recessions; (c) why basketball stars earn relatively large incomes; (d) why jobs that carry a health risk offer higher pay than jobs that do not, *ceteris paribus.*

6   Discuss the factors that might prevent the equalization of wage rates for identical or comparable jobs across labor markets.

7   Prepare a list of questions that an interviewer is likely to ask an interviewee in a job interview. Try to identify which of the questions are part of the interviewer's screening process.

8   Explain why the market demand curve for labor is not simply the horizontal "addition" of the firms' demand curves for labor.

9   Discuss the firm's objective, its constraints, and how it makes choices in its role as a buyer of resources.

10 Explain the relationship between each of the following pairs of concepts: (a) the elasticity of demand for a product and the elasticity of demand for the labor that produces the product; (b) the labor cost–total cost ratio and the elasticity of demand for labor; (c) the number of substitutes for labor and the elasticity of demand for labor.

working with numbers and graphs

1   Determine the appropriate numbers for the lettered spaces.

(1) Units of Factor X	(2) Quantity of Output	(3) Marginal Physical Product of X (MPP_X)	(4) Product Price, Marginal Revenue $(P = MR)$	(5) Total Revenue	(6) Marginal Revenue Product of X (MRP_X)
0	15	0	$8	F	L
1	24	A	8	G	M
2	32	B	8	H	N
3	39	C	8	I	O
4	45	D	8	J	P
5	50	E	8	K	Q

2   If the price of a factor is constant at $48, how many units of the factor will the firm buy?

3   On the same diagram, draw the *VMP* curve and the *MRP* curve for an oligopolist. Explain why the curves look the way you drew them.

4   Explain why the factor supply curve is horizontal for a factor price taker.

5   Look at the two factor demand curves in the following figure. Is the price of the product that labor goes to produce higher for MRP_2 than for MRP_1? Explain your answer.

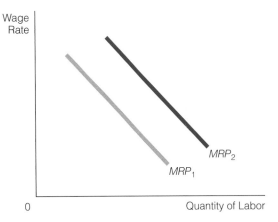

13

Wages, Unions, and Labor

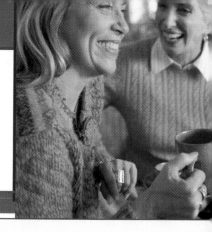

Setting the Scene

The following events occurred one day in November.

8:32 A.M.

The leaders of a union are sitting around a table, discussing what they should do in the current situation. One person says, "I think we should ask for a general wage increase of 7 percent."

"Why not more?" another person asks. "I don't think a 10 percent increase will cause much job loss."

10:04 A.M.

Sophie and Lily are having their morning coffee together at Sophie's house.

"Elliot is going to have to postpone his surgery again," Lily says. "Some union at the hospital is going on strike if the workers don't get a wage increase. The hospital is canceling all elective surgeries. Unions are always causing trouble. Too many workers in this country are members of unions."

"How many workers in the country *are* union members?" Sophie asks. "About half?"

"That would be my guess," answers Lily. "Somewhere around half."

12:46 P.M.

Tom and Carla Jenson have just finished their lunch in their company's cafeteria. They've been discussing their daughter's job prospects.

"I know Debbi has a good job that she likes, but I still think she should join the union," Tom says. "Union workers always get better wages."

"I know that's true in construction because my nephew's a union electrician," Carla replies. "But are you sure union wages are higher than nonunion wages in every industry?"

"I'm sure," replies Tom.

? Here are some questions to keep in mind as you read this chapter:

- *What does the wage increase a union seeks have to do with the number of union members working?*

- *What percentage of U.S. workers are members of unions?*

- *Are union wages always higher than nonunion wages in a given industry?*

See `analyzing the scene` at the end of this chapter for answers to these questions.

The Facts and Figures of Labor Unions

This section discusses the different types of labor unions and gives some statistics that place unions within the overall labor force.

Types of Unions

Economists often speak of three different types of labor unions: craft (trade) unions, industrial unions, and public employee unions. A **craft** or **trade union** is a union whose membership is made up of individuals who practice the same craft or trade. Examples include the plumbers', electricians', and musicians' unions.

An **industrial union** is a union whose membership is made up of workers who work in the same firm or industry but do not all practice the same craft or trade. Examples include the autoworkers' and the steelworkers' unions. For an industrial union to be successful, it must unionize all firms in an industry. If it does not, union firms will face competition from (possibly lower cost) nonunion firms, which may lead to a decrease in the number of union firms and workers.

A **public employee union** is a union whose membership is made up of workers who work for the local, state, or federal government. Examples include teachers', police, and firefighters' unions.

Besides these three types of unions, some economists hold that employee associations, such as the American Medical Association (AMA), the American Association of University Professors (AAUP), and the American Bar Association (ABA), are a type of union. An **employee association** is an organization whose members belong to a particular profession. Many people would probably not place professional employee associations into the union category. Some economists argue, however, that employee associations often have the same objectives and implement the same practices to meet those objectives as craft, industrial, and public employee unions; consequently, these associations should be considered unions.

> **Craft (Trade) Union**
> A union whose membership is made up of individuals who practice the same craft or trade.
>
> **Industrial Union**
> A union whose membership is made up of individuals who work in the same firm or industry but do not all practice the same craft or trade.
>
> **Public Employee Union**
> A union whose membership is made up of individuals who work for the local, state, or federal government.
>
> **Employee Association**
> An organization whose members belong to a particular profession.

Union Membership: The United States and Abroad

Union membership as a percentage of the U.S. labor force (total number of union members divided by total work force) was 5.6 percent in 1910, rising to about 12 percent in 1920. By 1930, it was down to about 7.4 percent, and in 1934, it fell to approximately 5 percent. From the late 1930s until the mid-1950s, union membership as a percentage of the labor force grew. It reached its peak of 25 percent in the mid-1950s. In recent years, union membership has declined. In 1983, it was 20.1 percent; in 1998, it was 13.9 percent; and in 2005, it was 12.5 percent.

Union membership as a percentage of the labor force is much higher in some countries than it is in the United States. For example, in 2001, it was more than 80 percent in Denmark, about 79 percent in Sweden, more than 40 percent in Ireland, about 39 percent in Austria, more than 30 percent in both Italy and Germany, and about 20 percent in Japan.

Objectives of Labor Unions

Labor unions usually seek one of three objectives: (1) to employ all their members, (2) to maximize the total wage bill, or (3) to maximize income for a limited number of union members.

Employment for All Members

One possible objective of a labor union is employment for all its members. To illustrate, suppose the demand curve in Exhibit 1 represents the demand for labor in a given union. Also assume the total membership of the union is Q_1. If the objective of the union is to have its total membership employed, then the wage rate that must exist in the market is W_1. At W_1, firms want to hire the total union membership.

Maximizing the Total Wage Bill

The total wage bill received by the membership of a union is equal to the wage rate multiplied by the number of labor hours worked. One possible objective of a labor union is to maximize this dollar amount—that is, to maximize the number of dollars coming *from* the employer *to* union members.

In Exhibit 1, the wage rate that maximizes the total wage bill is W_2. At W_2, the quantity of labor is Q_2 and the elasticity of demand for labor is equal to 1. Recall that total revenue (or total expenditure) is maximized when price elasticity of demand is equal to 1, or demand has unit elasticity. It follows that the total wage bill is maximized at that point where the demand for labor is unit elastic. Note, however, that less union labor is working at W_2 than at W_1, indicating that there is a tradeoff between higher wages and the employment of union members.

Maximizing Income for a Limited Number of Union Members

Some economists have suggested that a labor union might want neither total employment of its membership nor maximization of the total wage bill. Instead, it might prefer to maximize income for a *limited number* of union members, perhaps those with the most influence or seniority in the union. Suppose this group is represented by Q_3 in Exhibit 1. The highest wage at which this group can be employed is W_3; thus, the union might seek this wage rate instead of any lower wage.

Q&A

Wouldn't a higher wage than **W₂** *mean that more money was being transferred from the employer to the labor union?*

Think back to our discussion of price elasticity of demand in an earlier chapter. In that chapter, we learned that if demand (for a good) is elastic, raising the price of the good results in lower total revenue instead of greater total revenue. It is the same here with respect to the wage rate. If the demand for labor is elastic, then raising the wage rate will end up lowering the total amount employers spend on labor.

micro
Theme

In an earlier chapter, we said that economic agents (firms, individuals, etc.) have objectives. Once we know their objectives, it follows that we can predict their behavior. To illustrate, if the firm's objective is to maximize profit, then it will produce the quantity of output at which $MR = MC$. We also know that different behavior is a result of different objectives. For example, the firm will behave differently if it wants to maximize profit than if it wants to maximize sales.

The same idea holds with respect to labor unions. If the objective of the labor union is to, say, employ all the workers in the union, then it will behave differently from when its objective is to maximize the income for a limited number of individuals. In the first case, the wage rate the union seeks will be lower than in the second case.

Wage-Employment Tradeoff

Exhibit 1 suggests that a union can get higher wage rates, but some of the union members will lose their jobs in the process. Hence, a wage-employment tradeoff exists. This wage-employment tradeoff depends on the *elasticity of demand for labor.*

To illustrate, consider the demand for labor in two unions, A and B, in Exhibit 2. Suppose both unions bargain for a wage increase from W_1 to W_2. The quantity of labor

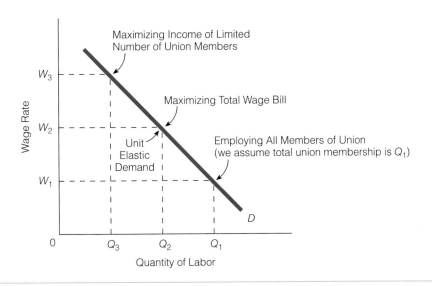

exhibit **1**

Labor Union Objectives

If total membership in the union is Q_1, and the union's objective is employment for all its members, it chooses W_1. If the objective is to maximize the total wage bill, it chooses W_2, where the elasticity of demand for labor equals 1. If the union's objective is to maximize the income of a limited number of union workers (represented by Q_3), it chooses W_3.

drops much more in union B, where demand for labor is elastic between the two wage rates, than in union A, where the demand for labor is inelastic between the two wage rates. We would expect union B to be less likely than union A to push for higher wages, *ceteris paribus*. The reason is that the wage-employment tradeoff is more pronounced for union B than for union A. It is simply costlier (in terms of union members' jobs) for union B to push for higher wages than it is for union A to do so.

micro
Theme   In an earlier chapter, we said that all economic agents face constraints. Different constraints will often bring about different behavior. For example, in our discussion of labor unions A and B, we noted that labor union B faces a sharper wage-employment tradeoff than labor union A. As a result, we predict that labor union B would be "less likely to push for higher wages, *ceteris paribus.*"

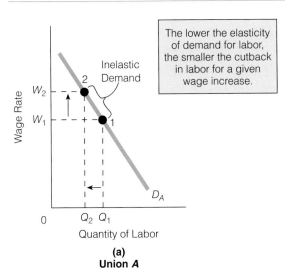

The lower the elasticity of demand for labor, the smaller the cutback in labor for a given wage increase.

(a)
Union A

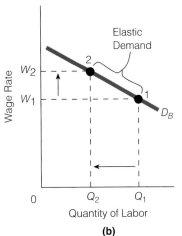

(b)
Union B

exhibit **2**

The Wage-Employment Tradeoff: Two Cases

For union A, which has an inelastic demand for its labor between W_1 and W_2, a higher wage rate brings about a smaller cutback in the quantity of labor than for union B, which has an elastic demand for its labor between W_1 and W_2. We predict that union B will be less likely to push for higher wages than union A because its wage-employment tradeoff is more pronounced.

Practices of Labor Unions

This section explains how labor unions try to meet their objectives by influencing one or more of the following factors: the elasticity of demand for labor, the demand for labor, and the supply of labor. We also discuss how unions can directly affect wages.

Affecting Elasticity of Demand for Union Labor

Exhibit 2 shows that the lower the elasticity of demand for labor, the smaller the cutback in labor for any given wage increase. Obviously, the smaller the cutback in labor for a given wage increase, the better it is from the viewpoint of the labor union. Given a choice between losing either 200 jobs or 50 jobs because of a wage rate increase of $2, the labor union prefers to lose the smaller number of jobs. Thus, a labor union looks for ways to lower the elasticity of demand for its labor. It does this mainly by attempting to reduce the availability of substitutes.

AVAILABILITY OF SUBSTITUTE PRODUCTS Consider the autoworkers' union, whose members produce American automobiles. We know that the lower the elasticity of demand for American automobiles, the lower the elasticity of demand for the labor that produces automobiles. We would expect, then, that unions would attempt to reduce the availability of substitutes for the products they produce through such means as import restrictions. The autoworkers' union, for example, has in past years proposed restrictions on the U.S. import of Japanese cars.

AVAILABILITY OF SUBSTITUTE FACTORS The fewer the substitute factors for union labor, the lower the elasticity of demand for union labor. There are two general substitutes for union labor: nonunion labor and certain types of machines. For example, a musical synthesizer (which can sound like many different instruments) is a substitute for a group of musicians playing different instruments. Labor unions have often attempted to reduce the availability of substitute factors—both the nonunion labor variety and the nonhuman variety. Thus, labor unions commonly oppose the relaxation of immigration laws, they usually favor the repatriation of illegal aliens, they generally are in favor of a high minimum wage (which increases the relative price of nonunion labor vis-à-vis union labor), and they usually oppose machines that can be substituted for their labor. Also, in the area of construction, unions usually specify that certain jobs are done by, say, electricians only (thus prohibiting substitute factors from being employed on certain jobs).

Affecting the Demand for Union Labor

Labor unions can try to meet their objectives by increasing the demand for union labor. All other things held constant, this leads to higher wage rates and more union labor employed. How can labor unions increase the demand for their labor? Consider the following possibilities.

INCREASING PRODUCT DEMAND Unions occasionally urge the buying public to buy the products produced by union labor. Union advertisements urge people to "look for the union label" or to look for the label that reads "Made in the U.S.A." As mentioned earlier, they sometimes also support legislation that either keeps out imports altogether or makes them more expensive.

INCREASING SUBSTITUTE FACTOR PRICES If union action leads to a rise in the relative price of factors that are substitutes for union labor, the demand for union labor rises. (Recall that if X and Y are substitutes and the price of X rises, so does the demand for Y.) For this reason, unions have often lobbied for an increase in the minimum wage—the wage received mostly by unskilled labor, which is a substitute for skilled union labor. The first minimum wage legislation was passed when many companies were moving from the unionized North to the nonunionized South. The minimum wage made the nonunionized, relatively unskilled labor in the South more expensive and is said to have slowed the movement of companies to the South.

INCREASING MARGINAL PHYSICAL PRODUCT If unions can increase the productivity of their members, the demand for their labor will rise. With this in mind, unions prefer to add skilled labor to their ranks, and they sometimes undertake training programs for new entrants.

Affecting the Supply of Union Labor

A third way labor unions try to meet their objectives is by decreasing the supply of labor. A decreased supply translates into higher wage rates. How might the labor union decrease the supply of labor from what it might be if the labor union did not exist? One possibility is to control the supply of labor in a market.

Craft unions, in particular, have been moderately successful in getting employers to hire only union labor. In the past, they were successful at turning some businesses into closed shops. A **closed shop** is an organization in which an employee must belong to the union before he or she can work. (In contrast, in an *open shop*, an employer may hire union or nonunion workers.) When unions can determine, or at least control in some way, the supply of labor in a given market, they can decrease it from what it would ordinarily have been. They can do this by restricting membership, by requiring long apprenticeships, or by rigid certification requirements. The closed shop was prohibited in 1947 by the Taft-Hartley Act.

The union shop, however, is legal in many states today. A **union shop** is an organization that does not require individuals to be union members to be hired but does require them to join the union within a certain period of time after becoming employed.

Today, unions typically argue for union shops, against open shops, and against the prohibition of closed shops. They also typically argue against state right-to-work laws (which some, but not all, states have), which make it illegal to require union membership for purposes of employment. (The Taft-Hartley Act allowed states to pass right-to-work laws and thus to override federal legislation that legalized union shops.) In short, the union shop is illegal in right-to-work states.

Closed Shop
An organization in which an employee must belong to the union before he or she can be hired.

Union Shop
An organization in which a worker is not required to be a member of the union to be hired but must become a member within a certain period of time after being employed.

Affecting Wages Directly: Collective Bargaining

Besides increasing wage rates indirectly by influencing the demand for and supply of their labor, unions can directly affect wage rates through collective bargaining. **Collective bargaining** is the process whereby wage rates are determined by the union bargaining with management on behalf of all its members. In collective bargaining, union members act together as a single unit to increase their bargaining power with management. On the other side of the market, the employers of labor may also band together and act as one unit. Their objective is the same as the union's: to increase their bargaining power.

From the viewpoint of the labor union, collective bargaining is unlikely to be successful unless the union can strike. A **strike** occurs when unionized employees refuse to work at a certain wage or under certain conditions. Exhibit 3 illustrates the effects of successful union collective bargaining.

Collective Bargaining
The process whereby wage rates and other issues are determined by a union bargaining with management on behalf of all union members.

Strike
The situation in which union employees refuse to work at a certain wage or under certain conditions.

exhibit 3

Successful Collective Bargaining by the Union

We start at a wage rate of W_1. The union's objective is to increase the wage rate to W_2. This means the union holds that the new supply curve of labor is $S'S$—the heavy supply curve. To convince management that the new supply curve looks as the union says it does, the union will have to either threaten a strike or call one. We assume that the union is successful at raising the wage rate to W_2. As a consequence, the quantity of labor employed is less than it would have been at W_1.

Suppose the initial wage rate that exists in the labor market is the competitive wage rate W_1. This is the wage rate that would exist if each employee were to bargain separately with management. The equilibrium quantity of labor is Q_1.

Management and the union (which represents all labor in this market) now sit down at a collective bargaining session. The union specifies that it wants a wage rate of W_2 and says that *none of its members will work at a lower wage rate*. This means the union holds that the new supply curve is $S'S$—the heavy supply curve in Exhibit 3. In effect, the union is telling management that it cannot hire anyone for a wage rate lower than W_2.

Whether the union can bring about this higher wage rate (W_2) depends on whether it can prevent labor from working at less than this wage. That is, if management does not initially agree to W_2, the union will have to call a strike and show management that it cannot hire any labor for a wage rate lower than W_2. It has to convince management that the new supply curve looks the way the union says it looks. We assume in Exhibit 3 that the strike threat, or actual strike, is successful for the union, and management agrees to the higher wage rate of W_2. As a result, the quantity of labor employed, Q_2, is less than it would have been at W_1. The new equilibrium is at point B instead of point A.

Strikes

The purpose of a strike is to convince management that the supply curve is what the union says it is. Often, this depends on the ability of striking union employees to prevent nonstriking and nonunion employees from working for management at a lower wage rate than the union is seeking through collective bargaining. For example, if management can easily hire individuals at a wage rate lower than W_2 in Exhibit 3, it will not be convinced that the heavy supply curve is the relevant supply curve.

chapter

14

The Distribution of Income and Poverty

Setting the Scene   Madison and Leslie, who have been friends since high school, are often on different sides of social and political issues. Today, they are discussing a report in the newspaper about the distribution of income in the country.

LESLIE:

The top one-fifth of income earners earned a larger percentage of the total income of the country this year than they did last year. The rich keep getting richer and the poor get poorer.

MADISON:

Just because the rich are getting richer doesn't mean the poor are getting poorer. The poor could be getting more income too.

LESLIE:

That's impossible. The rich have to be getting their larger percentage of income from somewhere—and they always get it from the poor.

MADISON:

Not necessarily. Everyone's income could rise if the national income of the country rises.

LESLIE:

Well, I still think everyone but the rich is worse off when incomes become more unequal.

MADISON:

I'm not sure about that. I seem to recall reading somewhere that whether or not people are better off depends on how many things—like goods and services—they can buy.

LESLIE:

Do you mean that if poor people can buy more things, then they're better off, even if they have a smaller percentage of the total income of the country?

MADISON:

That's exactly what I mean. An unequal income distribution isn't necessarily bad news for the poor.

? Here is a question to keep in mind as you read this chapter:

• *Can everyone become better off as the income distribution becomes more unequal?*

See analyzing the scene at the end of this chapter for an answer to this question.

© BANANASTOCK/JUPITER IMAGES

Some Facts About Income Distribution

In discussing public policy issues, people sometimes talk about a single fact when they should talk about facts. A single fact is usually not as informative as facts are, in much the same way that a single snapshot does not tell as much of a story as a moving picture—a succession of snapshots. This section presents a few facts about the distribution of income.

Who Are the Rich and How Rich Are They?

By many interpretations, the lowest fifth (lowest quintile) of households in the United States is considered poor, the top fifth is considered rich, and the three-fifths in between are considered middle income.[1]

In 2004, the lowest fifth (the poor) in the United States received 3.4 percent of the total money income, the second fifth received 8.9 percent, the third fifth received 14.7 percent, the fourth fifth received 23.0 percent, and the top fifth (the rich) received 50.0 percent (see Exhibit 1).[2]

Has the income distribution become more or less equal over time? Exhibit 2 shows the income shares of households in 1967 and 2004. In 1967, the highest fifth (top) of households accounted for 43.8 percent of all income; in 2004, the percentage had risen to 50.0 percent.

At the other end of the income spectrum, in 1967, the lowest fifth received 4.0 percent of all income; in 2004, the percentage had fallen to 3.4 percent. The middle groups—the three-fifths of income recipients between the lowest fifth and the highest fifth—accounted for 52.3 percent of all income in 1967 and 46.6 percent in 2004.

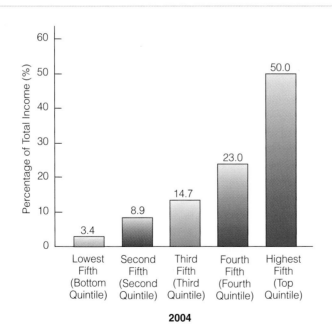

2004

Distribution of Household Income Shares, 2004

The annual income shares for different quintiles of households is shown here.

Source: U.S. Bureau of the Census.

---

[1] A household consists of all people who occupy a housing unit. It includes the related family members and all unrelated people.

[2] Percentages in this chapter do not always equal 100 percent due to rounding.

1967

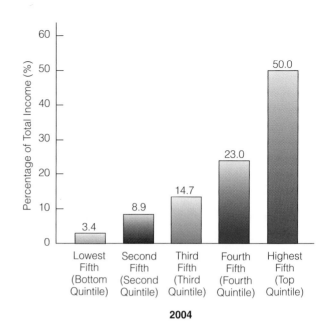

2004

exhibit **2**

Income Distribution, 1967 and 2004

Note that income shares have not been adjusted for such things as taxes and in-kind transfer payments, which are transfer payments made in terms of a specific good or service rather than in cash.

Keep in mind as you look at the data that most persons implicitly assume that the quintiles (the fifths) in income distributions contain equal shares of the population. But the official Bureau of the Census income "quintiles" do not contain equal shares of the population. The Census Bureau quintiles are unequal in size because they are based on a count of households rather than persons. In the United States, high-income households tend to be married couples with many members and earners. Low-income households tend to be single persons with little or no earnings. The average household in the top quintile contains 3.2 persons, and the average household in the bottom quintile contains 1.8 persons.

Some economists have argued that the unequal quintile populations skew the Census's measure of the income distribution. For example, in 2002, the top quintile contained 24.6 percent of the population, and the bottom quintile contained 14.3 percent of the population. Stated differently, there were 69.4 million persons in the highest "fifth" and 40.3 million persons in the lowest "fifth."

If we adjust the income distribution so that each quintile actually contains 20 percent of the population, then we get different results. In 2002, the income share of the lowest fifth rises from 3.5 percent to 9.4 percent, and the income share of the highest fifth falls from 49.7 percent to 39.6 percent.

Sometimes, economists make further adjustments to the income distribution. For example, the persons in each fifth do not all work the same number of hours. In 2002, individuals in the lowest fifth performed 4.3 percent of all work in the U.S. economy, and those in the highest fifth performed 33.9 percent. To be fair, the low levels of paid employment in the lowest fifth reflect the low numbers of working-age population in this group. In 2002, the lowest fifth contained only 11.2 percent of all working-age adults, and the highest fifth contained 27.6 percent. However, when we compare working-age adults in the lowest fifth with working-age adults in the highest fifth, we learn that the average working-age adult in the lowest fifth worked about half as many hours a year as the working-age adult in the highest fifth.

What was the median household income in the United States in 2004?

It was $44,389. You might also be interested in knowing that between 1967 and 2004, real median household income increased by 30 percent.

The Effect of Age on the Income Distribution

In analyzing the income distribution, it is important to distinguish between people who are poor for long periods of time (sometimes their entire lives) and people who are poor temporarily. Consider Sherri Holmer, who attends college and works part time as a waitress at a nearby restaurant. Currently, her income is so low that she falls into the lowest quintile of income earners. But it isn't likely that this will always be the case. After she graduates from college, Sherri's income will probably rise. If she is like most people, her income will rise during her twenties, thirties, and forties. In her late forties or early fifties, her income will take a slight downturn and then level off.

It is possible, in fact highly likely, that a person in her late twenties, thirties, or forties will have a higher income than a person in his early twenties or a person in her sixties, even though their total lifetime incomes will be identical. If we view each person over time, income equality is greater than if we view each person at a particular point in time (say, when one person is 58 years old and the other is 68 years old).

To illustrate, look at Exhibit 3, which shows the incomes of John and Stephanie in different years. In 2000, John is 18 years old and earning $10,000 per year, and Stephanie is 28 years old and earning $30,000 a year. The income distribution between John and Stephanie is unequal in 2000.

Ten years later, the income distribution is still unequal, with Stephanie earning $45,000 and John earning $35,000. In fact, the income distribution is unequal in every year shown in the exhibit. However, the total income earned by each person is $236,000, giving a perfectly equal income distribution over time.

In the United States, there seems to be quite a bit of upward income mobility over time. The University of Michigan's Panel Survey on Dynamics tracked 50,000 Americans for 17 years. Of the people in the lowest fifth of the income distribution in 1975, only 5.1 percent were still there in 1991—and 29 percent of them were in the highest fifth.

A Simple Equation

Before discussing the possible sources or causes of income inequality, we need to identify the factors that determine a person's income. The following simple equation combines four of these factors: labor income, asset income, transfer payments, and taxes:

Individual income = Labor income + Asset income + Transfer payments − Taxes

Year	John's Age	John's Income	Stephanie's Age	Stephanie's Income
2000	18 years	$10,000	28 years	$30,000
2010	28	35,000	38	45,000
2020	38	52,000	48	60,000
2030	48	64,000	58	75,000
2040	58	75,000	68	26,000
Total		$236,000		$236,000

Thinking like AN ECONOMIST *Many people believe that poor is poor. This is not the case for the economist. The economist wants to know why the person is poor. Is he poor because he is young and just starting out in life? Would he be poor if we were to consider the* **in-kind transfer payments** *or in-kind benefits he receives? Some people argue that when someone is poor, you don't ask questions, you simply try to help him. But the economist knows that not everyone is in the same situation for the same reason. The reason may determine whether or not you proceed with help, and if you do proceed, just how you do so. Both the elderly person with a disability and the young, smart college student may earn the same low income, but you may feel it is more important to help the elderly person with a disability than the college student.*

In-Kind Transfer Payments
Transfer payments, such as food stamps, medical assistance, and subsidized housing, that are made in a specific good or service rather than in cash.

exhibit 3

Income Distribution at One Point in Time and Over Time

In each year, the income distribution between John and Stephanie is unequal, with Stephanie earning more than John in 2000, 2010, 2020, and 2030 and John earning more than Stephanie in 2040. In the five years specified, however, both John and Stephanie earned the same total income of $236,000, giving a perfectly equal income distribution over time.

Labor income is equal to the wage rate an individual receives multiplied by the number of hours he or she works. Asset income consists of such things as the return to saving, the return to capital investment, and the return to land. **Transfer payments** refer to payments to persons that are not made in return for goods and services currently supplied (e.g., Social Security payments and cash welfare assistance are government transfer payments). Finally, from the sum of labor income, asset income, and transfer payments, we subtract taxes to see what an individual is left with (individual income). This equation provides a quick way of focusing on the direct and indirect factors that affect an individual's income and the degree of income inequality. The next section examines the conventional ways that income inequality is measured.

Transfer Payments

Payments to persons that are not made in return for goods and services currently supplied.

SELF-TEST

(Answers to Self-Test questions are in the Self-Test Appendix.)

1.   How can government change the distribution of income?

2.   Income inequality at one point in time is sometimes consistent with income equality over time. Comment.

3.   Smith and Jones have the same income this year, $40,000. Does it follow that their income came from the same sources? Explain your answer.

Lorenz Curve

A graph of the income distribution. It expresses the relationship between cumulative percentage of households and cumulative percentage of income.

Measuring Income Equality

Two commonly used measures of income inequality are the Lorenz curve and the Gini coefficient. We explain and discuss both measures in this section.

The Lorenz Curve

The **Lorenz curve** represents the distribution of income; it expresses the relationship between cumulative percentage of households and *cumulative percentage of income*. Exhibit 4 shows a hypothetical Lorenz curve.

exhibit **4**

A Hypothetical Lorenz Curve

The data in (a) were used to derive the Lorenz curve in (b). The Lorenz curve shows the cumulative percentage of income earned by the cumulative percentage of households. If all households received the same percentage of total income, the Lorenz curve would be the line of perfect income equality. The bowed Lorenz curve shows an unequal distribution of income. The more bowed the Lorenz curve is, the more unequal the distribution of income.

Quintile	Income Share (percent)	Cumulative Income Share (percent)
Lowest fifth	10%	10%
Second fifth	15	25
Third fifth	20	45
Fourth fifth	25	70
Highest fifth	30	100

(a)

(b)

The data in part (a) are used to plot the Lorenz curve in part (b). According to (a), the lowest fifth of households has an income share of 10 percent, the second fifth has an income share of 15 percent, and so on. The Lorenz curve in (b) is derived by plotting five points. Point *A* represents the cumulative income share of the lowest fifth of households (10 percent of income goes to the lowest fifth of households). Point *B* represents the cumulative income share of the lowest fifth plus the second fifth (25 percent of income goes to two-fifths, or 40 percent, of the income recipients). Point *C* represents the cumulative income share of the lowest fifth plus the second fifth plus the third fifth (45 percent of income goes to three-fifths, or 60 percent, of the income recipients). The same procedure is used for points *D* and *E*. Connecting these points gives the Lorenz curve that represents the data in (a); the Lorenz curve is another way of depicting the income distribution in (a). Exhibit 5 illustrates the Lorenz curve for the United States based on the (money) income shares in Exhibit 1.

What would the Lorenz curve look like if there were perfect income equality among different households? In this case, every household would receive exactly the same percentage of total income, and the Lorenz curve would be the line of perfect income equality illustrated in Exhibit 4(b). At any point on this 45-degree line, the cumulative percentage of income (on the vertical axis) equals the cumulative percentage of households (on the horizontal axis). For example, at point *F,* 60 percent of the households receive 60 percent of the total income.

The Gini Coefficient

The **Gini coefficient** is a measure of the degree of inequality in the income distribution and is used in conjunction with the Lorenz curve. It is equal to the area between the line of perfect income equality (or 45-degree line) and the actual Lorenz curve divided by the entire triangular area under the line of perfect income equality.

Gini Coefficient
A measure of the degree of inequality in the income distribution.

$$\text{Gini Coefficient} = \frac{\text{Area between the line of perfect income equality and actual Lorenz curve}}{\text{Entire triangular area under the line of perfect income equality}}$$

Exhibit 6 illustrates both the line of perfect income equality and an actual Lorenz curve. The Gini coefficient is computed by dividing the shaded area (the area between

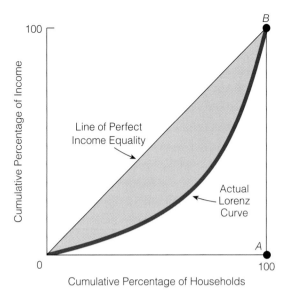

exhibit **6**

The Gini Coefficient

The Gini coefficient is a measure of the degree of income inequality. It is equal to the area between the line of perfect income equality and the actual Lorenz curve divided by the entire triangular area under the line of perfect income equality. In the diagram, this is equal to the shaded portion divided by the triangular area 0AB. A Gini coefficient of 0 means perfect income equality; a Gini coefficient of 1 means complete income inequality. The larger the Gini coefficient, the greater the income inequality; the smaller the Gini coefficient, the lower the income inequality

the line of perfect income equality and the actual Lorenz curve) by the area 0AB (the entire triangular area under the line of perfect income equality).

The Gini coefficient is a number between 0 and 1. At one extreme, the Gini coefficient equals 0 if the numerator in the equation is 0. A numerator of 0 means there is no area between the line of perfect income equality and the actual Lorenz curve, implying that they are the same. It follows that a Gini coefficient of 0 means perfect income equality.

At the other extreme, the Gini coefficient equals 1 if the numerator in the equation is equal to the denominator. If this is the case, the actual Lorenz curve is as far away from the line of perfect income equality as is possible. It follows that a Gini coefficient of 1 means complete income inequality. (What would the actual Lorenz curve look like if there were complete income inequality? In this situation, one person would have all the total income, and no one else would have any income. In Exhibit 4, a Lorenz curve representing complete income inequality would lie along the horizontal axis from 0 to A and then move from A to B.)

If a Gini coefficient of 0 represents perfect income equality and a Gini coefficient of 1 represents complete income inequality, then it follows that the larger the Gini coefficient, the higher the degree of income inequality, and the smaller the Gini coefficient, the lower the degree of income inequality. In 2004, the Gini coefficient in the United States was 0.450; in 1947, the Gini coefficient in the United States was 0.376.

A Limitation of the Gini Coefficient

Although we can learn the degree of inequality in the income distribution from the Gini coefficient, we have to be careful not to misinterpret it. For example, suppose the Gini coefficient is 0.33 in country 1 and 0.25 in country 2. We know the income distribution is more equal in country 2 than in country 1. But in which country does the lowest fifth of households receive the larger percentage of income? The natural inclination is to answer in the country with the more equal income distribution—country 2. However, this may not be true.

To see this, consider Exhibit 7, which shows two Lorenz curves. Overall, Lorenz curve 2 is closer to the line of perfect income equal-

Q&A

What is the Gini coefficient of various countries?

Argentina, 0.52 (in 2001); Brazil, 0.59 (2004); Canada, 0.33 (1998); China, 0.44 (2002); Denmark, 0.23 (2002); France, 0.33 (1995); Iran, 0.43 (1998); Ireland, 0.36 (1996); Israel, 0.34 (2005); Japan, 0.38 (2000); Mexico, 0.55 (2000); Turkey, 0.42 (2003).

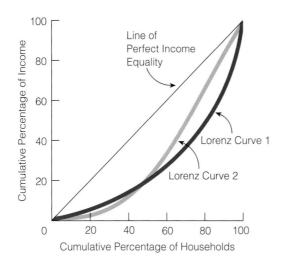

exhibit **7**

Limitation of the Gini Coefficient

By itself, the Gini coefficient cannot tell us anything about the income share of a particular quintile. Although there is a tendency to believe that the bottom quintile receives a larger percentage of total income the lower the Gini coefficient, this need not be the case. In the diagram, the Gini coefficient for Lorenz curve 2 is lower than the Gini coefficient for Lorenz curve 1. But, the bottom 20 percent of households obtains a smaller percentage of total income in the lower Gini coefficient case.

ity than Lorenz curve 1 is; thus, the Gini coefficient for Lorenz curve 2 is smaller than the Gini coefficient for Lorenz curve 1. But notice that the lowest 20 percent of households has a smaller percentage of total income with Lorenz curve 2 than with Lorenz curve 1.

Our point is that the Gini coefficient cannot tell us what is happening in different quintiles. We should not jump to the conclusion that because the Gini coefficient is lower in country 2 than in country 1, the lowest fifth of households has a greater percentage of total income in country 2 than in country 1.

SELF-TEST

1.   Starting with the top fifth of income earners and proceeding to the lowest fifth, suppose the income share of each group is 40 percent, 30 percent, 20 percent, 10 percent, and 5 percent. Can these percentages be right?

2.   Country *A* has a Gini coefficient of 0.45. What does this mean?

Why Income Inequality Exists

Why does income inequality exist? This question can be answered by focusing on our simple equation:

Individual income = Labor income + Asset income + Transfer payments – Taxes

Generally, income inequality exists because people do not receive the same labor income, asset income, and transfer payments, or pay the same taxes. But why don't they receive, say, the same labor income and asset income? This section discusses some of the specific reasons for income inequality by focusing on factors that often contribute to differences in labor and asset income. The next section looks at some of the proposed standards of income distribution.

Factors Contributing to Income Inequality

Six factors that contribute to income inequality are innate abilities and attributes, work and leisure, education and other training, risk taking, luck, and wage discrimination.

economics 24/7

WINNER-TAKE-ALL MARKETS[3]

Two economists, Robert Frank and Philip Cook, published a book in 1995 titled *The Winner-Take-All Society.* In the book, they argue that there are more winner-take-all markets today than in the past. A winner-take-all market is one in which the top producer or performer in the market earns appreciably more than others in the market earn. In fact, the top producers earn so much more than others that it is as if they "take it all."

For example, in making major movies, the producer, director, and leading actor may earn much more than anyone else involved in the movie. In the sports market, the sports stars earn more than their fellow players. For example, the last year that Michael Jordan played basketball with the Chicago Bulls, he earned 121 times the salary of the lowest paid player.

Frank and Cook state that there is nothing new about winner-take-all markets in sports and entertainment. What is new, they argue, is that winner-take-all is becoming a common feature of other markets. Winner-take-all is becoming increasingly more descriptive in such fields as law, journalism, design, investment banking, and medicine.

Do the data support what Frank and Cook are saying? Recent statistics show that "within-group" income inequality has been rising. In other words, the "winnings" have come to be concentrated on a smaller percentage of people in an industry. To illustrate, in 1980, major U.S. chief executive officers (CEOs) earned an average of 42 times the amount an average American production worker earned; by 2003, this multiple had jumped to 301.[4] There are other examples that illustrate the same phenomenon, prompting Frank and Cook to comment that we are increasingly coming to live in a winner-take-all society.

What has happened in recent years to bring about more winner-take-all markets and greater within-group income inequality? Frank and Cook identify two things: (1) developments in communications, manufacturing technology, and transportation costs that let top performers serve broader markets (a global marketplace) and (2) implicit and explicit rules that have led to more competition for top performers.

Let's look at the first cause identified by Frank and Cook. In a winner-take-all market, the demand for goods and services is focused on a small number of suppliers. This is not, as some

INNATE ABILITIES AND ATTRIBUTES Individuals are not all born with the same innate abilities and attributes. People vary in the degree of intelligence, good looks, and creativity they possess. Some individuals have more marketable innate abilities and attributes than others have. For example, the man or woman born with exceptionally good looks, the "natural" athlete, or the person who is musically gifted or mathematically adept is more likely to earn a higher income than someone with lesser abilities or attributes.

WORK AND LEISURE There is a tradeoff between work and leisure: More work means less leisure, and less work means more leisure. Some individuals will choose to work more hours (or take a second job) and thus have less leisure. This choice will be reflected in their labor income. They will earn a larger income than persons who choose not to work more, *ceteris paribus.*

EDUCATION AND OTHER TRAINING Economists usually refer to schooling and other types of training as an "investment in human capital." To buy a capital good or to invest in one, a person has to give up present consumption. A person does so in the hope that the capital good will increase his or her future consumption.

Schooling can be looked on as capital. First, one must give up present consumption to obtain it. Second, by providing individuals with certain skills and knowledge, schooling can increase their future consumption over what it would be without the schooling.

may think, because government is limiting our choices. According to Frank and Cook, we are simply focusing on "the best" suppliers to a greater degree than before because of changes in technology, communications, and transportation costs.

For example, consumers today do not have to settle for buying tires, cars, clothes, books, or much of anything else from regional or national producers of these items. They can buy these items from the best producers in the world. As Frank notes, while once a firm that produced a good tire in northern Ohio could be assured of selling tires in its regional market, today it cannot. Consumers buy tires from a handful of the best tire producers in the world.

Let's consider another example, one in which technological development plays an important part. Before there were records, tapes, or CDs, a person had to go to a concert to hear music. After the technology was developed for producing records, tapes, and CDs, this was no longer necessary. The best singers and bands in the world could simply put their music on a record, tape, or CD, and anyone in the world could listen to it. It was no longer necessary for a person living in a small town to go to a local concert to hear music performed by what may have been a very mediocre musician. Now, that person could listen to music performed by the best musicians in the world. His demand for music, and that of others, became focused on a smaller pool of musicians. As a consequence, these top musicians began to witness large increases in their earnings.

Now consider the second cause identified by Frank and Cook for the increase in within-group income inequality.

Frank and Cook argue that greater competition for top performers can be the result of a legal change. For example, consider the deregulation in airline, trucking, banking, brokerage, and other industries. Deregulation may have increased the salary competition for top performers, thus driving up their wages.

But why would this be an effect of deregulation? The answer is because in a deregulated environment, (market) competition comes to play a bigger role in determining outcomes—both "good" and "bad." Specifically, in a deregulated environment, the potential for both profits and losses is greater than in a regulated (less competitive) environment. To capture the higher potential profits and to guard against the increased likelihood of losses, talented professionals become more valuable to a firm.

Also, perhaps as a result of a less regulated, more fiercely competitive product market, the once widely accepted practice of companies promoting from within is today falling by the wayside. Increasingly, companies search for the top talent in other firms and industries and not just the top talent in their company pool. While once a top performer in a soft-drink company could expect only soft-drink companies to compete for his or her services, he or she can now expect to receive offers from soft-drink companies, computer companies, insurance companies, and more.

[3]This feature is based on Robert H. Frank, "Talent and the Winner-Take-All Society," in *The American Prospect*, no. 17 (Spring 1994): 97–107.
[4]The 2003 multiple is from *BusinessWeek*'s 54th Annual Executive Compensation Survey, April 2004.

Schooling, then, is human capital. In general, **human capital** refers to education, the development of skills, and anything else that is particular to the individual and increases his or her productivity.

Contrast a person who has obtained an education with a person who has not. The educated person is likely to have certain skills, abilities, and knowledge that the uneducated person lacks. Consequently, he or she is likely to be worth more to an employer. Most college students know this; it is part of the reason they attend college.

RISK TAKING Individuals have different attitudes toward risk. Some individuals are more willing to take on risk than others are. Some of the individuals who are willing to take on risk will do well and rise to the top of the income distribution, and others will fall to the bottom. Individuals who prefer to play it safe aren't as likely to reach the top of the income distribution or to hit the bottom.

LUCK When individuals can't explain why something has happened to them, they often say it was the result of good or bad luck. At times, the good or bad luck explanation makes sense; at other times, it is more a rationalization than an explanation.

Good and bad luck may influence incomes. For example, the college student who studies biology only to find out in her senior year that the bottom has fallen out of the biology market has experienced bad luck. The farmer who hits oil while digging a well

Human Capital
Education, development of skills, and anything else that is particular to the individual and increases his or her productivity.

has experienced good luck. An automobile worker who is unemployed owing to a recession he had no part in causing is experiencing bad luck. A person who trains for a profession in which there is an unexpected increase in demand experiences good luck.

Although luck can and does influence incomes, it is not likely to have (on average) a large or long-run effect. The person who experiences good luck today, and whose income reflects this fact, isn't likely to experience luck-boosting income increases time after time. In the long run, such factors as innate ability and attributes, education, and personal decisions (how much work, how much leisure?) are more likely to have a larger, more sustained effect on income than luck will have.

Wage Discrimination

The situation that exists when individuals of equal ability and productivity (as measured by their contribution to output) are paid different wage rates.

WAGE DISCRIMINATION Wage discrimination exists when individuals of equal ability and productivity, as measured by their marginal revenue products, are paid different wage rates by the same employer. It is a fact that in the period as a whole since World War II, the median income of African Americans has been approximately 60 percent that of whites. It is also a fact that since the late 1950s, females working full time have earned approximately 60-70 percent of the male median income. Are these differences between white and black incomes and between male and female incomes due wholly to discrimination? Most empirical studies show that approximately half the differences are due to differences in education, productivity, and job training (although one may ask if discrimination has anything to do with the education, productivity, and job training differences). The remainder of the wage differential is due to other factors, one of which is hypothesized to be discrimination.

Most people agree that discrimination exists, although they differ on the degree to which they think it affects income. We should also note that discrimination is not always directed at employees by employers. For example, consumers may practice discrimination—some white consumers may wish to deal only with white physicians and lawyers; some Asian Americans may wish to deal only with Asian American physicians and lawyers.

Income Differences: Some Are Voluntary, Some Are Not

Even in a world with no discrimination, differences in income would still exist. Other factors, which we have noted, account for this. Some individuals would have more marketable skills than others, some individuals would decide to work harder and longer hours than others, some individuals would take on more risk than others, and some individuals would undertake more schooling and training than others. Thus, some degree of income inequality occurs because individuals are innately different and make different choices. However, some degree of income inequality is also due to factors unrelated to innate ability or choices—such as discrimination or luck.

An interesting debate continues to be waged on the topic of discrimination-based income inequality. The opposing sides weight different factors differently. Some people argue that wage discrimination would be reduced if markets were allowed to be more competitive, more open, and freer. They believe that in an open and competitive market with few barriers to entry and no government protection of privileged groups, discrimination would have a high price. Firms that didn't hire the best and the brightest—regardless of a person's race, religion, or gender—would suffer. They would ultimately pay for their act of discrimination by having higher labor costs and lower profits. Individuals holding this view usually propose that government deregulate, reduce legal barriers to entry, and in general, not hamper the workings of the free market mechanism.

Others contend that even if the government were to follow this script, much wage discrimination would still exist. They think government should play an active legislative role in reducing both wage discrimination and other types of discrimination that they believe ultimately result in wage discrimination. The latter include discrimination in education and discrimination in on-the-job training. Proponents of an active role for government usually believe that such policy programs as affirmative action, equal pay for equal work, and comparable worth (equal pay for comparable work) are beneficial in reducing both the amount of wage discrimination in the economy and the degree of income inequality.

SELF-TEST

1. Jack and Harry work for the same company, but Jack earns more than Harry. Is this evidence of wage discrimination? Explain your answer.

2. A person decides to assume a lot of risk in earning an income. How could this affect his or her income?

Normative Standards of Income Distribution

For hundreds of years, economists, political philosophers, and political scientists, among others, have debated what constitutes a proper, just, or fair distribution of income and have proposed different normative standards. This section discusses three of the better known normative standards of income distribution: the marginal productivity normative standard, the absolute (complete) income equality normative standard, and the Rawlsian normative standard.

The Marginal Productivity Normative Standard

The marginal productivity theory of factor prices states that in a competitive setting, people tend to be paid their marginal revenue products.[5] The marginal productivity normative standard of income distribution holds that people *should* be paid their marginal revenue products.

This idea is illustrated in Exhibit 8(a). The first "income pie" in (a) represents the actual income shares of eight individuals, *A–H,* who work in a competitive setting and are paid their respective *MRP*s. The income distribution is unequal because the eight persons do not contribute equally to the productive process. Some individuals are more productive than others.

The second income pie in (a), which is the same as the first, is the income distribution that the proponents of the marginal productivity normative standard believe should exist. In short, individuals should be paid their marginal revenue products.

Proponents of this position argue that it is just for individuals to receive their contribution (high, low, or somewhere in between) to the productive process, no more and no less. In addition, paying people according to their productivity gives them an incentive to become more productive. For example, individuals have an incentive to learn more and to become better trained if they know they will be paid more as a consequence. According to this argument, without such incentives, work effort would decrease, laziness would increase, and in time, the entire society would feel the harmful effects. Critics respond that some persons are innately more productive than others and that rewarding them for innate qualities is unfair.

Keep in mind that this discussion assumes a competitive setting where people are paid their *MRP*s. Suppose a person is in a monopsony setting and is not being paid his or her *MRP.* Would the proponents of the marginal productivity normative standard argue that he or she should be? The answer is yes. People who propose normative standards think the marginal productivity standard should be applied regardless of the current

---

[5]Recall that in a competitive setting, value marginal product (*VMP*) equals marginal revenue product (*MRP*). Thus, the marginal productivity theory holds that in a competitive setting, people tend to be paid their *VMP*s, or *MRP*s.

(a) MARGINAL PRODUCTIVITY NORMATIVE STANDARD

Income Distribution That Is   Income Distribution That Should Be

(b) ABSOLUTE INCOME EQUALITY NORMATIVE STANDARD

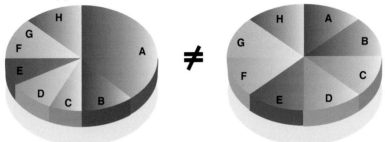

Income Distribution That Is   Income Distribution That Should Be

(c) RAWLSIAN NORMATIVE STANDARD

  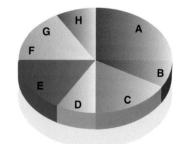

Income Distribution That Is   Income Distribution Agreed to   Income Distribution That Should Be
                                   Behind the Veil of Ignorance

situation. In other words, it is possible to be a proponent of the marginal productivity normative standard whether or not you believe people are currently being paid their marginal revenue products.

The Absolute Income Equality Normative Standard

Exhibit 8(b) illustrates the viewpoint of persons who advocate the absolute income equality normative standard. The first income pie represents the income distribution that exists—in which there is income inequality. The second income pie represents the income distribution that the persons who argue for absolute income equality believe should exist. Notice that each individual receives an equal percentage of the income pie. No one has any more or any less than anyone else.

Proponents of this position hold that an equal distribution of income will lead to the maximization of total utility (in society). The argument is as follows: (1) Individuals are alike when it comes to how much satisfaction they receive from an added increase in income. (2) Receiving additional income is subject to the law of diminishing marginal utility; that is, each additional dollar is worth less to the recipient than the dollar that preceded it. (3) From points 1 and 2, it follows that redistributing income from the rich to the poor will raise total utility. The rich will not lose as much utility from the redistribution as the poor will gain. Overall, total utility (of society) will rise through the redistribution of income from the rich to the poor. Total utility will be maximized when all persons receive the same income.

Opponents of this position hold that it is impossible to know if all individuals receive equal utility from an added dollar of income and that a rich person may receive far more utility from an added dollar of income than a poor person receives. If so, then redistributing income until it is equalized would not maximize total utility.

The Rawlsian Normative Standard

In *A Theory of Justice,* philosopher John Rawls states that individuals are less likely to argue for a different income distribution if they know what their position is in the current income distribution than if they don't know what their position is.[6]

To illustrate, Patricia Jevons is thought to be a rich person. Her income is $500,000 per year, so she is in the top 5 percent of income earners. Furthermore, the income distribution in which she occupies this position is largely unequal. There are few rich people and many poor people. Given that Patricia knows her position in the income distribution and considers it a comfortable position to occupy, she is less likely to argue for a more equal income distribution (and the high taxes that will be needed to bring it about) than if she were placed behind John Rawls's fictional *veil of ignorance.*

The **veil of ignorance** is the imaginary veil, or curtain, behind which a person does not know her position in the income distribution; that is, a person does not know whether she will be rich or poor when the veil is removed. Rawls argues that the "average" person would be more likely to vote for a more equal income distribution behind the veil than she would vote for without the veil.

Veil of Ignorance
The imaginary veil or curtain behind which a person does not know his or her position in the income distribution.

The full power of Rawls's veil of ignorance idea and its impact on income distribution can be seen in the following scenario. On Monday, everyone knows his position in the income distribution. Some people are arguing for more income equality, but a sizable group does not want this. They are satisfied with the status quo income distribution.

On Tuesday, everyone is somehow magically transported behind Rawls's veil of ignorance. Behind it, no one knows his position on the other side of the veil. No one knows whether he is rich or poor, innately talented or not, lucky or unlucky. As a group, the persons behind the veil must decide on the income distribution they wish to have when the veil is removed. Rawls believes that individuals are largely risk avoiders and will not want to take the chance that when the veil is removed, they will be poor. They will opt for an income distribution that will assure them that if they are (relatively) poor, their standard of living is not too low.

The Rawlsian normative standard is illustrated in Exhibit 8(c), which shows three income pies. The first represents the income distribution that currently exists. The second represents the income distribution that individuals behind the veil of ignorance would accept. The third and last income pie, which is the same as the second, represents the income distribution that Rawls holds should exist because it was agreed to in an

---

[6] John Rawls, *A Theory of Justice* (Cambridge: Harvard University Press, 1971).

The income pies in Exhibit 8 are drawn so that their size does not change no matter what the income distribution is. To an economist, the size of the pie is likely to change over time, and how much it changes may be related to the current income distribution. To illustrate, suppose government is determined to make all incomes the same, no matter how much income growth there is in a country. Given this, we would expect that the size of the income pie would not grow much at all. After all, individuals may not work as hard if they know that government is determined to make all incomes the same.

environment where individuals were, in a sense, equal: No one knew how he or she would fare when the veil was removed.

Critics of the Rawlsian position argue that individuals behind the veil of ignorance might not reach a consensus on the income distribution that should exist and that they might not be risk avoiders to the degree Rawls assumes they will be.

Furthermore, the individuals behind the veil of ignorance will consider the tradeoff between less income inequality and more output. In a world where the income distribution is likely to be unequal due to unequal individual productivities (sharply different marginal revenue products), reducing income inequality requires higher taxes and a lower reward for productive effort. In the end, this will lead to less productive effort being expended and less output for consumption. In short, the size of the income pie might change given different income distributions. Some of Rawls's critics maintain that individuals are likely to consider this information to a greater degree than Rawls assumes they will.

Poverty

This section presents some facts about poverty and examines its causes.

What Is Poverty?

There are principally two views of poverty. One view holds that poverty should be defined in absolute terms; the other holds that poverty should be defined in relative terms.

In absolute terms, poverty might be defined as follows: Poverty exists when the income of a family of four is less than $10,000 per year. In relative terms, poverty might be defined as follows: Poverty exists when the income of a family of four places it in the lowest 10 percent of income recipients.

Viewing poverty in relative terms means that poverty will always exist—unless, of course, there is absolute income equality. Given any unequal income distribution, some persons will always occupy the bottom rung of the income ladder; thus, there will always be poverty. This holds no matter how high the absolute standard of living of the members of the society. For example, in a society of ten persons where nine earn $1 million per year and one earns $400,000 per year, the person earning $400,000 per year is in the bottom 10 percent of the income distribution. If poverty is defined in relative terms, this person is considered to be living in poverty.

The U.S. government defines poverty in absolute terms. The absolute poverty measure was developed in 1964 by the Social Security Administration based on findings of the Department of Agriculture. Called the **poverty income threshold** or **poverty line**, this measure refers to the income below which people are considered to be living in poverty. Individuals or families with incomes below the poverty income threshold, or poverty line, are considered poor.

Poverty Income Threshold (Poverty Line)
Income level below which people are considered to be living in poverty.

In 2004, the poverty income threshold was $19,307 for a family of four. It was $9,827 for an individual under 65 years old. For an individual 65 years and older, it was $9,060.

The poverty threshold is updated yearly to reflect changes in the consumer price index. In 2004, 37 million people (in the United States), or 12.7 percent of the entire population, were living below the poverty line.

Limitations of the Official Poverty Income Statistics

The official poverty income statistics have certain limitations and shortcomings. First, the poverty figures are based solely on money incomes. Many money-poor persons receive in-kind benefits. For example, a family of four with a money income of $19,307 in 2004 was defined as poor, although it might have received in-kind benefits worth, say, $4,000. If the poverty figures are adjusted for in-kind benefits, the percentage of persons living in poverty drops.

Second, poverty figures are not adjusted for unreported income, leading to an overestimate of poverty. Third, poverty figures are not adjusted for regional differences in the cost of living, leading to both overestimates and underestimates of poverty.

Finally, government counters are unable to find some poor persons—such as some of the homeless—which leads to an underestimate of poverty.

What state has the highest poverty rate? the lowest poverty rate? What state has the largest number of people living in poverty?

In 2004, the state with the highest poverty rate (18.6 percent) was Mississippi. The state with the lowest poverty rate (5.4 percent) that year was New Hampshire. In 2004, the state with the most people living in poverty (4.7 million) was California.

Who Are the Poor?

Although the poor are persons of all religions, colors, genders, ages, and ethnic backgrounds, some groups are represented much more prominently in the poverty figures than others. For example, a greater percentage of African Americans and Hispanics than whites are poor. In 2004, 24.7 percent of African Americans, 21.9 percent of Hispanics, and 8.6 percent of whites lived below the poverty line.

A greater percentage of families headed by females than families headed by males are poor, and families with seven or more persons are much more likely to be poor than are families with fewer than seven persons. In addition, a greater percentage of young persons than others are poor, and the uneducated and poorly educated are more likely to be poor than are the educated. Overall, a disproportionate percentage of the poor are African American or Hispanic and live in large families headed by a female who is young and has little education.

If we look at poverty in terms of absolute numbers instead of percentages, then most poor persons are white, largely because there are more whites than other groups in the total population. In 2004, 25 million whites, 9.3 million African Americans, and 9.1 million Hispanics lived below the poverty line.

What Is the Justification for Government Redistributing Income?

Is there some justification for government redistributing income from the rich to the poor? Some individuals say there is no justification for government welfare assistance. In their view, playing Robin Hood is not a proper role of government. Persons who make this argument say they are not against helping the poor (e.g., they are usually in favor of private charitable organizations), but they are against government using its powers to take from some to give to others.

Some persons who believe in government welfare assistance usually present the *public good–free rider* justification or the *social-insurance* justification. Proponents of the public good–free rider position make the following arguments:

1.   Most individuals in society would feel better if there were little or no poverty. It is distressing to view the signs of poverty, such as slums, hungry and poorly clothed people, and the homeless. Therefore, there is a demand for reducing or eliminating poverty.

economics 24/7

MONKS, BLESSINGS, AND FREE RIDERS

A chief way to deal with poverty and the inequality of income is through government redistribution programs. In essence, the government can tax people with relatively high incomes and redistribute the funds—either directly or in the form of goods and services—to people with relatively low or no incomes. For example, government may use tax revenue to provide food, shelter, and medical care for the poor.

Almost all countries redistribute income in other ways too. In the United States, for example, there are private (nonreligious) and religious charities. A private organization may collect voluntary donations and use the funds to provide shelter for the homeless. Or a religious organization may collect donations from its members and use the funds to provide food and clothes for the poor.

In Thailand, Buddhist monks often play an important role in redistributing income.[7] By 10 A.M. each day, hundreds of Buddhist believers wait for the Buddhist monk, Luang Poh Koon, to emerge from his residence at the Ban Rai Temple.

When he arrives, the believers raise their right hands, which are holding (paper) money. Luang Poh Koon circulates through the crowd, taking the money from their upraised hands. He keeps one of the bills from each person; the others are returned as good-luck charms. As each person files past him to leave, he taps the person on the head with a wand of rolled-up paper as a blessing.

The believers come to Luang Poh Koon, it is reported, for two reasons. First, they believe that he will use their donations for worthwhile purposes. Luang Poh Koon collects approximately $1,000 a day, and there is strong evidence that he gives away most of the money to help build schools and hospitals. Speaking of the donors, he says, "The way I

see it, they entrust it (their money) to me to do things that are useful for the country." The second reason donors give is to be blessed. Moreover, they believe that the better the person receiving the offering, the more merit they will get.

Other monks in Thailand collect donations from believers too. Not all of them allocate the funds the way Luang Poh Koon does, however. Some of them use the money to enrich their lives. For example, some monks use the donations to purchase expensive cars and to furnish their monastery cells with high-tech audio and video equipment.

Before we conclude, think of how the "monk system" of redistributing income (to benefit the needy) solves the public good—free rider problem. Recall that the reduction or elimination of poverty is a public good; that is, when poverty is reduced or eliminated, everyone can share in the benefits of not having to view and feel the upsetting sights of poverty. But it is the public good aspect of poverty reduction and elimination that produces free riders. If no one can be excluded from experiencing the benefits of poverty reduction, then individuals will not have any incentive to pay for what they can get for free.

How does the "monk system" deal with the public good—free rider problem? If a person doesn't give funds to the monk—funds that are to be used for worthwhile purposes—then the person doesn't receive the monk's blessing. No donation, no blessing. In this way, the monks have tied something that people can receive only if they pay for it—the blessing—to a public good—the reduction or elimination of poverty.

---

[7]This feature is adapted from "Rich Are the Blessed," *Far Eastern Economic Review*, May 4, 1995. As of this writing, Luang Poh Koon is in very poor health, but he still blesses people who come to see him.

2.   The reduction or elimination of poverty is a *(nonexcludable) public good*—a good that if consumed by one person can be consumed by other persons to the same degree and the consumption of which cannot be denied to anyone. That is, when poverty is reduced or eliminated, everyone will benefit from no longer viewing the ugly and upsetting sights of poverty, and no one can be excluded from such benefits.

3.   If no one can be excluded from experiencing the benefits of poverty reduction, then individuals will not have any incentive to pay for what they can get for free. Thus, they will become free riders. Economist Milton Friedman sums up the force of the argument this way:

I am distressed by the sight of poverty. I am benefited by its alleviation; but I am benefited equally whether I or someone else pays for its alleviation; the benefits of other people's charity therefore partly accrue to me. To put it differently, we might all of us be willing to contribute to the relief of poverty, provided everyone else did it. We might not be willing to contribute the same amount without such assurance.[8]

Accepting the public good–free rider argument means that government is justified in taxing all persons to pay for the welfare assistance of some.

The social-insurance justification is a different type of justification for government welfare assistance. It holds that individuals currently not receiving welfare think they might one day need welfare assistance and thus are willing to take out a form of insurance for themselves by supporting welfare programs (with their tax dollars and votes).

SELF-TEST

1.   "Poor people will always exist." Comment.

2.   What percentage of the U.S. population was living in poverty in 2004?

3.   What is the general description of a disproportionate percentage of the poor?

A Reader Asks . . .

Are There Degrees of Poverty?

For a family of four, the poverty threshold or poverty line was $19,307 in 2004. This means that if a family of four earned less than $19,307 in 2004, it was living in poverty. But it seems that just setting a dollar figure below which someone is said to be living in poverty doesn't capture the severity or depth of poverty. After all, couldn't two four-person families have earned less than $19,307 in 2004, but still one family have earned much less than the other?

To focus in on the severity or depth of poverty, economists sometimes talk about the ratio of income to poverty.

$$\text{Ratio of income to poverty} = \frac{\text{Family's income}}{\substack{\text{Family's poverty} \\ \text{income threshold}}}$$

For example, consider two four-person families, *A* and *B*. In 2004, family *A* earned $16,000 and family *B* earned $9,000. The ratio of income to poverty for family *A* is:

$$\$16,000/\$19,307 = 0.83$$

The ratio of income to poverty for family *B* is:

$$\$9,000/\$19,307 = 0.47$$

In other words, both families are poor, but family *B* is poorer than family *A*. The depth or severity of family *B*'s poverty is greater than family *A*'s poverty.

Now suppose we consider family *C*, another four-person family, whose income was, say, $21,000 in 2004. The ratio of income to poverty for family *C* is:

$$\$21,000/\$19,307 = 1.08$$

Any time the ratio of income to poverty is greater than 1.00, a family is not considered to be living in poverty. However, if the ratio of income to poverty is between 1.00 and 1.25, the family is considered to be "near poor." Family *C*, therefore, is near poor.

As an aside, data show that one's chances of living in poverty decrease as one's educational level rises. To illustrate, 21.3 percent of the persons who did not have a high school diploma were living in poverty in 2003. This contrasts with 11.3 percent who had a high school diploma but no college, 8.5 percent who had some college but not a bachelor's degree, and 4.7 percent who had completed college and earned a bachelor's degree.

---

[8]Milton Friedman, *Capitalism and Freedom* (Chicago: University of Chicago Press, 1962), p. 191.

analyzing the scene

Can everyone become better off as the income distribution becomes more unequal?

Let's suppose that the income distribution has become more unequal and that the top one-fifth of all income earners has increased its income relative to all other fifths. Is it possible for everyone to be better off as the income distribution becomes more unequal? The answer is yes. To illustrate, suppose society is made up of five individuals, *A–E*. The yearly income for each individual is as follows: *A* earns $20,000, *B* earns $10,000, *C* earns $5,000, *D* earns $2,500, and *E* earns $1,250. The total yearly income in this society is $38,750, and the distribution of income is certainly unequal. *A* earns 51.61 percent of the income, *B* earns 25.81 percent, *C* earns 12.90 percent, *D* earns 6.45 percent, and *E* earns only 3.23 percent.

Now suppose each person earns additional real income. *A* earns $10,000 more real income for a total of $30,000, *B* earns $3,000 more real income for a total of $13,000,

C earns $2,000 more real income for a total of $7,000, *D* earns $1,000 more real income for a total of $3,500, and *E* earns $200 more real income for a total of $1,450. In terms of real income, each of the five persons is better off. But the income distribution has become even more unequal. For example, *A* (at the top fifth of income earners) now receives 54.60 percent of all income instead of 51.61 percent, and *E* (at the bottom fifth of income earners) now receives 2.64 percent instead of 3.22 percent. A newspaper headline might read, "The rich get richer as the poor get poorer." People reading this headline might naturally think that the poor in society are now worse off. But we know they are not worse off in terms of the goods and services they can purchase. They now have more real income than they had when the income distribution was less unequal. In short, it is possible for everyone to be better off even though the income distribution has become more unequal.

chapter summary

The Distribution of Income

- In 2004, the lowest fifth of households received 3.4 percent of the total money income, the second fifth received 8.9 percent, the third fifth received 14.7 percent, the fourth fifth received 23.0 percent, the top fifth received 50.0 percent.

- The government can change the distribution of income through taxes and transfer payments. Individual income = Labor income + Asset income + Transfer payments – Taxes. Government directly affects transfer payments and taxes.

- The Lorenz curve represents the income distribution. The Gini coefficient is a measure of the degree of inequality in the distribution of income. A Gini coefficient of 0 means perfect income equality; a Gini coefficient of 1 means complete income inequality.

- Income inequality exists because individuals differ in their innate abilities and attributes, their choices of work and leisure, their education and other training, their attitudes about risk taking, the luck they experience, and the amount of wage discrimination directed against them. Some income inequality is the result of voluntary choices, and some is not.

- There are three major normative standards of income distribution: (1) The marginal productivity normative standard holds that the income distribution should be based on workers being paid their marginal revenue products. (2) The absolute income equality normative standard holds that there should be absolute or complete income equality. (3) The Rawlsian normative standard holds that the income distribution decided on behind the veil of ignorance (where individuals are equal) should exist in the real world.

Poverty

- The income poverty threshold, or poverty line, is the income level below which a family or person is considered poor and living in poverty.

- It is important to be aware of the limitations of poverty income statistics. The statistics are usually not adjusted for (1) in-kind benefits, (2) unreported and illegal income, and (3) regional differences in the cost of living. Furthermore, the statistics do not count the poor who exist but are out of sight, such as some of the homeless.

- People who believe government should redistribute income from the rich to the poor usually base their argument on the public good–free rider justification or the social-insurance justification. The public good–free rider justification holds that many people are in favor of redistributing income from the rich to the poor and that the elimination of poverty is a public good. But unfortunately, it is a public good that individuals cannot "produce" because of the incentive everyone has to free ride on the contributions of others. Consequently, government is justified in taxing all persons to pay for the welfare assistance of some. The social-insurance justification holds that individuals not currently receiving

redistributed monies may one day find themselves in a position where they will need to, so they are willing to take out a form of insurance. In essence, they are willing to support redistribution programs today so that these programs exist if they should need them in the future.

key terms and concepts

Transfer Payments	Lorenz Curve	Human Capital	Veil of Ignorance
In-Kind Transfer Payments	Gini Coefficient	Wage Discrimination	Poverty Income Threshold (Poverty Line)

questions and problems

1 The Gini coefficient for country A is 0.35, and for country B, it is 0.22. From this, it follows that the bottom 10 percent of income recipients in country B have a greater percentage of the total income than the bottom 10 percent of the income recipients in country A. Do you agree or disagree? Why?

2 Would you expect greater income inequality in country A, where there is great disparity in age, or in country B, where there is little disparity in age? Explain your answer.

3 Has U.S. income inequality increased or decreased (if we compare the income distribution in 1967 with the income distribution in 2004)? What percentage of total money income did the top fifth of U.S. households receive in 2004?

4 What is a major criticism of the absolute income equality normative standard?

5 In what ways does the Rawlsian technique of hypothesizing individuals behind a veil of ignorance help or not

help us decide whether we should have a 65 mph speed limit or a higher one, a larger or smaller welfare system, and higher or lower taxes imposed on the rich?

6 Welfare recipients would rather receive cash benefits than in-kind benefits, but much of the welfare system provides in-kind benefits. Is there any reason for not giving recipients their welfare benefits the way they want to receive them? Would it be better to move to a welfare system that provides benefits only in cash?

7 What is the effect of age on the income distribution?

8 Can more people live in poverty at the same time that a smaller percentage of people live in poverty? Explain your answer.

9 Can luck partly explain income inequality? Explain your answer.

10 How would you determine whether or not the wage difference between two individuals is due to wage discrimination?

working with numbers and graphs

1 The lowest fifth of income earners have a 10 percent income share, the second fifth a 17 percent income share, the third fifth a 22 percent income share, the fourth fifth a 24 percent income share, and the highest fifth a 27 percent income share. Draw the Lorenz curve.

2 In Exhibit 7, using Lorenz curve 2, approximately what percentage of income goes to the second highest 20 percent of households?

3 Is it possible for real income for everyone in society to rise even though the income distribution has become more unequal? Prove your answer with a numerical example.

International Trade

Setting the Scene

The following events happened on a day in February.

9:33 A.M.

Daisy Castle, a reporter for a local newspaper, is in the office of Duncan Carlyle, president of a nearby steel company. Daisy is interviewing the president about his company's future.

"Your company has had some problems recently," comments Daisy. "You've had to lay off some workers because your sales have been down. Do things look better for the months ahead?"

"Much depends on what Congress does in the next few weeks," replies Duncan. "We would be greatly helped—and so would this community—if Congress imposes a tariff on steel imports. That would give us the breathing room we need right now."

"Steel imports have risen dramatically the last six months," says Daisy. "Can U.S. companies compete with foreign producers?"

"Not without the tariff," Duncan answers. "We need to level the playing field."

11:54 A.M.

Jack and Harry, engineers for a large telecommunications company, are sitting at lunch, passing the time.

"What do you think about the president's newest plan on immigration?" Jack asks.

"I think the president should be cutting back on the number of immigrants instead of increasing the numbers," Harry replies. "More immigrants in the country simply lead to lower wages for Americans."

"I guess that's true," comments Jack.

"Of course it's true. It's basic supply and demand," Harry says. "An increased supply of people means more people applying for jobs, and wages have to go down."

2:43 P.M.

A student in a college economics class asks her professor if economics is really nothing more than "good ol' common sense"? In response, the professor begins to talk about comparative advantage.

© GOODSHOOT/JUPITER IMAGES

? Here are some questions to keep in mind as you read this chapter:

- *How will a tariff help the domestic steel company?*

- *Do increased numbers of immigrants lower wages?*

- *Is economics nothing more than "good ol' common sense"?*

See analyzing the scene at the end of this chapter for answers to these questions.

International Trade Theory

International trade exists for the same reasons that trade at any level exists. Individuals trade to make themselves better off. Pat and Zach, both of whom live in Cincinnati, Ohio, trade because they both value something the other has more than they value some of their own possessions. On an international scale, Elaine in the United States trades with Cho in China because Cho has something that Elaine wants and Elaine has something that Cho wants.

Obviously, different countries have different terrains, climates, resources, worker skills, and so on. It follows that some countries will be able to produce some goods that other countries cannot produce or can produce only at extremely high costs.

For example, Hong Kong has no oil, and Saudi Arabia has a large supply. Bananas do not grow easily in the United States, but they flourish in Honduras. Americans could grow bananas if they used hothouses, but it is cheaper for Americans to buy bananas from Hondurans than to produce bananas themselves.

Major U.S. exports include automobiles, computers, aircraft, corn, wheat, soybeans, scientific instruments, coal, and plastic materials. Major imports include petroleum, automobiles, clothing, iron and steel, office machines, footwear, fish, coffee, and diamonds. Some of the countries of the world that are major exporters are the United States, Germany, Japan, France, and the United Kingdom. These same countries are some of the major importers in the world too.

How Do Countries Know What to Trade?

To explain how countries know what to trade, we need to review the concept of *comparative advantage,* an economic concept first discussed in Chapter 2. In this section, we discuss comparative advantage in terms of countries rather than in terms of individuals.

COMPARATIVE ADVANTAGE Assume a two country–two good world. The countries are the United States and Japan, and the goods are food and clothing. Both countries can produce the two goods in the four different combinations listed in Exhibit 1. For example, the United States can produce 90 units of food and 0 units of clothing, 60 units of food and 10 units of clothing, or other combinations. Japan can produce 15 units of food and 0 units of clothing, 10 units of food and 5 units of clothing, or other combinations.

Suppose the United States is producing and consuming the two goods in the combination represented by point *B* on its production possibilities frontier, and Japan is producing and consuming the combination of the two goods represented by point *F* on its production possibilities frontier. In this case, neither of the two countries is specializing in the production of one of the two goods, nor are the two countries trading with each other. We call this the *no specialization–no trade (NS-NT) case* (see column 1 in Exhibit 2).

Now suppose the United States and Japan decide to specialize in the production of a specific good and to trade with each other, called the *specialization–trade (S-T) case.* Will the two countries be better off through specialization and trade? A numerical example will help answer this question. But first, we need to find the answers to two other questions: What good should the United States specialize in producing? What good should Japan specialize in producing?

The general answer to both these questions is the same: *Countries specialize in the production of the good in which they have a comparative advantage.* A country has a **comparative advantage** in the production of a good when it can produce the good at lower opportunity cost than another country can.

For example, in the United States, the opportunity cost of producing 1 unit of clothing is 3 units of food (for every 10 units of clothing it produces, it forfeits 30 units of food). So the opportunity cost of producing 1 unit of food is 1/3 unit of clothing. In

Comparative Advantage
The situation when a country can produce a good at lower opportunity cost than another country can.

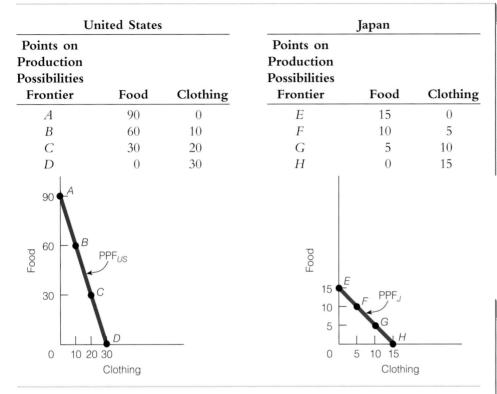

United States		
Points on Production Possibilities Frontier	Food	Clothing
A	90	0
B	60	10
C	30	20
D	0	30

Japan		
Points on Production Possibilities Frontier	Food	Clothing
E	15	0
F	10	5
G	5	10
H	0	15

exhibit 1

Production Possibilities in Two Countries

The United States and Japan can produce the two goods in the combinations shown. Initially, the United States is at point B on its PPF and Japan is at point F on its PPF. Both countries can be made better off by specializing in and trading the good in which each has a comparative advantage.

exhibit 2

Both Countries Gain from Specialization and Trade

Column 1: Both the United States and Japan operate independently of each other. The United States produces and consumes 60 units of food and 10 units of clothing. Japan produces and consumes 10 units of food and 5 units of clothing. Column 2: The United States specializes in the production of food; Japan specializes in the production of clothing. Column 3: The United States and Japan agree to the terms of trade of 2 units of food for 1 unit of clothing. They actually trade 20 units of food for 10 units of clothing. Column 4: Overall, the United States consumes 70 units of food and 10 units of clothing. Japan consumes 20 units of food and 5 units of clothing. Column 5: Consumption levels are higher for both the United States and Japan in the S-T case than in the NS-NT case.

Japan, the opportunity cost of producing 1 unit of clothing is 1 unit of food (for every 5 units of clothing it produces, it forfeits 5 units of food). To recap, in the United States, the situation is $1C = 3F$, or $1F = 1/3C$; in Japan the situation is $1C = 1F$, or $1F = 1C$.

The United States can produce food at a lower opportunity cost ($1/3C$ as opposed to $1C$ in Japan), whereas Japan can produce clothing at a lower opportunity cost ($1F$ as opposed to $3F$ in the United States). Thus, the United States has a comparative advantage in food, and Japan has a comparative advantage in clothing.

Suppose the two countries specialize in the production of the good in which they have a comparative advantage. That is, the United States specializes in the production of food (producing 90 units), and Japan specializes in the production of clothing (producing 15 units). In Exhibit 1, the United States locates at point A on its PPF, and Japan locates at point H on its PPF (see column 2 in Exhibit 2).

	No Specialization–No Trade *(NS-NT)* Case	Specialization-Trade *(S-T)* Case		
Country	(1) Production and Consumption in the *NS-NT* Case	(2) Production in the *S-T* Case	(3) Exports (−) Imports (+) Terms of Trade Are $2F = 1C$	(4) Consumption in the *S-T* Case (2) + (3)	(5) Gains from Specialization and Trade (4) − (1)
United States					
Food	60 } Point *B* in	90 } Point *A* in	−20	70	10
Clothing	10 } Exhibit 1	0 } Exhibit 1	+10	10	0
Japan					
Food	10 } Point *F* in	0 } Point *H* in	+20	20	10
Clothing	5 } Exhibit 1	15 } Exhibit 1	−10	5	0

Specialization and trade appear to allow a country's inhabitants to consume at a level beyond its production possibilities frontier. Is this correct?

Yes, that is correct. To see this, look at the PPF for the United States in Exhibit 1. In the NS–NT case, the United States consumes 60 units of food and 10 units of clothing—that is, the United States consumes at point B on its PPF. In the S-T case, however, it consumes 70 units of food and 10 units of clothing. A point that represents this combination of the two goods is beyond the country's PPF.

SETTLING ON THE TERMS OF TRADE After they have determined which good to specialize in producing, the two countries must settle on the terms of trade—that is, how much food to trade for how much clothing. The United States faces the following situation: For every 30 units of food it does not produce, it can produce 10 units of clothing, as shown in Exhibit 1. Thus, 3 units of food have an opportunity cost of 1 unit of clothing ($3F = 1C$), or 1 unit of food has a cost of 1/3 unit of clothing ($1F = 1/3C$). Meanwhile, Japan faces the following situation: For every 5 units of food it does not produce, it can produce 5 units of clothing. Thus, 1 unit of food has an opportunity cost of 1 unit of clothing ($1F = 1C$). Recapping, for the United States, $3F = 1C$, and for Japan, $1F = 1C$.

With these cost ratios, it would seem likely that both countries could agree on terms of trade that specify $2F = 1C$. The United States would benefit by giving up 2 units of food instead of 3 units for 1 unit of clothing, whereas Japan would benefit by getting 2 units of food instead of only 1 unit for 1 unit of clothing. Suppose the two countries agree to the terms of trade of $2F = 1C$ and trade, in absolute amounts, 20 units of food for 10 units of clothing (see column 3 in Exhibit 2). Will they make themselves better off? We'll soon see that they do.

RESULTS OF THE SPECIALIZATION–TRADE *(S-T)* CASE

Now the United States produces 90 units of food and trades 20 units to Japan, receiving 10 units of clothing in exchange. It consumes 70 units of food and 10 units of clothing. Japan produces 15 units of clothing and trades 10 to the United States, receiving 20 units of food in exchange. It consumes 5 units of clothing and 20 units of food (see column 4 in Exhibit 2).

Comparing the consumption levels in both countries in the two cases, the United States and Japan each consume 10 more units of food and no less clothing in the specialization–trade case than in the no specialization–no trade case (column 5 in Exhibit 2). We conclude that a country gains by specializing in producing and trading the good in which it has a comparative advantage.

How Do Countries Know When They Have a Comparative Advantage?

Government officials of a country do not analyze pages of cost data to determine what their country should specialize in producing and then trade. Countries do not plot production possibilities frontiers on graph paper or calculate opportunity costs. Instead, it is individuals' desire to earn a dollar, a peso, or a euro that determines the pattern of international trade. The desire to earn a profit determines what a country specializes in and trades.

To illustrate, consider Henri, an enterprising Frenchman who visits the United States. Henri observes that beef is relatively cheap in the United States (compared with the price in France) and perfume is relatively expensive. Noticing the price differences for beef and perfume between his country and the United States, he decides to buy some perfume in France, bring it to the United States, and sell it for the relatively higher U.S. price. With his profits from the perfume transaction, he buys beef in the United States, ships it to France, and sells it for the relatively higher French price. Obviously, Henri is buying low and selling high. He buys a good in the country where it is cheap and sells it in the country where the good is expensive.

What are the consequences of Henri's activities? First, he is earning a profit. The larger the price differences in the two goods

Is the desire to earn profit useful to society at large? In our example of Henri, his desire for profit ended up moving both the United States and France toward specializing in and trading the good in which they had a comparative advantage. And as we showed earlier in the chapter, when countries specialize and trade, they are better off than when they do neither.

economics 24/7

DIVIDING UP THE WORK

John and Veronica, husband and wife, have divided up their household tasks the following way: John usually does all the lawn work, fixes the cars, and does the dinner dishes, while Veronica cleans the house, cooks the meals, and does the laundry. Why have John and Veronica divided up the household tasks the way they have? Some sociologists might suggest that John and Veronica have divided up the tasks along gender lines: Men have for years done the lawn work, fixed the cars, and so on, and women have for years cleaned the house, cooked the meals, and so on. In other words, John is doing "man's work," and Veronica is doing "woman's work."

Well, maybe, but that leaves unanswered the question of why certain work became "man's work" and other work became "woman's work." Moreover, it doesn't explain why John and Veronica don't split every task evenly. In other words, why doesn't John clean half the house and Veronica clean half the house? Why doesn't Veronica mow the lawn on the second and fourth week of every month and John mow the lawn every first and third week of the month?

The law of comparative advantage may be the answer to all our questions. To illustrate, suppose we consider two tasks: cleaning the house and mowing the lawn. The following table shows how long John and Veronica take to complete the two tasks individually.

	Time to Clean the House	Time to Mow the Lawn
John	120 minutes	50 minutes
Veronica	60 minutes	100 minutes

Here is the opportunity cost of each task for each person.

	Opportunity Cost of Cleaning the House	Opportunity Cost of Mowing the Lawn
John	2.40 mowed lawns	0.42 clean houses
Veronica	0.60 mowed lawns	1.67 clean houses

In other words, John has a comparative advantage in mowing the lawn, and Veronica has a comparative advantage in cleaning the house.

Now let's compare two settings. In setting 1, John and Veronica each do half of each task. In setting 2, John only mows the lawn and Veronica only cleans the house.

In setting 1, John spends 60 minutes cleaning half of the house and 25 minutes mowing half of the lawn for a total of 85 minutes; Veronica spends 30 minutes cleaning half of the house and 50 minutes mowing half of the lawn for a total of 80 minutes. The total time spent by Veronica and John cleaning the house and mowing the lawn is 165 minutes.

In setting 2, John spends 50 minutes mowing the lawn, and Veronica spends 60 minutes cleaning the house. The total time spent by Veronica and John cleaning the house and mowing the lawn is 110 minutes.

In which setting, 1 or 2, are Veronica and John better off? John works 85 minutes in setting 1 and 50 minutes in setting 2, so he is better off in setting 2. Veronica works 80 minutes in setting 1 and 60 minutes in setting 2, so Veronica is better off in setting 2. Together, John and Veronica spend 55 fewer minutes in setting 2 than in setting 1. Getting the job done in 55 fewer minutes is the benefit of specializing in various duties around the house. Given our numbers, we would expect that John will mow the lawn (and nothing else) and Veronica will clean the house (and nothing else).

between the two countries and the more he shuffles goods between countries, the more profit Henri earns.

Second, Henri's activities are moving each country toward its comparative advantage. The United States ends up exporting beef to France, and France ends up exporting perfume to the United States. Just as the pure theory predicts, individuals in the two countries specialize in and trade the good in which they have a comparative advantage. The outcome is brought about spontaneously through the actions of individuals trying to make themselves better off; they are simply trying to gain through trade.

SELF-TEST

(Answers to Self-Test questions are in the Self-Test Appendix.)

1. Suppose the United States can produce 120 units of X at an opportunity cost of 20 units of Y, and Great Britain can produce 40 units of X at an opportunity cost of 80 units of Y. Identify favorable terms of trade for the two countries.

2. If a country can produce more of all goods than any other country, would it benefit from specializing and trading? Explain your answer.

3. Do government officials analyze data to determine what their country can produce at a comparative advantage?

Trade Restrictions

International trade theory shows that countries gain from free international trade—that is, from specializing in the production of the goods in which they have a comparative advantage and trading these goods for other goods. In the real world, however, there are numerous types of trade restrictions, which raise the question: If countries gain from international trade, why are there trade restrictions?

The answer to this question requires an analysis of costs and benefits; specifically, we need to determine who benefits and who loses when trade is restricted. But first, we need to discuss some pertinent background information.

The Distributional Effects of International Trade

The previous section explained that specialization and international trade benefit individuals in different countries. But this benefit occurs on net. Every individual person may not gain.

To illustrate, suppose Pam Dickson lives and works in the United States making clock radios. She produces and sells 12,000 clock radios per year at a price of $40 each. As the situation stands, there is no international trade. Individuals in other countries who make clock radios do not sell their clock radios in the United States.

Then one day, the U.S. market is opened to clock radios from China. It appears that the Chinese manufacturers have a comparative advantage in the production of clock radios. They sell their clock radios in the United States for $25 each. Pam realizes that she cannot compete at this price. Her sales drop to such a degree that she goes out of business. Thus, the introduction of international trade in this instance has harmed Pam personally.

The example of Pam Dickson raises the issue of the distributional effects of free trade. The benefits of international trade are not equally distributed to all individuals in the population. The topics of consumers' and producers' surplus are relevant to our analysis.

Consumers' and Producers' Surplus

The concepts of consumers' and producers' surplus were first discussed in Chapter 3. We review them briefly in this section.

Consumers' surplus is the difference between the maximum price a buyer is willing and able to pay for a good or service and the price actually paid.

Consumers' surplus = Maximum buying price − Price paid

Consumers' surplus is a dollar measure of the benefit gained by being able to purchase a unit of a good for less than one is willing to pay for it. For example, if Yakov would have paid $10 to see the movie at the Cinemax but paid only $4, his consumer surplus is $6. Consumers' surplus is the consumers' net gain from trade.

Producers' surplus (or sellers' surplus) is the difference between the price sellers receive for a good and the minimum or lowest price for which they would have sold the good.

Producers' surplus = Price received − Minimum selling price

Producers' surplus is a dollar measure of the benefit gained by being able to sell a unit of output for more than one is willing to sell it. For example, if Joan sold her knit sweaters for $24 each but would have sold them for as low as (but no lower than) $14 each, her producer surplus is $10 per sweater. Producers' surplus is the producers' net gain from trade.

Both consumers' and producers' surplus are represented in Exhibit 3. In part (a), consumers' surplus is represented by the shaded triangle. This triangle includes the area under the demand curve and above the equilibrium price. In part (b), producers' surplus is represented by the shaded triangle. This triangle includes the area above the supply curve and under the equilibrium price.

The Benefits and Costs of Trade Restrictions

There are numerous ways to restrict international trade. Tariffs and quotas are two of the more commonly used methods. We discuss these two methods using the tools of supply and demand. We concentrate on two groups: U.S. consumers and U.S. producers.

TARIFFS A **tariff** is a tax on imports. The primary effect of a tariff is to raise the price of the imported good for the domestic consumer. Exhibit 4 illustrates the effects of a tariff on cars imported into the United States.

Tariff
A tax on imports.

The world price for cars is P_W, as shown in Exhibit 4(a). At this price in the domestic (U.S.) market, U.S. consumers buy Q_2 cars, as shown in part (b). They buy Q_1 from U.S. producers and the difference between Q_2 and Q_1 ($Q_2 - Q_1$) from foreign producers. In other words, U.S. imports at P_W are $Q_2 - Q_1$.

What are consumers' and producers' surplus in this situation? Consumers' surplus is the area under the demand curve and above the world price, P_W. This is areas 1 + 2 +

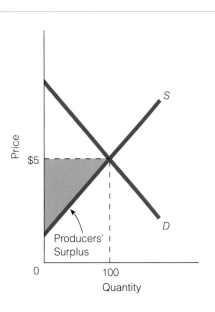

exhibit **3**

Consumers' and Producers' Surplus

(a) Consumers' surplus. As the shaded area indicates, the difference between the maximum or highest amount consumers would be willing to pay and the price they actually pay is consumers' surplus. (b) Producers' surplus. As the shaded area indicates, the difference between the price sellers receive for the good and the minimum or lowest price they would be willing to sell the good for is producers' surplus.

	Consumers' Surplus	Producers' Surplus	Government Tariff Revenue
Free trade (No tariff)	1 + 2 + 3 + 4 + 5 + 6	7	None
Tariff	1 + 2	3 + 7	5
Loss or Gain	− (3 + 4 + 5 + 6)	+3	+5

Result of Tariff = Loss to consumers + Gain to producers + Tariff revenue
$$= − (3 + 4 + 5 + 6) \qquad +3 \qquad +5$$
$$= − (4 + 6)$$

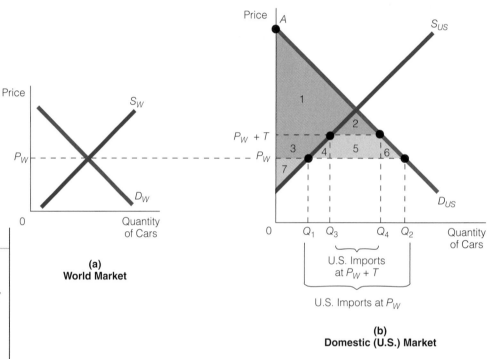

(a) World Market

(b) Domestic (U.S.) Market

exhibit 4

The Effects of a Tariff

A tariff raises the price of cars from P_W to $P_W + T$, decreases consumers' surplus, increases producers' surplus, and generates tariff revenue. Because consumers lose more than producers and government gain, there is a net loss due to the tariff.

3 + 4 + 5 + 6. Producers' surplus is the area above the supply curve and below the world price, P_W. This is area 7 (see Exhibit 4(b)).

　　Now suppose a tariff is imposed. The price for imported cars in the U.S. market rises to $P_W + T$ (the world price plus the tariff). At this price, U.S. consumers buy Q_4 cars: Q_3 from U.S. producers and $Q_4 − Q_3$ from foreign producers. U.S. imports are $Q_4 − Q_3$, which is a smaller number of imports than at the pretariff price. An effect of tariffs, then, is to reduce imports. What are consumers' and producers' surplus equal to after the tariff has been imposed? At price $P_W + T$, consumers' surplus is areas 1 + 2 and producers' surplus is areas 3 + 7.

　　Notice that consumers receive more consumers' surplus when tariffs do not exist and less when they do exist. In our example, consumers received areas 1 + 2 + 3 + 4 + 5 + 6 in consumers' surplus when the tariff did not exist but only areas 1 + 2 when the tariff did exist. Because of the tariff, consumers' surplus was reduced by an amount equal to areas 3 + 4 + 5 + 6.

　　Producers, though, receive less producers' surplus when tariffs do not exist and more when they do exist. In our example, producers received producers' surplus equal to area 7 when the tariff did not exist, but they received producers' surplus equal to areas 3 + 7 with the tariff. Because of the tariff, producers' surplus increased by an amount equal to area 3.

The government collects tariff revenue equal to area 5. This area is obtained by multiplying the number of imports $(Q_4 - Q_3)$ by the tariff, which is the difference between $P_W + T$ and P_W.[1]

In conclusion, the effects of the tariff are a decrease in consumers' surplus, an increase in producers' surplus, and tariff revenue for government. Because the loss to consumers (areas $3 + 4 + 5 + 6$) is greater than the gain to producers (area 3) plus the gain to government (area 5), it follows that *a tariff results in a net loss*. The net loss is areas $4 + 6$.

QUOTAS A **quota** is a legal limit on the amount of a good that may be imported. For example, the government may decide to allow no more than 100,000 foreign cars to be imported, or 10 million barrels of OPEC oil, or 30,000 Japanese television sets. A quota reduces the supply of a good and raises the price of imported goods for domestic consumers (Exhibit 5).

Quota
A legal limit on the amount of a good that may be imported.

---

[1]For example, if the tariff is $100 and the number of imports is 50,000, then the tariff revenue is $5 million.

	Consumers' Surplus	Producers' Surplus	Revenue of Importers
Free trade (No quota)	$1 + 2 + 3 + 4 + 5 + 6$	7	8
Quota	$1 + 2$	$3 + 7$	$5 + 8$
Loss or Gain	$- (3 + 4 + 5 + 6)$	$+3$	$+5$

Result of Quota $=$ Loss to consumers $+$ Gain to producers $+$ Gain to importers
$= - (3 + 4 + 5 + 6) \qquad +3 \qquad\qquad +5$
$= - (4 + 6)$

exhibit **5**

The Effects of a Quota

A quota that sets the legal limit of imports at $Q_4 - Q_3$ causes the price of cars to increase from P_W to P_Q. A quota raises price, decreases consumers' surplus, increases producers' surplus, and increases the total revenue importers earn. Because consumers lose more than producers and importers gain, there is a net loss due to the quota.

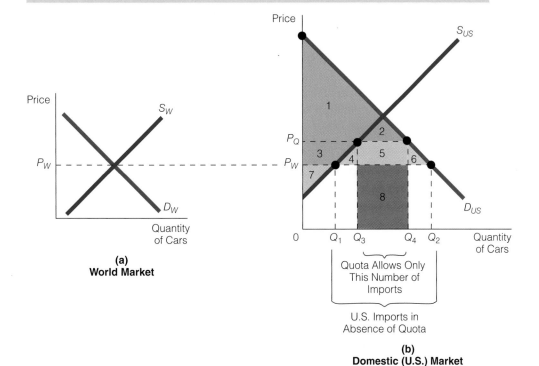

(a)
World Market

(b)
Domestic (U.S.) Market

Once again, we consider the situation in the U.S. car market. At a price of P_W (established in the world market for cars), U.S. consumers buy Q_1 cars from U.S. producers and $Q_2 - Q_1$ cars from foreign producers. Consumers' surplus is equal to areas $1 + 2 + 3 + 4 + 5 + 6$. Producers' surplus is equal to area 7.

Suppose now that the U.S. government sets a quota equal to $Q_4 - Q_3$. Because this is the number of foreign cars U.S. consumers imported when the tariff was imposed (see Exhibit 4), the price of cars rises to P_Q in Exhibit 5 (which is equal to $P_W + T$ in Exhibit 4). At P_Q, consumers' surplus is equal to areas $1 + 2$ and producers' surplus is areas $3 + 7$. The decrease in consumers' surplus due to the quota is equal to areas $3 + 4 + 5 + 6$; the increase in producers' surplus is equal to area 3.

But what about area 5? Is this area transferred to government, as was the case when a tariff was imposed? No, it isn't. This area represents the additional revenue earned by the importers (and sellers) of $Q_4 - Q_3$. Look at it this way: Before the quota, importers were importing $Q_2 - Q_1$, but only part of this total amount, or $Q_4 - Q_3$, is relevant here. Only $Q_4 - Q_3$ is relevant because this is the amount of imports now that the quota has been established. So what dollar amount did the importers receive for $Q_4 - Q_3$ before the quota was established? The answer is $P_W \times (Q_4 - Q_3)$, or area 8. Because of the quota, the price rises to P_Q and they now receive $P_Q \times (Q_4 - Q_3)$, or areas $5 + 8$. The difference between the total revenues on $Q_4 - Q_3$ with a quota and without a quota is area 5.

In conclusion, the effects of a quota are a decrease in consumers' surplus, an increase in producers' surplus, and an increase in total revenue for the importers who sell the allowed number of imported units. Because the loss to consumers (areas $3 + 4 + 5 + 6$) is greater than the increase in producers' surplus (area 3) plus the gain to importers (area 5), there is a *net loss as a result of the quota*. The net loss is equal to areas $4 + 6$.[2]

If Free Trade Results in Net Gain, Why Do Nations Sometimes Restrict Trade?

Based on the analysis in this chapter so far, the case for free trade (no tariffs or quotas) appears to be a strong one. The case for free trade has not gone unchallenged, however. Some persons maintain that at certain times, free trade should be restricted or suspended. In almost all cases, they argue that it is in the best interest of the public or country as a whole to do so. In short, they advance a public interest argument. Other persons contend that the public interest argument is only superficial; down deep, they say, it is a special interest argument clothed in pretty words. As you might guess, the debate between the two groups is often heated.

The following sections describe some arguments that have been advanced for trade restrictions.

THE NATIONAL-DEFENSE ARGUMENT It is often stated that certain industries—such as aircraft, petroleum, chemicals, and weapons—are necessary to the national defense. Suppose the United States has a comparative advantage in the production of wheat and country X has a comparative advantage in the production of weapons. Should the United States

---

[2]It is perhaps incorrect to imply that government receives nothing from a quota. Although it receives nothing directly, it may gain indirectly. Economists generally argue that because government officials are likely to be the persons who will decide which importers will get to satisfy the quota, they will naturally be lobbied by importers. Thus, government officials will likely receive something, if only dinner at an expensive restaurant while the lobbyist makes his or her pitch. In short, in the course of the lobbying, resources will be spent by lobbyists as they curry favor with government officials or politicians who have the power to decide who gets to sell the limited number of imported goods. In economics, lobbyists' activities geared toward obtaining a special privilege are referred to as rent seeking.

economics 24/7

OFFSHORE OUTSOURCING, OR OFFSHORING

Outsourcing is the term used to describe work done for a company by another company or by people other than the original company's employees. It entails purchasing a product or process from an outside supplier rather than producing this product or process in house. To illustrate, suppose company X has, in the past, hired employees for personnel, accounting, and payroll services within the company. Currently, though, it has these duties performed by a company in another state. Company X, then, has outsourced certain work activities.

When a company outsources certain work activities to individuals in another country, it is said to be engaged in offshore outsourcing, or *offshoring.* Consider a few examples. A New York securities firm replaces 800 software engineering employees with a team of software engineers in India. A computer company replaces 200 on-call technicians in its headquarters in Texas with 150 on-call technicians in India.

The benefits of offshoring for a U.S. firm are obvious; it pays lower wages to individuals in other countries for the same work that U.S. employees do for higher wages. Benefits also flow to the employees hired in the foreign countries. The costs of offshoring are said to fall on persons who lose their jobs as a result, such as the software engineer in New York or the on-call computer technician in Texas. Some have argued that offshoring will soon become a major political issue and that it could bring with it a wave of protectionism.

There is no doubt that there will be both proponents of and opponents to offshoring. But what are the effects of offshoring on net? Are there more benefits than costs or more costs than benefits? Consider a U.S. company that currently employs Jones as a software engineer, paying her $X a year. Then, one day, the company tells Jones that it has to let her go; it is replacing her with a software engineer in India who will work for $Z a year (where $Z is less than $X).

Now some have asked why Jones doesn't simply say that she will work for $Z. That is, why doesn't she offer to work for the same wage as that agreed to by the Indian software engineer? The obvious answer is because Jones can work elsewhere for some wage between $X and $Z. Assume this wage is $Y. Thus, while offshoring has moved Jones from earning $X to earning $Y, $Y is still more than $Z.

In short, the U.S. company is able to lower its costs from $X to $Z, and Jones's income falls from $X to $Y. Notice that the U.S. company lowers its costs more than Jones's income falls. That's because the difference between $X and $Z is greater than the difference between $X and $Y.

If the U.S. company operates within a competitive environment, its lower costs will shift its supply curve to the right and end up lowering prices. In other words, offshoring can end up reducing prices for U.S. consumers. The political fallout from offshoring might, in the end, depend on how visible to the average American the employment effects of offshoring are relative to the price reduction effects.

specialize in the production of wheat and then trade wheat to country X in exchange for weapons? Many Americans would answer no. It is too dangerous, they maintain, to leave weapons production to another country.

The national-defense argument may have some validity. But even valid arguments may be abused. Industries that are not really necessary to the national defense may maintain otherwise. In the past, the national-defense argument has been used by some firms in the following industries: pens, pottery, peanuts, papers, candles, thumbtacks, tuna fishing, and pencils.

THE INFANT-INDUSTRY ARGUMENT Alexander Hamilton, the first U.S. secretary of the treasury, argued that "infant," or new, industries often need protection from older, established foreign competitors until they are mature enough to compete on an equal basis. Today, some persons voice the same argument. The infant-industry argument is clearly an argument for temporary protection. Critics charge, however, that after an industry is protected from foreign competition, removing the protection is almost impossible. The once infant industry will continue to maintain that it isn't old enough to go it alone. Critics of the infant-industry argument say that political realities make it unlikely that a benefit once bestowed will be removed.

Finally, the infant-industry argument, like the national-defense argument, may be abused. It may well be that all new industries, whether they could currently compete successfully with foreign producers or not, would argue for protection on infant-industry grounds.

Dumping
The sale of goods abroad at a price below their cost and below the price charged in the domestic market.

THE ANTIDUMPING ARGUMENT Dumping is the sale of goods abroad at a price below their cost and below the price charged in the domestic market. If a French firm sells wine in the United States for a price below the cost of producing the wine and below the price charged in France, it is said to be dumping wine in the United States. Critics of dumping maintain that it is an unfair trade practice that puts domestic producers of substitute goods at a disadvantage.

In addition, critics charge that dumpers seek only to penetrate a market and drive out domestic competitors; then they will raise prices. However, some economists point to the infeasibility of this strategy. After the dumpers have driven out their competition and raised prices, their competition is likely to return. The dumpers, in turn, would have obtained only a string of losses (owing to their selling below cost) for their efforts. Opponents of the antidumping argument also point out that domestic consumers benefit from dumping because they pay lower prices.

THE FOREIGN-EXPORT-SUBSIDIES ARGUMENT Some governments subsidize the firms that export goods. If a country offers a below-market (interest rate) loan to a company, it is often argued that the government subsidizes the production of the good the firm produces. If, in turn, the firm exports the good to a foreign country, that country's producers of substitute goods call foul. They complain that the foreign firm has been given an unfair advantage that they should be protected against.[3]

Others say that one should not turn one's back on a gift (in the form of lower prices). If foreign governments want to subsidize their exports, and thus give a gift to foreign consumers at the expense of their own taxpayers, then the recipients should not complain. Of course, the recipients are usually not the ones who are complaining. Usually, the ones complaining are the domestic producers who can't sell their goods at as high a price because of the gift domestic consumers are receiving from foreign governments.

THE LOW-FOREIGN-WAGES ARGUMENT It is sometimes argued that American producers can't compete with foreign producers because American producers pay high wages to their workers and foreign producers pay low wages to their workers. The American producers insist that international trade must be restricted or they will be ruined. However, the argument overlooks the reason American wages are high and foreign wages are low in the first place: productivity. High productivity and high wages are usually linked, as are low productivity and low wages. If an American worker, who receives $20 per hour, can produce (on average) 100 units of X per hour, working with numerous capital goods, then the cost per unit may be lower than when a foreign worker, who receives $2 per hour, produces (on average) 5 units of X per hour, working by hand. In short, a coun-

---

[3]Words are important in this debate. For example, domestic producers who claim that foreign governments have subsidized foreign firms say that they are not asking for *economic protectionism,* but only *retaliation,* or *reciprocity,* or simply *tit-for-tat*—words that have less negative connotation than the words their opponents use.

try's high-wage disadvantage may be offset by its productivity advantage; a country's low-wage advantage may be offset by its productivity disadvantage. High wages do not necessarily mean high costs when productivity (and the costs of nonlabor resources) is included.

THE SAVING-DOMESTIC-JOBS ARGUMENT Sometimes, the argument against completely free trade is made in terms of saving domestic jobs. Actually, we have already discussed this argument in its different guises. For example, the low-foreign-wages argument is one form of it. That argument continues along this line: If domestic producers cannot compete with foreign producers because foreign producers pay low wages and domestic producers pay high wages, domestic producers will go out of business and domestic jobs will be lost. The foreign-export-subsidies argument is another form of this argument. Its proponents generally state that if foreign-government subsidies give a competitive edge to foreign producers, not only will domestic producers fail, but as a result of their failure, domestic jobs will be lost. Critics of the saving-domestic-jobs argument (in all its guises) often argue that if a domestic producer is being outcompeted by foreign producers and domestic jobs in a particular industry are being lost as a result, the world market is signaling that those labor resources could be put to better use in an industry in which the country holds a comparative advantage.

The World Trade Organization (WTO)

The international trade organization, the *World Trade Organization (WTO)*, came into existence on January 1, 1995. It is the successor to the General Agreement on Tariffs and Trade (GATT), which was set up in 1947. In mid-2006, 149 countries in the world were members of the WTO.

According to the WTO, its "overriding objective is to help trade flow smoothly, freely, fairly, and predictably." It does this by administering trade agreements, acting as a forum for trade negotiations, settling trade disputes, reviewing national trade policies, assisting developing countries in trade policy issues, and cooperating with other international organizations. Perhaps its most useful and controversial role is adjudicating trade disputes. For example, suppose the United States claims that the Canadian government is preventing U.S. producers from openly selling their goods in Canada. The WTO will look at the matter, consult with trade experts, and then decide the issue. A country that is found engaging in unfair trade can either desist from this practice or face appropriate retaliation from the injured country.

In theory, at least, the WTO is supposed to lead to freer international trade, and there is some evidence that it has done just this. The critics of the WTO often say that it has achieved this objective at some cost to a nation's sovereignty. For example, in the past, some of the trade disputes between the United States and other countries have been decided against the United States.

Also, some of the critics of the WTO often argue that the member countries often put trade issues above environmental issues and do not do enough to help the poor in the world. In the past, some of the critics of the WTO have taken to the streets to demonstrate against it. In a few cases, riots have broken out.

Thinking like **AN ECONOMIST** *International trade often becomes a battleground between economics and politics. The simple tools of supply and demand and consumers' and producers' surplus show that there are net gains from free trade. On the whole, tariffs and quotas make living standards lower than they would be if free trade were permitted.*

On the other side, though, are the realities of business and politics. Domestic producers may advocate quotas and tariffs to make themselves better off, giving little thought to the negative effects felt by foreign producers or domestic consumers.

Perhaps the battle over international trade comes down to this: Policies are largely advocated, argued, and lobbied for based more on their distributional effects than on their aggregate or overall effects. On an aggregate level, free trade produces a net gain for society, whereas restricted trade produces a net loss. But economists understand that just because free trade in the aggregate produces a net gain, it does not necessarily follow that every single person benefits more from free trade than from restricted trade. We have just shown how a subset of the population (producers) gains more, in a particular instance, from restricted trade than from free trade. In short, economists realize that the crucial question in determining real-world policies is more often "How does it affect me?" than "How does it affect us?"

SELF-TEST

1. Who benefits and who loses from tariffs? Explain your answer.

2. Identify the directional change in consumers' surplus and producers' surplus when we move from free trade to tariffs. Is the change in consumers' surplus greater than, less than, or equal to the change in producers' surplus?

3. What is a major difference between the effects of a quota and the effects of a tariff?

4. Outline the details of the infant-industry argument for trade restriction.

A Reader Asks . . .

Why Does the Government Impose Tariffs and Quotas?

If tariffs and quotas result in higher prices for U.S. consumers, then why does the government impose them?

The answer is that government is sometimes more responsive to producer interests than to consumer interests. But then, we have to wonder why. To explain, consider the following example.

Suppose there are 100 U.S. producers of good X and 20 million U.S. consumers of good X. The producers want to protect themselves from foreign competition, so they lobby for and receive a quota on foreign goods that compete with good X. As a result, consumers must pay higher prices. For simplicity's sake, let's say that consumers must pay $40 million more. Thus, producers receive $40 million more for good X than they would have if the quota had not been imposed.

If the $40 million received is divided equally among the 100 producers, each producer receives $400,000 more as a result of the quota. If the additional $40 million paid is divided equally among the 20 million consumers, each customer pays $2 more as a result of the quota.

A producer is likely to think, "I should lobby for the quota because if I'm effective, I'll receive $400,000." A consumer is likely to think, "Why should I lobby against the quota? If I'm effective, I'll only save $2. Saving $2 isn't worth the time and trouble my lobbying would take."

In short, the benefits of quotas are concentrated on relatively few producers, and the costs of quotas are spread out over relatively many consumers. This makes each producer's gain relatively large compared with each consumer's loss. We predict that producers will lobby government to obtain the relatively large gains from quotas but that consumers will not lobby government to keep from paying the small additional cost due to quotas.

Politicians are in the awkward position of hearing from people who want the quotas but not hearing from people who are against them. It is likely the politicians will respond to the vocal interests. Politicians may mistakenly assume that consumers' silence means that the consumers accept the quota policy, when in fact they may not. Consumers may simply not find it worthwhile to do anything to fight the policy.

! analyzing the scene

How will a tariff help the domestic steel company?

The domestic steel company gains producers' surplus from a tariff, government gains tariff revenue, and consumers lose consumers' surplus. More important, consumers lose more than what producers and government gain. It is sometimes thought that private producers are always promarket. Not so. A domestic company is often better off operating in an environment where its foreign competition has been stifled (as is the case through tariffs).

Do increased numbers of immigrants lower wages?

Some residents of the United States argue that increased immigration will cause wages in the United States to decline. Their argument is based on simple supply-and-demand analysis: Increased immigration leads to a greater supply of workers and lower wages.

There is little doubt that increased immigration will affect the supply of labor in the country. But it will affect the demand for labor too. The demand for labor is a derived demand—derived from the demand for the product that labor produces. With increased immigration, there will be more people living in the United States. A larger population translates into higher demand for food, housing, clothes, entertainment services, and so on. A higher demand for these goods translates into a higher demand for the workers who produce these goods.

In summary, increased immigration will affect both the supply of and demand for labor. What will be the effect on wages? It depends on whether the increase in demand is greater than, less than, or equal to the increase in supply.

If demand increases by more than supply, wages will rise; if supply increases by more than demand, wages will fall; if demand rises by the same amount as supply rises, wages will not change.

Is economics nothing more than "good ol' common sense"?

Many people think economics requires only common sense. But common sense often leads us to accept what sounds reasonable and sensible, and much in economics is counterintuitive—that is, it is different from what we might expect. Consider the discussion of comparative advantage. One country—the United States—is better than another country—Japan—at producing both food and clothing. Common sense might lead us to conclude that because the United States is better than Japan at producing both food and clothing, the United States could not gain by specializing and trading with Japan. But our analysis shows differently. For many people, that conclusion is counterintuitive; it goes against what intuition or good ol' common sense indicates.

chapter summary

Specialization and Trade

- A country has a comparative advantage in the production of a good if it can produce the good at a lower opportunity cost than another country can.

- Individuals in countries that specialize and trade have a higher standard of living than would be the case if their countries did not specialize and trade.

- Government officials do not analyze cost data to determine what their country should specialize in and trade. Instead, the desire to earn a dollar, peso, or euro guides individuals' actions and produces the unintended consequence that countries specialize in and trade the good(s) in which they have a comparative advantage. However, trade restrictions can change this outcome.

Tariffs and Quotas

- A tariff is a tax on imports. A quota is a legal limit on the amount of a good that may be imported.

- Both tariffs and quotas raise the price of imports.

- Tariffs lead to a decrease in consumers' surplus, an increase in producers' surplus, and tariff revenue for the government. Consumers lose more through tariffs than producers and government (together) gain.

- Quotas lead to a decrease in consumers' surplus, an increase in producers' surplus, and additional revenue for the importers who sell the amount specified by the quota. Consumers lose more through quotas than producers and importers (together) gain.

Arguments for Trade Restrictions

- The national-defense argument states that certain goods—such as aircraft, petroleum, chemicals, and weapons—are necessary to the national defense and should be produced domestically whether the country has a comparative advantage in their production or not.

- The infant-industry argument states that "infant," or new, industries should be protected from free (foreign) trade so that they may have time to develop and compete on an equal basis with older, more established foreign industries.

- The antidumping argument states that domestic producers should not have to compete (on an unequal basis) with foreign producers that sell products below cost and below the prices they charge in their domestic markets.

- The foreign-export-subsidies argument states that domestic producers should not have to compete (on an unequal basis) with foreign producers that have been subsidized by their governments.

- The low-foreign-wages argument states that domestic producers cannot compete with foreign producers that pay low wages to their employees when domestic producers pay high wages to their employees. For high-paying domestic firms to survive, limits on free trade are proposed.

- The saving-domestic-jobs argument states that through low foreign wages or government subsidies (or dumping etc.), foreign producers will be able to outcompete domestic producers, and therefore, domestic jobs will be lost. For domestic firms to survive and domestic jobs not to be lost, limits on free trade are proposed.

- Everyone does not accept the arguments for trade restrictions as valid. Critics often maintain that the arguments can be and are abused and, in most cases, are motivated by self-interest.

key terms and concepts

Comparative Advantage

Tariff

Quota

Dumping

questions and problems

1 Although a production possibilities frontier is usually drawn for a country, one could be drawn for the world. Picture the world's production possibilities frontier. Is the world positioned at a point on the PPF or below it? Give a reason for your answer.

2 "Whatever can be done by a tariff can be done by a quota." Discuss.

3 Consider two groups of domestic producers: those that compete with imports and those that export goods. Suppose the domestic producers that compete with imports convince the legislature to impose a high tariff on imports—so high, in fact, that almost all imports are eliminated. Does this policy in any way adversely affect domestic producers that export goods? If so, how?

4 Suppose the U.S. government wants to curtail imports. Would it be likely to favor a tariff or a quota to accomplish its objective? Why?

5 Suppose the landmass known to you as the United States of America had been composed, since the nation's founding, of separate countries instead of separate states. Would you expect the standard of living of the people who inhabit this landmass to be higher, lower, or equal to what it is today? Why?

6 Even though Jeremy is a better gardener and novelist than Bill is, Jeremy still hires Bill as his gardener. Why?

7 Suppose a constitutional convention was called tomorrow, and you were chosen as one of the delegates from your state. You and the other delegates must decide whether it will be constitutional or unconstitutional for the federal government to impose tariffs and quotas or restrict international trade in any way. What would be your position?

8 Some economists have argued that because domestic consumers gain more from free trade than domestic producers gain from (import) tariffs and quotas, consumers should buy out domestic producers and rid themselves of costly tariffs and quotas. For example, if consumers save $400 million from free trade (through paying lower prices) and producers gain $100 million from tariffs and quotas, consumers can pay producers something more than $100 million but less than $400 million and get producers to favor free trade too. Assuming this scheme were feasible, what do you think of it?

9 If there is a net loss to society from tariffs, why do tariffs exist?

working with numbers and graphs

1   Using the data in the table, answer the following questions: (a) For which good does Canada have a comparative advantage? (b) For which good does Italy have a comparative advantage? (c) What might be a set of favorable terms of trade for the two countries? (d) Prove that both countries would be better off in the specialization–trade case than in the no specialization–no trade case.

Points on Production Possibilities Frontier	Canada		Italy	
	Good X	Good Y	Good X	Good Y
A	150	0	90	0
B	100	25	60	60
C	50	50	30	120
D	0	75	0	180

2   In the following figure, P_W is the world price and $P_W + T$ is the world price plus a tariff. Identify the following:

a   The level of imports at P_W
b   The level of imports at $P_W + T$
c   The loss in consumers' surplus as a result of a tariff
d   The gain in producers' surplus as a result of a tariff
e   The tariff revenue as the result of a tariff
f   The net loss to society as a result of a tariff
g   The net benefit to society of moving from a tariff situation to a no-tariff situation

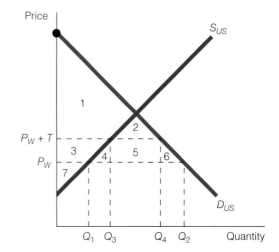

19

International Finance

Setting the Scene

The following events occurred on a day in December.

12:01 P.M.

Karen Sullivan is packing for a trip. Tomorrow, at 7:05 A.M., she'll be on a plane headed for London. She'll spend five days in London and then go to Oxford, where she'll spend two days. Then she'll board a train for Scotland and spend four days in Edinburgh. After Edinburgh, she'll head back down to England and spend a day in Harrogate, two days in Birmingham, and finally, two days in Cambridge. She's been saving for this trip for three years, and even though the dollar has been falling relative to the pound, she's still going on the trip.

1:56 P.M.

Robert Ivans owns a furniture business in North Carolina. In a given year, he exports 25 percent of the furniture he produces. This year, he expects his export business will boom because the U.S. dollar is falling in value. In fact, in four minutes, he'll begin to interview individuals for two new positions in his company.

3:06 P.M.

Winona Murphy-Collins, a business columnist for a local newspaper, just wrote the following headline: U.S. Balance of Payments at Record High.

6:11 P.M.

The president of the United States is speaking with one of his economic advisors. The advisor is telling the president that the recent run of big budget deficits is likely to affect interest rates, the value of the dollar, exports and imports, and the merchandise trade balance. The president looks at the economic advisor for a few seconds and then says, "I didn't realize things were so interconnected when it comes to the economy."

? Here are some questions to keep in mind as you read this chapter:

What does the value of the dollar have to do with Karen's trip?

What does the value of the dollar have to do with Robert Ivans's business?

Is anything wrong with the headline that the business columnist wrote?

Do big budget deficits really affect as many things as the president's economic advisor indicates?

See **analyzing the scene** at the end of this chapter for answers to these questions.

The Balance of Payments

Countries keep track of their domestic level of production by calculating their gross domestic product (GDP). Similarly, they keep track of the flow of their international trade (receipts and expenditures) by calculating their balance of payments.

The **balance of payments** is a periodic statement (usually annual) of the money value of all transactions between residents of one country and residents of all other countries. The balance of payments provides information about a nation's imports and exports, domestic residents' earnings on assets located abroad, foreign earnings on domestic assets, gifts to and from foreign countries (including foreign aid), and official transactions by governments and central banks.

Balance of payments accounts record both debits and credits. A debit is indicated by a minus (–) sign, and a credit is indicated by a plus (+) sign. *Any transaction that supplies the country's currency in the foreign exchange market is recorded as a* **debit**. (The **foreign exchange market** is the market in which currencies of different countries are exchanged.) For example, suppose a U.S. retailer wants to buy Japanese television sets so that he can sell them in his stores in the United States. To buy the TV sets from the Japanese, the retailer first has to supply U.S. dollars (in the foreign exchange market) in return for Japanese yen. Then he will turn over the yen to the Japanese in exchange for the television sets.

Any transaction that creates a demand for the country's currency in the foreign exchange market is recorded as a **credit**. For example, suppose a Russian retailer wants to buy computers from U.S. computer producers. Can she pay the U.S. producers in Russian rubles? Probably not; U.S. producers want U.S. dollars. So the Russian retailer must supply rubles (in the foreign exchange market) in return for dollars. Then she will turn over the dollars to the U.S. producers in exchange for the computers. Exhibit 1 presents a summary of debits and credits.

The international transactions that occur, and that are summarized in the balance of payments, can be grouped into three categories, or three accounts—the current account, the capital account, and the official reserve account—and a statistical discrepancy. Exhibit 2 illustrates a U.S. balance of payments account for year Z. The data in the exhibit are hypothetical (to make the calculations simpler) but not unrealistic. In this section, we describe and explain each of the items in the balance of payments using the data in Exhibit 2 for our calculations.

Balance of Payments
A periodic statement (usually annual) of the money value of all transactions between residents of one country and residents of all other countries.

Debit
In the balance of payments, any transaction that supplies the country's currency in the foreign exchange market.

Foreign Exchange Market
The market in which currencies of different countries are exchanged.

Credit
In the balance of payments, any transaction that creates a demand for the country's currency in the foreign exchange market.

Q&A

When Americans buy Japanese goods, they supply dollars and demand yen. When the Japanese buy American goods, they supply yen and demand dollars. Thus, the first transaction is recorded as a debit (it supplies U.S. currency), and the second transaction is recorded as a credit (it increases demand for U.S. currency) in the U.S. balance of payments. Is this correct?

Yes, that is correct.

exhibit **1**

Debits and Credits

Item	Definition	Example
Debit (–)	Any transaction that supplies the country's currency.	Jim, an American, supplies dollars in exchange for yen so that he can use the yen to buy Japanese goods.
Credit (+)	Any transaction that creates a demand for the country's currency.	Svetlana, who is Russian and living in Russia, supplies rubles in order to demand dollars so that she can use the dollars to buy U.S. goods.

CURRENT ACCOUNT

1. EXPORTS OF GOODS AND SERVICES   +340
   a. Merchandise exports (including military sales)   +220
   b. Services   +30
   c. Income from U.S. assets abroad   +90
2. IMPORTS OF GOODS AND SERVICES   -390
   a. Merchandise imports (including military purchases)   -300
   b. Services   -40
   c. Income from foreign assets in U.S.   -50

Merchandise Trade Balance
Difference between value of merchandise exports (item 1a)
and value of merchandise imports (item 2a): +220 − 300 = −80

3. NET UNILATERAL TRANSFERS ABROAD   −11

Current Account Balance
Items 1, 2, 3: +340 − 390 − 11 = ⟶   −61

CAPITAL ACCOUNT   −16
4. OUTFLOW OF U.S. CAPITAL
5. INFLOW OF FOREIGN CAPITAL   +60

Capital Account Balance
Items 4 and 5: − 16 + 60 = ⟶   +44

OFFICIAL RESERVE ACCOUNT   −4
6. INCREASE (−) IN U.S. OFFICIAL RESERVE ASSETS
7. INCREASE (+) IN FOREIGN OFFICIAL ASSETS IN U.S.   +3

Official Reserve Balance
Items 6 and 7: −4 + 3 = ⟶   −1

STATISTICAL DISCREPANCY   +18

TOTAL $0 $0
                                                                        (always zero)

BALANCE OF PAYMENTS =

Summary statistic of all ⟨ ⟩ items (items 1−7 and the statistical discrepancy)

+$340 − $390 − $11 − $16 + $60 − $4 + $3 + $18 = $0
or

Summary statistic of all ▢ items (current account balance, capital account balance,
official reserve balance, and the statistical discrepancy)

−$61 + $44 − $1 + $18 = $0

Note: The pluses (+) and the minuses (−) in the exhibit serve two purposes. First, they
distinguish between credits and debits. A plus is always placed before a credit, and a
minus is always placed before a debit. Second, in terms of the calculations, the pluses
and minuses are viewed as operational signs. In other words, if a number has a plus in
front of it, it is added to the total. If a number has a minus in front of it, it is subtracted
from the total.

---

exhibit **2**

U.S. Balance of Payments, Year *Z*

The data in this exhibit are hypothetical, but not unrealistic. All numbers
are in billions of dollars. The plus and
minus signs in the exhibit should be
viewed as operational signs.

Current Account

The **current account** includes all payments related to the purchase and sale of goods
and services. The current account has three major components: exports of goods and
services, imports of goods and services, and net unilateral transfers abroad.

Current Account

Includes all payments related to the
purchase and sale of goods and
services. Components of the account
include exports, imports, and net
unilateral transfers abroad.

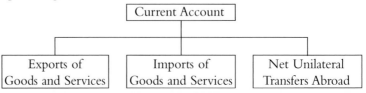

1. **Exports of goods and services.** Americans export goods (e.g., cars), they export services (e.g., insurance, banking, transportation, and tourism), and they receive income on assets they own abroad. All three activities increase the demand for U.S. dollars at the same time that they increase the supply of foreign currencies in the foreign exchange market; thus, they are recorded as credits (+). For example, if a foreigner buys a U.S. computer, payment must ultimately be made in U.S. dollars. Thus, she is required to supply her country's currency when she demands U.S. dollars. (We use foreigner in this chapter to refer to a resident of a foreign country.)

2. **Imports of goods and services.** Americans import goods and services, and foreigners receive income on assets they own in the United States. These activities increase the demand for foreign currencies at the same time that they increase the supply of U.S. dollars to the foreign exchange market; thus, they are recorded as debits (–). For example, if an American buys a Japanese car, payment must ultimately be made in Japanese yen. Thus, he is required to supply U.S. dollars when he demands Japanese yen.

In Exhibit 2, exports of goods and services total +$340 billion in year Z, and imports of goods and services total −$390 billion.[1] Before discussing the third component of the current account—net unilateral transfers abroad—we define some important relationships between exports and imports.

Look at the difference between the *value of merchandise exports* (1a in Exhibit 2) and the *value of merchandise imports* (2a in the exhibit). This difference is the merchandise trade balance or the balance of trade. Specifically, the **merchandise trade balance** is the difference between the value of merchandise exports and the value of merchandise imports. In year Z, the merchandise trade balance is $220 billion − $300 billion = −$80 billion.

> Merchandise trade balance = Value of merchandise exports
> − Value of merchandise imports

Merchandise Trade Balance
The difference between the value of merchandise exports and the value of merchandise imports.

If the value of a country's merchandise exports is less than the value of its merchandise imports, it is said to have a **merchandise trade deficit.**

> Merchandise trade deficit: Value of merchandise exports
> < Value of merchandise imports

Merchandise Trade Deficit
The situation where the value of merchandise exports is less than the value of merchandise imports.

If the value of a country's merchandise exports is greater than the value of its merchandise imports, it is said to have a **merchandise trade surplus**.

> Merchandise trade surplus: Value of merchandise exports
> > Value of merchandise imports

Merchandise Trade Surplus
The situation where the value of merchandise exports is greater than the value of merchandise imports.

Exhibit 3 shows the U.S. merchandise trade balance from 1990 to 2005. Notice that there has been a merchandise trade deficit in each of these years.

3. **Net unilateral transfers abroad.** Unilateral transfers are one-way money payments. They can go from Americans or the U.S. government to foreigners or foreign governments. If an American sends money to a relative in a foreign country, if the U.S. government gives money to a foreign country as a gift or grant, or if an American retires in a foreign country and receives a Social Security check there, all these transactions are referred to as unilateral transfers. If an American or the U.S. government makes a unilateral transfer abroad, this gives rise to a demand for foreign currency and a supply of U.S. dollars; thus, it is entered as a debit item in the U.S. balance of payments accounts.

---

[1] In everyday language, people do not say, "Exports are a positive $X billion and imports are a negative $Y billion." Placing a plus sign (+) in front of exports and a minus sign (–) in front of imports simply reinforces the essential point that exports are credits and imports are debits. This will be useful later when we calculate certain account balances.

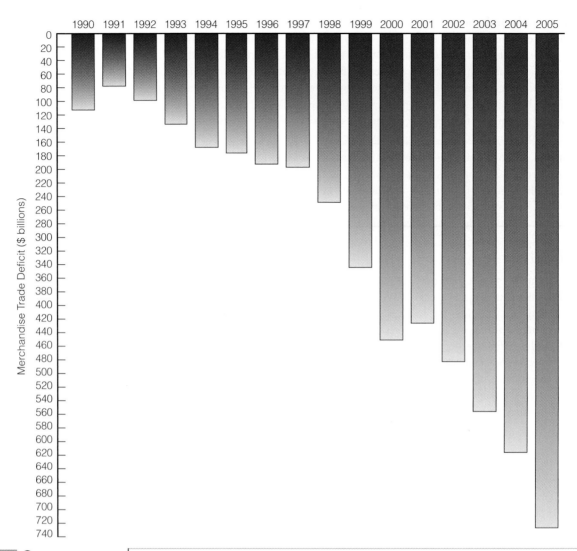

exhibit 3

U.S. Merchandise Trade Balance

In each of the years shown, 1990–2005, a merchandise trade deficit has existed.

Source: U.S. Department of Commerce, Bureau of Economic Analysis.

Unilateral transfers can also go from foreigners or foreign governments to Americans or to the U.S. government. If a foreign citizen sends money to a relative living in the United States, this is a unilateral transfer. If a foreigner makes a unilateral transfer to an American, this gives rise to a supply of foreign currency and a demand for U.S. dollars; thus, it is entered as a credit item in the U.S. balance of payments accounts.

Net unilateral transfers abroad include both types of transfers—from the United States to foreign countries and from foreign countries to the United States. The dollar amount of net unilateral transfers is negative if U.S. transfers are greater than foreign transfers. It is positive if foreign transfers are greater than U.S. transfers.

For year Z in Exhibit 2, we have assumed that unilateral transfers made by Americans to foreign citizens are greater than unilateral transfers made by foreign citizens to Americans. Thus, there is a *negative* net dollar amount, −$11 billion, in this case.

Items 1, 2, and 3 in Exhibit 2—exports of goods and services, imports of goods and services, and net unilateral transfers abroad—comprise the current account. The **current account balance** is the summary statistic for these three items. In year Z, it is −$61 billion. The news media sometimes call the current account balance the balance of payments. To an economist, this is incorrect; the balance of payments includes several more items.

Current Account Balance

The summary statistic for exports of goods and services, imports of goods and services, and net unilateral transfers abroad.

Capital Account

The **capital account** includes all payments related to the purchase and sale of assets and to borrowing and lending activities. Its major components are outflow of U.S. capital and inflow of foreign capital.

1. **Outflow of U.S. capital.** American purchases of foreign assets and U.S. loans to foreigners are outflows of U.S. capital. As such, they give rise to a demand for foreign currency and a supply of U.S. dollars on the foreign exchange market. Hence, they are considered a debit. For example, if an American wants to buy land in Japan, U.S. dollars must be supplied to purchase (demand) Japanese yen.

2. **Inflow of foreign capital.** Foreign purchases of U.S. assets and foreign loans to Americans are inflows of foreign capital. As such, they give rise to a demand for U.S. dollars and to a supply of foreign currency on the foreign exchange market. Hence, they are considered a credit. For example, if a Japanese citizen buys a U.S. Treasury bill, Japanese yen must be supplied to purchase (demand) U.S. dollars.

Items 4 and 5 in Exhibit 2—outflow of U.S. capital and inflow of foreign capital—comprise the capital account. The **capital account balance** is the summary statistic for these two items. It is equal to the difference between the outflow of U.S. capital and the inflow of foreign capital. In year Z, it is $44 billion.

Official Reserve Account

A government possesses official reserve balances in the form of foreign currencies, gold, its reserve position in the **International Monetary Fund**, and **special drawing rights (SDRs)**. Countries that have a deficit in their combined current and capital accounts can draw on their reserves. For example, if the United States has a deficit in its combined current and capital accounts of $5 billion, it can draw down its official reserves to meet this deficit.

Item 6 in Exhibit 2 shows that the United States increased its reserve assets by $4 billion in year Z. This is a debit item because if the United States acquires official reserves (say, through the purchase of a foreign currency), it has increased the demand for the foreign currency and supplied dollars. Thus, an increase in official reserves is like an outflow of capital in the capital account and appears as a payment with a negative sign. It follows that an increase in foreign official assets in the United States is a credit item.

Statistical Discrepancy

If someone buys a U.S. dollar with, say, Japanese yen, someone must sell a U.S. dollar. Thus, dollars purchased equal dollars sold.

In all the transactions discussed earlier—exporting goods, importing goods, sending money to relatives in foreign countries, buying land in foreign countries—dollars were bought and sold. The total number of dollars sold must always equal the total number of dollars purchased. However, balance of payments accountants do not have complete information; they can record only credits and debits that they observe. There may be more debits or credits than those observed in a given year.

Suppose in year Z, all debits are observed and recorded, but not all credits are observed and recorded—perhaps because of smuggling activities, secret bank accounts,

Capital Account

Includes all payments related to the purchase and sale of assets and to borrowing and lending activities. Components include outflow of U.S. capital and inflow of foreign capital.

Capital Account Balance

The summary statistic for the outflow of U.S. capital. It is equal to the difference between the outflow of U.S. capital and the inflow of foreign capital.

International Monetary Fund (IMF)

An international organization created to oversee the international monetary system. The IMF does not control the world's money supply, but it does hold currency reserves for member nations and make loans to central banks.

Special Drawing Right (SDR)

An international money, created by the IMF, in the form of bookkeeping entries; like gold and currencies, that can be used by nations to settle international accounts.

people living in more than one country, and so on. To adjust for this, balance of payments accountants use the *statistical discrepancy*, which is the part of the balance of payments that adjusts for missing information. In Exhibit 2, the statistical discrepancy is +$18 billion. This means that $18 billion worth of credits (+) went unobserved in year Z. There may have been some hidden exports and unrecorded capital inflows that year.

What the Balance of Payments Equals

The balance of payments is the summary statistic for the following:

- Exports of goods and services (item 1 in Exhibit 2)
- Imports of goods and services (item 2)
- Net unilateral transfers abroad (item 3)
- Outflow of U.S. capital (item 4)
- Inflow of foreign capital (item 5)
- Increase in U.S. official reserve assets (item 6)
- Increase in foreign official assets in the United States (item 7)
- Statistical discrepancy

Calculating the balance of payments in year Z using these items, we have (in billions of dollars) $+340 - 390 - 11 - 16 + 60 - 4 + 3 + 18 = 0$.

Alternatively, the balance of payments is the summary statistic for the following:

- Current account balance
- Capital account balance
- Official reserve balance
- Statistical discrepancy

Calculating the balance of payments in year Z using these items, we have (in billions of dollars) $-61 + 44 - 1 + 18 = 0$. The balance of payments for the United States in year Z equals zero.

Q&A

Why does the balance of payments always equal zero?

The reason the balance of payments always equals zero is that the three accounts that comprise the balance of payments, when taken together, plus the statistical discrepancy, include all of the sources and all of the uses of dollars in international transactions. And because every dollar used must have a source, adding the sources (+) to the uses (−) necessarily gives us zero.

SELF-TEST

(Answers to Self-Test questions are in the Self-Test Appendix.)

1. If an American retailer buys Japanese cars from a Japanese manufacturer, is this transaction recorded as a debit or a credit? Explain your answer.

2. Exports of goods and services equal $200 billion and imports of goods and services equal $300 billion. What is the merchandise trade balance?

3. What is the difference between the merchandise trade balance and the current account balance?

The Foreign Exchange Market

If a U.S. buyer wants to purchase a good from a U.S. seller, the buyer simply gives the required number of U.S. dollars to the seller. If, however, a U.S. buyer wants to purchase a good from a seller in Mexico, the U.S. buyer must first exchange her U.S. dollars for Mexican pesos. Then, with the pesos, she buys the good from the Mexican seller.

As mentioned earlier, the market in which currencies of different countries are exchanged is the foreign exchange market. In the foreign exchange market, currencies are bought and sold for a price; an **exchange rate** exists. For instance, it might take 96 cents to buy a euro, 10 cents to buy a Mexican peso, and 13 cents to buy a Danish krone.

Exchange Rate
The price of one currency in terms of another currency.

In this section, we explain why currencies are demanded and supplied in the foreign exchange market. Then we discuss how the exchange rate expresses the relationship between the demand for and supply of currencies.

The Demand for Goods

To simplify our analysis, we assume that there are only two countries in the world, the United States and Mexico. This, then, means there are only two currencies in the world, the U.S. dollar (USD) and the Mexican peso (MXN). We want to answer the following two questions:

1. What creates the demand for and supply of dollars on the foreign exchange market?
2. What creates the demand for and supply of pesos on the foreign exchange market?

Suppose an American wants to buy a couch from a Mexican producer. Before he can purchase the couch, the American must buy Mexican pesos; hence, Mexican pesos are demanded. But the American buys Mexican pesos with U.S. dollars; that is, he supplies U.S. dollars to the foreign exchange market to demand Mexican pesos. We conclude that *the U.S. demand for Mexican goods leads to (1) a demand for Mexican pesos and (2) a supply of U.S. dollars on the foreign exchange market* (see Exhibit 4(a)). Thus, the demand for pesos and the supply of dollars are linked:

Demand for pesos ↔ Supply of dollars

The result is similar for a Mexican who wants to buy a computer from a U.S. producer. Before she can purchase the computer, the Mexican must buy U.S. dollars; hence, U.S. dollars are demanded. The Mexican buys the U.S. dollars with Mexican pesos. We conclude that *the Mexican demand for U.S. goods leads to (1) a demand for U.S. dollars and (2) a supply of Mexican pesos on the foreign exchange market* (see Exhibit 4(b)). Thus, the demand for dollars and the supply of pesos are linked:

Demand for dollars ↔ Supply of pesos

The Demand for and Supply of Currencies

Now let's look at Exhibit 5, which shows the markets for pesos and dollars. Part (a) shows the market for Mexican pesos. The quantity of pesos is on the horizontal axis, and the exchange rate—stated in terms of the dollar price per peso—is on the vertical axis. Exhibit 5(b) shows the market for U.S. dollars, which mirrors what is happening in the market for Mexican pesos. Notice that the exchange rates in (a) and (b) are reciprocals of each other. If 0.10 USD = 1 MXN, then 10 MXN = 1 USD.

exhibit 4

The Demand for Goods and the Supply of Currencies

In Exhibit 5(a), the demand curve for pesos is downward sloping, indicating that as the dollar price per peso increases, Americans buy fewer pesos, and as the dollar price per peso decreases, Americans buy more pesos.

Dollar price per peso ↑	Americans buy fewer pesos
Dollar price per peso ↓	Americans buy more pesos

For example, if it takes 0.10 dollars to buy a peso, Americans will buy more pesos than they would if it takes 0.20 dollars to buy a peso. (It is analogous to buyers purchasing more soft drinks at $3 a six-pack than at $5 a six-pack.) Simply put, the higher the dollar price per peso, the more expensive Mexican goods are for Americans and the fewer Mexican goods Americans will buy. Thus, a smaller quantity of pesos is demanded.

The supply curve for pesos in Exhibit 5(a) is upward sloping. It is easy to understand why when we recall that the supply of Mexican pesos is linked to the Mexican demand for U.S. goods and U.S. dollars. Consider a price of 0.20 dollars for 1 peso compared with a price of 0.10 dollars for 1 peso. At 0.10 USD = 1 MXN, a Mexican buyer gives up 1 peso and receives 10 cents in return. But at 0.20 USD = 1 MXN, a Mexican buyer gives up 1 peso and receives 20 cents in return. At which exchange rate are U.S. goods cheaper for Mexicans? The answer is at the exchange rate of 0.20 USD = 1 MXN.

To illustrate, suppose a U.S. computer has a price tag of $1,000. At an exchange rate of 0.20 USD = 1 MXN, a Mexican will have to pay 5,000 pesos to buy the American computer; but at an exchange rate of 0.10 USD = 1 MXN, a Mexican will have to pay 10,000 pesos for the computer:

Translating U.S. Demand for Pesos into U.S. Supply of Dollars and Mexican Demand for Dollars into Mexican Supply of Pesos

(a) The market for pesos. (b) The market for dollars. The demand for pesos in (a) is linked to the supply of dollars in (b): When Americans demand pesos, they supply dollars. The supply of pesos in (a) is linked to the demand for dollars in (b): When Mexicans demand dollars, they supply pesos. In (a), the exchange rate is 0.10 USD = 1 MXN, which is equal to 10 MXN = 1 USD in (b). Exchange rates are reciprocals of each other.

0.20 USD = 1 MXN	0.10 USD = 1 MXN
1 USD = (1/0.20) MXN	1 USD = (1/0.10) MXN
1,000 USD = (1,000/0.20) MXN	1,000 USD = (1,000/0.10) MXN
= 5,000 MXN	= 10,000 MXN

To a Mexican buyer, the American computer is cheaper at the exchange rate of 0.20 dollars per peso than at 0.10 dollars per peso.

Exchange Rate	Dollar Price	Peso Price
0.20 USD = 1 MXN	1,000 USD	5,000 MXN [(1,000/0.20) MXN]
0.10 USD = 1 MXN	1,000 USD	10,000 MXN [(1,000/0.10) MXN]

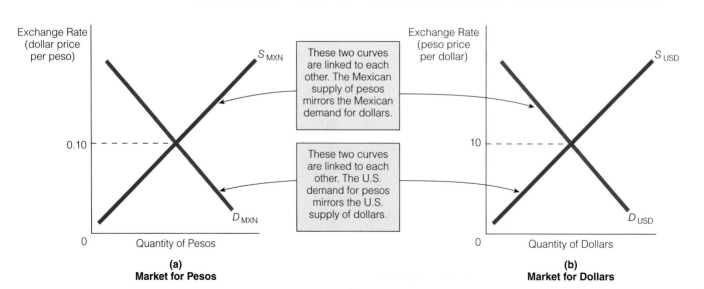

(a)
Market for Pesos

(b)
Market for Dollars

economics 24/7

THE NOBEL PRIZE IN ECONOMICS AND FOREIGN EXCHANGE MARKETS

Do winners of the Nobel Prize in Economics care what is happening on foreign exchange markets? Because the prize money they win is paid in Swedish kronor, should they care?[2]

Consider the case of Robert Mundell, the 1999 winner of the prize. Mundell received a prize of 7.9 million Swedish kronor. In mid-October, when he was informed that he had won the prize, the prize money was worth nearly $1 million. Mundell, however, decided not to take the prize money in kronor and then exchange it for dollars. Instead, he asked the Nobel Foundation to deposit the funds in his bank account in euros because he expected that over the next few months, the euro would appreciate relative to the dollar.

Gary Becker was the 1992 winner of the Nobel Prize in Economics. Like all winners, he was notified of his winning the coveted prize in mid-October. He would not actually collect the prize money, however, until late December. In mid-October, the prize money (at current exchange rates)

was worth $1.2 million. Becker thought that the Swedish kronor was likely to depreciate in the near future, and so intended to buy dollars on the futures market. He never got around to doing so, though. Two weeks after he had been notified that he had won the Nobel Prize, there was a currency crisis in Sweden. As a result, his prize money shrank to $900,000.

Ronald Coase, who won the Nobel Prize in Economics in 1991, was to be paid his prize money at the end of 1991. Coase suspected that the kronor was about to appreciate in value relative to the dollar, so he asked the foundation to pay him part of his prize money in January 1992, to which the foundation agreed. In January, the kronor appreciated in value, giving Coase more dollars per kronor.

[2]This feature is based on Sylvia Nasar, "Nobel Economics: Spending the Check," *The New York Times*, December 5, 1999.

It follows, then, that the higher the dollar price per peso, the greater the quantity demanded of dollars by Mexicans (because U.S. goods will be cheaper), and therefore, the greater the quantity supplied of pesos to the foreign exchange market. The upward-sloping supply curve for pesos illustrates this.

Flexible Exchange Rates

In this section, we discuss how exchange rates are determined in the foreign exchange market when the forces of supply and demand are allowed to rule. Economists refer to this as a **flexible exchange rate system**. In the next section, we discuss how exchange rates are determined under a fixed exchange rate system.

The Equilibrium Exchange Rate

In a completely flexible exchange rate system, the exchange rate is determined by the forces of supply and demand. In our two country–two currency world, suppose the equilibrium exchange rate (dollar price per peso) is 0.10 USD = 1 MXN, as shown in Exhibit 6. At this dollar price per peso, the quantity demanded of pesos equals the quantity supplied of pesos. There are no shortages or surpluses of pesos. At any other exchange rate, however, either an excess demand for pesos or an excess supply of pesos exists.

> ### Thinking like AN ECONOMIST
>
> *The demand for dollars is linked to the supply of pesos, and the demand for pesos is linked to the supply of dollars. Economists often think in terms of one activity being linked to another because economics, after all, is about exchange. In an exchange, one gives (supply) and gets (demand): John "supplies" $25 to demand the new book from the shopkeeper; the shopkeeper supplies the new book so that he may "demand" the $25. In such a transaction, we usually diagrammatically represent the demand for and supply of the new book—but we could also diagrammatically represent the demand for and supply of money. Of course, in international exchange, where monies are bought and sold before goods are bought and sold, this is exactly what we do.*

Flexible Exchange Rate System
The system whereby exchange rates are determined by the forces of supply and demand for a currency.

exhibit **6**

A Flexible Exchange Rate System

The demand curve for pesos is downward-sloping. The higher the dollar price for pesos, the fewer pesos will be demanded; the lower the dollar price for pesos, the more pesos will be demanded. At 0.12 USD = 1 MXN, there is a surplus of pesos, placing downward pressure on the exchange rate. At 0.08 USD = 1 MXN, there is a shortage of pesos, placing upward pressure on the exchange rate. At the equilibrium exchange rate, 0.10 USD = 1 MXN, the quantity demanded of pesos equals the quantity supplied of pesos.

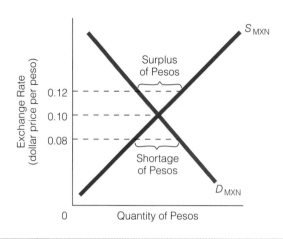

Q&A

Are the demand and supply curves in Exhibit 6 related to the U.S. balance of payments in Exhibit 2?

Yes, they are. For example, U.S. exports represent a demand for U.S. dollars by foreigners (and therefore constitute the supply of foreign currencies), while U.S. imports represent the U.S. demand for foreign currencies (and therefore constitute the supply of U.S. dollars). In fact, any dollar amount with a plus sign (+) in front of it in Exhibit 2 represents a demand for U.S. dollars and a supply of foreign currencies, and any dollar amount with a minus sign (–) in front of it represents a demand for foreign currencies and a supply of U.S. dollars.

Appreciation

An increase in the value of one currency relative to other currencies.

Depreciation

A decrease in the value of one currency relative to other currencies.

At the exchange rate of 0.12 USD = 1 MXN, a surplus of pesos exists. As a result, downward pressure will be placed on the dollar price of a peso (just as downward pressure will be placed on the dollar price of an apple if there is a surplus of apples). At the exchange rate of 0.08 USD = 1 MXN, there is a shortage of pesos, and upward pressure will be placed on the dollar price of a peso.

Changes in the Equilibrium Exchange Rate

Chapter 3 explains that a change in the demand for a good, in the supply of a good, or in both will change the equilibrium price of the good. The same holds true for the price of currencies. A change in the demand for pesos, in the supply of pesos, or in both will change the equilibrium dollar price per peso. If the dollar price per peso rises—say, from 0.10 USD = 1 MXN to 0.12 USD = 1 MXN—the peso is said to have **appreciated** and the dollar to have **depreciated**.

A currency has appreciated in value if it takes more of a foreign currency to buy it. A currency has depreciated in value if it takes more of it to buy a foreign currency. For example, a movement in the exchange rate from 0.10 USD = 1 MXN to 0.12 USD = 1 MXN means that it now takes 12 cents instead of 10 cents to buy a peso, so the dollar has depreciated. The other side of the "coin," so to speak, is that it takes fewer pesos to buy a dollar, so the peso has appreciated. That is, at an exchange rate of 0.10 USD = 1 MXN, it takes 10 pesos to buy $1, but at an exchange rate of 0.12 USD = 1 MXN, it takes only 8.33 pesos to buy $1.

Factors That Affect the Equilibrium Exchange Rate

If the equilibrium exchange rate can change owing to a change in the demand for and supply of a currency, then it is important to understand what factors can change the demand for and supply of a currency. Three are presented in this section.

A DIFFERENCE IN INCOME GROWTH RATES An increase in a nation's income will usually cause the nation's residents to buy more of both domestic and foreign goods. The increased demand for imports will result in an increased demand for foreign currency.

Suppose U.S. residents experience an increase in income, but Mexican residents do not. As a result, the demand curve for pesos shifts rightward, as illustrated in Exhibit 7.

economics 24/7

BACK TO THE FUTURES

Meet (the fictional) Bill Whatley, owner of a Toyota dealership in Tulsa, Oklahoma. It is currently May, and Bill is thinking about a shipment of Toyotas he plans to buy in August. He knows that he must buy the Toyotas from Japan with yen, but he has a problem. At the present time, the price of 1 yen is 0.008 dollars. Bill wonders what the dollar price of a yen will be in August when he plans to make his purchase. Suppose the price of 1 yen rises to 0.010 dollars. If this happens, then instead of paying $20,000 for a Toyota priced at 2.5 million yen, he would have to pay $25,000.[3] This difference of $5,000 may be enough to erase his profit on the sale of the Toyotas.

What is Bill to do? He could purchase a futures contract today for the needed quantity of yen in August. A futures contract is a contract in which the seller agrees to provide a particular good (in this example, a particular currency) to the buyer on a specified future date at an agreed-on price. In short, Bill can buy yen today at a specified dollar price and take delivery of the yen at a later date (in August).

But suppose the price of 1 yen falls to 0.007 dollars in August. If this happens, Bill would have to pay only $17,500 (instead of $20,000) for a Toyota priced at 2.5 million yen. Although he could increase his profit in this case, Bill, like other car dealers, might not be interested in assuming the risk associated with changes in exchange rates. He may prefer to lock in a sure thing.

Who would sell yen to Bill? The answer is someone who is willing to assume the risk of changes in the value of currencies—for example, Julie Jackson. Julie thinks to herself, "I think the dollar price of a yen will go down between now and August. Therefore, I'll enter into a contract with Bill stating that I'll give him 2.5 million yen in August for $20,000—the exchange rate specified in the contract being 1 JPY = 0.008 USD. If I'm right, and the actual exchange rate in August is 1 JPY = 0.007 USD, then I can purchase the 2.5 million yen for $17,500 and fulfill my contract with Bill by turning the yen over to him for $20,000. I walk away with $2,500 in profit."

Many economists argue that futures contracts offer people a way of dealing with the risk associated with a flexible exchange rate system. If a person doesn't know what next month's exchange rate will be and doesn't want to take the risk of waiting to see, then he or she can enter into a futures contract and effectively shift the risk to someone who voluntarily assumes it.

---

[3]If 1 yen equals 0.008 dollars, then a Toyota with a price of 2.5 million yen costs $20,000 because 2.5 million × 0.008 dollars = $20,000. If 1 yen equals 0.010 dollars, then a Toyota with a price of 2.5 million yen costs $25,000 dollars because 2.5 million × 0.010 dollars equals $25,000.

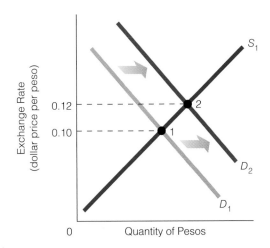

Exchange Rate (dollar price per peso)

0.12

0.10

S_1

D_2

D_1

0   Quantity of Pesos

This causes the equilibrium exchange rate to rise from 0.10 USD = 1 MXN to 0.12 USD = 1 MXN. *Ceteris paribus,* if one nation's income grows and another's lags behind, the currency of the higher-growth-rate country *depreciates,* and the currency of the lower-growth-rate country *appreciates.* To many persons, this seems paradoxical; nevertheless, it is true.

DIFFERENCES IN RELATIVE INFLATION RATES Suppose the U.S. price level rises 10 percent at a time when Mexico experiences stable prices. An increase in the U.S. price level will make Mexican goods relatively less expensive for Americans and U.S. goods relatively more expensive for Mexicans. As a result, the U.S. demand for Mexican goods will increase, and the Mexican demand for U.S. goods will decrease.

How will this affect the demand for and supply of Mexican pesos? As shown in Exhibit 8, the demand for Mexican pesos will increase (Mexican goods are relatively cheaper than they were before the U.S. price level rose), and the supply of Mexican pesos will decrease (American goods are relatively more expensive, so Mexicans will buy fewer American goods; thus, they demand fewer U.S. dollars and supply fewer Mexican pesos).

As Exhibit 8 shows, the result of an increase in the demand for Mexican pesos and a decrease in the supply of Mexican pesos is an *appreciation* in the peso and a *depreciation* in the dollar. It takes 11 cents instead of 10 cents to buy 1 peso (dollar depreciation); it takes 9.09 pesos instead of 10 pesos to buy $1 (peso appreciation).

An important question is: How much will the U.S. dollar depreciate as a result of the rise in the U.S. price level? (Recall that there is no change in Mexico's price level.) The **purchasing power parity (PPP) theory** predicts that the U.S. dollar will depreciate by 10 percent as a result of the 10 percent rise in the U.S. price level. This requires the dollar price of a peso to rise to 11 cents (10 percent of 10 cents is 1 cent, and 10 cents + 1 cent = 11 cents). A 10 percent depreciation in the dollar restores the *original relative prices of American goods to Mexican customers.*

Consider a U.S. car with a price tag of $20,000. If the exchange rate is 0.10 USD = 1 MXN, a Mexican buyer of the car will pay 200,000 pesos. If the car price increases by 10 percent to $22,000 and the dollar depreciates 10 percent (to 0.11 USD = 1 MXN), the Mexican buyer of the car will still pay only 200,000 pesos.

Purchasing Power Parity (PPP) Theory

States that exchange rates between any two currencies will adjust to reflect changes in the relative price levels of the two countries.

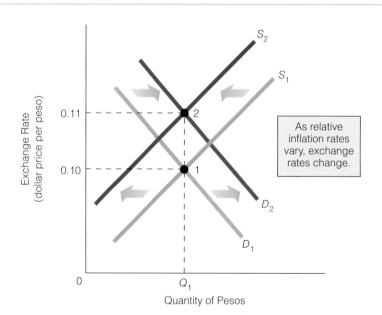

Exchange Rate	Dollar Price	Peso Price
0.10 USD = 1 MXN	20,000 USD	200,000 MXN [(20,000/0.10) MXN]
0.11 USD = 1 MXN	22,000 USD	200,000 MXN [(22,000/0.11) MXN]

In short, the PPP theory predicts that *changes in the relative price levels of two countries will affect the exchange rate in such a way that 1 unit of a country's currency will continue to buy the same amount of foreign goods* as it did before the change in the relative price levels. In our example, the higher U.S. inflation rate causes a change in the equilibrium exchange rate and leads to a depreciated dollar, but 1 peso continues to have the same purchasing power it previously did.

On some occasions, the PPP theory of exchange rates has predicted accurately, but on others, it has not. Many economists suggest that the theory does not always predict accurately because the demand for and supply of a currency are affected *by more than the difference in inflation rates between countries.* For example, we have already noted that different income growth rates affect the demand for a currency and therefore the exchange rate. In the *long run,* however, and in particular, when there is a *large difference in inflation rates across countries,* the PPP theory does predict exchange rates accurately.

CHANGES IN REAL INTEREST RATES As shown in the U.S. balance of payments in Exhibit 2, more than goods flow between countries. Financial capital also moves between countries. The flow of financial capital depends on different countries' *real interest rates*—interest rates adjusted for inflation.

To illustrate, suppose initially that the real interest rate is 3 percent in both the United States and Mexico. Then the real interest rate in the United States increases to 4.5 percent. What will happen? Mexicans will want to purchase financial assets in the United States that pay a higher real interest rate than financial assets in Mexico. The Mexican demand for dollars will increase, and therefore, Mexicans will supply more pesos. As the supply of pesos increases on the foreign exchange market, the exchange rate (dollar price per peso) will change; fewer dollars will be needed to buy pesos. In short, the dollar will appreciate, and the peso will depreciate.

SELF-TEST

1. In the foreign exchange market, how is the demand for dollars linked to the supply of pesos?

2. What could cause the U.S. dollar to appreciate against the Mexican peso on the foreign exchange market?

3. Suppose the U.S. economy grows while the Swiss economy does not. How will this affect the exchange rate between the dollar and the Swiss franc? Why?

4. What does the purchasing power parity theory say? Give an example to illustrate your answer.

Fixed Exchange Rates

The major alternative to the flexible exchange rate system is the **fixed exchange rate system**. This system works the way it sounds. Exchange rates are fixed; they are not allowed to fluctuate freely in response to the forces of supply and demand. Central banks buy and sell currencies to maintain agreed-on exchange rates. The workings of the fixed exchange rate system are described in this section.

Fixed Exchange Rate System

The system where a nation's currency is set at a fixed rate relative to all other currencies, and central banks intervene in the foreign exchange market to maintain the fixed rate.

Fixed Exchange Rates and Overvalued/Undervalued Currency

Once again, we assume a two country–two currency world. Suppose this time, the United States and Mexico agree to fix the exchange rate of their currencies. Instead of letting the dollar depreciate or appreciate relative to the peso, the two countries agree to set the price of 1 peso at 0.12 dollars; that is, they agree to the exchange rate of 0.12 USD = 1 MXN. Generally, we call this the fixed exchange rate or the *official price* of a peso.[4] We will deal with more than one official price in our discussion, so we refer to 0.12 USD = 1 MXN as official price 1 (Exhibit 9).

Overvaluation

A currency is overvalued if its price in terms of other currencies is above the equilibrium price.

If the dollar price of pesos is above its equilibrium level (which is the case at official price 1), a surplus of pesos exists, and the peso is said to be **overvalued**. This means that the peso is fetching more dollars than it would at equilibrium. For example, if in equilibrium, 1 peso trades for 0.10 dollars, but at the official exchange rate, 1 peso trades for 0.12 dollars, then the peso is said to be overvalued.

It follows that if the peso is overvalued, the dollar is undervalued, which means it is fetching fewer pesos than it would at equilibrium. For example, if in equilibrium, $1 trades for 10 pesos, but at the official exchange rate, $1 trades for 8.33 pesos, then the dollar is undervalued.

Undervaluation

A currency is undervalued if its price in terms of other currencies is below the equilibrium price.

Similarly, if the dollar price of pesos is below its equilibrium level (which is the case at official price 2 in Exhibit 9), a shortage of pesos exists, and the peso is **undervalued**. This means that the peso is not fetching as many dollars as it would at equilibrium. It follows that if the peso is undervalued, the dollar must be overvalued.

Overvalued peso ↔ Undervalued dollar
Undervalued peso ↔ Overvalued dollar

A Fixed Exchange Rate System

In a fixed exchange rate system, the exchange rate is fixed—and it may not be fixed at the equilibrium exchange rate. The exhibit shows two cases. (1) If the exchange rate is fixed at official price 1, the peso is overvalued, the dollar is undervalued, and a surplus of pesos exists. (2) If the exchange rate is fixed at official price 2, the peso is undervalued, the dollar is overvalued, and a shortage of pesos exists.

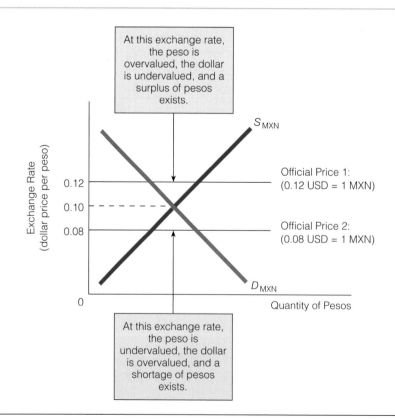

At this exchange rate, the peso is overvalued, the dollar is undervalued, and a surplus of pesos exists.

S_{MXN}

Official Price 1:
(0.12 USD = 1 MXN)

0.12

0.10

0.08

Official Price 2:
(0.08 USD = 1 MXN)

Exchange Rate (dollar price per peso)

D_{MXN}

0

Quantity of Pesos

At this exchange rate, the peso is undervalued, the dollar is overvalued, and a shortage of pesos exists.

[4]If the price of 1 peso is 0.12 dollars, it follows that the price of $1 is approximately 8.33 pesos. Thus, setting the official price of a peso in terms of dollars automatically sets the official price of a dollar in terms of pesos.

What Is So Bad About an Overvalued Dollar?

Suppose you read in the newspaper that the dollar is overvalued. You also read that economists are concerned about the overvalued dollar. "But why are economists concerned?" you ask.

Economists are concerned because the exchange rate—and hence, the value of the dollar in terms of other currencies—affects the amount of U.S. exports and imports. Because it affects exports and imports, it naturally affects the merchandise trade balance.

To illustrate, suppose the demand for and supply of pesos are represented by D_1 and S_1 in Exhibit 10. With this demand curve and supply curve, the equilibrium exchange rate is 0.10 USD = 1 MXN. Let's also suppose the exchange rate is fixed at this exchange rate. In other words, the equilibrium exchange rate and the fixed exchange rate are initially the same.

Time passes and eventually the demand curve for pesos shifts to the right, from D_1 to D_2. Under a flexible exchange rate system, the exchange rate would rise to 0.12 USD = 1 MXN. But a flexible exchange rate is not operating here—a fixed one is. Therefore, the exchange rate stays fixed at 0.10 USD = 1 MXN. This means the fixed exchange rate (0.10 USD = 1 MXN) is below the new equilibrium exchange rate (0.12 USD = 1 MXN).

Recall that if the dollar price per peso is below its equilibrium level (which is the case here), the peso is undervalued and the dollar is overvalued. At equilibrium (point 2 in Exhibit 10), 1 peso would trade for 0.12 dollars, but at its fixed rate (point 1), it trades for only 0.10 dollars—so the peso is undervalued. At equilibrium (point 2), $1 would trade for 8.33 pesos, but at its fixed rate (point 1), it trades for 10 pesos—so the dollar is overvalued.

But what is so bad about an overvalued dollar? The answer is that it makes U.S. goods more expensive (for foreigners to buy), which in turn can affect the U.S. merchandise trade balance.

For example, suppose a U.S. good costs $100. At the equilibrium exchange rate (0.12 USD = 1 MXN), a Mexican would pay 833 pesos for the good; but at the fixed exchange rate (0.10 USD = 1 MXN), he will pay 1,000 pesos.

Exchange Rate	Dollar Price	Peso Price
0.12 USD = 1 MXN (equilibrium)	100 USD	833 MXN [(100/0.12) MXN]
0.10 USD = 1 MXN (fixed)	100 USD	1,000 MXN [(100/0.10) MXN]

The higher the prices of U.S. goods (exports), the fewer of those goods Mexicans will buy, and as just shown, an overvalued dollar makes U.S. export goods higher in price.

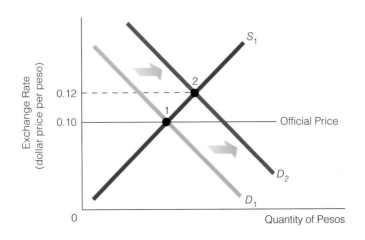

exhibit **10**

Fixed Exchange Rates and an Overvalued Dollar

Initially, the demand for and supply of pesos are represented by D_1 and S_1, respectively. The equilibrium exchange rate is 0.10 USD = 1 MXN, which also happens to be the official (fixed) exchange rate. In time, the demand for pesos rises to D_2, and the equilibrium exchange rate rises to 0.12 USD = 1 MXN. The official exchange rate is fixed, however, so the dollar will be overvalued. As explained in the text, this can lead to a trade deficit.

Ultimately, an overvalued dollar can affect the U.S. merchandise trade balance. As U.S. exports become more expensive for Mexicans, they buy fewer U.S. exports. If exports fall below imports, the result is a U.S. trade deficit.[5]

Government Involvement in a Fixed Exchange Rate System

Look back at Exhibit 9. Suppose the governments of Mexico and the United States agree to fix the exchange rate at 0.12 USD = 1 MXN. At this exchange rate, a surplus of pesos exists. What becomes of the surplus of pesos?

To maintain the exchange rate at 0.12 USD = 1 MXN, the Federal Reserve System (the Fed) could buy the surplus of pesos. But what would it use to buy the pesos? The Fed would buy the surplus of pesos with dollars. Consequently, the demand for pesos will increase and the demand curve will shift to the right, ideally, by enough to raise the equilibrium rate to the current fixed exchange rate.

Alternatively, instead of the Fed buying pesos (to mop up the excess supply of pesos), the Banco de Mexico (the central bank of Mexico) could buy pesos with some of its reserve dollars. (Why doesn't it buy pesos with pesos? Using pesos would not reduce the surplus of pesos on the market.) This action by the Banco de Mexico will also increase the demand for pesos and raise the equilibrium rate.

Finally, the two actions could be combined; that is, both the Fed and the Banco de Mexico could buy pesos.

Options Under a Fixed Exchange Rate System

Suppose there is a surplus of pesos in the foreign exchange market—indicating that the peso is overvalued and the dollar is undervalued. The Fed and the Banco de Mexico each attempt to rectify this situation by buying pesos. But suppose this combined action is not successful. The surplus of pesos persists for weeks, along with an overvalued peso and an undervalued dollar. What is left to do? There are a few options.

DEVALUATION AND REVALUATION Mexico and the United States could agree to reset the official price of the dollar and the peso. This entails *devaluation* and *revaluation*.

A **devaluation** occurs when the official price of a currency is lowered. A **revaluation** occurs when the official price of a currency is raised. For example, suppose the first official price of a peso is 0.10 USD = 1 MXN. It follows that the first official price of $1 is 10 pesos.

Now suppose Mexico and the United States agree to change the official price of their currencies. The second official price is 0.12 USD = 1 MXN. This means that the second official price of $1 is 8.33 pesos.

Moving from the first official price to the second, the peso has been revalued. That's because it takes *more dollars to buy a peso* (12 cents instead of 10 cents). Of course, moving from the first official price to the second means the dollar has been devalued. That's because it takes *fewer pesos to buy a dollar* (8.33 pesos instead of 10 pesos).

Devaluation
A government act that changes the exchange rate by lowering the official price of a currency.

Revaluation
A government act that changes the exchange rate by raising the official price of a currency.

[5]The other side of the coin, so to speak, is that if the dollar is overvalued, the peso must be undervalued. An undervalued peso makes Mexican goods cheaper for Americans. So while the overvalued dollar is causing Mexicans to buy fewer U.S. exports, the undervalued peso is causing Americans to import more goods from Mexico. In conclusion, U.S. exports fall, U.S. imports rise, and we move closer to a trade deficit, or if one already exists, it becomes larger.

© CHARLES PERTWEE/BLOOMBERG NEWS/LANDOV

economics 24/7

BIG MACS AND EXCHANGE RATES

In an earlier chapter, we explained why goods that can be easily transported from one location to another usually sell for the same price in all locations. For example, if a candy bar can be moved from Atlanta to Seattle, then we would expect the candy bar to sell for the same price in both locations. Why? Because if the candy bar is priced higher in Seattle than Atlanta, people will move candy bars from Atlanta (where the price is relatively low) to Seattle to fetch the higher price. In other words, the supply of candy bars will rise in Seattle and fall in Atlanta. These changes in supply in the two locations affect the price of the candy bars in the two locations. In Seattle, the price will fall, and in Atlanta, the price will rise. This price movement will stop when the price of a candy bar is the same in the two locations.

Now consider a good that is sold all over the world, McDonald's Big Mac. Suppose the exchange rate between the dollar and the yen is $1 = ¥100 and the price of a Big Mac in New York City is $3 and ¥400 in Tokyo. Given the exchange rate, is a Big Mac selling for the same price in the two cities? The answer is no. In New York, it is $3, but in Tokyo it is $4 (the price in Tokyo is ¥400, and $1 = ¥100). Stated differently, in New York, $1 buys one-third of a Big Mac, but in Tokyo, $1 buys only one-fourth of a Big Mac.

Will Big Macs be shipped from New York to Tokyo to fetch the higher price? No. The exchange rate is likely to adjust in such a way that the price of a Big Mac is the same in both cities.

Now ask yourself what the exchange rate has to be between the dollar and yen before the Big Mac is the same dollar price in New York and Tokyo. Here are three different exchange rates. Pick the correct one.

(a) $1 = ¥133.33
(b) $1 = ¥150.00
(c) $1 = ¥89.00

The answer is (a), $1 = ¥133.33. At this exchange rate, a Big Mac in New York is $3 (as we stated earlier), and a Big Mac in Tokyo that is ¥400 is $3 (once we have computed its price in dollars). Here are the steps: (1) The exchange rate is $1 = ¥133.33; (2) 1 yen is equal to $0.0075; (3) $0.0075 × 400 yen is $3.

The *purchasing power parity theory* in economics predicts that the exchange rate between two currencies will adjust so that, in the end, $1 buys the same amount of a given good in all places around the world. Thus, if the exchange rate is initially $1 = ¥100 when a Big Mac is $3 in New York and ¥400 in Tokyo, it will change to become $1 = ¥133.33. That is, the dollar will soon appreciate relative to the yen.

The Economist, a well-known economics magazine, publishes what it calls the "Big Mac index" each year. It shows what exchange rates currently are, and it shows what a Big Mac costs in different countries (just as we did here). Then it predicts which currencies will appreciate and depreciate based on this information. *The Economist* does not always predict accurately, but it does do so in many cases.

If you want to predict whether the euro, pound, or peso is going to appreciate or depreciate in the next few months, looking at exchange rates in terms of the price of Big Mac will be a useful source of information.

Might one country want to devalue its currency but another country not want to revalue its currency? For example, suppose Mexico wants to devalue its currency relative to the U.S. dollar. Would U.S. authorities always willingly comply? Not necessarily.

To see why, we have to understand that the United States will not sell as many goods to Mexico if the dollar is revalued. That's because, as we stated earlier, revaluing the dollar means Mexicans have to pay more for it—instead of paying, say, 8.33 pesos for $1, Mexicans might have to pay 10 pesos. At a revalued dollar (higher peso price for a dollar), Mexicans will find U.S. goods more expensive and not want to buy as many.

Americans who produce goods to sell to Mexico may see that a revalued dollar will hurt their pocketbooks, and so they will argue against it.

PROTECTIONIST TRADE POLICY (QUOTAS AND TARIFFS) Recall that an overvalued dollar can bring on or widen a trade deficit. How can a country deal with both the trade deficit and the overvalued dollar at once? Some say it can impose quotas and tariffs to reduce domestic consumption of foreign goods. (The previous chapter explains how both tariffs and quotas meet this objective.) A drop in the domestic consumption of foreign goods goes hand in hand with a decrease in the demand for foreign currencies. In turn, this can affect the value of the country's currency on the foreign exchange market. In this case, it can get rid of an overvalued dollar.

Economists are quick to point out, though, that trade deficits and overvalued currencies are sometimes used as an excuse to promote trade restrictions—many of which simply benefit special interests (e.g., U.S. producers that compete for sales with foreign producers in the U.S. market).

CHANGES IN MONETARY POLICY Sometimes, a nation can use monetary policy to support the exchange rate or the official price of its currency. Suppose the United States is continually running a merchandise trade deficit; year after year, imports are outstripping exports. To remedy this, the United States might enact a tight monetary policy to retard inflation and drive up interest rates (at least in the short run). The tight monetary policy will reduce the U.S. rate of inflation and thereby lower U.S. prices relative to prices in other nations. This will make U.S. goods relatively cheaper than they were before (assuming other nations didn't also enact a tight monetary policy) and promote U.S. exports and discourage foreign imports. It will also generate a flow of investment funds into the United States in search of higher real interest rates.

Some economists argue against fixed exchange rates because they think it unwise for a nation to adopt a particular monetary policy simply to maintain an international exchange rate. Instead, they believe domestic monetary policies should be used to meet domestic economic goals—such as price stability, low unemployment, low and stable interest rates, and so forth.

The Gold Standard

If nations adopt the gold standard, they *automatically fix* their exchange rates. Suppose the United States defines a dollar as equal to 1/10 of an ounce of gold and Mexico defines a peso as equal to 1/100 of an ounce of gold. This means that 1 ounce of gold could be bought with either 10 dollars or 100 pesos. What, then, is the exchange rate between dollars and pesos? It is 10 MXN = 1 USD or 0.10 USD = 1 MXN. This is the fixed exchange rate between dollars and pesos.

To have an international gold standard, countries must do the following:

1. Define their currencies in terms of gold.

2. Stand ready and willing to convert gold into paper money and paper money into gold at the rate specified (e.g., the United States would buy and sell gold at $10 an ounce).

3. Link their money supplies to their holdings of gold.

With this last point in mind, consider how a gold standard would work. Let's again look at Mexico and the United States and initially assume that the gold-standard (fixed) exchange rate of 0.10 USD = 1 MXN is the equilibrium exchange rate. Then, a change occurs: Inflation in Mexico raises prices there by 100 percent. A Mexican table that was priced at 2,000 pesos before the inflation is now priced at 4,000 pesos. At the gold-standard (fixed) exchange rate, Americans now have to pay $400 (4,000 pesos/10 pesos per dollar) to buy the table, whereas before the inflation Americans had to pay only $200 (2,000 pesos/10 pesos per dollar) for the table. As a result, Americans buy fewer Mexican tables; Americans import less from Mexico.

At the same time, Mexicans import more from the United States because American prices are now relatively lower than before inflation hit Mexico. A quick example illustrates our point. Suppose that before inflation hit Mexico, an American pair of shoes cost $200, and as before, a Mexican table cost 2,000 pesos. At 0.10 USD = 1 MXN, the $200 American shoes cost 2,000 pesos and the 2,000-peso Mexican table cost $200. In other words, 1 pair of American shoes traded for (or equaled) 1 Mexican table.

Now look at things after inflation has raised the price of the Mexican table to 4,000 pesos, or $400. Because the American shoes are still $200 (there has been no inflation in the United States) and the exchange rate is still fixed at 0.10 USD = 1 MXN, 1 pair of American shoes no longer equals 1 Mexican table; instead, it equals 1/2 of a Mexican table. In short, the inflation in Mexico has made U.S. goods *relatively cheaper* for Mexicans. As a result, Mexicans buy more U.S. goods; Mexicans import more from the United States.

To summarize: The inflation in Mexico has caused Americans to buy fewer goods from Mexico and Mexicans to buy more goods from the United States. What does this mean in terms of the merchandise trade balance for each country? In the United States, imports decline (Americans are buying less from Mexico) and exports rise (Mexicans are buying more from the United States), so the U.S. trade balance is likely to move into surplus. Contrarily, in Mexico, exports decline (Americans are buying less from Mexico) and imports rise (Mexicans are buying more from the United States), so Mexico's trade balance is likely to move into deficit.

On a gold standard, Mexicans have to pay for the difference between their imports and exports with gold. Gold is therefore shipped to the United States. An increase in the supply of gold in the United States expands the U.S. money supply. A decrease in the supply of gold in Mexico contracts the Mexican money supply. Prices are affected in both countries. In the United States, prices begin to rise; in Mexico, prices begin to fall.

As U.S. prices go up and Mexican prices go down, the earlier situation begins to reverse itself. American goods look more expensive to Mexicans, and they begin to buy less, whereas Mexican goods look cheaper to Americans, and they begin to buy more. Consequently, American imports begin to rise and exports begin to fall; Mexican imports begin to fall and exports begin to rise. Thus, by changing domestic money supplies and price levels, the gold standard begins to correct the initial trade balance disequilibrium.

The change in the money supply that the gold standard sometimes requires has prompted some economists to voice the same argument against the gold standard that is often heard against the fixed exchange rate system; that is, it subjects domestic monetary policy to international instead of domestic considerations. In fact, many economists cite this as part of the reason many nations abandoned the gold standard in the 1930s. At a time when unemployment was unusually high, many nations with trade deficits felt that matters would only get worse if they contracted their money supplies to live by the edicts of the gold standard.

SELF-TEST

1. Under a fixed exchange rate system, if one currency is overvalued, then another currency must be undervalued. Explain why this is true.

2. How does an overvalued dollar affect U.S. exports and imports?

3. In each case, identify whether the U.S. dollar is overvalued or undervalued.

    a. The fixed exchange rate is $2 = 1 pound and the equilibrium exchange rate is $3 = 1 pound.
    b. The fixed exchange rate is $1.25 = 1 euro and the equilibrium exchange rate is $1.10 = 1 euro.
    c. The fixed exchange rate is $1 = 10 pesos and the equilibrium exchange rate is $1 = 14 pesos.

4. Under a fixed exchange rate system, why might the United States want to devalue its currency?

Fixed Exchange Rates Versus Flexible Exchange Rates

As is the case in many economic situations, there are both costs and benefits to any exchange rate system. This section discusses some of the arguments and issues surrounding fixed exchange rates and flexible exchange rates.

Promoting International Trade

Which are better at promoting international trade, fixed or flexible exchange rates? This section presents the case for each.

THE CASE FOR FIXED EXCHANGE RATES Proponents of a fixed exchange rate system often argue that fixed exchange rates promote international trade, whereas flexible exchange rates stifle it. A major advantage of fixed exchange rates is certainty. Individuals in different countries know from day to day the value of their nation's currency. With flexible exchange rates, individuals are less likely to engage in international trade because of the added risk of not knowing from one day to the next how many dollars, euros, or yen they will have to trade for other currencies. Certainty is a necessary ingredient in international trade; flexible exchange rates promote uncertainty, which hampers international trade.

Economist Charles Kindleberger, a proponent of fixed exchange rates, believes that having fixed exchange rates is analogous to having a single currency for the entire United States instead of having a different currency for each of the 50 states. One currency in the United States promotes trade, whereas 50 different currencies would hamper it. In Kindleberger's view:

> The main case against flexible exchange rates is that they break up the world market. . . . Imagine trying to conduct interstate trade in the USA if there were fifty different state monies, none of which was dominant. This is akin to barter, the inefficiency of which is explained time and again by textbooks.[6]

THE CASE FOR FLEXIBLE EXCHANGE RATES Advocates of flexible exchange rates, as we have noted, maintain that it is better for a nation to adopt policies to meet domestic economic goals than to sacrifice domestic economic goals to maintain an exchange rate. They also say that there is too great a chance that the fixed exchange rate will diverge greatly from the equilibrium exchange rate, creating persistent balance of trade problems. This leads deficit nations to impose trade restrictions (tariffs and quotas) that hinder international trade.

---

[6]Charles Kindleberger, *International Money* (London: Allen and Unwin, 1981), p. 174.

Optimal Currency Areas

As of 2006, the European Union (EU) consists of 25 member states. According to the European Union, its ultimate goal is "an ever closer union among the peoples of Europe, in which decisions are taken as closely as possible to the citizen." As part of meeting this goal, the EU established its own currency—the euro—on January 1, 1999.[7] Although euro notes and coins were not issued until January 1, 2002, certain business transactions were made in euros beginning January 1, 1999.

The European Union and the euro are relevant to a discussion of an *optimal currency area*. An **optimal currency area** is a geographic area in which exchange rates can be fixed or a *common currency* used without sacrificing domestic economic goals, such as low unemployment. The concept of an optimal currency area originated in the debate over whether fixed or flexible exchange rates are better. Most of the pioneering work on optimal currency areas was done by Robert Mundell, the winner of the 1999 Nobel Prize in Economics.

Before discussing an optimal currency area, we need to look at the relationships among labor mobility, trade, and exchange rates. Labor mobility means that it is easy for the residents of one country to move to another country.

TRADE AND LABOR MOBILITY Suppose there are only two countries, the United States and Canada. The United States produces calculators and soft drinks, and Canada produces bread and muffins. Currently, the two countries trade with each other, and there is complete labor mobility between the two countries.

One day, the residents of both countries reduce their demand for bread and muffins and increase their demand for calculators and soft drinks. In other words, there is a change in relative demand. Demand increases for U.S. goods and falls for Canadian goods. Business firms in Canada lay off employees because their sales have plummeted. Incomes in Canada begin to fall, and the unemployment rate begins to rise. In the United States, prices initially rise because of the increased demand for calculators and soft drinks. In response to the higher demand for their products, U.S. business firms begin to hire more workers and increase their production. Their efforts to hire more workers drive wages up and reduce the unemployment rate.

Because labor is mobile, some of the newly unemployed Canadian workers move to the United States to find work. This will ease the economic situation in both countries. It will reduce some of the unemployment problems in Canada, and with more workers in the United States, more output will be produced, thus dampening upward price pressures on calculators and soft drinks. Thus, changes in relative demand pose no major economic problems for either country if labor is mobile.

TRADE AND LABOR IMMOBILITY Now let's change things. Suppose that relative demand has changed, but this time, labor is not mobile between the United States and Canada (labor immobility). There are either political or cultural barriers to people moving between the two countries. What happens in the economies of the two countries if people cannot move? The answer depends largely on whether exchange rates are fixed or flexible.

If exchange rates are flexible, the value of U.S. currency changes vis-à-vis Canadian currency. If Canadians want to buy more U.S. goods, they will have to exchange their domestic currency for U.S. currency. This increases the demand for U.S. currency on the foreign exchange market at the same time that it increases the supply of Canadian currency. Consequently, U.S. currency appreciates and Canadian currency depreciates. Because Canadian currency depreciates, U.S. goods become relatively more expensive for Canadians, so they buy fewer. And because U.S. currency appreciates, Canadian goods become relatively cheaper for Americans, so they buy more. Canadian business firms

Optimal Currency Area

A geographic area in which exchange rates can be fixed or a common currency used without sacrificing domestic economic goals, such as low unemployment.

[7]So far, 12 of the 25 member states have adopted the euro as their official currency.

begin to sell more goods, so they hire more workers, the unemployment rate drops, and the bad economic times in Canada begin to disappear.

If exchange rates are fixed, however, U.S. goods will not become relatively more expensive for Canadians, and Canadian goods will not become relatively cheaper for Americans. Consequently, the bad economic times in Canada (high unemployment) might last for a long time indeed instead of beginning to reverse. Thus, if labor is immobile, changes in relative demand may pose major economic problems when exchange rates are fixed but not when they are flexible.

COSTS, BENEFITS, AND OPTIMAL CURRENCY AREAS There are both costs and benefits to flexible exchange rates. The benefits we have just discussed. The costs include the cost of exchanging one currency for another (there is a charge to exchange, say, U.S. dollars for Canadian dollars or U.S. dollars for Japanese yen) and the added risk of not knowing what the value of one's currency will be on the foreign exchange market on any given day. For many countries, the benefits outweigh the costs, and so they have flexible exchange rate systems.

Suppose some of the costs of flexible exchange rates could be eliminated, while the benefits were maintained. Under what conditions could two countries have a fixed exchange rate or adopt a common currency and retain the benefits of flexible exchange rates? The answer is when labor is mobile between the two countries. Then, there is no reason to have separate currencies that float against each other because resources (labor) can move easily and quickly in response to changes in relative demand. There is no reason the two countries cannot fix exchange rates or adopt the same currency.

When labor in countries within a certain geographic area is mobile enough to move easily and quickly in response to changes in relative demand, the countries are said to constitute an *optimal currency area*. Countries in an optimal currency area can either fix their currencies or adopt the same currency and thus keep all the benefits of flexible exchange rates without any of the costs.

It is commonly argued that the states within the United States constitute an optimal currency area. Labor can move easily and quickly between, say, North Carolina and South Carolina in response to relative demand changes. Some economists argue that the countries that compose the European Union are within an optimal currency area and that adopting a common currency—the euro—will benefit these countries. Other economists disagree. They argue that while labor is somewhat more mobile in Europe today than in the past, there are still certain language and cultural differences that make labor mobility less than sufficient to truly constitute an optimal currency area.

The Current International Monetary System

Today's international monetary system is best described as a managed flexible exchange rate system, sometimes referred to more casually as a **managed float**. In a way, this system is a rough compromise between the fixed and flexible exchange rate systems. The current system operates under flexible exchange rates, but not completely. Nations now and then intervene to adjust their official reserve holdings to moderate major swings in exchange rates.

Proponents of the managed float system stress the following advantages:

Managed Float

A managed flexible exchange rate system, under which nations now and then intervene to adjust their official reserve holdings to moderate major swings in exchange rates.

1. **It allows nations to pursue independent monetary policies.** Under a (strictly) fixed exchange rate system, fixed either by agreement or by gold, a nation with a merchandise trade deficit might have to enact a tight monetary policy to retard inflation and promote its exports. This would not be the case with the managed float. Its proponents argue that it is better to solve trade imbalances by adjusting one price—the exchange rate—than by adjusting the price level.

2. **It solves trade problems without trade restrictions.** As stated earlier, under a fixed exchange rate system, nations sometimes impose tariffs and quotas to solve trade imbalances. For example, a deficit nation might impose import quotas so that exports and imports of goods will be more in line. Under the current system, trade imbalances are usually solved through changes in exchange rates.

3. **It is flexible and therefore can easily adjust to shocks.** In 1973–1974, the OPEC nations dramatically raised the price of oil, which resulted in many oil-importing nations running trade deficits. A fixed exchange rate system would have had a hard time accommodating such a major change in oil prices. The current system had little trouble, however. Exchange rates took much of the shock (there were large changes in exchange rates) and thus allowed most nations' economies to weather the storm with a minimum of difficulty.

Opponents of the current international monetary system stress the following disadvantages:

1. **It promotes exchange rate volatility and uncertainty and results in less international trade than would be the case under fixed exchange rates.** Under a flexible exchange rate system, volatile exchange rates make it riskier for importers and exporters to conduct business. As a result, there is less international trade than there would be under a fixed exchange rate system. Proponents respond that the futures market in currencies allows importers and exporters to shift the risk of fluctuations in exchange rates to others. For example, if an American company wants to buy a certain quantity of a good from a Japanese company three months from today, it can contract today for the desired quantity of yen it will need at a specified price. It will not have to worry about a change in the dollar price of yen during the next three months. There is, of course, a cost to purchasing a futures contract, but it is usually modest.

2. **It promotes inflation.** As we have seen, the monetary policies of different nations are not independent of one another under a fixed exchange rate system. For example, a nation with a merchandise trade deficit is somewhat restrained from inflating its currency because this will worsen the deficit problem. It will make the nation's goods more expensive relative to foreign goods and promote the purchase of imports. In its attempt to maintain the exchange rate, a nation with a merchandise trade deficit would have to enact a tight monetary policy.

    Under the current system, a nation with a merchandise trade deficit does not have to maintain exchange rates or try to solve its deficit problem through changes in its money supply. Opponents of the current system argue that this frees nations to inflate. They predict more inflation will result than would occur under a fixed exchange rate system.

3. **Changes in exchange rates alter trade balances in the desired direction only after a long time; in the short run, a depreciation in a currency can make the situation worse instead of better.** It is often argued that soon after a depreciation in a trade-deficit nation's currency, the trade deficit will increase (not decrease, as was hoped). The reason is that import demand is inelastic in the short run: Imports are not very responsive to a change in price. For example, suppose Mexico is running a trade deficit with the United States at the present exchange rate of 0.12 USD = 1 MXN. At this exchange rate, the peso is overvalued. Mexico buys 2,000 television sets from the United States, each with a price tag of $500. Assume Mexico therefore spends 8.33 million pesos on imports of American television sets. Now suppose the overvalued peso begins to depreciate, say, to 0.11 USD = 1 MXN. Furthermore, in the short run, Mexican customers buy only 100 fewer American television sets; that is, they import 1,900 television sets. At a price of $500

each and an exchange rate of 0.11 USD = 1 MXN, Mexicans now spend 8.63 million pesos on imports of American television sets. In the short run, then, a depreciation in the peso has widened the trade deficit because imports fell by only 5 percent while the price of imports (in terms of pesos) increased by 9.09 percent. As time passes, imports will fall off more (it takes time for Mexican buyers to shift from higher priced American goods to lower priced Mexican goods), and the deficit will shrink.

SELF-TEST

1.   What is an optimal currency area?

2.   Country 1 produces good X and country 2 produces good Y. People in both countries begin to demand more of good X and less of good Y. Assume there is no labor mobility between the two countries and that a flexible exchange rate system exists. What will happen to the unemployment rate in country 2? Explain your answer.

3.   How important is labor mobility in determining whether or not an area is an optimal currency area?

$\mathcal{A}$ $\mathcal{R}eader$ $\mathcal{A}sks$...

How Do I Convert Currencies?

I plan to travel to several different countries during the summer. How do I convert prices of products in other countries into dollars?

Here is the general formula you would use:

Price of the product in dollars = Price of the product in foreign currency × Price of the foreign currency in dollars

For example, suppose you travel to Mexico and see something priced at 100 pesos. You'd change the general formula into a specific one:

Price of the product in dollars = Price of the product in pesos × Price of a peso in dollars

If the dollar price of a peso is, say, 0.12 dollars, then the dollar price of the product is $12. Here is the calculation:

Price of the product in dollars = 100 × 0.12 = 12

Or suppose you are in Tokyo and you see a product for 10,000 yen. What is the price in dollars? At the exchange rate of 0.008 USD = 1 JPY, it is $80.

Price of the product in dollars = 10,000 × 0.008 = 80

Now let's suppose you are in Russia and you don't know what the exchange rate is between dollars and rubles. You pick up a newspaper to find out (often, exchange rates are quoted in the newspaper). But instead of finding the exchange rate quoted in terms of the dollar price of a ruble (e.g., 0.0318 dollars for 1 ruble), you find the ruble price of a dollar (31.4190 rubles for 1 dollar). What do you do now?

Perhaps the easiest thing to do is first convert rubles per dollar into dollars per ruble and then use the earlier formula to find the price of the Russian product in dollars. Recall that exchange rates are reciprocals, so:

$$\text{Dollars per ruble} = \frac{1}{\text{Rubles per dollar}}$$

To illustrate, if it takes 31.4190 rubles to purchase $1, then it takes 0.0318 dollars to buy 1 ruble. Here is the computation:

$$\text{Dollars per ruble} = \frac{1}{31.41990} = 0.0318$$

Now, because you know that 0.0318 dollars = 1 ruble, it follows that, say, a Russian coat that costs 10,000 rubles costs $318:

Price of the product in dollars = 10,000 × 0.0318 = 318

! analyzing the scene

What does the value of the dollar have to do with Karen's trip? What does the value of the dollar have to do with Robert Ivans's business?

These questions show two sides of how a fall in the value of the dollar affects people's lives. In Karen's case, the dollar is falling relative to the pound. So the dollar is depreciating and the pound is appreciating. Karen will now have to pay more in dollars and cents to buy a pound, so everything she buys on her trip (denominated in pounds) will be more expensive for her.

For Robert Ivans, if the dollar is depreciating, then some other currency is appreciating—say, the pound. An appreciating pound makes it cheaper for the British to buy U.S. goods, such as Robert Ivans's goods. If the British demand for U.S. goods is elastic, we can expect the British to spend more on U.S. goods as their currency appreciates.

Is anything wrong with the headline that the business columnist wrote?

The business columnist could not have been referring to the balance of payments because the balance of payments *always* equals zero. The reason the balance of payments always equals zero is that the three accounts that comprise the balance of payments, when taken together, plus the statistical discrepancy, include all of the *sources* and all of the *uses* of dollars in international transactions. And because every dollar used must have a source, adding the sources (+) to the uses (–) necessarily gives us zero. The columnist probably meant that the merchandise trade deficit was at a record high. Often, the news media erroneously use the term *balance of payments* to refer to the current account balance or the merchandise trade balance.

Do big budget deficits really affect as many things as the president's economic advisor indicates?

When the economic advisor tells the president that the recent run of big budget deficits is likely to affect interest rates, the value of the dollar, exports and imports, and the merchandise trade balance, he is probably thinking that big budget deficits will mean the federal government will have to borrow more funds, which will increase the demand for credit. This will push up the interest rate. As the U.S. interest rate rises relative to interest rates in other countries, foreigners will want to purchase financial assets in the United States that pay a higher return. This will increase the demand for dollars, the dollar will appreciate, and foreign currencies will depreciate. In turn, this will affect both import and export spending, and therefore, it will affect the merchandise trade balance.

chapter summary

Balance of Payments

- The balance of payments provides information about a nation's imports and exports, domestic residents' earnings on assets located abroad, foreign earnings on domestic assets, gifts to and from foreign countries, and official transactions by governments and central banks.

- In a nation's balance of payments, any transaction that supplies the country's currency in the foreign exchange market is recorded as a debit (–). Any transaction that creates a demand for the country's currency is recorded as a credit (+).

- The three main accounts of the balance of payments are the current account, the capital account, and the official reserve account.

- The current account includes all payments related to the purchase and sale of goods and services. The three major components of the account are exports of goods and services, imports of goods and services, and net unilateral transfers abroad.

- The capital account includes all payments related to the purchase and sale of assets and to borrowing and lending activities. The major components are outflow of U.S. capital and inflow of foreign capital.

- The official reserve account includes transactions by the central banks of various countries.

- The merchandise trade balance is the difference between the value of merchandise exports and the value of merchandise imports. If exports are greater than imports, a nation has a trade surplus; if imports are greater than exports, a nation has a trade deficit.

- The balance of payments equals current account balance + capital account balance + official reserve balance + statistical discrepancy.

The Foreign Exchange Market

- The market in which currencies of different countries are exchanged is called the foreign exchange market. In this market, currencies are bought and sold for a price; an exchange rate exists.

- If Americans demand Mexican goods, they also demand Mexican pesos and supply U.S. dollars. If Mexicans demand American goods, they also demand U.S. dollars and supply Mexican pesos. When the residents of a nation demand a foreign currency, they must supply their own currency.

Flexible Exchange Rates

- Under flexible exchange rates, the foreign exchange market will equilibrate at the exchange rate where the quantity demanded of a currency equals the quantity supplied of the currency; for example, the quantity demanded of U.S. dollars equals the quantity supplied of U.S. dollars.

- If the price of a nation's currency increases relative to a foreign currency, the nation's currency is said to have appreciated. For example, if the price of a peso rises from 0.10 USD = 1 MXN to 0.15 USD = 1 MXN, the peso has appreciated. If the price of a nation's currency decreases relative to a foreign currency, the nation's currency is said to have depreciated. For example, if the price of a dollar falls from 10 MXN = 1 USD to 8 MXN = 1 USD, the dollar has depreciated.

- Under a flexible exchange rate system, the equilibrium exchange rate is affected by a difference in income growth rates between countries, a difference in inflation rates between countries, and a change in (real) interest rates between countries.

Fixed Exchange Rates

- Under a fixed exchange rate system, countries agree to fix the price of their currencies. The central banks of the countries must then buy and sell currencies to maintain the agreed-on exchange rate.

- If a persistent deficit or surplus in a nation's combined current and capital account exists at a fixed exchange rate, the nation has a few options to deal with the problem: devalue or revalue its currency, enact protectionist trade policies (in the case of a deficit), or change its monetary policy.

- A gold standard automatically fixes exchange rates. To have an international gold standard, nations must do the following: (1) define their currencies in terms of gold; (2) stand ready and willing to convert gold into paper money and paper money into gold at a specified rate; and (3) link their money supplies to their holdings of gold. The change in the money supply that the gold standard sometimes requires has prompted some economists to voice the same argument against the gold standard that is often heard against the fixed exchange rate system: It subjects domestic monetary policy to international instead of domestic considerations.

The Current International Monetary System

- Today's international monetary system is described as a managed flexible exchange rate system, or managed float. For the most part, the exchange rate system is flexible, although nations do periodically intervene in the foreign exchange market to adjust exchange rates. Because it is a managed float system, it is difficult to tell if nations will emphasize the "float" part or the "managed" part in the future.

- Proponents of the managed flexible exchange rate system believe it offers several advantages: (1) It allows nations to pursue independent monetary policies. (2) It solves trade problems without trade restrictions. (3) It is flexible and therefore can easily adjust to shocks. Opponents of the managed flexible exchange rate system believe it has several disadvantages: (1) It promotes exchange rate volatility and uncertainty and results in less international trade than would be the case under fixed exchange rates. (2) It promotes inflation. (3) It corrects trade deficits only a long time after a depreciation in the currency; in the interim, it can make matters worse.

key terms and concepts

Balance of Payments	Merchandise Trade Surplus	Exchange Rate	Overvaluation
Debit	Current Account Balance	Flexible Exchange Rate System	Undervaluation
Foreign Exchange Market	Capital Account	Appreciation	Devaluation
Credit	Capital Account Balance	Depreciation	Revaluation
Current Account	International Monetary Fund (IMF)	Purchasing Power Parity (PPP) Theory	Optimal Currency Area
Merchandise Trade Balance	Special Drawing Right (SDR)	Fixed Exchange Rate System	Managed Float
Merchandise Trade Deficit			

questions and problems

1 Suppose the United States and Japan have a flexible exchange rate system. Explain whether each of the following events will lead to an appreciation or depreciation in the U.S. dollar and Japanese yen. (a) U.S. real interest rates rise above Japanese real interest rates. (b) The Japanese inflation rate rises relative to the U.S. inflation rate. (c) Japan imposes a quota on imports of American radios.

2 Give an example that illustrates how a change in the exchange rate changes the relative price of domestic goods in terms of foreign goods.

3 Suppose the media report that the United States has a deficit in its current account. What does this imply about the U.S. capital account balance and official reserve account balance?

4 Suppose Canada has a merchandise trade deficit and Mexico has a merchandise trade surplus. The two countries have a flexible exchange rate system, so the Mexican peso appreciates and the Canadian dollar depreciates. It is noticed, however, that soon after the depreciation of the Canadian dollar, Canada's trade deficit grows instead of shrinks. Why might this occur?

5 What are the strong and weak points of the flexible exchange rate system? What are the strong and weak points of the fixed exchange rate system?

6 Individuals do not keep a written account of their balance of trade with other individuals. For example, John doesn't keep an account of how much he sells to Alice

and how much he buys from her. In addition, neither cities nor any of the 50 states calculate their balance of trade with all other cities and states. However, nations do calculate their merchandise trade balance with other nations. If nations do it, should individuals, cities, and states do it? Why or why not?

7 Every nation's balance of payments equals zero. Does it follow that each nation is on an equal footing in international trade and finance with every other nation? Explain your answer.

8 Suppose your objective is to predict whether the euro (the currency of the European Union) and the U.S. dollar will appreciate or depreciate on the foreign exchange market in the next two months. What information would you need to help make your prediction? Specifically, how would this information help you predict the direction of the foreign exchange value of the euro and dollar? Next, explain how a person who could accurately predict exchange rates could become extremely rich in a short time.

9 Suppose the price of a Big Mac always rises by the percentage rise in the price level of the country in which it is sold. According to the purchasing power parity (PPP) theory, we would expect the price of a Big Mac to be the same everywhere in the world. Why?

10 If everyone in the world spoke the same language, would the world be closer to or further from being an optimal currency area? Explain your answer.

working with numbers and graphs

1 The following foreign exchange information appeared in a newspaper:

	U.S. Dollar Equivalent		Currency per U.S. Dollar	
	THURS.	**FRI.**	**THURS.**	**FRI.**
Russia (ruble)	0.0318	0.0317	31.4190	31.5290
Brazil (real)	0.3569	0.3623	2.8020	2.7601
India (rupee)	0.0204	0.0208	48.9100	47.8521

a Between Thursday and Friday, did the U.S. dollar appreciate or depreciate against the Russian ruble?

b Between Thursday and Friday, did the U.S. dollar appreciate or depreciate against the Brazilian real?

c Between Thursday and Friday, did the U.S. dollar appreciate or depreciate against the Indian rupee?

2 If $1 equals 0.0093 yen, then what does 1 yen equal?

3 If $1 equals 7.7 krone (Danish), then what does 1 krone equal?

4 If $1 equals 31 rubles, then what does 1 ruble equal?

5 If the current account is −$45 billion, the capital account is +$55 billion, and the official reserve balance is −$1 billion, what does the statistical discrepancy equal?

6 Why does the balance of payments always equal zero?

Globalization

Setting the Scene

The following events occurred one day in September.

10:13 A.M.

The leaders of some of the richest countries in the world were gathering for a meeting in a small town in Switzerland. The topic for discussion was economic globalization. Outside the meeting, hundreds of people from all over the world screamed slogans and held up signs. One of the most common signs read, "Globalization hurts the poor." One of the chants heard there was, "Hey, Hey, Ho, Ho. Globalization has got to go!"

6:14 P.M.

Ken works as a software engineer for a large firm in New York City. He just walked into his house after a hard day at work. His wife, Alexis, who usually gets home about 7:00, is already home. She says to Ken, "What's got you so down? You look as if you lost your job today." "I did," says Ken. "The company is sending my job out of the country."

7:45 P.M.

Diane is watching a television news show. Here is what the TV news reporter is currently saying: "People are somewhat afraid that with globalization, their jobs and their livelihoods will be determined by forces outside their control, perhaps by forces emanating from halfway around in the world. This is the scary side of globalization. But on the other hand, some people look upon this new and global economy with optimism. They say that with globalization come opportunities—opportunities to end poverty and to turn a turbulent and hostile world into a peaceful one. We'll just have to wait and see. For WTYX News, this is Tabitha Sherman."

11:54 P.M.

Elizabeth lives in Kentucky. Last week, she bought a computer online from a U.S. company. She is having a little trouble with the computer, so she calls the customer service number. It is a 1-800 number. A voice on the other end of the line asks for her service tag number. She gives it to the person. The person she is speaking with is in India.

? Here are some questions to keep in mind as you read this chapter:

- *What is globalization and does it hurt the poor?*

- *Will globalization lead to some people losing jobs?*

- *Does everyone agree as to what the benefits and costs of globalization are?*

- *Why does Elizabeth's customer service call connect to a person in India?*

See analyzing the scene at the end of this chapter for answers to these questions.

What Is Globalization?

What is this thing called **globalization**? Many economists define it as (1) a phenomenon by which individuals and businesses in any part of the world are much more affected by events elsewhere in the world than before. Globalization can also be defined as (2) the growing integration of the national economies of the world to the degree that we may be witnessing the emergence and operation of a single worldwide economy. These factors—people and businesses across the world having greater impact on each other, creating a smaller world, and the movement toward a worldwide economy—are repeated in the many different definitions of globalization. Let's take a closer look at these key features of globalization.

Globalization

A phenomenon by which economic agents in any given part of the world are more affected by events elsewhere in the world than before; the growing integration of the national economies of the world to the degree that we may be witnessing the emergence and operation of a single worldwide economy.

A Smaller World

The first definition emphasizes that economic agents in any given part of the world are affected by events elsewhere in the world. If you live in the United States, you are not only affected by what happens in the United States but also by what happens in Brazil, Russia, and China. For example, in 2005, the Chinese government was taking much of the money it earned in trade with the United States and buying bonds issued by the U.S. government. As a result of Chinese purchases of U.S. bonds, interest rates in the United States ended up being lower than they would have been. Because of lower interest rates, some people took out mortgage loans to buy a house who otherwise would not have. Some people took out car loans to buy a car who otherwise would not have.

But can you see how, in a sense, globalization makes the world smaller? China hasn't moved physically; it isn't any closer to the United States (in terms of distance) than it was 100 years ago. Still, what happens in distant China today, because of globalization, has an effect on you as, in the past, what happened between locations only 10 miles or 100 miles away. For all practical purposes, we live in a "smaller world" today than people did 100 years ago.

A World Economy

Globalization is closely aligned with a movement toward more free enterprise, freer markets, and more freedom of movement for people and goods. Thomas Friedman, author of several books on globalization, states that "globalization means the spread of free-market capitalism in the world." Economic globalization is essentially a free enterprise activity, and to the degree that many countries are "globalizing," they are moving toward greater free enterprise practices. Much of this globalization, and much of the movement toward freer markets, is occurring in the world today.

With globalization, the world is moving from hundreds of national economies toward *one large world economy*. In this world economy, it does not make as much sense to speak of *different* economic systems as it once did. It makes sense to speak of "the" economic system for that one world economy. And as we said, the economic system that best describes what is happening in the world economy is free enterprise or capitalism.

Q&A

I've heard that globalization is bad for U.S. workers. After all, can't globalization lead to a lot of Americans losing their jobs to people in other countries?

You will learn more about this later in the chapter, but for now, keep two points in mind: (1) Yes, globalization can lead to some American workers losing jobs, but (2) during a relatively intense period of globalization in the United States (during the 1990s and early 2000s), the U.S. unemployment rate was at historic lows. If globalization necessarily led to large numbers of Americans losing their jobs and staying unemployed, we would expect the unemployment rate in the country to be much higher than it was during the period of, say, 1990 to 2006. Instead, we find that for this period in the United States, globalization and lower unemployment rates seem to have gone together.

Two Ways to "See" Globalization

Sometimes, a definition is not as good as a picture to describe and explain something. Let's try to create two mental pictures that should give you a good idea of what globalization is about. The first picture is of a world without any barriers to trade, where the cost of dealing with anyone in the world is essentially the same.

No Barriers

Suppose land was not divided into nation states—no United States, no China, no Russia. Also suppose physical, economic, or political barriers to trade did not exist. Essentially, then, you could trade with whomever you wanted to trade with, no matter where in the world this person lived. You could trade with a person living 5,000 miles away as easily as you could trade with your next-door neighbor.

In this pretend world, businesses could hire workers and set up factories anywhere in the world. People could open savings accounts in banks 7,000 miles away or buy stock in companies located on the other side of the globe.

Now, in a sense, our world—the world that we live in today—is moving in the direction of this pretend world just described. As this movement proceeds, a nation's economy (e.g., the U.S. economy) becomes more and more a part of the world economy. As this process continues, it becomes more and more relevant to speak of a world or global economy rather than the Russian, U.S., or Chinese economies.

A Union of States

The second way to see globalization is familiar to people who reside in the United States. We know that the United States is made up of 50 states. Today, it is easy to move goods and services between these states. If a person wants to, he can produce goods in, say, North Carolina and then transport those goods (with only a few exceptions) for sale to every state in the country. In addition, a person living anywhere in the United States can move to any state and work, save, purchase, sell, and so on. In other words, within the United States, free movement of people and goods is possible.

Some people will argue today that economic globalization is, in a way, similar to changing countries (of the world) into states of one country. It is similar to taking independent countries such as the United States, Russia, China, Brazil, and Japan and turning them into the United States of the World.

Globalization Facts

How do we know globalization is occurring? What do you need to see happening in the world before you could say that globalization was taking place?

You would see countries in the world opening up to more trade with each other. You would see people in one country investing some of their money in other countries. You would see companies in one country hiring people in other countries. Essentially, you would see people in the world acting more like they once acted only within their individual countries. Some evidence suggests that all these things are happening.

Q&A

What specifically is the difference between a national economy and a global economy?

Think of an invisible string connecting you and everyone you have an economic relationship with. If you buy something from someone, a string connects the two of you; if you work for someone, a string connects you. Now, perhaps the best way to think of a national economy is to think of strings only linking people who reside in the same country. In a world or global economy, however, strings link individuals with people in their own country and in other countries too. Their economic relationships extend beyond the nation's borders. In the past, a few strings extended outside country borders, but only a few, and for a long time, the strings only went to certain countries. With globalization, more and more strings, a seemingly unlimited number of strings, are being connected across borders. And these strings are being connected between people in more and more countries.

International Trade

The average **tariff** rate in the United States was 40 percent in 1946. According to the 2006 *Economic Report of the President,* the average tariff today is about 1.4 percent. You may also be interested in knowing that federal government revenue from tariffs in the early 1900s accounted for half of all federal government revenues, whereas today they account for less than 2 percent. Exhibit 1 presents average tariff rates in the United States during the period 1930–2005.

What has been occurring in the United States (a decline in tariff rates) has also been happening in countries such as India, China, Brazil, and many others. For example, in 2000, the average tariff rate in China was 18.7 percent; one year later, it was 12.8 percent. In 2000, the average tariff rate in India was 30.2 percent; one year later, it was 21 percent. Furthermore, both India and China are trading more with other countries. For example, 15 years ago, China did not trade much with the countries of Europe. Today, for most European countries, China is one of their top five trading partners.

As further evidence of globalization, between 1973 and 2006, countries exported and imported more goods. Exports became a larger percentage of a country's total output. To explain these changes, think of an analogy. Suppose you produce computers. Last year, all the computers you produced were purchased by residents of the country in which you live. This year, half the computers you produced are purchased by residents of the country in which you live, and the other half are purchased by persons who live in foreign countries. In 2006, U.S. exports and imports were more like the second scenario; in 1973, things were closer to the first scenario.

Foreign Exchange Trading

When people of one country want to trade with people of another country or invest in a foreign company, they have to buy the currency used in the other country. So if globalization occurred, we would expect a lot more currency exchanges to take place. In economics, *foreign exchange trading* is a term that means "buying and selling foreign currencies." In 1995, daily foreign exchange trading was 60 times higher than it was in 1977. In 1992, daily foreign exchange trading amounted to $820 billion. In 1998, this amount had risen to $1.5 trillion, close to doubling in just 6 years.

Foreign Direct Investment

If a U.S. company wants to invest in a company in, say, Russia, it undertakes what is called *foreign direct investment.* The more foreign direct investment there is, the more likely

Tariff
A tax on imports.

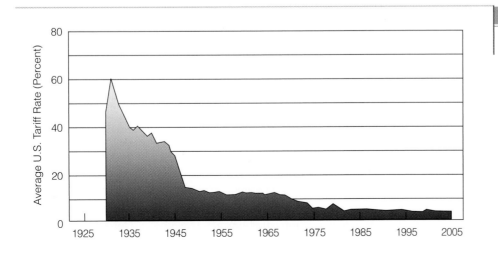

exhibit **1**

Average U.S. Tariff Rates, 1930–2005

© INDEX STOCK IMAGERY/JUPITER IMAGES

economics 24/7

HOW HARD WILL IT BE TO GET INTO HARVARD IN 2025?

The Indian Institute of Technology (in India) is one of the hardest universities in the world to be admitted to, largely because of its reputation. It has been compared to putting Harvard, MIT (Massachusetts Institute of Technology), and Princeton together.

In an average year, about 178,000 high school seniors in India take the exam necessary to apply to the Indian Institute of Technology. Just over 3,500 students (only 1.96 percent of all applicants) are admitted. In comparison, the admission rate of Harvard University is nearly 10 percent. Often, students from India who are admitted to MIT, Princeton, and Cal Tech (all of which are listed in the top 10 of U.S. colleges and universities) cannot gain admission to the Indian Institute of Technology.

Now consider some highly prestigious U.S. universities and colleges, such as Brown, Columbia, Cornell, Dartmouth, Harvard, the University of Pennsylvania, Princeton, Yale, Stanford, Northwestern, and Duke. These schools have some of the most selective admission criteria of all colleges and universities in the country. Each year, students who have the grade point average and standardized test scores to (potentially) be admitted to these universities are turned away.

This phenomenon has been occurring at the same time that college tuition has been increasing rapidly. For example, during the period 1990 to 2003, college tuition went up by 130 percent, considerably more than medical care costs, the price of housing, food, gasoline, cars, and so on.

If we look around the world at other prestigious institutions of higher learning, we see the same theme: The admission rate is usually low, and the cost is usually high.

Consider how grades (one major admissions criterion) and money actually function in this situation: They are rationing devices. We know that because of scarcity, some mechanism has to ration the available resources, goods, and services. Still we have to ask: Why have these two rationing

devices—grades and money—become stiffer when it comes to being admitted to the top universities in the world? Why ever higher grades and ever more money? The answer is twofold.

First, the population of the world increased at the same time that the number of Harvards did not. Harvard cannot clone itself, nor can Yale, the Indian Institute of Technology, or MIT. To a large degree, the world has only one Harvard, Oxford (in the United Kingdom), and Indian Institute of Technology. We can produce more computers, houses, and dining room chairs as the population of the world increases, but it seems much more difficult to produce more Harvards. So, what happens over time is a heightened scarcity of top-notch, one-of-a-kind educational institutions. As a result, the rationing devices for such institutions must do more work to ration, which essentially means that it will become harder and more expensive to get admitted to such places.

The second reason involves globalization. One of things that pays a high dividend in a global economy is education. "Brains" seem to matter more than "brawn," which will increase the overall demand for a college education—and not just at Harvard but at all levels of higher education (from community colleges to 4-year state and private universities). So, will the premium placed on education in a global economy cause the demand at the most prestigious educational establishments to rise at a faster rate than at other colleges? It would be similar to asking: If the premium for playing music were to rise, would the demand to be at Juilliard (one of the premier music institutions in the world) rise faster than the demand to study with the local piano teacher down the street? The likely answer is yes. With a growing world population, and with the global economy paying a high premium to those who are educated (compared to those who are not), we can expect it to get increasingly more difficult and more expensive to be admitted to the world's best institutions of higher learning.

the process of globalization is at work. In 1975, foreign direct investment amounted to $23 billion. In 1997, it had risen to $644 billion, a 30-fold increase. In 1980, 6.2 percent of the U.S. population was foreign born; in 2005, it was 12 percent. Between 1984 and 2003, U.S. investment holdings in foreign companies tripled while foreign investment in the U.S. increased six-fold.

Personal Investments

Many people in the United States own stocks. If you own a number of stocks, you are said to have a stock portfolio. In 1980, these stock portfolios were comprised of no more than 2 percent of foreign stocks. Today, it is 14 percent. Thus, Americans are increasingly buying stock in foreign companies.

The World Trade Organization

The World Trade Organization (sometimes called the WTO) is an international organization whose mission is to promote international free trade (trade between countries). In 1948, only 23 countries of the world chose to be members of the precursor to the WTO, GATT (General Agreement on Tariffs and Trade); in mid-2006, that number had risen to 149 countries.

Business Practices

It is becoming increasingly common for Americans to work for foreign companies that have offices in the United States. For example, the number of Americans working for foreign companies (with offices in the United States) grew from 4.9 million in 1991 to 6.5 million in 2001, an increase of 1.6 million.

Movement Toward Globalization

How did we come to live in a global economy? Did someone push a button years ago and start the process of globalization? No, things don't happen that way.

Globalization did not just appear on the world stage two decades ago. The world has gone through different globalization periods. For example, during the period from the mid-1800s to the late-1920s, globalization was occurring. Some people today refer to it as the First Era of globalization. In some ways, that world was a freer world when it came to the movement of people than the world today, as evidenced by the fact that many people moved from country to country without a passport, which was not required.

This early era of globalization was largely ended by the two world wars (World War I and World War II) and the Great Depression. Even though the Great Depression and both world wars were over by 1945, globalization did not start anew. The Cold War essentially divided the world into different camps (free vs. unfree, capitalist vs. communist), which led to relatively high political and economic barriers. The visible symbol of these barriers—the Berlin Wall—separated not only East from West Germany but one group of countries living under one political and economic system from another group of countries living under a different political and economic system.

The more recent period of globalization that we speak about today has several causal factors. Not everyone agrees as to what all the factors are, and not everyone agrees as to the weight one assigns to each of the factors. For example, some people will argue that one factor means more to globalization than another factor. Still, it is important that you are aware of the causal factors of globalization most often mentioned.

The End of the Cold War

The Cold War intensified after World War II and, most agree, ended with the visible fall of the Berlin Wall in 1989. This event, while historic in and of itself, occurred at the time when the Soviet empire was beginning to crumble and many of the communist East European countries were breaking away from the Soviet Union. As some explain it, the end of the Cold War resulted in turning two different worlds (the capitalist and communist worlds) into one world. It resulted in a thawing of not only political but economic relations between former enemies. You might not trade with your enemy, but once that person or country is no longer your enemy, you don't feel the same need to cut him or it out of your political and economic life.

At the beginning of this section, we asked you to imagine a world where no barriers affected your trading with anyone in the world. The barriers might be distance, culture, politics, or anything else. The Cold War acted as a political barrier between certain groups of countries; once it ended, one barrier standing in the way of trade was no longer there.

One way to view the current period of economic liberalization (freer markets, lower tariffs) and globalization is to ask whether it would be occurring as it is today if the United States and the Soviet Union were still engaged in the Cold War. This is doubtful. Even though the end of the Cold War might not be the full and only cause for the current period of globalization, it is probably true that if the Cold War had not ended, globalization would not be accelerating at the pace it is today.

Advancing Technology

In the past, innovations such as the internal combustion engine, steamship, telephone, and telegraph led to increased trade between people in different countries. All of these inventions led to lower transportation or communication costs, and lower costs mean fewer barriers to trade. What technology often does is lower the hindrances (of physical distance) that act as stumbling blocks to trade. For example, the cost of a 3-minute telephone call from New York to London in 1930 was $250. In 1960, it was $60.42; in 1980, it was $6.32; and in 2000, it was 40 cents. Today, the cost is even less. As the costs of communicating continue to fall, in some sense, the hindrance of physical distance (to trade) is overcome. Businesspeople in the United States, for example, can more cheaply talk with businesspeople in China.

Now consider the price of a computer in various years. What was the cost of a computer in 1960, one comparable to the desktop computer that many people today have on their desk at home? The answer is $1.8 million. That computer was $199,983 in 1970, $27,938 in 1980, $7,275 in 1990, and only $1,000 in 2000. People today not only use computers for their work, but they communicate with others via the Internet. This computer and Internet technology makes it possible for people to communicate with others over long distances, thus increasing the probability that people will trade with each other.

Today, even farmers in poor developing countries can have access to people and information they didn't have access to only a few years ago. A farmer in the Ivory Coast can check agricultural prices in the world with a cell phone—something that was unheard of a decade ago. Or consider such innovations as online banking. Years ago, it was common to have "your bank" just down the road from you. Today, it is possible to open up an account with an online bank, many of which are located nowhere near you.

Policy Changes

Governments have the power to slow down the process of globalization if they want. Suppose two countries, *A* and *B,* have free economic relations with each other. Neither country imposes tariffs on the goods of the other country. Neither country prevents its citizens from going to the other country to live and work. Neither country hampers its citizens from investing in the other country. Then, one day, for whatever reason, the government of country *A* decides to impose tariffs on the goods of country *B* and limit its citizens from traveling to and investing in country *B*. In other words, the government of country *A* decides to close its political and economic doors.

Well, just as a government of one country can close the door on another country, it can open that door too. It can open that door a little, more than a little, or a lot. In

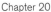

economics 24/7

© FRANK MICELOTTA/GETTY IMAGES FOR UNIVERSAL MUSIC

WILL GLOBALIZATION CHANGE THE SOUND OF MUSIC?

Suppose you had only 100 people to whom you could sell some good. Given this small number, if you want to sell something, you had better sell something that some of these 100 people want to buy. For example, if these 100 people don't like fruit salad, then you better not produce and offer to sell fruit salad; if some of these 100 people like bread, then perhaps you should produce and offer to sell bread.

Now increase the number of people from 100 to 1 million. Is it more or less likely that some people in a group of 1 million will like fruit salad than in a group of 100? The answer is that as the size of the potential customer base increases, the number of things you can sell increases too. In a world of 100 people, you can only sell bread, but in a world of 1 million people, you can sell fruit salad or bread.

Now suppose you are a musician. As a musician, you can play different styles of music: jazz, pop, classical, hard rock, metal, hip hop, and so on. If you are limited to selling your music to the people of a single state of the United States, you would have fewer styles of music you could offer to sell than if you could sell your music to the people who reside throughout the United States.

Our general point is a simple one: The larger the size of the potential customer base (simply put, the more people you can possibly sell to), the greater is the variety of goods we are likely to see.

Globalization is, to a large degree, expanding everyone's ability to potentially sell to more people. American companies aren't limited to selling only to Americans; they can sell to others in the world too. Chinese firms aren't limited to selling only to Chinese; they can sell to others in the world too.

As an example, consider some musician in the United States who is experimenting with a new style of music. With a population of only the United States as a potential customer base (the population of the U.S. is 300 million), the musician might not yet have enough actual customers to make it worth producing and offering to sell this particular, unique, and narrowly defined music. However, if the musician can draw on the population of the world (population: 6.4 billion), then the musician might then be able to find enough people who are willing to buy this particular new type of music.

As we move toward a world economy, we see a greater variety of goods within almost every category of goods you can think of: a greater variety of music to listen to, books to read, types of television shows to watch, and so on. Today, the greater variety of goods you see in your world is an effect of globalization.

recent decades, governments of many countries have been opening their doors to other countries. China has opened its door, India has opened its door, and Russia has opened its door.

The driving forces of this most recent period of globalization have been (1) the end of the Cold War, (2) technological changes that lower the costs of transporting goods and communicating with people, and (3) government policy changes that express an openness toward freer markets and long–distance trade.

SELF-TEST

(Answers to Self-Test questions are in the Self-Test Appendix.)

1. Some have said that the end of the Cold War has led to greater globalization. Explain the reasoning here.

2. What is globalization?

3. How might advancing technology lead to increased globalization?

Benefits and Costs of Globalization

Some people believe that globalization is, in general, a good thing and that its benefits outweigh its costs. Other people take the opposite view and believe that the costs of globalization are greater than the benefits. Let's look at what those who favor globalization say are its benefits and what those who oppose it say are its costs. As you read, you will probably begin to form your own opinion.

The Benefits

TRADE To say that the world is undergoing the process of globalization is really no more than saying that people are trading with more people, at greater distances, than they once did. They are trading different things: money for goods, their labor services for money, their savings for expected returns, and so on. Expanding trade—which is what globalization is about—is no more than extending the benefits of trading to people one might not have traded with earlier.

Economist David Friedman compared free international trade to a technology. He says that you can produce, say, cars in two ways. You can set up factories in Detroit, Michigan, and produce cars. Or you can harvest wheat in the Midwest, load it on ships and send it to Japan, and then wait for the ships to return with cars.

Looking at things the second way sometimes brings out the "magic" of trade. After all, with free trade across countries, wheat gets turned into cars, an accomplishment that really is magical. The lesson Friedman is trying to communicate is that we all think a technological improvement is a good thing because it often leads to a higher standard of living. Well, then, trading with people across the world really is nothing more than a technology of sorts; it is a way to turn wheat into cars. The more we trade with others, the more magic we witness.

INCOME PER PERSON Now let's consider the benefits of globalization in a slightly more concrete way. As both India and China opened up their economies to globalization in recent decades, they experienced increases in income per person. For example, between 1980 and 2000, income per person doubled in India. Between 1940 and 2000, income per person increased by 400 percent in China, much of this increase coming in recent years. According to the International Monetary Fund, these dramatic increases in income per person accompanied the expansion of free international trade (which is a key component of globalization).

Q&A *Isn't it the case that prices can fall even if they are not traded between countries? If so, how do we identify whether a good's price has fallen because of, say, technology or because it is a good that is traded between countries?*

One way is to compare prices between more and less traded goods. According to the 2006 Economic Report of the President, *"a clear divergence in price trends emerges when products are split this way. Internationally traded products tend to experience lower inflation rates—even real price declines—while nontraded goods tend to experience price increases."*

PRICES Numerous studies have established a link between lower prices and the degree of international trade and globalization. Simply put, international trade (a key component of globalization) lowers prices. For example, in Exhibit 2, we show the CPI (consumer price index) and an import price index for the period 1990–2004. You will notice that the CPI (which contains domestic goods and imported goods) has risen faster than the import price index (which contains only imported goods). Also, between 1977 and 2004, the inflation-adjusted prices for an array of goods traded between countries fell while the inflation-adjusted prices for an array of goods not traded between countries actually increased. Some of the traded goods whose prices fell include audio equipment (−26 percent), TV sets (−51 percent), toys (−34 percent), and clothing (−9 percent); some of the nontraded goods whose prices increased include whole milk (+28 percent), butter (+23 percent), ice cream (+18 percent), peanut butter (+9 percent).

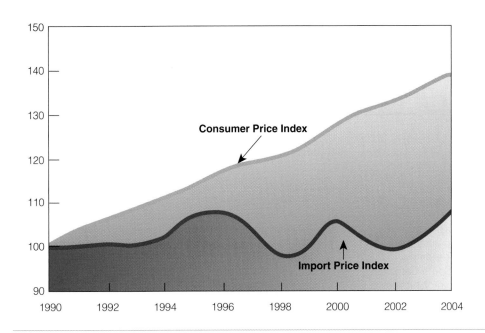

exhibit **2**

CPI and Import Price Index,
1990–2004

The CPI increased at a faster rate
during the period 1990–2004 than
the import price index (which both
increased and decreased during the
period).

Source: Bureau of Labor Statistics.

PRODUCTIVITY AND INNOVATION Firms that face global competition are often pushed to increase their productivity and to innovate more. According to the 2006 *Economic Report of the President*, "Studies show that firms exposed to the world's best practices demonstrate higher productivity through many channels, such as learning from these best practices, and also creating new products and processes in response to this exposure." For example, one study from the United Kingdom showed that almost 3 times as many firms that faced global competition reported product or process innovations than firms that did not face global competition.

Or consider an extreme case, North and South Korea. The two countries share a people and a culture, but North Korea avoided the process of globalization during the period in which South Korea embraced it. What we observe is that South Koreans enjoy a much higher standard of living than North Koreans.

Q&A *How do we know that the benefits you say are a result of globalization are, in fact, caused by globalization? Couldn't they be caused by something else?*

Economists are fairly sure that globalization leads to an increased standard of living based on their comparisons of countries with similar characteristics, except for the fact that one set of countries is globalizing while the other set is not. For example, take a look at Exhibit 3, which shows that the annual percentage change during the 1990s in output per person (a measure of material standard of living) is positive in globalized developing countries but negative in less globalized countries.

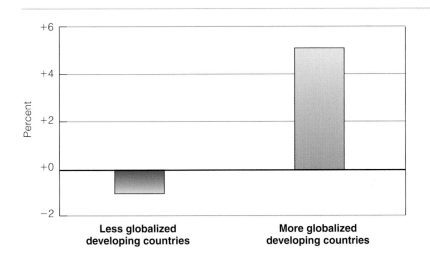

exhibit **3**

Annual Average Percentage Change
in Output per Person in the 1990s

economics 24/7

SHOULD YOU LEAVE A TIP?

In the United States, tipping in restaurants amounts to $16 billion a year. Even though tipping in the United States is common today, 24 percent of the individuals in one study said that they thought tipping was unfair to customers. In the past, some states prohibited tipping. For example, in the early 1900s, Arkansas, Mississippi, Iowa, South Carolina, Tennessee, and Washington passed laws to prohibit tipping.

What about the rest of the world? Do people around the world have the same tipping practices as Americans? Some do, but certainly not all. For example, it is increasingly more customary in European restaurants to have an automatic service charge added to a restaurant bill than to tip the server. Little tipping of any sort goes on in Argentina and Vietnam. Much less tipping occurs (fewer service providers expect tips) in Australia, New Zealand, and Italy than in the United States, and more tipping goes on in Mexico and Egypt than in the United States.

In several studies, researchers looked at the number of different service providers (out of a total of 33) for which tipping is customary in a given country. The more service providers it was customary to tip in a country, the higher the country's "prevalence of tipping." For example, if it was customary to tip 31 different service providers in country *A* but only 15 in country *B*, then country *A* would have a higher prevalence of tipping than country *B*.

The conclusion of these studies is that countries where success and materialism were highly valued had a higher prevalence to tip than countries where caring and personal relationships were highly valued. In addition, the prevalence of tipping increased as the national need for achievement and recognition rose. In one study, tipping was more prevalent in countries with lower taxes than in countries with higher taxes.

If it becomes increasingly relevant to speak of a world economy instead of hundreds of national economies, will tipping practices around the world become more common? If they do become more common, toward what degree of tipping will they gravitate?

We do not know the answer to these questions, so you might then wonder: Why ask? The answer is twofold. First, it gets us to think about what *changes* we are likely to see in our everyday lives as globalization continues forward and whether those changes will only be in the strictly economic realm (e.g., we can buy more clothes from China) or will disperse outward into the social and cultural realms too. Second, it forces us to separate into categories things that are so deeply embedded in the character of a people (and therefore unlikely to change) from things that are somewhat superficial (and therefore more likely to change). Which is a rock (incapable of absorbing), and which is a sponge (capable of absorbing)?

The Costs

INCREASED INCOME INEQUALITY Globalization's critics often point out that globalization seems to go hand in hand with increased income inequality in the world. Has income inequality increased? Yes it has. For example, 100 years ago, people in rich countries had about 10 times more income than people in poor countries. Today, they have about 75 times more income. Without a doubt, globalization and income inequality (between rich and poor countries) are strongly correlated. The question, though, is whether globalization causes the income inequality. The critics of globalization say it does, whereas the supporters say it does not.

The supporters of globalization argue that it is much like a train. Economic systems that get on the train will benefit (and reach their economic destinies faster), but those that don't will get left increasingly farther behind. In other words, it may not be globalization that delivers greater income inequality but a combination of some countries globalizing while others are not. (If everyone is walking, some faster than others, then some will always be in front of others. If those who are walking fast start to run while the others continue their slow walking pace, the gap between the ones in front and the ones in back will grow.)

Of course, it is not only a matter of choosing to get on the train of globalization. Sometimes, a "conductor" on the train doesn't let some people on. Some rich countries work against some poor countries when it comes to the poor countries' globalization efforts. For example, tariffs on goods imported from the poor, developing world are 30 percent above the global average for all tariffs.

LOSING AMERICAN JOBS Many critics of globalization argue that globalization can result in Americans losing certain jobs. Suppose a U.S. company hires engineers in India to do jobs that once were done by Americans. This practice of hiring people in other countries is often called **offshoring**.

It is true that some Americans may lose their jobs to workers in other countries due to globalization. It has already happened. Over the past few years, a major New York securities firm replaced its team of 800 American software engineers, who earned about $150,000 per year, with an equally competent team in India earning an average of about $20,000 a year. Additionally, the number of radiologists in the United States is expected to fall significantly because it is now possible to send the data (that U.S. radiologists analyze) over the Internet to Asian radiologists who can analyze the data at a fraction of the cost.

Keep in mind, though, that offshoring is a two-way street: The United States might offshore certain jobs to, say, India or China, but foreign countries around the world offshore jobs to the United States too. Although some Americans do lose jobs due to globalization efforts, we also need to keep in mind that jobs are always being lost (and found) in a dynamic economy that is responding to market changes. Even if the degree of offshoring in the United States was zero, people would still be losing old jobs and getting new jobs every day.

MORE POWER TO BIG CORPORATIONS Many critics of globalization argue that the process will simply "turn over" the world (and especially the developing countries of the world) to large Western corporations (corporations headquartered in the United States, the United Kingdom, Canada, and etc.). In fact, in the minds of many people, globalization is not what we have defined it as in this chapter, but rather, it is the process of *corporatizing* the world. Instead of governments deciding what will and will not be done, large corporations will assume the responsibility.

The proponents of globalization often point out a major difference between a corporation and a government. First, a government can force people to do certain things (pay taxes, join the military). No corporation can do the same; instead, corporations can simply produce goods that they hope customers will buy. Additionally, the proponents of globalization often argue that the critics overestimate the influence and reach of large transnational companies. For example, in 2000, the top 100 transnational companies produced only 4.3 percent of the entire world's output, which is about as much as what one country, the United Kingdom, produced in 2000.

The Continuing Globalization Debate

Many (but certainly not all) economists argue that the worldwide benefits of globalization are likely to be greater than the worldwide costs. Of course, it doesn't mean that everyone is going to see the beneficial side of globalization. To a large degree, whether one supports or criticizes globalization seems to depend on where "one is sitting." Globalization doesn't affect everyone in the same way, and often, *how* it affects *you* determines how you feel about it. For example, suppose Sanders, an American worker residing in

Offshoring
Work done for a company by persons other than the original company's employees in a country other than the one in which the company is located.

New York, loses his job to an Indian worker in New Delhi, India, who will do Sanders's job for less pay. In this case, Sanders incurs real costs, but what about Sanders's company and the company's customers? For the company, this change means lower costs and higher profits. For the company's customers, prices for the company's products may go down. So in this case, Sanders is probably a strong opponent of offshoring, while his company and its customers are probably supporters.

When it comes to globalization, it is often much more difficult to see the benefits than it is to see the costs. For example, the supporters of globalization argue that it brings greater economic wealth, lower prices (than would otherwise exist), more innovation, less poverty, and so on. Yet sometimes, it is difficult for us to see all these benefits. When you buy cheaper goods or different goods because of globalization, you probably never say, "Wow, I can't believe all the benefits I get from globalization!" In fact, you might not even connect the lower priced goods with globalization at all. The benefits of globalization tend to be difficult to see, partly because they are so widely dispersed.

The costs of globalization, in contrast, are more visible, often because they are so concentrated. A person who loses a job because of freer international trade in the world knows exactly what is to blame for the predicament he or she is in. This person surely could receive some benefits from globalization (in the role of a consumer), but this person also could, for a time, incur some rather high costs from globalization (in the role of a worker). It is likely that this person will know of the costs but be unaware of the benefits.

In the end, things may stack up this way: The people who receive only benefits from globalization might not be able to see the benefits or to connect them with globalization. The people who receive benefits and costs from globalization may only be aware of the costs. This one-sided view could create strong antiglobalization sentiment in a country.

More or Less Globalization: A Tug of War?

Is increased globalization inevitable? Will the day come when all countries in the world are similar to all 50 states in the United States—part of one global economy with easy movement of people, resources, financial capital, goods, and services among the countries? Or will the conditions that prevented globalization reappear and reverse the recent trend?

Think of this struggle as a tug of war. We have the forces of globalization pulling in one direction, and we have the forces of antiglobalization pulling in the other direction. As of today, the forces of globalization are moving things in their direction. Will this trend continue uninterrupted? Well, maybe not, some say. Surely, at any time, the forces of antiglobalization could get a burst of energy and make an extra strong tug on the rope.

To answer the question, let's go back to what we stated were the driving forces of the most recent era of globalization: the end of the Cold War, changes in technology (which lowered the costs of transportation and communication), and policy changes that opened up countries' economies to each other.

Less Globalization

INCREASED POLITICAL TENSION The end of the Cold War is a historical fact that we cannot "undo." We could, however, enter a period when political tensions among countries, or among groups of countries, emerge. We are not suggesting that such a period of tension will happen, only that it could. If it did, it could slow down globalization or, depending on the severity of the tension, even reverse it.

Terrorism. Another inhibiting factor to globalization is global terrorism. Global terrorism tends to motivate certain countries into closing borders and into being much more careful about the people and goods that cross their borders.

Technology. We cannot undo our technology. We cannot go from a world with the Internet to one without it. So it is unlikely that anything on the technological front will slow down or reverse globalization.

Government Policies. However, we can witness policy changes that will slow down or reverse globalization. Governments of countries that opened up their economies to others could reverse their course; doors that opened to others can be closed. We cannot say whether this sort of isolationism will happen in the future.

More Globalization

Still, some will argue that even with the forces of antiglobalization looming on the horizon, the forces of globalization are stronger. In the end, these individuals say, the forces of globalization will win the tug of war. They believe that in the long run, economics is what influences politics rather than the other way around. To give some proof to what they are saying, they often point to the former Soviet Union and to China. Both were strongly communist countries. Both countries saw, in the end, that they were worse off by holding themselves outside the orbit of free market forces. You might say that they found themselves "out of step" with the economic forces that were loudly playing on the world stage.

Thomas Friedman states that "globalization is not just some economic fad, and it is not a passing trend." He also argues that the "relevant market today is planet Earth." The basic globalization force that will probably not be overcome—no matter how strong the political forces may be against it—is the human inclination that the founder of modern economics, Adam Smith, noticed more than 200 years ago. Smith said that human beings want to trade with each other. In fact, it is the desire to trade that separates us from all other species, he says. In his words, "Man is an animal that makes bargains: no other animal does this—no dog exchanges bones with another."

We want to trade with people: our next-door neighbor, the person down the street, the person on the other side of town, the person in the next state, the person on the other side of the country, and finally, the person on the other side of the world. Some economists go on to suggest that this "trading" inclination we possess is a good thing in that, when we trade with people, we not only tolerate them but we have much less reason to fight with them. Robert Wright, a visiting scholar at the University of Pennsylvania, argues that it is not a coincidence that religious toleration is high in the United States, a country that is open to trade and globalization. What we often see, he argues, is that people who live in countries that trade with other people, people who live in countries that are open to other people, end up being countries that tolerate different types of people.

In a similar vein, Thomas Friedman advanced his "Golden Arches theory of conflict prevention," which says that "no two countries that both had McDonald's had fought a war against each other since each got its McDonald's." The United States will not fight Germany since both countries have McDonald's. France won't fight Mexico since both countries have McDonald's. Certainly, it is not the sheer presence of a McDonald's in a country that prevents people from fighting with other people. It's because McDonald's is symbolic of certain things being present in the country. For Friedman, it is a symbol for a certain degree of economic globalization and a level of economic development sufficient enough to support a large middle class.

SELF-TEST

1.   Identify some of the benefits of globalization.

2.   Identify some of the costs of globalization.

A Reader Asks...

Will My Job Be Sent Overseas?

One hears much these days about out-sourcing or offshoring jobs. Are some jobs more likely to be sent overseas than others?

When it comes to some jobs, location matters. But when it comes to other jobs, location does not seem to matter. First, let's look at some jobs where location matters.

If you are sick and need a doctor, you prefer to have a doctor close to you. If you live in Ithaca, New York, you will probably want a doctor who works in Ithaca, New York, not in Bangkok, 8,553 miles away.

If you need a plumber, you will probably want a plumber close by, not one on the other side of the world. If you want to go out to eat, you will most likely go to a restaurant near where you live, not one on the other side of the world.

Now when it comes to buying a book, location may not matter: It may not matter to you where the bookseller resides, as long as you can get the book fairly quickly. When it comes to someone answering your technical computer questions, it may not matter where the technician lives. As long as the technician speaks your language, listens well, and gives clear and concise instructions, you probably don't care where he or she is located.

In short, when a provider's (supplier's, worker's) location is important to you, you can be fairly sure that the kind of job the provider performs will not be offshored to another country. When a provider's location is not important to you, the probability of the provider's job being offshored rises.

In 2004, *Forbes* magazine ran a story titled "Ten Professions Not Likely to Be Outsourced." Here is the list:

- Chief Executive Officer
- Physician and Surgeon
- Pilot, Copilot, and Flight Engineer
- Lawyer
- Computer and Information Systems Manager
- Sales Manager
- Pharmacist
- Chiropractor
- Physician's Assistant
- Education Administrator, Elementary and Secondary School

! analyzing the scene

What is globalization and does it hurt the poor?

Globalization is a phenomenon by which economic agents in any given part of the world are affected by events elsewhere in the world; it represents the growing integration of the national economies of the world to the degree that we may be witnessing the emergence and operation of a single worldwide economy. So far, most of the evidence shows that globalization does not hurt the poor. For example, output per person (a measure of one's material standard of living) grew at positive rates during the 1990s in more globalized developing countries but declined in less globalized countries (see Exhibit 3). Also both India and China, countries that have been opening up their economies to globalization, have seen their income per person increase in recent decades. According to the International Monetary Fund, in the past 30 years, hunger and child labor have been cut in half and life expectancy has increased in developing countries. Work done by economists Gary Hufbauer and Paul L. E. Grieco shows that globalization increases U.S. income by roughly $1 trillion a year, or $10,000 per household.

Will globalization lead to some people losing jobs?

Yes. Globalization is not a static process in which everything stays the same from day to day. Globalization will cause some people to lose jobs, but even without globalization, some people will lose jobs. Even in a country without any trade with other countries, people's preferences would change for goods and services, and some people would lose their jobs as a consequence.

Does everyone agree as to what the benefits and costs of globalization are?

No, but this chapter tries to give you some idea of the nature of the debate over globalization.

Why does Elizabeth's customer service call connect to a person in India?

It could be because the U.S. company found it cheaper to hire the person in India than to hire a person in, say, the United States, the United Kingdom, or some other country to answer customers' calls.

chapter summary

What Is Globalization?

- Globalization is a phenomenon by which individuals and businesses in any part of the world are much more affected by events elsewhere in the world than before; it is the growing integration of national economies of the world to the degree that we may be witnessing the emergence and operation of a single worldwide economy.

- There are certain facts that provide evidence that globalization is occurring. Some of these facts are (1) lower tariff rates in many countries; (2) many countries exporting and importing more goods than in the past; (3) greater foreign exchange trading; (4) more foreign direct investment; (5) many more people own foreign stocks; (6) many more countries have joined the WTO in recent years; (7) a greater number of Americans working for foreign companies that have offices in the United States.

Movement Toward Globalization

- What has caused this most recent push toward globalization? In the chapter we identified (1) the end of the Cold War, (2) advancing technology, and (3) policy changes as causal factors.

Benefits and Costs of Globalization

- Some of the benefits of globalization include (1) benefits from increased international trade, (2) greater income per person, (3) lower prices for goods, (4) greater product variety, and (5) increased productivity and innovation.

- Some of the costs of globalization include (1) increased income inequality (although there is some debate here), (2) offshoring, and (3) increased economic power for large corporations (although there is some debate here too).

- When it comes to globalization, it is often much more difficult to see the benefits than the costs. The benefits are largely dispersed over a large population while the costs (e.g., offshoring) might be concentrated on relatively few.

The Future of Globalization

- There is a debate over the future of globalization. Some persons argue that globalization will continue; others say it will stall and (perhaps) backtrack.

key terms and concepts

Globalization

Tariff

Offshoring

questions and problems

1 Why might it be easier to recognize the costs of globalization than the benefits?

2 If globalization continues over the next few decades, how might your life be different?

3 How might governments impact globalization?

4 Identify and explain two of the benefits and two of the costs of globalization.

5 What effect might advancing technology have on globalization?

6 Some have argued that the end of the Cold War acted as a catalyst toward greater globalization. How so?

7 What is Thomas Friedman's "Golden Arches theory of conflict prevention"?

8 David Friedman said that free (international) trade is a technology. Explain what he means.

9 Will globalization lead to some people losing jobs? Explain your answer.

10 How do tariff rates in the United States today compare with 1946?

Self-Test Appendix

Chapter 1

CHAPTER 1, PAGE 5

1 False. It takes two things for scarcity to exist: finite resources and infinite wants. If people's wants were equal to or less than the finite resources available to satisfy their wants, there would be no scarcity. Scarcity exists only because people's wants are greater than the resources available to satisfy their wants. Scarcity is the condition of infinite wants clashing with finite resources.

2 Because of scarcity, there is a need for a rationing device. People will compete for the rationing device. For example, if dollar price is the rationing device, people will compete for dollars.

3 Because our unlimited wants are greater than our limited resources—that is, because scarcity exists—some wants must go unsatisfied. We must choose which wants we will satisfy and which we will not.

CHAPTER 1, PAGE 12

1 Every time a person is late to history class, the instructor subtracts one-tenth of a point from the person's final grade. If the instructor raised the opportunity cost of being late to class—by subtracting one point from the person's final grade—economists predict there would be fewer persons late to class. In summary, the higher the opportunity cost of being late to class, the less likely people will be late to class.

2 Yes. To illustrate, suppose the marginal benefits and marginal costs (in dollars) are as follows for various hours of studying.

Hours	Marginal Benefits	Marginal Costs
First hour	$20.00	$10.00
Second hour	$14.00	$11.00
Third hour	$13.00	$12.00
Fourth hour	$12.10	$12.09
Fifth hour	$11.00	$13.00

Clearly, you will study the first hour because the marginal benefits are greater than the marginal costs. Stated differently, there is a net benefit of $10 (the difference between the marginal benefits of $20 and the marginal costs of $10) for studying the first hour. If you stop studying after the first hour and do not proceed to the second, then you will forfeit the net benefit of $3 for the second hour. To maximize your net benefits of studying, you must proceed until the marginal benefits and the marginal costs are as close to equal as possible. (In the extreme, this is an epsilon away from equality. However, economists simply speak of "equality" between the two for convenience.) In this case, you will study through the fourth hour. You will not study the fifth hour because it is not worth it; the marginal benefits of studying the fifth hour are less than the marginal costs. In short, there is a net cost to studying the fifth hour.

3 You might feel sleepy the next day, you might be less alert while driving, and so on.

Chapter 2

CHAPTER 2, PAGE 38

1 A straight-line PPF represents constant opportunity costs between two goods. For example, for every unit of X produced, one unit of Y is forfeited. A bowed-outward PPF represents increasing opportunity costs. For example, we may have to forfeit one unit of X to produce the eleventh unit of Y, but we have to forfeit two units of X to produce the one hundredth unit of Y.

2 A bowed-outward PPF is representative of increasing costs. In short, the PPF would not be bowed outward if increasing costs did not exist. To prove this, look back at Exhibits 1 and 2. In Exhibit 1, costs are constant (not increasing), and the PPF is a straight line. In Exhibit 2, costs are increasing, and the PPF is bowed outward.

3 The first condition is that the economy is currently operating *below* its PPF. It is possible to move from a point below the PPF to a point on the PPF and get more of all goods. The second condition is that the economy's PPF shifts outward.

4 False. Take a look at Exhibit 5. There are numerous productive efficient points, all of which lie on the PPF.

CHAPTER 2, PAGE 42

1 Transaction costs are the costs associated with the time and effort needed to search out, negotiate, and consummate a trade. The transaction costs are likely to be higher for buying a house than for buying a car because buying a house is a more detailed and complex process.

2 Under certain conditions, Smith will buy good X from Jones. For example, suppose Smith and Jones agree on a price of, say, $260, and neither person incurs transaction costs greater than $40. If transaction costs are zero for each person, then each person benefits $40 from the trade. Specifically, Smith buys the good for $40 less than his maximum price, and Jones sells the good for $40 more than his minimum price. But suppose each person incurs a transaction cost of, say, $50. Smith would be unwilling to pay $260 to Jones and $50 in transaction costs (for a total of $310) when he is only willing to pay a maximum price of $300 for good X. Similarly, Jones would be unwilling to sell good X for $260 and incur $50 in transaction costs (leaving him with only $210, or $10 less than his minimum selling price).

3 Answers will vary. Sample answer: John buys a magazine and reads it. There is no third-party effect. Sally asks a rock band to play at a party. Sally's next-door neighbor (a third party) is disturbed by the loud music.

CHAPTER 2, PAGE 46

1 If George goes from producing 5X to 10X, he gives up 5Y. This means the opportunity cost of 5 more X is 5 fewer Y. It follows that the opportunity cost of 1X is 1Y. Conclusion: The opportunity cost of 1X is 1Y.

2 If Harriet produces 10 more X she gives up 15Y. It follows that the opportunity cost of 1X is 1.5Y, and the opportunity cost of 1Y is 0.67X. If Bill produces 10 more X, he gives up 20Y. It follows that the opportunity cost of 1X is 2Y, and the opportunity cost of 1Y is 0.5X. Harriet is the lower cost producer of X, and Bill is the lower cost producer of Y. In short, Harriet has the comparative advantage in the production of X; Bill has the comparative advantage in the production of Y.

Chapter 3

CHAPTER 3, PAGE 60

1 Popcorn is a normal good for Sandi. Prepaid telephone cards are an inferior good for Mark.

2 Asking why demand curves are downward sloping is the same as asking why price and quantity demanded are inversely related (as one rises, the other falls). There are two reasons mentioned in this section: (1) As price rises, people substitute lower priced goods for higher priced goods. (2) Because individuals receive less utility from an additional unit of a good they consume, they are only willing to pay less for the additional unit. The second reason is a reflection of the law of diminishing marginal utility.

3 Suppose only two people, Bob and Alice, have a demand for good X. At a price of $7, Bob buys 10 units and Alice buys 3 units; at a price of $6, Bob buys 12 units and Alice buys 5 units. One point on the market demand curve represents a price of $7 and a quantity demanded of 13 units; another point represents $6 and 17 units. A market demand curve is derived by adding the quantities demanded at each price.

4 A change in income, preferences, prices of related goods, number of buyers, and expectations of future price can change demand. A change in the price of the good changes the quantity demanded of the good. For example, a change in *income* can change the *demand* for oranges, but only a change in the *price* of oranges can directly change the *quantity demanded* of oranges.

CHAPTER 3, PAGE 65

1 It would be difficult to increase the quantity supplied of houses over the next ten hours, so the supply curve in (a) is vertical, as in Exhibit 7. It is possible to increase the quantity supplied of houses over the next 3 months, however, so the supply curve in (b) is upward sloping.

2 **a** The supply curve shifts to the left.
   b The supply curve shifts to the left.
   c The supply curve shifts to the right.

3 False. If the price of apples rises, the *quantity supplied* of apples will rise—not the *supply* of apples. We are talking about a *movement* from one point on a supply curve to a point higher up on the supply curve and not about a shift in the supply curve.

CHAPTER 3, PAGE 73

1 Disagree. In the text, we plainly saw how supply and demand work at an auction. Supply and demand are at work in the grocery store, too, although no auctioneer is present. The essence of the auction example is the auctioneer raising the price when there was a shortage and lowering the price when there was a surplus. The same thing happens at the grocery store. For example, if there is a surplus of corn flakes, the manager of the store is likely to have a sale (lower prices) on corn flakes. Many markets without auctioneers act *as if* there are auctioneers raising and lowering prices in response to shortages and surpluses.

2 No. It could be the result of a higher supply of computers. Either a decrease in demand or an increase in supply will lower price.

3 **a** Lower price and quantity
   b Lower price and higher quantity
   c Higher price and lower quantity
   d Lower price and quantity

4 At equilibrium quantity, the maximum buying price and the minimum selling price are the same. For example, in Exhibit 14, both prices are $40 at the equilibrium quantity 4. Equilibrium quantity is the only quantity at which the maximum buying price and the minimum selling price are the same.

5 $46; $34.

CHAPTER 3, PAGE 77

1 Yes, if nothing else changes—that is, yes, *ceteris paribus*. If some other things change, though, they may not. For example, if the government imposes an effective price ceiling on gasoline, Jamie may pay lower gas prices at the pump but have to wait in line to buy the gas (due to first come, first served trying to ration the shortage). It is not clear if Jamie is better off paying a higher price and not waiting in line or paying a lower price and waiting in line. The point, however, is that buyers don't necessarily prefer lower prices to higher prices unless everything else (quality, wait, service, etc.) stays the same.

2   Disagree. Both long-lasting shortages and long lines are caused by price ceilings. First, the price ceiling is imposed, creating the shortage; then, the rationing device first come, first served emerges because price isn't permitted to fully ration the good. There are shortages every day that don't cause long lines to form. Instead, buyers bid up price, output and price move to equilibrium, and there is no shortage.

3   Buyers might argue for price ceilings on the goods they buy—especially if they don't know that price ceilings have some effects they may not like (e.g., fewer exchanges, FCFS used as a rationing device, etc.). Sellers might argue for price floors on the goods they sell—especially if they expect their profits to rise. Employees might argue for a wage floor on the labor services they sell—especially if they don't know that they may lose their jobs or have their hours cut back as a result.

Chapter 4

CHAPTER 4, PAGE 83

1   If supply and tuition are constant and demand rises, the shortage of openings at the university will become greater. The university will continue to use its nonprice rationing devices (GPA, SAT scores, ACT scores) but will have to raise the standards of admission. Instead of requiring a GPA of, say, 3.5 for admission, it may raise the requirement to 3.8.

2   Not likely. A university that didn't make admission easier in the face of a surplus of openings might not be around much longer. When tuition cannot be adjusted directly—in other words, when the rationing device of price cannot be adjusted—it is likely that the nonprice rationing device (standards) will be.

CHAPTER 4, PAGE 84

1   Price will fall.

2   Quantity will rise.

CHAPTER 4, PAGE 86

1   The recording industry is trying to raise the "price" of downloading music.

2   The recording industry has to consider the costs and expected benefits of various actions. It will follow the path that it thinks will have the biggest bang for the buck. The industry likely believes that trying to lower demand will have fewer positive results than either trying to reduce supply or trying to raise price.

CHAPTER 4, PAGE 86

1   A higher expected price for houses would likely raise the (current) demand for houses. The reasoning: Buy now before the price rises.

2   A lower expected price for cars would likely lower the (current) demand for cars. The reasoning: Buy later when the price is lower.

CHAPTER 4, PAGE 88

1   Yes. At the equilibrium wage rate, the quantity demanded of labor equals the quantity supplied. At a higher wage (the minimum wage), the quantity supplied stays constant (given the vertical supply curve), but the quantity demanded falls. Thus, a surplus results.

2   The person is assuming that the labor demand curve is vertical (no matter what the wage rate is, the quantity demanded of labor is always the same).

CHAPTER 4, PAGE 91

1   Agree. At any price below equilibrium price, a shortage exists: The quantity demanded of kidneys is greater than the quantity supplied of kidneys. As price rises toward its equilibrium level, quantity supplied rises and quantity demanded falls until the two are equal.

2   It depends on whether or not $0 is the equilibrium price of kidneys. If it is—that is, if the kidney demand and supply curves intersect at $0—then there is no shortage of kidneys. But if, at $0, the quantity demanded of kidneys is greater than the quantity supplied, then a shortage exists.

CHAPTER 4, PAGE 92

1   Moving from a system where patients cannot sue their HMOs to one where they can gives patients something they didn't have before (the right to sue) at a higher price (higher charges for healthcare coverage). The "free lunch"—the right to sue—isn't free after all.

2   If the students get the extra week and nothing else changes, then the students will probably say they are better off. In other words, more of one thing (time) and no less of anything else makes one better off. But if because of the extra week, the professor grades their papers harder than she would have otherwise, then some or all of the students may say that they weren't made better off by the extra week.

CHAPTER 4, PAGE 93

1   A demand curve exists, and it is downward sloping, if the law of demand holds. If the law of demand holds for using foul language, then there is a downward-sloping demand curve for using foul language.

2   There probably is not a downward-sloping demand curve for sneezing because sneezing is an automatic response. In other words, it is hard to control your sneezing in such a way that you sneeze less when the price of sneezing rises.

CHAPTER 4, PAGE 94

1   The answer can be either the shifting supply of gold or the attempt to earn profit. Consider the first answer. If the price of gold is higher in one location than another, the supply of gold shifts from the lower priced location to the higher priced location. In the process, the gold prices in the two locations converge. Now, if we want to know what causes the shifting supply of gold, the answer is the attempt to earn profit. Specifically, the attempt to earn profit prompts people to buy gold in the lower priced location and sell it in the higher priced location.

2   You can move a Honda Pilot from one place to another in response to a rising price. What holds for gold holds for Honda Pilots too.

CHAPTER 4, PAGE 94

1   One possible answer is: There are two cities, one with clean air and the other with dirty air. The demand to live in the clean-air city is higher than the demand to live in the dirty-air city. As a result, housing prices are higher in the clean-air city than in the dirty-air city.

2   Ultimately, the person who owns the land in the good-weather city receives the payment. Look at it this way: People have a higher demand for houses in good-weather cities than they do for houses in bad-weather cities. As a result, house builders receive higher prices for houses built and sold in good-weather cities. Because of the higher house prices in good-weather cities, house builders have a higher demand for land in good-weather cities. In the end, higher demand for land translates into higher land prices or land rents for landowners.

CHAPTER 4, PAGE 96

1   The shortage is greater in computer science. If (1) supply in each field is the same, (2) the wage rate is the same, and (3) demand is greater in computer science than in biology, then the horizontal difference (which measures the degree of shortage) between the demand curve and supply curve is greater in computer science than in biology. Draw this and see.

2   Under the condition that demand and supply are the same in all fields. Stated differently, under the condition that the equilibrium wage in each field is the same.

CHAPTER 4, PAGE 97

1   Look at the demand curve and the supply curve between Q_2 and Q_1. Notice that the demand curve lies *above* the supply curve in this area. This means that buyers are willing to pay more for each of the units between Q_2 and Q_1 (more, say, for the $Q_2 + 1$ unit) than sellers need to receive for them to place these units on the market. In short, moving from an equilibrium price to a price floor lowers the number of mutually beneficial trades that will be made. As discussed in Chapter 3, price floors lead to fewer exchanges.

2   It is likely that producers care more about how a change affects them than how it affects society. At the price floor, they receive more producers' surplus than they receive at the equilibrium price, even though consumers lose, in terms of consumers' surplus, more than producers gain. Look at it like this: Producers gain $10 and consumers lose $12. The sum of positive $10 and negative $12 is negative $2. Producers may not care about the sum (–$2); they care about their $10 gain.

CHAPTER 4, PAGE 99

1   Suppose University X gives a full scholarship to every one of its football players (all of whom are superathletes). In addition, suppose that the full scholarship (translated into wages) is far below the equilibrium wage of each of the football players. (Think of it this way: Each football player gets a wage, or full scholarship, of $10,000 a year, when his equilibrium wage is $40,000 a year.) Paying lower than the equilibrium wage will end up transferring dollars and other benefits from the football players to the university to the new field house and track and perhaps to you if you use the track for exercise.

2   If paying student athletes (a wage above the full scholarship) lowers consumers' demand for college athletics, then the equilibrium wage for college athletes is not as high as shown in Exhibit 7.

CHAPTER 4, PAGE 100

1   Any price above 70 cents.

2   Assuming that tolls are not used, freeway congestion will worsen. An increase in driving population simply shifts the demand curve for driving to the right.

CHAPTER 4, PAGE 101

1   A person's time is worth something. For example, if a person spends one hour doing something instead of working and has a wage rate of $10 an hour, then one hour of her time is worth $10. When we know a person's wage rate, we can convert "time spent" into "dollars forfeited."

2   If demand rises more than supply and price is held constant, there will be a shortage of parking. Some non-price rationing device will emerge to allocate parking spaces along with dollar price. It will probably be first come, first served (whoever gets to an empty parking spot first gets to park).

CHAPTER 4, PAGE 103

1   Answers will vary. Students sometimes say that it is "fairer" if everyone is charged the same price. Is it unfair then that moviegoers pay less if they go to the 2 P.M. movie than if they go to the 8 P.M. movie?

CHAPTER 4, PAGE 104

1   It is not necessarily the case that if government places a tax on the seller of a good that the seller of the good will end up paying the full tax. The key word here is *full* tax. In other words, some of the tax may be paid for by the buyer of the good. We showed this explicitly in Exhibit 10. Government placed the $1 tax fully on the seller. This resulted in the supply curve shifting upward and leftward. As a result, there was a new equilibrium price that was, in our example, 50 cents higher than the old equilibrium price. Conclusion: Although the tax was placed fully on the seller of the good, the buyer of the good ended up paying a part of the tax in terms of a higher price for the good.

2   What matters to sellers is how much they keep for each DVD sold, not how much buyers pay. If sellers are keeping $15 per DVD for Q_1 DVDs before the tax is imposed, then they want to keep $15 per DVD for Q_1 DVDs after the tax is imposed. But if the tax is $1, the only way they can keep $15 per DVD for Q_1 DVDs is to receive $16 per DVD. They receive $16 per DVD from buyers, turn over $1 to the government, and keep $15. In other words, each quantity on the new supply curve, S_2, corresponds to a $1 higher price than it did on the old supply curve, S_1.

Chapter 5

CHAPTER 5, PAGE 119

1   $E_d = 1.44$

2   It means that if there is a change in price, quantity demanded will change (in the opposite direction) by 0.39 times the percentage change in price. For example, if price rises 10 percent, then quantity demanded will fall 3.9 percent. If price rises 20 percent, then quantity demanded will fall 7.8 percent.

3   **a** Total revenue falls.
    b Total revenue falls.
    c Total revenue remains constant.
    d Total revenue rises.
    e Total revenue rises.

4   Alexi is implicitly assuming that demand is inelastic. If, however, she is wrong and demand is elastic, then a rise in price will actually lower total revenue.

CHAPTER 5, PAGE 123

1   No. Moving from 7 to 9 substitutes doesn't necessarily change demand from being inelastic to elastic. It simply leads to a rise in price elasticity of demand, *ceteris paribus*. For example, if price elasticity of demand is 0.45 when there are 7 substitutes, it will be higher than this when there are 9 substitutes, *ceteris paribus*. Higher could be 0.67. If this is the case, demand is still inelastic (but less so than before).

2   **a** Dell computers
    b Heinz ketchup
    c Perrier water

    In all three cases, the good with the higher price elasticity of demand is the more specific of the two goods; therefore, it has more substitutes.

CHAPTER 5, PAGE 127

1   It means that the good (in question) is a normal good and that it is income elastic—that is, as income rises, the quantity demanded rises by a greater percentage. In this case, quantity demanded rises by 1.33 times the percentage change in income. If income rises by 10 percent, the quantity demanded of the good will rise by 13.3 percent.

2   A change in price does not change quantity supplied.

Chapter 6

CHAPTER 6, PAGE 137

1   The paradox is that water, which is essential to life, is cheap, and diamonds, which are not essential to life, are expensive. The solution to the paradox depends on knowing the difference between total and marginal utility and the law of diminishing marginal utility. By saying that water is essential to life and diamonds are not essential to life, we signify that water gives us high total utility relative to diamonds. But then someone asks, "Well, if water gives us greater total utility than diamonds do, why isn't the price of water greater than the price of diamonds?" The answer is, "Price isn't a reflection of total utility; it is a reflection of marginal utility. The marginal utility of water is less than the marginal utility of diamonds." This answer raises another question, "How can the total utility of water be greater than the total utility of diamonds, but the marginal utility of water be less than the marginal utility of diamonds?" The answer is based on the fact that water is plentiful and diamonds are not and on the law of diminishing marginal utility. There is so much more water relative to diamonds that the next (additional) unit of water gives us less utility (lower marginal utility) than the next unit of diamonds.

2   If total utility declines, marginal utility must be negative. For example, if total utility is 30 utils when Lydia consumes 3 apples and 25 utils when she consumes 4 apples, it must be because the fourth apple had a marginal utility of minus 5 utils. Chapter 1 explains that something that takes utility away from us (or gives us disutility) is called a *bad*. For Lydia, the fourth apple is a bad, not a good.

3   The total and marginal utility of a good are the same for the first unit of the good consumed. For example, before Tomas eats his first apple, he receives no utility or disutility from apples. Eating the first apple, he receives 15 utils. So the total utility (*TU*) for 1 apple is 15 utils,

and the marginal utility (*MU*) for the first apple is 15 utils. Exhibit 1 shows that *TU* and *MU* are the same for the first unit of good *X*.

CHAPTER 6, PAGE 140

1 Alesandro is not in consumer equilibrium because the marginal utility per dollar of *X* is 16 utils and the marginal utility per dollar of *Y* is 13.14 utils. To be in equilibrium, a consumer has to receive the same marginal utility per dollar for each good consumed.

2 It means the marginal utility-price ratio for one of the goods is higher than the ratio for the other good.

CHAPTER 6, PAGE 144

1 Yes, Brandon is compartmentalizing. He is treating $100 that comes from his grandmother differently from $100 that comes from his father.

2 The endowment effect relates to individuals valuing *X* more highly when they possess it than when they don't have it but are thinking of acquiring it. Friedman argues that if we go back in time to a hunter-gatherer society when there were no well-established property rights (no rules as to what is "mine" and "thine"), individuals who would fight hard to keep what they possessed, but wouldn't fight as hard to acquire what they did not possess, would have a higher probability of surviving than individuals who would fight hard at both times. Thus, those who would fight hard only to keep what they possessed would have a higher probability of reproductive success. The characteristic of "holding on to what you have" has been passed down from generation to generation, and although it may not be as important today as it was in a hunter-gatherer society, it still influences behavior.

Chapter 7

CHAPTER 7, PAGE 163

1 No. Individuals will only form teams or firms when the sum of what they can produce as a team (or firm) is greater than the sum of what they can produce working alone.

2 The person earning the low salary has lower implicit costs and so is more likely to start his or her own business. He or she gives up less to start a business.

3 Accounting profit is larger. Only explicit costs are subtracted from total revenue in computing accounting profit, but both explicit and implicit costs are subtracted from total revenue in computing economic profit. If implicit costs are zero, then accounting profit and economic profit are the same. Economic profit is never greater than accounting profit.

4 When he is earning (positive) accounting profit but his total revenue does not cover the sum of his explicit and implicit costs. For example, suppose Brad earns total revenue of $100,000 and has explicit costs of $40,000

and implicit costs of $70,000. His accounting profit is $60,000, but his total revenue of $100,000 is not large enough to cover the sum of his explicit and implicit costs ($110,000). Brad's economic profit is a negative $10,000. In other words, while Brad earns an accounting profit, he takes an economic loss.

CHAPTER 7, PAGE 168

1 No. The short run and the long run are not "lengths of time." The short run is that period of time when some inputs are fixed, and therefore, the firm has fixed costs. The long run is that period of time when no inputs are fixed (i.e., all inputs are variable), and thus, all costs are variable costs. It's possible for the short run to be, say, 6 months and the long run to be a much shorter period of time. In other words, the time period when there are no fixed inputs can be shorter than the time period when there are fixed inputs.

2 The law of diminishing marginal returns holds only when we add more of one input to a given (fixed) quantity of another input. The statement does not identify one input as fixed (it says that both increase), and so the law of diminishing marginal returns is not relevant in this situation.

3 When *MC* is declining, *MPP* is rising; when *MC* is constant, *MPP* is constant; and when *MC* is rising, *MPP* is falling.

CHAPTER 7, PAGE 178

1 $ATC = TC/Q$ and $ATC = AFC + AVC$

2 Yes. Suppose a business incurs a cost of $10 to produce a product. Before it can sell the product, though, the demand for the product falls and moves the market price from $15 to $6. Does the owner of the business say, "I can't sell the product for $6 because I'd be taking a loss"? If she does, she chooses to let a sunk cost affect her current decision. Instead, she should ask herself, "Do I think the market price of the product will rise or fall?" If she thinks it will fall, she should sell the product today for $6.

3 Unit costs are another name for average total costs (*ATC*), so the question is: What happens to *ATC* as *MC* rises? You might be inclined to say that as *MC* rises, so does *ATC*—but this is not necessarily so (see Region 1 in Exhibit 5(b)). What matters is whether or not *MC* is greater than *ATC*. If it is, then *ATC* will rise. If it is not, then *ATC* will decline. This is a trick question of sorts. There is a tendency to misinterpret the average-marginal rule and to believe that as marginal cost rises, average total cost rises; and as marginal cost falls, average total cost falls. But this is not what the average-marginal rule says. The rule says that when *MC* is above *ATC, ATC* rises; and when *MC* is below *ATC, ATC* falls.

4 Yes. As marginal physical product (*MPP*) rises, marginal cost (*MC*) falls. If *MC* falls enough to move below unit cost (which is the same as average total cost), then unit cost declines. Similarly, as *MPP* falls, *MC* rises. If *MC* rises enough to move above unit cost, then unit cost rises.

CHAPTER 7, PAGE 181

1   It currently takes 10 units of X and 10 units of Y to produce 50 units of good Z. Let both X and Y double to 20 units each. As a result, the output of Z more than doubles—say, to 150 units. When inputs are increased by some percentage and output increases by a greater percentage, then economies of scale are said to exist. When economies of scale exist, unit costs fall. And another name for unit costs is average total costs.

2   The $LRATC$ curve would be horizontal. When there are constant returns to scale, output doubles if inputs double. If this happens, unit costs stay constant. In other words, they don't rise and they don't fall, so the $LRATC$ curve is horizontal.

3   Unit costs must have been lower when it produced 200 units than when it produced 100 units. That is, there were economies of scale between 100 units and 200 units. To explain further: Profit per unit is the difference between price per unit and cost per unit (or unit costs): Profit per unit = Price per unit − Cost per unit. Suppose the unit cost is $3 when the price is $4—giving a profit per unit of $1. Next, there are economies of scale as the firm raises output from 100 units to 200 units. It follows that unit costs fall—let's say to $2 per unit. If price is $3, then there is still a $1 per-unit profit.

Chapter 8

CHAPTER 8, PAGE 193

1   It means the firm cannot change the price of the product it sells by its actions. For example, if firm A cuts back on the supply of what it produces and the price of its product does not change, then we'd say that firm A cannot control the price of the product it sells. In other words, if price is independent of a firm's actions, that firm does not have any control over price.

2   The easy, and incomplete, answer is that a perfectly competitive firm is a price taker because it is in a market where it cannot control the price of the product it sells. But this simply leads to the question: Why can't it control the price of the product it sells? The answer is because it is in a market where its supply is small relative to the total market supply, it sells a homogeneous good, and all buyers and sellers have all relevant information.

3   If a perfectly competitive firm tries to charge a price higher than equilibrium price, all buyers will know this (assumption 3). These buyers will then simply buy from another firm that sells the same (homogeneous) product (assumption 2).

4   No. A market doesn't have to perfectly match all assumptions of the theory of perfect competition for it to be labeled a perfectly competitive market. What is important is whether or not it acts *as if* it is perfectly competitive. You know the old saying, "If it walks like a duck and it quacks like a duck, it's a duck." Well, if it acts like a perfectly competitive market, it's a perfectly competitive market.

CHAPTER 8, PAGE 199

1   No. Whether a firm earns profits or not depends on the relationship between price (P) and average total cost (ATC). If $P > ATC$, then the firm earns profits. To understand this, remember that profits exist when total revenue (TR) minus total cost (TC) is a positive number. Total revenue is simply price times quantity ($TR = P \times Q$), and total cost is average total cost times quantity ($TC = ATC \times Q$). Because quantity (Q) is common to both TR and TC, if $P > ATC$, then $TR > TC$, and the firm earns profits.

2   In the short run, whether or not a firm should shut down operations depends on the relationship between price and average variable cost (AVC), not between price and ATC. It depends on whether price is greater than or less than average variable cost. If $P > AVC$, the firm should continue to produce; if $P < AVC$, it should shut down.

3   As long as $MR > MC$—for example, $MR = \$6$ and $MC = \$4$—the firm should produce and sell additional units of a good because this adds more to TR than it does to TC. It's adding $6 to TR and $4 to TC. Whenever you add more to TR than you do to TC, the gap between the two becomes larger.

4   We start with the upward-sloping market supply curve and work backward. First, market supply curves are upward sloping because they are the "addition" of individual firms' supply curves—which are upward sloping. Second, individual firms' supply curves are upward sloping because they are that portion of their marginal cost curves above their average variable cost curves, and this portion of the MC curve is upward sloping. Third, marginal cost curves have upward-sloping portions because of the law of diminishing marginal returns. In conclusion, market supply curves are upward sloping because of the law of diminishing marginal returns.

CHAPTER 8, PAGE 207

1   According to the theory of perfect competition, the profits will draw new firms into the market. As these new firms enter the market, the market supply curve will shift to the right. As a result of a larger supply, price will fall. As price declines, profit will decline until firms in the market are earning (only) normal (or zero economic) profit. When there is zero economic profit, there is no longer an incentive for firms to enter the market.

2   No. The market is only in long-run competitive equilibrium when (1) there is no incentive for firms to enter or exit the industry, (2) there is no incentive for firms to produce more or less output, and (3) there is no incentive for firms to change their plant size. If any of these conditions is not met, then the market is not in long-run equilibrium.

3   Initially, price will rise. Recall from Chapter 3 that when demand increases, *ceteris paribus*, price rises. In time, though, price will drop because new firms will enter the industry due to the positive economic profits generated by the higher price. How far the price drops

depends on whether the firms are in a constant-cost, an increasing-cost, or a decreasing-cost industry. In a constant-cost industry, price will return to its original level; in an increasing-cost industry, price will return to a level above its original level; and in a decreasing-cost industry, price will return to a level below its original level.

4   Maybe initially, but probably not after certain adjustments are made. If firm *A* really has a genius on its payroll and, as a result, earns higher profits than firm *B*, then firm *B* might try to hire the genius away from firm *A* by offering the genius a higher income. To keep the genius, firm *A* will have to match the offer. As a result, the costs of firm *A* will rise, and if nothing else changes, its profits will decline.

CHAPTER 8, PAGE 208

1   It depends on how many firms in the market witness higher costs. If it is only one, then it is doubtful that the market supply curve will shift enough to bring about a higher price. If, however, many firms in the market witness higher costs, then the market supply curve will shift left, and price will rise.

2   No. Perfectly competitive firms that sell homogeneous products won't advertise individually, but this doesn't mean that the industry won't advertise in the hope of pushing the market (industry) demand curve (for their product) to the right.

Chapter 9

CHAPTER 9, PAGE 216

1   Let's assume that John is right when he says that there are always some close substitutes for the product a firm sells. The question, however, is: How close does the substitute have to be before the theory of monopoly is not useful? For example, a "slightly close" substitute for a seller's product may not be close enough to matter. The theory of monopoly may still be useful in predicting a firm's behavior.

2   Economies of scale exist when a firm doubles inputs and its output more than doubles, lowering its unit costs (average total costs) in the process. If economies of scale exist only when a firm produces a large quantity of output and one firm is already producing this output, then new firms (that start off producing less output) will have higher unit costs than those of the established firm. Some economists argue that this will make the new firms uncompetitive when compared to the established firm. In other words, economies of scale will act as a barrier to entry, effectively preventing firms from entering the industry and competing with the established firm.

3   In a monopoly, there is a single seller of a good for which there are no close substitutes, and there are extremely high barriers to competing with the single seller. If a movie superstar has so much talent that the moviegoing public puts her in a class by herself, she might be considered a monopolist. Can anyone compete with her? They can try, but she may have such great talent (relative to everyone else) that no one will be able to effectively compete with her. Her immense talent acts as a barrier to entry in the sense that even if someone does try to compete with her, they won't be a close substitute for her.

CHAPTER 9, PAGE 222

1   The single-price monopolist has to lower price to sell an additional unit of its good (this is what a downward-sloping demand curve necessitates). As long as it has to lower price to sell an additional unit, its marginal revenue will be below its price. A demand curve plots price (P) and quantity (Q), and a marginal revenue curve plots marginal revenue (MR) and quantity (Q). Because $P > MR$ for a monopolist, its demand curve will lie above its marginal revenue curve.

2   No. Profit depends on whether or not price is greater than average total cost. It is possible for a monopolist to produce the quantity of output at which $MR = MC$, charge the highest price per unit possible for the output, and still have its unit costs (ATC) greater than price. If this is the case, the monopolist incurs losses; it does not earn profits.

3   No. The last chapter explains that a firm is resource allocative efficient when it charges a price equal to its marginal cost ($P = MC$). The monopolist does not do this; it charges a price above marginal cost. Profit maximization ($MR = MC$) does not lead to resource allocative efficiency ($P = MC$) because for the monopolist, $P > MR$. This is not the case for the perfectly competitive firm, where $P = MR$.

4   A monopolist is searching for the highest price at which it can sell its product. In contrast, the perfectly competitive firm doesn't have to search; it simply takes the equilibrium price established in the market. For example, suppose Nancy is a wheat farmer. She gets up one morning and wants to know at what price she should sell her wheat. She simply turns on the radio, listens to the farm report, and finds out that the equilibrium price per bushel of wheat is, say, $5. Being a price taker, she knows she can't sell her wheat for a penny more than this ($5 is the highest price), and she won't want to sell her wheat for a penny less than this. The monopoly firm doesn't know what the highest price is for the product it sells. It has to search for it; it has to experiment with different prices before it finds the "highest" price.

CHAPTER 9, PAGE 229

1   There are three in particular:

a   A monopoly firm produces too little output relative to a perfectly competitive firm; this causes the deadweight loss of monopoly.

b   The profits of the monopoly are sometimes subject to rent-seeking behavior. Rent seeking, while rational for an individual firm, wastes society's resources. What good does society receive if one firm expends resources to take over the monopoly position of another firm? Answer: none. Resources that could have been used to produce goods (e.g., computers, software, shoes, houses, etc.) are instead used to transfer profits from one firm to another.

    c A monopolist may not produce its products at the lowest possible cost. Again, this wastes society's resources.

2 An example helps to illustrate this concept. Suppose a perfectly competitive firm would produce 100 units of good *X,* but a monopoly firm would produce only 70 units of good *X.* This is a difference of 30 units. Buyers value these 30 units by more than it would cost the monopoly firm to produce them, yet the monopoly firm chooses not to produce the units. The net benefit (benefits to buyers minus costs to the monopolist) of producing these 30 units is said to be the deadweight loss of monopoly. It represents how much buyers lose because the monopolist chooses to produce less than the perfectly competitive firm.

3 If a seller is not a price searcher, then he is a price taker. A price taker can sell his product at only one price, the market equilibrium price.

Chapter 10

CHAPTER 10, PAGE 239

1 It is like a monopolist in that it faces a downward-sloping demand curve; it is a price searcher, $P > MR;$ and it is not resource allocative efficient. It is like a perfect competitor in that it sells to many buyers and competes with many sellers, and there is easy entry into and exit from the market.

2 Essentially, because they face downward-sloping demand curves. Because the demand curve is downward sloping, it cannot be tangent to the lowest point on a U-shaped *ATC* curve (see Exhibit 3).

CHAPTER 10, PAGE 246

1 The incentive in both cases is the same: profit. Firms have an incentive to form a cartel to increase their profits. After the cartel is formed, however, each firm has an incentive to break the cartel to increase its profits even further. This is illustrated in Exhibit 5. If there is no cartel agreement, the firm is earning zero profits by producing $q_1.$ After the cartel is formed, it earns CP_CAB in profits by producing $q_C.$ But it can earn even higher profits (FP_CDE) by cheating on the cartel and producing $q_{CC}.$

2 There is a kink because the demand curve for an oligopolist is more elastic above the kink than it is below the kink. The difference in elasticity is based on the assumption that rival (oligopoly) firms will not match a price hike but will match a price decline. Thus, if a given oligopolist raises product price, it is assumed that its quantity demanded will fall a lot, but if it lowers price, its quantity demanded will not rise much.

3 The dominant firm tries to figure out the price that would exist if it were not in the market. Suppose this price is $10. Then it figures out how much it would supply at this price (the answer is zero) and at all prices less than this. For example, suppose the firm supplies 0 units at $10, 20 units at $9, and 30 units at $8. These, then, are three points on the dominant firm's demand curve—sometimes called the residual demand curve. Next, the dominant firm produces the level of output at which $MR = MC$ and charges the highest price per unit consistent with this output.

Chapter 11

CHAPTER 11, PAGE 271

1 The way a market is defined will help determine whether or not a particular firm is considered a monopoly. If a market is defined broadly, it will include more substitute goods, and so the firm is less likely to be considered a monopolist. If a market is defined narrowly, it will include fewer substitute goods, and so the firm is more likely to be considered a monopolist.

2 The four-firm concentration ratio is 20 percent; the Herfindahl index is 500. The formulas in Exhibit 1 show how each is computed.

3 The Herfindahl index provides information about the dispersion of firm size in an industry. For example, suppose the top four firms in an industry have 15 percent, 10 percent, 9 percent, and 8 percent market shares. The four-firm concentration ratio will be the same for an industry with 15 firms as it is for an industry with 150 firms. The Herfindahl index will be different in the two situations.

CHAPTER 11, PAGE 278

1 Average cost pricing is the same as profit regulation. The regulators state that the natural monopolist must charge a price equal to its average total costs $(P = ATC).$ Under this pricing policy, there is no incentive for the natural monopolist to keep costs down. In fact, there may be an incentive to deliberately push costs up. Higher costs—in the form of higher salaries or more luxurious offices—simply mean higher prices to cover the higher costs.

2 No matter what the motive for initially regulating an industry, eventually, the regulating agency will be "captured" by the special interests (the firms) in the industry. In the end, the regulatory body will not so much regulate the industry as serve the interests of the firms in the industry.

3 According to the capture theory, the outcomes of the regulatory process will favor the regulated firms. According to the public choice theory, the outcomes of the regulatory process will favor the regulators.

4 Sometimes, they favor regulation, and at other times, they do not. Economists make the point that regulation involves both costs and benefits, and whether the particular regulation in question is worthwhile depends on whether the costs are greater than or less than the benefits.

Chapter 12

CHAPTER 12, PAGE 289

1 $MRP = MR \times MPP$. For a perfectly competitive firm, $MR = P$, so MR is $10. MPP in this case is 19 units. It follows that $MRP = \$190$.

2 There is no difference between MRP and VMP if the firm is perfectly competitive. In this situation, $P = MR$, and because $MRP = MR \times MPP$ and $VMP = P \times MPP$, the two are the same. If the firm is a price searcher—monopolist, monopolistic competitor, or oligopolist—$P > MR$; therefore, $VMP > MRP$.

3 It can buy all it wants of a factor at the equilibrium price, and it will not cause factor price to rise. For example, if firm X is a factor price taker in the labor market, it can buy all the labor it wants at the equilibrium wage, and it will not cause this wage to rise.

4 It should buy that quantity at which MRP of labor = MFC of labor.

CHAPTER 12, PAGE 300

1 The MRP curve is the firm's factor demand curve. $MRP = P \times MPP$ for a perfectly competitive firm, so if either the price of the product that labor produces rises or the MPP of labor rises (reflected in a shift in the MPP curve), the factor demand curve shifts rightward.

2 It means that for every 1 percent change in the wage rate, the quantity demanded of labor changes by 3 times this percentage. For example, if wage rates rise 10 percent, then the quantity demanded of labor falls 30 percent.

3 The short answer is because supply-and-demand conditions differ among markets. But this raises the question: Why do supply-and-demand conditions differ? This question is answered in Exhibit 11.

4 We can't answer this question specifically without more information. We know that under four conditions, wage rates would not differ. These conditions are: (1) the demand for every type of labor is the same; (2) there are no special nonpecuniary aspects to any job; (3) all labor is ultimately homogeneous and can costlessly be trained for different types of employment; and (4) all labor is mobile at zero cost. For wage rates to differ, one or more of these conditions is not being met. For example, perhaps labor is not mobile at zero cost.

Chapter 13

CHAPTER 13, PAGE 313

1 The demand for union labor is lowered by (a) a decline in the demand for the product union labor produces, (b) a decline in the price of substitute factors, and (c) a decline in the marginal physical product of union labor.

2 A closed shop requires an employee to be a member of the union before he or she can be hired; a union shop does not. The union shop does require employees to join the union within a certain period of time after becoming employed.

3 To prove to management that union members will not work for a wage rate that is lower than the rate specified by the union. In terms of Exhibit 3, it is to prove that union members will not work for less than W_2.

CHAPTER 13, PAGE 320

1 A monopsonist cannot buy additional units of a factor without increasing the price it pays for the factor. A factor price taker can.

2 Under the following conditions: (1) The firm hiring the labor is a monopsonist and (2) the minimum wage is above the wage it is already paying and below the wage that corresponds to the point where $MFC = MRP$. To understand this completely, look at Exhibit 4(c). Suppose the firm is currently purchasing Q_1 labor and paying W_1. Then, W_2 becomes the minimum wage the monopsonist can pay to workers. Now it hires Q_2 workers. Notice, however, that if the monopsonist had to pay a wage higher than the wage that equates MFC and MRP, it would employ fewer workers than Q_1.

3 If the higher wage rate reduces the number of people working in the unionized sector and the people who lose their jobs in the unionized sector move to the nonunionized sector, then the supply of labor will increase in the nonunionized sector and wage rates will fall. This is illustrated in Exhibit 6.

Chapter 14

CHAPTER 14, PAGE 328

1 It can change the distribution of income through transfer payments and taxes. Look at this equation: Individual income = Labor income + Asset income + Transfer payments − Taxes. By increasing one person's taxes and increasing another person's transfer payments, government can change people's incomes.

2 The statement is true. For example, two people can have unequal incomes at any one point in time and still earn the same incomes over time. For example, in year 1, Patrick earns $40,000 and Francine earns $20,000. In year 2, Francine earns $40,000 and Patrick earns $20,000. In each year, there is income inequality, but over the 2 years, Patrick and Francine earn the same income ($60,000).

3 No. Individual income = Labor income + Asset income + Transfer payments − Taxes. It is possible for Smith's income to come entirely from labor income and Jones's income to come entirely from asset income. The same dollar income does not necessitate the same source of income.

CHAPTER 14, PAGE 331

1 No. The income shares total 105 percent.

2 A Gini coefficient of 0 represents perfect income equality and a Gini coefficient of 1 represents complete income

inequality, so we are sure that country *A* has neither perfect income equality nor complete income inequality. Beyond this, it is difficult to say anything. Usually, the Gini coefficient is used as a comparative measure. For example, if country *A*'s Gini coefficient is 0.45 and country *B*'s is 0.60, we could then conclude that country *A* has a more equal (less unequal) distribution of income than country *B* has.

CHAPTER 14, PAGE 335

1 The simple fact that Jack earns more than Harry is not evidence of wage discrimination. We lack the information necessary to know whether wage discrimination exists. For example, we don't know if Jack and Harry work the same job, we don't know how productive each person is, and so on.

2 It could affect it negatively or positively. There is a higher probability of both higher and lower income if a person assumes a lot of risk than if a person simply plays it safe. To illustrate, suppose Nancy has decided she wants to be an actress, although her parents want her to be an accountant. The chances of her being successful in acting are small, but if she is successful, she will earn a much higher income than if she had been an accountant (a top actress earns more than a top accountant). Of course, if she isn't successful, she will earn less income as an actress than she would have as an accountant (the average actress earns less than the average accountant).

CHAPTER 14, PAGE 341

1 Whether poor people always exist or not depends on how we define poor. If we define poor in relative terms and we assume that there is not absolute income equality, then there must be some people who fall into, say, the lowest 10 percent of income earners. We could refer to these persons as poor. Remember, though, these persons are relatively poor—they earn less than a large percentage of the income earners in the country—but we do not know anything about their absolute incomes. In a world of multimillion-dollar income earners, a person who earns $100,000 might be considered poor.

2 12.7 percent

3 An African American or Hispanic female who is the head of a large family and who is young and has little education.

Chapter 15

CHAPTER 15, PAGE 350

1 Because there is a monetary incentive for them to be equal. To illustrate, suppose the return on capital is 12 percent, and the price for loanable funds is 10 percent. In this case, a person could borrow loanable funds at 10 percent and invest in capital goods to earn the 12 percent return. As this happens, though, the amount of capital increases and its return falls. If the interest rates are reversed and the return on capital is lower than the price for a loanable fund, no one will borrow to invest in capital goods. Over time, then, the stock of capital will diminish and its return will rise.

2 Because the real interest rate is the rate paid by borrowers and received by lenders. For example, if a person borrows funds at a 12 percent interest rate and the inflation rate is 4 percent, he will be paying only an 8 percent (real) interest rate to the lender. Stated differently, the lender has 8 percent, not 12 percent, more buying power because he made the loan.

3 $907.03. The formula is $PV = \$1,000/(1 + 0.05)^2$.

4 No. The present value of $2,000 a year for 4 years at an 8 percent interest rate is $6,624.25. [$PV = \$2,000/(1 + 0.08)^1 + \$2,000/(1 + 0.08)^2 + \$2,000/(1 + 0.08)^3 + \$2,000/(1 + 0.08)^4$]. The present value is less than the cost of the capital good, so it is not worth purchasing.

CHAPTER 15, PAGE 354

1 Jones earns $2 million a year as a news anchor for KNBC. His next best alternative in the news industry is earning $1.9 million a year as a news anchor for KABC. If Jones were not working in the news industry, his next best alternative would be as a journalism professor earning $100,000 a year. Within the news industry, Jones earns $100,000 economic rent (which is the difference between $2 million and $1.9 million). If we move beyond the news industry, Jones earns $1.9 million economic rent (which is the difference between $2 million and $100,000).

2 It is zero dollars.

3 When a firm competes for artificial rents, it expends resources to simply transfer economic rent from another firm to itself. In other words, resources are used to bring about a transfer only. There are no additional goods and services produced as a part of the process. But when a firm competes for real rents, resources are used to produce additional goods and services.

CHAPTER 15, PAGE 358

1 A probability cannot be assigned to uncertainty; a probability can be assigned to risk.

2 There are many different theories that purport to explain profit. One theory states that profit exists because uncertainty exists. No uncertainty, no profit. Another theory states that profit exists because arbitrage opportunities exist (the opportunities to buy low and sell high), and some people are alert to these opportunities. Still another theory states that profit exists because some people (called entrepreneurs) are capable of creating profit opportunities by devising a new product, production process, or marketing strategy.

3 Profit can be a signal, especially if the profit is earned in a competitive market. Specifically, profit signals that buyers value a good (as evidenced by the price they are willing and able to pay for the good) by more than the factors that go to make the good.

Chapter 16

CHAPTER 16, PAGE 368

1 The market output does not reflect or adjust for either external costs (in the case of a negative externality) or external benefits (in the case of a positive externality). The socially optimal output does.

2 Certainly, if there are no costs incurred by moving from the market output to the socially optimal output, the answer is yes. But this isn't likely to be the case. The economist considers whether the benefits of moving to the socially optimal output are greater than or less than the costs of moving to the socially optimal output. If the benefits are greater than the costs, then yes; if the benefits are less than the costs, then no.

CHAPTER 16, PAGE 373

1 It means to adjust the private cost by the external cost. To illustrate, suppose someone's private cost is $10 and the external cost is $2. If the person internalizes the externality, the external cost becomes his cost, which is now $12.

2 Transaction costs are associated with the time and effort needed to search out, negotiate, and consummate an exchange. These costs are higher for buying a house than they are for buying a hamburger. It takes more time and effort to search out a house to buy, negotiate a price, and consummate the deal than it takes to search out and buy a hamburger.

3 Under certain conditions, no. Specifically, if transaction costs are zero or trivial, the property rights assignment that a court makes is irrelevant to the resource allocative outcome. Of course, if transaction costs are not zero or trivial, then the property rights assignment a court makes does matter.

4 If there is a negative externality, there is a marginal external cost. The marginal external cost (MEC) plus the marginal private cost (MPC) equals the marginal social cost (MSC): $MSC = MPC + MEC$. If a corrective tax (t) is to correctly adjust for the marginal external cost associated with the negative externality, it must be equal to the marginal external cost—in other words, tax = MEC. With this condition fulfilled, MPC + tax = $MSC = MPC + MEC$.

CHAPTER 16, PAGE 375

1 All other things held constant, less pollution is preferable to more pollution. Zero pollution is the least amount of pollution possible; therefore, zero pollution is best. But in reality, all other things are not held constant. Sometimes, when we reduce pollution, we also eliminate some of the things we want. The economist wants to eliminate pollution as long as the benefits of eliminating pollution are greater than the costs. When the benefits equal the costs, the economist would stop eliminating pollution. If society has eliminated so much pol-

lution that the costs of eliminating it are greater than the benefits, then society has gone too far. It has eliminated too much pollution. Some units of pollution were simply not worth eliminating.

2 Under market environmentalism, the entities that can eliminate pollution at least cost are the ones that eliminate the pollution. This is not the case under standards, where both the low-cost and high-cost eliminators of pollution must reduce pollution.

3 The dollar price of the pollution permits is a cost for firm Z, but it is not a cost to society. As far as society is concerned, firm Z simply paid $660 to firms X and Y. Firm Z ended up with $660 less, and firms X and Y ended up with $660 more; the amounts offset. Only when resources are used in eliminating pollution is the dollar cost of those resources counted as a cost to society of eliminating pollution.

CHAPTER 16, PAGE 378

1 Because after a nonexcludable public good is produced, the individual or firm that produced it wouldn't be able to collect payment for it. When a nonexcludable public good is provided to one person, it is provided to everyone. Because an individual can consume the good without paying for it, he is likely to take a free ride. Another way of answering this question is simply to say, "The market fails to produce nonexcludable public goods because of the free rider problem."

2 (a) A composition notebook is a private good. It is rivalrous in consumption; if one person is using it, someone else cannot. (b) A Shakespearean play performed in a summer theater is an excludable public good. It is nonrivalrous in consumption (everyone in the theater can see the play) but excludable (a person must pay to get into the theater). (c) An apple is a private good. It is rivalrous in consumption; if one person eats it, someone else cannot. (d) A telephone in service is a private good. One person using the phone (e.g., in your house) prevents someone else from using it. (e) Sunshine is a nonexcludable public good. It is nonrivalrous in consumption (one person's consumption of it doesn't reduce its consumption by others) and nonexcludable (it is impossible to exclude free people from consuming the sunshine).

3 A concert is an example. If one person consumes the concert, this does not take away from others consuming it to the same degree. However, people can be excluded from consuming it.

CHAPTER 16, PAGE 384

1 Consider a fictional product, X. The sellers of X know that the good could, under certain conditions, cause health problems, but they do not release this information to the buyers. Consequently, the demand for good X is likely to be greater than it would be if there were symmetric information. The quantity consumed of good X is likely to be higher when there is asymmetric information than when there is symmetric information.

2 To illustrate, consider again the used car market discussed in the text. If there are two types of used cars—good used cars and "lemons"—and asymmetric information, the market price for a used car may understate the value of a good used car and overstate the value of a lemon. This will induce sellers of lemons to enter the market and sellers of good cars to leave it. (The owners of good used cars will not want to sell their cars for less than their cars are worth.) In theory, the used car market may consist of nothing but lemons. In other words, a used car market for good cars does not exist.

3 A college professor tells her students that she does not believe in giving grades of D or F. As a result, her students do not take as many "precautionary" measures to guard against receiving low grades. Does your example have the characteristic of this example—namely, one person's assurance affects another person's incentive?

Chapter 17

CHAPTER 17, PAGE 395

1 No. The model doesn't say every politician has to do these things; it simply predicts that politicians who do these things have an increased chance of winning the election in a two-person race.

2 Voters may want more information from politicians, but supplying that information is not always in the best interests of politicians. When they speak in specific terms, politicians are often labeled as being at one end or the other of the political spectrum. But politicians don't win elections by being in the right wing or left wing; they win elections by being in the middle.

3 Yes. In the cost equation of voting, we included (1) the cost of driving to the polls, (2) the cost of standing in line, and (3) the cost of filling out the ballot. Bad weather (heavy rain, snow, ice) would likely raise the cost of driving to the polls and the cost of standing in line, therefore raising the cost of voting. The higher the cost of voting, the less likely people will vote, *ceteris paribus*.

CHAPTER 17, PAGE 397

1 2 units

2 In Example 2 with equal taxes, 1 unit received a simple majority of the votes. Person *C* was made worse off because his *MPB* for the first unit of good *Y* was $100, but he ended up paying a tax of $120 and was worse off by $20.

CHAPTER 17, PAGE 402

1 Both farmers and consumers are affected by federal agricultural policy—but not in the same way and not to the same degree. Federal agricultural policy directly affects farmers' incomes, usually by a large amount. It indirectly affects consumers' costs, but not as much as it affects farmers' incomes. Simply put, farmers have more at stake than consumers when it comes to federal agricultural policy. People tend to be better informed about matters that mean more to them.

2 The legislation is more likely to pass when group *A* includes 10 million persons because the wider the dispersal of the costs of the legislation, the greater the likelihood of passage. When costs are widely dispersed, the cost to any one individual is so small that she or he is unlikely to lobby against the legislation.

3 Examples include teachers saying that more money for education will help the country compete in the global marketplace; domestic car manufacturers saying that tariffs on foreign imports will save American jobs and U.S. manufacturing; farmers saying that subsidies to farmers will preserve the "American" farm and a way of life that Americans cherish. Whether any of these groups is right or wrong is not the point. The point is that special interest groups are likely to advance their arguments (good or bad) with public interest talk.

4 Rent seeking is socially wasteful because the resources that are used to seek rent could instead be used to produce goods and services.

Chapter 18

CHAPTER 18, PAGE 414

1 For the United States, $1X = 1/6Y$ or $1Y = 6X$. For England, $1X = 2Y$ or $1Y = 1/2X$. Let's focus on the opportunity cost of $1X$ in each country. In the United States, $1X = 1/6Y$, and in Great Britain, $1X = 2Y$. Terms of trade that are between these two endpoints would be favorable for the two countries. For example, suppose we choose $1X = 1Y$. This is good for the United States because it would prefer to give up $1X$ and get $1Y$ in trade than to give up $1X$ and only get $1/6Y$ (without trade). Similarly, Great Britain would prefer to give up $1Y$ and get $1X$ in trade than to give up $1Y$ and get only $1/2X$ (without trade). Any terms of trade between $1X = 1/6Y$ and $1X = 2Y$ will be favorable to the two countries.

2 Yes; this is what the theory of comparative advantage shows. Exhibit 1 shows that the United States could produce more of both food and clothing than Japan. Still, the United States benefits from specialization and trade, as shown in Exhibit 2. In column 5 of this exhibit, the United States can consume 10 more units of food by specializing and trading.

3 No. It is the desire to buy low and sell high (earn a profit) that pushes countries into producing and trading at a comparative advantage. Government officials do not collect cost data and then issue orders to firms in the country to produce *X*, *Y*, or *Z*. We have not drawn the PPFs in this chapter and identified the cost differences between countries to show what countries actually do in the real world. We described things technically to simply show how countries benefit from specialization and trade.

CHAPTER 18, PAGE 422

1 Domestic producers benefit because producers' surplus rises; domestic consumers lose because consumers' surplus falls. Also, government benefits in that it receives the tariff revenue. Moreover, consumers lose more than producers and government gain, so that there is a net loss resulting from tariffs.

2 Consumers' surplus falls by more than producers' surplus rises.

3 With a tariff, the government receives tariff revenue. With a quota, it does not. In the latter case, the revenue that would have gone to government goes, instead, to the importers who get to satisfy the quota.

4 Infant or new domestic industries need to be protected from older, more established competitors until they are mature enough to compete on an equal basis. Tariffs and quotas provide these infant industries the time they need.

Chapter 19

CHAPTER 19, PAGE 432

1 A debit. When an American enters into a transaction in which he has to supply U.S. dollars in the foreign exchange market (to demand a foreign currency), the transaction is recorded as a debit.

2 We do not have enough information to answer this question. The merchandise trade balance is the difference between the value of *merchandise* exports and *merchandise* imports. The question gives only the value of exports and imports. *Exports* is a more inclusive term than merchandise exports. Exports include (a) merchandise exports, (b) services, and (c) income from U.S. assets abroad (see Exhibit 2). Similarly, *imports* is a more inclusive term than merchandise imports. It includes (a) merchandise imports, (b) services, and (c) income from foreign assets in the United States.

3 The merchandise trade balance includes fewer transactions than are included in the current account balance. The merchandise trade balance is the summary statistic for merchandise exports and merchandise imports. The current account balance is the summary statistic for exports of goods and services (which include merchandise exports), imports of goods and services (which include merchandise imports), and net unilateral transfers abroad (see Exhibit 2).

CHAPTER 19, PAGE 439

1 As the demand for dollars increases, the supply of pesos increases. For example, suppose someone in Mexico wants to buy something produced in the United States. The American wants to be paid in dollars, but the Mexican doesn't have any dollars—she has pesos. So she has to buy dollars with pesos; in other words, she has to supply pesos to buy dollars. Thus, as she demands more dollars, she will necessarily have to supply more pesos.

2 The dollar is said to have appreciated (against the peso) when it takes more pesos to buy a dollar and fewer dollars to buy a peso. For this to occur, either the demand for dollars must increase (which means the supply of pesos increases) or the supply of dollars must decrease (which means the demand for pesos decreases). To see this graphically, look at Exhibit 5(b). The only way for the peso price per dollar to rise (on the vertical axis) is for either the demand curve for dollars to shift to the right or the supply curve of dollars to shift to the left. Each of these occurrences is mirrored in the market for pesos in part (a) of the exhibit.

3 *Ceteris paribus,* the dollar will depreciate relative to the franc. As incomes for Americans rise, the demand for Swiss goods rises. This increases the demand for francs and the supply of dollars on the foreign exchange market. In turn, this leads to a depreciated dollar and an appreciated franc.

4 The theory states that the exchange rate between any two currencies will adjust to reflect changes in the relative price levels of the two countries. For example, suppose the U.S. price level rises 5 percent and Mexico's price level remains constant. According to the PPP theory, the U.S. dollar will depreciate 5 percent relative to the Mexican peso.

CHAPTER 19, PAGE 445

1 The terms *overvalued* and *undervalued* refer to the equilibrium exchange rate: the exchange rate at which the quantity demanded and quantity supplied of a currency are the same in the foreign exchange market. Let's suppose the equilibrium exchange rate is 0.10 USD = 1 MXN. This is the same as saying that 10 pesos = $1 If the exchange rate is fixed at 0.12 USD = 1 MXN (which is the same as 8.33 pesos = $1), the peso is overvalued and the dollar is undervalued. Specifically, a currency is overvalued if 1 unit of it fetches more of another currency than it would in equilibrium; a currency is undervalued if 1 unit of it fetches less of another currency than it would in equilibrium. In equilibrium, 1 peso would fetch 0.10 dollars and at the current exchange rate it fetches 0.12 dollars—so the peso is overvalued. In equilibrium, $1 would fetch 10 pesos, and at the current exchange rate, it fetches only 8.33 pesos—so the dollar is undervalued.

2 An overvalued dollar means some other currency is undervalued—let's say it is the Japanese yen. An overvalued dollar makes U.S. goods more expensive for the Japanese, so they buy fewer U.S. goods. This reduces U.S. exports. On the other hand, an undervalued yen makes Japanese goods cheaper for Americans, so they buy more Japanese goods; the U.S. imports more. Thus, an overvalued dollar reduces U.S. exports and raises U.S. imports.

3 **a** Dollar is overvalued.

   b Dollar is undervalued.

   c Dollar is undervalued.

4 When a country devalues its currency, it makes it cheaper for foreigners to buy its products.

CHAPTER 19, PAGE 450

1 An optimal currency area is a geographic area in which exchange rates can be fixed or a common currency used without sacrificing any domestic economic goals.

2 As the demand for good Y falls, the unemployment rate in country 2 will rise. This increase in the unemployment rate is likely to be temporary, though. The increased demand for good X (produced by country 1) will increase the demand for country 1's currency, leading to an appreciation in country 1's currency and a depreciation in country 2's currency. Country 1's good (good X) will become more expensive for the residents of country 2, and they will buy less. Country 2's good (good Y) will become less expensive for the residents of country 1, and they will buy more. As a result of the additional purchases of good Y, country 2's unemployment rate will begin to decline.

3 Labor mobility is very important to determining whether or not an area is an optimal currency area. If there is little or no labor mobility, an area is not likely to be an optimal currency area. If there is labor mobility, an area is likely to be an optimal currency area.

Chapter 20

CHAPTER 20, PAGE 461

1 As some explain it, the end of the Cold War resulted in turning two different worlds (the capitalist and communist worlds) into one world. It resulted in a thawing of not only political but economic relations between former enemies. You might not trade with your enemy, but once that person or country is no longer your enemy, you don't feel the same need to cut him or it out of your political and economic life.

2 Globalization is the phenomenon by which individuals and businesses in any part of the world are much more affected by events elsewhere in the world than before; it is the growing integration of the national economies of the world to the degree that we may be witnessing the emergence and operation of a single worldwide economy.

3 Advancing technology can reduce both transportation and communication costs, thus making it less costly to trade with people around the world.

CHAPTER 20, PAGE 467

1 Benefits identified in the section include (a) benefits from increased international trade, (b) greater income per person, (c) lower prices for goods, (d) greater product variety, and (e) increased productivity and innovation.

2 Costs identified in the section include (a) increased income inequality, (b) offshoring, and (c) more power for big corporations.

Chapter 21

CHAPTER 21, PAGE 482

1 30

2 Stocks are purchased either for the dividends that the stocks may pay, the expected gain in price (of the stock), or both.

3 The dividend per share (of the stock) divided by the closing price per share.

4 It means that the stock is selling for a share price that is 23 times its earnings per share.

CHAPTER 21, PAGE 486

1 A bond is an IOU or a promise to pay. The issuer of a bond is borrowing funds and promising to pay back those funds (with interest) at a later date.

2 $0.07X = \$400$, so $X = \$400/0.07$, or $\$5,714.29$.

3 $\$1,000/\$9,500 = 10.53$ percent

4 Municipal bonds are issued by state and local governments, and a Treasury bond is issued by the federal government.

CHAPTER 21, PAGE 489

1 A futures contract is a contract in which the seller agrees to provide a good to the buyer on a specified future date at an agreed-upon price.

2 You can buy a call option, which sells for a fraction of the cost of the stock. A call option gives the owner of the option the right to buy shares of a stock at a specified price within the time limits of the contract.

3 A put option gives the owner the right, but not the obligation, to *sell* (rather than buy, as in a call option) shares of a stock at a strike price during some period of time.

Web Chapter 34

CHAPTER 34, PAGE 745

1 She does so through the futures market. Specifically, she enters into a futures contract with someone who will guarantee to take delivery of her foodstuff (in the future) for a stated price. Then, if the price goes up or down between the present and the future, the farmer does not have to worry. She has locked in the price of her foodstuff.

2 If the farmer faces an inelastic demand curve, the order of preference would be (b)-(a)-(c). That is, he prefers (b) to (a) and he prefers (a) to (c). If all farmers except himself have bad weather (b), then the market supply curve of the individual farmer's product shifts to the left. This brings about a higher price. But the individual farmer's supply curve doesn't shift to the left; it stays where it is. Thus, the individual farmer sells the same amount of output at the higher price. Consequently, his total revenue rises. In (a), both the market supply curve and the

individual farmer's supply curve shift left, so the farmer has less to sell at a higher price. Again, if the demand is inelastic, the individual farmer will increase his total revenue but not as much as in (b) where the individual farmer's output did not fall. Finally, in (c), the market supply curve shifts to the right, lowering price. If demand is inelastic, this lowers total revenue.

3   Increased productivity will lead to higher total revenue when demand is elastic. To illustrate, increased productivity shifts the supply curve to the right. This lowers price. If demand is elastic, then the percentage rise in quantity sold is greater than the percentage fall in price; therefore, total revenue rises. In summary, increased productivity leads to higher total revenue when demand is elastic.

CHAPTER 34, PAGE 750

1   Because the deficiency payment is the difference between the target price and the market price, the answer depends on what the market price is. If the market price is, say, $4, and the target price is $7, then the deficiency payment is $3.

2   A farmer pledges a certain number of bushels of foodstuff to obtain a loan—say, 500 bushels. He receives a loan equal to the number of bushels times the designated loan rate per bushel. For example, if the loan rate is $2 per bushel and 500 bushels are pledged, then the loan is $1,000. The farmer ends up paying back the loan with interest or keeping the loan and forfeiting the bushels of the crop. Which course of action the farmer takes depends on the market price of the crop. If the market price of the crop is higher than the loan rate, he or she pays back the loan and sells the crop. If the market price is less than the loan rate, he or she forfeits the crop. A nonrecourse loan guarantees that the farmer will not receive less than the loan rate for each bushel of his crop.

3   The effects of a price support are (a) a surplus, (b) fewer exchanges (less bought by private citizens), (c) higher prices paid by consumers of the crop (on which the support exists) and (d) government purchase and storage of the surplus crop (for which taxpayers pay).

Web Chapter 35

CHAPTER 35, PAGE 756

1   In country *A,* there is an economic expansion, and real income in the country rises. As a result, residents of the country buy more imports from country *B.* In country *B,* exports rise relative to imports, thus increasing net exports. As net exports in country *B* rise, the *AD* curve for country *B* shifts to the right, increasing Real GDP.

2   If the dollar appreciates, the Japanese yen depreciates. U.S. products become more expensive for the Japanese, and Japanese products become cheaper for Americans. U.S. imports will rise, U.S. exports will fall, and consequently, U.S. net exports will fall. As a result, the *AD* curve in the United States will shift leftward, pushing down Real GDP.

CHAPTER 35, PAGE 759

1   Foreign input prices can change directly as a result of supply conditions in the foreign country, or they can change indirectly as a result of a change in the exchange rate. In either case, as foreign input prices rise—either directly or as a result of a depreciated dollar—the U.S. *SRAS* curve shifts leftward. If foreign input prices fall—either directly or as a result of an appreciated dollar—the *SRAS* curve shifts rightward.

2   The higher real interest rates in the United States attract capital to the United States. This increases the demand for the dollar. As a result, the dollar appreciates and the yen depreciates. An appreciated dollar shifts the U.S. *AD* curve leftward and the U.S. *SRAS* curve rightward. The *AD* curve shifts leftward by more than the *SRAS* curve shifts rightward, so the price level falls.

CHAPTER 35, PAGE 763

1   When the money supply is raised, the *AD* curve shifts rightward, pushing up Real GDP. Also, as a result of the increased money supply, interest rates may decline in the short run. This promotes U.S. capital outflow and a depreciated dollar. As a result of the depreciated dollar, imports become more expensive for Americans, and U.S. exports become cheaper for foreigners. Imports fall and exports rise, thereby increasing net exports and *again* shifting the *AD* curve to the right. Real GDP rises.

2   Expansionary fiscal policy pushes the *AD* curve rightward and (under certain conditions) raises Real GDP. If the expansionary fiscal policy causes a deficit, then the government will have to borrow to finance the deficit, and interest rates will be pushed upward. As a result of the higher interest rates, there will be increased foreign capital inflows and dollar appreciation, thus pushing the *AD* curve leftward and the *SRAS* curve rightward.

A

Absolute (Money) Price   The price of a good in money terms.

Absolute Real Economic Growth   An increase in Real GDP from one period to the next.

Accounting Profit   The difference between total revenue and explicit costs.

Adverse Selection   Exists when the parties on one side of the market, who have information not known to others, self-select in a way that adversely affects the parties on the other side of the market.

Antitrust Law   Legislation passed for the stated purpose of controlling monopoly power and preserving and promoting competition.

Appreciation   An increase in the value of one currency relative to other currencies.

Arbitrage   Buying a good at a low price and selling the good for a higher price.

Asymmetric Information   Exists when either the buyer or the seller in a market exchange has some information that the other does not have.

Average Fixed Cost (AFC)   Total fixed cost divided by quantity of output: $AFC = TFC / Q$.

Average Total Cost (ATC), or Unit Cost   Total cost divided by quantity of output: $ATC = TC / Q$.

Average Variable Cost (AVC)   Total variable cost divided by quantity of output: $AVC = TVC / Q$.

Average–Marginal Rule   When the marginal magnitude is above the average magnitude, the average magnitude rises; when the marginal magnitude is below the average magnitude, the average magnitude falls.

B

Bad   Anything from which individuals receive disutility or dissatisfaction.

Balance of Payments   A periodic statement (usually annual) of the money value of all transactions between residents of one country and residents of all other countries.

Bond   An IOU, or promise to pay.

Budget Constraint   All the combinations or bundles of two goods a person can purchase given a certain money income and prices for the two goods.

Business Firm   An entity that employs factors of production (resources) to produce goods and services to be sold to consumers, other firms, or the government.

C

Capital   Produced goods that can be used as inputs for further production, such as factories, machinery, tools, computers, and buildings.

Capital Account   Includes all payments related to the purchase and sale of assets and to borrowing and lending activities. Components include outflow of U.S. capital and inflow of foreign capital.

Capital Account Balance   The summary statistic for the outflow of U.S. capital. It is equal to the difference between the outflow of U.S. capital and the inflow of foreign capital.

Capture Theory of Regulation   Holds that no matter what the motive is for the initial regulation and the establishment of the regulatory agency, eventually, the agency will be "captured" (controlled) by the special interests of the industry being regulated.

Cartel   An organization of firms that reduces output and increases price in an effort to increase joint profits.

Cartel Theory   In this theory of oligopoly, oligopolistic firms act as if there were only one firm in the industry.

Ceteris Paribus   A Latin term meaning "all other things constant" or "nothing else changes."

Closed Shop   An organization in which an employee must belong to the union before he or she can be hired.

Coase Theorem   In the case of trivial or zero transaction costs, the property rights assignment does not matter to the resource allocative outcome.

Collective Bargaining   The process whereby wage rates and other issues are determined by a union bargaining with management on behalf of all union members.

Comparative Advantage   The situation when a person or country can produce a good at lower opportunity cost than another person or country can.

Complements   Two goods that are used jointly in consumption. If two goods are complements, the demand for one rises as the price of the other falls (or the demand for one falls as the price of the other rises).

Concentration Ratio   The percentage of industry sales (or assets, output, labor force, or some other factor) accounted for by x number of firms in the industry.

Conglomerate Merger   A merger between companies in different industries.

Constant Returns to Scale   Exist when inputs are increased by some percentage and output increases by an equal percentage, causing unit costs to remain constant.

Constant-Cost Industry   An industry in which average total costs do not change as (industry) output increases or decreases when firms enter or exit the industry, respectively.

Consumer Equilibrium   Occurs when the consumer has spent all income and the marginal utilities per dollar spent on each good purchased are equal: $MU_A/P_A = MU_B/P_B = \ldots = MU_Z/P_Z$, where the letters $A–Z$ represent all the goods a person buys.

Consumers' Surplus (CS)   The difference between the maximum price a buyer is willing and able to pay for a good or service and the price actually paid. $CS =$ Maximum buying price − Price paid.

Contestable Market   A market in which entry is easy and exit is costless, new firms can produce the product at the same cost as current firms, and exiting firms can easily dispose of their fixed assets by selling them.

Craft (Trade) Union   A union whose membership is made up of individuals who practice the same craft or trade.

Credit   In the balance of payments, any transaction that creates a demand for the country's currency in the foreign exchange market.

Cross Elasticity of Demand   Measures the responsiveness in quantity demanded of one good to changes in the price of another good.

Current Account   Includes all payments related to the purchase and sale of goods and services. Components of the account include exports, imports, and net unilateral transfers abroad.

Current Account Balance   The summary statistic for exports of goods and services, imports of goods and services, and net unilateral transfers abroad.

D

Deadweight Loss   The loss to society of not producing the competitive, or supply-and-demand-determined, level of output.

Deadweight Loss of Monopoly   The net value (value to buyers over and above costs to suppliers) of the difference between the monopoly quantity of output (where $P > MC$) and the competitive quantity of output (where $P = MC$). The loss of not producing the competitive quantity of output.

Debit   In the balance of payments, any transaction that supplies the country's currency in the foreign exchange market.

Decisions at the Margin   Decision making characterized by weighing the additional (marginal) benefits of a change against the additional (marginal) costs of a change with respect to current conditions.

Decreasing-Cost Industry   An industry in which average total costs decrease as output increases and increase as output decreases when firms enter and exit the industry, respectively.

Demand   The willingness and ability of buyers to purchase different quantities of a good at different prices during a specific time period.

Demand Schedule   The numerical tabulation of the quantity demanded of a good at different prices. A demand schedule is the numerical representation of the law of demand.

Depreciation   A decrease in the value of one currency relative to other currencies.

Derived Demand   Demand that is the result of some other demand. For example, factor demand is the result of the demand for the products that the factors go to produce.

Devaluation   A government act that changes the exchange rate by lowering the official price of a currency.

Diamond-Water Paradox   The observation that things that have the greatest value in use sometimes have little value in exchange and things that have little value in use sometimes have the greatest value in exchange.

Directly Related   Two variables are directly related if they change in the same way.

Diseconomies of Scale   Exist when inputs are increased by some percentage and output increases by a smaller percentage, causing unit costs to rise.

Disequilibrium   A state of either surplus or shortage in a market.

Disequilibrium Price   A price other than equilibrium price. A price at which quantity demanded does not equal quantity supplied.

Disutility   The dissatisfaction one receives from a bad.

Dividend   A share of the profits of a corporation distributed to stockholders.

Dow Jones Industrial Average (DJIA)   The most popular, widely cited indicator of day-to-day stock market activity. The DJIA is a weighted average of 30 widely traded stocks on the New York Stock Exchange.

(Downward-Sloping) Demand Curve   The graphical representation of the law of demand.

Dumping   The sale of goods abroad at a price below their cost and below the price charged in the domestic market.

E

Economic Profit   The difference between total revenue and total cost, including both explicit and implicit costs.

Economic Rent   Payment in excess of opportunity costs.

Economics   The science of scarcity; the science of how individuals and societies deal with the fact that wants are greater than the limited resources available to satisfy those wants.

Economies of Scale   Exist when inputs are increased by some percentage and output increases by a greater percentage, causing unit costs to fall.

Efficiency   Exists when marginal benefits equal marginal costs.

Elastic Demand   The percentage change in quantity demanded is greater than the percentage change in price. Quantity demanded changes proportionately more than price changes.

Elasticity of Demand for Labor   The percentage change in the quantity demanded of labor divided by the percentage change in the wage rate.

Employee Association   An organization whose members belong to a particular profession.

Entrepreneurship   The particular talent that some people have for organizing the resources of land, labor, and capital to produce goods, seek new business opportunities, and develop new ways of doing things.

Equilibrium   Equilibrium means "at rest." Equilibrium in a market is the price-quantity combination from which there is no tendency for buyers or sellers to move away. Graphically, equilibrium is the intersection point of the supply and demand curves.

Equilibrium Price (Market-Clearing Price)   The price at which quantity demanded of the good equals quantity supplied.

Equilibrium Quantity   The quantity that corresponds to equilibrium price. The quantity at which the amount of the good that buyers are willing and able to buy equals the amount that sellers are willing and able to sell, and both equal the amount actually bought and sold.

Ex Ante   Phrase that means "before," as in before a trade.

Ex Post   Phrase that means "after," as in after a trade.

Excess Capacity Theorem   States that a monopolistic competitor in equilibrium produces an output smaller than the one that would minimize its costs of production.

Exchange (Trade)   The process of giving up one thing for something else.

Exchange Rate   The price of one currency in terms of another currency.

Excludability   A good is excludable if it is possible, or not prohibitively costly, to exclude someone from receiving the benefits of the good after it has been produced.

Explicit Cost   A cost incurred when an actual (monetary) payment is made.

Externality   A side effect of an action that affects the well-being of third parties.

F

Face Value   Dollar amount specified on a bond. The total amount the issuer of the bond will repay to the buyer of the bond.

Factor Price Taker   A firm that can buy all of a factor it wants at the equilibrium price. It faces a horizontal (flat, perfectly elastic) supply curve of factors.

Fixed Costs   Costs that do not vary with output; the costs associated with fixed inputs.

Fixed Exchange Rate System   The system where a nation's currency is set at a fixed rate relative to all other currencies, and central banks intervene in the foreign exchange market to maintain the fixed rate.

Fixed Input   An input whose quantity cannot be changed as output changes.

Flexible Exchange Rate System
The system whereby exchange rates are determined by the forces of supply and demand for a currency.

Foreign Exchange Market   The market in which currencies of different countries are exchanged.

Free Rider   Anyone who receives the benefits of a good without paying for it.

Futures Contract   Agreement to buy or sell a specific amount of something (commodity, currency, financial instrument) at a particular price on a stipulated future date.

G

Game Theory   A mathematical technique used to analyze the behavior of decision makers who try to reach an optimal position for themselves through game playing or the use of strategic behavior, are fully aware of the interactive nature of the process at hand, and anticipate the moves of other decision makers.

Gini Coefficient   A measure of the degree of inequality in the income distribution.

Globalization   A phenomenon by which economic agents in any given part of the world are more affected by events elsewhere in the world than before; the growing integration of the national economies of the world to the degree that we may be witnessing the emergence and operation of a single worldwide economy.

Good   Anything from which individuals receive utility or satisfaction.

Government Bureaucrat   An unelected person who works in a government bureau and is assigned a special task that relates to a law or program passed by the legislature.

H

Herfindahl Index   Measures the degree of concentration in an industry. It is equal to the sum of the squares of the market shares of each firm in the industry.

Horizontal Merger   A merger between firms that are selling similar products in the same market.

Human Capital   Education, development of skills, and anything else that is particular to the individual and increases his or her productivity.

I

Implicit Cost   A cost that represents the value of resources used in production for which no actual (monetary) payment is made.

Income Elastic   The percentage change in quantity demanded of a good is greater than the percentage change in income.

Income Elasticity of Demand
Measures the responsiveness of quantity demanded to changes in income.

Income Inelastic   The percentage change in quantity demanded of a good is less than the percentage change in income.

Income Unit Elastic   The percentage change in quantity demanded of a good is equal to the percentage change in income.

Increasing-Cost Industry   An industry in which average total costs increase as output increases and decrease as output decreases when firms enter and exit the industry, respectively.

Independent   Two variables are independent if as one changes, the other does not.

Indifference Curve   Represents an indifference set. A curve that shows all the bundles of two goods that give an individual equal total utility.

Indifference Curve Map   Represents a number of indifference curves for a given individual with reference to two goods.

Indifference Set   Group of bundles of two goods that give an individual equal total utility.

Industrial Union   A union whose membership is made up of individuals who work in the same firm or industry but do not all practice the same craft or trade.

Inelastic Demand   The percentage change in quantity demanded is less than the percentage change in price. Quantity demanded changes proportionately less than price changes.

Inferior Good   A good the demand for which falls (rises) as income rises (falls).

Initial Public Offering (IPO)   A company's first offering of stock to the public.

In-Kind Transfer Payments   Transfer payments, such as food stamps, medical assistance, and subsidized housing, that are made in a specific good or service rather than in cash.

Internalizing Externalities   An externality is internalized if the persons or group that generated the externality incorporate into their own private or internal cost-benefit calculations the external benefits (in the case of a positive externality) or the external costs (in the case of a negative externality) that third parties bear.

International Monetary Fund (IMF)
An international organization created to oversee the international monetary system. The IMF does not control the world's money supply, but it does hold currency reserves for member nations and make loans to central banks.

Interpersonal Utility Comparison
Comparing the utility one person receives from a good, service, or activity with the utility another person receives from the same good, service, or activity.

Inversely Related Two variables are inversely related if they change in opposite ways.

Investment Bank Firm that acts as an intermediary between the company that issues the stock and the public that wishes to buy the stock.

J

J-Curve The curve that shows a short-run worsening in net exports after a currency depreciation, followed later by an improvement.

K

Kinked Demand Curve Theory A theory of oligopoly that assumes that if a single firm in the industry cuts prices, other firms will do likewise, but if it raises price, other firms will not follow suit. The theory predicts price stickiness or rigidity.

L

Labor The physical and mental talents people contribute to the production process.

Land All natural resources, such as minerals, forests, water, and unimproved land.

Law of Demand As the price of a good rises, the quantity demanded of the good falls, and as the price of a good falls, the quantity demanded of the good rises, *ceteris paribus*.

Law of Diminishing Marginal Returns As ever-larger amounts of a variable input are combined with fixed inputs, eventually, the marginal physical product of the variable input will decline.

Law of Diminishing Marginal Utility
The marginal utility gained by consuming equal successive units of a good will decline as the amount consumed increases.

Law of Increasing Opportunity Costs
As more of a good is produced, the opportunity costs of producing that good increase.

Law of Supply As the price of a good rises, the quantity supplied of the good rises, and as the price of a good falls, the quantity supplied of the good falls, *ceteris paribus*.

Least-Cost Rule Specifies the combination of factors that minimizes costs. This requires that the following condition be met: $MPP_1/P_1 = MPP_2/P_2 = \ldots = MPP_N/P_N$, where the numbers stand for the different factors.

Loanable Funds Funds that someone borrows and another person lends, for which the borrower pays an interest rate to the lender.

Lock-In Effect Descriptive of the situation where a particular product or technology becomes settled upon as the standard and is difficult or impossible to dislodge as the standard.

Logrolling The exchange of votes to gain support for legislation.

Long Run A period of time in which all inputs in the production process can be varied (no inputs are fixed).

Long-Run Average Total Cost (LRATC) Curve A curve that shows the lowest (unit) cost at which the firm can produce any given level of output.

Long-Run Competitive Equilibrium
The condition where $P = MC = SRATC = LRATC$. There are zero economic profits, firms are producing the quantity of output at which price is equal to marginal cost, and no firm has an incentive to change its plant size.

Long-Run (Industry) Supply (LRS) Curve Graphic representation of the quantities of output that the industry is prepared to supply at different prices after the entry and exit of firms are completed.

Lorenz Curve A graph of the income distribution. It expresses the relationship between cumulative percentage of households and cumulative percentage of income.

M

Macroeconomics The branch of economics that deals with human behavior and choices as they relate to highly aggregate markets (e.g., the goods and services market) or the entire economy.

Managed Float A managed flexible exchange rate system, under which nations now and then intervene to adjust their official reserve holdings to moderate major swings in exchange rates.

Managerial Coordination The process in which managers direct employees to perform certain tasks.

Marginal Benefits Additional benefits. The benefits connected to consuming an additional unit of a good or undertaking one more unit of an activity.

Marginal Cost (MC) The change in total cost that results from a change in output: $MC = \Delta TC/\Delta Q$.

Marginal Costs Additional costs. The costs connected to consuming an additional unit of a good or undertaking one more unit of an activity.

Marginal Factor Cost (MFC) The additional cost incurred by employing an additional factor unit.

Marginal Physical Product (MPP)
The change in output that results from changing the variable input by one unit, holding all other inputs fixed.

Marginal Productivity Theory States that firms in competitive or perfect product and factor markets pay their factors their marginal revenue products.

Marginal Rate of Substitution The amount of one good an individual is willing to give up to obtain an additional unit of another good and maintain equal total utility.

Marginal Revenue (MR) The change in total revenue that results from selling one additional unit of output.

Marginal Revenue Product (MRP)
The additional revenue generated by employing an additional factor unit.

Marginal Social Benefits (MSB) The sum of marginal private benefits (*MPB*) and marginal external benefits (*MEB*): $MSB = MPB + MEB$.

Marginal Social Costs (MSC) The sum of marginal private costs (*MPC*) and marginal external costs (*MEC*): MSC = MPC + MEC.

Marginal Utility The additional utility a person receives from consuming an additional unit of a particular good.

Market Any place people come together to trade.

Market Coordination The process in which individuals perform tasks, such as producing certain quantities of goods, based on changes in market forces, such as supply, demand, and price.

Market Failure A situation in which the market does not provide the ideal or optimal amount of a particular good.

Market Structure The particular environment of a firm, the characteristics of which influence the firm's pricing and output decisions.

Median Voter Model Suggests that candidates in a two-person political race will move toward matching the preferences of the median voter (i.e., the person whose preferences are at the center, or in the middle, of the political spectrum).

Merchandise Trade Balance The difference between the value of merchandise exports and the value of merchandise imports.

Merchandise Trade Deficit The situation where the value of merchandise exports is less than the value of merchandise imports.

Merchandise Trade Surplus The situation where the value of merchandise exports is greater than the value of merchandise imports.

Microeconomics The branch of economics that deals with human behavior and choices as they relate to relatively small units—an individual, a firm, an industry, a single market.

Minimum Efficient Scale The lowest output level at which average total costs are minimized.

Monitor Person in a business firm who coordinates team production and reduces shirking.

Monopolistic Competition A theory of market structure based on three assumptions: many sellers and buyers, firms producing and selling slightly differentiated products, and easy entry and exit.

Monopoly A theory of market structure based on three assumptions: There is one seller, it sells a product for which no close substitutes exist, and there are extremely high barriers to entry.

Monopsony A single buyer in a factor market.

Moral Hazard Exists when one party to a transaction changes his or her behavior in a way that is hidden from and costly to the other party.

N

Natural Monopoly The condition where economies of scale are so pronounced that only one firm can survive.

Negative Externality Exists when a person's or group's actions cause a cost (adverse side effect) to be felt by others.

Network Good A good whose value increases as the expected number of units sold increases.

Neutral Good A good the demand for which does not change as income rises or falls.

Nominal Interest Rate The interest rate actually charged (or paid) in the market; the market interest rate. The nominal interest rate = Real interest rate + Expected inflation rate.

Nonexcludability A good is nonexcludable if it is impossible, or prohibitively costly, to exclude someone from receiving the benefits of the good after it has been produced.

Nonrivalrous in Consumption A good is nonrivalrous in consumption if its consumption by one person does not reduce its consumption by others.

Normal Good A good the demand for which rises (falls) as income rises (falls).

Normal Profit Zero economic profit. A firm that earns normal profit is earning revenue equal to its total costs (explicit plus implicit costs). This is the level of profit necessary to keep resources employed in that particular firm.

Normative Economics The study of "what should be" in economic matters.

O

Offshoring Work done for a company by persons other than the original company's employees in a country other than the one in which the company is located.

Oligopoly A theory of market structure based on three assumptions: few sellers and many buyers, firms producing either homogeneous or differentiated products, and significant barriers to entry.

Opportunity Cost The most highly valued opportunity or alternative forfeited when a choice is made.

Optimal Currency Area A geographic area in which exchange rates can be fixed or a common currency used without sacrificing domestic economic goals, such as low unemployment.

Option Contract that gives the owner the right, but not the obligation, to buy or sell shares of a stock at a specified price on or before a specified date.

Overvaluation A currency is overvalued if its price in terms of other currencies is above the equilibrium price.

Own Price The price of a good. For example, if the price of oranges is $1, this is (its) own price.

P

Perfect Competition A theory of market structure based on four assumptions: There are many sellers and buyers, sellers sell a homogeneous good, buyers and sellers have all relevant information, and there is easy entry and exit from the market.

Perfect Price Discrimination Occurs when the seller charges the highest price each consumer would be willing to pay for the product rather than go without it.

Perfectly Elastic Demand   A small percentage change in price causes an extremely large percentage change in quantity demanded (from buying all to buying nothing).

Perfectly Inelastic Demand   Quantity demanded does not change as price changes.

Positive Economics   The study of "what is" in economic matters.

Positive Externality   Exists when a person's or group's actions cause a benefit (beneficial side effect) to be felt by others.

Positive Rate of Time Preference   Preference for earlier availability of goods over later availability of goods.

Poverty Income Threshold (Poverty Line)   Income level below which people are considered to be living in poverty.

Present Value   The current worth of some future dollar amount of income or receipts.

Price Ceiling   A government-mandated maximum price above which legal trades cannot be made.

Price Discrimination   Occurs when the seller charges different prices for the product it sells and the price differences do not reflect cost differences.

Price Elasticity of Demand   A measure of the responsiveness of quantity demanded to changes in price.

Price Elasticity of Supply   Measures the responsiveness of quantity supplied to changes in price.

Price Floor   A government-mandated minimum price below which legal trades cannot be made.

Price Leadership Theory   In this theory of oligopoly, the dominant firm in the industry determines price, and all other firms take their price as given.

Price Searcher   A seller that has the ability to control to some degree the price of the product it sells.

Price Taker   A seller that does not have the ability to control the price of the product it sells; it takes the price determined in the market.

Producers' (Sellers') Surplus (PS)   The difference between the price sellers receive for a good and the minimum or lowest price for which they would have sold the good. PS = Price received − Minimum selling price.

Production Possibilities Frontier (PPF)   Represents the possible combinations of the two goods that can be produced in a certain period of time under the conditions of a given state of technology and fully employed resources.

(Production) Subsidy   A monetary payment by government to a producer of a good or service.

Productive Efficiency   The condition where the maximum output is produced with given resources and technology; The situation that exists when a firm produces its output at the lowest possible per-unit cost (lowest ATC).

Productive Inefficiency   The condition where less than the maximum output is produced with given resources and technology. Productive inefficiency implies that more of one good can be produced without any less of another good being produced.

Profit   The difference between total revenue and total cost.

Profit-Maximization Rule   Profit is maximized by producing the quantity of output at which $MR = MC$.

Public Choice   The branch of economics that deals with the application of economic principles and tools to public sector decision making.

Public Choice Theory of Regulation   Holds that regulators are seeking to do, and will do through regulation, what is in their best interest (specifically to enhance their power and the size and budget of their regulatory agencies).

Public Employee Union   A union whose membership is made up of individuals who work for the local, state, or federal government.

Public Franchise   A right granted to a firm by government that permits the firm to provide a particular good or service and excludes all others from doing the same.

Public Good   A good the consumption of which by one person does not reduce the consumption by another person—that is, a public good is characterized by nonrivalry in consumption. There are both excludable and nonexcludable public goods. An excludable public good is a good that while nonrivalrous in consumption can be denied to a person who does not pay for it. A nonexcludable public good is a good that is nonrivalrous in consumption and that cannot be denied to a person who does not pay for it.

Public Interest Theory of Regulation   Holds that regulators are seeking to do, and will do through regulation, what is in the best interest of the public or society at large.

Purchasing Power Parity (PPP) Theory   States that exchange rates between any two currencies will adjust to reflect changes in the relative price levels of the two countries.

Pure Economic Rent   A category of economic rent where the payment is to a factor that is in fixed supply, implying that it has zero opportunity costs.

Q

Quota   A legal limit on the amount of a good that may be imported.

R

Rational Ignorance   The state of not acquiring information because the costs of acquiring the information are greater than the benefits.

Rationing Device   A means for deciding who gets what of available resources and goods.

Real Interest Rate   The nominal interest rate minus the expected inflation rate. When the expected inflation rate is zero, the real interest rate equals the nominal interest rate.

Regulatory Lag   The time period between when a natural monopoly's costs change and when the regulatory agency adjusts prices for the natural monopoly.

Relative Price   The price of a good in terms of another good.

Rent Seeking   Actions of individuals and groups who spend resources to influence public policy in the hope of redistributing (transferring) income to themselves from others.

Residual claimant   Persons who share in the profits of a business firm.

Resource Allocative Efficiency   The situation that exists when firms produce the quantity of output at which price equals marginal cost: $P = MC$.

Revaluation   A government act that changes the exchange rate by raising the official price of a currency.

Rivalrous in Consumption   A good is rivalrous in consumption if its consumption by one person reduces its consumption by others.

Roundabout Method of Production The production of capital goods that enhance productive capabilities to ultimately bring about increased consumption.

S

Scarcity   The condition in which our wants are greater than the limited resources available to satisfy those wants.

Screening   The process used by employers to increase the probability of choosing "good" employees based on certain criteria.

Second-Degree Price Discrimination Occurs when the seller charges a uniform price per unit for one specific quantity, a lower price for an additional quantity, and so on.

Shirking   The behavior of a worker who is putting forth less than the agreed-to effort.

Short Run   A period of time in which some inputs in the production process are fixed.

Short-Run (Firm) Supply Curve The portion of the firm's marginal cost curve that lies above the average variable cost curve.

Short-Run Market (Industry) Supply Curve   The horizontal "addition" of all existing firms' short-run supply curves.

Shortage (Excess Demand)   A condition in which quantity demanded is greater than quantity supplied. Shortages occur only at prices below equilibrium price.

Slope   The ratio of the change in the variable on the vertical axis to the change in the variable on the horizontal axis.

Socially Optimal Amount (Output) An amount that takes into account and adjusts for all benefits (external and private) and all costs (external and private). The socially optimal amount is the amount at which $MSB = MSC$. Sometimes, the socially optimal amount is referred to as the efficient amount.

Special Drawing Right (SDR)   An international money, created by the IMF, in the form of bookkeeping entries; like gold and currencies, that can be used by nations to settle international accounts.

Special Interest Groups   Subsets of the general population that hold (usually) intense preferences for or against a particular government service, activity, or policy. Often, special interest groups gain from public policies that may not be in accord with the interests of the general public.

Stagflation   The simultaneous occurrence of high rates of inflation and unemployment.

Stock   A claim on the assets of a corporation that gives the purchaser a share of the corporation.

Store of Value   The ability of an item to hold value over time. A function of money.

Strike   The situation in which union employees refuse to work at a certain wage or under certain conditions.

Structural Deficit   The part of the budget deficit that would exist even if the economy were operating at full employment.

Structural Unemployment   Unemployment due to structural changes in the economy that eliminate some jobs and create other jobs for which the unemployed are unqualified.

Substitutes   Two goods that satisfy similar needs or desires. If two goods are substitutes, the demand for one rises as the price of the other rises (or the demand for one falls as the price of the other falls).

Sunk Cost   A cost incurred in the past that cannot be changed by current decisions and therefore cannot be recovered.

Supply   The willingness and ability of sellers to produce and offer to sell different quantities of a good at different prices during a specific time period.

Supply Schedule   The numerical tabulation of the quantity supplied of a good at different prices. A supply schedule is the numerical representation of the law of supply.

Surplus (Excess Supply)   A condition in which quantity supplied is greater than quantity demanded. Surpluses occur only at prices above equilibrium price.

T

Tariff   A tax on imports

Technology   The body of skills and knowledge concerning the use of resources in production. An advance in technology commonly refers to the ability to produce more output with a fixed amount of resources or the ability to produce the same output with fewer resources.

Terms of Trade   How much of one thing is given up for how much of something else.

Theory   An abstract representation of the real world designed with the intent to better understand the world.

Third-Degree Price Discrimination Occurs when the seller charges different prices in different markets or charges a different price to different segments of the buying population.

Tie-in Sale   A sale whereby one good can be purchased only if another good is also purchased.

Total Cost (TC)   The sum of fixed costs and variable costs.

Total Revenue (TR)   Price times quantity sold.

Total Surplus (TS)   The sum of consumers' surplus and producers' surplus. $TS = CS + PS$

Total Utility   The total satisfaction a person receives from consuming a particular quantity of a good.

Transaction Costs   The costs associated with the time and effort needed to search out, negotiate, and consummate an exchange.

Transfer Payment   A payment to a person that is not made in return for goods and services currently supplied.

Trust   A combination of firms that come together to act as a monopolist.

U

Undervaluation   A currency is undervalued if its price in terms of other currencies is below the equilibrium price.

Unemployment Rate   The percentage of the civilian force that is unemployed: Unemployment rate = Number of unemployed persons/Civilian labor force.

Union Shop   An organization in which a worker is not required to be a member of the union to be hired but must become a member within a certain period of time after being employed.

Unit Elastic Demand   The percentage change in quantity demanded is equal to the percentage change in price. Quantity demanded changes proportionately to price changes.

(Upward-Sloping) Supply Curve   The graphical representation of the law of supply.

Util   An artificial construct used to measure utility.

Utility   The satisfaction one receives from a good.

Value Marginal Product (VMP)   The price of the good multiplied by the marginal physical product of the factor: $VMP = P \times MPP$.

Variable Costs   Costs that vary with output; the costs associated with variable inputs.

Variable Input   An input whose quantity can be changed as output changes.

Veil of Ignorance   The imaginary veil or curtain behind which a person does not know his or her position in the income distribution.

Vertical Merger   A merger between companies in the same industry but at different stages of the production process.

Wage Discrimination   The situation that exists when individuals of equal ability and productivity (as measured by their contribution to output) are paid different wage rates.

X-Inefficiency   The increase in costs and organizational slack in a monopoly resulting from the lack of competitive pressure to push costs down to their lowest possible level.

Yield   Equal to the annual coupon payment divided by the price paid for the bond.

A

absolute income equality normative standard, 336–337
absolute prices, 53
accounting profit, 162
account representatives, 478
Adelman, Irma, 27
adverse selection, 381–382
advertising
  monopolistic competition and, 239
  perfect competition and, 207
advertising, elasticity and, 121
African Americans, poverty and, 339
"after the bell," 489
age, income distribution and, 327
agricultural price floors, supply and demand, 96–97
AIDS, antitrust and, 260, 279
airline industry
  deregulation and, 277–278, 279
  hub-and-spoke system of, 277
  supply and demand, 69, 82, 106
"air pocket stock," 489
Akerlof, George, 476
Alchian, Armen, 158
Aluminum Company of America (Alcoa), 215
Amazon, 189, 227
American Stock Exchange (AMEX), 473–474
antidumping, trade restrictions and, 420
antitrust issues, 260–282
  AIDS example, 260, 279
  antitrust law, defined, 261
    cases and actions, 266–268
    Celler-Kefauver Antimerger Act (1950), 262
    Clayton Act (1914), 261–262, 266
    Federal Trade Commission Act (1914), 262
    "hidden fee" economy and, 267
    mergers and, 265–266
    network monopolies, 269
    regulation and, 260, 271–278, 279
    Robinson-Patman Act (1936), 262
    Sherman Act (1890), 261, 270–271
    Sherman Act, civil action complaint, 270–271
    Thomas Edison and Hollywood example, 264
    trust, defined, 261
    unsettled policy, 262–265
    Wheeler-Lea Act (1938), 262
Apple Computer Corporation, 204–205
appreciation, 436

arbitrage, 225, 356
arms race, game theory and, 254
artificial rents, 354
asymmetric information
  adverse selection, 381–382, 381–383
  as cause of market failure, 380–381
    defined, 379
    in factor markets, 380
    as market failure cause, 380–381
    moral hazard, 383
    in product markets, 379–380
athletic scholarships, supply and demand, 97–99
attainable region, 35, 47
auction houses, price fixing and, 278
average fixed cost (AFC), 170
average-marginal rule, 171–174
average physical product, 168
average total cost (ATC), 170, 196–197
average variable cost (AVC), 170, 195–196, 199

B

bads, 2
Bailey, Martin, 371
balance of payments
  calculating, 432
    capital account, 431
    current account, 428–430
    defined, 427–428
    official reserve account, 431
    statistical discrepancy, 431–432
bar graphs, 21, 22
Barnes & Noble, 189
barriers, monopoly and, 214–215
barter, 345
"bear" market, 489
Becker, Gary, 27, 435
behavior, opportunity cost and, 5–6
behavioral economics, 140–144, 177–178, 182
benefits
  costs and, 6–7
    marginal benefits (MB), 8
    net benefits, maximizing, 9–10
Bezos, Jeff, 189
"big board," 489
"Big Mac index" (Economist), 443
"Bo Derek," 489
Boeing, 268
bonds, 471, 472, 482–486, 489–492
  components of, 482
    defined, 482
    how to read bond market page, 484–486

prices and yields, 483
  ratings of, 482–483
  types of, 483–484
Boston Tea Party, monopoly and, 215
bowed-outward production possibilities frontier (PPF), 33–34
British East India Company, 215
brokers, 478
Brooks, Diana, 278
Buchanan, James, 389, 404
Buddhism, 340
"bull" market, 489
bureaucrats, defined, 402–403
business, study of, 28
business firms
  corporate power and globalization, 465
    defined, 158
    globalization and, 459
    monopoly and, 219–220
    profit objective of, 160–163
    purpose of, 158–160
Business Week, 13, 28
buyers, demand of goods and, 58

C

calculators, for interest, 358
call option, 488–489
capital, 2
capital account, 431
capital account balance, 431
capital goods, interest and, 350
capture theory of regulation, 275
cars, interest and, 349
cartel theory, 215, 240–243, 319
cartel, defined, 240
  defined, 240
    New Year's resolution example, 242
"casino finance," 489
celebrities, advertising and, 121
Celler-Kefauver Antimerger Act (1950), 262
change in demand, 55–59
cheating
  cartel theory and, 242–243
    cost example, 157, 182–183
    fear of guilt example, 255–256
    Mafia example, 244
children, elasticity example, 124
China, 468
choices, 3–4. see also scarcity
Christie's, 278
churches, competition and, 191
cigarette tax, elasticity and, 118
cigars, utility and, 135
Cipla, 279

Chapter 1
What Economics Is About

What This Chapter Is About

This chapter is an introduction to economics. Economics is defined and a few of the important concepts in economics are discussed – such as scarcity, opportunity cost, and more. Also, this chapter introduces you to the economic way of thinking.

Key Concepts in the Chapter

    a.   good
    b.   bad
    c.   scarcity
    d.   opportunity cost
    e.   decisions made at the margin
    f.   efficiency
    g.   exchange or trade
    h.   positive and normative economics

- A **good** is anything that gives a person utility or satisfaction.
- A **bad** is anything that gives a person disutility or dissatisfaction.
- **Scarcity** is the condition under which people's wants (for goods) are greater than the resources available to satisfy those wants.
- **Opportunity cost** is the most highly valued opportunity or alternative forfeited when a choice is made.
- When we make **decisions at the margin**, we compare the marginal benefits and marginal costs of things.
- Efficiency exists when the marginal benefits of doing something equal the marginal costs of doing that something.
- **Exchange** or **trade** is the process of giving up one thing for something else.
- **Positive economics** deals with "what is," and **normative economics** deals with what someone thinks "should be."

Review Questions

1.   Is scarcity the condition under which people have infinite wants?

2.   What is the difference between a *good* and a *bad*?

3.   Give an example of when something is a good one day, and a bad some other day?

4.   What is the opportunity cost of your reading this study guide?

5.   If the opportunity cost of smoking cigarettes rises, fewer people will smoke. Why?

6.   What is a synonym (in economics) for the word *additional*?

7.   If Harriet is thinking of studying for one more hour, she considers the marginal benefits and marginal costs of studying for one more hour—not the total benefits and total costs. Why does she consider marginal benefits and costs and not total benefits and costs?

8.   In the text the author discussed the unintended effects of wearing seatbelts. Come up with an example of an unintended effect of something.

9.   What is the relationship between scarcity and choice? Between scarcity and opportunity cost?

10.   What is the relationship between thinking in terms of "what would have been" and opportunity cost?

11.   Is it possible to study too much? Explain your answer.

12.   What are the four categories of resources?

13.   Why do people enter into exchanges or trades?

Problems

1.   Draw a flow chart that shows the relationship between scarcity, choice, and opportunity cost.

2.   Jim is considering going to college. He knows there are benefits and costs to attending college. In the table below you will see various factors identified in the first column. Determine whether the factor relates to the cost of going to college or to the benefit of going to college. Next, identify whether the specified change in the factor raises or lowers the cost or benefit of going to college. If it raises the benefit of going to college, place an upward arrow ($\uparrow$) in the benefits column; if it lowers the benefit of going to college, place a downward arrow ($\downarrow$) in the benefits column. Do the same for the costs column. Finally, identify whether the change in the factor makes it more likely (Yes or No) Jim will go to college.

Factor	Benefits of attending college	Costs of attending college	More likely to go to college? Yes or No
Jim thought he would earn $20 an hour if he didn't go to college, but learns that he will earn $35 an hour instead.			
His friends are going to college and he likes being around his friends.			
The salary gap between college graduates and high school graduates has widened.			
Jim learns something about himself: he doesn't like to study.			
The college he is thinking about attending just opened a satellite campus near Jim's home.			
The economy has taken a downturn and it looks like there are very few jobs for high school graduates right now.			

3.   Identify each of the following questions as related to either a microeconomic or macroeconomic topic.

   a.   Why did that firm charge a higher price?

   b.   When will the economy slow down?

   c.   When will the unemployment rate fall?

   d.   Are interest rates rising?

   e.   How does that firm decide how many cars it will produce this year?

   f.   What is the price of a really fast computer?

   g.   Why did that restaurant go out of business?

4. There is an opportunity cost to everything you do. In the first column you will see an activity identified. In the second column, identify what you think the opportunity cost (for you) would be if you undertook that particular activity.

Activity	Opportunity Cost
Study one more hour each night	
Take a trip to someplace you have always wanted to visit	
Sit in the back of the room in one of your classes	
Talk up more in class	
Get a regular medical checkup	
Surf the Web more	

What Is Wrong?

In each of the statements below, something is wrong. Identify what is wrong in the space provided.

1. People have finite wants and infinite resources.

2. People prefer more bads to fewer bads.

3. Scarcity is an effect of competition.

4. The lower the opportunity cost of playing tennis, the less likely a person will play tennis.

5. Microeconomics is the branch of economics that deals with human behavior and choices as they relate to highly aggregate markets or the entire economy.

6. Positive economics is to normative economics as opinion is to truth.

7. Because there are rationing devices, there will always be scarcity.

8.   The four factors of production, or resources, are land, labor, capital, and profit.

9.   In a two-person exchange, one person is made better off while the other person is made worse off.

10.   If X is a good for Smith, it must then be a good for Jones too.

Multiple Choice
Circle the correct answer.

1. Economics is the science of
    a.   human relationships in an economic setting.
    b.   business and prices.
    c.   scarcity.
    d.   goods and services.

2. Scarcity exists
    a.   in only poor countries of the world.
    b.   in all countries of the world
    c.   only when society does not employ all its resources in an efficient way.
    d.   only when society produces too many frivolous or silly goods.

3. Which of the following statements is true?
    a.   Both a millionaire and a poor person must deal with scarcity.
    b.   People would have to make choices even if scarcity did not exist.
    c.   Scarcity is a relatively new problem in the world's history; it has not always existed.
    d.   It is likely that one day scarcity will no longer exist.

4. Which of the following statements is true?
    a.   Coca-Cola is a good for everyone, even someone who has an allergy to Coca-Cola.
    b.   If you pay someone to take X off your hands, then it is likely that X is a bad.
    c.   It is possible, but not likely, that someone can obtain both utility and disutility from a bad.
    d.   If there is more of good A than people want at zero price, then good A is an economic good.

5. Kristin Taylor had a safety inspection performed on her car last week and it passed with flying colors. How is this likely to affect her future driving behavior, compared to a situation in which cars did not get safety inspections at all?
    a.   She will probably drive faster, and the probability of having an accident is reduced.
    b.   She will probably drive slower, and the probability of having an accident is reduced.
    c.   She will probably drive faster, and the probability of having an accident is increased.
    d.   She will probably drive slower, and the probability of having an accident is increased.

6. Frank is 19 years old and is an actor in a soap opera, "One Life to Ruin." He earns $100,000 a year. Cassandra is also 19 years old and works in a local clothing store. She earns $9 an hour. Which of the two persons is more likely to attend college and for what reason?
    a.   Cassandra, because she is smarter.
    b.   Frank, because he has higher opportunity costs of attending college than Cassandra.
    c.   Cassandra, because she has lower opportunity costs of attending college than Frank.
    d.   Frank, because he earns a higher income than Cassandra.

7. Which of the following is an example of a *positive* statement?
    a. If you drop a quarter off the top of the Sears building in Chicago, it will fall to the ground.
    b. The minimum wage should be raised to eight dollars an hour.
    c. There is too much crime in the United States; something should be done about it.
    d. People should learn to get along with each other.

8. Which of the following topics is a microeconomics topic?
    a. the study of what influences the nation's unemployment rate
    b. the study of how changes in the nation's money supply affect the nation's output
    c. the study of prices in the automobile market
    d. the study of what affects the inflation rate

9. "Productive resources" include which of the following?
    a. land, labor, money, management
    b. land, labor, money, entrepreneurship
    c. land, labor, capital, entrepreneurship
    d. land, labor, natural resources, entrepreneurship

10. Efficiency exists if
    a. marginal benefits are greater than marginal costs.
    b. marginal costs are greater than marginal benefits.
    c. marginal costs equal zero.
    d. marginal costs equal marginal benefits.
    e. none of the above

True-False
Write a "T" or "F" after each statement.

11. A good is anything from which individuals receive utility. _____

12. If there is no explicit charge for a good, it is not a scarce good. _____

13. Scarcity implies that choices will be made. _____

14. The higher a person's opportunity cost of time, the more likely a person will stand in a long line to buy a ticket to a concert or some other event, *ceteris paribus.* _____

15. As economists use the term, a "good" is a tangible item that you can see and touch (rather than an intangible service). _____

Fill in the Blank
Write the correct word in the blank.

16. _____ is the branch of economics that deals with highly aggregated markets or the entire economy.

17. One more unit of something is the _____ unit.

18. A good that is used to produce other goods, yet is not a natural resource, is called a _____ good.

19. The person who organizes production in a firm and is responsible for recognizing new business opportunities is an _____ .

20. _____ is the process of giving up one thing for something else.

Chapter 2
Economic Activities: Producing and Trading

What This Chapter Is About
People do it everyday—produce goods and enter into trades. They might produce a desk, computer, or book. They might trade $10 for a book or $2 for a loaf of bread. This chapter is about both producing and trading.

Key Concepts in the Chapter
- a.   exchange
- b.   terms of exchange
- c.   transaction costs
- d.   comparative advantage
- e.   production possibilities frontier
- f.   efficiency
- g.   inefficiency

- **Exchange** is the process of trading one thing for another.
- The **terms of exchange** refer to how much of one thing is traded for how much of something else. For example, the terms of exchange may be $2,000 for one computer.
- **Transaction costs** are the costs associated with the time and effort needed to search out, negotiate, and consummate an exchange.
- **Comparative advantage** refers to the situation in which someone can produce a good at lower opportunity cost than someone else. For example, if Jones can produce good Z at lower cost than Smith, then Jones has a comparative advantage in the production of good Z.
- A **production possibilities frontier (PPF)** represents the possible combination of two goods that an economy can produce in a certain period of time, under the conditions of a given state of technology, no unemployed resources, and efficient production.
- **Efficiency** implies the impossibility of gains in one area without losses in another.
- **Inefficiency** implies the possibility of gains in one area without losses in another.

Review Questions

1.   José is thinking of buying a house. Is he in the *ex ante* or *ex post* position with respect to exchange?

2.   How is economic growth represented in the production possibilities frontier framework?

3. How are choice and opportunity cost represented in the production possibilities frontier framework?

4. Consumers prefer terms of exchange in their favor. What does this mean?

5. Are the transaction costs of buying a hamburger at a fast food restaurant higher or lower than the transaction costs of selling a house? Explain your answer.

6. Give an example of an exchange with a third-party negative effect.

7. Janet can produce either (a) 10 units of X and 20 units of Y, or (b) 20 units of X and 5 units of Y. What is the cost (to Janet) of producing one unit of X? One unit of Y?

8. Why does specialization and trade benefit people?

9. Why do people trade? What is the necessary condition for trade to take place?

10. Give an example that illustrates the law of increasing costs.

11. What does a straight-line production possibilities frontier (PPF) indicate about costs?

12. What does a bowed-outward (concave downward) PPF indicate about costs?

13. A country can be at either point A or B on its PPF. What does this fact have to do with the economic concept of *tradeoff*?

14. Identify two things that can shift a PPF outward (to the right).

    a.

    b.

15. Give an example of an advance in technology.

Problems

1. Vernon bought a hat for $40. Identify more favorable terms of exchange for Vernon.

2. Karen's maximum buying price is $400 for good X. Randy's minimum selling price is $350 for good X. Currently, Karen and Randy have to each pay $60 in transaction costs to buy and sell good X. If an entrepreneur charges both the buyer and the seller $5, what is the minimum reduction in transaction costs that that entrepreneur must bring about (for each person) before the trade will be actualized at a price of $370?

3. Can you draw a PPF for grades? Use the data (that follow) to draw a production possibilities frontier for grades.

Hours spent studying Sociology	Grade in Sociology	Hours spent studying Economics	Grade in Economics
6	90	0	60
5	85	1	65
4	80	2	70
3	75	3	75
2	70	4	80
1	65	5	85
0	60	6	90

Grade in
Sociology

Grade in Economics

4. Using the data in the previous question, what is the opportunity cost of earning a 65 instead of a 60 in Economics?

5. Identify the points on the PPF that are efficient.

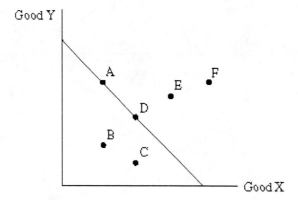

6. Which points on the PPF (in the previous question) are inefficient?

7. Which points on the PPF (in question 5) are unattainable?

8. Suppose that point C, with 100 units of good X and 200 units of good Y, is an efficient point. Could point D, with 75 units of good X and 250 units of good Y, also be an efficient point? Explain your answer.

9. Within a PPF framework, diagrammatically represent the effect of a war that destroys people and property.

10. Within a PPF framework, diagrammatically represent the effect of an advance in technology.

What Is Wrong?
In each of the statements below, something is wrong. Identify what is wrong in the space provided.

1. If costs are increasing, the PPF is a straight (downward-sloping) line.

2. If Jones can produce either (a) 100 units of X and 100 units of Y or (b) 200 units of X and zero units of Y, then he has a comparative advantage in the production of Y.

3. The following PPF represents a two-for-one opportunity cost of apples.

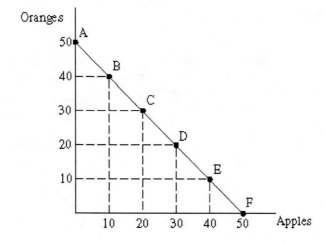

4.   There are probably more unemployed resources at point A than at point D.

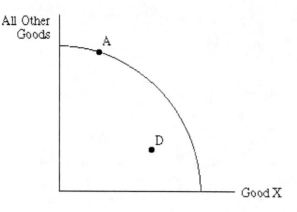

5.   Efficiency implies the possibility of gains in one area without losses in another area.

6.   If Georgina reads one more book, she will have to give up doing something else. This shows that Georgina is inefficient.

7.   If Bobby can produce either (a) 100 units of good X and 50 units of good Y, or (b) 25 units of good X and 80 units of good Y, then the cost of 1 unit of good X is 1.5 units of good Y.

8.   John says, "I bought this sweater yesterday and I think I got a bad deal." It follows that in the *ex ante* position John thought he would be better off with the sweater than with the money he paid for it, but in the *ex post* position he prefers the money to the sweater.

Multiple Choice
Circle the correct answer.

1.   Which of the following statements is true?
    a.   The production possibilities frontier is always bowed outward.
    b.   The production possibilities frontier is usually bowed outward.
    c.   The production possibilities frontier is never bowed outward.
    d.   The production possibilities frontier is usually a straight line.

2. Which of the following statements is false?
    a. A straight-line production possibilities frontier represents increasing costs.
    b. A bowed outward production possibilities frontier represents constant costs.
    c. An efficient point is located on the production possibilities frontier.
    d. a and b

3. If there is always a constant tradeoff between goods A and B, the production possibilities frontier between A and B is
    a. circular.
    b. a downward-sloping curve bowed toward the origin.
    c. a downward-sloping straight line.
    d. a downward-sloping straight line that is broken at one point.

4. Consider two points on the production possibilities frontier: point X, at which there are 100 cars and 78 trucks, and point Y, at which there are 90 cars and 70 trucks. If the economy is currently at point X, the opportunity cost of moving to point Y is
    a. 12 cars.
    b. 1 truck.
    c. 10 cars.
    d. 79 trucks.
    e. none of the above

5. If it is possible to increase production of one good without getting less of another, then currently the economy is
    a. operating efficiently.
    b. sluggish.
    c. operating inefficiently.
    d. operating at technological inferiority.

6. The production possibilities frontier represents the possible combinations of two goods that an economy can produce
    a. in a certain time.
    b. in a certain time, under the condition of a given state of resources.
    c. given that there are not unemployed resources.
    d. under the condition of efficient production.
    e. None of the answers is complete enough.

7. When the economy exhibits inefficiency, it is not producing the
    a. maximum output with the available resources and technology.
    b. minimum output with minimum resources and technology.
    c. the goods and services consumers wish to buy.
    d. b and c

8. When Beverly trades $60 for good X, economists assume that she is trading something
    a. of less value to her for something of more value to her.
    b. of more value to her for something of less value to her.
    c. that gives her less utility for something that gives her more utility.
    d. a and c
    e. none of the above

9. The _____ refer(s) to how much of one thing is traded for how much of something else.
    a. exchange process
    b. terms of exchange
    c. duality prices
    d. non-monetary pricing process
    e. double pricing process

10. Transaction costs are
    a.   the costs associated with the time and effort needed to search out, negotiate, and consummate an exchange.
    b.   the costs a consumer pays in the *ex ante* position.
    c.   the costs a seller pays in the *ex post* position.
    d.   identical to the terms of exchange.
    e.   always higher for buyers than sellers.

11. If Mark and Bob are not currently trading $10 for a book, it may be because
    a.   transaction costs are too high.
    b.   transaction costs are too low.
    c.   at least one of the two individuals does not think he would be made better off by the trade.
    d.   both individuals think they will be made worse off by the trade.
    e.   a, c, and d

12. If Sean can bake bread at a lower cost than Jason, and Jason can produce paintings at a lower cost then Sean, it follows that
    a.   Sean has a comparative advantage in paintings and Jason has a comparative advantage in baking bread.
    b.   Both Sean and Jason have a comparative advantage in baking bread.
    c.   Both Sean and Jason have a comparative advantage in producing paintings.
    c.   Sean has a comparative advantage in baking bread and Jason has a comparative advantage in producing paintings.
    d.   There is not enough information to answer the question.

13. Vernon can produce the following combinations of X and Y: 100X and 20Y, 50X and 30Y, or 0X or 40Y. The opportunity cost of one unit of Y for Vernon is
    a.   five units of Y.
    b.   two units of Y.
    c.   three units of Y.
    d.   one-half unit of Y.
    e.   none of the above

True-False
Write a "T" or "F" after each statement.

14. Because scarcity exists, individuals and societies must make choices. ____

15. If the production of good X comes in terms of increasing costs of good Y, then the production possibilities frontier between the two goods is a downward-sloping straight line. ____

16. Economic growth shifts the production possibilities frontier inward. ____

17. Productive efficiency is diagrammatically represented as a point on the production possibilities frontier. ____

18. Without scarcity, there would be no production possibilities frontier. ____

Fill in the Blank

Write the correct word in the blank.

19. _____ implies it is possible to obtain gains in one area without losses in another.

20. _____ implies it is impossible to obtain gains in one area without losses in another.

21. At point A on a production possibilities frontier there are 50 apples and 60 oranges. At point B there are 49 apples and 68 oranges. If the economy is currently at point B, the opportunity cost of moving to point A is _____oranges.

22. The higher the _____ _____ of making an exchange, the less likely the exchange will be made.

23. The higher the _____ _____ of doing X, the less likely X will be done.

24. A point on a PPF is considered to represent a combination of two goods that is _____.

25. A _____ _____ PPF represents constant costs.

Chapter 3
Supply and Demand: Theory

What This Chapter Is About
This chapter is about markets. A market has two sides—a demand side and a supply side. The chapter first discusses demand, then supply, then it puts both sides of the market together and discusses the price and quantity of goods.

Key Concepts in the Chapter
- a. demand
- b. law of demand
- c. supply
- d. law of supply
- e. equilibrium price
- f. shortage
- g. surplus
- h. consumers' surplus
- i. producers' surplus

- **Demand** is the willingness and ability to buy different quantities of a good at different prices over some period of time. Keep in mind that if a person doesn't have both the willingness and ability to buy a good, then there is no demand.
- The **law of demand** states that price and quantity demanded are inversely related, *ceteris paribus*. This means that as price rises, quantity demanded falls, and as price falls, quantity demanded rises, *ceteris paribus*.
- **Supply** is the willingness and ability to produce and offer to sell different quantities of a good at different prices over some period of time.
- The **law of supply** states that price and quantity supplied are directly related, *ceteris paribus*. This means that as price rises, quantity supplied rises, and as price falls, quantity supplied falls, *ceteris paribus*.
- **Equilibrium price** is the price at which the quantity demanded of a good equals the quantity supplied. For example, if, at $40, the quantity supplied of good X is 100 units, and quantity demanded of good X is also 100 units, then $40 is the equilibrium price.
- **Equilibrium quantity** is the quantity that corresponds to equilibrium price. At equilibrium, quantity demanded = quantity supplied = equilibrium quantity.
- A **shortage** exists in a market if quantity demanded is greater than quantity supplied. If buyers want to buy 100 units of good X, and sellers only want to sell 30 units, then there is a shortage.
- A **surplus** exists in a market if quantity supplied is greater than quantity demanded. If buyers want to buy 100 units of good X, and sellers want to sell 300 units, then there is a surplus.
- **Consumers' surplus** is the difference between the maximum buying price and price paid. For example, if Smith is willing to pay a maximum of $40 for good X, and he only has to pay $10, then the difference, or $30, is consumers' surplus.
- **Producers' surplus** is the difference between the price paid and the minimum selling price. For example, if Jones is willing to sell good X for $10, but is paid $50, then the difference, or $40, is producers' surplus.

Review Questions

1.   What does the law of demand state?

2. What does it mean to say that price and quantity demanded are inversely related?

3. What is quantity demanded?

4. How does quantity demanded differ from demand?

5. Demand is a function of five factors. Stated differently, if there is a change in any of these five factors, demand will either increase or decrease. What are these five factors?

   a.

   b.

   c.

   d.

   e.

6. If demand for a good increases, will the demand curve (that represents the good) shift to the right or to the left?

7. If demand for a good decreases, will the demand curve (that represents the good) shift to the right or to the left?

8. What is quantity supplied?

9. If a supply curve is vertical, what does this mean?

10. If a supply curve is upward-sloping, what does this mean?

11. Supply is a function of six factors. Stated differently, if there is a change in any of these six factors, supply will either increase or decrease. What are these six factors?

    a.

    b.

    c.

    d.

    e.

    f.

12. If the supply of a good increases, will the supply curve (that represents the good) shift to the right or to the left?

13. If the supply of a good decreases, will the supply curve (that represents the good) shift to the right or to the left?

14. Consider the standard supply and demand diagram. The demand curve is downward-sloping and the supply curve is upward-sloping.

    What is on the horizontal axis?

    What is on the vertical axis?

15. What is the difference between the relative price of a good and the absolute price of a good?

16. Demand rises and supply is constant. What happens to equilibrium price and quantity?

17. Supply rises and demand is constant. What happens to equilibrium price and quantity?

18. Demand rises by more than supply rises. What happens to equilibrium price and quantity?

19. Supply falls by more than demand rises. What happens to equilibrium price and quantity?

20. If price rises, what happens to consumers' surplus?

Problems

1. There are many factors that can directly affect supply and demand and indirectly affect price and quantity. In the first column we identify a change in a given factor. How does the change in the factor affect supply or demand? How does it affect price and quantity? Draw an upward arrow (↑) in the demand column if demand rises and a downward arrow (↓) if demand falls. The same holds for supply, equilibrium price, and equilibrium quantity.

Factor	Demand	Supply	Equilibrium Price	Equilibrium Quantity
Price of a substitute rises				
Price of a complement falls				
Income rises (normal good)				
Income falls (inferior good)				
Price of relevant resource rises				
Technology advances				
Quota				
Number of buyers rises				
Number of sellers rises				
Buyers expect higher price				
Sellers expect higher price				
Tax on production				
Preferences become more favorable with respect to the good				

2.   Draw a rise in demand that is greater than a rise in supply.

3.   Draw a fall in supply that is greater than an increase in demand.

4.   What area(s) does consumers' surplus equal at 100 units?

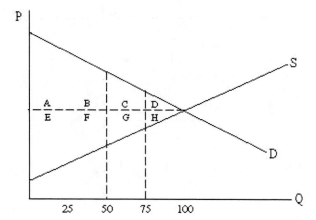

5. What area(s) does producers' surplus equal at equilibrium quantity?

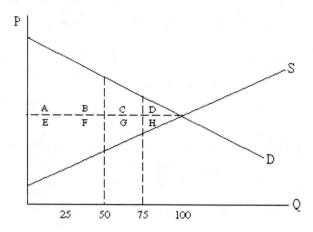

6. What is the shortage equal to at a price ceiling of $6?

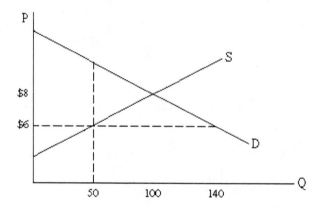

7. What is the surplus equal to at a price floor of $10?

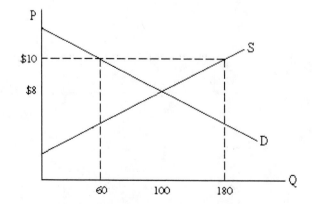

8. There are two buyers in a market, John and Mary. Below you see the quantity demanded for each at various prices. What is the quantity demanded (on the market demand curve) at each price specified? Write in the various quantities demanded in the spaces provided in the table.

Price	Quantity demanded by John	Quantity demanded by Mary	Quantity demanded (market demand)
$10	100	130	
$12	80	120	
$14	50	100	

9. If the price ceiling for good X is $4, and the maximum buying price for good X is $10, what is the highest price for a good that is "tied" to good X (as in a tie-in sale)?

10. Give an example that illustrates the law of diminishing marginal utility.

What Is Wrong?
In each of the statements below, something is wrong. Identify what is wrong in the space provided.

1. If the price of a good rises, the demand for the good will fall.

2. Consumers' surplus is equal to the minimum selling price minus the price paid.

3. As income rises, demand for a normal good rises; as income falls, demand for an inferior good falls.

4. The supply curve for Picasso paintings is upward-sloping.

5. As price rises, supply rises; as price falls, supply falls.

6. Quantity demanded is greater than supply when there is a shortage.

7. If supply rises, and demand is constant, equilibrium price rises and equilibrium quantity rises.

8. The law of diminishing marginal utility states that as a consumer consumes additional units of a good, each successive unit gives him or her more utility than the previous unit.

9. According to the law of demand, as the price of a good rises, the quantity demanded of the good rises, *ceteris paribus*.

Multiple Choice
Circle the correct answer.

1. The law of demand states that
    a. price and demand are inversely related, *ceteris paribus*.
    b. price and demand are directly related, *ceteris paribus*.
    c. price and quantity demanded are directly related, *ceteris paribus*.
    d. price and quantity demanded are inversely related, *ceteris paribus*.

2. Which of the following persons would be most likely to prefer first-come-first-served (FCFS) as a rationing device?
    a. A person who has just returned from visiting a busy city.
    b. A person who has just returned from visiting a small town.
    c. A person with low opportunity cost of time.
    d. A person with high opportunity cost of time.

3. At a price ceiling (below equilibrium price),
    a. there is a surplus.
    b. quantity supplied is greater than quantity demanded.
    c. quantity demanded equals quantity supplied.
    d. supply equals demand.
    e. quantity demanded is greater than quantity supplied.

4. Which of the following statements is true?
    a. A demand schedule is the same thing as a demand curve.
    b. A downward-sloping demand curve is the graphical representation of the law of demand.
    c. Quantity demanded is a relationship between price and demand.
    d. Quantity demanded is the same as demand.

5. Because of a price ceiling on light bulbs, the quantity demanded of light bulbs exceeds the quantity supplied. The owner of the light bulbs decided to sell them on a first-come-first-served basis. This is an example of a
   a. surplus.
   b. tie-in sale.
   c. nonprice rationing device.
   d. black market.
   e. none of the above.

6. A neutral good is a good
   a. the demand for which does not change as income falls.
   b. the demand for which does not change as income rises.
   c. the demand for which rises as income falls.
   d. the demand for which falls as income rises.
   e. a and b.

7. If the absolute price of good X is $600 and the absolute price of good Y is $400, then the relative price of good Y is
   a. 2 units of X.
   b. 2/3 unit of X.
   c. 1-1/3 unit of X.
   d. 1-1/2 unit of X.
   e. none of the above.

8. If an increase in income leads to an increase in the demand for sausage, then sausage is
   a. an essential good.
   b. a normal good.
   c. a luxury good.
   d. a discretionary good.

9. Which of the following can shift the demand curve rightward?
   a. an increase in income
   b. an increase in the price of a substitute good
   c. an increase in the price of a complementary good
   d. all of the above
   e. a and b

10. Which of the following cannot increase the demand for good X?
    a. an increase in income
    b. a decrease in the price of good X
    c. an increase in the price of a substitute good
    d. more buyers
    e. a change in preferences in favor of good X

11. The law of supply states that price and quantity supplied are
    a. directly related.
    b. inversely related.
    c. inversely related, *ceteris paribus*.
    d. directly related, *ceteris paribus*.

12. A change in the quantity supplied of a good is directly brought about by a
    a. change in the good's own price.
    b. decrease in income.
    c. technological advance.
    d. fall in the price of resources needed to produce the good.
    e. none of the above.

13. Five dollars is the equilibrium price for good Z. At a price of $2, there is
    a.   a shortage.
    b.   surplus.
    c.   excess supply.
    d.   aggregate demand.

14. If supply rises by a greater amount than demand rises,
    a.   equilibrium price rises and equilibrium quantity falls.
    b.   equilibrium price falls and equilibrium quantity falls.
    c.   equilibrium price rises and equilibrium quantity rises.
    d.   equilibrium price falls and equilibrium quantity rises.

15. If supply rises and demand is constant,
    a.   equilibrium price rises and equilibrium quantity falls.
    b.   equilibrium price falls and equilibrium quantity falls.
    c.   equilibrium price rises and equilibrium quantity rises.
    d.   equilibrium price falls and equilibrium quantity rises.

True-False
Write a "T" or "F" after each statement.

16. One of the effects of a price ceiling is that quantity supplied is greater than quantity demanded. ____

17. Demand is more important to the determination of market price than supply. ____

18. At the equilibrium price for good X, good X is scarce. ____

19. "Supply" is a specific amount of a good, such as 50 units of good Y. ____

20. There is a tendency for price to rise when the quantity demanded of a good is greater than the quantity supplied. ____

Fill in the Blank
Write the correct word in the blank.

21. As price rises, quantity demanded _____ and quantity supplied _____.

22. A _____ is any arrangement by which people exchange goods and services.

23. If Matt's demand for motorcycles rises as his income falls, then motorcycles are a(n)
    _____ good for Matt.

24. If demand rises more than supply falls, then equilibrium quantity _____.

25. At equilibrium, the quantity demanded of a good _____ the quantity supplied of the good.

26. Suppose you live in New York City and are required to rent the furniture in an apartment before you can rent the apartment. This is called a _____ - _____ sale.

Chapter 4
Supply and Demand: Practice

What This Chapter Is About
In the last chapter you learned the basic theory of supply and demand. You learned what a demand curve is, what factors will shift it right and left, what a supply curve is, what factors will shift it right and left, and so on. The theory of supply and demand is worth little unless you can apply it. That is what we do in this chapter. We present a series of applications of supply and demand.

Key Concepts in the Chapter
    a.   law of demand
    b.   law of supply
    c.   nonprice rationing device
    d.   minimum wage
    e.   price floor
    f.   price ceiling

- The **law of demand** states that price and quantity demanded are inversely related, *ceteris paribus*.
- The **law of supply** states that price and quantity supplied are directly related, *ceteris paribus*.
- Just as price can serve as a rationing device, so can other things. These other things we call **nonprice rationing devices**. First-come-first-served (FCFS) is a nonprice rationing device.
- The **minimum wage** is the lowest wage a worker can be paid. The minimum wage is an example of a price floor.
- The **price floor** is a government-mandated minimum price below which legal trades cannot be made.
- A **price ceiling** is a government-mandated maximum price above which legal trades cannot be made.

Review Questions

1. The tuition students pay at University X (T_1) is lower than the equilibrium tuition (T_E). If the tuition students pay remains constant, and demand to attend University X rises, what do you predict will happen to the requirements for admission? Explain your answer.

2. "If marijuana is legalized, the price of marijuana will fall." What does this statement assume about the supply of and demand for marijuana after legalization?

3. How would kidneys (for transplants) be rationed in a free market?

4. The recording industry files suit against hundreds of persons who download music (without paying). Explain this action in terms of a supply-and-demand framework.

5. How can the pricing scheme that a college chooses to allocate student parking spots have anything to do with whether or not a student is late to class?

6. There is freeway congestion on Interstate 5 at 8 a.m. on Monday morning. What are three solutions to the problem of freeway congestion at this time?

7. Why are gold prices the same everywhere?

8. Will patients pay more for health care if they have the right to sue their provider than if they don't have the right to sue? Explain your answer.

9. In the text it was argued that people pay for good weather. How do they pay for good weather?

10. Why do people pay a tip to be seated at many shows in Las Vegas, but do not pay a tip to be seated at a major league baseball game?

11. If the Olympics are being viewed on Channel 9, then why will Channel 11 be more likely to place a rerun on the schedule (opposite the Olympics) than a new episode of a television show?

12. Who feeds Cleveland?

Problems

1. Use the law of demand to explain why Yvonne loses her temper with her mother but not with her father.

2. Older people tend to drive more slowly than younger people. For example, a 68-year-old retired person may drive more slowly than a working 32-year-old person. Some people say this is because as people age, their reflexes slow down, their eyesight becomes less clear, and so on. All this may be true. Still, might there be an explanation that has to do with the price of driving? If so, what is this explanation?

3. Suppose the equilibrium tuition at college X is $2,000 a semester, but students only pay $800 a semester. The state taxpayers pay the $1,200 difference. Do you think professors will teach differently knowing their students paid a below-equilibrium tuition instead of the equilibrium tuition? Why or why not?

4. Richard Posner states, "The law of demand doesn't operate just on goods with explicit prices. Unpopular teachers sometimes try to increase enrollment by raising the average grade of the students in their courses, thereby reducing the price of the course to the student." In other words, unpopular teachers give away grades, thus becoming more popular. Do you think the same holds, with necessary changes, for unpopular people? Do unpopular people try to change the price of being around them? Or are they unpopular because the price they charge to be around them is too high?

5. Under what condition will the decriminalization of marijuana lead to an unchanged price for marijuana?

6. Some people argue that an increase in the minimum wage will lead to a large cutback in the number of unskilled workers employed, while others argue that it will lead to only a small cutback in the number of unskilled workers employed. Are the two groups of people arguing over a change in direction or a change in magnitude?

7. "The same number of kidneys will be forthcoming for transplants no matter what the price paid for a kidney." For this statement to be true, what must the supply curve of kidneys look like?

8. Why does a candy bar sell for the same price (or nearly the same price) everywhere in the country, but houses do not?

9. Jones has tried to sell his car for six months. No buyers. Does Jones have a really bad car that no one wants to buy?

10. "Professors in economics, sociology, and biology all lecture, grade papers, meet with students, and so on. It follows, then, that economists and sociologists should be paid the same dollar salary." What does the person who makes this statement forget, overlook, or ignore?

What May Have Been Overlooked?
In each of the statements below, something may have been overlooked or ignored. Identify what may have been overlooked or ignored.

1. The higher the demand for something, the greater the quantity demanded.

2. I think how I behave is independent of the setting that I am in. I act the same way no matter what the setting.

3. If there were no flea markets or garage sales (where people can buy old furniture), new furniture companies would sell more (new) furniture.

4. The rock band has the best interest of its fans in mind. It knows it can charge $80 a ticket, but it charges only $20 a ticket so that its fans won't have to pay so much.

5. If my university doesn't charge for student parking, then I am definitely better off than I would be if it did charge for student parking.

6. The tuition at Harvard is very high, so Harvard must be charging the equilibrium tuition to students. Still, Harvard uses such things as GPA, SAT and ACT scores for admission purposes. It must be wrong that these nonprice rationing devices (GPA, etc.) are only used by colleges and universities that charge below-equilibrium tuition.

7. If a good doesn't have a money price, it has no price at all.

Multiple Choice
Circle the correct answer.

1. There is no toll charge to drive on freeway A. If there is freeway congestion at 9 a.m., there will be greater freeway congestion at 11 a.m. if
    a. the demand to drive on the freeway is the same at both times.
    b. the demand to drive on the freeway at 11 a.m. is less than the demand to drive on the freeway at 9 a.m.
    c. the demand to drive on the freeway at 9 a.m. is greater than the demand to drive on the freeway at 11 a.m.
    d. fewer people carpool at 11 a.m. than at 9 a.m.
    e. none of the above

2. If goods are not rationed according to price, it follows that
    a. they won't get rationed at all.
    b. something will ration the goods.
    c. first-come-first-served will necessarily be the rationing device.
    d. there will be surpluses in the market.
    e. none of the above

3. Market X can be divided into two submarkets, A and B. The supply in each submarket is the same, but
    the demand in A is greater than the demand in B. If submarket B is in equilibrium, it follows that
    a. A is in equilibrium.
    b. there is a shortage in A.
    c. there is a surplus in A.
    d. there is a shortage in B only if there is a surplus in A.
    e. none of the above

4. The demand to attend a certain college is represented by a downward-sloping demand curve. The
    supply of spots at the college is represented by a vertical supply curve. At the tuition that students are
    charged, there is a shortage of spots at the college. If the demand to attend the college falls, but the
    tuition stays constant, if follow that the
    a. GPA required to attend the college will probably rise.
    b. GPA required to attend the college will probably fall.
    c. SAT score required to attend the college will probably not change.
    d. a and c
    e. There is not enough information to answer the question.

5. There are two groups of workers, A and B, who are equally productive. Currently, employers
    discriminate against workers in group B. It follows that
    a. the demand for workers in group B is higher than the demand for workers in group A.
    b. the demand for workers in groups A and B is the same.
    c. the demand for workers in group A is higher than the demand for workers in group B.
    d. There is not enough information to answer the question.

6. If the minimum wage is the same as the equilibrium wage, then
    a. there will be a shortage of labor.
    b. there will be a surplus of labor.
    c. quantity demanded of labor will equal quantity supplied of labor.
    d. fewer people will be working than if the minimum wage were lower than the equilibrium wage.
    e. none of the above

7. If there is a price ceiling in the kidney (available for transplant) market , and the price ceiling is lower
    than the equilibrium price, it follows that
    a. the supply of kidneys will be vertical.
    b. the quantity demanded of kidneys will be greater than it would be at equilibrium price.
    c. the quantity demanded of kidneys will be smaller than it would be at equilibrium price.
    d. a and b
    e. a and c

8. The recording industry runs a television ad showing all the people in the industry that are hurt by
    music piracy. This is an attempt to:
    a. raise the price of music piracy.
    b. lower the demand for music piracy.
    c. lower the quantity supplied of songs.
    d. raise the demand for music piracy.
    e. none of the above

9. A seller's minimum price for providing a good rises. It follows that
    a. the supply curve does not change.
    b. the supply curve shifts upward and to the left.
    c. the supply curve shifts downward and to the right.
    d. equilibrium price will end up falling.
    e. b and d

10. The supply for sociologists and economists is the same, but the demand for sociologists is higher. If both sociologists and economists are paid the same salary, it follows that
    a. there is a shortage of sociologists.
    b. there is a surplus of economists.
    c. there is neither a shortage of, nor surplus of, sociologists or economists.
    d. a and b
    e. There is not enough information to answer the question.

11. If there is freeway congestion at 8 a.m., we can reduce (or eliminate) the congestion by
    a. building more freeways.
    b. raising the price to drive on the freeway at 8 a.m.
    c. giving people an incentive to carpool
    d. a and b
    e. a, b, and c

12. If parking spots on campus were auctioned to the highest bidder,
    a. the closest spots to buildings would probably fetch the highest prices.
    b. the people with the lowest time costs would park the closest to the buildings.
    c. there would always be shortages.
    d. a and b
    e. a, b, and c

13. The university offers "free" seat cushions to any football fan that will arrive at least an hour before the game starts. It is correct to say that these cushions are offered at
    a. zero price.
    b. zero money price.
    c. zero nominal price.
    d. either a or b.
    e. none of the above

14. Aisle seats on commercial airplanes are priced the same as window seats. If the demand for aisle seats is greater than the demand for window seats, the supply of each kind of seat is the same, and the window-seat market is in equilibrium, it follows that
    a. the aisle-seat market is in equilibrium, too.
    b. there is a shortage of aisle seats.
    c. there is a surplus of aisle seats.
    d. There is not enough information to answer the question.

15. The price of speeding (on a highway) is equal to the price of a speeding ticket times the probability of being caught speeding. If the demand curve for speeding is downward-sloping, it follows that
    a. a higher probability of getting caught speeding will reduce speeding.
    b. a higher ticket price will reduce speeding
    c. a lower ticket price combined with a higher probability of getting caught speeding will reduce speeding.
    d. a and b.
    e. a, b, and c

True–False
Write a "T" or "F" after each statement.

16. The higher the demand to attend a given college or university, the higher its equilibrium tuition, *ceteris paribus*. ____

17. If there is a price ceiling in the kidney market, and the price ceiling is below the equilibrium price for a kidney, there will be a shortage of kidneys available for transplant. ____

18. If both A and B are bicycles, but A can be resold and B cannot, then the demand for A is likely to be higher than the demand for B, *ceteris paribus*. ____

19. Law 1 gives tenants three months to vacate an apartment, and Law 2 gives tenants six months. Apartment rent is likely to be higher under Law 1. ____

20. The price of pencils is more likely to be the same everywhere than the price of houses. ____

Fill in the Blank
Write the correct word in the blank.

21. At a given price, the greater demand is, the greater _____ _____ is.

22. If there is good weather in City X and bad weather in City Y, and everything is the same about the two cities except the weather, the demand to live in City X will be _____ than the demand to live in City Y.

23. First-come-first-served is a _____ _____ device.

24. NCAA rules often end up raising a colleges _____ _____ signing a college athlete.

25. John earns $100 an hour and Bill earns $20 an hour. If it takes time to make friends, then the _____ price of friendship is higher and, *ceteris paribus*, _____ will make more friends.

Chapter 5
Elasticity

What This Chapter Is About

Elasticity is one of the most important topics in economics. There are different types of elasticity—price elasticity of demand, cross elasticity of demand, income elasticity of demand, and price elasticity of supply. All four of these concepts are discussed in this chapter.

Key Concepts in the Chapter
    a.   price elasticity of demand
    b.   cross elasticity of demand
    c.   income elasticity of demand
    d.   price elasticity of supply

- **Price elasticity of demand** measures the responsiveness in quantity demanded to a change in price.
- **Cross elasticity of demand** measures the responsiveness in quantity demanded of one good to a change in price of another good.
- **Income elasticity of demand** measures the responsiveness in quantity demanded to a change in income.
- **Price elasticity of supply** measures the responsiveness in quantity supplied to a change in price.

Review Questions

1.   What is price elasticity of demand?

2.   What is the relationship between price elasticity of demand and the number of substitutes for a good?

3.   If a good has many substitutes, does it follow that demand for the good is elastic?

4. What is the relationship between time (since a change in price) and price elasticity of demand?

5. What is the relationship between the percentage of one's budget spent on a good and price elasticity of demand?

6. What does cross elasticity of demand measure?

7. What does it mean if a good is income inelastic?

8. What is price elasticity of supply?

Problems

1. Fill in the blanks in the table.

Price and quantity demanded at point A	Price and quantity demanded at point B	Price elasticity of demand is equal to	Is demand (elastic, unit elastic, or inelastic)?
$10 100	$8 140		
$8 200	$15 120		
$7 40	$10 33		

2. Fill in the blanks in the table.

Price elasticity of demand is	Change	Price elasticity of demand (rises, falls, remains unchanged)
0.34	more substitutes for the good	
1.99	more time passes since change in price	
2.20	smaller percentage of one's budget spent on the good	

3. Fill in the blanks in the table.

Demand is	Price (rises, falls)	Total revenue (rises, falls, remains unchanged)
elastic	falls	
inelastic	rises	
unit elastic	rises	
inelastic	falls	
elastic	rises	

4. Fill in the blanks in the table.

Price of good X (rises, falls)	Quantity demanded of good Y (rises, falls)	Cross elasticity of demand is	The two goods, X and Y, are (substitutes, complements)
rises by 10 percent	falls by 5 percent		
falls by 20 percent	rises by 4 percent		
rises by 8 percent	rises by 5 percent		

5. Fill in the blanks in the table.

Income (rises, falls)	Quantity demanded (rises, falls)	Income elasticity of demand is
rises by 20 percent	rises by 10 percent	
falls by 10 percent	falls by 15 percent	
rises by 5 percent	rises by 20 percent	

6. Fill in the blanks in the table.

Price (rises, falls)	Quantity supplied (rises, falls)	Is supply (elastic, inelastic, unit elastic)?
rises 3 percent	rises 4 percent	
rises 1 percent	rises 6 percent	
falls 20 percent	falls 10 percent	

7. Fill in the blanks in the table.

Initial equilibrium price and quantity	New equilibrium price and quantity (after $1 tax has been placed on supplier)	Percentage of the tax paid by the seller in terms of a higher price	Percentage of the tax paid by the seller in terms of a lower price kept
$40 100	$40.44 90		
$9 87	$9.57 80		
$10 200	$10.76 150		

What Is the Question?
Identify the question for each of the answers that follow.

1. Measures the responsiveness of quantity demanded given a change in price.

2. Price and total revenue are directly related.

3. Quantity demanded changes by 20 percent if price changes by 10 percent.

4.   There is no change in quantity demanded as price changes.

5.   The number of substitutes, the percentage of one's budget spent on the good, time (since the change in price), and luxury vs. necessity.

6.   Price of one good rises and quantity demanded for another good rises.

What Is Wrong?
In each of the statements that follow, something is wrong. Identify what is wrong in the space provided.

1.   If price rises, and total revenue falls, then demand is inelastic.

2.   The elasticity coefficient is greater than 1 for a good that is income inelastic.

3.   Cars have more substitutes than Ford cars.

4.   As we move down a demand curve, price elasticity of demand rises.

5.   For inelastic demand, quantity demanded changes proportionately more than price changes.

6. A perfectly inelastic demand curve can be downward-sloping.

7. The elasticity coefficient is greater than zero for goods that are complements.

8. If demand is inelastic, buyers pay the full tax that is placed on sellers.

9. If income elasticity of demand is 1.24, it means that for every 1 percent change in income there is a 1.24 percent change in price.

10. Price elasticity of supply measures the responsiveness of quantity supplied to changes in income.

Multiple Choice
Circle the correct answer.

1. In general, elasticity deals with
   a. the responsiveness in one variable to a change in another variable.
   b. price and quantity demanded.
   c. income and quantity demanded.
   d. supply and demand.
   e. b and c

2. Price elasticity of demand is a measure of the responsiveness of quantity demanded to changes in
   a. interest rates.
   b. supply.
   c. price.
   d. demand.

3. If quantity demanded rises by 27 percent as price falls by 30 percent, price elasticity of demand equals
   a. 2.4.
   b. 0.9.
   c. 1.1.
   d. 1.7.
   e. none of the above.

4. Price rises from $12 to $14 and the quantity demanded falls from 80 units to 60 units. What is the price elasticity of demand between the two prices?
    a. approximately 1.86
    b. approximately 0.80
    c. approximately 0.53
    d. 1.00
    e. none of the above

5. If the percentage change in quantity demanded is greater than the percentage change in price, demand is
    a. inelastic.
    b. unit elastic.
    c. elastic.
    d. perfectly elastic.
    e. perfectly inelastic.

6. If quantity demanded is completely unresponsive to changes in price, demand is
    a. inelastic.
    b. unit elastic.
    c. elastic.
    d. perfectly inelastic.
    e. perfectly elastic.

7. If the price of good X falls and the demand for good X is elastic, then
    a. the percentage rise in quantity demanded is greater than the percentage fall in price and total revenue rises.
    b. the percentage rise in quantity demanded is less than the percentage fall in price and total revenue falls.
    c. the percentage rise in quantity demanded is greater than the percentage fall in price and total revenue falls.
    d. the percentage fall in quantity demanded is greater than the percentage fall in price and total revenue rises.
    e. the percentage rise in quantity demanded is equal to the percentage fall in price and total revenue remains constant

8. The more substitutes a good has, *ceteris paribus*,
    a. the higher its price elasticity of demand.
    b. the lower its price elasticity of demand.
    c. the less elastic the demand for the good.
    d. the more inelastic the demand for the good.

9. *Ceteris paribus*, the price elasticity of demand is lowest for which of the following goods?
    a. McDonald's hamburgers
    b. hamburgers
    c. Wendy's hamburgers
    d. Burger King hamburgers
    e. it is between a, c, and d

10. _____ measures the responsiveness of changes in the quantity demanded of one good to changes in the price of another good.
    a. Price elasticity of demand
    b. Income elasticity of demand
    c. Price elasticity of supply
    d. Cross elasticity of demand

11. _____ measures the responsiveness of changes in the quantity demanded of a good to changes in income.
    a.   Price elasticity of demand
    b.   Price elasticity of supply
    c.   Income elasticity of demand
    d.   Cross elasticity of demand

12. Income elasticity of demand for an inferior good is
    a.   less than zero.
    b.   greater than zero.
    c.   equal to zero.
    d.   none of the above

13. The price of X rises by 10 percent and the quantity demanded of Y falls by 25 percent. Cross elasticity of demand equals
    a.   1.25.
    b.   0.25.
    c.   2.50.
    d.   0.40.
    e.   none of the above

14. If price and total revenue move in the opposite direction, then
    a.   demand is elastic.
    b.   demand is inelastic.
    c.   demand is unit elastic.
    d.   supply is elastic.
    e.   supply is inelastic.

15. If price and total revenue move in the same direction, then
    a.   demand is elastic.
    b.   demand is inelastic.
    c.   demand is unit elastic.
    d.   supply is elastic.
    e.   supply is inelastic.

True-False
Write "T" of "F" after each statement.

16. The greater the percentage of one's budget spent on a good, the higher the price elasticity of demand. ____

17. The less time that passes (after a change in price), the lower the price elasticity of demand. ____

18. A normal good can be income inelastic but not income elastic. ____

19. Supply is elastic if price changes by a greater percent than quantity supplied.

20. Total revenue always rises when price rises. ____

Fill in the Blank
Write the correct word in the blank.

21. If the percentage in quantity demanded is greater than the percentage change in price, the
    _____ _____ is greater than 1, and demand is _____.

22. If price rises and total revenue rises, too, demand is _____.

23. As we move up a straight-line downward-sloping demand curve from lower to higher prices, price
    elasticity of demand _____.

24. The short-run price elasticity of demand for gasoline is likely to be _____ than the long-
    run price elasticity of demand for gasoline.

25. If price falls and total revenue rises, then demand is _____.

Chapter 6
Consumer Choice: Maximizing Utility and Behavioral Economics

What This Chapter Is About

How do consumers make decisions? How do they decide how many units of a good to buy? This chapter answers these questions and more. In a way, this chapter gives you a deeper understanding of demand, discussed in an earlier chapter. It also introduces you to the marginal benefits-marginal costs framework of analysis, which is used extensively in economics.

Key Concepts in the Chapter

    a.   utility
    b.   total utility
    c.   marginal utility
    d.   law of diminishing marginal utility
    e.   consumer equilibrium

- **Utility** is a measure of satisfaction, happiness, or benefit that results from the consumption of a good.
- **Total utility** is the total satisfaction a person receives from consuming a particular quantity of a good.
- **Marginal utility** is the additional utility a person receives from consuming an additional unit of a particular good.
- The **law of diminishing marginal utility** states that the marginal utility gained by consuming equal successive units of a good will decline as the amount consumed increases.
- **Consumer equilibrium** exists when the consumer has spent all income and the marginal utility-price ratios (MU-P ratios) are the same.

Review Questions

1.   Give an example to illustrate the difference between total utility and marginal utility.

2.   Give an example to illustrate the law of diminishing marginal utility.

3. Give an example of a person making an interpersonal utility comparison. Define what it means to make an interpersonal utility comparison.

4. What is the diamond-water paradox?

5. What is the solution to the diamond-water paradox?

6. What does this say: $MU_a/P_a > MU_b/P_b$? Of what significance is this condition to a buyer?

7. Explain how consumers achieve consumer equilibrium.

8. Describe the experiments of the economists Zizzo and Oswald.

9. What does it mean if a person compartmentalizes?

10. What is the endowment effect?

Problems

1. Fill in the blank spaces in the table.

Unit	Total utility (utils)	Marginal utility (utils)
1st	100	
2nd	146	
3rd		28

2. At what quantity of X and Y is the consumer in equilibrium if the price of X is $2, the price of Y is $1, and the consumer has $7?

Good X (units)	Total utility (utils)	Good Y (units)	Total utility (utils)
1	60	1	80
2	110	2	100
3	150	3	110

3. Fill in the blank spaces in the table.

Number of hours playing baseball	Total benefits (in utils)	Marginal benefits (in utils)
1	100	
2	178	
3	210	

4. If the marginal utility of good X is 40 utils, the price of good X is $10, the marginal utility of good Y is 50 utils and the price of good Y is $12, then which good will a consumer be more likely to purchase more of and why?

5. If the total utility of two units of good Z is 130 utils, is it possible to determine the marginal utility of the second unit? Why or why not?

What Is the Question?
Identify the question for each of the answers that follow.

1. The additional utility gained from consuming an additional unit of good X.

2. Marginal utility turns negative.

3. The consumer will buy more of good X and less of good Y.

4. It slopes downward (left to right) because of the law of diminishing marginal utility.

5. Ownership makes things more valuable.

What Is Wrong?
In each of the statements that follow, something is wrong. Identify what is wrong in the space provided.

1. If total utility is falling, then marginal utility is greater than zero.

2. A millionaire gets less utility from an additional $100 than a poor person receives from an additional $100.

3. If total benefits rise, then marginal benefits must rise, too.

4. If the marginal utility-price ratio for good A is greater than the marginal utility-price ratio for good B, then a consumer will buy more of both good A and B.

5. If Smith has a greater income than Jones, then Smith necessarily receives less utility from earning an additional dollar than Jones receives from earning an additional dollar.

Multiple Choice
Circle the correct answer.

1. If Fiona says that drinking soda gives her utility, what specifically does she mean?
    a.   That there are things worse than drinking soda.
    b.   That drinking soda is tasty.
    c.   That drinking soda is something that gives her satisfaction or pleasure.
    d.   That there is nothing better than drinking soda.
    e.   b and d

2. Suppose Will consumes 5 units of good X and receives 20 utils from the first unit, 18 from the second, 12 from the third, 7 from the fourth, and 1 from the fifth. The total utility Will receives from consuming 5 units is
    a.   50 utils.
    b.   58 utils.
    c.   40 utils.
    d.   45 utils.
    e.   none of the above

3. Suppose Bob received 123 utils from consuming one banana and 159 utils from consuming two bananas. What is the marginal utility of the second banana?
    a. 282 utils.
    b. 30 utils.
    c. 0 utils.
    d. 36 utils.
    e. none of the above.

4. The law of diminishing marginal utility says that the marginal utility gained by consuming equal _____ units of a good will _____ as the amount consumed _____.
    a. successive; decline; decreases
    b. successive; decline; increases
    c. large; decline; decreases
    d. small; decline; increases
    e. none of the above

5. Which of the following is false?
    a. It is impossible for total utility to rise as marginal utility falls.
    b. Marginal utility is the same as average utility.
    c. Marginal utility is greater than total utility for the first unit of a good consumed.
    d. a and c
    e. a, b, and c

6. In which of the following settings is an interpersonal utility comparison not being made?
    a. Brady says to Armand, "I get a lot more satisfaction from eating hamburgers than you do."
    b. Francis says, "I don't know what he is feeling or thinking; I can't read a person's heart or mind."
    c. Ida ways to Lucy, "I know you like this course a lot more than I do."
    d. a and b
    e. a, b, and c

7. Suppose for a consumer the marginal utility of pickles is 50 utils and the MU of milk is 30 utils; the price of pickles is $1.00 and the price of milk is $1.25. Given this,
    a. the same amount of utility per penny is gained from consuming milk as pickles.
    b. more utility per penny is gained from consuming milk than pickles.
    c. more utility penny is gained from consuming pickles than milk.
    d. the consumer is in consumer equilibrium.

8. The price of good Y, a normal good, falls from $10 to $8. As a result, the quantity demanded of good Y rises from 125 units to 155 units. Holding real income constant, the quantity demanded of good Y rises 20 units. Which of the following is true?
    a. The consumer consumes 20 more units of Y because it has become relatively cheaper; therefore this is the income effect.
    b. The consumer consumes 10 more units of Y because he or she has more real income; therefore this is the income effect.
    c. The consumer consumes 20 more units of Y because it has become relatively cheaper; therefore this is the substitution effect.
    d. The consumer consumes 10 more units of Y because it has become relatively more expensive; therefore this is the income effect.

9. In the study of the "buying" behavior of two white rats, as the "relative price" of one beverage was raised,
    a. one white rat began to consume more of the higher priced beverage and the other began to consume less.
    b. both white rats began to consume less of the higher priced beverage.
    c. both white rats began to consume more of the higher priced beverage.
    d. both white rats continued consuming the same amount of the beverage as before its price was raised.

10. Which of the following statements is false?
   a. If Tracy receives 30 utils from consuming one hamburger and 55 utils from consuming two hamburgers, the marginal utility of the second hamburger is 25 utils.
   b. The law of diminishing marginal utility says that the more of a particular good one consumes, the more utility one receives from the consumption of that good.
   c. The consumption of gold probably takes place at relative high marginal utility, since there is little gold in the world.
   d. b and c
   e. none of the above

11. We would expect the total utility of diamonds to be _____ than the total utility of water, and the marginal utility of diamonds to be _____ than the marginal utility of water.
   a. higher; higher
   b. lower; lower
   c. higher; lower
   d. lower; higher

12. In order for an individual to achieve consumer equilibrium through the consumption of two goods, A and B, that individual must fulfill the condition
   a. $TU_A = TU_B$
   b. $TU_A/P_A = TU_B/P_B$
   c. $MU_A = MU_B$
   d. $MU_A/P_A = MU_B/P_B$
   e. $MU_B/P_A = MU_A/P_B$

13. If the marginal utility of a good is negative, then consumers
   a. should buy less of it.
   b. will only consume it if it is free.
   c. should buy more of it to make its marginal utility rise.
   d. either b or c
   e. none of the above

14. If total utility of a good is high while the price of the good is low, it is likely that the good
   a. is plentiful.
   b. is inferior.
   c. is rare.
   d. has high marginal utility.

15. If marginal utility is rising, then
   a. total utility is falling.
   b. total utility is rising.
   c. total utility is constant.
   d. b or c.
   e. there is not enough information to answer the question.

True-False
Write "T" or "F" after each statement.

16. One makes an interpersonal utility comparison if he or she compares the utility one person receives from a good with the utility another person receives from the same good. ____

17. Total utility may increase if marginal utility is negative. ____

18. A consumer is in disequilibrium if she receives different marginal utility per dollar for different goods she purchases. _____

19. Total utility may increase as marginal utility decreases. _____

20. The law of diminishing marginal utility can be used to make interpersonal utility comparisons. _____

Fill in the Blank
Write the correct word in the blank.

21. The _____ – _____ _____ states that that which sometimes has great value in use has little value in exchange, and that which has little value in use sometimes has great value in exchange.

22. When the consumer has spent all his income, and the marginal utilities per dollar spent on each good purchased are equal, the consumer is said to be in _____.

23. The _____ _____ states that someone values something more if he owns it or possesses it than if he doesn't own or possess it.

24. Prices reflect _____ _____.

25. If total utility for two units of a good is more than double what it is for one unit, then the marginal utility of the second unit is _____ than the marginal utility of the first unit.

Chapter 7
Production and Costs

What This Chapter Is About
This chapter is about why the firm exists. In addition, this chapter is about the production and cost side of the firm. In later chapters, the revenue side of the firm will be discussed.

Key Concepts in the Chapter
- a. shirking
- b. explicit cost
- c. implicit cost
- d. normal profit
- e. sunk cost
- f. fixed costs
- g. variable costs
- h. marginal cost
- i. law of diminishing marginal returns
- j. average-marginal rule

- **Shirking** refers to the behavior of a worker who is putting forth less than the agreed-effort.
- An **explicit cost** is a cost that is incurred when an actual monetary payment is made.
- An **implicit cost** is a cost that represents the value of resources used in production for which no actual monetary payment is made.
- **Normal profit** is zero economic profit. A firm that earns normal profit is earning revenues equal to its total opportunity costs (explicit plus implicit costs).
- **Sunk cost** is a cost incurred in the past that cannot be changed by current decisions and therefore cannot be recovered.
- **Fixed costs** are costs that do not vary with output.
- **Variable costs** are costs that vary with output.
- **Marginal cost** is the change in total cost that results from a change in output. It is the additional cost of producing additional output.
- The **law of diminishing marginal returns** states that as ever larger amounts of a variable input are combined with fixed inputs, eventually the marginal physical product of the variable input will decline.
- The **average-marginal rule** states that if the marginal magnitude is below the average magnitude, the average magnitude is declining; if the marginal magnitude is above the average magnitude, the average magnitude is rising.

Review Questions

1. According to Alchian and Demsetz, what condition is necessary before teams (firms) are formed?

2. What affects how much a person shirks?

3.   What is a residual claimant?

4.   Give an example of an explicit cost.

5.   Give an example of an implicit cost.

6.   Why is economic profit smaller than accounting profit?

7.   A firm that earns zero economic profit is likely to stay in business. Why?

8.   Give an example of sunk cost.

9.   When making decisions, economists say it is better to ignore sunk cost. Give an example that illustrates why it would be better to ignore sunk cost than not to ignore it.

10. Give an example of a fixed input.

11. Give an example of a variable input.

12. What is the difference between average total cost and marginal cost?

13. Give an example that illustrates the law of diminishing marginal returns.

14. How are diminishing marginal returns related to rising marginal cost?

15. What is the difference between marginal productivity and average productivity?

16. What do diminishing marginal returns (in production) have to do with rising average total costs?

17. Give an example that illustrates the average-marginal rule.

18. What is the long-run average total cost (LRATC) curve?

19. What does it mean if a firm experiences economies of scale?

20. Explain how a change in taxes can affect a firm's cost curves.

21. Why does the AFC curve continually decline over output?

Problems
1. Fill in the blanks in the table.

Explicit costs	Implicit costs	Total revenue	Economic profit	Accounting profit
$40,000		$100,000	$20,000	$60,000
	$30,000	$230,000	$50,000	
$30,000	$40,000	$300,000		

2. Fill in the blank spaces in the table.

Variable cost	Fixed cost	Units of output produced	Average variable cost	Average fixed cost
$500	$1,000	100		
$400	$500	200		
$1,000	$200	400		

3. Fill in the blank spaces in the table.

Variable cost	Fixed cost	Units of output produced	Average total cost
$500	$200	100	
$300	$400	50	
$400	$1,000	75	

4. Fill in the blank spaces in the table.

Average total cost is	Marginal cost is	Average total cost is (rising, fall, remaining unchanged)
$40	$45	
$30	$20	
$20	$37	

5. Fill in the blank spaces in the table.

Variable input (units)	Fixed input (units)	Quantity of output	Marginal physical product of variable input
0	1	0	0
1	1	20	
2	1	45	

6. Fill in the blank spaces in the table.

Marginal physical product (units)	Variable cost	Marginal cost
20	$400	
18	$360	
33	$660	

7. Diagrammatically represent a TFC curve. Explain why you drew the curve the way you did.

8. Diagrammatically represent an AFC curve. Explain why you drew the curve the way you did.

9. In the following diagram the ATC curve is drawn. Draw the MC curve in relation to the ATC curve. Why did you draw the MC curve the way you did?

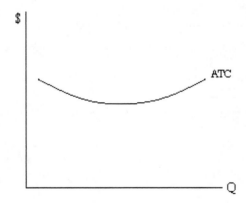

10. A firm initially faces increasing marginal returns, then constant marginal returns, and finally diminishing marginal returns. Draw the marginal cost curve that would reflect these changes in production. Explain why you drew the MC curve the way you did.

What Is the Question?
Identify the question for each of the answers that follow.

1. These economists suggest that firms are formed when benefits can be obtained from individuals working as a team.

2. The process in which managers direct employees to perform certain tasks.

3. This rises as the costs of shirking falls.

4. This is the person in a business firm who coordinates team production and reduces shirking.

5. Persons who share in the profits of a business firm.

6. A cost that is incurred when an actual monetary payment is made.

7. It is a cost that cannot be recovered.

8. When marginal physical product is rising, this cost is declining.

9. These costs do not vary with output.

10. Total cost divided by output.

11. When this cost is above average total cost, average total cost is rising.

12. As output increases, the difference between average variable cost and this cost becomes smaller.

13. The lowest output level at which average total costs are minimized.

14. This exists when inputs are increased by some percentage and output increases by a smaller percentage, causing unit costs to rise.

What Is Wrong?
In each of the statements or diagrams that follow, something is wrong. Identify what is wrong in the space provided.

1. Economic profit is the difference between total revenue and explicit costs.

2. When a firm earns zero economic profit it has not covered its total opportunity costs.

3. The difference between the ATC curve and the AVC curve gets larger as output rises.

4. Marginal physical product is equal to output divided by units of the variable input.

5. When marginal physical product falls, marginal cost falls, too.

6.

7.

8.

9.

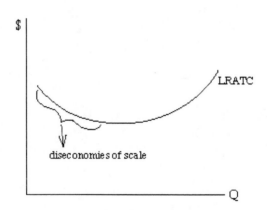

Multiple Choice
Circle the correct answer.

1. Which of the following statements is true?
    a. Implicit costs are necessarily higher than explicit costs.
    b. Explicit costs are necessarily higher than implicit costs.
    c. Tammy owns a restaurant; she paid Jack $15,000 for the curtains he installed in the restaurant. The $15,000 for curtains is an explicit cost.
    d. An implicit cost is a cost that represents actual monetary payment.
    e. none of the above

2. Which of the following is false?
    a. Economic profit is always higher than accounting profit.
    b. Accounting profit is the difference between total revenue and explicit costs.
    c. Economic profit is the difference between total revenue and implicit costs.
    d. a and c
    e. a, b, and c

3. Here is some information that relates to a business Max opened last year (all data relate to a year): price = $5; quantity sold = 15,000; implicit cost = $4,500; explicit cost = $8,500. What did economic profits equal for the year?
    a. $66,500
    b. $62,000
    c. $52,000
    d. $70,500

4. You purchased a lamb chop from the grocery store yesterday for $5. The store has a no-return policy. The $5 purchase of the lamb chop is best described as
    a. an average cost.
    b. a normal cost.
    c. a sunk cost.
    d. a low fixed cost.

5. Evie recently went into the business of producing and selling greeting cards. For this business, which of the following is likely to be a fixed cost?
    a. paper costs
    b. labor costs
    c. the six-month lease for the factory
    d. long distance telephone costs
    e. a, b, and d

6. Which of the following statements is true?
    a. Since fixed costs are constant as output changes in the short run, it follows that average fixed cost is constant in the short run, too.
    b. Marginal cost is the additional cost of producing an additional unit of output.
    c. Changes in variable costs are reflected dollar-for-dollar in total cost.
    d. b and c
    e. a and b

7. The law of diminishing marginal returns states that
    a. as ever larger amounts of a variable input are combined with fixed inputs, eventually the marginal physical product of the variable input will increase.
    b. as ever smaller amounts of a variable input are combined with fixed inputs, eventually the marginal physical product of the variable input will increase.
    c. as ever larger amounts of a fixed input are combined with a variable input, eventually the marginal physical product of the fixed input will decline.
    d. as ever larger amounts of a variable input are combined with a fixed input, eventually the marginal physical product of the variable input will decline

8. The production of a good usually requires two types of inputs,
    a. variable and fixed.
    b. long-run and short-run.
    c. total and unit.
    d. sunk and fixed.
    e. none of the above

Exhibit A

(1) Variable input	(2) Fixed input	(3) Quantity of output	(4) MPP of variable input
0	1	0	
1	1	40	A
2	1	62	B
3	1	80	C
4	1	96	D
5	1	106	E
6	1	114	F

Note: MPP = marginal physical product

9. In Exhibit A above, the numbers that go in blanks A and B are, respectively,
   a. 40; 22
   b. 0; 22
   c. 20; 20
   d. 1; 2
   e. 20; 22

10. In Exhibit A above, the numbers that go in blanks C and D are, respectively,
   a. 18; 16
   b. 20; 16
   c. 40; 184
   d. 20; 22
   e. none of the above

11. If the average variable cost curve is falling,
   a. the marginal cost (MC) curve must be above it.
   b. MC must be less than AVC.
   c. the MC curve is necessarily rising.
   d. the MC curve is horizontal (neither rising nor falling).

Exhibit B

(1) Variable input	(2) Price per variable input	(3) Fixed cost	(4) Output	(5) Marginal cost
1	$15	$100	30	
2	$15	$100	31	A
3	$15	$100	33	B
4	$15	$100	36	C
5	$15	$100	38	D

12. In Exhibit B above, the dollar amounts that go in blanks A and B are, respectively,
   a. $10.00; $7.50
   b. $10.00; $5.00
   c. $15.00; $7.50
   d. $5.00; $5.00
   e. $2.00; $12.00

13. In Exhibit B above, the dollar amounts that go in blanks <u>C</u> and <u>D</u> are, respectively,
    a. $5.00; $7.50
    b. $10.00; $3.33
    c. $5.00; $10.00
    d. $10.00; $10.00
    e. $9.33; $10.00

14. If, in the production process, inputs are increased by 18 percent and output increases by more than 18 percent, _____ are said to exist.
    a. economies of scale
    b. diminishing marginal returns
    c. diseconomies of scale
    d. constant returns to scale
    e. none of the above

15. If, in the production process, inputs are increased by 10 percent and output increases by less than 10 percent, _____ are said to exist.
    a. economies of scale
    b. diminishing marginal returns
    c. diseconomies of scale
    d. constant returns to scale
    e. none of the above

True-False
Write "T" or "F" at the end of each statement.

16. Accounting profit equals economic profit if there are no implicit costs. ____

17. Accounting profit is the difference between total revenue and explicit costs. ____

18. A firm that earns zero economic profit is earning a normal profit. ____

19. In the long run, there are only fixed costs. ____

20. The average-marginal rule states that if the marginal magnitude is below the average magnitude, the average magnitude rises. ____

Fill in the Blank
Write the correct word in the blank.

21. The _____ – _____ _____ _____ _____ curve shows the lowest unit cost at which the firm can produce any given level of output.

22. The _____ _____ _____ is the lowest output level at which average total costs are minimized.

23. If inputs are increased by some percentage and output increases by a smaller percentage, unit costs _____, and _____ _____ _____ are said to exist.

24. Assume labor and some fixed input are used to produce good X. As the marginal physical product of labor increases, marginal cost _____.

25. The _____ _____ _____ of the variable input is equal to the change in output that results from changing the variable input by one unit, holding all other inputs fixed.

Chapter 8
Perfect Competition

What This Chapter Is About
Beginning in this chapter, and continuing for the next two chapters, market structures are discussed. Think of a market structure as the setting in which a firm finds itself. That setting relates to the number of buyers and sellers in the market, the good being produced, whether or not there is easy entry into the market, and more.

Key Concepts in the Chapter
    a.   price taker
    b.   marginal revenue
    c.   profit-maximization rule
    d.   resource allocative efficiency

- A **price taker** is a seller that does not have the ability to control the price of the product it sells; it takes the price determined in the market.
- **Marginal revenue** is the change in total revenue that results from selling one additional unit of output.
- The **profit-maximization rule** states that profit is maximized by producing the quantity at which MR = MC.
- **Resource allocative efficiency** exists when the firm produces the quantity of output at which price equals marginal cost, P = MC.

Review Questions

1. What are the four assumptions in the theory of perfect competition?

2. Firm A is a price taker when it comes to selling its good. What does this mean?

3. Why are the demand curve and marginal revenue curve the same curve for the perfectly competitive firm?

4. Explain why a perfectly competitive firm is resource-allocative efficient.

5. The MR curve is downward sloping and the MC curve is upward sloping. Why will a profit-maximizing firm produce the quantity of output at which MR = MC instead of producing the quantity of output at which there is the greatest difference between MR and MC?

6. What does a firm consider when deciding whether or not to shut down (its operation) in the short run?

7. If a firm produces the quantity of output at which MR = MC, is it guaranteed to earn profit? Explain your answer.

8. The firm's supply curve is that portion of its MC curve that is above its AVC curve. Why isn't the entire MC curve the firm's supply curve instead of only a portion of it?

9. How is the market supply curve derived?

10. What is the link between the market supply curve and the law of diminishing marginal returns?

11. What conditions does a perfectly competitive firm satisfy when it is in long-run equilibrium?

12. If price is above short-run average total cost, the perfectly competitive firm is not in long-run equilibrium. Why?

13. If SRATC is greater than LRATC, the perfectly competitive firm is not in long-run equilibrium. Why?

14. What is a constant cost industry?

15. There are positive economic profits in a perfectly competitive market. Explain what happens as a result.

16. Will a perfectly competitive firm advertise its product? Why or why not?

17. Firm X is not productive efficient. What does this mean?

Problems

1. Fill in the blank spaces in the table.

Price	Quantity	Total revenue	Marginal revenue
$10	1		
$10	2		
$10	3		

2. Assuming the firm is a perfectly competitive firm, fill in the blank spaces in the table.

Price	Quantity	Total revenue
$40		$4,000
	50	
	80	

3. Assuming the firm is a perfectly competitive firm, fill in the blank spaces in the table.

Price	Quantity	Marginal revenue
$15	1	
	2	
	3	

4. Fill in the blank spaces in the table.

Price	Quantity	Average variable cost	Average total cost	Total variable cost	Will the firm (continue to produce, shut down)
$10	100	$7	$9		
$15	50	$13	$16		
$23	1,000	$24	$26		

5. Fill in the blank spaces in the table.

Price	Quantity	Average variable cost	Average total cost	Average fixed cost	Total cost
$10	100	$4	$6		
$40	2,000	$45	$46		
$25	198	$21	$23		

6. Fill in the blank spaces in the table.

Price	Marginal cost	ATC	Is the perfectly competitive firm earning profits? (yes, no)	Is the perfectly competitive firm in long-run equilibrium? (yes, no)
$40	$40	$30		
$30	$30	$35		
$25	$25	$23		

7. Fill in the blank spaces in the table.

Price	Quantity	ATC	AVC	Profit (+) or Loss (−)
$33	1,234	$31	$30	
$55	2,436	$25	$20	
$100	1,000	$110	$99	

What Is the Question?

1. A seller that does not have the ability to control the price of the product it sells.

2. The firm sells its good at market equilibrium price.

3. When price is below average variable cost.

4. That portion of its MC curve above its AVC curve.

5. The horizontal summation of the individual firms' supply curves.

6. There is no incentive for firms to enter or exit the industry, there is no incentive for firms to produce more or less output, and there is no incentive for firms to change plant size.

7. P = SRATC, P = MC, and SRATC = LRATC.

8.   The long-run supply curve is upward sloping.

9.   The long-run supply curve is downward-sloping.

10. P = MC.

11. The firm produces its output at the lowest possible per-unit cost.

What Is Wrong?
In each of the statements that follow, something is wrong. Identify what is wrong in the space provided.

1.   Firms in a perfectly competitive market have easy entry into the market and costly exit from the market.

2.   In long-run competitive equilibrium, the average or representative firm may earn positive economic profit.

3.   Price is greater than marginal revenue for a perfectly competitive firm.

4.   A perfectly competitive firm will shut down in the short run if its price is below average total cost.

5. If a firm produces the quantity of output at which MR = MC, it is guaranteed to earn profits.

6. The market supply curve is the vertical summation of the individual firms' supply curves.

7. If SRATC = LRATC for a firm, there is no incentive for the firm to enter or exit the industry.

8. The long-run supply curve is downward-sloping for an increasing cost industry.

9. When average fixed cost is positive, average total cost is usually, but not always, greater than average variable cost.

10. A firm that produces its output at the lowest possible per unit cost is said to exhibit resource allocative efficiency.

Multiple Choice
Circle the correct answer.

1. Which of the following is one of the assumptions upon which the theory of perfect competition is built?
    a.   there are few buyers and few sellers
    b.   there are many buyers and few sellers
    c.   there are few buyers and many sellers
    d.   there are many buyers and many sellers

2. Which of the following markets comes closest to being a perfectly competitive market?
    a.   the corn market
    b.   the cigarette market
    c.   the insurance market
    d.   the soft drink market

3. In a perfectly competitive market there are
   a. neither barriers to entry nor to exit.
   b. barriers to entry, but not to exit.
   c. barriers to exit, but not to entry.
   d. barriers to both entry and exit.

4. A firm that is a price taker is a firm that
   a. has the ability to control the price of the product it sells.
   b. has the ability, albeit limited, to control the price of the product it sells.
   c. can raise the price of the product it sells and still sell some units of its product.
   d. sells a high-quality product.
   e. none of the above

5. Which of the following statements is true?
   a. In the theory of perfect competition, the single firm's demand curve is downward-sloping.
   b. In the theory of perfect competition, the market demand curve is downward-sloping.
   c. In the theory of perfect competition, the single firm's demand curve is horizontal.
   d. In the theory of perfect competition, the market demand curve is horizontal.
   e. b and c

6. If the firm produces the quantity of output at which marginal revenue (MR) equals marginal cost (MC), is it guaranteed of maximizing profit?
   a. Yes, when MR=MC, it follows that total revenue (TR) is greater than total cost (TC), and thus the firm maximizes profit.
   b. Yes, since it is always the case that if the MC curve is rising, the average variable total cost curve lies below it and thus profit is earned.
   c. No, when the firm produces the quantity at which MR = MC, it could be the case that average total cost is greater than price. If this is the case, the firm will take a loss, not earn a profit.
   d. No, at the quantity of output at which MR = MC, it could be the case that average total cost is greater than price. If this is the case, the firm will take a loss, not earn a profit.

7. Consider the following data: equilibrium price = $12, quantity of output produced = 100 units, average total cost = $9, and average variable cost = $6. Given this, total revenue is _____, total cost is _____ and fixed cost is _____.
   a. $1,200; $900; $300
   b. $1,200; $700; $100
   c. $1,200; $900; $600
   d. $1,000; $800; $200
   e. none of the above

8. Consider the following data: equilibrium price = $12, quantity of output produced = 50 units, average total cost = $9, and average variable cost = $8. What will the firm do, and why?
   a. Shut down in the short run, since it is taking a loss of $150.
   b. Continue to produce in the short run, since firms are always stuck with having to produce in the short run.
   c. Shut down in the short run, since average total cost is greater than average variable cost.
   d. Continue to produce in the short run, since price is greater than average variable cost.

9. The perfectly competitive firm's short-run supply curve is that portion of its
   a. average variable cost curve above its marginal revenue curve.
   b. marginal cost curve above its average total cost curve.
   c. marginal cost curve above its average variable cost curve.
   d. average total cost curve above price.
   e. none of the above

10. Which of the following conditions does not characterize long-run competitive equilibrium?
    a. Economic profit is positive.
    b. Firms are producing the quantity of output at which price is greater than marginal cost.
    c. No firm has an incentive to change its plant size.
    d. a and b
    e. a, b and c

11. The following holds: (1) there is no incentive for firms to enter or exit the industry; (2) for some firms in the industry short-run average total cost is greater than long-run average total cost at the level of output where marginal revenue equals marginal cost; (3) all firms in the industry are currently producing the quantity of output at which marginal revenue equals marginal cost; (4) all firms in the industry are producing a homogeneous product. Is the industry in long-run competitive equilibrium?
    a. Yes.
    b. No, because of numbers 1 and 2.
    c. No, because of numbers 2 and 3.
    d. No, because of number 2.
    e. No, because of numbers 1, 2, 3 and 4.

12. An increasing-cost industry has a long-run (industry) supply curve that is
    a. upward-sloping
    b. downward-sloping
    c. horizontal
    d. vertical

13. Demand increases in a decreasing-cost industry that is initially in long-run competitive equilibrium. After full adjustment, price will be
    a. equal to its original level.
    b. below its original level.
    c. above its original level.
    d. There is not enough information to answer the question.

14. The change in total revenue which results from selling one additional unit of output is called
    a. average revenue.
    b. median revenue.
    c. marginal revenue.
    d. standard revenue.

15. Which of the following conditions about a firm in long-run competitive equilibrium is false?
    a. $P = AVC$
    b. $P = MC$
    c. $P = SRATC$
    d. $P = LRATC$

True-False
Write "T" or "F" after each statement.

16. A real-world market has to meet all the assumptions of the theory of perfect competition before the theory predicts well. ____

17. In the theory of perfect competition, price is greater than marginal revenue. ____

18. A perfectly competitive firm is a price searcher. ____

19. A decreasing-cost industry is an industry in which average total costs decrease as industry output increases. ____

20. If price is above average total costs, the firm earns profits and will continue to operate in the short run.
    ____

Fill in the Blank
Write the correct word in the blank.

21. A firm that produces the quantity of output at which price equals marginal cost is said to exhibit

_____ _____ _____.

22. In the long run in perfect competition, profits are _____.

23. Firms attempt to produce that quantity of output at which (the condition) _____ = _____
    holds.

24. The firm's _____ – _____ _____ curve is that portion of its marginal
    cost curve that lies above the average variable cost curve.

25. The greater the fixed cost-total cost ratio, the _____ likely the firm will operate in the short
    run.

Chapter 9
Monopoly

What This Chapter Is About
This chapter discusses the theory of monopoly.

Key Concepts in the Chapter
   a.   price searcher
   b.   deadweight loss of monopoly
   c.   rent seeking

   • A **price searcher** is a seller that has the ability to control to some degree the price of the product it sells.
   • **Deadweight loss of monopoly** refers to the net value of the difference between the monopoly quantity of output and the competitive quantity of output.
   • **Rent seeking** refers to the actions of individuals and groups who spend resources to influence public policy in the hope of redistributing (transferring) income to themselves from others.

Review Questions

1.   What are the three assumptions of the theory of monopoly?

2.   What is a natural monopoly?

3.   Why is a monopoly a price searcher?

4. How does the monopoly seller decide what quantity of output to produce?

5. Compared with a perfectly competitive seller, a monopoly seller produces too little output and charges too high a price. Explain.

6. Economist Gordon Tullock has argued that rent-seeking behavior is individually rational but socially wasteful. What does this mean?

7. Identify and define the three types of price discrimination.

8. What are the necessary conditions for price discrimination?

9. Is the perfectly price-discriminating monopolist resource allocative efficient? Explain your answer.

Problems

1. Fill in the blank spaces in the table.

Price	Quantity	Total revenue	Marginal revenue
$10	1		
$9	2		
$8	3		

2. Using the diagram that follows, identify the consumers' surplus under perfect competition and monopoly.

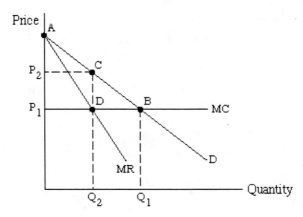

Consumers' surplus under perfect competition = _____

Consumers' surplus under monopoly = _____

3. Using the diagram that follows, identify the deadweight loss triangle of monopoly.

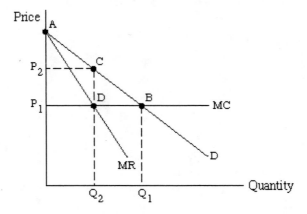

4.   Diagrammatically represent the quantity of output the monopolist produces and the price it charges.

5.   Diagrammatically represent a monopolist that incurs losses.

What Is the Question?
Identify the question for each of the answers that follow.

1.   A right granted to a firm by government that permits the firm to provide a particular good or service and excludes all others from doing the same.

2.   An exclusive right to sell something.

3.   Price is greater than marginal revenue.

4. Actions of individuals and groups who spend resources to influence public policy in the hope of redistributing (transferring) income to themselves from others.

5. This occurs when the seller charges a uniform price per unit for one specific quantity, a lower price for an additional quantity, and so on.

6. The increase in costs and organizational slack in a monopoly resulting from the lack of competitive pressure to push costs down to their lowest possible level.

7. Total revenue is greater if the monopolist can do this.

8. If it does this, the monopolist will be resource allocative efficient.

What Is Wrong?
In each of the statements that follow, something is wrong. Identify what is wrong in the space provided.

1. The single-price monopolist exhibits resource allocative efficiency.

2. One of the assumptions in the theory of monopoly is that the single seller sells a product for which there are no perfect substitutes.

3. For the monopolist, price is equal to marginal revenue.

4. If fixed costs exist, then a firm that maximizes revenue automatically maximizes profit, too.

5. The monopoly seller produces the quantity of output at which MR = P and charges the highest price per unit for this quantity.

6. A monopoly seller cannot incur losses, since it is the single seller of a good.

7. Perfect price discrimination occurs when the seller charges a uniform price per unit for one specific quantity, a lower price for an additional quantity, and so on.

8. A monopoly seller can charge any price it wants for the good it produces and sells.

Multiple Choice
Circle the correct answer.

1. Which of the following is *not* an assumption of the theory of monopoly?
    a. There is only one seller in the industry.
    b. The seller sells a product for which there are no close substitutes.
    c. The seller has high variable costs.
    d. There are high barriers to entry into the industry.

2. Which of the following is the best example of a barrier to entry into a monopolistic industry?
    a. diminishing returns
    b. economies of scale
    c. comparative advantage
    d. high elasticity of demand

3. In the United States, patents are granted to inventors of a product or process for a period of
    a. 2 years.
    b. 12 years.
    c. 20 years.
    d. 22 years.
    e. none of the above.

4. A price searcher
    a. faces a horizontal demand curve.
    b. is a seller that searches for good employees and pays them a low wage.
    c. is a seller that searches for the best price at which to buy its nonlabor inputs.
    d. is a seller that has the ability to control, to some degree, the price of the product it sells.
    e. a and c

5. Which of the following statements is true?
    a. A price searcher must raise price to sell an additional unit of its product.
    b. For a price searcher, price equals marginal revenue for all units except the first.
    c. For a price searcher, price is less than marginal revenue for all units except the first.
    d. A price searcher, like a price taker, produces that quantity of output for which marginal revenue equals marginal cost.
    e. c and d

6. The marginal revenue curve lies above the demand curve for a
    a. monopoly firm.
    b. price taker.
    c. price searcher.
    d. a and c
    e. none of the above

7. Economic or monopoly rent is a payment in excess of
    a. price.
    b. average variable cost.
    c. opportunity cost.
    d. explicit cost, but not necessarily a payment in excess of implicit cost.
    e. none of the above

8. When a seller charges different prices for the product he sells and the price differences do not reflect cost differences, the seller is engaging in
    a. rent seeking.
    b. arbitrage.
    c. the capitalization of profits.
    d. price discrimination.

9. A seller who charges the highest price each consumer would be willing to pay for the product rather than go without that product is practicing
    a. perfect price discrimination.
    b. disciplined price discrimination.
    c. ideal price discrimination.
    d. competitive price discrimination.

10. For a firm that perfectly price discriminates,
    a. price equals marginal revenue.
    b. price is less than marginal cost.
    c. price is greater than average total cost.
    d. There is not enough information to answer the question.

11. Which of the following is a rent-seeking activity?
    a. Carol produces shoes that will be purchased by the Army.
    b. Mick produces blankets that are sold in Egypt.
    c. Jackie produces suntan lotion that is sold exclusively in Hawaii.
    d. a and b
    e. none of the above

12. According to Gordon Tullock,
    a.   monopoly profits or rents are subject to rent seeking.
    b.   the welfare cost triangle is subject to rent seeking.
    c.   X-inefficiency is something that differentiates government monopolies from private monopolies.
    d.   the theory of monopoly is superior to the theory of perfect competition.

13. (Single-price) monopoly firms produce
    a.   the resource allocative efficient output.
    b.   more than the resource allocative efficient output.
    c.   less that the resource allocative efficient output.
    d.   where P = MC.

14. The monopolist will maximize profits at a level of output at which marginal revenue equals
    a.   average fixed cost.
    b.   average variable cost.
    c.   average total cost.
    d.   marginal cost.

15. Perfect price discrimination is sometimes called discrimination among
    a.   buyers.
    b.   sellers.
    c.   quantities.
    d.   units.

True-False
Write "T" or "F" after each statement.

16. If a firm is a price searcher, it necessarily cannot price discriminate. ____

17. The revenue-maximizing price is the profit-maximizing price when there are no variable costs. ____

18. A monopoly firm charges a higher price and produces more output than a perfectly competitive firm with the same cost conditions. ____

19. Monopoly profits can turn out to be zero in the long run through the capitalization of profits. ____

20. In perfect competition, P = MC; in monopoly, P < MC. ____

Fill in the Blank
Write the correct word in the blank.

21. _____ _____ is the condition where economies of scale are so pronounced in an industry that only one firm can survive.

22. _____ _____ is a seller that has the ability to control to some degree the price of the product it sells.

23. Buying a good in a market where its price is low, and selling the good in another where its price is higher, is called _____.

24. _____ – _____ is the increase in costs and organization slack in a monopoly resulting from the lack of competitive pressure to push costs down to their lowest possible level.

25. The major developer of the theory or rent seeking is _____ _____.

Chapter 10
Monopolistic Competition, Oligopoly, and Game Theory

What This Chapter Is About
We have discussed two market structures so far—perfect competition and monopoly. In this chapter we discuss two more market structures—monopolistic competition and oligopoly. We also discuss game theory.

Key Concepts in the Chapter
    a.   monopolistic competition
    b.   oligopoly
    c.   game theory

- The theory of **monopolistic competition** is based on three assumptions: (1) many sellers and buyers, (2) firms produce and sell slightly differentiated products, (3) easy entry and exit.
- The theory of **oligopoly** is based on three assumptions: (1) few sellers and many buyers, (2) firms produce either homogeneous of differentiated products, (3) significant barriers to entry.
- **Game theory** is a mathematical technique used to analyze the behavior of decision makers who try to reach an optimal position for themselves through game playing or the use of strategic behavior, are fully aware of the interactive nature of the process at hand, and anticipate the moves of other decision makers.

Review Questions

1. What are the three assumptions of the theory of monopolistic competition?

2. How is a monopolistic competitor like a perfectly competitive firm?

3. How is a monopolistic competitor like a monopoly firm?

4. What quantity of output will the monopolistic competitor produce?

5. Is a monopolistic competitor resource allocative efficient? Explain your answer.

6. Why does a monopolistic competitor have excess capacity?

7. What are the three assumptions of the theory of oligopoly?

8. What is a four-firm concentration ratio?

9. What is the essence of the prisoner's dilemma game? Stated differently, how do we know something is a prisoner's dilemma game?

10. What is the objective of a cartel?

11. Why might cartel members try to cheat on each other (break their agreement not to compete)?

12. What conditions does a contestable market satisfy?

13. Explain the arms race between the U.S. and the (former) Soviet Union in game theoretic terms.

Problems

1. Diagrammatically represent a monopolistic competitive firm incurring losses.

Price

Quantity

2. Diagrammatically represent the excess capacity for a monopolistic competitive firm.

Price

Quantity

3. Several firms form a cartel. Before the cartel, each firm earns normal profit. As a part of the cartel, each firm charges P_1 in the diagram that follows. What are profits equal to for the firm that holds to the cartel? What are profits equal to for the firm if it cheats on the cartel agreement while no other firms cheat on the cartel agreement.

Profits if the firm holds to the cartel agreement =

_____

Profits if the firm cheats on the cartel agreement while no other firms cheat on the agreement =

_____

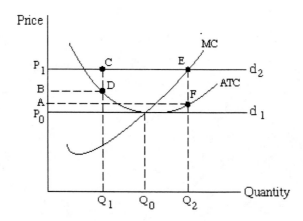

4. Give an example that illustrates how to compute the four-firm concentration ratio.

5.   What are the four problems associated with a cartel?

What Is the Question?
Identify the question for each of the answers that follow.

1.   States that a monopolistic competitor in equilibrium produces an output smaller than the one that would minimize its costs of production.

2.   It does not produce at the lowest point on its ATC curve because the demand curve it faces is downward-sloping.

3.   There are significant barriers to entry in this market structure.

4.   Individually rational behavior leads to a jointly inefficient outcome.

5.   The key behavioral assumption is that oligopolists in an industry act as if there is only one firm in the industry.

6.   This is a way out of the prisoner's dilemma for two firms trying to form a cartel.

7.   If a single firm lowers price, other firms will do likewise, but if a single firm raises price, other firms will not follow suit.

8.   The theory fails to explain how the original price comes about.

9.   One firm determines price and the all other firms take this price as given.

10. There is easy entry into the market and costless exit from the market, new firms entering the market can produce the product at the same cost as current firms, and firms exiting the market can easily dispose of their fixed assets by selling them elsewhere.

What Is Wrong?
In each of the statements that follow, something is wrong. Identify what is wrong in the space provided.

1.   The monopolistic competitor is a price taker and the oligopolist is a price searcher.

2.   For the monopolistic competitor, price lies below marginal revenue.

3.   When profits are normal, the monopolistic competitor exhibits resource allocative efficiency.

4.   The cartel theory assumes that firms in an oligopolistic industry act in a manner consistent with there being only a few firms in the industry.

5.   The kinked demand curve theory assumes that if a single firm raises price, other firms will do likewise, but if a single firm lowers price, other firms will not follow.

6.   The price leadership theory assumes that the dominant firm in the industry determines price and all other firms sell below this price.

7.   Both monopolistic competitive firms and oligopolistic firms produce the quantity of output at which price equals marginal revenue.

8. A contestable market is one in which there is easy entry into the market and costless exit from the market, new firms entering the market can produce the product at the same costs as current firms, and firms exiting the market only have to suffer the loss of their fixed assets.

Multiple Choice
Circle the correct answer.

1. Which of the following is *not* an assumption of the theory of monopolistic competition?
   a. There are high barriers to entry.
   b. There are many sellers and many buyers.
   c. Each firm in the industry produces and sells a highly differentiated product.
   d. a and c
   e. all of the above

2. The monopolistic competitor
   a. is a price searcher.
   b. is a price taker.
   c. is a mix between a price taker and a price searcher (it has elements of competition and monopoly).
   d. produces that quantity of output at which MR > MC.

3. Total industry sales for Year 1 are $10 million. The top four firms, A, B, C, and D, account for sales of $2 million, $2.5 million, $3.1 million, and $0.5 million, respectively. What is the four-firm concentration ratio?
   a. 0.91
   b. 0.55
   c. 0.69
   d. 0.81
   e. none of the above

4. Concentration ratios are not perfect guides to industry concentration because they do not
   a. take into account foreign competition and competition from substitute goods.
   b. adjust for inflation.
   c. adjust for quality of products.
   d. adjust for price.

5. If a single firm lowers price, other firms will do likewise, but it a single firm raises price, other firms will not necessarily follow suit. This is the behavioral assumption in the
   a. cartel theory.
   b. price leadership theory.
   c. kinked demand curve theory.
   d. price discrimination theory.
   e. none of the above

6. Which of the following statements is true?
   a. According to the kinked demand curve theory, the marginal cost (MC) curve can shift within a certain region and the firm will continue to produce the same quantity but charge a different price.
   b. According to the kinked demand curve theory, the marginal cost (MC) curve can shift within a certain region and the firm will continue to produce the same quantity and charge the same price.
   c. According to the kinked demand curve theory, the demand curve can shift within a certain region and the firm will continue to produce the same quantity and charge the same price.
   d. According to the kinked demand curve theory, the demand curve can shift within a certain region and the firm will continue to produce the same quantity but charge a different price.

7. The top firm in the industry determines price and all other firms take this price as given. This is the behavioral assumption of the
    a. kinked demand curve theory.
    b. price leadership theory.
    c. both the cartel and price leadership theories.
    d. monopolistic competitive theory.

8. In the price leadership theory, at a price of $5 per unit, the fringe firms supply the entire market. At a price of $4, the (market) quantity demanded is 900 units and the quantity supplied by fringe firms is 430. Given this, which of the following quantity-price combinations is represented by a point on the dominant firm's demand curve?
    a. 1,330 units at $5
    b. 230 units at $4
    c. 470 units at $4
    d. 470 units at $5
    e. 1 unit at $5

9. The key behavioral assumption of the cartel theory is that oligopolists in an industry
    a. try to maximize revenue instead of profits.
    b. act as if they are perfect monopolistic competitors.
    c. act in a manner consistent with there being only one firm in the industry.
    d. try to manipulate government into subsidizing their activities.
    e. b and d

10. Which of the following is an example of an oligopoly?
    a. a law partnership
    b. a local gas company
    c. a dental firm
    d. General Motors Company
    e. none of the above

11. Product differentiation is most likely a form of
    a. advertising.
    b. nonprice competition.
    c. lowering variable costs.
    d. lowering the fixed costs to total cost ratio.
    e. none of the above

12. *Ceteris paribus*, the free rider problem is more serious
    a. the smaller the number of potential cartel members.
    b. the larger the number of potential cartel members.
    c. the higher total costs.
    d. the lower total costs.
    e. b and c

13. Which of the following statements is true? .   .
    a. One of the developers of contestable markets theory is William Baldwin.
    b. Orthodox market structure theory places much greater weight than contestable markets theory on the number of firms in an industry as a major factor in determining a firm's behavior.
    c. Contestable markets theory emphasizes product differentiation; orthodox market structure theory does not.
    d. Contestable markets theory emphasizes nonprice competition; orthodox market structure theory does not.
    e. a and b

14. The prisoner's dilemma game illustrates that
    a. what is good for you and me individually may be bad for us collectively.
    b. what is good for me is good for you.
    c. cartels are likely to be stable in the long run.
    d. what is high is low and what is low is high.
    e. none of the above.

15. A monopolistic competitor has a demand curve that is
    a. more elastic than a perfectly competitive firm.
    b. less elastic than a perfectly competitive firm.
    c. less elastic than a monopoly firm.
    d. b and c

True-False
Write "T" or "F" after each statement.

16. There is easy entry but costly exit in monopolistic competition. ____

17. In monopolistic competition, the marginal revenue curve lies below the demand curve. ____

18. In equilibrium a monopolistic competitor produces an output smaller than the one that would minimize its costs of production.

19. Third-degree price discrimination is sometimes seen in the form of cents-off coupons. ____

20. There are few sellers and few buyers in oligopoly. ____

Fill in the Blank
Write the correct word in the blank.

21. The economist _____ _____ found no evidence that the oligopolists he examined were more reluctant to match price increases than price cuts.

22. A _____ is an organization of firms that reduces output and increases price in an effort to increase joint profits.

23. Once a cartel agreement is made, there is an incentive for cartel members to _____ on the agreement.

24. The _____ _____ _____ states that a monopolistic competitor will, in equilibrium, produce an output smaller than the one at which average total costs (unit costs) are minimized.

25. The tactic of _____ – _____ – _____ is possible in a contestable market.

Chapter 11
Government and Product Markets: Antitrust and Regulation

What This Chapter Is About
This chapter deals with government involvement in product markets. Essentially, it looks at government's attempts to apply the antitrust laws and to regulate.

Key Concepts in the Chapter
a. antitrust law
b. network good
c. lock-in effect

- **Antitrust law** is legislation passed for the stated purpose of controlling monopoly power and preserving and promoting competition.
- A **network good** is a good whose value increases as the expected number of units sold increases.
- The **lock-in effect** is descriptive of the situation where a particular product or technology becomes settled upon as the standard and is difficult or impossible to dislodge as the standard.

Review Questions

1. What is exclusive dealing?

2. Of what relevance to antitrust policy is how broadly or narrowly a market is defined?

3. Give an example to illustrate how the Herfindahl index is computed.

4.   What is the difference between a vertical merger and a horizontal merger?

5.   What antitrust issue was relevant to the Utah pie case?

6.   What is the relevance of switching costs to a network monopoly?

7.   Outline the details of the capture theory of regulation.

8.   What is a criticism of profit regulation (with respect to a natural monopolist)?

9.   How do economists view regulation? Are they pro-regulation, anti-regulation, or neither pro- nor anti-regulation? Explain your answer.

Problems

1. Fill in the blank spaces in the table.

Provision of the antitrust act	Name of the Act
Every person who shall monopolize, or attempt to monopolize, or combine or conspire with any other person or persons to monopolize any part of the trade or commerce…shall be guilty of a misdemeanor.	
Prohibits suppliers from offering special discounts to large chain stores unless they also offer the discounts to everyone else.	
Empowers the Federal Trade Commission to deal with false and deceptive acts or practices.	
Declares illegal unfair methods of competition in commerce.	
Declares illegal exclusive dealing and tying contracts.	

2. Fill in the blank spaces in the table.

Number of firms in the industry	Market shares of the firms, in order from top to bottom	Herfindahl index
6	20, 20, 20, 20, 10, 10	
10	20, 10, 10, 10, 10, 10, 10, 10, 5, 5	
10	10, 10, 10, 10, 10, 10, 10, 10, 10, 10	

3. Fill in the blank spaces in the table.

Proposed merger	What type of merger? (horizontal, vertical, conglomerate)
Between two firms, each of which produces and sells tires.	
Between two firms, one of which produces and sells houses and the other which produces and sells wood.	
Between two firms, one of which produces and sells books and one of which produces and sells bottled water.	

4. Using the diagram that follows, what price will the natural monopoly charge if it is resource allocative efficient?

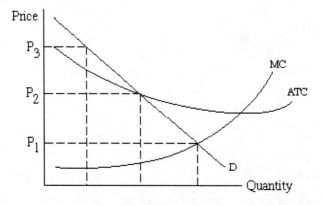

5. Using the diagram in question 4, what price will the natural monopoly charge under profit regulation?

6. Diagrammatically show that price regulation can lead to a natural monopoly incurring losses.

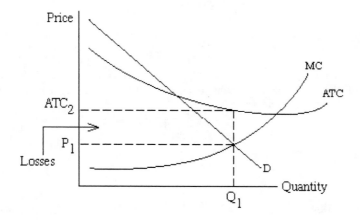

What Is the Question?
Identify the question for each of the answers that follow.

1. This antitrust act made interlocking directorates illegal.

2. One advantage is that it provides information about the dispersion of firm size in an industry.

3. This is descriptive of the situation where a particular product or technology becomes settled upon as the standard and is difficult or impossible to dislodge as the standard.

4. This is the time period between when a natural monopoly's costs change and when the regulatory agency adjusts prices of the natural monopoly.

5.   Holds that regulators are seeking to do, and will do through regulation, what is in their best interest.

6.   One criticism is that it does not explain which specific acts constitute "restraint of trade."

7.   This theory holds that regulators are seeking to do, and will do through regulation, what is in the best interest of the public or society at larger.

What Is Wrong?
In each of the statements that follow, something is wrong. Identify what is wrong in the space provided.

1.   The size of the market is irrelevant to whether a firm is a monopolist or not.

2.   A conglomerate merger is a merger between companies in the same market.

3.   For a network good, its value increases as the expected number of units bought decreases.

4.   The lock-in effect reduces switching costs.

5.   The more broadly a market is defined, the more likely a firm will be considered a monopolist.

6. George Stigler and Claire Friedland studied both unregulated and regulated electric utilities and found a small difference in the rates charged by them.

7. The federal government looks more closely at proposed vertical mergers than horizontal mergers.

8. A profit-maximizing natural monopoly will produce the quantity of output at which MR = MC and charge the price that equals its ATC.

9. The capture theory of regulation holds that no matter what the motive for the initial regulation and the establishment of the regulatory agency, eventually the bureaucrats that run the agency will control the industry.

Multiple Choice
Circle the correct answer.

1. The Clayton Act made
    a. price discrimination illegal.
    b. price discrimination legal.
    c. mergers between companies in the same industry illegal.
    d. union strikes illegal in certain states.

2. Selling to a retailer on the condition that the seller not carry any rival products is called _____, and it was made illegal by the _____ Act.
    a. exclusive dealing; Robinson-Patman
    b. exclusive dealing; Clayton
    c. a tying contract; Wheeler-Lea
    d. price discrimination; Clayton

3. The piece of antitrust legislation which declares illegal "unfair methods of competition in commerce" is the _____ Act.
    a. Sherman
    b. Federal Trade Commission
    c. Clayton
    d. Robinson-Patman
    e. none of the above

4. Which of the following statements is true?
    a. In the Dupont case in 1956, the market relevant to Dupont was ruled to be the cellophane market, rather than the broader flexible wrapping materials market.
    b. In 1975, a court ruled that Alcoa was a monopoly.
    c. The way a market is defined can have much to say as to whether a firm is viewed as a monopoly or not.
    d. a and c
    e. a, b, and c

5. The advantage of the Herfindahl index over the four-firm and eight-firm concentration ratios is that it provides information about
    a. the dispersion of firm size in an industry.
    b. the price effects of industry concentration.
    c. merger acquisitions.
    d. b and c
    e. none of the above

6. Consider a merger between Firm A, with a market share of 19 percent, and Firm B, with a market share of 16 percent. Will the Antitrust Division of the Justice Department file suit against these two firms if they enter into a merger?
    a. No, because together they have 35 percent of the market.
    b. Yes, because the Herfindahl index is 617 (which is more than 200).
    c. No, because the difference between the Herfindahl index when the two firms are not merged and the Herfindahl index when they are merged is more than 200.
    d. No, because neither firm has a market share under 10 percent.
    e. No, because the Herfindahl index is 139 (which is more than 100).

7. When one firm can supply the entire output demanded at lower cost than two or more firms can, we have a(an)
    a. natural market.
    b. natural monopoly.
    c. regulated firm.
    d. efficient firm.
    e. none of the above

Exhibit 12

(1) Firm	(2) Quantity	(3) Average total cost
A	200 units	$5
B	400 units	$4
	600 units	$7

8. In Exhibit 12 above, the resource-allocative efficient output is 600 units. Currently, Firm B is the only firm supplying the good; it is supplying 400 units. Based on the data presented in Exhibit 12, is Firm B a natural monopoly? If so, why?
    a. No, because Firm A can supply 200 units at a lower average total cost than Firm B can supply 400 units.
    b. No, because it is not the only firm that can supply the good.
    c. Yes, because it can supply the entire output.
    d. No, because it cannot supply the entire output (600 units) at lower cost ($4,200) than the two firms together (where Firm A produces 200 units at $5 per unit and Firm B produces 400 units at $4 per unit).

9. In marginal-cost price regulation of the natural monopoly firm, the objective is to set a price
    a. that will guarantee zero economic profit.
    b. equal to average total cost.
    c. consistent with the maximization of profits.
    d. equal to the quantity of output at which demand intersects marginal cost.
    e. none of the above

10. One of the criticisms of average-cost pricing regulation of the natural monopoly firm is:
    a. if the natural monopoly firm knows it is guaranteed a price equal to average total cost, it will cut costs and decrease quality.
    b. the natural monopoly firm is forced into taking a loss.
    c. the natural monopoly is guaranteed a positive economic profit.
    d. none of the above

11. Which of the following is usually noted as a natural monopoly?
    a. a firm that builds houses
    b. a company that sells electricity
    c. a bank
    d. a cruise ship company
    e. none of the above

12. Under Civil Aeronautics Board (CAB) chairman _____, the airline industry began to be deregulated in 1978.
    a. Alfred Kahn
    b. R. T. McClow
    c. Everett George
    d. Michael Kennedy
    e. none of the above

13. George Stigler is closely associated with the _____, which says _____.
    a. public interest theory of regulation; regulators work hard to benefit the public interest
    b. capture hypothesis; regulatory agencies are "captured" by the special interests of the industry that are being regulated
    c. capture hypothesis; eventually the public "captures" the benefits of regulation through lower prices
    d. public interest theory or regulation; the public is dissatisfied with the efforts of the regulatory agencies but can do little about this situation.

14. One of the major criticisms of the antitrust laws is that
    a. certain antitrust acts hinder, rather than promote, competition.
    b. they are too short in length.
    c. they do not all employ the Herfindahl index.
    d. they do not all employ the four-firm concentration ratio.

15. Which of the following is a way of regulating a natural monopoly firm?
    a. output regulation
    b. average-cost regulation
    c. marginal-cost price regulation
    d. a, b, and c
    e. none of the above

True-False
Write "T" or "F" after each statement.

16. A criticism of profit regulation is that firms have no incentive to hold costs down. _____

17. The Herfindahl index is equal to the sum of the squares of the market shares of each firm in the industry divided by two. _____

18. Antitrust law is legislation passed for the stated purpose of increasing monopoly power and reducing competition. _____

19. The Wheeler-Lea Act empowered the Federal Trade Commission to deal with false and deceptive acts or practices. _____

20. The Clayton Act made tying contracts illegal. _____

Fill in the Blank
Write the correct word in the blank.

21. The _____ _____ _____ _____ _____ holds that regulators are seeking to do and will do through regulation what is in the best interest of the public or society at large.

22. The _____ _____ _____ _____ declared illegal "unfair methods of competition in commerce."

23. The local gas company is usually cited as an example of a _____ _____.

24. The way a _____ is defined will help determine whether a particular firm is considered a monopoly or not.

25. The Herfindahl index and the four- and eight-firm concentration ratios have been criticized from implicitly arguing from _____ to _____ _____.

Chapter 12
Factor Markets: With Emphasis on the Labor Market

What This Chapter Is About
There are many markets in an economy. This chapter is about a market that most people are particularly interested in—the labor market.

Key Concepts in the Chapter
    a.   derived demand
    b.   marginal revenue product
    c.   factor price taker
    d.   least-cost rule
    e.   marginal productivity theory

- **Derived demand** is demand that is the result of some other demand. For example, factor demand is the result of the demand for the products that factors go to produce.
- **Marginal revenue product** is the additional revenue generated by employing an additional factor unit.
- A **factor price taker** is a firm that can buy all of a factor it wants at the equilibrium price.
- The **least-cost rule** specifies the combination of factors that minimizes costs. It requires that the MPP/P ratio for each factor be the same.
- **Marginal productivity theory** states that firms in competitive or perfect product and factor markets pay factors their marginal revenue products.

Review Questions

1.   Give an example that illustrates what derived demand is.

2.   When is the factor demand curve downward sloping?

3.   When is value marginal product the same as marginal revenue product?

4.   How many units of a factor should a firm buy? Explain your answer.

5.   How are costs minimized if the least-cost rule is observed?

6.   What are three main determinants of elasticity of demand for labor?

7.   As the wage rate rises, the quantity supplied of labor rises. Does it follow that the income effect does not occur? Explain your answer.

8.   What affects the demand for labor?

9.   What affects the supply of labor?

10. Explain how what appears to be employer discrimination may be an information problem instead.

Problems

1.   Fill in the blank spaces in the table.

Quantity of factor Z	Quantity of output	Product price	Total revenue	Marginal revenue product
1	30	$40		
2	50	$40		
3	60	$40		

2.   Fill in the blank spaces in the table.

Quantity of factor Z	Price of factor Z	Total cost	Marginal factor cost
1	$10		
2	$10		
3	$10		

3.   Fill in the blank spaces in the table.

MPP of factor X (units)	Price of factor X	MPP of factor Y (units)	Price of factor Y	Should the firm buy more of factor X or factor Y?
30	$2	40	$1.25	
50	$4	100	$5	
100	$30	100	$40	

4.   Fill in the blank spaces in the table.

Change	Does this affect the demand for labor (yes, no)?	Does this affect the supply of labor (yes, no)?	Effect on wage (up, down, no change)
product supply falls			
product demand rises			
training costs rise			
positive change in the nonpecuniary aspects of the job			

5. Diagrammatically represent the VMP and MRP curves for a monopolist, monopolistic competitor, and oligopolist.

6. Diagrammatically represent the factor supply curve for a factor price taker.

What Is the Question?
Identify the question for each of the answers that follow.

1. The additional revenue generated by employing an additional factor unit.

2. It is also the factor demand curve.

3. It slopes downward because the MPP of the factor eventually declines.

4. It will buy the number of factor units for which MRP = MFC.

5. The firm will buy more of factor X and less of factor Y.

6. It is equal to the MPP of the factor divided by the cost of the factor.

7. The percentage change in the quantity demanded of labor divided by the percentage change in the wage rate.

8. It is upward sloping because the substitution effect outweighs the income effect.

9. One of the reasons is that jobs have different nonpecuniary qualities.

10. States that firms in competitive or perfect product and factor markets pay factors their marginal revenue products.

What Is Wrong?
In each of statements that follow, something is wrong. Identify what is wrong in the space that is provided.

1. If price equals marginal revenue, then VMP is greater than MRP.

2. The factor demand curve usually lies above the MRP curve.

3. The firm will purchase the quantity of a factor at which the difference between the MRP and MFC of the factor are maximized.

4. An increase in MPP will shift the factor demand curve to the left.

5. If the demand for the product that labor produces is highly elastic, a small percentage increase in price will decrease quantity demanded of the product by a relatively small percentage.

6. The more substitutes for labor, the lower the elasticity of demand for labor; the fewer substitutes for labor, the higher the elasticity of demand for labor.

7. Screening is the process used by employers to increase the probability of choosing good employees (to promote) from within the firm.

8. A firm minimizes costs by buying factors in the combination at which the MPP-to-price ratio for the expensive factors is greater than the MPP-to-price ratio for the less expensive factors.

9. The supply curve is upward-sloping for a factor price taker.

10. The higher the labor cost-total cost ratio, the lower the elasticity of demand for labor.

Multiple Choice
Circle the correct answer.

1. A factor price taker is a firm that
   a. can buy all of a factor it wants at the equilibrium price.
   b. can sell all of a product it wants at the equilibrium price.
   c. must pay a higher price to buy an additional unit of a factor.
   d. must lower price to sell an additional unit of the good it produces.

2. A firm that is a price taker in a factor market faces
   a. an upward-sloping supply curve of factors.
   b. a vertical supply curve of factors.
   c. a downward-sloping supply curve of factors.
   d. a horizontal supply curve of factors.

3. The demand for factors is
   a. a derived demand.
   b. an extra demand.
   c. an indirect demand.
   d. a distinct demand.
   e. none of the above

Exhibit 14

(1) Units of Factor X	(2) Quantity of output	(3) Product price	(4) Marginal revenue product
0	10	$12	
1	20	$12	A
2	29	$12	B
3	36	$12	C
4	41	$12	D

4. In Exhibit 14, the collar amounts that go in blanks A, B, C, and D are, respectively,
   a. $120; $108; $84; $60
   b. $100; $204; $30; $40
   c. $190; $180; $70; $40
   d. $105; $140; $40; $30

5. Suppose a factor price searcher purchases one unit of factor X for $15. What would it purchase the second unit of factor X for, and what would marginal factor cost (MFC) equal?
   a. It would purchase the second unit for $15, and MFC equals $15.
   b. There is not enough information to know what it would purchase the second unit for, and thus we do not know what MFC equals.
   c. It would purchase the second unit for $15, but there is not enough information to know what MFC equals.
   d. There is not enough information to know what it would purchase the second unit for, but MFC equals $15.
   e. none of the above

6. The marginal factor cost (MFC) curve is
   a. vertical for a factor price taker.
   b. horizontal for a factor price taker.
   c. horizontal for a factor price searcher.
   d. upward-sloping for a factor price searcher.
   e. b and d

7. For a product price searcher,
   a. VMP = MRP.
   b. VMP < MRP.
   c. VMP > MRP.
   d. There is not enough information to answer the question.

8. For a price taker in both the product and factor markets, at the profit-maximizing factor quantity,
   a. VMP = MRP > MFC = factor price
   b. VMP < MRP = MFC = factor price
   c. VMP > MRP = MFC = factor price
   d. VMP = MRP = MFC = factor price

9. The wage rate increases 30 percent and the quanitity demanded of labor falls by 90 percent. The elasticity of demand for labor is _____.
   a. 1.33
   b. 2.40
   c. 1.50
   d. 3.00
   e. none of the above

10. The lower the elasticity of demand for a product,
    a. the higher the ratio of labor costs to total costs.
    b. the lower the ratio of labor costs to total costs.
    c. the lower the elasticity of demand for the labor that produces the product.
    d. the higher the elasticity of demand for the labor that produces the product.
    e. none of the above

11. A rise in the wage rate
    a. shifts the supply curve of labor rightward.
    b. increases the quantity supplied of labor.
    c. shifts the supply curve of labor leftward.
    d. decreases the quantity supplied of labor.

12. The supply of labor curve will slope upward if the
    a. substitution effect outweighs the income effect.
    b. income effect outweighs the substitution effect.
    c. wage rises.
    d. wage falls.

13. Marginal factor cost is
    a. the additional cost incurred by employing an additional factor unit.
    b. the additional revenue generated by employing an additional factor unit.
    c. always equal to marginal revenue product.
    d. constant in the long run.
    e. a and d

14. The marginal revenue product (MRP) curve is the firm's
    a. marginal output curve.
    b. factor supply curve.
    c. average revenue curve.
    d. factor demand curve.

15. The more substitutes there are for labor,
    a. the more sensitive buyers of labor will be to a change in the price of labor.
    b. the less sensitive buyers of labor will be to a change in the price of labor.
    c. the higher costs will rise in the short run.
    d. the greater marginal revenue will be in the long run.
    e. none of the above

True-False
Write "T" or "F" after each statement.

16. The firm minimizes costs by buying factors in the combination at which the MPP-price ratio for each
    is the same. _____

17. Marginal productivity theory states that firms in competitive or perfect product and factor markets pay
    factors their marginal revenue products. _____

18. A factor price taker faces a horizontal supply curve of factors. _____

19. A firm can be a product price taker and a factor price searcher, but it cannot be a product price searcher
    and a factor price taker. _____

20. If the demand curve for the product that labor produces shifts rightward, the demand curve for labor
    shifts leftward. _____

Fill in the Blank
Write the correct word in the blank.

21. _____   _____   _____ = P x MPP.

22. The process used by employers to increase the probability of choosing "good" employees based on
    certain criteria is called _____.

23. The elasticity of demand for labor is defined as the percentage change in the _____
    _____ _____ _____ divided by the percentage change in the
    _____ _____.

24. The firm buys and employs the factor quantity at which (the condition) _____ = _____
    holds.

25. The demand for labor is _____.

Chapter 14
The Distribution of Income and Poverty

What This Chapter Is About
In an earlier chapter we discussed the factors that determine income. In this chapter we discuss the income distribution—specifically, how the income that is earned in society is distributed. We also discuss the issue of poverty. What are its causes? Why are some people poor and other people rich? What are the policies used to deal with poverty?

Key Concepts in the Chapter
    a.   Lorenz curve
    b.   Gini coefficient
    c.   human capital
    d.   wage discrimination
    e.   poverty income threshold

- The **Lorenz curve** is a graph of the income distribution. It expresses the relationship between cumulative percentage of households and cumulative percentage of income.
- The **Gini coefficient** is a measurement of the degree of inequality in the income distribution.
- **Human capital** refers to education, the development of skills, and anything else that is particular to the individual and increases his or her productivity.
- **Wage discrimination** is the situation that exists when individuals of equal ability and productivity are paid different wage rates.
- The **poverty income threshold** is the income level below which people are considered to be living in poverty.

Review Questions

1.   What are the four components of individual income?

2.   Explain how a Lorenz curve is constructed.

3.   What is a limitation of the Gini coefficient?

4. Identify the factors that contribute to income inequality.

5. What is the Rawlsian normative standard of the income distribution?

6. What is absolute poverty? What is relative poverty?

7. How does age affect the income distribution?

8. What is the marginal productivity normative standard of income distribution?

9. What is the public good-free rider argument for taxing persons to pay for the welfare assistance of some?

Problems

1. Fill in the blank spaces in the table.

Quintile	Percentage of total income, 2004
Lowest fifth	
Second fifth	
Third fifth	
Fourth fifth	
Highest fifth	

2. Fill in the blank spaces in the table.

Quintile	Income share (percent)	Cumulative percentage of income	Cumulative percentage of households
Lowest fifth	10		
Second fifth	12		
Third fifth	22		
Fourth fifth	25		
Highest fifth	31		

3. Diagrammatically represent the Lorenz curve if there is a perfectly equal income distribution.

Cumulative
Percentage
of Income

Quantity Percentage
of Households

4. Use the first table to fill in the blank spaces in the second table.

Cumulative percentage of households	Cumulative percentage of income
20	10
40	30
60	51
80	73
100	100

Quintile	Income share
Lowest fifth	
Second fifth	
Third fifth	
Fourth fifth	
Highest fifth	

What Is the Question?
Identify the question for each of the answers that follow.

1. Payments to persons that are not made in return for goods and services currently supplied.

2. Labor income plus asset income plus transfer payments minus taxes.

3. This exists when individuals of equal ability and productivity are paid different wage rates.

4. It is determined in factor markets.

5. The Gini coefficient is 1.

6. The income level below which people are considered to be living in poverty.

7. An example is that everyone who earns less than $5,000 is living in poverty.

8. An example is that the bottom one-tenth of income earners are living in poverty.

9. It holds that individuals currently not receiving welfare think they might one day need welfare assistance and thus are willing to take out a form of insurance for themselves by supporting welfare programs.

What Is Wrong?
In each of the statements that follow, something is wrong. Identify what is wrong in the space provided.

1. The government can change the distribution of income through taxes, but not through transfer payments.

2. The Lorenz curve is a measurement of the degree of inequality in the distribution of income.

3. The Rawlsian normative standard of the income distribution holds that there should be complete income equality.

4. Asset income is equal to the wage rate an individual receives multiplied by the number of hours he or she works.

5. In general, human capital refers to the increases in productivity brought about by humans when they use physical capital goods.

6. The Gini coefficient is zero (0) if there is an unequal income distribution.

Multiple Choice
Circle the correct answer.

1. Which of the following statements is true?
   a. In 2004, the top fifth of income earners earned 50.0% of total income.
   b. In 1967, the lowest 20% of all income earners earned over 10% of the total money income.
   c. The people that make up the highest fifth of all income earners are millionaires.
   d. a and c
   e. a, b, and c

2. The U.S. income distribution is likely to be less unequal if it is
   a. adjusted for in-kind transfer payments and taxes.
   b. adjusted for the capital appreciation allowance.
   c. not adjusted for taxes.
   d. not adjusted for in-kind transfer payments.
   e. none of the above

3. The smaller the Gini coefficient, the
   a. greater the degree of income inequality.
   b. greater the degree of income equality.
   c. higher the birth rate.
   d. larger the population.
   e. none of the above

4. Which of the following statements is false?
   a. Economists agree that it is better for a country to have a lower Gini coefficient than a higher one.
   b. Economists agree that it is better for a country to have a higher Gini coefficient than a lower one.
   c. There is greater income equality in the United States than Sweden.
   d. Because the Gini coefficient is lower in Country A than Country B, the lowest income group in Country A has a greater percentage of total income than the lowest income group in Country B.
   e. all of the above

5. One way to increase the degree of income inequality is to
   a. decrease transfer payments going to people with low labor and asset incomes and decrease taxes on people with high labor and asset incomes.
   b. increase transfer payments going to people with low labor and asset incomes and decrease taxes on people with high labor and asset incomes.
   c. increase transfer payments going to people with low labor and asset incomes by more than you increase taxes on the same people.
   d. increase transfer payments going to people with high labor and asset incomes by less than you increase taxes on the same people.
   e. a and d

6. Which of the following statements is true?
    a. If people were alike in terms of their marketable innate abilities and attributes, there would be less income inequality.
    b. Some degree of income inequality can be attributed to the fact that some people consume more leisure than others.
    c. Schooling is referred to as human capital.
    d. a and c
    e. a, b, and c

7. Human capital refers to
    a. equal pay.
    b. education and development of skills.
    c. factories and computers.
    d. a and c
    e. none of the above

8. The proponents of absolute income equality sometimes argue that an equal income distribution of income will maximize total utility. Their argument goes like this:
    a. Individuals are alike when it comes to how much satisfaction they receive from an increase in income; receiving additional income is subject to the law of diminishing marginal utility, redistributing income from the rich to the poor helps the poor less than it hurts the rich, so total utility rises.
    b. Individuals are alike when it comes to how much satisfaction they receive from an increase in income; receiving additional income is subject to the law of constant marginal costs, redistributing income from the rich to the poor helps the poor more than it hurts the rich, so total utility rises.
    c. Individuals are not alike when it comes to how much satisfaction they receive from an increase in income; receiving additional income is subject to the law of diminishing marginal utility, redistributing income from the rich to the poor helps the poor less than it hurts the rich, so total utility rises.
    d. Individuals are alike when it comes to how much satisfaction they receive from an increase in income; receiving additional income is subject to the law of diminishing marginal utility, redistributing income from the rich to the poor helps the poor more than it hurts the rich, so total utility rises.

9. Which of the following is a definition of poverty in relative terms?
    a. A family is in poverty if it receives less than $10,000 a year.
    b. A family is in poverty if it receives an income that places it in the lowest 5 percent of family income recipients.
    c. A family is in poverty if the majority of families receive more income than it receives.
    d. b and c
    e. a, b, and c

10. Which of the following leads to an underestimate of the number of persons in poverty?
    a. illegal income
    b. unreported income
    c. some poor persons can't be found, therefore they can't be counted
    d. a and b
    c. a, b, and c

True-False
Write "T" or "F" at the end of each statement.

11. The *ex ante* distribution of income is the before-tax and before-transfer distribution of income. ____

12. The Lorenz curve is a graphical representation of the distribution of income. ____

13. The *ex post* distribution of income (in the U.S.) is more equal than the *ex ante* distribution of income. ____

14. John Rawls wrote *A Theory of Justice.* ____

15. The acceptance of the public good-free rider argument leads individuals to conclude that government is justified in taxing all persons to pay for welfare assistance for some. ____

Fill in the Blank
Write the correct word in the blank.

16. _____ _____ are payments to persons that are not made in return for goods and services currently supplied.

17. The _____ _____ is a measurement of the degree of inequality in the income distribution.

18. _____ _____ exists when individuals of equal ability and productivity, as measured by their marginal revenue products, are paid different wage rates.

19. The closer the Gini coefficient is to _____, the greater the degree of income inequality.

20. The _____ _____ distribution of income is the before-tax-and-transfer payment distribution of income.

Chapter 18
International Trade

What This Chapter Is About
This chapter is about international trade—why people in different countries trade with each other, the effects of tariffs and quotas, and more.

Key Concepts in the Chapter
    a.   comparative advantage
    b.   consumers' surplus
    c.   producers' surplus

- **Comparative advantage** is the situation in which a country can produce a good at lower opportunity cost than another country.
- **Consumers' surplus** is the difference between the maximum buying price and the price paid.
- **Producers' surplus** is the difference between the price received (by the seller) and the minimum selling price.

Review Questions

1. Why do people in different countries trade with each other?

2. Why are countries better off specializing and trading (with each other) than not specializing and not trading?

3. How will a tariff affect (domestic) consumers' surplus?

4. How will a quota affect (domestic) producers' surplus?

5. Why might quotas be imposed even when the benefits of quotas (to the beneficiaries) are less than the costs of the quotas?

6. Outline the details of the infant-industry argument for trade restrictions.

7. What is the antidumping argument for trade restrictions?

8. Suppose a tariff or quota saves some domestic jobs. Would an economist say it is worth it? Explain your answer.

9.   What is the role of the WTO?

10.   There is a net loss from tariffs. What does this mean?

Problems

1.   Fill in the blank spaces in the second table, based on the information in the first table.

Country A can produce these combinations of X and Y	Country B can produce these combinations of X and Y
120X, 0Y	60X, 0Y
80X, 60Y	40X, 20Y
40X, 120Y	20X, 40Y
0X, 180Y	0X, 60Y

Opportunity cost of one unit of X for Country A	Opportunity cost of one unit of Y for Country A	Opportunity cost of one unit of X for Country B	Opportunity cost of one unit of Y for Country B

2.   Using the diagram that follows, identify the area of consumers' surplus.

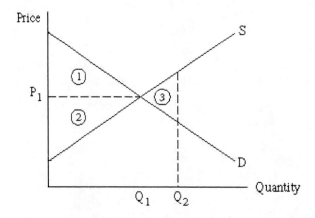

3. Using the diagram that follows, identify the area of producers' surplus.

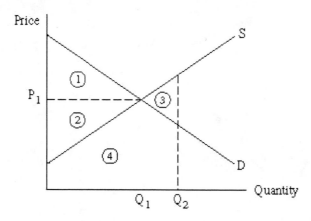

4. In the diagram (that follows), the world price is P_W. The price after a tariff has been imposed is P_T. Identify the change in consumers' surplus due to the tariff. Identify the change in producers' surplus due to the tariff.

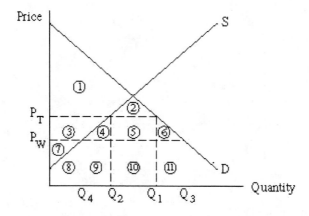

5. In the diagram (that follows), identify the gain due to the tariff. Next, identify the loss due to the tariff.

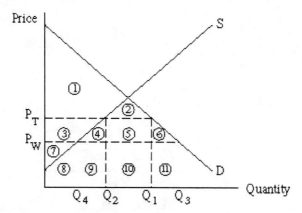

6.   In the diagram (that follows), identify the net loss due to the tariff.

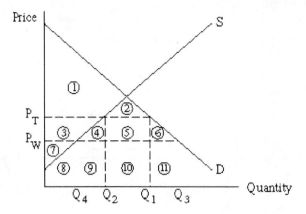

7.   In the diagram (that follows), P_W is the world price and P_Q is the price after a quota has been imposed. Identify the increase in additional revenue received by importers due to the quota.

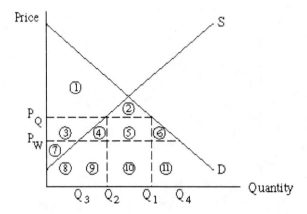

8.   Using the diagram that follows, fill in the blank spaces in the table below.

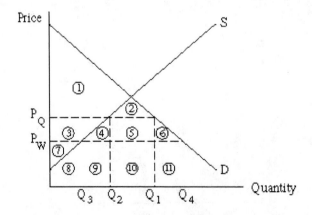

Price after quota	Loss in consumers' surplus due to the quota	Gain in producers' surplus due to the quota	Increase in revenue received by importers due to the quota	Net loss due to the quota
P_Q				

What is the Question?
Identify the questions for each of the answers that follow.

1.   This will allow the country to consume beyond its production possibilities frontier (PPF).

2.   As a result, imports decrease.

3.   The sale of goods abroad at a price below their cost and below the price charged in the domestic market.

4.   The situation in which a country can produce a good at lower opportunity cost than another country.

5.   The gains are less than the losses plus the tariff revenues.

What Is Wrong?
In each of the statements that follow, something is missing. Identify what is wrong in the space provided.

1.   A PPF for the world can be drawn when 1) countries do not specialize and trade and 2) when they do specialize and trade. The world PPF will be the same in both cases.

2. The national-defense argument states that certain goods are necessary to the national defense and therefore should be produced only by allies.

3. A quota raises more government revenue than a tariff.

4. Consumers' surplus and producers' surplus fall as a result of a tariff being imposed on imported goods.

5. What producers gain from a quota is greater than what consumers lose from a quota.

6. If the United States sells a good for less in France than it does in Brazil, then the United States is said to be dumping goods in France.

7. A voluntary export restraint is an agreement between two countries in which importing countries voluntarily agree to limit their imports of a good from another country.

8. A quota is a tax on the amount of a good that may be imported into a country.

Multiple Choice
Circle the correct answer.

EXHIBIT A

United States		Japan	
Good X	Good Y	Good X	Good Y
120	0	30	0
80	10	20	10
40	20	10	20
0	30	0	30

1. In Exhibit A, the opportunity cost of one unit of Y for the United States is _____, whereas the opportunity cost of one unit of Y for Japan is _____.
    a.   2X; 5X
    b.   10X; 2X
    c.   4X; 1X
    d.   6X; 5X
    e.   none of the above

2. In Exhibit A, the United States is the lower opportunity cost producer of _____ and Japan is the lower opportunity cost producer of _____.
    a.   good X; good Y
    b.   both goods; neither good
    c.   neither good; both goods.
    d.   good Y; good X

3. Considering the data in Exhibit A, which of the following terms of trade would both countries agree to?
    a.   5.5X = 1Y
    b.   0.5X = 1Y
    c.   5X = 1Y
    d.   2X = 1Y

4. Jack paid $40 for good X and gained $10 consumers' surplus. What is the highest price Jack would have paid for the good?
    a. $50
    b. $30
    c. $60
    d. $65
    e.   There is not enough information to answer the question.

5. Producers' surplus is the difference between the price _____ receive for a good and the _____ price for which they would have _____ the good.
    a.   sellers; minimum; sold
    b.   buyers; maximum; bought
    c.   sellers; maximum; sold
    d.   buyers; minimum; bought

6. The national defense argument for trade restriction contends that
    a.   the president should have the authority to erect trade barriers in case of war or national emergency.
    b.   free trade makes a country dependent on other countries and this weakens the national defense.
    c.   a country should produce those goods necessary fro national defense purposes even if it doesn't have a comparative advantage in them.
    d.   if your enemy erects trade restrictions, so should you.
    e.   b and c

7. Dumping refers to
   a. buying goods at low prices in foreign countries and selling them at high prices in the United States.
   b. expensive goods being sold for low prices.
   c. government actions to remedy "unfair" trade practices.
   d. the sale of goods abroad at a price below their cost and below the price charged in the domestic market.

8. A tariff is a
   a. restriction on the number of people that can work in an export business.
   b. legal limit on the amount of a good that may be imported.
   c. business fee incurred to ship goods abroad.
   d. tax on imports.
   e. none of the above

9. Under a policy of prohibiting exports,
   a. domestic consumers have greater consumers' surplus than under a policy of permitting exports.
   b. domestic consumers have less consumers' surplus than under a policy of permitting exports.
   c. domestic producers have greater producers' surplus than under a policy of permitting exports.
   d. a and c
   e. b and c

10. Under a tariff policy,
   a. domestic consumers have greater consumers' surplus than under a policy of free trade.
   b. domestic consumers have less consumers' surplus than under a policy of free trade.
   c. domestic producers have greater producers' surplus than under a policy of free trade.
   d. a and c
   e. b and c

11. Company A is a new company that produces a good that is already produced in many foreign countries and sold in the United States. Most likely, the argument it will voice in its attempt to be protected from foreign competition is the
   a. antidumping argument.
   b. low-foreign-wages argument.
   c. job creating argument.
   d. infant industry argument.
   e. national defense argument.

12. Tariffs and quotas are
   a. beneficial for producers in a protected industry, but not beneficial for the workers in the industry.
   b. beneficial for producers in a protected industry, but not beneficial for consumers.
   c. beneficial for workers in a protected industry, but not beneficial for consumers.
   d. not beneficial for the workers in a protected industry or for consumers.
   e. b and c

13. A tariff is imposed on good X. The tariff will _____ the price of good X in the domestic market, _____ the number of units of good X imported into the domestic market, and _____ consumers' surplus.
   a. lower; raise; raise
   b. raise; lower; lower
   c. raise; lower; raise
   d. lower; raise; lower
   e. none of the above

14. Tariffs and quotas are often imposed when government is responsive to _____ interests, and the benefits of tariffs and quotas are often _____.
    a. consumer; dispersed
    b. consumer; concentrated
    c. producer; dispersed
    d. producer; concentrated

15. Which of the following is not an example of a trade restriction?
    a. tariff
    b. quota
    c. dumping
    d. a and b
    e. a, b, and c

True-False
Write "T" or "F" at the end of each statement.

16. Consumers' surplus is greater at higher prices than lower prices. ____

17. There is a net loss from tariffs. ____

18. Specialization and trade allow a country's inhabitants to consume at a level beyond its production possibilities frontier. ____

19. If the price received is $40 and producers' surplus is $10, then the minimum selling price is $30. ____

20. A quota is a legal limit on the amount of a good that may be imported. ____

Fill in the Blank
Write the correct word in the blank.

21. The _____ argument states that domestic producers should not have to compete (on an unequal basis) with foreign producers that sell products below cost and below the prices they charge in their domestic markets.

22. As a result of a quota, the number of imported goods will _____.

23. As a result of a tariff, consumers' surplus _____.

24. The gains from a quota are _____ than the losses from a quota.

25. The gains from free trade are _____ than the losses from protected (non-free) trade.

Chapter 19
International Finance

What This Chapter Is About
The main subject of this chapter is exchange rates. What are exchange rates? How are exchange rates determined? What are the effects of changes in exchange rates? These questions and more are answered in this chapter.

Key Concepts in the Chapter
    a.   balance of payments
    b.   current account balance
    c.   capital account balance
    d.   merchandise trade balance
    e.   exchange rate
    f.   appreciation
    g.   depreciation
    h.   optimal currency area

- The **balance of payments** is a periodic statement of the money value of all transactions between residents of one country and residents of all other countries.
- The **current account balance** is the summary statistic for exports of goods and services, imports of goods and services, and net unilateral transfers abroad.
- The **capital account balance** is the summary statistic for the outflow of U.S. capital and the inflow of foreign capital. It is equal to the difference between the outflow of U.S. capital and the inflow of foreign capital.
- The **merchandise trade balance** is the difference between the value of merchandise exports and the value of merchandise imports.
- The **exchange rate** is the price of one currency in terms of another currency.
- **Appreciation** refers to an increase in the value of one currency relative to other currencies.
- **Depreciation** refers to a decrease in the value of one currency relative to other currencies.
- An **optimal currency area** is a geographic area in which exchange rates can be fixed or a common currency used without sacrificing domestic economic goals—such as low unemployment.

Review Questions

1.   Give an example of a transaction that would be considered a debit item in the balance of payments.

2.   Give an example of a transaction that would be considered a credit item in the balance of payments.

3.   What is the difference between the current account balance and the merchandise trade balance?

4.   What items compose the capital account?

5.   What is the difference between a flexible and a fixed exchange rate system?

6.   The demand for pounds is related to the supply of dollars. How so?

7. The supply of pounds is related to the demand for dollars. How so?

8. It took 106 yen to buy 1 dollar on Tuesday and 110 yen to buy 1 dollar on Wednesday. Has the dollar appreciated or depreciated from Tuesday to Wednesday? Explain your answer.

9. What factors can lead to a change in exchange rates?

10. Give an example of a currency that is overvalued.

11. What is the difference between a currency that is devalued and one that has depreciated?

Problems

Answer questions 1 through 5 based on the table that follows.

Item	Dollar amount
Merchandise exports	+ 400
Income from U.S. assets abroad	+ 36
Services (exports)	+ 80
Outflow of U.S. capital	− 33
Statistical discrepancy	− 20
Inflow of foreign capital	+ 50
Increase in U.S. official reserve assets	− 5
Decrease in foreign official assets in the U.S.	+ 4
Merchandise imports	− 410
Services (imports)	− 34
Net unilateral transfers abroad	− 18
Income from foreign assets in U.S.	− 50

1. What does the merchandise trade balance equal?

2. What does the current account balance equal?

3. What does the capital account balance equal?

4. What does the official reserve balance equal?

5. What does the balance of payments equal?

6. Suppose there are only two currencies in the world, pesos and dollars. Fill in the blank spaces in the table.

If the	Then the
demand for dollars rises in the foreign exchange market	
	supply of dollars falls on the foreign exchange market
	supply of pesos rises on the foreign exchange market

7. Fill in the blank spaces where a question mark appears in the table.

If	Then
$1 = 106 yen	1 yen = ?
$1 = 74 Kenyan shillings	1 shilling = ?
$1 = 1,500 Lebanese pounds	1 pound = ?

8. Fill in the blank spaces in the table.

The exchange rate is	And the item costs	What does the item cost in dollars?
$1 = 106 yen	18,000 yen	
$1 = £0.50	£ 34.00	
$1 = 9.44 pesos	89 pesos	

9. Fill in the blank spaces in the table.

The exchange rate changes from	Has the dollar appreciated or depreciated?
$2 = £1 to $2.50 = £1	
109 yen = $1 to 189 yen = $1	
10 pesos = $1 to 8 pesos = $1	

10. Fill in the blank spaces in the table.

If ...	The dollar will (appreciate, depreciate)
the real interest rate in the U.S. rises relative to real interest rates in other countries	
income in foreign countries (that trade with the U.S.) rises relative to income in the United States	
the inflation rate in the U.S. rises and the inflation rate in all other countries falls	

11. Fill in the blank spaces in the table.

If the equilibrium exchange rate is $1 = £ 0.50 and the official exchange rate is	Then the dollar is (overvalued, undervalued)
$1 = £ 0.60	
$1 = £ 0.30	

What is the Question?

Identify the question for each of the answers that follow.

1. Any transaction that supplies the country's currency in the foreign exchange market.

2. Any transaction that creates a demand for the country's currency in the foreign exchange market.

3. The summary statistic for the exports of goods and services, imports of goods and services, and net unilateral transfers abroad.

4. The difference between the value of merchandise exports and the value of merchandise imports.

5. One-way money payments.

6. The price of one currency in terms of another currency.

7. It predicts that the exchange rates between any two currencies will adjust to reflect changes in the relative price levels of the two countries.

8. Raising the official price of a currency.

What Is Wrong?

In each of the statements that follow, something is wrong. Identify what is wrong in the space provided.

1. The balance of payments is the summary statistic for the current account balance, capital account balance, net unilateral transfers abroad, and statistical discrepancy.

2. The demand for dollars on the foreign exchange market is linked to the supply of dollars on the foreign exchange market. In short, if the demand for dollars rises, the supply of dollars rises, too.

3. There are two countries, A and B. The income of Country B rises and the income of Country A remains constant. As a result, the currency of Country B appreciates.

4. There are two countries, C and D. The price level in Country C rises 10 percent and the inflation rate in Country D is zero percent. As a result, the demand for Country C's goods rises, and the supply of its currency falls.

5. A change in real interest rates across countries cannot change the exchange rate.

6. If the equilibrium exchange rate is £1 = $1.50, and the official exchange rate is £1 = $1.60, then the dollar is overvalued and the pound is undervalued.

7. An international monetary fund right is a special international money created by the IMF.

Multiple Choice
Circle the correct answer.

1. An international transaction that supplies the nation's currency also creates a
    a. supply of foreign currency, and is recorded as a credit in the balance of payments.
    b. demand for foreign currency, and is recorded as a credit in the balance of payments.
    c. demand for foreign currency, and is recorded as a debit in the balance of payments.
    d. supply of the nation's currency, and is recorded as a debit in the balance of payments.

2. If the French buy American computers, they
    a. demand U.S. dollars and supply French francs.
    b. demand U.S. dollars and demand French francs.
    c. supply U.S. dollars and demand French francs.
    d. supply both U.S. dollars and French francs.

Exhibit A

Components of the Balance of Payments	($ billions)
Exports of goods and services	+ 330
Merchandise exports (including military sales)	+ 150
Export services	+ 40
Income from U.S. assets abroad	+ 140
Imports of goods and services	− 390
Merchandise imports (including military sales)	− 220
Import services	− 80
Income from foreign assets abroad	− 90
Net unilateral transfers abroad	− 21
Outflow of U.S. capital	− 46
Inflow of foreign capital	+ 60
Increase in U.S. official reserve assets	− 21
Increase in foreign official assets in U.S.	+ 23
Statistical discrepancy	+ 65

3. In Exhibit A, the merchandise trade balance equals _____ billion dollars.
    a. − 80
    b. + 100
    c. − 70
    d. + 60
    e. none of the above

4. In Exhibit A, the current account balance equals _____ billion dollars.
    a. − 111
    b. − 81
    c. − 60
    d. + 63
    e. none of the above

5. In Exhibit A, the capital account balance equals _____ billion dollars.
    a. + 15
    b. − 10
    c. + 14
    d. − 14
    e. none of the above

6. In Exhibit A, the official reserve balance equals _____ billion dollars.
    a. + 2
    b. − 1
    c. + 10
    d. + 17
    e. none of the above

7. The three major components of the current account are
    a. exports of goods and services, imports of goods and services, and statistical discrepancy.
    b. outflow of U.S. foreign capital, inflow of foreign capital, and statistical discrepancy.
    c. merchandise exports, merchandise imports, and net unilateral transfers abroad
    d. exports of goods and services, imports of goods and services, and inflow of foreign capital.
    e. none of the above

8. The lower the dollar price per yen, the _____ Japanese goods are for Americans and the _____ Japanese goods Americans will buy; thus _____ yen will be demanded.
    a. more expensive; more; fewer
    b. more expensive; fewer; fewer
    c. less expensive; more; more
    d. less expensive; more; fewer
    e. none of the above

9. An American computer is priced at $5,500. If the exchange rate between the U.S. dollar and the British pound is $1.70 = £1, approximately how many pounds will a British buyer pay for the computer?
    a. £3,235
    b. £3,052
    c. £2,543
    d. £6,599

10. If the dollar price per pound moves from $1.90 = £1 to $1.40 = £1, the pound is said to have _____ and the dollar to have _____.
    a. depreciated; appreciated
    b. appreciated; appreciated
    c. appreciated; depreciated
    d. depreciated; depreciated

11. The U.S. dollar has appreciated relative to the French franc if it takes
    a. fewer francs to buy a dollar.
    b. fewer dollars to buy a franc.
    c. more dollars to buy a franc.
    d. a and c
    e. none of the above

12. Suppose the current exchange rate between the dollar and British pound is $1.70 = £1. Furthermore, suppose the price level in the United States rises 25 percent at a time when the British price level is stable. According to the purchasing power parity theory, what will be the new equilibrium exchange rate?
    a. $2.72 = £1
    b. $1.55 = £1
    c. $1.86 = £1
    d. $2.13 = £1

13. The purchasing power parity theory predicts less nearly accurately in the _____ run, and when there is
    a _____ difference in inflation rates across countries.
    a. long; small
    b. short; large
    c. long; large
    d. short; small

14. Under a fixed exchange rate system, if the Mexican peso is overvalued then there exists
    a. a shortage of pesos.
    b. a surplus of pesos.
    c. the equilibrium level of pesos.
    d. there is not enough information to answer the question (we need to know the actual exchange rate)

15. One of the things a nation must do if it is on an international gold standard is
    a. link its money supply to its gold holdings.
    b. increase taxes.
    c. declare itself to be on a flexible exchange rate system.
    d. revalue its currency.
    e. none of the above

True-False
Write "T" or "F" after each statement.

16. If more euros are needed to buy a dollar, then the dollar has appreciated. ____

17. If fewer euros are needed to buy a peso, the euro has depreciated. ____

18. Any transaction that supplies the nation's currency is recorded as a debit in the balance of payments.

    ____

19. The current account balance is the summary statistic for exports of goods and services, imports of
    goods and services, and the statistical discrepancy. ____

20. Any transaction that supplies a foreign currency is recorded as a credit in the balance of payments.

    ____

Fill in the Blank
Write the correct word in the blank.

21. The _____ _____ _____ is the difference between the value of
    merchandise exports and the value of merchandise imports.

22. The _____ _____ _____ _____ predicts that
    changes in the relative price levels of two countries will affect the exchange rate in such a way that one
    unit of nation's currency will continue to buy the same amount of foreign goods as it did before the
    change in the relative price levels.

23. When nations adopt the gold standard, they automatically _____ their exchange rates.

24. A _____ occurs when the official price of currency (under the fixed exchange rate
    system) is lowered.

25. Central banks play a much larger role under a _____ exchange rate system than under a
    _____ exchange rate system.

Chapter 20
Globalization

What This Chapter Is About
This chapter is about the costs and the benefits of globalization.

Key Concepts in the Chapter
    a.   globalization
    b.   offshoring

- **Globalization** is a phenomenon by which economic agents in any given part of the world are more affected by events elsewhere in the world than before; it refers to the growing integration of the national economies of the world to the degree that we may be witnessing the emergence and operation of a single worldwide economy.
- **Offshoring** is the term used to describe work done for a company by persons other than the company's original employees in a country other than the one in which the company is located.

Review Questions

1. Globalization is a process by which the world "becomes smaller." What does this mean?

2. Give an example of something happening in one country that affects the people in another country.

3. Identify and explain the two ways (identified in the text) with which to "see" globalization.

4. Is globalization unique to the end of the 20th century and beginning of the 21st century?

5. What is the "end-of-the-Cold-War" explanation for current globalization?

6. How can technological advancements promote globalization?

7. Give an example of an economic policy that acts to retard globalization.

8. Identify a few of the potential benefits of globalization.

9. When it comes to globalization, it is often much more difficult to see the benefits than the costs. Why?

What Is the Question?
Identify the question for each of the answers that follow.

1. During a rather intense period of globalization during the 1990s and early 2000s, the unemployment rate in the U.S. was low.

2. Forty percent in 1946 and about 1.4 percent today.

3. In 1995 it was 60 times higher than it was in 1977.

4. In 1946, only 18 countries were members; in 2006, 149 countries were members.

5. The end of the Cold War.

6. The end of the Cold War, technological changes that lower the costs of transporting goods and communicating with people, and government policy changes that express an openness toward freer markets and long-distance trade.

7. Because the benefits are spread over many people and the costs are concentrated on relatively few.

What Is Wrong?

In each of the statements that follow, there is something wrong. Identify what is wrong in the space provided.

1. Globalization is closely aligned with a movement toward more free enterprise, restrained markets, and more freedom of government for people and goods.

2. Tariff rates are higher in the United States today than they were in 1946.

3. The cost of a three-minute telephone call from New York to London was $250; in 2000, it was $10

4. Between 1980 and 2000, income per person increased 20 percent in India.

5. Between 1990 and 2005, the CPI rose more slowly than the import price index.

6. Globalization causes greater income inequality.

7. The benefits of globalization tend to be difficult to see, partly because they are so concentrated.

Multiple Choice

Circle the correct answer.

1. A characteristic of globalization is
   a. a greater world population.
   b. a greater number of economic links with people outside the country.
   c. a physically smaller world.
   d. less offshoring.
   e. a and b

2. Globalization was occurring between 1990 and 2006. If globalization takes jobs away from Americans (without replacing them, in whole or in part), then we would expect to see during this period
   a. a declining unemployment rate.
   b. a rising unemployment rate.
   c. declining U.S. ownership of foreign stocks.
   d. less foreign direct investment.
   e. none of the above

3. As evidence of increased globalization,
   a. in 2000 the average tariff was 18.7 percent and one year later it was lower.
   b. daily foreign trading has increased.
   c. fewer countries are members of the WTO.
   d. a and b
   e. b and c

4. Which of the following statements is false?
   a. During the period from the mid-1800s to the late-1920s, globalization was occurring.
   b. According to Thomas Friedman, globalization is not an economic fad.
   c. Globalization is closely aligned with a movement toward more free enterprise, freer markets, and more freedom of movement for people and goods.
   d. The average tariff rate in the United States is higher today than it was in 1946.
   e. none of the above

5. Some of the signs of globalization include:
   a. tariff rates rising.
   b. greater foreign exchange trading.
   c. less foreign direct investment.
   d. more residents in one country working for companies located in other countries.
   e. b and d

6. The Internet is most likely something that
   a. does not affect globalization.
   b. promotes globalization.
   c. leads to a change in government policy toward more protectionism.
   d. b and c
   e. none of the above

7. Some of the benefits of globalization often cited include:
   a. friendlier relations between countries.
   b. a homogeneous world culture.
   c. higher income per person.
   d. less stressful life.
   e. none of the above

8. Some of the costs of globalization often cited include:
   a. increased income inequality.
   b. offshoring (losing jobs).
   c. more stressful life.
   d. a and b
   e. a, b, and c

9. A debate wages on as to whether there will be more or less globalization in the future. One of the factors that could result in less globalization is
    a. a change in government policy toward, say, greater protectionism.
    b. less global terrorism.
    c. technological advances.
    d. b and c
    e. none of the above

10. Which of the following statements is false?
    a. Robert Wright argues that it is not a coincidence that religious tolerance is high in the United States, a country that is open to trade and globalization.
    b. One of the benefits of globalization is increased trade.
    c. Between 1977 and 2004, the inflation-adjusted prices for an array of goods traded between countries increased while the inflation-adjusted prices for an array of goods not traded between countries actually decreased.
    d. b and c
    e. none of the above

True-False
Write "T" or "F" at the end of each statement.

11. A U.K. study showed that almost three times as many firms that faced global competition reported product or process innovations than those firms that did not face global competition. _____

12. Increased income inequality is sometimes cited as one of the costs of globalization. _____

13. Globalization is often associated with less free enterprise. _____

14. Foreign direct investment relates to a company in one country investing in a company in another country. _____

15. In 1948, 10 countries of the world were members of the WTO. _____

Fill in the Blank
Write the correct word in the blank.

16. The _____ _____ _____ is an international organization whose mission it is to promote international free trade.

17. _____ _____ by governments can affect globalization.

18. One of the benefits of globalization is _____ _____ for goods.

19. _____ is the practice of hiring people in other countries.

20. According to _____ _____ "Man is an animal that makes bargains: no other animal does this — no dog exchanges bones with another."

Answer Key

Chapter 1
Answers

Review Questions
1. Yes and no. This is only part of scarcity. Scarcity is the condition in which people have infinite wants *and* there are not enough resources (finite resources) to satisfy those wants.
2. A good gives a person utility or satisfaction; a bad gives a person disutility or dissatisfaction. People want goods and they don't want bads.
3. Josie likes to play music on Friday night. Music is a good on Friday night. Josie doesn't like to play music when she is studying for an exam. At that time, music is a bad.
4. The opportunity cost of your reading this study guide is whatever you would be doing if you weren't reading it. If you would be watching television, then watching television is the opportunity cost of your reading this study guide.
5. People are interested in only doing things when the benefits are greater than the costs. As the cost of smoking rises, it will be the case (for some people) that the benefits of smoking will no longer be greater than the costs, and therefore they will quit smoking.
6. marginal
7. Harriet considers what is relevant. Only the benefits of the next hour and the costs of the next hour are relevant to her. Costs and benefits in the past are not relevant. What does it matter what the costs and benefits have been? What matters is what they are expected to be. Marginal benefits and marginal costs deal with "additions," hence they deal with benefits and costs to come.
8. Answers will vary. Here is a sample answer. Someone takes a sleeping pill at night in order to get a restful sleep. Getting a restful sleep is the intended effect. The person does get a restful sleep, but also feels rather groggy for the first two hours she is up in the morning. Feeling groggy is an unintended effect.
9. Because scarcity exists—because our wants are greater than the resources available to satisfy them— we must decide (choose) which of our wants we will satisfy and which of our wants we won't satisfy. When we make choices, we necessarily incur an opportunity cost. After all, to choose to do X is to choose not to do Y. Y is the opportunity cost of doing X.
10. To think in terms of what would have been is to think in terms of opportunity cost. For example, you choose to go for a jog by the beach. What might have been had you not decided to jog by the beach? What would you have done instead? Whatever it was, it was the opportunity cost of your jogging by the beach.
11. The right amount of time to study—or the efficient amount of time to study—is the amount of time at which the marginal benefits of studying equal the marginal costs.
12. Land, labor, capital, and entrepreneurship.

Theory on a Television Show

Problems
1.

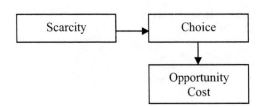

203

2.

Factor	Benefits of attending college	Costs of attending college	More likely to go to college? Yes or No
Jim thought he would earn $20 an hour if he didn't go to college, but learns that he will earn $35 an hour instead.		↑	No
His friends are going to college and he likes being around his friends.	↑		Yes
The salary gap between college graduates and high school graduates has widened.	↑		Yes
Jim learns something about himself: he doesn't like to study.		↑	No
The college he is thinking about attending just opened a satellite campus near Jim's home.		↓	Yes
The economy has taken a downturn and it looks like there are very few jobs for high school graduates right now.		↓	Yes

4. a. microeconomics, b. macroeconomics, c. macroeconomics, d. macroeconomics, e. microeconomics, f. microeconomics, g. microeconomics

5. Answers will vary. In each case, you want to ask yourself what you would do if you chose not to do the activity specified. The following are some sample answers.

Activity	Opportunity Cost
Study one more hour each night	Watch television
Take a long trip to someplace you have always wanted to visit	Buy a new car
Sit in the back of the room in one of your classes	Sit in the middle of the room
Talk up more in class	Daydream
Get a regular medical checkup	Play tennis
Surf the Web more	Watch television

What Is Wrong?

1. People have finite wants and infinite resources.

    People have infinite wants and resources are finite. This is scarcity.

2. People prefer more bads to fewer bads.

    Since people receive disutility from bads, they want fewer bads. Alternatively, you could say that people prefer more goods to fewer goods.

3. Scarcity is an effect of competition.

    Competition is an effect of scarcity.

4. The lower the opportunity cost of playing tennis, the less likely a person will play tennis.

    The lower the opportunity cost of playing tennis, the more likely a person will play tennis. The higher the opportunity cost of playing tennis, the less likely a person will play tennis.

5. Microeconomics is the branch of economics that deals with human behavior and choices as they relate to highly aggregate markets or the entire economy.

    Macroeconomics is the branch of economics that deals with human behavior and choices as they relate to highly aggregate markets or the entire economy.

6. Positive economics is to normative economics what opinion is to truth.

    Positive economics and truth are more closely aligned, as are normative economics and opinion.

7. Because there are rationing devices, there will always be scarcity.

    Because there is scarcity, there will always be rationing devices.

8. The four factors of production, or resources, are land, labor, capital, and profit.

    Profit is not a factor of production, it is a payment to a factor of production. The missing factor of production is entrepreneurship.

9. In a two-person exchange, one person is made better off while the other person is made worse off.

    In a two-person exchange, both persons are made better off.

10. If X is a good for Smith, it must then be a good for Jones too.

    If X is a good for Smith, it does not necessarily follow that X is good for Jones too.

Multiple Choice
   1. c
   2. b
   3. a
   4. b
   5. c
   6. c
   7. a
   8. c
   9. c
   10. d

True-False
   11. T
   12. F
   13. T
   14. F
   15. F

Fill in the Blank
   16. Macroeconomics
   17. fails to reject
   18. marginal
   19. capital
   20. entrepreneur
   21. Exchange

Chapter 2
Answers

Review Questions

1. *Ex ante* position. *Ex ante* means before the exchange.
2. Economic growth is represented as a shift rightward in the PPF.
3. Choice is represented by any point on or below the PPF. Opportunity cost is (best) represented as a movement from one point on the PPF to another point on the PPF.
4. It means consumers prefer low to high prices for what they buy.
5. The transaction costs of buying a hamburger are lower than selling a house. There are many things involved in selling a house—finding an agent to list the house, signing contracts, etc.
6. Jake buys a cigarette from George and then smokes the cigarette while sitting next to Tabitha. Tabitha is allergic to cigarette smoke.
7. $1X = 1.5Y$; $1Y = 0.66X$
8. Through specialization and trade people can consume more goods. But this doesn't answer why this happens. It happens because when people specialize, they produce those things that they can produce at a lower cost than other people. In other words, they are doing what they do best and then trading with others. If everyone does what he or she does best, you would naturally think that everyone has to be better off—at least as compared to the situation where no one does his or her best.
9. People trade to make themselves better off. The necessary condition: People have to value what they will trade for more than what they will trade with. For example, if Yvonne trades $10 for a book, she values the book (which she doesn't currently have) more than the $10 (which she currently does have).
10. We have to give up 10 units of X to produce the first 10 units of Y, but we have to give up 20 units of X to produce the second 10 units of Y.
11. It indicates constant costs.
12. It indicates increasing costs.
13. These are two points *on* its PPF, which means the two points are efficient. Efficiency implies the impossibility of gains in one area without losses in another. This is what a tradeoff is about: more of one thing, but less of something else.
14. An advance in technology; more resources.
15. Answers will vary. The example you come up with should make it possible to produce more goods with the same resources.

Problems

1. 1 hat = $30 or 1 hat = $20. Any price lower than $40 gives us the correct answer.
2. If the entrepreneur can lower Karen's transaction costs from $60 to $24 (a reduction of $36), then Karen will make the trade. Karen will think this way: I pay $370 to the seller, and $5 to the entrepreneur, for a total of $375. My maximum buying price is $400, so I will receive $25 net benefit. But what about transaction costs? As long as my transaction costs are not more than, say, $24, I will receive at least $1 net benefit and the exchange is worth it to me. The entrepreneur will have to lower Randy's transaction costs from $60 to $14 (a reduction of $46). Randy will think this way: I receive $370 from the buyer and I pay $5 to the entrepreneur. This leaves me with $365. My minimum selling price is $350, so I receive $15 net benefit. But what about transaction costs? As long as my transaction costs are not higher than, say, $14, I will receive $1 net benefit and the exchange is worth it to me.

3.

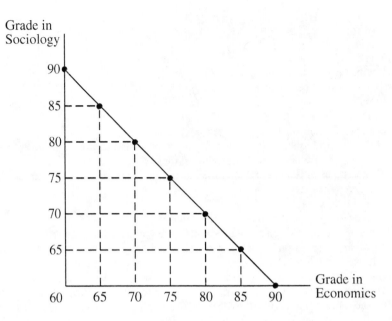

4. 5 fewer points in sociology.
5. Points A and D
6. Points B and C
7. Points E and F
8. Yes, point D could be efficient. The reason why is that there are tradeoffs moving from one efficient point to another. In other words, more of one good comes with less of another good.
9.

10.

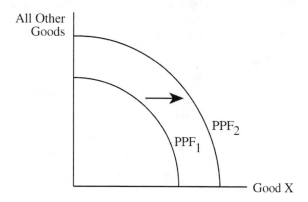

What Is Wrong?

1. If costs are increasing, the PPF is a straight (downward-sloping) line.

    If costs are increasing, the PPF is bowed outward. Alternatively you could say: If costs are constant, the PPF is a straight line.

2. If Jones can produce either (a) 100 units of X and 100 units of Y or (b) 200 units of X and zero units of Y, then he has a comparative advantage in the production of Y.

    We don't know whether he has a comparative advantage in Y or not. To know this, we have to compare his costs to someone else's costs.

3. The following PPF represents a 2-for-1 opportunity cost of apples.

    It is a 1-for-1 opportunity cost of apples. For every apple produced, one orange is not produced. For every one orange produced, one apple is not produced.

4. There are probably more unemployed resources at point A than at point D.

    There are more unemployed resources at D, a point below the PPF.

5. Efficiency implies the possibility of gains in one area without losses in another area.

    Efficiency implies the impossibility of gains in one area without losses in another area. Alternatively, you could have written, Inefficiency implies the possibility of gains in one area without losses in another area.

6. If Georgina reads one more book, she will have to give up doing something else. This shows that Georgina is inefficient.

    When there is efficiency, there are tradeoffs. Georgina cannot do more of one thing without doing less of something else.

7. If Bobby can produce either (a) 100 units of good X and 50 units of good Y, or (b) 25 units of good X and 80 units of good Y, then the cost of 1 unit of good X is 1.5 units of good Y.

    The cost of 1 unit of good X is 0.4 units of good Y.

8.   John says, "I bought this sweater yesterday and I think I got a bad deal." It follows that in the *ex ante* position John thought he would be better off with the sweater than with the money he paid for it, but in the *ex post* position he prefers the money to the sweater.

> *This could be true, but it could be that John is not disheartened about the trade (of money for the sweater), but about the terms of exchange. He may simply have preferred to pay less for the sweater.*

Multiple Choice
   1.   b
   2.   d
   3.   c
   4.   c
   5.   c
   6.   e
   7.   a
   8.   d
   9.   b
   10. a
   11. e
   12. d
   13. e

True-False
   14. T
   15. F
   16. F
   17. T
   18. T

Fill in the Blank
   19. Inefficiency
   20. Efficiency
   21. 8
   22. transaction costs
   23. opportunity costs
   24. efficient
   25. straight line

Chapter 3
Answers

Review Questions

1. Price and quantity demanded are inversely related, *ceteris paribus*.
2. Price and quantity demanded move in opposite directions: as price rises, quantity demanded falls, and as price falls, quantity demanded rises.
3. Amount of a good buyers are willing and able to buy at a particular price. For example, quantity demanded may be 100 units at $10 per unit.
4. Quantity demanded is a specific number—such as 100 units. Demand is a relationship between various prices and various quantities demanded.
5. income, preferences, prices of related goods (substitutes and complements), number of buyers, expectations of future price.
6. to the right
7. to the left
8. Amount of a good sellers are willing and able to produce at a particular price.
9. Quantity supplied is constant as price changes. Stated differently, quantity supplied is independent of (does not depend on) changes in price.
10. Price and quantity supplied are directly related.
11. prices of relevant resources, technology, number of sellers, expectations of future price, taxes and subsidies, government restrictions
12. to the right
13. to the left
14. Quantity of the good is on the horizontal axis, price is on the vertical axis.
15. The absolute price of a good is the money price of a good—such as $3,000 for a computer. The relative price of a good is the price of the good in terms of some other good. For example, if the absolute price of a computer is $3,000, and the absolute price of a TV set is $1,000, then the relative price of a computer (in terms of TV sets) is 3 TV sets.
16. Equilibrium price and quantity rise.
17. Equilibrium price falls and equilibrium quantity rises.
18. Equilibrium price and quantity rise.
19. Equilibrium price rises and equilibrium quantity falls.
20. Consumers' surplus falls. Consumers' surplus equals maximum buying price minus price paid, so if price paid rises, consumers' surplus must fall.

Problems

1.

Factor	Demand	Supply	Equilibrium Price	Equilibrium Quantity
Price of a substitute rises	↑		↑	↑
Price of a complement falls	↑		↑	↑
Income rises (normal good)	↑		↑	↑
Income falls (inferior good)	↑		↑	↑
Price of relevant resource rises		↓	↑	↓
Technology advances		↑	↓	↑
Quota		↓	↑	↓
Number of buyers rises	↑		↑	↑
Number of sellers rises		↑	↓	↑
Buyers expect higher price	↑		↑	↑
Sellers expect higher price		↓	↑	↓
Tax on production		↓	↑	↓
Preferences become more favorable with respect to the good	↑		↑	↑

2.

3.

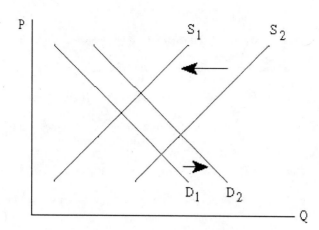

4.   A + B + C + D
5.   E + F + G + H
6.   140 – 50 = 90 units
7.   180 – 60 = 120 units
8.

Price	Quantity demanded by John	Quantity demanded by Mary	Quantity demanded (market demand)
$10	100	130	230
$12	80	120	200
$14	50	100	150

9. $6
10. Jack's first candy bar gives him more utility than the second; the second gives him more utility than the third; and so on.

What Is Wrong?

1.   If the price of a good rises, the demand for the good will fall.

     If the price of a good rises, the quantity demanded of the good will fall. (not demanded)

2.   Consumers' surplus is equal to the minimum selling price minus price paid.

     Consumers' surplus is equal to the maximum buying price minus price paid.

3.   As income rises, demand for a normal good rises; as income falls, demand for an inferior good falls.

     …as income falls, demand for an inferior good rises.

4.   The supply curve for Picasso paintings is upward-sloping.

     The supply curve for Picasso paintings is vertical.

5.   As price rises, supply rises; as price falls, supply falls.

     As price rises, quantity supplied rises; as price falls, quantity supplied falls.

6. Quantity demanded is greater than supply when there is a shortage.

   Quantity demanded is greater than quantity supplied when there is a shortage.

7. If supply rises, and demand is constant, equilibrium price rises and equilibrium quantity rises.

   If supply rises, and demand is constant, equilibrium price falls and equilibrium quantity rises.

8. The law of diminishing marginal utility states that as a consumer consumes additional units of a good, each successive unit gives him or her more utility than the previous unit.

   ...each successive unit gives him or her less utility than the previous unit.

9. According to the law of demand, as the price of a good rises, the quantity demanded of the good rises, *ceteris paribus*.

   According to the law of demand, as the price of a good rises, the quantity demanded of the good falls, ceteris paribus.

Multiple Choice
1. d
2. c
3. e
4. b
5. c
6. b
7. b
8. b
9. e
10. b
11. d
12. a
13. a
14. d
15. d

True-False
16. F
17. F
18. T
19. F
20. T

Fill in the Blank
21. falls; rises
22. market
23. inferior
24. increases
25. equals
26. tie-in

Chapter 4
Answers

Review Questions

1. Requirements for admission (scores on standardized tests, grade point averages) will rise. As student tuition remains constant in the face of rising demand, the gap between the student tuition and equilibrium tuition will increase. Or, the shortage of spaces at the university will increase. There will be "more work" for the nonprice rationing devices to do.

2. To get a lower price, (1) demand can fall, (2) demand can fall and supply can rise, (3) demand can rise by less than supply rises, or (4) supply can rise.

3. By price.

4. The recording industry's action raises the price of music piracy and therefore lowers the quantity demanded of music piracy.

5. If the university charges a below-equilibrium price for parking, there will be a shortage of parking spaces. Something will have to ration the available parking spots. It is more likely to be first-come-first-served (FCFS). What happens if you're not one of the first in line to park? You might end up being late to class.

6. Raise price, raise supply, lower demand. The freeway congestion is evidence of a shortage. There are three ways to get rid of a shortage. The first is to allow price to move up to its equilibrium level, where quantity demanded is equal to quantity supplied. The second is to raise supply enough so that there is no more shortage. The third is to lower demand enough so that there is no more shortage. Increasing supply, in the context of freeway congestion, means adding more freeways. Lowering demand means, perhaps, giving people an incentive to carpool to a greater degree.

7. Because if, at any point in time, gold prices weren't the same everywhere in the world, there would exist an opportunity to buy gold in one location at a low price and sell it in another location at a high price. This difference in gold prices would lead to a reallocation of gold supply and, eventually, the same price for gold everywhere.

8. Yes, patients will pay more for health care when they have the right to sue their provider than when they do not have the right to sue. That's because when patients have the right to sue, the costs to the provider of providing health care are higher, and thus the supply curve of health care is closer to the origin. This results in a higher price for health care.

9. The price (people pay) for good weather is one component of the overall price for housing in a good-weather city.

10. The athlete receives lower pay for playing his or her sport (than he or she would at equilibrium) and the college receives greater consumers' surplus.

Problems

1. Suppose there is a downward-sloping demand for losing one's temper. If so, the higher the price to lose one's temper, the less one will lose one's temper. Yvonne's father charges her a higher price to lose her temper than Yvonne's mother charges her. Notice that people don't often lose their tempers with their bosses (the price you would have to pay is too high), but will lose their tempers with family members, etc.

2. Driving takes time. For example, it might take 20 minutes, going at 50 mph, to go from point X to point Y. The more valuable time is, the more a person will want to economize on time. How valuable time is may be a function of one's wage rate. The higher one's wage rate, the more valuable time is, and the more one will want to economize on time. The 68-year-old retired person may face a lower wage rate than the 32-year-old working person and so time is less valuable to the older person than to the younger person. We would expect the 68-year-old to care less about whether or not he drives slowly because time is less valuable to him or her.

3. Answers will vary. Here is a sample answer. When students pay the equilibrium, professors know that the quantity demanded of spots at the university equals the quantity supplied. If they do something that students don't like, then the demand curve may fall (for education at the university) and, at the given tuition, quantity supplied will be greater than quantity demanded. In other words, there will be a surplus. Will the university get rid of some professors when this happens? Now consider the case when students pay below-equilibrium tuition. Professors know that there is a shortage of space at the university. If they do something that some of their students don't like, and the students leave the university, there are others to take their places (because of the shortage). We predict the following. *If there is a difference between the way a professor wants to teach a class and the way students want it taught, the professor is more likely to respond to the preferences of the students in the first setting (where students pay equilibrium tuition) than in the second setting (where there is a shortage of students due to a below-equilibrium tuition being charged).*

4. Answers will vary. This is a good question to think about.

5. After decriminalization, the demand for marijuana increases by the same amount as the supply of marijuana.

6. Both believe there will be a cutback in employment, so there is no disagreement as to direction (down). The argument is over the magnitude of the downward change.

7. It must be vertical. The supply curve of kidneys discussed in the text was upward-sloping, not vertical. An upward-sloping supply curve illustrates a direct relationship between price and quantity supplied.

8. If a candy bar sells for more in location X than Y, candy bars will be moved from Y to X in search of the higher price. In other words, the supply of candy bars will be reallocated in such a way that no candy bar (in any location) will sell for more or less than any other candy bar. It is not as easy to reallocate houses on land. In short, if a house sells for more in location X than Y, it is difficult (if not impossible) to pick up the house (attached to the land it is on) and move it from Y to X. Since the supply of houses on land cannot be reallocated as easily as candy bars, we would expect that housing prices may differ between locations whereas candy bar prices will not.

9. A car that does not sell does not mean "a bad car." It could simply mean a higher-than-equilibrium price. Jones's car may be a great car, for which the equilibrium price may be, say, $30,000. However, if Jones is charging $100,000 for the car, no one will buy it.

10. He or she forgets, overlooks, or ignores that professors in different fields do not all face the same market conditions. The demand for economists may be higher than the demand for sociologists, and if the supply of each is the same, the equilibrium wage for economists will be higher than the equilibrium wage for sociologists. Suppose we pay economists the same as sociologists, and that the salary we pay each is midway between the equilibrium wage of economists and the equilibrium wage of sociologists. What happens now? There will be a shortage of economists and a surplus of sociologists.

11. The management of Channel 11 will be more likely to view a rerun (instead of a new episode of a television show) because it expects many people to be watching the Olympics on Channel 9. Stated differently, it feels that the demand for a show that competes with the Olympics is likely to be low. Low demand translates into low advertising rates, and so the management at Channel 11 saves its new TV episodes for a time when demand is likely to be high.

12. The market — consisting of buyers and sellers of food — is what feeds Cleveland.

What May Have Been Overlooked?

1. The higher the demand for something, the greater the quantity demanded.

   This is true at a given price. However, a lower price and lower demand can generate a greater quantity demanded than a higher price and higher demand.

2. I think how I behave is independent of the setting that I am in. I act the same way no matter what the setting.

   The person has overlooked the fact that the price of acting a certain way may be different in different settings and that people usually respond to changes in price.

3. If there were no flea markets or garage sales (where people can buy old furniture), new furniture companies would sell more (new) furniture.

   This is the used-car-market example in disguise. The person sees one fact that affects the demand for new furniture, but not another. She sees the fact that if there were fewer buyers of old furniture, there would be more buyers of new furniture. What she doesn't see is that the demand for new furniture is higher if furniture (purchased) can be resold.

4. The rock bank has the best interest of its fans in mind. It knows it can charge $80 a ticket, but it charges only $20 a ticket so that its fans won't have to pay so much.

   What the rock band forgets is that people pay in money or in something else. If $80 is the equilibrium price, then $20 is a below-equilibrium price, at which there will be a shortage of tickets. How will the tickets be rationed? By a combination of first-come-first-served (FCFS). FCFS will no doubt lead to fans standing in long lines to get tickets, some of whom will end up not getting the tickets. Fans will pay by standing in line instead of more money.

5. If my university doesn't charge for student parking, then I am definitely better off than I would be if it did charge for student parking.

   Not necessarily. If there is some positive equilibrium price for parking, then a zero price will create a shortage of parking spots and some nonprice rationing device will come into play. It will probably be first-come-first-served (FCFS), which will cause students to have to pay for parking spots in time instead of money.

6. The tuition at Harvard is very high, so Harvard must be charging the equilibrium tuition to students. Still, Harvard uses such things as GPA, SAT and ACT scores for admission purposes. It must be wrong that these nonprice rationing devices (GPA, etc.) are used only by colleges and universities that charge below-equilibrium tuition.

   The demand for Harvard may be very high, such that even at the high tuition charged, there still is a shortage of spots at Harvard. In other words, Harvard can still charge a high tuition and the high tuition may still not be high enough to equal the equilibrium tuition.

7. If a good doesn't have a money price, it has no price at all.

   Price connotes sacrifice, or giving up something to get something. Someone offers you free tickets to a concert if you will drive to his house and pick up the tickets and later that week mow his lawn. No money has changed hands, but if you accept the deal you will have to pay a nonmoney price for the tickets.

Multiple Choice
   1. e
   2. b
   3. b
   4. b
   5. c
   6. c
   7. b
   8. b
   9. b
   10. e
   11. e
   12. a
   13. b
   14. b
   15. d

True-False

16. T
17. T
18. T
19. F
20. T

Fill in the Blank

21. quantity demanded
22. higher
23. nonprice rationing
24. consumers' surplus
25. John's; Bill

Chapter 5
Answers

Review Questions

1. Price elasticity of demand is equal to the percentage change in quantity demanded divided by the percentage change in price. It is a measure of the responsiveness in quantity demanded to a change in price.
2. The more substitutes for a good, the higher the price elasticity of demand. The fewer substitutes for a good, the lower the price elasticity of demand.
3. No. The more substitutes for a good, the higher the price elasticity of demand, but still the elasticity coefficient can be less than 1 (which makes demand for the good inelastic).
4. The more time that has passed (since a change in price), the higher price elasticity of demand.
5. The larger one's budget that goes for the purchase of a good, the higher price elasticity of demand.
6. Cross elasticity of demand measures the responsiveness in quantity demanded of one good given a change in the price of another good.
7. It means that the percentage change in quantity demanded of a good is less than the percentage change in income. For example, if income rises by 10 percent and quantity demanded for good A rises by 5 percent, then good A is income inelastic.
8. It is a measure of the responsiveness in quantity supplied to a change in price.

Problems

1.

Price and quantity demanded at point A		Price and quantity demanded at point B		Price elasticity of demand is equal to	Is demand (elastic, unit elastic, or inelastic)?
$10	100	$8	140	3.0	elastic
$8	200	$15	120	0.82	inelastic
$7	40	$10	33	0.54	inelastic

2.

Price elasticity of demand is	Change	Price elasticity of demand (rises, falls, remains unchanged)
0.34	more substitutes for the good	rises
1.99	more time passes since change in price	rises
2.20	smaller percentage of one's budget spent on the good	falls

3.

Demand is	Price (rises, falls)	Total revenue (rises, falls, remains unchanged)
elastic	falls	rises
inelastic	rises	rises
unit elastic	rises	remains unchanged
inelastic	falls	falls
elastic	rises	falls

219

4.

Price of good X (rises, falls)	Quantity demanded of good Y (rises, falls)	Cross elasticity of demand is	The two goods, X and Y, are (substitutes, complements)
rises by 10 percent	falls by 5 percent	0.5	complements
falls by 20 percent	rises by 4 percent	5	substitutes
rises by 8 percent	rises by 5 percent	0.625	complements

5.

Income (rises, falls)	Quantity demanded (rises, falls)	Income elasticity of demand is
rises by 20 percent	rises by 10 percent	0.5
falls by 10 percent	falls by 15 percent	1.5
rises by 5 percent	rises by 20 percent	4.0

6.

Price (rises, falls)	Quantity supplied (rises, falls)	Is supply (elastic, inelastic, unit elastic)?
rises 3 percent	rises 4 percent	elastic
rises 1 percent	rises 6 percent	elastic
falls 20 percent	falls 10 percent	inelastic

7.

Initial equilibrium price and quantity		New equilibrium price and quantity (after $1 tax has been placed on supplier)		Percentage of the tax paid by the seller in terms of a higher price	Percentage of the tax paid by the seller in terms of a lower price kept
$40	100	$40.44	90	44 percent	56 percent
$9	87	$9.57	80	57 percent	43 percent
$10	200	$10.76	150	76 percent	24 percent

What Is the Question?

1. Measures the responsiveness of quantity demanded given a change in price.

    What is price elasticity of demand?

2. Price and total revenue are directly related.

    What is the relationship between price and total revenue if demand is inelastic?

3. Quantity demanded changes by 20 percent if price changes by 10 percent.

    What does price elasticity of demand equal to 2 mean?

4. There is no change in quantity demanded as price changes.

    What is the relationship between price and quantity demanded if demand is perfectly inelastic?

5.   The number of substitutes, the percentage of one's budget spent on the good, time (since the change in price), and luxury vs. necessity.

What are the four determinants of price elasticity of demand?

6.   Price of one good rises and quantity demanded for another good rises.

What does it mean if cross elasticity of demand is greater than zero and two goods are substitutes?

What Is Wrong?

1.   If price rises, and total revenue falls, then demand is inelastic.

If price rises, and total revenue falls, then demand is elastic.

2.   The elasticity coefficient is greater than 1 for a good that is income inelastic.

The elasticity coefficient is greater than 1 for a good that is income elastic. Alternatively, you could write: The elasticity coefficient is less than 1 for a good that is income inelastic.

3.   Cars have more substitutes than Ford cars.

Cars have fewer substitutes than Ford cars.

4.   As we move down a demand curve, price elasticity of demand rises.

As we move down a demand curve, price elasticity of demand falls. Alternatively, you could write: As we move up a demand curve, price elasticity of demand rises.

5.   For inelastic demand, quantity demanded changes proportionately more than price changes.

For inelastic demand, quantity demanded changes proportionately less than price changes. Alternatively, you could write: For elastic demand, quantity demanded changes proportionately more than price changes.

6.   A perfectly inelastic demand curve can be downward-sloping.

A perfectly inelastic demand curve is vertical. Alternatively, you could write: An inelastic demand curve is downward-sloping.

7.   The elasticity coefficient is greater than zero for goods that are complements.

The elasticity coefficient is less than zero for goods that are complements. Alternatively, you could write: The elasticity coefficient is greater than zero for goods that are substitutes.

8.   If demand is inelastic, buyers pay the full tax that is placed on sellers.

If demand is perfectly inelastic, buyers pay the full tax that is placed on sellers.

9.   If income elasticity of demand is 1.24, it means that for every 1 percent change in income there is a 1.24 percent change in price.

If income elasticity of demand is 1.24, it means that for every 1 percent change in income there is a 1.24 percent change in quantity demanded.

10. Price elasticity of supply measures the responsiveness of quantity supplied to changes in income.

   Price elasticity of supply measures the responsiveness of quantity supplied to changes in price.

Multiple Choice
1. a
2. c
3. b
4. e
5. c
6. d
7. a
8. a
9. b
10. d
11. c
12. a
13. c
14. a
15. b

True-False
16. T
17. T
18. F
19. F
20. F

Fill in the Blank
21. elasticity coefficient, elastic
22. inelastic
23. increases
24. lower
25. elastic

Chapter 6
Answers

Review Questions

1. John eats the first apple and receives 10 utils of utility. He eats the second apple and receives 8 utils of utility. The total utility he receives from eating two apples is 18 utils. The marginal utility of the first apple is 10 utils; the marginal utility of the second apple is 8 utils.
2. Yvonne gets more utility from walking the first mile than the second mile and more utility from the second mile than the third mile.
3. If a person makes an interpersonal utility comparison, he states that one person receives more utility from doing X than another person receives from doing X. For example, John watches April and Rebecca, two young children, playing in the sandbox. John says that April gets more utility from playing in the sandbox than Rebecca. John is making an interpersonal utility comparison. How does John know how much utility each of the two children receive? The answer is, he doesn't.
4. Diamonds, which are not necessary for life, sell for a higher price than water, which is necessary for life. Water, which has more use value than diamonds, sells for less than diamonds.
5. Goods that have high total utility (a reflection of high use value) may have lower marginal utility than goods that have relatively low total utility. Price is a reflection of marginal utility, not total utility.
6. It says that a person receives more utility per unit of money (say, $1) buying A than B. When the consumer has not equated MU-P ratios, he will rearrange his purchases until he has equated MU-P ratios and is in consumer equilibrium.
7. They buy more of some goods and less of other goods until the MU-P ratio of all the goods they purchase is the same.
8. Zizzo and Oswald set up a series of experiments in which four groups of people were given equal sums of money and asked to gamble with their new money. At the end of each act of gambling, two of the four persons in each group had more money, and two had less. Each of the four persons was then given the opportunity to pay some money to reduce the take of the others in the group. Sixty-two percent of the participants did just this: they made themselves worse off in order to make someone else worse off. The explanation for this type of behavior is that individuals are concerned with relative rank and status more than with absolute well-being.
9. A person who compartmentalizes values things of equal value differently in different settings. Example: Smith earns $1,000 by working hard at a job and $1,000 at the roulette table in Las Vegas. Does he treat the two $1,000 amounts the same? If not, then he is compartmentalizing. If he would be more likely to spend the $1,000 winnings than the hard-earned $1,000, then he is compartmentalizing.
10. The endowment effect states that people value things they own (or have) more than things they do not own (or have). For example, a person value his sweater $40, but not be willing to pay $40 for an identical sweater.

Problems

1.

Unit	Total utility (utils)	Marginal utility (utils)
1st	100	100
2nd	146	46
3rd	174	28

2. 3 units of X and 2 units of Y.

3.

Number of hours playing baseball	Total benefits (in utils)	Marginal benefits (in utils)
1	100	100
2	178	78
3	210	32

4. The person is more likely to buy good Y because the MU-P ratio for good Y is higher than the MU-P ratio for good X. In other words, the consumer receives more utility per $1 buying good Y than Y.

5. No, it is not possible to determine the marginal utility of the second unit. To do this, we would need to know the total utility received from the first unit. If it is, say, 80 utils, and then the total utility for two units is 130 utils, we would know that the marginal utility of the second (additional) unit is 50 utils.

What Is the Question?

1. The additional utility gained from consuming an additional unit of good X.

    What is marginal utility?

2. Marginal utility turns negative.

    What happens to marginal utility when total utility declines?

3. The consumer will buy more of good X and less of good Y.

    If $MU_X/P_X > MU_Y/P_Y$ what will the consumer do?

4. It slopes downward (left to right) because of the law of diminishing marginal utility.

    What is the shape of the marginal utility or marginal benefit curve?

5. Ownership makes things more valuable.

    What is the endowment effect?

What Is Wrong?

1. If total utility is falling, then marginal utility is greater than zero.

    If total utility is falling, then marginal utility is negative.

2. A millionaire gets less utility from an additional $100 than a poor person receives from an additional $100.

    We don't know if this is true or not. A millionaire may get less utility, more utility, or the same amount of utility from an additional $100 as a poor person receives.

3. If total benefits rise, then marginal benefits must rise, too.

    Marginal benefits don't have to rise as total benefits rise. For example, if total benefit is 100 utils for one unit of a good and 180 utilis for two units of the good, marginal benefit goes from 100 to 80. In other words, marginal benefit is falling as total benefit is rising.

4. If the marginal utility-price ratio for good A is greater than the marginal utility-price ratio for good B, then a consumer will buy more of both good A and B.

    If the marginal utility-price ratio for good A is greater than the marginal utility-price ratio for good B, then a consumer will buy more of good A. The person may reallocate dollars from the purchase of B to A.

5. If Smith has a greater income than Jones, then Smith necessarily receives less utility from earning an additional dollar than Jones receives from earning an additional dollar.

    If Smith has a greater income than Jones, it does necessarily hold that Smith receives less utility from earning an additional dollar than Jones receives from earning an additional dollar.

Multiple Choice
1. c
2. b
3. d
4. b
5. e
6. b
7. c
8. c
9. b
10. b
11. d
12. d
13. a
14. a
15. b

True-False
16. T
17. F
18. T
19. T
20. F

Fill in the Blank
21. diamond-water paradox
22. (consumer) equilibrium
23. endowment effect
24. marginal utility
25. higher (or greater)

Chapter 7
Answers

Review Questions

1. The sum of what individuals can produce as a team is greater than the sum of what the individuals can produce working alone.
2. The benefits and costs of shirking. This chapter focused on the costs of shirking and stated that the lower the costs of shirking (to the individual), the more likely the individual will shirk.
3. A person who takes the profits or incurs the losses of the firm.
4. A producer of a good pays $100 to buy some inputs necessary to produce the good.
5. An accountant who works for a firm, and earns $70,000 a year, quits her job to start her own accounting business. The forfeited $70,000 salary is an implicit cost of her new accounting business.
6. Economic profit is smaller than accounting profit because when calculating economic profit both explicit and implicit costs are subtracted from total revenue. When calculating accounting profit only explicit costs are subtracted from total revenue.
7. It is covering all its opportunity costs; stated differently, it is covering both its explicit costs and implicit costs.
8. Examples will vary here. Your example should be consistent with the definition of sunk cost. A sunk cost is a cost incurred in the past, that cannot be undone, and cannot be recovered.
9. James buys a pair of shoes that cannot be resold or returned to the store from which he purchased the shoes. The shoes are a sunk cost. The shoes hurt his feet but he decides to wear them anyway because he wants to get his money's worth out of the shoes. Really, he wants to recover the cost of the shoes somehow. He is trying to undo a sunk cost. He is worse off doing this than simply ignoring the sunk cost and choosing not to wear the shoes. When he wears the shoes, he increases the probability that he will have problems with his feet and have to visit a podiatrist. If he doesn't wear the shoes, he doesn't have this problem. He has lost the money he spent to buy the shoes in either case, so why not lose the money and have comfortable feet than lose the money and have uncomfortable feet.
10. The factory a producer rents.
11. The labor a producer hires.
12. Average total cost is total cost divided by output. Marginal cost is the change in total cost divided by the change in output. Marginal cost considers all "changes," average total cost does not.
13. With the addition of the sixth unit of a variable input, output rises from 100 to 120 units. With the addition of the seventh unit of a variable input, output rises from 120 to 135. The marginal physical product falls from 20 to 15.
14. As diminishing marginal returns set in (and marginal physical product is declining), marginal cost begins to rise.
15. Marginal productivity is the change in output divided by the change in the variable input. Average productivity is output divided by the number of units of the variable input used to produce the output.
16. As diminishing marginal returns set in, marginal cost rises. At some point as marginal cost rises, it will rise above average total cost. When this happens, average total cost will rise.
17. The temperature in San Diego has been 70 degrees each day for the seven days. The average temperature for the week is 70 degrees. Then, the temperature falls to 60 degrees one day. Since the temperature on the additional day (the marginal day) is less than the average temperature, the average temperature will fall. The new average for the last seven days is 68 degrees.
18. It is a curve that shows the lowest unit cost at which the firm can produce any given level of output.
19. It means that its output increases by a greater percentage than the increase in its inputs, causing unit costs to fall.
20. A tax may affect fixed costs but not variable costs. Also, a tax may affect variable costs but not fixed costs. To illustrate, suppose a firm has to pay a lump-sum tax, no matter how much it produces. This tax will raise the firm's fixed costs. If a firm has to pay a tax per unit of output it produces, then this tax affects its variable costs.

21. The AFC curve continually declines (over output) because AFC = TFC/Q. TFC is constant, so that as Q rises, AFC must decline. The more Q rises, the smaller AFC becomes.

Problems

1. Fill in the blanks in the table.

Explicit costs	Implicit costs	Total revenue	Economic profit	Accounting profit
$40,000	$40,000	$100,000	$20,000	$60,000
$150,000	$30,000	$230,000	$50,000	$80,000
$30,000	$40,000	$300,000	$230,000	$270,000

2. Fill in the blank spaces in the table.

Variable cost	Fixed cost	Units of output produced	Average variable cost	Average fixed cost
$500	$1,000	100	$5.00	$10.00
$400	$500	200	$2.00	$2.50
$1,000	$200	400	$2.50	$0.50

3. Fill in the blank spaces in the table.

Variable cost	Fixed cost	Units of output produced	Average total cost
$500	$200	100	$7.00
$300	$400	50	$14.00
$400	$1,000	75	$18.67

4. Fill in the blank spaces in the table.

Average total cost is	Marginal cost is	Average total cost is (rising, fall, remaining unchanged)
$40	$45	rising
$30	$20	falling
$20	$37	rising

5. Fill in the blank spaces in the table.

Variable input (units)	Fixed input (units)	Quantity of output	Marginal physical product of variable input
0	1	0	0
1	1	20	20
2	1	45	25

6. Fill in the blank spaces in the table.

Marginal physical product (units)	Variable cost	Marginal cost
20	$400	$20
18	$360	$20
33	$660	$20

7. TFC does not change as output changes (rises or falls).

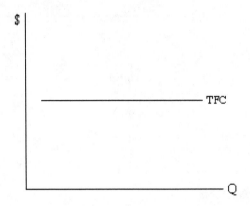

8. AFC is TFC/Q. TFC does not change as Q rises, so AFC must continually decline.

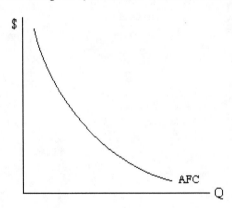

9. The MC curve must cut the ATC curve at its low point.

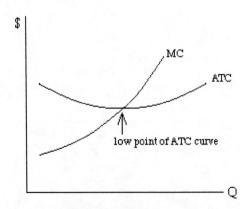

10. When the firm experiences increasing marginal returns, MC is falling; when it experiences constant marginal returns, MC is stable and neither rising nor falling; and when it experiences diminishing marginal returns, MC is rising.

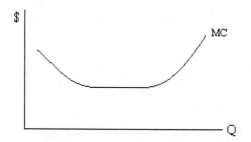

What Is the Question?

1. These economists suggest that firms are formed when benefits can be obtained from individuals working as a team.

    Who are Alchian and Demsetz?

2. The process in which managers direct employees to perform certain tasks.

    What is managerial coordination?

3. This rises as the costs of shirking falls.

    What happens to the amount of shirking as the cost of shirking falls?

4. This is the person in a business firm who coordinates team production and reduces shirking.

    Who is the monitor?

5. Persons who share in the profits of a business firm.

    Who are residual claimants?

6. A cost that is incurred when an actual monetary payment is made.

    What is an explicit cost?

7. It is a cost that cannot be recovered.

    What is a sunk cost?

8. When marginal physical product is rising, this cost is declining.

    What is marginal cost?

9. These costs do not vary with output.

    What are fixed costs?

10. Total cost divided by output.

    What is average total cost or unit cost?

11. When this cost is above average total cost, average total cost is rising.

    What is marginal cost?

12. As output increases, the difference between average variable cost and this cost becomes smaller.

    What is average total cost?

13. The lowest output level at which average total costs are minimized.

    What is the minimum efficient scale?

14. This exists when inputs are increased by some percentage and output increases by a smaller percentage, causing unit costs to rise.

    What are diseconomies of scale?

What Is Wrong?

1. Economic profit is the difference between total revenue and explicit costs.

   Economic profit is the difference between total revenue and the sum of explicit and implicit costs. Alternatively, you could write: Accounting profit is the difference between total revenue and explicit costs.

2. When a firm earns zero economic profit it has not covered its total opportunity costs.

   When a firm earns zero economic profit it has covered its total opportunity costs. Alternatively, you could write: When a firm earns less than zero economic profit it has not covered its total opportunity costs.

3. The difference between the ATC curve and the AVC curve gets larger as output rises.

   The difference between the ATC and the AVC curves gets smaller as output rises.

4. Marginal physical product is equal to output divided by units of the variable input.

   Marginal physical product is equal to the change in output divided by a change in the units of the variable input. Alternatively, you could write: Average physical product is equal to output divided by units of the variable input.

5. When marginal physical product falls, marginal cost falls, too.

   When marginal physical product falls, marginal cost rises. Alternatively, you could write: When marginal physical product rises, marginal cost falls.

6.

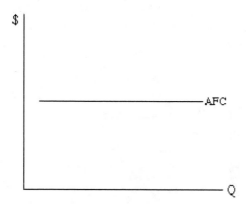

AFC curve is not supposed to be horizontal. It declines as output rises.

7.

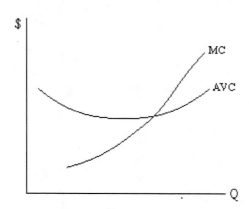

MC cuts AVC at wrong point. MC is supposed to cut AVC at the low point of AVC.

8.

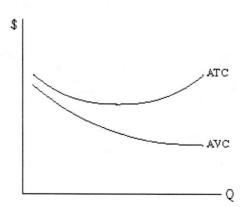

AVC is supposed to be closer to ATC as output rises.

9.

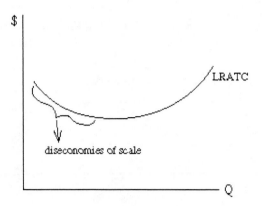

Diseconomies of scale is misrepresented. The area shown represents what happens to LRATC if economies of scale exist, not diseconomies of scale.

Multiple Choice
1. c
2. d
3. b
4. c
5. c
6. d
7. d
8. a
9. a
10. a
11. b
12. c
13. a
14. a
15. c

True-False
16. T
17. T
18. T
19. F
20. T

Fill in the Blank
21. long-run average total cost (LRATC)
22. minimum efficient scale
23. rise; diseconomies of scale
24. falls
25. marginal physical product

Chapter 8
Answers

Review Questions

1. There are many sellers and many buyers, none of which are large in relation to total sales or purchases. Each firm produces and sells a homogeneous product. Buyers and sellers have all relevant information about prices, product quality, sources of supply, and so forth. Firms have easy entry and exit.

2. It means that the seller does not have the ability to control the price of the product it sells; it takes (or sells its good at) the price determined in the market.

3. Plotting price against quantity derives a demand curve. Plotting marginal revenue against quantity derives a marginal revenue curve. Since, for a perfectly competitive firm, price equals marginal revenue, the two curves are the same.

4. To be resource-allocative efficient, price equals marginal cost at the quantity of output the firm produces. A firm will try to maximize profits by producing the quantity of output at which MR = MC. Since, for a perfectly competitive firm, MR = P, it follows that when a firm maximizes profit, it also meets the resource-allocative condition, P = MC.

5. Suppose MR declines and MC rises. Also suppose that the quantity at which MR = MC is 120 units. It follows then that for any quantity less than 120, MR > MC. Why then stop producing where the biggest difference between MR and MC appears? To do this would be to ignore the net benefit derived anytime MR is greater than MC. Take a look at Exhibit 3 in your text chapter. If the firm stops producing at 50 units, where the largest difference between MR and MC appears, it forfeits all net benefits derived by producing the next 75 units of the good.

6. It considers how much it loses if it shuts down and compares this to how much it loses (or earns) if it doesn't shut down. Essentially, this means it compares the price at which it sells the good to its average variable cost. If price is greater than average variable cost, it continues to produce in the short run. If price is less than average variable cost, it shuts down in the short run.

7. No. The firm earns profit only if, at the quantity of output at which MR = MC, price is greater than average total cost.

8. The firm will not produce if price is below AVC, so that portion of the MC curve that is below the AVC curve is not relevant to production.

9. The market supply curve is the horizontal summation of the individual firms' supply curves. For example, if there are two firms in the industry, A and B, and Firm A supplies 10 units at a $10 price, and Firm B supplies 20 units at a $10 price, then one point on the market supply curve represents $10 and 30 units.

10. The market supply curve is upward sloping. This is because the individual firm's supply curve is upward sloping. The firm's supply curve is upward sloping because its supply curve is that portion of its MC curve above its AVC curve, and this portion of its MC curve is upward sloping. But why do MC curves slope up at all? In the last chapter we learned that MC rises when marginal physical product declines (or, in other words, when diminishing marginal returns set in).

11. Here are the three conditions: P = MC, P = SRATC, and LRATC = SRATC.

12. If price is above short-run average total cost, the firm is earning positive economic profits and there is an inconsistency with one of the long-run equilibrium conditions (specifically, P = SRATC).

13. If SRATC is greater than LRATC, then the firm is not producing its output at the lowest possible cost, which is one of the conditions of long-run equilibrium (specifically SRATC = LRATC).

14. A constant-cost industry is one in which average total costs do not change as industry output increases or decreases, and when firms enter or exit the industry, respectively.

15. The firms in the market will increase output and new firms will enter the market. In time, price will fall and the profits will be no longer. In the long run, there will be only normal profits (zero economic profit) in the market.

16. No, because it sells a homogeneous good and to advertise its product is to advertise its competitors' products, too. While a firm may not advertise, the industry may advertise. The industry advertises in the hopes of increasing the market demand for the goods that the sellers produce and sell.

17. It means that the firm is not producing its output at the lowest per unit costs possible.

Problems

1.

Price	Quantity	Total revenue	Marginal revenue
$10	1	$10	$10
$10	2	$20	$10
$10	3	$30	$10

2.

Price	Quantity	Total revenue
$40	100	$4,000
$40	50	$2,000
$40	80	$3,200

3.

Price	Quantity	Marginal revenue
$15	1	$15
$15	2	$15
$15	3	$15

4.

Price	Quantity	Average variable cost	Average total cost	Total variable cost	Will the firm (continue to produce, shut down)
$10	100	$7	$9	$700	continue to produce
$15	50	$13	$16	$650	continue to produce
$23	1,000	$24	$26	$2,400	shut down

5.

Price	Quantity	Average variable cost	Average total cost	Average fixed cost	Total cost
$10	100	$4	$6	$2	$600
$40	2,000	$45	$46	$1	$92,000
$25	198	$21	$23	$2	$4,554

6.

Price	Marginal cost	ATC	Is the perfectly competitive firm earning profits? (yes, no)	Is the perfectly competitive firm in long-run equilibrium? (yes, no)
$40	$40	$30	yes	no
$30	$30	$35	no	no
$25	$25	$23	yes	no

7.

Price	Quantity	ATC	AVC	Profit (+) or Loss (−)
$33	1,234	$31	$30	+ $2,468
$55	2,436	$25	$20	+ $73,080
$100	1,000	$110	$99	− $10,000

What Is the Question?

1. A seller that does not have the ability to control the price of the product it sells.

   What is a price taker?

2. The firm sells its good at market equilibrium price.

   At what (per unit) price does the perfectly competitive firm sell its good?

3. When price is below average variable cost.

   When does the firm shut down in the short run?

4. That portion of its MC curve above its AVC curve.

   What portion of the firm's MC curve is its supply curve?

5. The horizontal summation of the individual firms' supply curves.

   What is the market supply curve equal to?

6. There is no incentive for firms to enter or exit the industry, there is no incentive for firms to produce more or less output, and there is no incentive for firms to change plant size.

   What are the conditions that specify long-run competitive equilibrium?

7. P = SRATC, P = MC, and SRATC = LRATC: ·

   What are the conditions that specify long-run competitive equilibrium?

8. The long-run supply curve is upward sloping.

   What does the long-run supply curve look like for an increasing-cost industry?

9. The long-run supply curve is downward-sloping.

    What does the long-run supply curve look like for a decreasing-cost industry?

10. P = MC.

    What condition specifies resource allocative efficiency?

11. The firm produces its output at the lowest possible per unit cost.

    If a firm is productive efficient, what condition holds?

What Is Wrong?

1. Firms in a perfectly competitive market have easy entry into the market and costly exit from the market.

    Firms in a perfectly competitive market have easy entry into the market and easy exit from the market.

2. In long-run competitive equilibrium, the average or representative firm may earn positive economic profit.

    In long-run competitive equilibrium, the average or representative firm earns zero economic profit (or normal profit).

3. Price is greater than marginal revenue for a perfectly competitive firm.

    Price is equal to marginal revenue for a perfectly competitive firm.

4. A perfectly competitive firm will shut down in the short run if its price is below average total cost.

    A perfectly competitive firm will shut down in the short run if its price is below average variable cost. Alternatively, you could write: A perfectly competitive firm will not necessarily shut down if its price is below average total cost.

5. If a firm produces the quantity of output at which MR = MC, it is guaranteed to earn profits.

    If a firm produces the quantity of output at which MR = MC, it is not guaranteed to earn profits. It only earns profits if price is greater than average total cost.

6. The market supply curve is the vertical summation of the individual firms' supply curves.

    The market supply curve is the horizontal summation of the individual firms' supply curves.

7. If SRATC = LRATC for a firm, there is no incentive for the firm to enter or exit the industry.

    If SRATC = LRATC for a firm, there is no incentive for a firm to change plant size. Alternatively, you could write: If P = SRATC, there is no incentive for the firm to enter or exit the industry.

8. The long-run supply curve is downward-sloping for an increasing-cost industry.

    The long-run supply curve is downward-sloping for a decreasing-cost industry. Alternatively, you could write: The long-run supply curve is upward-sloping for an increasing-cost industry.

9. When average fixed cost is positive, average total cost is usually, but not always, greater than average variable cost.

    When average fixed cost is positive, average total cost is always greater than average variable cost.

10. A firm that produces its output at the lowest possible per-unit cost is said to exhibit resource allocative efficiency.

    A firm that produces its output at the lowest possible per-unit cost is said to exhibit productive efficiency.

Multiple Choice
1. d
2. a
3. a
4. e
5. e
6. d
7. a
8. d
9. c
10. d
11. d
12. a
13. b
14. c
15. a

True-False
16. F
17. F
18. F
19. T
20. T

Fill in the Blank
21. resource allocative efficiency
22. zero
23. MR = MC
24. short-run supply
25. more

Chapter 9
Answers

Review Questions

1. There is one seller; the single seller sells a product for which there are no close substitutes; there are extremely high barriers to entry.
2. A natural monopoly is a firm for which economies of scale are so pronounced that it will end up being the only firm that will survive in the industry.
3. A price searcher is a seller that can, to some degree, control the price of the product it sells. A monopolist fits this description. A monopoly can sell different quantities at different prices. It can raise price and still sell some of its output; it can lower price and sell more of its output. Contrast this with a perfectly competitive firm (which is a price taker). If the perfectly competitive firm raises price above market equilibrium, it sells nothing.
4. It produces the quantity of output at which MR = MC.
5. Look at Exhibit 6 in your text chapter. The perfectly competitive seller produces and sells the quantity at which the demand curve intersects the marginal cost curve, or Q_{PC}. The monopoly seller produces and sells the quantity at which the marginal revenue curve intersects the marginal cost curve, or Q_M. The perfectly competitive seller charges P_{PC} and the monopoly seller charges P_M.
6. It is rational for the individual to seek monopoly rents if the expected benefits of the rents are greater than the costs of obtaining the rents. However, from society's perspective, resources are wasted because resources that could be used to produce goods and services are instead used to bring about transfers.
7. Perfect price discrimination occurs when the seller charges the highest price each consumer would be willing to pay for the product rather than go without. Second-degree price discrimination occurs when the seller charges a uniform price per unit for one specific quantity, a lower price for an additional quantity, and so on. Third-degree price discrimination occurs when the seller charges different prices in different markets or charges a different price to different segments of the buying population.
8. The seller must exercise some control over price (it must be a price searcher); the seller must be able to distinguish among buyers who would be willing to pay different prices; it must be impossible or too costly for one buyer to resell the good to other buyers.
9. Yes. A perfectly price-discriminating monopolist charges the highest price for each unit of the good it sells. This means its price is always equal to marginal revenue. In short, its demand curve and marginal revenue curve are the same (as is the case for the perfectly competitive firm, which is resource allocative efficient). The perfectly price-discriminating monopolist will produce the quantity of output at which MR = MC, and since P = MR, then P = MC. P = MC is the condition that must be satisfied before a seller is resource allocative efficient.

Problems

1.

Price	Quantity	Total revenue	Marginal revenue
$10	1	$10	$10
$9	2	$18 .	$8
$8	3	$24	$6

2. Consumers' surplus under perfect competition = P_1AB
    Consumers' surplus under monopoly = P_2AC

3. The triangle is CBD.

4. It produces the quantity at which MR = MC (which is Q_1 in the exhibit) and charges the highest (per unit) price consistent with this quantity (which is P_1 in the exhibit).

5.

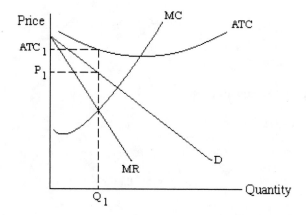

What Is the Question?

1. A right granted to a firm by government that permits the firm to provide a particular good or service and excludes all others from doing the same.

    What is a public franchise?

2. An exclusive right to sell something.

    What was the original meaning of the word monopoly?

3. Price is greater than marginal revenue.

   What is the relationship between price and marginal revenue for the monopolist?

4. Actions of individuals and groups who spend resources to influence public policy in the hope of redistributing (transferring) income to themselves from others.

   What is rent seeking?

5. This occurs when the seller charges a uniform price per unit for one specific quantity, a lower price for an additional quantity, and so on.

   What is second-degree price discrimination?

6. The increase in costs and organizational slack in a monopoly resulting from the lack of competitive pressure to push costs down to their lowest possible level.

   What is X-inefficiency?

7. Total revenue is greater if the monopolist can do this.

   What happens to total revenue for the monopolist if it can go from being a single-price monopolist to a price-discriminating monopolist?

8. If it does this, the monopolist will be resource allocative efficient.

   What will happen if a single-price monopolist becomes a perfectly price-discriminating monopolist?

What Is Wrong?

1. The single-price monopolist exhibits resource allocative efficiency.

   The single-price monopolist does not exhibit resource allocative efficiency. Alternatively, you could write: The perfectly price-discriminating monopolist exhibits resource allocative efficiency. Or, from the last chapter: The perfectly competitive firm exhibits resource allocative efficiency.

2. One of the assumptions in theory of monopoly is that the single seller sells a product for which there are no perfect substitutes.

   One of the assumptions in theory of monopoly is that the single seller sells a product for which there are no close substitutes.

3. For the monopolist, price is equal to marginal revenue.

   For the monopolist, price is greater than marginal revenue.

4. If fixed costs exist, then a firm that maximizes revenue automatically maximizes profit, too.

   If fixed costs exist, then a firm that maximizes revenue does not automatically maximize profit.

5. The monopoly seller produces the quantity of output at which MR = P and charges the highest price per unit for this quantity.

    The monopoly seller produces the quantity of output at which MC = MR and charges the highest price per unit for this quantity.

6. A monopoly seller cannot incur losses, since it is the single seller of a good.

    A monopoly seller can incur losses; it will incur losses if the highest price at which it can sell its output is less than its ATC.

7. Perfect price discrimination occurs when the seller charges a uniform price per unit for one specific quantity, a lower price for an additional quantity, and so on.

    Second-degree price discrimination occurs when the seller charges a uniform price per unit for one specific quantity, a lower price for an additional quantity, and so on. Alternatively, you could write: Perfect price discrimination occurs when the seller charges the highest price each consumer would be willing to pay for the product rather than go without it.

8. A monopoly seller can charge any price it wants for the good it produces and sells.

    A monopoly seller cannot charge any price it wants for the good it produces and sells; it is limited by the height of the demand curve it faces.

Multiple Choice
1. c
2. b
3. c
4. d
5. d
6. e
7. c
8. d
9. a
10. a
11. e
12. a
13. c
14. d
15. d

True-False
16. F
17. T
18. F
19. T
20. F

Fill in the Blank
21. Natural monopoly
22. Price searcher
23. arbitrage
24. X-inefficiency
25. Gordon Tullock

Chapter 10
Answers

Review Questions
1. There are many buyers and sellers, each firm produces and sells a slightly differentiated product, there is easy entry and exit.
2. A perfectly competitive firm and a monopolistic competitive firm face many rivals.
3. A monopolistic competitive firm and a monopoly firm face a downward-sloping demand curve and each is a price searcher.
4. The quantity at which MR = MC.
5. No. To be resource allocative efficient, a firm must produce the quantity of output at which P = MC. For the quantity of output the monopolistic competitive firm faces, P > MC.
6. Essentially because it faces a downward-sloping demand curve.
7. There are few sellers and many buyers, firms produce and sell either homogeneous or differentiated products, there are significant barriers to entry.
8. The percentage of industry sales accounted for by the four largest firms.
9. The essence is that individually rational behavior leads to an outcome that is less-than-best for all parties concerned.
10. To act as if there is only one seller so that monopoly profits can be captured.
11. If a firm cheats, and other firms do not cheat, it earns higher profits.
12. There is easy entry into the market and costless exit from the market, new firms entering the market can produce the product at the same cost as current firms, firms exiting the market can easily dispose of their fixed assets by selling them elsewhere.
13. Initially, the U.S. and Soviet Union are competing in an arms race. Each then realizes it can be better if both countries stop the race. They enter into a cooperative agreement to stop the arms race, but once the agreement has been made, each country realizes it can be made better off if it continues to build up its arms while the other country holds to the agreement. In the end, each country adopts the "strategy" of building up its arms and hoping the other does not. In the end, both countries are back in the arms race. In short, the two countries are in a prisoner's dilemma setting.

Problems
1.

2.

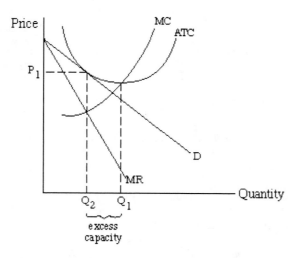

3. P_1CDB; P_1EFA
4. The top four firms in the industry have 12 percent, 10 percent, 8 percent, and 3 percent of industry sales, respectively. The four-firm concentration ratio is 33 percent.
5. The problem of forming the cartel, the problem of formulating policy, the problem of entry into the industry, and the problem of cheating.

What Is the Question?

1. States that a monopolistic competitor in equilibrium produces an output smaller than the one that would minimize its costs of production.

    What does the excess capacity theorem state?

2. It does not produce at the lowest point on its ATC curve because the demand curve it faces is downward-sloping.

    Why doesn't a monopolistic competitive firm produce at the lowest point on its ATC curve?

3. There are significant barriers to entry in this market structure.

    What is oligopoly?

4. Individually rational behavior leads to a jointly inefficient outcome.

    What is a prisoner's dilemma (game)?

5. The key behavioral assumption is that oligopolists in an industry act as if there is only one firm in the industry.

    What is the key behavioral assumption of cartel theory?

6. This is a way out of the prisoner's dilemma for two firms trying to form a cartel.

    What role does the enforcer play in a prisoner's dilemma (game)?

7.   If a single firm lowers price, other firms will do likewise, but if a single firm raises price, other firms will not follow suit.

     What is the key behavioral assumption of the kinked demand curve theory?

8.   The theory fails to explain how the original price comes about.

     What is a criticism of the kinked demand curve theory?

9.   One firm determines price and the all other firms take this price as given.

     What is the key behavioral assumption of the price leadership theory?

10. There is easy entry into the market and costless exit from the market, new firms entering the market can produce the product at the same cost as current firms, and firms exiting the market can easily dispose of their fixed assets by selling them elsewhere.

     What are the conditions that characterize a contestable market?

What Is Wrong?

1.   The monopolistic competitor is a price taker and the oligopolist is a price searcher.

     Both the monopolistic competitor and the oligopolist are price searchers.

2.   For the monopolistic competitor, price lies below marginal revenue.

     For the monopolistic competitor, price lies above marginal revenue.

3.   When profits are normal, the monopolistic competitor exhibits resource allocative efficiency.

     It doesn't matter whether profits are normal are not, the monopolistic competitor does not exhibit resource allocative efficiency.

4.   The cartel theory assumes that firms in an oligopolistic industry act in a manner consistent with there being only a few firms in the industry.

     The cartel theory assumes that firms in an oligopolistic industry act in a manner consistent with there being only one firm in the industry.

5.   The kinked demand curve theory assumes that if a single firm raises price, other firms will do likewise, but if a single firm lowers price, other firms will not follow.

     The kinked demand curve theory assumes that if a single firm raises price, other firms will not follow, but if a single firm lowers price, other firms will do likewise.

6.   The price leadership theory assumes that the dominant firm in the industry determines price and all other firms sell below this price.

     The price leadership theory assumes that the dominant firm in the industry determines price and all other firms will sell at this price.

7. Both monopolistic competitive firms and oligopolistic firms produce the quantity of output at which price equals marginal revenue.

    Both monopolistic competitive firms and oligopolistic firms produce the quantity of output at which marginal cost equals marginal revenue.

8. A contestable market is one in which there is easy entry into the market and costless exit from the market, new firms entering the market can produce the product at the same costs as current firms, and firms exiting the market only have to suffer the loses of their fixed assets.

    A contestable market is one in which there is easy entry into the market and costless exit from the market, new firms entering the market can produce the product at the same costs as current firms, and firms exiting the market can easily dispose of their fixed assets (less depreciation).

Multiple Choice
1. d
2. a
3. d
4. a
5. c
6. b
7. b
8. c
9. c
10. d
11. b
12. b
13. b
14. a
15. b

True-False
16. F
17. T
18. T
19. T
20. F

Fill in the Blank
21. George Stigler
22. cartel
23. cheat
24. excess capacity theorem
25. hit-and-run

Chapter 11
Answers

Review Questions
1. Selling to a retailer on the condition that the retailer will not carry any rivals' products.
2. The more broadly the market is defined, the more substitutes that exist for the good that a firm produces, and the less likely the antitrust authorities will identify the firm as a monopolist.
3. Suppose there are four firms in an industry and each firm has 25 percent of the market. The Herfindahl index is the sum of each firm's market share squared, or $25^2 + 25^2 + 25^2 + 25^2$.
4. A vertical merger is between two firms in the same industry, but at different stages of production. For example, a car manufacturer could merge with a tire manufacturer. A horizontal merger is between two firms in the same industry that sell the same good. For example, two companies that sell office-supply products could merge.
5. price discrimination
6. The higher switching costs are, the greater the permanency of the network monopoly.
7. An agency initially regulates an industry but, in time, the industry ends up controlling the agency.
8. If a firm is guaranteed a profit rate, then it has no incentive to keep its costs down.
9. Economists believe that there are both costs and benefits to regulation and that regulation, should only be undertaken if the benefits are greater than the costs.

Problems

1.

Provision of the antitrust act	Name of the Act
Every person who shall monopolize, or attempt to monopolize, or combine or conspire with any other person or persons to monopolize any part of the trade or commerce…shall be guilty of a misdemeanor.	Sherman Act
Prohibits suppliers from offering special discounts to large chain stores unless they also offer the discounts to everyone else.	Robinson-Patman Act
Empowers the Federal Trade Commission to deal with false and deceptive acts or practices.	Wheeler-Lea Act
Declares illegal unfair methods of competition in commerce.	Federal Trade Commission Act
Declares illegal exclusive dealing and tying contracts.	Clayton Act

2.

Number of firms in the industry	Market shares of the firms, in order from top to bottom	Herfindahl index
6	20, 20, 20, 20, 10, 10	1,800
10	20, 10, 10, 10, 10, 10, 10, 10, 5, 5	1,150
10	10, 10, 10, 10, 10, 10, 10, 10, 10, 10	1,000

3.

Proposed merger	What type of merger? (horizontal, vertical, conglomerate)
Between two firms, each of which produces and sells tires.	horizontal
Between two firms, one of which produces and sells houses and the other which produces and sells wood.	vertical
Between two firms, one of which produces and sells books and one of which produces and sells bottled water.	conglomerate

4. P_1
5. P_2
6.   If the firm charges P_1 it will incur losses. Losses are identified.

What Is the Question?

1.   This antitrust act made interlocking directorates illegal.

    What is the Clayton Act?

2.   One advantage is that it provides information about the dispersion of firm size in an industry.

    What is one advantage of the Herfindahl index over the four- or eight-firm concentration ratio?

3.   This is descriptive of the situation where a particular product or technology becomes settled upon as the standard and is difficult or impossible to dislodge as the standard.

    What is the lock-in effect?

4.   This is the time period between when a natural monopoly's costs change and when the regulatory agency adjusts prices of the natural monopoly.

    What is regulatory lag?

5.   Holds that regulators are seeking to do, and will do through regulation, what is in their best interest.

    What is the essence of the public choice theory of regulation?

6.   One criticism is that it does not explain which specific acts constitute "restraint of trade."

    What is one criticism of the Sherman Act?

7.   This theory holds that regulators are seeking to do, and will do through regulation, what is in the best interest of the public or society at larger.

    What is the public interest theory of regulation?

What Is Wrong?

1.   The size of the market is irrelevant to whether a firm is a monopolist or not.

    No, the size of the market matters. The more broadly the market is defined (and therefore the larger the market is), the less likely a firm will be considered a monopolist.

2. A conglomerate merger is a merger between companies in the same market.

    A horizontal merger is a merger between companies in the same market. Alternatively, you could write: A conglomerate merger is a merger between companies in different markets (or industries).

3. For a network good, its value increases as the expected number of units bought decreases.

    For a network good, its value increases as the expected number of units sold increases.

4. The lock-in effect reduces switching costs.

    The lock-in effect increases switching costs.

5. The more broadly a market is defined, the more likely a firm will be considered a monopolist.

    The more broadly a market is defined, the less likely a firm will be considered a monopolist.

6. George Stigler and Claire Friedland studied both unregulated and regulated electric utilities and found a small difference in the rates charged by them.

    George Stigler and Claire Friedland studied both unregulated and regulated electric utilities and found no difference in the rates charged by them.

7. The federal government looks more closely at proposed vertical mergers than horizontal mergers.

    The federal government looks more closely at proposed horizontal mergers than vertical mergers.

8. A profit-maximizing natural monopoly will produce the quantity of output at which MR = MC and charge the price that equals its ATC.

    A profit-maximizing natural monopoly will produce the quantity of output at which MR = MC and charge the highest (per unit) price possible.

9. The capture theory of regulation holds that no matter what the motive for the initial regulation and the establishment of the regulatory agency, eventually the bureaucrats that run the agency will control the industry.

    The capture theory of regulation holds that no matter what the motive for the initial regulation and the establishment of the regulatory agency, eventually the regulated industry will control the regulators.

Multiple Choice
1. a
2. b
3. b
4. d
5. a
6. c
7. b
8. d
9. d
10. d
11. b
12. a
13. b
14. a
15. d

True-False

16. T
17. F
18. F
19. T
20. T

Fill in the Blank

21. public interest theory of regulation
22. Federal Trade Commission Act
23. natural monopoly
24. market
25. size; market power

Chapter 12
Answers

Review Questions
1. There is a demand for restaurant meals. If the demand for restaurant meals increases, the demand for restaurant workers will increase. The demand for restaurant workers is a derived demand—it depends on changes in the demand for restaurant meals.
2. The factor demand curve is the MRP curve. MRP is equal to MR x MPP. At some point, MPP will decline, which will make MRP decline, which will cause the factor demand curve to be downward sloping.
3. When P = MR.
4. It should buy the quantity at which MRP = MFC. As long as MRP > MFC, the benefits of purchasing another factor unit are greater than the costs, that is, there is a net benefit of purchasing another factor unit.
5. The least-cost rule states that the MPP-to-factor price ratio is the same for all factors. If the ratio is higher for factor X than Y, then it is cheaper to buy less of Y and more of X. Why? Because there is a greater change in output for a $1 expenditure on X than Y. That is essentially what a higher MPP-to-factor price ratio says.
6. Elasticity of demand for the product that labor produces, ratio of labor costs to total costs, and number of substitute factors.
7. No, the income effect may arise, but simply be outweighed by the substitution effect.
8. Product demand and supply (and therefore product price and marginal revenue), and the MPP of labor. See relevant exhibit in the text chapter.
9. Wage rates in other markets, nonpecuniary aspects of the job, number of persons who can do the job, training costs, and moving costs.
10. It may be too costly for an employer to generate full information on a potential employee, and therefore the employer may make a decision to hire (not to hire) based on less than full information. Had the employer known more, the decision might have been different.

Problems
1.

Quantity of factor Z	Quantity of output	Product price	Total revenue	Marginal revenue product
1	30	$40	$1,200	$1,200
2	50	$40	$2,000	$800
3	60	$40	$2,400	$400

2.

Quantity of factor Z	Price of factor Z	Total cost	Marginal factor cost
1	$10	$10	$10
2	$10	$20	$10
3	$10	$30	$10

3.

MPP of factor X (units)	Price of factor X	MPP of factor Y (units)	Price of factor Y	Should the firm buy more of factor X or factor Y?
30	$2	40	$1.25	Y
50	$4	100	$5.00	Y
100	$30	100	$40.00	X

4.

Change	Does this affect the demand for labor (yes, no)?	Does this affect the supply of labor (yes, no)?	Effect on wage (up, down, no change)
product supply falls	yes	no	up
product demand rises	yes	no	yes
training costs rise	no	yes	up
positive change in the nonpecuniary aspects of the job	no	yes	down

5.

6.

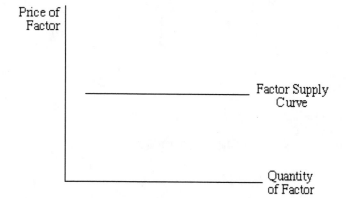

What Is the Question?

1. The additional revenue generated by employing an additional factor unit.

    What is marginal revenue product?

2. It is also the factor demand curve.

    What is the MRP curve?

3. It slopes downward because the MPP of the factor eventually declines.

    Why does the factor demand curve (or MRP curve) slope downward?

4. It will buy the number of factor units for which MRP = MFC.

    What quantity of factor units will the firm purchase?

5. The firm will buy more of factor X and less of factor Y.

    What will the firm do if the MPP-to-price ratio for factor X is greater than the MPP-to-price ratio for factor Y?

6. It is equal to the MPP of the factor divided by the cost of the factor.

    What does output produced per $1 of cost equal?

7. The percentage change in the quantity demanded of labor divided by the percentage change in the wage rate.

    What does elasticity of demand for labor equal?

8. It is upward sloping because the substitution effect outweighs the income effect.

    Why is the supply of labor curve upward sloping?

9. One of the reasons is that jobs have different nonpecuniary qualities.

    Why are supply conditions in different labor markets different?

10. States that firms in competitive or perfect product and factor markets pay factors their marginal revenue products.

    What does the marginal productivity theory state?

What Is Wrong?

1. If price equals marginal revenue, then VMP is greater than MRP.

    If price equals marginal revenue, then VMP equals MRP.

2. The factor demand curve usually lies above the MRP curve.

    The factor demand curve is the MRP curve.

3. The firm will purchase the quantity of a factor at which the difference between the MRP and MFC of the factor are maximized.

    The firm will purchase the quantity of a factor at which MRP = MFC.

4. An increase in MPP will shift the factor demand curve to the left.

    An increase in MPP will shift the factor demand curve to the right. Alternatively, you could write, A decrease in MPP will shift the factor demand curve to the left.

5. If the demand for the product that labor produces is highly elastic, a small percentage increase in price will decrease quantity demanded of the product by a relatively small percentage.

    If the demand for the product that labor produces is highly elastic, a small percentage increase in price will decrease quantity demanded of the product by a relatively large percentage.

6. The more substitutes for labor, the lower the elasticity of demand for labor; the fewer substitutes for labor, the higher the elasticity of demand for labor.

    The more substitutes for labor, the higher the elasticity of demand for labor; the fewer substitutes for labor, the lower the elasticity of demand for labor.

7. Screening is the process used by employers to increase the probability of choosing good employees (to promote) from within the firm.

    Screening is the process used by employers to increase the probability of choosing good employees—from within or outside the firm.

8. A firm minimizes costs by buying factors in the combination at which the MPP-to-price ratio for the expensive factors is greater than the MPP-to-price ratio for the less expensive factors.

    A firm minimizes costs by buying factors in the combination at which the MPP-to-price ratio for all factors is the same.

9. The supply curve is upward-sloping for a factor price taker.

    The supply curve is horizontal for a factor price taker.

10. The higher the labor cost-total cost ratio, the lower the elasticity of demand for labor.

    The higher the labor cost-total cost ratio, the higher the elasticity of demand for labor. Alternatively, you could write: The lower the labor cost-total cost ratio, the lower the elasticity of demand for labor.

Multiple Choice
1. a
2. d
3. a
4. a
5. b
6. e
7. c
8. d
9. d
10. c
11. b
12. a
13. a
14. d
15. a

True-False
16. T
17. T
18. T
19. F
20. F

Fill in the Blank
21. Value marginal product (VMP)
22. screening
23. quantity demanded of labor; wage rate
24. MRP = MFC
25. derived

Chapter 14
Answers

Review Questions

1. Labor income, asset income, transfer payments, taxes.
2. The income share of different quintiles is identified. Then cumulative quintile (households) is plotted against cumulative income share. For example, suppose the lowest fifth (of households) has an income share of 10 percent and the second fifth (of households) has an income share of 15 percent. One point on the Lorenz curve identifies 20 percent of households against a 10 percent income share. A second point on the Lorenz curve identifies 40 percent of households against a 25 percent income share. For more details, see the relevant exhibit in the text chapter.
3. By comparing Gini coefficients, we cannot identify the percentage of income earned by a particular income group. For example, even though Country A may have a lower Gini coefficient than Country B, we don't know if the lowest fifth of households in Country A do, or do not, earn more income than the lowest fifth of households in Country B.
4. Innate abilities and attributes, work and leisure, education and other training, risk taking, luck, and wage discrimination.
5. The income distribution that should exist is the income distribution that people would agree to behind the veil of ignorance, where they do not know their position in the income distribution.
6. A person is said to be in absolute poverty if he or she earns an income below a certain dollar amount. A person is said to be in relative poverty if he or she is one of the lowest income earners. For example, if 95 percent of individuals earn more than Smith, Smith might be said to be falling into relative poverty. In short, absolute dollar amounts are relevant to absolute poverty and percentages are relevant to relative poverty.
7. People tend to earn more in middle age than in their youth. A very youthful population, therefore, might skew the income distribution toward greater inequality.
8. It argues that people should be paid their marginal revenue products.
9. It holds that the reduction or elimination of poverty is a public good and therefore everyone will take a free ride on someone else's efforts at trying to eliminate poverty. In this setting, very little poverty will be reduced or eliminated. It follows, then, that government is justified in taxing all persons to pay for the welfare assistance of some.

Problems

1.

Quintile	Percentage of total income, 2004
Lowest fifth	3.4
Second fifth	8.9
Third fifth	14.7
Fourth fifth	23.0
Highest fifth	50.0

2.

Quintile	Income share (percent)	Cumulative percentage of income	Cumulative percentage of households
Lowest fifth	10	10	20
Second fifth	12	22	40
Third fifth	22	44	60
Fourth fifth	25	69	80
Highest fifth	31	100	100

3.

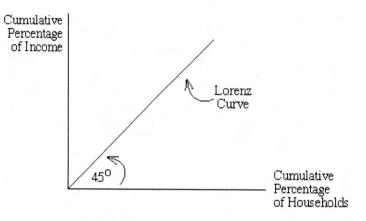

4.

Quintile	Income share
Lowest fifth	10 percent
Second fifth	20 percent
Third fifth	21 percent
Fourth fifth	22 percent
Highest fifth	27 percent

What Is the Question?

1. Payments to persons that are not made in return for goods and services currently supplied.

    What are transfer payments?

2. Labor income plus asset income plus transfer payments minus taxes.

    What does an individual's income equal?

3. This exists when individuals of equal ability and productivity are paid different wage rates.

    What is wage discrimination?

4. It is determined in factor markets.

    Where is the income distribution determined?

5. The Gini coefficient is 1.

    What is the Gini coefficient if there is complete income inequality?

6. The income level below which people are considered to be living in poverty.

    What is the poverty income threshold or poverty line?

7. An example is that everyone who earns less than $5,000 is living in poverty.

    What is absolute poverty?

8. An example is that the bottom one-tenth of income earners are living in poverty.

    What is relative poverty?

9. It holds that individuals currently not receiving welfare think they might one day need welfare assistance and thus are willing to take out a form of insurance for themselves by supporting welfare programs.

    What is the social insurance justification of welfare assistance?

What Is Wrong?

1. The government can change the distribution of income through taxes, but not through transfer payments.

    The government can change the distribution of income through taxes and transfer payments.

2. The Lorenz curve is a measurement of the degree of inequality in the distribution of income.

    The Gini coefficient is a measurement of the degree of inequality in the distribution of income. Alternatively, you could write: The Lorenz curve is the graphical representation of the income distribution.

3. The Rawlsian normative standard of the income distribution holds that there should be complete income equality.

    The absolute income equality standard holds that there should be complete income equality. Alternatively, you could write, The Rawlsian normative standard holds that the income distribution should be what is decided behind the veil of ignorance.

4. Asset income is equal to the wage rate an individual receives multiplied by the number of hours he or she works.

    Labor income is equal to the wage rate an individual receives multiplied by the number of hours he or she works. Alternatively, you could write: Asset income consists of such things as the return to saving, the return to capital investment, and the return to land.

5. In general, human capital refers to the increases in productivity brought about by humans when they use physical capital goods.

    In general, human capital refers to the labor productivity brought about through education, developing one's skills, and so on.

6. The Gini coefficient is zero (0) if there is an unequal income distribution.

    The Gini coefficient is zero if there is an absolutely equal income distribution. Alternatively, you could write: The Gini coefficient is between 0 and 1 if there is an unequal income distribution.

Multiple Choice
1. a
2. b
3. b
4. e
5. a
6. e
7. b
8. d
9. d
10. c

True-False
11. T
12. T
13. T
14. T
15. T

Fill in the Blank
16. Transfer payments
17. Gini coefficient
18. Wage discrimination
19. One (1)
20. *ex ante*

Chapter 18
Answers

Review Questions
1. People in different countries trade with each other for the same reason that people within a country trade with each other—to make themselves better off.
2. Through specialization, countries (as a group) can end up producing more than if they don't specialize. Since they can produce more through specialization, the possibility certainly exists that they can consume more, too. This is accomplished by their trading with each other.
3. A tariff will lower consumers' surplus.
4. A quota will raise producers' surplus.
5. The benefits of the tariff may be concentrated over relatively few producers and the costs of the tariff may be dispersed over relatively many consumers. As a result, the average producer may receive more in gains than the average consumer loses, although consumers (as a group) lose more than producers (as a group) gain. This means the average producer has a sharper incentive to lobby for the tariff than the average consumer has to lobby against it.
6. Industries that are new (infants) in one country may have a hard time competing against their counterparts in other countries that have been around for awhile (and therefore are adults). The infant industries may need some assistance (protection) until they grow up and mature and are ready to compete on an equal basis.
7. A country is said to be dumping goods if it sells a good for less than its cost and below the price charged in the domestic market. Some people argue that this is unfair to domestic industries and therefore they should be protected from this action.
8. No, not necessarily. An economist might ask: What was the price to save the domestic job? If consumers have to pay $60,000 (in higher prices) to save every $40,000 job, it isn't worth saving those jobs.
9. The WTO's objective is to help trade flow "smoothly, freely, fairly, and predictably." It does this by administering trade agreements, assisting developing countries in trade-policy issues, and cooperating with other international organizations.
10. It means that the gains to the winners (or beneficiaries) of tariffs are less than the costs (or losses) to the losers.

Problems
1.

Opportunity cost of one unit of X for Country A	Opportunity cost of one unit of Y for Country A	Opportunity cost of one unit of X for Country B	Opportunity cost of one unit of Y for Country B
1.5Y	0.67X	1Y	1X

2. Area 1
3. Area 2
4. Change in consumers' surplus is the loss of areas 3, 4, 5, 6. Change in producers' surplus is the gain of area 3.
5. Gain from the tariff is area 3 (for producers) and area 5 (for government). Loss is the areas 3, 4, 5, and 6 (for consumers).
6. Net loss is the areas 4 and 6.
7. Area 5

8.

Price after quota	Loss in consumers' surplus due to the quota	Gain in producers' surplus due to the quota	Increase in revenue received by importers due to the quota	Net loss due to the quota
P_Q	Areas 3, 4, 5, 6	Area 3	Area 5	Areas 4 and 6

What Is the Question?

1. This will allow the country to consume beyond its production possibilities frontier (PPF).

    What will specialization and trade do for a country (in terms of its consumption)?

2. As a result, imports decrease.

    What will happen to imports as a tariff or quota is imposed.

3. The sale of goods abroad at a price below their cost and below the price charged in the domestic market.

    What is dumping?

4. The situation in which a country can produce a good at lower opportunity cost than another country.

    What does comparative advantage refer to?

5. The gains are less than the losses plus the tariff revenues.

    What is the net effect of a tariff?

What Is Wrong?

1. A PPF for the world can be drawn when 1) countries do not specialize and trade and 2) when they do specialize and trade. The world PPF will be the same in both cases.

    The world PPF will be further to the right when countries specialize and trade than when they do not.

2. The national-defense argument states that certain goods are necessary to the national defense and therefore should be produced only by allies.

    The national-defense argument states that certain goods are necessary to the national defense and therefore should be produced only by the domestic country.

3. A quota raises more government revenue than a tariff.

    A quota doesn't raise tariff revenue.

4. Consumers' surplus and producers' surplus fall as a result of a tariff being imposed on imported goods.

    Only consumers' surplus falls as a result of a tariff. Producers' surplus rises.

5.   What producers gain from a quota is greater than what consumers lose from a quota.

     What producers gain from a quota is less than what consumers lose from a quota.

6.   If the United States sells a good for less in France than it does in Brazil, then the United States is said to be dumping goods in France.

     The United States may not be dumping goods in this situation. Dumping requires the United States to sell goods for less than cost and less than the price charged in the domestic economy.

7.   A voluntary export restraint is an agreement between two countries in which importing countries voluntarily agree to limit their imports of a good from another country.

     A voluntary export restraint is an agreement between two countries in which the exporting country voluntarily agrees to limit its exports of a good to another country.

8.   A quota is a tax on the amount of a good that may be imported into a country.

     A tariff is a tax on the amount of a good that may be imported into a country.

Multiple Choice
1.   c
2.   a
3.   d
4.   a
5.   a
6.   c
7.   d
8.   d
9.   a
10. e
11. d
12. e
13. b
14. d
15. c

True-False
16. F
17. T
18. T
19. T
20. T

Fill in the Blank
21. antidumping
22. fall
23. falls
24. less
25. more (greater)

Chapter 19
Answers

Review Questions

1. A person in the United States wants to buy a British good. The American has to supply dollars in the foreign exchange market in order to buy pounds.
2. A German wants to buy a U.S. good. The German has to supply marks (in the foreign exchange market) in order to demand dollars.
3. The current account balance takes into account more items than the merchandise trade balance. The merchandise trade balance looks at the difference between merchandise exports and merchandise imports. The merchandise account balance takes into account exports of goods and services (one component of which is merchandise exports), imports of goods and services (one component of which is merchandise imports) and net unilateral transfers abroad.
4. Outflow of U.S. capital and inflow of foreign capital.
5. With a flexible exchange rate system, the demand for and supply of currencies determine equilibrium exchange rates. It is no different than supply and demand determining the price of corn, television sets, or houses. In this case supply and demand simply determine the price of one currency in terms of another currency. With a fixed exchange rate system, governments determine the exchange rate. Under a fixed exchange rate system, exchange rates are determined by government edict, not market forces.
6. If a person in the United States wants to buy a British good, he must pay for the British good with pounds. Thus he will have a demand for pounds. How will he get these pounds? He will have to supply dollars in order to demand pounds in order to buy the British good.
7. If a person in the UK wants to buy a U.S. good, he must pay for good with dollars. Thus he will have a demand for dollars. How will he get these dollars? He will have to supply pounds in order to demand dollars in order to buy the U.S. good.
8. The dollar has appreciated. When it takes less of currency X to buy currency Y, currency X is said to have appreciated. It took $0.0094 to buy one yen on Tuesday, and $0.0090 to buy one yen on Wednesday.
9. A difference in income growth rates (among countries), a difference in relative inflation rates (among countries), and changes in real interest rates (among countries).
10. Suppose the equilibrium exchange rate is $1 = 106 yen and the official exchange rate is $1 = 150 yen. The dollar is overvalued.
11. Devaluation is an act of government; depreciation is an act of markets.

Problems
1. − $10
2. + $4
3. + $17
4. − $1
5. $ 0
6.

If the	Then the
demand for dollars rises in the foreign exchange market	supply of pesos rises on the foreign exchange market
demand for pesos falls on the foreign exchange market	supply of dollars falls on the foreign exchange market
demand for dollars rises in the foreign exchange market	supply of pesos rises on the foreign exchange market

7.

If	Then
$1 = 106 yen	1 yen = $0.0094
$1 = 74 Kenyan shillings	1 shilling = $0.135
$1 = 1,500 Lebanese pounds	1 pound = $0.000667

8.

The exchange rate is	And the item costs	What does the item cost in dollars?
$1 = 106 yen	18,000 yen	$169.81
$1 = £0.50	£ 34	$68
$1 = 9.44 pesos	89 pesos	$9.43

9.

The exchange rate changes from	Has the dollar appreciated or depreciated?
$2 = £1 to $2.50 = £1	depreciated
109 yen = $1 to 189 yen = $1	appreciated
10 pesos = $1 to 8 pesos = $1	depreciated

10.

If ...	The dollar will (appreciate, depreciate)
the real interest rate in the U.S. rises relative to real interest rates in other countries	appreciate
income in foreign countries (that trade with the U.S.) rises relative to income in the United States	appreciate
the inflation rate in the U.S. rises and the inflation rate in all other countries falls	depreciate

11.

If the equilibrium exchange rate is $1 = £ 0.50 and the official exchange rate is	Then the dollar is (overvalued, undervalued)
$1 = £ 0.60	overvalued
$1 = £ 0.30	undervalued

What is the Question?

1. Any transaction that supplies the country's currency in the foreign exchange market.

    What is a debit?

2. Any transaction that creates a demand for the country's currency in the foreign exchange market.

    What is a credit?

3. The summary statistic for the exports of goods and services, imports of goods and services, and net unilateral transfers abroad.

    What is the current account balance?

4. The difference between the value of merchandise exports and the value of merchandise imports.

    What is the merchandise trade balance?

5. One-way money payments.

    What are unilateral transfers?

6. The price of one currency in terms of another currency.

    What is the exchange rate?

7. It predicts that the exchange rates between any two currencies will adjust to reflect changes in the relative price levels of the two countries.

    What does the purchasing power parity theory predict?

8. Raising the official price of a currency.

    What is revaluation?

What Is Wrong?

1. The balance of payments is the summary statistic for the current account balance, capital account balance, net unilateral transfers abroad, and statistical discrepancy.

    The balance of payments is the summary statistic for the current account balance, capital account balance, official reserve balance, and statistical discrepancy.

2. The demand for dollars on the foreign exchange market is linked to the supply of dollars on the foreign exchange market. In short, if the demand for dollars rises, the supply of dollars rises, too.

    The demand for dollars on the foreign exchange market is linked to the supply of other currencies on the foreign exchange market. In short, if the demand for dollars rises, the supply of other currencies rise, too.

3. There are two countries, A and B. The income of Country B rises and the income of Country A remains constant. As a result, the currency of Country B appreciates.

    There are two countries, A and B. The income of Country B rises and the income of Country A remains constant. As a result, the currency of Country B depreciates.

4. There are two countries, C and D. The price level in Country C rises 10 percent and the inflation rate in Country D is zero percent. As a result, the demand for Country C's goods rises and the supply of its currency falls.

    There are two countries, C and D. The price level in Country C rises 10 percent and the inflation rate in Country D is zero percent. As a result, the demand for Country C's goods falls and the supply of other countries' currencies fall. Alternatively, you could write: As a result, the demand for Country C's goods falls and the demand for its currency falls.

5. A change in real interest rates across countries cannot change the exchange rate.

    A change in real interest rates across countries can change the exchange rate.

6. If the equilibrium exchange rate is £1 = $1.50, and the official exchange rate is £1 = $1.60, then the dollar is overvalued and the pound is undervalued.

    If the equilibrium exchange rate is £1 = $1.50, and the official exchange rate is £1 = $1.60, then the dollar is undervalued and the pound is overvalued.

7. A international monetary fund right is a special international money crated by the IMF.

    A special drawing right is an international money crated by the IMF.

Multiple Choice
1. c
2. a
3. c
4. b
5. c
6. a
7. e
8. c
9. a
10. a
11. b
12. d
13. d
14. b
15. a

True-False
16. T
17. F
18. T
19. F
20. T

Fill in the Blank
21. merchandise trade balance
22. purchasing power parity theory
23. fix
24. devaluation
25. fixed; flexible

Chapter 20
Answers

Review Questions

1. If the world is "becoming smaller," then what happens in other countries is "closer" to you than before, and more likely to affect you. Saying that globalization is similar to the world becoming smaller signifies that with globalization what happens in other countries is more likely than ever to affect us.

2. Examples will vary, but the example we used in the text concerned the Chinese buying U.S., thus affecting interest rates in the United States.

3. Globalization may be viewed as a world in which there are no physical, economic, or political barriers to trade. It also may be viewed the same way the 50 states are viewed within the context of the United States. Just as the residents in the 50 states can trade with each other, in a global economy, countries can easily trade with each other. Economic globalization is, in a way, similar to changing countries (of the world) into states of one country. It is similar to taking independent countries such as the United States, Russia, China, Brazil, and Japan and turning them into the United States of the World.

4. No, there have been other times when globalization was present. For example, during the mid-1880s.

5. During the Cold War, there were political barriers standing between individuals in different countries. For example, between people in the Soviet Union and people in the United States. When the Cold War ended, these barriers no longer existed, thus opening up both political and economic transactions between people in the formerly communist world and those in the capitalist world. The end-of-the Cold-War explanation of globalization today suggests that globalization would not be occurring to the degree it is if the Cold War were still going on.

6. What technological advancements can do is lower the hindrances of physical distances that act as stumbling blocks to trade. Also, computer and Internet technology makes it possible for people to communicate with others over long distances, thus increasing the probability that people will trade with each other.

7. Answers will vary, but certainly one example is a policy of either implementing tariffs or raising tariff rates.

8. Benefits of globalization include (1) increased trade and the benefits that come with trade, (2) greater income per person, (3) lower prices, (4) greater productivity and innovation.

9. The benefits are usually spread over many people while the costs are usually concentrated on certain individuals. Take a specific person, George. Some of the benefits of globalization include lower prices. One of the costs might be that George loses a job to a person living in another country. For George, his loss is very visible, while the benefits he receives from globalization (like lower prices) are relatively invisible (For example, how does he know for sure that the lower prices are due to globalization and not something else?).

What Is the Question?

1. During a rather intense period of globalization during the 1990s and early 2000s, the unemployment rate in the U.S. was low.

   Is there any evidence that increased globalization does not cause many Americans to lose jobs?

2. Forty percent in 1946 and about 1.4 percent today.

   What was the average tariff rate in the United States in 1946 and what is it today.

3. In 1995 it was 60 times higher than it was in 1977.

   How many times higher was foreign exchange trading in 1995 than in 1977?

4. In 1946, only 18 countries were members; in 2006, 149 countries were members.

    How many countries of the world were members of the WTO (World Trade Organization)in 1946 and in 2006?

5. The end of the Cold War.

    According to some, what has intensified the move toward globalization in recent decades?

6. The end of the Cold War, technological changes that lower the costs of transporting goods and communicating with people, and government policy changes that express an openness toward freer markets and long distance trade.

    What are the driving forces of this most recent period of globalization?

7. Because the benefits are spread over many people and the costs are concentrated on relatively few.

    Why is it often harder to see the benefits of globalization than the costs?

What Is Wrong?

1. Globalization is closely aligned with a movement toward more free enterprise, restrained markets, and more freedom of government for people and goods.

    Globalization is closely aligned with a movement toward more free enterprise, freer markets, and more freedom of government for people and goods.

2. Tariff rates are higher in the United States today than they were in 1946.

    Tariff rates are lower in the United States today than they were in 1946.

3. The cost of a three-minute telephone call from New York to London was $250; in 2000, it was $10

    The cost of a three-minute telephone call from New York to London was $250; in 2000, it was 40 cents.

4. Between 1980 and 2000, income per person increased 20 percent in India.

    Between 1980 and 2000, income per person doubled in India.

5. Between 1990 and 2005, the CPI rose less fast than the import price index.

    Between 1990 and 2005, the CPI rose more quickly than the import price index.

6. Globalization causes greater income inequality.

    Globalization may cause some degree of greater income inequality, but it is a point still debated among economists.

7. The benefits of globalization tend to be difficult to see, partly because they are so concentrated.

    The benefits of globalization tend to be difficult to see, partly because they are so widely dispersed.

Multiple Choice
1. b
2. b
3. e
4. d
5. d
6. b
7. c
8. d
9. a
10. c

True-False
11. T
12. T
13. F
14. T
15. F

Fill in the Blank
16. World Trade Organization
17. Policy changes
18. lower prices
19. Offshoring
20. Adam Smith